KANDINSKY IN PARIS: 1934-1944

KANDINSKY IN PARIS
1934-1944

This exhibition and catalogue are supported by a grant from the National Endowment for the Humanities.

Additional funding for the exhibition has been provided by the National Endowment for the Arts.

Solomon R. Guggenheim Museum, New York

Kandinsky Society

Library of Congress Cataloging in Publication Data

Kandinsky, Wassily, 1866–1944.
Kandinsky in Paris, 1934–1944.
Exhibition catalogue.
Bibliography: p. 258.
Includes index.
1. Kandinsky, Wassily, 1866–1944—Exhibitions.
2. Concrete art—France—Paris—Exhibitions. 3. Art, Abstract—France—Paris—Exhibitions. I. Solomon R. Guggenheim Museum. II. Solomon R. Guggenheim Foundation. III. Title.
N6999.K33A4 1985 760'.092'4 84-27627
ISBN: 0-89207-049-8

Published by

The Solomon R. Guggenheim Foundation, New York, 1985

Cover: Kandinsky, *Sky Blue*. March 1940 (cat. no. 116)

LENDERS TO THE EXHIBITION

Anni Albers and the Josef Albers Foundation

Fondation Arp, Clamart

Archiv Baumeister, Stuttgart

Max Bill, Zürich

The Blue Rider Research Trust

The Colin Collection, New York

Collection Domela

Lillian H. Florsheim Foundation for Fine Arts

Mark Goodson, New York

Latner Family Collection

Mr. and Mrs. Adrien Maeght

Alberto and Susi Magnelli

Megatrends, Limited

Marina Picasso

The Hilla von Rebay Foundation Archive

Lawrence D. Saidenberg, New York

Arnold A. Saltzman, New York

Madame Schimek-Reichel, Paris

Thyssen-Bornemisza Collection, Lugano, Switzerland

Mr. and Mrs. Burton Tremaine, Meriden, Connecticut

Association-Fondation Christian et Yvonne Zervos, Vézelay

The Baltimore Museum of Art

Bibliothèque Nationale, Paris

Esbjerg Kunstforening, Esbjerg, Denmark

Peggy Guggenheim Collection, Venice

Solomon R. Guggenheim Museum, New York

Haags Gemeentemuseum, The Hague, The Netherlands

Kunstmuseum Basel

Kunstmuseum Bern

Kunstsammlung Nordrhein-Westfalen, Düsseldorf

Gabriele Münter-und Johannes Eichner-Stiftung, Städtische Galerie im Lenbachhaus, Munich

Musée National d'Art Moderne, Centre Georges Pompidou, Paris

Musée National Fernand Léger, Biot

Musée National du Louvre, Paris

Musée de Vallauris, France

Museum Boymans-van Beuningen, Rotterdam

The Museum of Modern Art, New York

The Museum of Modern Art, Seibu Takanawa

Museum Moderner Kunst, Vienna

Philadelphia Museum of Art

The Phillips Collection, Washington, D.C.

Staatsgalerie Stuttgart

Statens Museum for Kunst, Copenhagen

American Literature, The Beinecke Rare Book and Manuscript Library, Yale University

Galerie Beyeler, Basel

Galerie Jeanne Bucher, Paris

Davlyn Gallery, New York

Galerie Rosengart, Lucerne

TABLE OF CONTENTS

Christian Derouet's essay was translated by Eleanor Levieux

PREFACE AND ACKNOWLEDGEMENTS

Kandinsky in Paris completes a tripartite project that began in 1982 with *Kandinsky in Munich* and continued in 1983 with *Kandinsky: Russian and Bauhaus Years.* Together, the three exhibitions and their accompanying catalogues constitute what is certainly the most extensive investigation in exhibition form of Kandinsky's lifework and beyond this probably one of the most far-reaching probes ever undertaken with respect to a twentieth-century master. Few artists in modern times could sustain so relentless an analysis, and the method applied here does not, therefore, lend itself to easy reapplication. For, in addition to the great quantity and quality of Kandinsky's oeuvre and the importance of his contacts with contemporaries, there is in his case the somewhat unusual circumstance of a life divided into separate phases, each of which is linked to an artistic style that has its own clearly recognizable attributes.

Thus, the Munich period culminates in the first abstract expressionist paintings which differ visibly from the abstract constructivist works fully developed by Kandinsky at the Bauhaus—a development that would remain inexplicable but for the stylistic transition that took place while Kandinsky weathered the war and postwar years in pre- and post-Revolutionary Russia. The break between his work of Weimar and Dessau and that of his last years in Paris, which is the subject of the current effort, if less marked, is nevertheless easily perceived by the attentive viewer. Like the earlier transition, it is the result of complex internal and external factors that are at least partially subject to analysis and demonstration.

The Guggenheim, largely for historical reasons noted in the catalogues of the previous installments of this project, assumes an inimitable position among American museums with respect to Kandinsky. The strength of its own collection is paralleled only by those of Munich's Städtische Galerie im Lenbachhaus and the Musée National d'Art Moderne, Centre Georges Pompidou in Paris. Its pioneering history as it relates to Kandinsky and abstract art in general has provided the Guggenheim with the well-nigh unchallengeable claim to primacy in the execution of the Vasily Kandinsky trilogy. Such an assessment does not in any sense reduce the originating institution's dependence upon the above-named sister institutions and upon many other museums, galleries and individuals, without whose generous readiness to participate none of the three Kandinsky chapters could have been written. As in the earlier Kandinsky catalogues, lenders to the exhibition are listed separately. Although our gratitude is expressed to them collectively herewith, it is nevertheless directed to each and every one of them. In addition we extend our special thanks to Dominique Bozo and Germain Viatte, Musée National d'Art Moderne, Centre Georges Pompidou, Paris, for their major loans. We wish to single out the following lenders for their exceptional generosity: Mme Arp and Greta Ströh, Fondation Arp, Clamart; Max Bill; Pierre Bruguière; Dr. Christian Geelhaar, Kunstmuseum Basel; Anne d'Harnoncourt, Philadelphia Museum of Art; Jean-François Jaeger, Galerie Jeanne Bucher, Paris; Christian Limousin, Association-Fondation Christian et Yvonne Zervos, Vézelay; Mr. and Mrs. Adrien Maeght; Susi Magnelli; Dr. Werner Schmalenbach, Kunstsammlung Nordrhein-Westfalen, Düsseldorf; Dr. Hans Christoph von Tavel, Kunstmuseum Bern; and Dr. Armin Zweite, Städtische Galerie im Lenbachhaus, Munich.

Basic to the organization of the threefold exhibition sequence was a working pattern that would correspond to the existing continuity as well as distinctions that mark the periods in Kandinsky's art. Throughout this cycle specialized guest curators therefore have worked more closely with the Guggenheim's curatorial staff than normally would be the case. In the current instance Christian Derouet was charged with the conceptualization and the selection of the exhibition, as well as with the authorship of the principal essay for this catalogue. Mr. Derouet is a curator at the Centre Pompidou whose special responsibility is the documentation and publication of information on Nina Kandinsky's bequest to his museum. His unequalled access to material on Kandinsky's Paris years and his deep involvement with the same subject made him the obvious choice for the project's closing *étape*. Mr. Derouet received essential help in executing his task from Jean K. Benjamin, Jessica Boissel and Christiane Rojouan of the Musée National d'Art Moderne, Paris, César Domela, Jean Hélion, Richard Mortensen and Mmes Ivanov and Koustnetzoff. As was the case with his predecessors in this series, Mr. Derouet was ably and extensively supported by highly qualified Museum Staff members. This assistance was extended primarily but not exclusively by Curator Vivian Endicott Barnett, as the Project Coordinator; Assistant Curator Susan B. Hirschfeld, as Exhibition Coordinator; and Carol Fuerstein, in her capacity as the Guggenheim's Editor, all of whom, thanks to their analogous involvement in all three installments, made valuable and determinative contributions to the *Kandinsky in Paris* exhibition. Mrs. Barnett has also enriched the catalogue by writing a searching essay. The following Staff members are also thanked for their assistance: Diana Murphy,

Editorial Coordinator, Lewis Kachur and Nancy Spector, Curatorial Assistants.

A gesture of appreciation on this occasion should be extended to my colleagues serving as members of the Kandinsky Society—an organization created by the late Nina Kandinsky to assume responsibility for the safeguarding of her husband's spiritual legacy. The current show, indeed the threefold exhibition and series of publications as a whole, enjoyed the moral support of the Society and of its President Mme Claude Pompidou.

It would be unthinkable to conclude an undertaking of such magnitude without stressing the enabling part played by sponsors. The large sums of money required nowadays for the realization of major museum shows and publications have long since outstripped the financial capacities of most originating museums. It is a pleasure, therefore, to acknowledge here the key support received from the National Endowment for the Humanities, which, in sponsoring *Kandinsky in Paris,* has assumed such burdens for the second time within the Vasily Kandinsky sequence. The Humanities grant, in keeping with that federal agency's special purposes, has been directed toward the catalogue and other interpretative aspects of the exhibition, while the National Endowment for the Arts, which provided a grant for the second show in our series, has once again generously given much needed support for the exhibition. To these federal agencies I take pleasure in extending the deeply felt gratitude of the Guggenheim's Trustees and Staff.

Lastly, it should be noted here that, although the Solomon R. Guggenheim Museum originated the three exhibitions devoted to Kandinsky's lifework, the public range of the project extended far beyond the presentations that opened in New York. No fewer than eight major museums in five different countries will have shared parts of the cycle with us by the conclusion of the present show, and it is a pleasure, therefore, to salute Peter C. Marzio, Director, The Museum of Fine Arts, Houston, and Dieter Ronte, Director, Museum des 20. Jahrhunderts, Vienna, who, in presenting *Kandinsky in Paris* will importantly enlarge the scale and scope of the exhibition.

THOMAS M. MESSER, *Director*
The Solomon R. Guggenheim Foundation

KANDINSKY IN PARIS: 1934-1944

Christian Derouet

I would particularly like to thank all those who made it possible for me to work on this subject and helped me carry out my research. In 1979, after *Kandinsky, trente tableaux des musées soviétiques* was presented at the Musée National d'Art Moderne, Centre Georges Pompidou, Paris (MNAM), I had the good fortune to undertake specific research into certain aspects of Kandinsky's years in Paris, with the blessing and assistance of Nina Kandinsky. She very generously lent me books and archives so that I could photocopy them, and she wrote letters of recommendation to facilitate my reconstruction of Kandinsky's correspondence. She took keen interest in the compilation of the catalogue of Kandinsky's works in the MNAM collection, a project broken off and deferred by tragic circumstances. Despite all of its flaws, this essay is a tribute to the warm and constructive reception Nina Kandinsky gave everyone who shared her admiration for her husband's work.

My thanks go to Thomas M. Messer for his faith in my ability to deal with the Paris period, for his understanding and patience while this essay was in preparation, to Vivian Endicott Barnett and Susan B. Hirschfeld, both of whom so painstakingly organized this exhibition, and to Carol Fuerstein for her thoughtful editing of the catalogue. I am grateful to Dominique Bozo for allowing me to carry out this task along with my duties at MNAM, where I had the benefit of friendly assistance and encouragement from Jessica Boissel, Olga Makhroff and Christiane Rojouan. And, finally, I am indebted to two of my former mentors — Jacques Thuillier, professor at the Collège de France, and Francis Haskell, professor of the history of art at Oxford University—for the inspiration for this essay, which has more to do with history than with aesthetics.

Kandinsky in Munich: 1896-1914 (significantly, the exhibition was not entitled *Kandinsky and Munich)* showed how splendid the artistic life of the Bavarian capital was in its twilight period and revealed how European painting discovered abstraction. *Kandinsky: Russian and Bauhaus Years, 1915-1933* attempted not so much to appraise Kandinsky's role in the Russian cultural revolution as to show what enormous influence he wielded over the Bauhaus, that astonishing school of decorative arts and legitimate pride of the Weimar Republic. *Kandinsky in Paris: 1934-1944* covers the last decade in a lifetime of adventure in the arts. It is Kandinsky's least-known and least-popular decade, the final chapter in the biography of an artistic genius who has left his mark on the twentieth century. As a last step in evaluating what Kandinsky did or did not do, we must weigh in the balance what Paris owes to him and what he extracted from the Parisian art-world of the 1930s.

How important were those years, extending from the start of the Depression, in 1929, to the beginning of the German Occupation? It has often been said that artistic life in Paris at that time was lifeless or at best dozing, that a few giants harking back to a timeworn avant-garde—the Cubists—cast a long shadow over all attempts at other forms of expression, that only Surrealism was able to lay claim to a few innovations. For over twenty years the museums of France upheld that view and entrenched it: today it is being thoroughly revised. The 1930s may have been a confused grab bag of aesthetics, but they were not a vacuum. Interest in them has recently revived, if only because many of the ideas that seem important to us today echo that recent past: we are witnessing a return to figurative art, arguing about what the relationship between art and politics can or should be, asking whether art should be socially committed, coming to the end of abstract art and going beyond it.[1] Half a century later, we are getting used to the 1930s again. Not long ago we decreed that those gray years were beyond recovery; today we linger over them gladly.

Braque's late painting, very much "in the French manner," arouses interest; selections from Picasso's last works draw the masses like a magnet; recent articles on the products of Mondrian's New York years have praised them to the skies. Even what seemed unthinkable a few years ago has been achieved: de Chirico's last paintings, those from 1920 until his death in 1978, have been rehabilitated. So it has become fashionable to listen to the great masters' swan songs and abandon the idea of the avant-garde in art history. In this context we can scrutinize the output of Kandinsky's last ten years, and take a closer look at what little the critics have said about it. They generally dismiss the last decade as a period of only secondary importance, a phase that we can skip even if we wish to grasp his work as a whole. Clement Greenberg, for instance, disposed of it in these terms:

> *There is a great variety of manner, motif, scheme and configuration in Kandinsky's later works, but it is a mechanical variety, ungoverned by style or by the development of style. The works in themselves remain fragments, and fragments of fragments, whose ultimate significance is mostly in what they allude to: peasant design, East European color, Klee, the world of machinery—and in the fact that they contain almost nothing spurious. Kandinsky may have betrayed his gifts but he did not falsify them, and his honesty, at his own as well as art's expense, is utterly unique. For this reason alone if for no other, we shall have to go on reckoning with him as a large phenomenon if not as a large artist.*[2]

This is a double-edged judgement: it singles out an artist's approach and elevates it to the rank of a moral example, yet it looks dubiously at a type of painting that American critics of the 1950s may not have been prepared to understand. During that period, American Abstract Expressionism was their darling, and their attitude was a sign of the times. Hans Konrad Roethel, a German scholar of the same generation, was one of those responsible for the founding of the Gabriele Münter- und Johannes Eichner-Stiftung in Munich and devoted his life to studying Kandinsky's work—yet he wrote relatively little on Kandinsky's final decade.

He got around the problem by quoting the painter's last writings, the last positions he took, and merely raised the issue of continuity, asking what thread ran through Kandinsky's lifetime output: ". . . what kind of harmony could link the early landscapes and Art Nouveau works, with their contemplation of the past; the expressionistic abstractions completed before World War I; the geometric constructions of the Bauhaus period; and the cool, cryptic conjurations of Paris?"[3] The two adjectives he uses, "cool" (that is, devoid of sensitivity) and "cryptic" (meaningless, or hard to understand), grossly underestimate Kandinsky's Parisian period.

Will Grohmann also dodged the issue. From 1923 on he was one of Kandinsky's close friends and his champion, responsible for all of the important writings; Kandinsky imposed him on the Paris critics. In the monograph on

1. Concerning the historical context, see Jean-Pierre Azema, *De Munich à la libération, 1938-1944,* Paris, 1979, and Henri Dubief, *Le Déclin de la troisième république (1929-1938),* Paris, 1976. Concerning the artistic context, see *L'Art face à la crise: L'Art en occident 1929-1939,* Saint-Etienne, 1980; *Paris 1937-Paris 1957: créations en France,* exh. cat., Paris, 1981; *Cahiers du Musée National d'Art Moderne,* no. 9, 1982, special issue devoted to above exhibition; although it concerns Paris only indirectly, see also Serge Guilbaut, *How New York Stole the Idea of Modern Art, Abstract Expressionism, Freedom and the Cold War,* Chicago, 1983.
2. Clement Greenberg, *Art and Culture: Critical Essays,* Boston, 1961, p. 113.
3. Hans K. Roethel in collaboration with Jean K. Benjamin, *Kandinsky,* New York, 1979, p. 15.

Kandinsky he was asked to write in 1958, he did not dwell on the Paris years, and acknowledged that he did not understand them very clearly. He brandished the idea of synthesis, which he borrowed from Kandinsky's last writings. In "La Valeur d'une oeuvre concrète," Kandinsky urges once again that the distinctions between knowledge and art, and between one art and another, be removed. He notes that "the vast wall between art and science is tottering" and that the time has come for "the Great Synthesis."[4] Grohmann is only too happy to follow suit, and lumps together the idea of synthesis with that of "serenity" and "wisdom"—qualities always credited to ageing geniuses by their worshipful biographers.

Few French critics have written anything about Kandinsky lately. They have felt called upon to defend his Parisian period, but none of them is an historian, or has the training in aesthetics of the German critics. They are all brilliant preface-writers, used to drafting a few short paragraphs for some exhibition or other. All of them question Grohmann's idea of "synthesis." In an essay entitled "Symbols and Masks," Gaëtan Picon—a veritable rationalistic doubting Thomas—very skillfully puts down Kandinsky's so-called synthesis and serenity.[5] Michel Conil Lacoste, however, in his *Kandinsky*, takes a less gingerly approach to the problem of the Parisian period and quite frankly lists all the doubts voiced about it.[6] Like Greenberg, the French *littérateurs* actually emphasize Kandinsky's moral qualities so as to avoid discussing his painting. André Breton set the example in 1938, when he was asked to produce a preface for the Kandinsky show Peggy Guggenheim organized in London; he paid more attention to Kandinsky's gaze than to the paintings on exhibit: "His admirable eye, merging with his faint veil of glass to form perfect crystal lights up with the sudden iridescent glitter of quartz. It is the eye of one of the first and one of the greatest revolutionaries of vision."[7]

Why all of this beating about the bush? It actually sheds light on one of the difficulties inherent in Kandinsky's career: his work is the work of a stateless man, uprooted repeatedly and forced again and again to find a new public and new critics each time. The German critics turned away from him as soon as he settled in France, and the French critics have had trouble giving their stamp of approval to the final years of an artist whose impact is rooted in Germanic culture. Even today we can feel the consequences of the critics' disarray: whereas a number of doctoral theses have covered the Munich and Bauhaus periods, the Paris period has stimulated no such study and so has not been properly evaluated.

This catalogue has a mission, therefore, to fill a bibliographical void. Our first aim is to provide the historical background necessary for situating Kandinsky's Paris period and measuring its influence. We will not attempt to look beyond the limits defined by the dates 1934 to 1944 and see how Kandinsky's final works affected *Art Informel* in Paris or Abstract Expressionism in New York. We merely note—with some satisfaction—that an artist such as Frank Stella has attempted, in recent lectures at Harvard and in a commentary on *Complexité simple (Complex-Simple)*, to reevaluate Kandinsky's Parisian period.[8]

4. Vassily Kandinsky, "La Valeur d'une oeuvre concrète," *XXe Siècle*, vol. 1, no. 5-6, Winter-Spring 1939, pp. 48-50, translated as "The Value of a Concrete Work" in Kenneth C. Lindsay and Peter Vergo, eds., *Kandinsky: Complete Writings on Art*, Boston, 1982, vol. II, p. 827.
5. Gaëtan Picon, "Symbols and Masks" in *Kandinsky, Parisian Period, 1934-1944*, exh. cat., New York, 1969, pp. 7-14.
6. Michel Conil Lacoste, *Kandinsky*, New York, 1979, p. 82: "It is his most controversial period, and it is remarkable that it has never been wholeheartedly accepted by even fervent admirers of the earlier works, who find it difficult to see in it any connections with what went before. The large number of names which have been given to the style perhaps reflect the conflicting feelings it has aroused . . . ."
7. André Breton, "Some Appreciations of the Work of Wassily Kandinsky" in *Wassily Kandinsky*, exh. cat., London, 1938. Breton's twenty-two-line preface for the catalogue for the show, which opened at Guggenheim Jeune on Feb. 17, 1938, was translated by Samuel Beckett, according to Peggy Guggenheim's letter to Kandinsky dated Feb. 15, 1938: "Mr. Beckett, who has done all of the other translations, and who will send it to you . . . ." The letters to Kandinsky cited in these notes are preserved in the Kandinsky Archive, MNAM.
8. Frank Stella, "Complexité simple-Ambiguïté" in *Kandinsky: Album de l'exposition*, exh. cat., Paris, 1984, pp. 84-90.
9. Will Grohmann, *Kandinsky*, New York, 1958, pp. 246-247: "Kandinsky continued working until March 1944, then he fell ill. Nine months later, at 8 p.m. on December 13, he died. The cause of death was sclerosis of the cerebellum . . . . He was buried in the cemetery in Neuilly, only a few persons being present at the funeral. On the large stone slab that covers his grave appear these words only: 'Wassily Kandinsky, 1866-1944.'" Burial is in the Cimetière nouveau de Neuilly, rue Vimy, Nanterre, 16e division, série 53, tombe no. 5.
10. Kandinsky's correspondence frequently has to do with money. In France the connection between money and art is considered not quite decent. Kandinsky can easily be excused for talking about money at such length in his letters because he had to fight a hard battle in order to earn any in Paris. Not one Paris dealer wanted to

A simple set of facts will help us grasp the essential ambiguity of those years. Born of Russian parents in Moscow in 1866, Kandinsky died a French citizen, in Neuilly-sur-Seine, a Paris suburb, in 1944. He is buried, not in the shade of the chestnut trees that line the street he lived on in Neuilly (see cat. no. 16), nor in the Bois or Bagatelle park (see cat. no. 18), where he went walking every day, but in the new Neuilly cemetery, an enclave within the city limits of Nanterre, hemmed in by superhighways and the skyscrapers of the new Défense district.[9]

Sources

This essay is based on widely varying but specific sources. It does not have to rely on the sort of supposition to which art history is all too often reduced: "Kandinsky doubtless saw such and such, Kandinsky must certainly have read this or that." But we do not claim that our interpretation of the material available is necessarily the best.

The Kandinsky Archive at the Musée National d'Art Moderne, Centre Georges Pompidou in Paris is now being classified. It includes manuscripts, a record of the artist's correspondence, press cuttings, his famous Handlists *(Hauskataloge)*, the books that were in his library in Paris, samples of the materials he used, hundreds of drawings and sketchbooks from which we can reconstitute at least to some extent the process that led to the finished paintings of this period.

The Archive also contains the letters Kandinsky received; as we would expect of an artist of his age and talent, there are numerous letters from his dealers settling the details of sales and exhibitions.[10] There are fewer letters from fellow artists, but they do testify warmly to the relationships Kandinsky managed to establish in a new setting and in the relatively short period of six years, 1933 to 1939. Few letters from abroad are here, of course, since the war made it impossible, or at best extremely difficult, to receive mail from outside the country. As for the artists who lived in Paris, they of course did not write; they telephoned, and hardly any trace remains of their calls. There are only two letters from Hans Arp, for instance, but the telephone bills show that phone calls from Meudon were frequent. The collection of snapshots includes few group pictures and is of only middling interest with regard to the period of 1933 to 1944. Some minute prints are mementos of an excursion made to Varengeville, in Normandy, in 1939, while Kandinsky was visiting Joan Miró; the other photographs shed little light on Kandinsky's contacts with artists.

In addition to Kandinsky's correspondence with Josef Albers, Katherine Dreier, Grohmann, Hilla Rebay, Paul Klee, Hermann Rupf and Hans Thiemann, with which students are already familiar, there are reconstituted collections of more specifically Parisian letters: the correspondence in Russian between the painter and his nephew, Alexandre Kojève, a philosophy professor at the Ecole Pratique des Hautes-Etudes in Paris;[11] between Kandinsky and Christian Zervos, who edited *Cahiers d'Art*; between Kandinsky and André Dézarrois, curator of the Musée des Ecoles Etrangères at the Jeu de

handle him. Therefore, he was his own dealer and refused to sell for low prices even though his market had collapsed in Germany. When he arrived in Paris, no specific value was attached to his works. On Apr. 12, 1933, at a sale at the Hôtel Drouot for the benefit of *Cahiers d'Art*, a Kandinsky watercolor of 1913 sold for the same price as a banal watercolor by Raoul Dufy. In a letter to Christian Zervos dated Feb. 24, 1933, Kandinsky wrote about his future prices: "You told me I could align my prices according to Léger's, more or less." He did so, and seldom sold any large paintings. But the decision was vital. Letter from Kandinsky to Grohmann dated Aug. 6, 1935: "My exhibition here at the Cahiers [d'Art] was inaugurated on June 21 .... I stood firm and refused to lower my prices .... Two years ago I lowered them by 50% and I will not go lower." Peggy Guggenheim wrote mockingly, "No one looked less like an artist than Kandinsky, who resembled a Wall Street broker." *Out of This Century: Confessions of an Art Addict*, New York, 1979, p. 170. But gradually Kandinsky won his battle; in a letter to Hans Arp dated July 28, 1942, Kandinsky wrote: "I've been having a show at the Galerie Jeanne Bucher since July 21. It was very sad that you weren't at the opening; the show is going satisfactorily, even favorably. You remember that business about prices, my dear Arp. Now I know that I was right; they really have gone up 30% or 40%." Letters to Zervos cited in these notes are preserved in private collections; those to Grohmann are in the Archiv Will Grohmann, Staatsgalerie Stuttgart; and those to Arp are in the Archives of the Fondation Arp, Clamart, France.

11. Kandinsky's half-nephew, Aleksandr Kozhevnikov (1902-68), changed his name to Alexandre Kojève once he was naturalized a French citizen in 1937. Educated in German universities, he taught at the Ecole Pratique des Hautes-Etudes in Paris (where he replaced Alexandre Koyre) and there introduced the practice of reading Hegel's philosophical works. Among his students were Georges Bataille, Maurice Merleau-Ponty and Raymond Queneau. Urged by his students, Editions Gallimard in Paris are publishing Kojève's courses as *Essai d'une histoire raisonnée de la philosophie païenne*. During the German Occupation of France, Kojève fled to Marseilles where, in 1943, he wrote *Esquisse d'une phénoménologie du droit*.

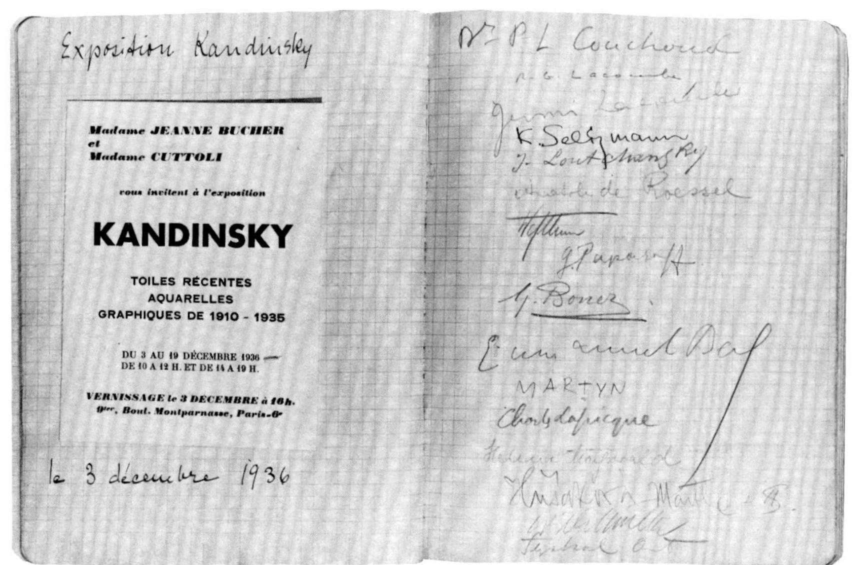

LA GALERIE PIERRE
2, RUE DES BEAUX-ARTS
PRÉSENTE DU 2 AU 14 MAI
DES ŒUVRES RÉCENTES DE

ARP
FERREN
GIACOMETTI
HARTUNG
HÉLION
KANDINSKY
NELSON
PAALEN
TAEUBER-ARP

fig. 1
Invitation and guest book from first Kandinsky exhibition at Galerie Jeanne Bucher, Paris, 1936
Courtesy Galerie Jeanne Bucher, Paris

fig. 2
Brochure for group exhibition at Pierre Loeb's Galerie Pierre, Paris, 1936
Collection Musée National d'Art Moderne, Centre Georges Pompidou, Paris, Kandinsky Bequest

Paume; between Kandinsky and Pierre Bruguière, an art collector. All of these are valuable sources; from them we learn about the painter's daily life in the Paris of the 1930s, about what he thought of the opening of this show and that, about the exhibitions he attended. What Kandinsky does not often write about, unfortunately, is his own work.

The information we find in his correspondence about events of only everyday importance is borne out by other archives—for instance, the letters from the painter Jean Hélion to the art collector Albert Gallatin, preserved at The New York Historical Society; or the correspondence (now in the process of being compiled) of the Galerie Jeanne Bucher, where Kandinsky exhibited from 1936 to 1944 (fig. 1).[12] These scattered writings convey the tone of that period. His widow's memoirs, *Kandinsky et moi,* provide the links, and let us see how she and her husband lived in Paris from day to day; Nina Kandinsky frequently quotes from the Kandinsky-Grohmann letters—without always showing where her quotes begin and end.[13]

Pierre Loeb wrote a marvelous series of verbal portraits and an essay entitled "Où va la peinture?," included in *Voyages à travers la peinture.* Although he did not discuss Kandinsky as such, these pieces constitute one of the best (and also one of the most elliptical) introductions to life in the Paris art world in the period between the two world wars (fig. 2).[14] The material available at the Fondation Arp in Clamart and at the Fondation Christian et Yvonne Zervos in Vézelay also makes us feel the spirit of the times.

Settling Down in Paris

The accidents of history brought Vasily and Nina Kandinsky to Paris. The Bauhaus in Berlin had closed. Kandinsky rightly felt threatened by the Nazi dictatorship. Leaving Germany for Paris was, for him, a veritable exile, even though he had been wooing the Paris market for a while (he had shown in

12. Jeanne Bucher ran a small gallery which attracted the most important artists—Cubists, Surrealists, abstract painters—between 1925 and 1946. With the kind cooperation of Jean-François Jaeger, director of the gallery, Marie Blanche Pouradier-Duteil and I have undertaken to reconstitute Jeanne Bucher's archives. This research has been very helpful in verifying certain theories concerning the way Kandinsky's work was received in Paris between the two world wars.
13. Nina Kandinsky, *Kandinsky et moi,* Paris, 1978.
14. Pierre Loeb, *Voyages à travers la peinture,* Paris, 1945. This book consists of notes the art dealer wrote in Cuba, where he lived during World War II.

two small galleries in 1929 and 1930) and was not unknown in France; *Cahiers d'Art* had published a monograph on his work in 1931.[15] But Kandinsky feared the stress of Parisian life, an agitation unknown in his remote and verdant Berlin suburb. Their decision to emigrate was shaped by the Reichstag fire, the threats of physical violence and the xenophobic slogans, and one of Hitler's harangues. Nina Kandinsky explained in her memoirs, *Kandinsky et moi*: "In July 1933 we went to the area near Toulon, in France, for our summer vacation. Early in September we spent some time in Paris and it was at the Hôtel des Saints-Pères that we heard Hitler's speech. . . . A few days later we had lunch with Marcel Duchamp. . . . When we went back to Berlin we had the lease and our identification papers with us. . . . On January 2, 1934, our apartment was finished and ready for us to move into. Our furniture arrived in Paris that day." But she immediately added, "When we moved . . . we intended to spend only a year in Paris, to begin with, and then return to Germany. . . . We thought about it for a long time, wondering whether it might not be be better to go to Switzerland, Italy or America."[16]

So the Kandinskys' arrival in Paris was only halfhearted.[17] As far as the French administration and the bourgeoisie were concerned, they were emigrants, driven out by the new German regime. As far as the avant-garde of the French art world was concerned, they were victims of a dictatorship that had expelled modern art from its museums. As their new acquaintances had other linguistic backgrounds, they gradually stopped speaking German.[18] Only Jeanne Bucher, Arp, César Domela and a few others knew how to speak it. Kandinsky was amused when he attended the openings of Paris art shows to hear such a Babel-like blend of Russian, German, English and French. His French was good, and he used it to communicate with the English and Americans, the Spaniards and the Italians.

In Paris Kandinsky regained his Russian identity. The French did not pay much attention to his German passport; they considered him Russian, or at least Germanified Russian. For that one reason the art journalists fell into the habit of linking him with Marc Chagall, who had an unshakeable reputation in the art world of the period.[19] Kandinsky even had to remind his Italian translator, Colonna di Cesarò, that Chagall never belonged to the *Blaue Reiter*.[20]

When the time came to open his first show in Paris, Kandinsky invited the Russian emigré colony of Paris.[21] He asked Kojève to find out several addresses, including Stravinsky's.[22] But he was soon disenchanted by the welcome he received from those members of the colony who frequented the Russian church on the rue Daru;[23] they appreciated old, familiar styles of painting and were not prepared to understand his abstract works. Alexandre Benois, painter, former designer for the *Ballets Russes* and an important critic for the Russian-language newspapers in Paris, expressed his unequivocal disapproval of the works Kandinsky exhibited at the Galerie Jeanne Bucher in 1936:

> *Allow me to be altogether sincere. Yesterday I went to see your show, I looked at everything very carefully, and I came away convinced that I*

15. The exhibitions were Paris, Galerie Zak, *Wassily Kandinsky* (watercolors), Jan. 15-31, 1929, and Paris, Galerie de France, *Kandinsky*, Mar. 14-31, 1930; the monograph, Will Grohmann, *Kandinsky*, Paris, 1931, the sixth in the series *Les Grands peintres d'aujourd'hui*, published by Editions des Cahiers d'Art.
16. Nina Kandinsky, pp. 171, 174, 182.
17. In a letter to Zervos dated Apr. 3, 1933, Kandinsky wrote: "But it is easier to say, 'once we're in Paris,' than to actually go there."
18. In a letter to Grohmann dated Feb. 15, 1939, Kandinsky said he was happy to have heard a Bavarian radio program and to have understood it all; he preferred the Bavarian dialect and listened frequently to the German radio.
19. The replies of both Chagall and Kandinsky to an inquiry by Maurice Raynal and E. Tériade regarding the similarities between 1830 and 1930 were published in *L'Intransigeant*, Dec. 2, 1929, p. 5.
20. In 1929 Colonna di Cesarò began to translate *On the Spiritual in Art* into Italian. In 1934 he wrote a preface for the translation, discussed in a letter to Kandinsky dated Nov. 19, 1934.
21. Paris, Galerie des "Cahiers d'Art," *Kandinsky, peintures de toutes les époques, aquarelles et dessins*, May 23-June 23, 1934, organized by Yvonne Zervos.
22. Letter from Kandinsky to Kojève dated May 12, 1934. Letters to Kojève cited in these notes were provided by Mme Nina Ivanov and Mme Koustnetzoff, who also supplied their French translations.
23. The Russian metropolitan church of Paris, Alexandre Nevski, rue Daru, Paris 8e.

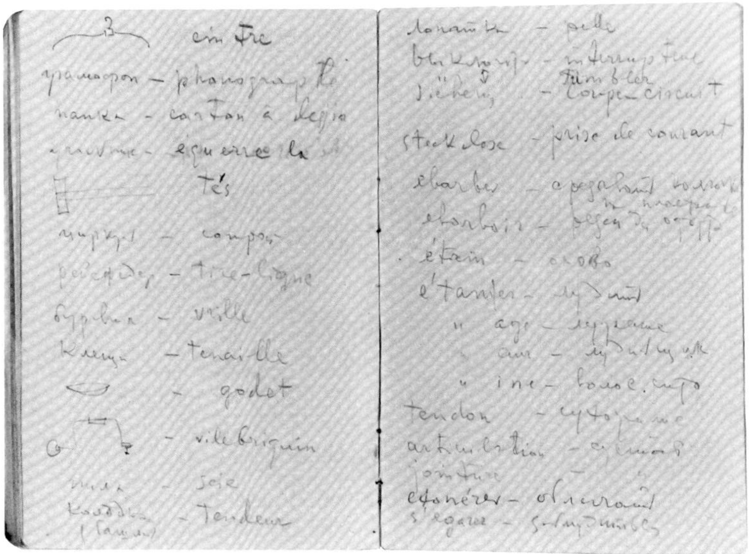

fig. 3
Kandinsky's notebook with Russian-French vocabulary
Collection Musée National d'Art Moderne, Centre Georges Pompidou, Paris, Kandinsky Bequest

didn't understand a bit of it! Especially since art gives me a queasy feeling. Obviously there is some organic deficiency involved. For I am perfectly willing to admit that in theory, in principle, art such as that can exist. In fact it is entirely possible that yours is the true art, just as we say of certain types of music that it is "pure music." But it has not been granted to me to understand and enjoy such art. And if art does not give me any pleasure, I simply do not understand and do not accept it. I am an incorrigible "celebrator of things." If I am to feel that special thrill "that makes life worth living," I need images that are comprehensible to my rational self or at least to my conscious or even my subconscious. And that is precisely what I do not find in your work. . . . I am also ready to admit that what you create may have a great future ahead of it. I would not be at all surprised if, as I looked into the future, I saw a type of art very similar to yours, or even stemming from yours. . . . As I say, I would not be surprised but I would be profoundly saddened.[24]

Kandinsky and Nina were so shocked by the way the Russian emigré colony behaved that they refused to attend a concert given by their friend Thomas de Hartmann and his wife, so that they would not have to run into the leading Russian figures of Paris.[25] Only from time to time did Kandinsky keep in touch with Aleksei Remizov, the writer, whom he wanted Jeanne Bucher to publish,[26] and with the Russian sculptor Antoine Pevsner, whose work he recommended for inclusion in various exhibitions.[27] But as he aged, the urge to speak Russian became stronger; he spoke Russian with Nina, and it was in Russian that he liked to swap ideas with his nephew Kojève. And it became natural for him, when jotting down indications of color on a preliminary drawing, to use Russian abbreviations instead of the German names (fig. 3). Renewing relations with his half-nephews and half-nieces, he plunged into a certain nostalgia for his native country.[28] The political situation

24. Letter from Benois (1870 [St. Petersburg]—1960 [Paris]), to Kandinsky, in Russian, dated Dec. 8, 1936. Several drawings by Benois were acquired by the Jeu de Paume before 1930; these were shown in Paris, MNAM, *Paris-Moscou,* June 27-Sept. 3, 1979, in the permanent collections, *Artistes russes à Paris de 1919 à 1939: oeuvres dans les collections nationales,* no cat.

25. Letter from Olga Hartmann to Kandinsky, in Russian, dated June 1937: "I tried in vain to talk to her [Nina Kandinsky] about how annoyed she was about the Russian newspapers, and to convince her that it was much more trying for us to see that our friends did not want to hear Thomas's new pieces than it was for her to see that certain people on the Russian papers did not understand your art." Among the items in Kandinsky's library preserved in the Kandinsky Archive is a concert program that includes poems by K. Balmont, Adamovitch and Marina Zwetaeva that were set to music by de Hartmann; these are listed under the heading, "Works by Th. de Hartmann, sung by Madame Hartmann; at the piano: the composer."

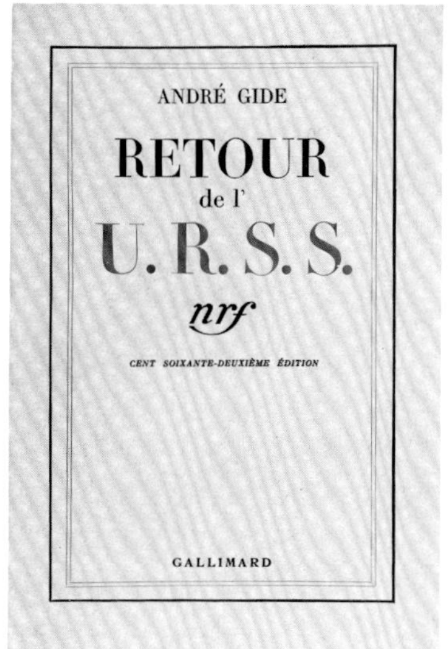

ANDRÉ GIDE

RETOUR
de l'
U. R. S. S.

nrf

CENT SOIXANTE-DEUXIÈME ÉDITION

GALLIMARD

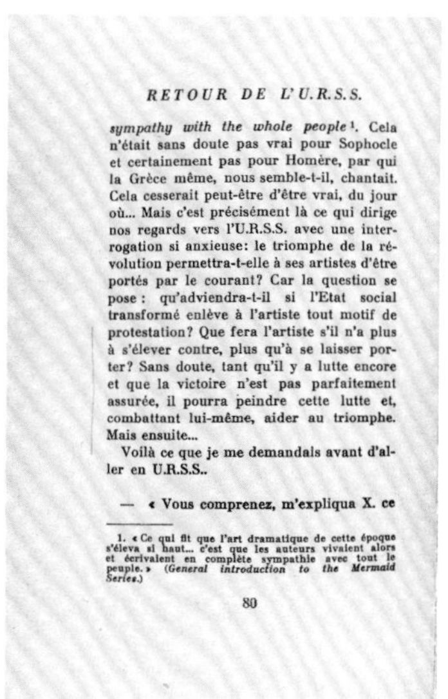

RETOUR DE L'U.R.S.S.

sympathy with the whole people[1]. Cela n'était sans doute pas vrai pour Sophocle et certainement pas pour Homère, par qui la Grèce même, nous semble-t-il, chantait. Cela cesserait peut-être d'être vrai, du jour où... Mais c'est précisément là ce qui dirige nos regards vers l'U.R.S.S. avec une interrogation si anxieuse: le triomphe de la révolution permettra-t-elle à ses artistes d'être portés par le courant? Car la question se pose : qu'adviendra-t-il si l'Etat social transformé enlève à l'artiste tout motif de protestation? Que fera l'artiste s'il n'a plus à s'élever contre, plus qu'à se laisser porter? Sans doute, tant qu'il y a lutte encore et que la victoire n'est pas parfaitement assurée, il pourra peindre cette lutte et, combattant lui-même, aider au triomphe. Mais ensuite...

Voilà ce que je me demandais avant d'aller en U.R.S.S..

— « Vous comprenez, m'expliqua X. ce

1. « Ce qui fit que l'art dramatique de cette époque s'éleva si haut... c'est que les auteurs vivaient alors et écrivalent en complète sympathie avec tout le peuple. » (*General introduction to the Mermaid Series.*)

80

fig. 4
Gide, *Retour de l'U.R.S.S.*, 1936, cover and p. 80, scored by Kandinsky
Collection Musée National d'Art Moderne, Centre Georges Pompidou, Paris, Kandinsky Bequest

in Russia worried him, and although he was usually very circumspect about politics, he let himself go in clearly anti-Communist remarks—as in this letter to his nephew dated October 6, 1932: "It seems things are going very badly in Russia. They're expecting a real famine. And so, as in a bad pun, instead of coming to a station called 'prosperity for all,' they unexpectedly arrive at 'annihilation of all.' But I do not hold out much hope that the logically minded materialists will come a cropper once and for all. The muddy waters are spreading farther and farther, in every direction. . . ."

By 1936, adopting an attitude that was common enough then but somewhat short on analysis and comprehension, he lumped together Communists and Fascists, criticizing the Moscow trials and the Führer's auto da fés.

Just as he had done in 1906, when he first stayed in Paris and Sèvres, Kandinsky lived in France with Russia—a certain Russia—always in mind. His Russia was composed of memories of a country that had disappeared, and he tended to gild his outdated, picturesque images of it. It had been the continent of his childhood, and all that was left to him was an immense sadness. He devoured André Gide's pamphlet *Retour de l'U.R.S.S.* and underlined everything in it that the author had noted was a limitation on artistic freedom and on spirituality (fig. 4). Kandinsky was less sensitive to news about the *Entartete Kunst* (degenerate art) exhibitions in Munich than to the description of the antireligious museums Gide had visited. Gide wrote:

> *I did not see the antireligious museums in Moscow but I did visit the one in Leningrad, in Saint Isaac's Cathedral, whose golden dome glows exquisitely over the city. On the outside, the cathedral is very beautiful; on the inside it is appalling. The large, pious paintings it harbors could tempt one into blasphemy, so hideous are they. The museum itself is far less impertinent than I might have feared. Its purpose was to contrast the myth spun by religion with the mightiness of science. Cicerones are*

26. Letter from Remizov to Kandinsky dated Feb. 3, 1937.

27. Pevsner had been living in Paris since 1927. Kandinsky had no eye for sculpture. In 1937 he wrote to Dézarrois to advise him to separate sculpture and painting at the Jeu de Paume, and specifically to set aside the ground floor "for sculpture, which often gets in the way of painting."

28. In a letter to Grohmann dated Feb. 19, 1939, Kandinsky discussed a visit by his niece from Greece in the near future and his and Nina's plans for a trip to Athens.

on hand to convince those whose indolent minds may not be impressed by the various optical instruments or the tables on astronomy or natural history or anatomy or statistics. The overall effect is decent enough and not too defamatory.[29]

Over-mistrustful of leftwing tyrannies, Kandinsky neglected to dissociate himself from those on the far right. He took a disconcertingly wait-and-see attitude toward the Nazis. For a long time he believed he would be able to go back to Germany and when Kojève traveled to Berlin, Kandinsky asked him to plead his case before the administration of the Third Reich and the banks: "... although Germany was my permanent place of residence even before the war, I traveled very often, not only in northern and southern Germany but also abroad, and at one point lived abroad for four consecutive years (in France, Belgium, Tunisia and Italy). So the reasons why I have not been in Germany for almost two years now have nothing to do with politics but only with art."[30]

In 1936 Sophie Taeuber-Arp reported to him in the most disturbing terms on the precarious condition of modern art in Germany, and soon afterward Arp wrote him a letter about "degenerate art," enclosing newspaper articles on the removal from German museums of works that had been in their collections and on the smear campaign launched against every modern form of expression.[31]

In 1938 Kandinsky's attitude changed. He signed a petition in support of Otto Freundlich, a Jewish artist living in Paris; one of his sculptures had been reproduced on the cover of the catalogue of the *Entartete Kunst* exhibition in Munich.[32] Kandinsky attended the vernissage of the show that Jeanne Bucher organized in Freundlich's honor and helped to buy one of Freundlich's works so that it could be given to the Jeu de Paume (fig. 5). At the urging of Peggy Guggenheim and Herbert Read, Kandinsky agreed to lend several paintings to the *Twentieth Century German Art* exhibition in London devoted to artists who had been banished from Germany.[33] When Otto Dix exhibited his antiwar painting *Flanders* at the show, Kandinsky protested about mixing politics and art. Herbert Read agreed with him, writing on November 9, 1938:

I do not think you would be well advised to exhibit in future with the German expressionists. Not only is your art so different in spirit, but most of them are so determined to make political capital out of their unhappy fate that they antagonise the only people who are likely to buy their paintings. I do not say this in a mood of cynicism or of compromise. Politically and intellectually I am totally opposed to fascism and continually fight against it. But there are political realities and there are aesthetic realities, and it is necessary to preserve the distinction. I mean, that if one strives for the freedom of art, one does not at the same time strive for the politisation of art.

Already, at the huge *Exposition Internationale* of 1937 Picasso had come out of his artistic ivory tower by showing *Guernica,* that memorable protest

29. André Gide, *Retour de l'U.R.S.S.,* Paris, 1936, p. 88.

30. Letter from Kandinsky to Kojève; this letter is undated, but since it was written at La Napoule, it must date from the summer of 1935, when Kandinsky stayed there.

31. Letter from Arp to Kandinsky dated Sept. 18, 1936, reproduced in MNAM, *Kandinsky,* coll. cat., Paris, 1984, p. 365. Nina Kandinsky, p. 186: "In 1936 we received a clipping from *Die Essener National Zeitung* that terrified us. That was where we came across the diabolical expression, 'degenerate art.' "

32. Three paintings and two watercolors by Kandinsky were shown in *Entartete Kunst: Bildersturm vor 25 Jahren* at the Haus der Kunst, Munich, in the summer of 1937.

33. London, New Burlington Galleries, *Exhibition of Twentieth Century German Art,* July 7-31, 1938. All of the artists represented had been included in the notorious *Entartete Kunst* show the previous summer.

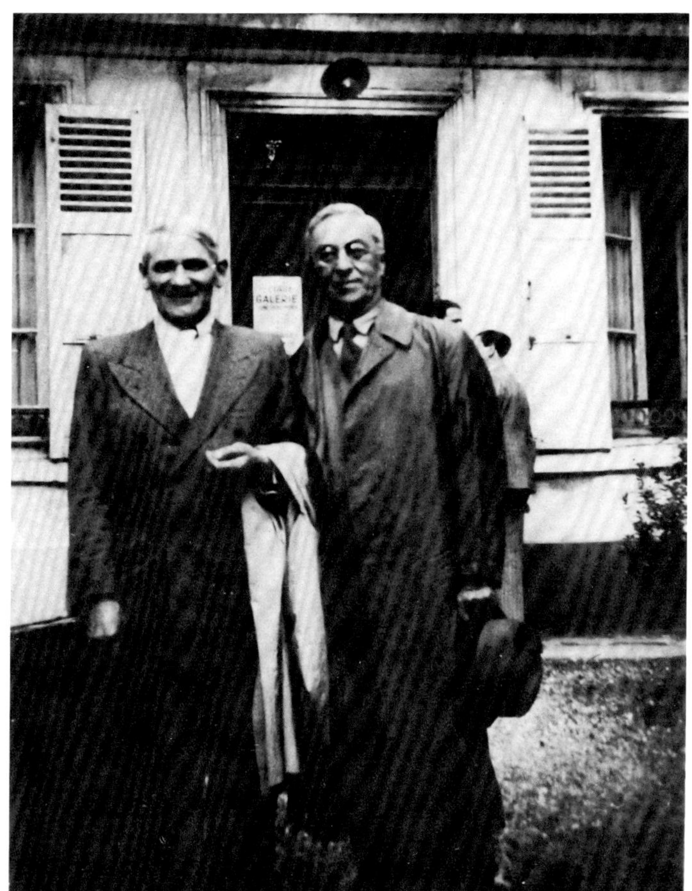

fig. 5
Freundlich and Kandinsky on occasion of *Hommage à Freundlich,* Galerie Jeanne Bucher, Paris, 1938
Collection Musée National d'Art Moderne, Centre Georges Pompidou, Paris, Kandinsky Bequest

against the Putsch and Franco's military repression, the only masterpiece of any consequence left by this failed exhibition. Miró, though timid, painted *The Reaper* and produced the lithograph *Aidez L'Espagne.* The sculptor Jacques Lipchitz created a monstrous *Prometheus Strangling the Vulture*; commissioned by the government, it was considered a gesture of solidarity with the Jews of Central Europe and their suffering under the Nazis and set off a virulent campaign in the reactionary French newspapers. Kandinsky observed that crowds of visitors streamed to the German pavilion at the exposition and he told Grohmann how pleased he was that it was receiving so many official awards.[34] But how can we tell how ironic Kandinsky was being?

His political blindness ended the following year: his German passport expired, and the German embassy in Paris refused to renew it.[35] Kandinsky immediately began taking steps to obtain French naturalization (see cat. no. 224). In support of his application he produced letters from Dézarrois, curator at the Jeu de Paume, and Jean Cassou, deputy curator of the Musée du Luxembourg. By the time war was declared, Kandinsky had become French—which spared him from being interned in a camp as were many other artists who were citizens of enemy countries. His only somewhat daring gesture—not a very bold one, to be sure—of opposition to tyranny was to contribute to illustrations for a poem by Stephen Spender, which was translated by Louis

34. Letter from Kandinsky to Grohmann dated Dec. 3, 1937.
35. Kandinsky's eyes were finally opened by the sales of "degenerate art" carried out surreptitiously by Swiss painters or officially at public sales in Lucerne, to which the French weekly *Beaux-Arts* devoted numerous articles. See *Beaux-Arts,* no. 329, Apr. 21, 1939, p. 1; no. 340, July 7, 1939, pp. 1, 7; no. 341, July 14, 1939, p. 8.

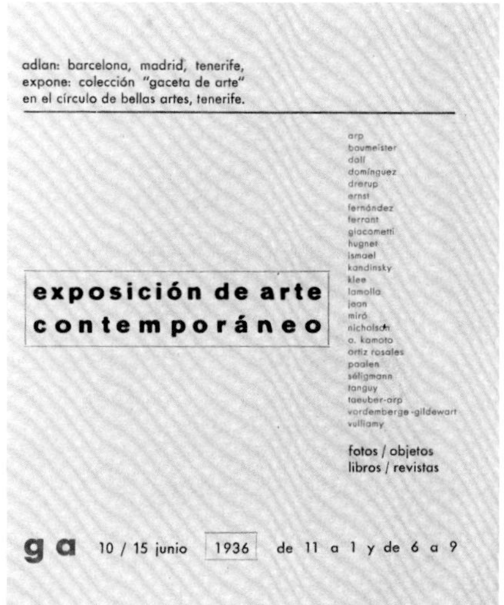

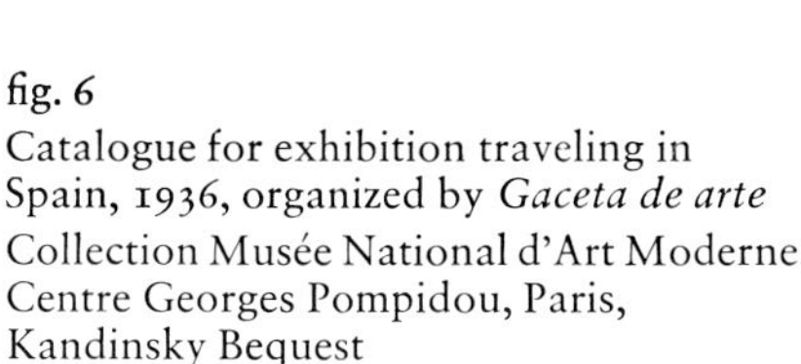

fig. 6
Catalogue for exhibition traveling in Spain, 1936, organized by *Gaceta de arte*
Collection Musée National d'Art Moderne, Centre Georges Pompidou, Paris, Kandinsky Bequest

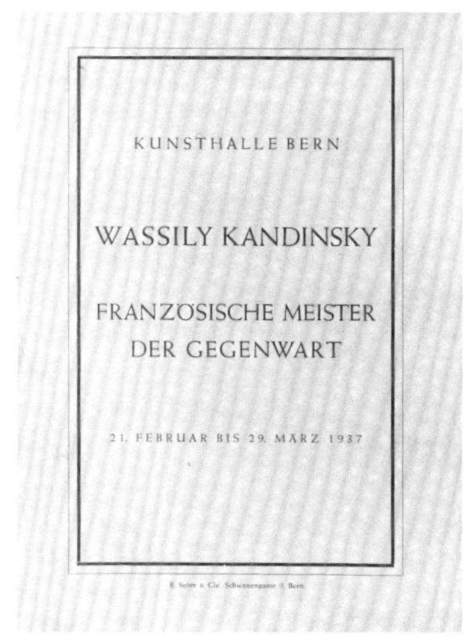

fig. 7
Catalogue and Kandinsky's installation plan for *Wassily Kandinsky: Französische Meister der Gegenwart,* Kunsthalle Bern, 1937
Collection Musée National d'Art Moderne, Centre Georges Pompidou, Paris, Kandinsky Bequest

Aragon and published in 1939 by the American engraver Stanley William Hayter (cat. no. 42). This stance, as the quiet man of the art world, was doubtless what made it possible for him to work and exhibit regularly during the Occupation without being hindered.

Kandinsky's Geographical World

The USSR was forbidden him; Germany had rejected him. Spain, where some critics had begun to pay attention to him in 1936 (fig. 6), had collapsed quickly under Franco's dictatorship.[36] Italy still appealed to him strongly but was in disgrace. Europe had shrunk to France, Switzerland (fig. 7) and England.[37] Beyond that, there was only imaginary geography: China, but by now he was too old to go there, and America, from which he derived most of his income (fig. 8).

On several occasions he made plans to go to America and began studying English. In 1931 he wanted to deliver lectures in Chicago.[38] In 1933 his friends Anni and Josef Albers left for America, to teach at Black Mountain, and they began urging him repeatedly to join them.[39] But America also meant the new Bauhaus, re-created in Chicago by László Moholy-Nagy, and Kandinsky, like many former pupils of the German Bauhaus—the only authentic one—assumed that the new one was only a mediocre imitation. He also considered that Rudolf Bauer was, as he saw it, unfairly competing with him for the attention of Hilla Rebay and Solomon Guggenheim.[40] Kandinsky preferred to stay in Paris, "the city that gave artistic activity its resonance."

36. On Dec. 14, 1936, the Canary Islands fell to the seditious troops; the editorial staff of Eduardo Westerdahl's *Gaceta de arte* was dispersed.
37. The Kunsthalle Bern gave Kandinsky an opportunity to organize a genuine retrospective in 1937. Between 1939 and 1940, Rupf (a collector and Kandinsky's banker) was virtually the only person outside France with whom Kandinsky corresponded; see the annotated edition of their correspondence by Sandor Kuthy in *Bulletin des Musées des Beaux-Arts de Berne,* no. 150-151, May-June 1979; no. 152-153, Aug.-Sept. 1979.
38. Letter from Solomon R. Guggenheim to Kandinsky dated June 6, 1931: "You have to say about coming to America, Chicago, lecturing. . . ."
39. Kandinsky may have dreamed of Indian landscapes and art when Albers wrote him enthusiastic letters about Mexico and the pre-Colombian civilizations (he even sent Kandinsky little pottery figures that arrived in Paris in bits) and when Breton visited Trotsky in Mexico City in 1938.
40. It was a work by Bauer that adorned the cover of the *Second Enlarged Catalogue of the Solomon R. Guggenheim Collection of Non-Objective Paintings.* The catalogue, which accompanied an exhibition at the Philadelphia Art Alliance presented Feb. 8-28, 1937, listed sixty-nine works by Bauer and thirty-four by Kandinsky. Concerning the relationship between Rebay and Kandinsky, see Joan M. Lukach, *Hilla Rebay: In Search of the Spirit in Art,* New York, 1983.

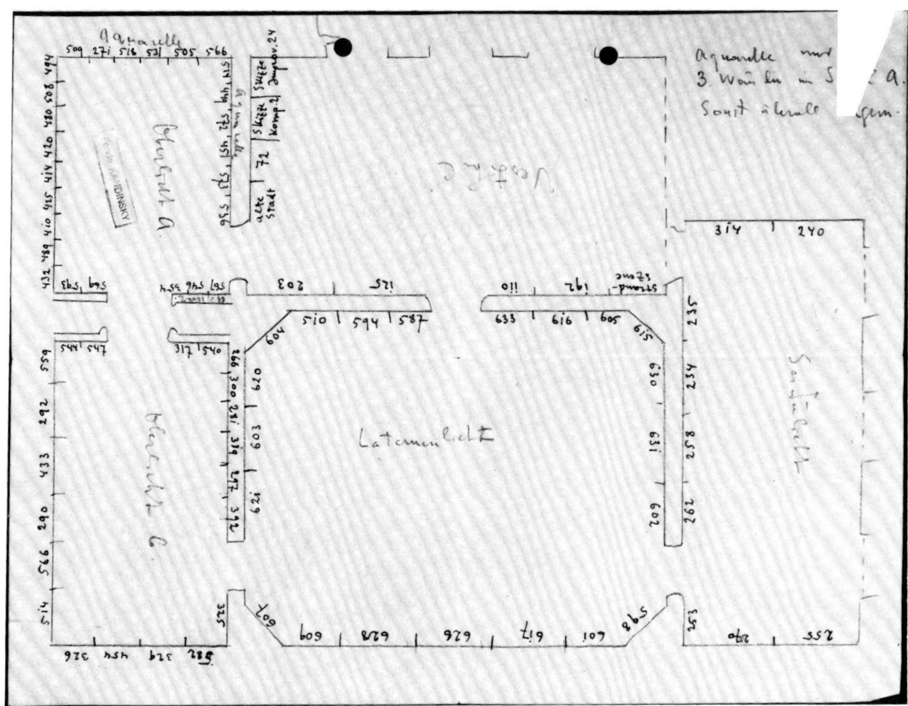

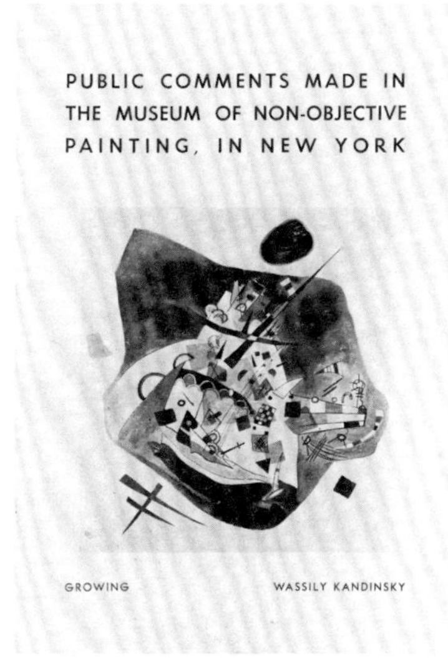

fig. 8
Pamphlet published by Museum of Non-Objective Painting, New York
Collection Musée National d'Art Moderne, Centre Georges Pompidou, Paris, Kandinsky Bequest

Kandinsky felt that neither *Cubism and Abstract Art* nor the 1938 Bauhaus exhibition—both organized by Alfred Barr at The Museum of Modern Art in New York—showed him in his best light. He was simply glad to know that much of his work was in safekeeping with Karl Nierendorf, a dealer in New York, out of danger of being destroyed by the war.[41] While the northern half of France was occupied, Varian Fry in Marseilles regularly sent Kandinsky messages from Barr (referred to as "cousin Barr" to fool the censors) urging him to leave for America—and bring his old paintings with him.[42] But Kandinsky remained in Neuilly, and New York remained forever in the realm of dreams: "Nothing gigantic about it, no hint of its limitless possibilities. To me New York is like a pretty little garden-city, a strange dream."[43] His only traveling was prosaic: daily walks in the Bois de Boulogne or at Bagatelle, with an occasional expedition as far as the Parc Monceau.

A Relatively Isolated Existence

Although Kandinsky was not a recluse, he did live alongside Paris rather than in it.[44] He was getting older, fearing the onset of illness. His apartment was far from the center of Paris and its art life. He missed his friends from earlier days—Paul Klee, Will Grohmann, Anni and Josef Albers. The Paris he had known in 1906—the Post-Impressionists' Paris, the world of parks that the Nabis had painted—was gone. At least he was able to see some Gauguins again at Wildenstein's and remember how dazzled he had been by the

41. Letter from Kandinsky to Homer Saint-Gaudens, director of the Museum of Art, Carnegie Institute, Pittsburgh, dated Feb. 5, 1940. Xerox preserved in the Kandinsky Archive, MNAM.

42. Fry was in charge of the Centre Américain de Secours in Marseilles. In particular, letter dated May 7, 1941.

43. Nina Kandinsky, p. 230.

44. In a letter to Grohmann dated Feb. 11, 1935, and in a letter to Arnold Schönberg dated July 1, 1936, Kandinsky said he wished to keep aloof from the atmosphere of intrigue that flourished in the Paris art world but that at the same time it was not very advantageous to keep aloof because there, more than anywhere else that he knew of, it was important to know the right people.

Gauguin retrospective at the Salon d'Automne in 1906.[45] He was also glad to find some paintings by the Douanier Rousseau he had never seen before, at Paul Rosenberg's gallery. But of the friendships dating from the *Blaue Reiter* period few were left. Matisse was now in Nice. Pierre Girieud had given way to academicism—and was now executing frescoes for the university hall in Poitiers. Albert Gleizes was living hermit-like in Serrière and teaching pottery to a few disciples who were attempting a sort of return to nature. Kandinsky had to build up a whole network of acquaintances from scratch, especially since what he had thought would be a merely intermediate stage was proving to be the longest period he had ever spent in one place, and indeed in the same apartment: eleven years.

The Apartment-cum-Painter's Studio

A number of critics, art historians and curators went as on pilgrimages to Kandinsky's small, cozy seventh-floor apartment at 135, boulevard de la Seine (now du général Koenig) in Neuilly (fig. 9). The building had just been finished when he moved into it. The pilgrims did not find much to look at on the walls of his place—it was nothing like the huge, baroque, very turn-of-the-century apartment on the rue La Boétie that Picasso had turned into a studio in 1920.[46] Kandinsky managed to fit into his small rooms the jumble of furniture from his Munich days that Gabriele Münter had given back to him in 1926.[47] It was all pretty old-fashioned except for the Breuer table and chairs in the dining room. Kandinsky painted the walls black and white and pink, the way they had been in Dessau. Grohmann wrote in his monograph, "... he furnished his apartment with great care, making the tiny dining room look exactly like the one in Dessau ...."[48] In her memoirs, Nina Kandinsky wrote:

> *Kandinsky had decided to use the largest room in the apartment as his studio; but once the paintings, the shelves, the three easels and the rest of his professional equipment had been fitted in, there was very little room left for him to paint in. ... Since Kandinsky died, I have changed hardly anything in the apartment. The collection of little multicolored Chinese figurines still stands on the bookshelves in the living room, just the way Kandinsky had arranged them, and the antique icons in his studio continue to hang where he hung them. He did not want anything but those icons in his studio, and especially not his own creations; nothing was supposed to distract him from his work; with bare walls he was sure he would be able to concentrate.*[49]

Kandinsky does not seem to have attached a great deal of importance to this apartment; most often it is mentioned in his correspondence in connection with heating problems. Only the windows were important: he loved to look at the sky, watch the light, the clouds that played with the smoke rising from the factories at Puteaux, the fishermen waiting at the water's edge, the rowers on the Seine.[50] He admired the flowering chestnut trees (see cat. nos. 15–17).[51]

45. Paris, [Wildenstein's] Galerie de la Gazette des Beaux-Arts, *La Vie ardente de Paul Gauguin,* Paris, Dec. 1936. This was accompanied by a catalogue by Raymond Cogniat with an introduction by Henri Focillon. The same year *Le Cinquantenaire du Symbolisme,* an exhibition of manuscripts, autographs, prints, paintings, sculptures, rare editions, portraits and objets d'art, was presented by the Bibliothèque Nationale, Paris.

46. Kandinsky's apartment was rented from the Caisse nationale des dépôts et consignations.

47. Nina Kandinsky, p. 250: "The furniture arrived from Munich in 1926. To the furniture and the everyday household objects, Gabriele Münter added fourteen paintings and several sketches."

48. Grohmann, p. 221.

49. Nina Kandinsky, pp. 24, 190.

50. The view from the window often provided the metaphors for Kandinsky's writings, for example, "Line and Fish" in *Axis,* no. 2, Apr. 1935, p. 6, and the theme of the poem "La Promenade" published in *L'Art abstrait, ses origines, ses premiers maîtres,* Paris, 1950, p. 167. The correspondence with Grohmann is studded with references to light and the view, for example letters dated Jan. 7, 1934, and Dec. 3, 1937.

51. In a letter to Alberto Magnelli dated May 9, 1942: "Our boulevard de la Seine is a real poem, because of its chestnut trees."

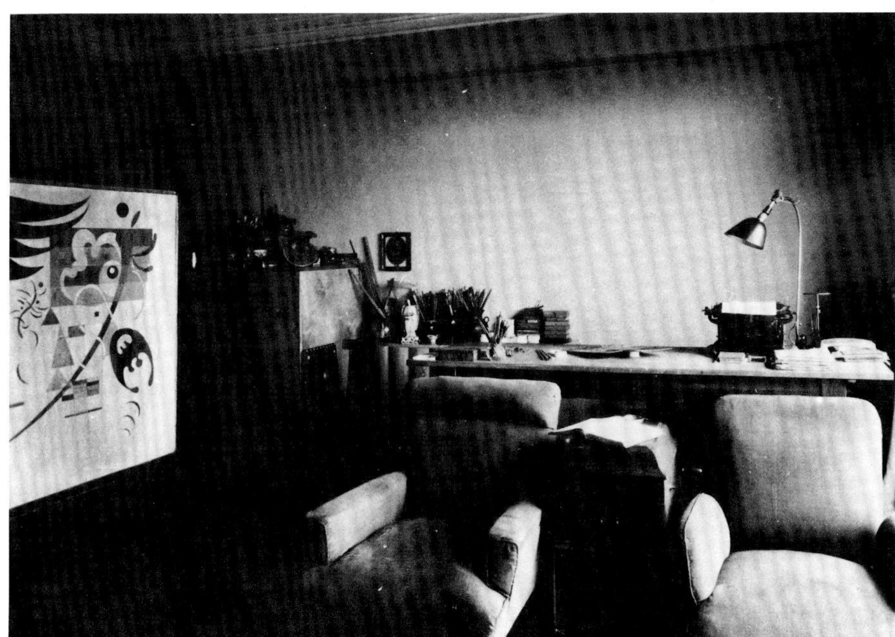

fig. 9
Kandinsky's studio in Neuilly-sur-Seine, photographed shortly after his death
Collection Musée National d'Art Moderne, Centre Georges Pompidou, Paris, Kandinsky Bequest

He worked regularly and lived entirely for his painting. No event stands out in his life, except for a few weeks' summer vacation.[52] His Paris years can be divided into two phases. First, from 1933 to 1939, he kept up with what was happening in the art world, took part in shows, wrote and painted a great deal. His studio was an international pole of attraction; any artist or critic visiting Paris had to go there. Then, starting in 1940, life became more difficult. There were restrictions on food, heating, everything; materials for drawing and painting became scarce.[53] Most artists, dealers and critics left the city. Visitors were rare in the extreme. Yet, despite the war and the risks it entailed, Kandinsky was abundantly optimistic—as witness these two excerpts from his correspondence with Pierre Bruguière, an art collector who was a judge at that time in Tours:[54]

> *March 14, 1942*
> *. . . By and large, we personally have nothing serious to complain about. From our windows we had a very clear view of the bombardment on March 3 and for some time we were naive enough to think it was a marvelous display of fireworks. My wife is somewhat worried because of the number of factory smokestacks at Puteaux, just across the river, but I am confident that the English will not bomb a built-up area where houses surround the factories on all sides and come up very close to them; besides the factories in Puteaux are quite small affairs. But after a long "intermission" we can hear the sirens' song again, a very strange and disturbing type of music. None of this prevents me from getting a lot of work done, and it is with the greatest of pleasure that I will show you my new paintings.*

52. Letter from Kandinsky to Grohmann dated June 25, 1943. Correspondence between France and Germany had become possible again, and Kandinsky was happy to be able to write to Grohmann, who had remained in Germany. Kandinsky told him that in 1942 he and Nina had not been able to go away on summer vacation and had to make do with the Bois de Boulogne and the Parc de Bagatelle, both within walking distance.
53. Food rationing had no influence on the themes Kandinsky chose. Not so with Georges Braque, who in 1940 painted a tempting *Ham,* a sumptuous *Kitchen Table* and the portrait of his *Stove.*
54. These are included in the twenty-five letters from Kandinsky to Bruguière published by the author in *Les Cahiers du Musée Nationale d'Art Moderne,* no. 9, 1982, pp. 84-109. This correspondence sheds light on little-known aspects of life in the Paris art world during the German Occupation of 1940-44.

April 7, 1943
As you heard yesterday or the day before, the bombardment spared us. While I was writing you those hypothetical questions I completely forgot the bombing, though it made a violent impression on us. We had just finished lunch when we heard the planes, definitely not German, they must have been British or American. The alert sounded too late; the two explosions at the racetrack claimed so many victims. A little later we could see from our windows a tremendous fire in the direction of Saint-Cloud: the Coty factory was burning. The bomb explosions at the Raynault [sic] *factory could not be heard from our place; the damage is supposed to be terrible. I was sorry, after you came to see us, that I had forgotten to show you the drawings you wanted to see.*

The Pleasure of Painting

In the course of his eleven years in Neuilly, Kandinsky produced 144 paintings, about 250 watercolors and gouaches and many India ink and pencil drawings.[55] His last canvas, *Delicate Tensions* (cat. no. 130), dates from the summer of 1942. After that he stopped doing easel painting and gouaches and produced only hybrids of the techniques, a series of Lilliputian gouache-and-oils on cardboard that were halfway between paintings and "colored drawings." Why did Kandinsky revert to the kinds of tempera works he had exhibited at the Salon d'Automne from 1904 to 1907? Was it easier for him, less tiring, to paint flat on a table? Was he anxious to go faster? It would seem, judging from two or three paintings on board left unfinished, that he undertook regular series of such works during this period.

Most of the time there is no relationship between the gouache-watercolors and the paintings. Whereas the watercolor *Reunited Surfaces* of August 1934 (cat. no. 55) can be considered a very detailed preliminary study for *Two Green Points* of the following April (cat. no. 54), many other gouaches, on the contrary, merely reproduce, with some variations, details from the painted compositions. For instance, the untitled gouache entered as cat. no. 638 in Kandinsky's Handlist of watercolors, actually shows the details of the lower left portion of the canvas *Complex-Simple* painted the year before, 1939. But most of the gouaches and watercolors are authentically original works in their own right, with their own series of preliminary drawings leading up to them. The troubled years just before and at the beginning of the war gave Kandinsky an insatiable appetite for works on paper, to the detriment of easel painting. To produce a series of "colored drawings" took less room and cost less. When Kandinsky first settled in Paris, he began with watercolors: thirty-four of them in one year, compared with twelve paintings. By 1940 the year's output was ten oil paintings and sixty gouache-watercolors—to which he stopped giving titles.

It was logical for Kandinsky's work to fall into two categories, major and minor. Kandinsky was trying to broaden his market. He asked very high prices for the oil paintings, which made them unattainable for Parisian and other European art collectors. But the gouaches were still within reach of the

55. Nina Kandinsky, pp. 207, 247. According to Nina Kandinsky, her husband stopped painting in July 1944. But on May 24 Jeanne Bucher had already written to Nina Kandinsky: "Let's hope Kandinsky gets well again."

art lovers who frequented such circles as the Galerie des "Cahiers d'Art" or the Galerie Jeanne Bucher—which "placed" several of the works on paper with some of the "occupants" during the war.

We have to keep this split-level market in mind in order to understand what Kandinsky produced in Paris. The canvases are never repetitious and incorporate all of his plastic research. They remained piled up in his studio until 1939, when they were sent south for safekeeping to the Aveyron region.[56]

After the summer of 1942 he devoted all his time to gouaches and works combining several techniques; less dense than the paintings, conveying less tension, they were close relatives or iridescent reflections of the "bagatelles" of his earlier days. They were meant to be instantly appealing. As such, they were probably more influenced by the spirit of the times than the paintings were.

Kandinsky did not go into detail about his methods. While his letters are full of allusions to his leisure activities, his walks and excursions, he was very secretive when it came to his creative life. We have to rely on what Nina Kandinsky wrote: "It was Kandinsky's practice, unlike Klee's, to concentrate on only one work at a time; he never began a new painting until the previous one was finished."[57] This was chiefly true for the large canvases but we must not assume that it was an inflexible rule. Zervos pointed out in his "Notes sur Kandinsky" in 1934 that "sometimes he works on three different paintings at the same time."[58]

It would be interesting to know how long each step in the process of maturation took: first, the conceptual discovery of a given form, then rough versions of it in a sketchbook, then letting it decant from line drawing to line drawing as Kandinsky envisaged its pictorial projection, and finally the execution of the painting itself. In some instances the preliminary sketches were followed very quickly by the final composition; in others—as in the earlier periods—years might go by between the first step and the last. In a note he sent to Freundlich in 1938, Kandinsky used his work as an excuse for not attending a party. Those few lines give us an idea of Kandinsky's enthusiasm for his art and also a glimpse of how he went about it: "I have just finished one painting and am already at work on the preliminary drawings for the next one. I must do something in order to get rid of such habits or I won't manage to find time for any vacation. I have had this new painting in my mind since January, and must get it down on canvas !"[59]

The formats Kandinsky used for his paintings had always varied widely, and at no point more than during the Paris years. Some of his formats were disconcerting, ones not usually found at a Paris art-supply shop; after 1941 this can be explained by the difficulty of finding the right materials, but for the earlier years there must be some other explanation.[60] A sort of seasonal rhythm emerged as large formats alternated with small. It also seems that Kandinsky was determined, by means of this alternating pattern, to avoid the risk of repeating himself; whenever he became too used to any given format, he abandoned it and adopted another, more eccentric one, making him look at his own compositions with a fresh eye.

56. Sixty-five paintings were placed in the care of M. Emile Redon, at Saint-Félix de Sorgues, Aveyron, on Sept. 27, 1939.

57. Nina Kandinsky, p. 225.

58. Christian Zervos, "Notes sur Kandinsky: à propos de sa récente exposition à la Galerie des 'Cahiers d'Art,'" *Cahiers d'Art,* 9e année, no. 5-8, 1934, pp. 149-157. This article is actually a long interview, transcribed and modified by Zervos.

59. Letter from Kandinsky to Freundlich dated July 15, 1938. Letters to Freundlich cited in these notes are preserved in the Archives de la donation Freundlich au Musée de Pontoise.

60. Concerning the standard dimensions for stretchers and frames in use among art suppliers, see Xavier de Langlais, *La Technique de la peinture à l'huile,* Paris, 1959, pp. 406-407.

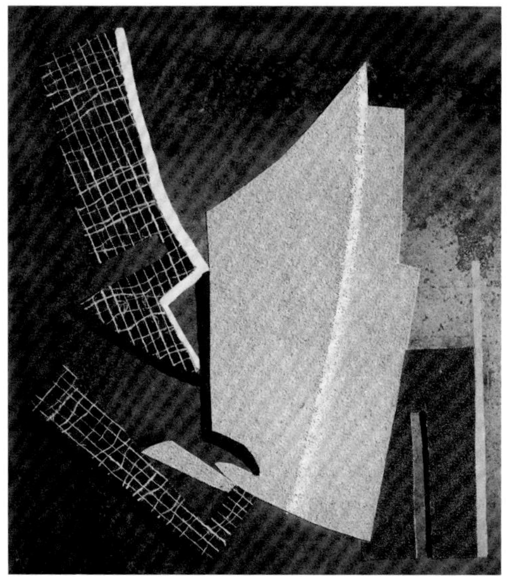

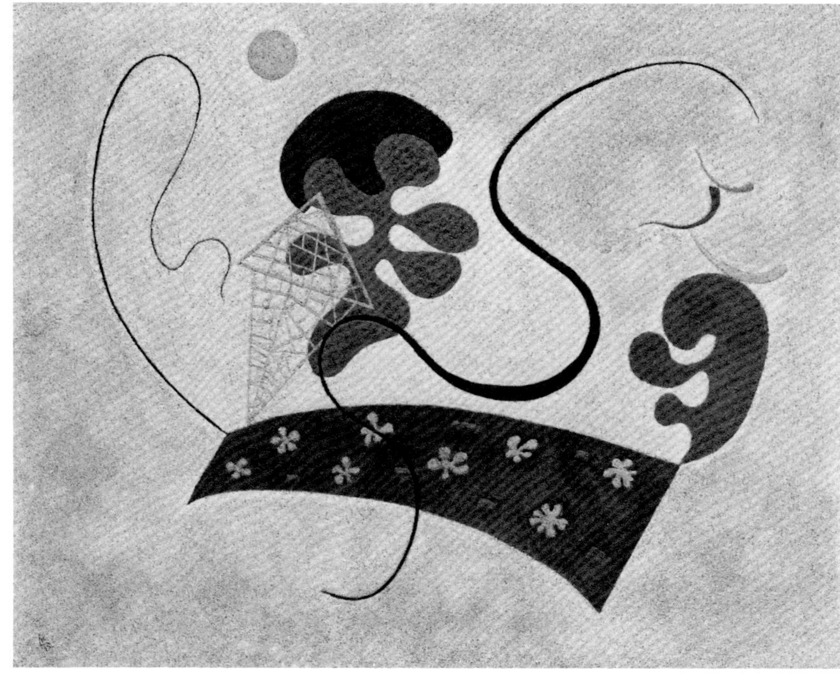

fig. 10
Alberto Magnelli
Collage on Sheet-Iron. 1938
Whereabouts unknown

fig. 11
Vasily Kandinsky
Balancing Act. February 1935
Oil with sand on canvas
Private Collection

From 1935 to 1938, a sort of golden age within his Paris period, Kandinsky clearly preferred two large formats referred to in the trade in Paris as "*40 figure*" (100 x 81 cm., or 39⅜ x 31⅞") and "*50 figure*" (116 x 89 cm., or 45⅝ x 35"). He usually used them horizontally. Twelve of his paintings were *40 figure,* twenty-two were *50 figure.* So these were all fairly large canvases, considerably larger than those of the Bauhaus period; yet none of the paintings from his final decade in Paris approached the sizes of his large compositions of 1913.

In his inventory Kandinsky listed two paintings from this Paris period in the category of *Compositions*: *Composition IX* (cat. no. 7), painted in 1936 and purchased in 1939 by the Musée du Jeu de Paume, and *Composition X* (cat. no. 105), begun late in 1938, completed in 1939, and now in the Kunstsammlung Nordrhein-Westfalen, Düsseldorf. Oddly enough, Kandinsky did not include in the same category another *120 figure* (195 x 140 cm., or 76¾ x 55⅛"), the largest Parisian commercial format, which he rightly considered one of his most beautiful creations of that period. It is *Dominant Curve,* 1936 (cat. no. 6), which Peggy Guggenheim bought immediately after she organized the Kandinsky show of 1939 in her London gallery, and now in the Solomon R. Guggenheim Museum Collection.

Kandinsky did not choose his formats on the basis of any contract with the dealers nor, apparently, with any future exhibition in mind. The choice was strictly up to him and his "inner necessity." He bought his stretchers one by one, as the need arose, partly to avoid spending much at any one time, even though he had enough money, and partly because he did not have room to store anything cumbersome. As a result, he was caught unprepared by the

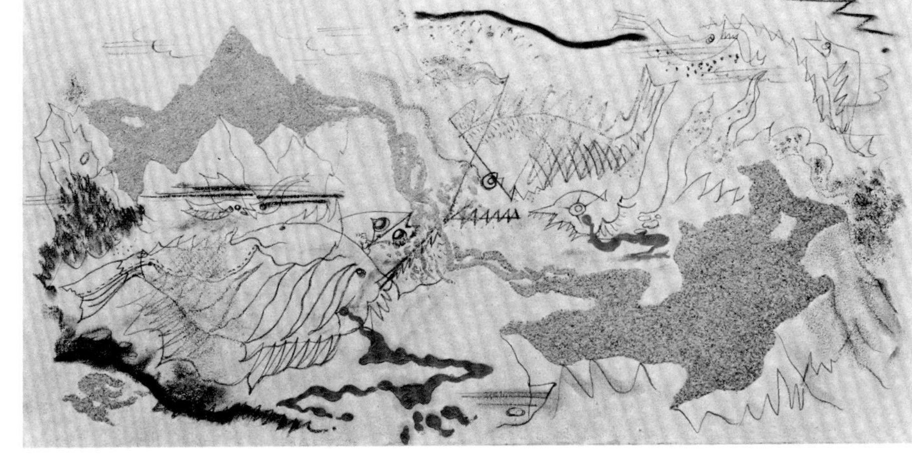

fig. 12
André Masson
Battle of Fishes. 1926
Sand, gesso, oil, pencil and charcoal on canvas
Collection The Museum of Modern Art, New York. Purchase
Reproduced in *La Révolution Surréaliste,* 1927

war and had run out of unused canvas by 1941.[61] He did not solve the problem until 1943, when by some unexplained means he acquired a stock of German cardboard of medium format (42 x 58 cm., or 16½ x 22⅞")—it was on this he painted most of his last works.

Kandinsky was somewhat hesitant about trying out new materials and remained faithful to the German art-suppliers. Every time his nephew Kojève went to Berlin, Kandinsky asked him to bring back tempera paints.[62] Kandinsky made few changes in his technique. He continued to flout the rules taught in all the art schools by mixing tempera and oils, drawing on painted surfaces with India ink, using enamel, and so on. But he did not try his hand at collages, which had become fashionable again in Paris around 1930 (fig. 10), nor at frottages, which he admired in Max Ernst's work. He took part in the collage and photomontage show organized in London in 1939 by Peggy Guggenheim and Hans Arp—by exhibiting a sand painting called *Rayé (Striped)* (cat. no. 29).[63] Sand painting was the only technical innovation Kandinsky adopted upon his arrival in Paris (fig. 11); by 1936 he had exhausted its possibilities. He knew some of Masson's sand paintings, which had been reproduced in the Surrealist magazines (fig. 12),[64] and had seen the very thick, hard-baked surfaces of Braque's most recent works. He was also in touch with Willi Baumeister, who specialized in large mural painting projects. Kandinsky contacted as well the organizers of the first *Salon de l'art mural* in Paris.[65] It is surprising to find Kandinsky's name among the participants in a salon that brought together what were for the most part academic painters—Aman-Jean and Paul Colin, for example—conformist critics and figures from the museum world. An ephemeral affair, the Salon was presided over by Eugenio d'Ors and by Amédée Ozenfant, who must have been the hard worker behind it all. Curiously enough, the two important decorators of 1937, Fernand Léger and Robert Delaunay, are not included in the list.

To assert his new Paris manner Kandinsky sent his multitechnique paintings to the shows of the period. They caused a sensation at *Thèse-Antithèse-Synthèse,* the international exhibition in Lucerne in 1935.[66] Among the principal organizers of this show, one of the most complete and best documented

61. In a notebook Kandinsky kept track of the orders he placed for stretchers and canvas: on Mar. 24, 1942, two *50 figure,* one *50 paysage,* two *40 figure* and one *80 figure* ordered from Lefèbvre-Foinet; one *50 figure* and one *40 figure* ordered from Sennelier. It seems that these orders were not delivered in full.
62. Letter from Kandinsky to Kojève dated May 18, 1934.
63. London, Guggenheim Jeune, *Exhibition of Collages, Papiers Collés, and Photo-Montages,* Nov. 3-26, 1938.
64. *La Révolution Surréaliste,* no. 9-10, Oct. 1, 1927, p. 10 (Masson [sable]); no. 11, Mar. 15, 1928, p. 23 (Masson, "une métamorphose").
65. Paris, 64 bis, rue La Boétie, *Salon de l'art mural,* May 31-June 30, 1935.
66. Zervos reported in *Cahiers d'Art,* 9e année, no. 9-10, 1934, p. 272, that the exhibition ranged from "the subtle, infinitely mobile, sparkling works by Kandinsky" to "Mondrian's limpid, taut, pitiless compositions."

exhibitions of abstract art in the 1930s, was Hans Erni, a Swiss painter whose own work at the time was abstract. In his report on the exhibition in the English magazine *Axis,* Erni placed more emphasis on Kandinsky's technical innovation than on the new plastic vocabulary he was developing in Paris: ". . . While the works 'Monde bleu' (1934), 'Violet dominant' (1934), 'Deux entourages' (1934) with their delicate, pale-coloured surface shapes on an even, clear background, and the flat-toned pictures carried out in a fine sand technique, must be considered as illustrations full of the meaning of his prudent existence in Paris."[67]

Also in 1935 Parisians were able to see Kandinsky's recent works in *Nouvelles toiles, aquarelles, dessins,* the second show Yvonne Zervos organized in his honor at the Galerie des "Cahiers d'Art."[68] Several of the works shown were reproduced in the first issue of *Cahiers d'Art* published after the exhibition. Shortly thereafter, Kandinsky granted an interview to the Italian daily *Il lavoro fascista.* Among other things, he discussed technique:

> *But let us not speak anymore of books and theories on paper. Now then, did you see my exhibition? As you may remember, I gathered in* Cahiers d'Art *ten very recent paintings, twenty-five gouaches and watercolors, also recent, and twenty-eight drawings that span the period from 1910–1934. In the majority of the compositions on canvas I used a sand technique more or less consistently, but I usually don't distinguish between traditional oil painting, gouache, tempera and watercolor, and I even simultaneously use the various techniques in the same work. What is essential for me is to be able to clearly convey what I want,* to recount my dream. *I consider both technique and form to be mere instruments of expression, and my stories, furthermore, are not narrative or historical in character, but purely pictorial.*[69]

Kandinsky used a sort of dry technique in Paris, evenly, patiently, carefully spreading a thin coat of color. His tones were mat and perfectly smooth. Every detail was colored with infinite thoroughness, which contributed to the tense construction of the whole. Shapes and colors participated equally in the play of balance and imbalance among the motifs, conceived as a battle of great bipartite antagonists (fig. 13). Kandinsky made instability interact with inextricableness. In bringing together the infinitely small with the infinitely large, he was not overly concerned with the scale of the elements he brought into play: in *Sky Blue* (cat. no. 116) a scattering of microbian creatures is sown over the blueness of space like snowflakes suddenly motionless in a winter sky.

With *Each for Himself* (cat. no. 22), one of the first canvases Kandinsky painted after moving to Neuilly, he clearly demonstrated his aesthetics of complexity. "Since the winter of 1933, [Kandinsky] has been working in Paris. The first of his Paris paintings, *Each for Himself,* was done in tempera and oils; it is composed of nine entities, so to speak, each with its own life. The difficulty lay in linking these nine independent existences so as to make a unified painting out of them. Kandinsky succeeded by using signs and tones that bring his canvas into perfect balance."[70]

67. Hans Erni, "The Lucerne Exhibition," *Axis,* no. 2, Apr. 1935, pp. 27, 28.

68. The exhibition opened on June 21, 1935. In his review in *La Bête noire,* no. 4, July 1935, p. 5, Maurice Raynal wrote: "Why didn't the organizers of the Salon de l'art mural invite Kandinsky or Miró, if they really intended to show us walls on which something could happen." A. Bognard noted in his review in *Beaux-Arts,* no. 131, July 5, 1935: "One is aware not so much of the peculiar substance these panels are made of, as of the decoratively graceful hieroglyphics that cover them."

69. *Il lavoro fascista,* vol. XIII, July 28, 1935, p. 4. On the occasion of the same show Arp's poem on Kandinsky was published in the Danish magazine *Konkretion,* no. 1, Sept. 15, 1935, pp. 4–5.

70. Zervos, "Notes sur Kandinsky," p. 154.

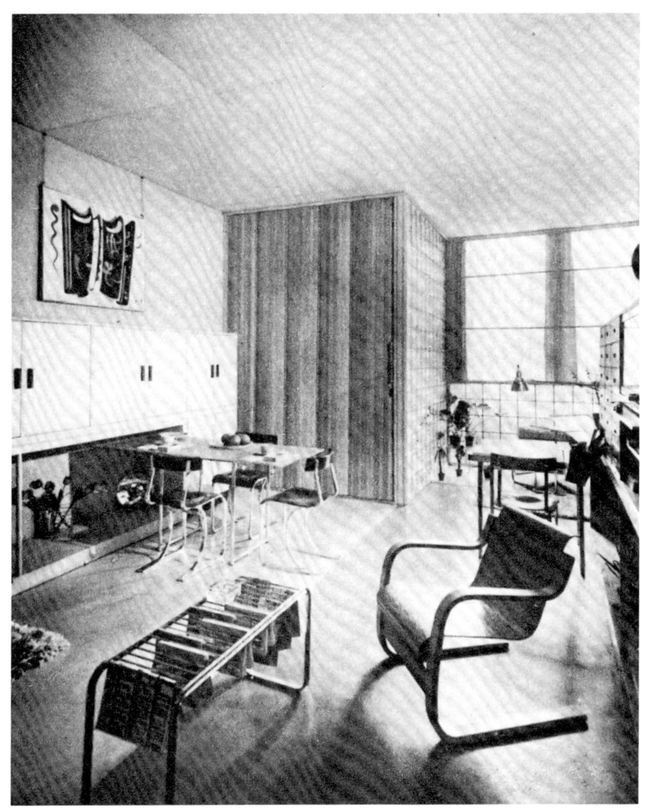

fig. 13
Kandinsky's *Brown with Supplement* (cat. no. 53) in photograph of "Intellectual's Living Room" in P. D'Uckerman, *L'Art dans la vie moderne,* Paris, 1937, p. 115, fig. 5

The novel aspect here is the reversion to drawing, to meticulously defined shapes. Earlier, in his Murnau period, drawing had been submerged by painting; his composition was based on the equilibrium among spots of color. Although it would be an exaggeration to say that as Kandinsky grew older he became above all a draftsman, it is true that during his Paris period line and color became equally important.

He did not scribble any more. His line was less lyrical, less rapid, less open than in the notes he had earlier jotted down on paper for *Composition IV* or *Composition VII.* He actually sketched a great deal less, hesitated less over what he wanted. Although the Kandinsky Archive houses several hundred drawings from the Paris period alone, there are seldom more than one or two preparatory sketches for his most important compositions: only one in pen and ink for *Composition IX,* none at all for *Composition X.* Possibly Kandinsky destroyed some of his preliminary drawings, since no one was supposed to see them.

They are generally done in pencil and are very deliberate, with even the least important detail worked out once and for all. No effect of light and shadow, of course; no trace of blurring, no erasure. They are definitive drawings, ready to be squared. Sometimes Kandinsky did a second drawing, in India ink, in which he rearranged various elements. His choice of colors was already made and indicated on the drawing in Russian abbreviations. Each drawing was like a musical score, ready to be played. They are rarely dated and initialled—which clearly shows that in Kandinsky's mind they were totally different from the drawings that were shown on their own merits at various exhibitions. Kandinsky exhibited drawings in order to prove that he was capable of drawing and to lay to rest the somewhat simplistic notion that "the abstract painters" used colors because they did not know how to use line. He says so explicitly in his *Il lavoro fascista* interview:

> *I must first of all assure you that drawing has a much stronger significance in my art than in realistic or figurative painting and that the errors in drawing of the so-called* abstractionists *are more easily perceptible than the imperfections in drawing of the others. The graphic essays that I exhibited tend to belie the opinion of those who believe that abstract painting consists only of chromatic whims. In fact, more than one observor has discovered coloristic value in my black and white drawings that include extreme linear simplifications and complicated and imaginary forms.*[71]

Like many other painters, Kandinsky drew when it was impossible for him to paint. Every year he allowed himself a few weeks' vacation—and took along his pads and colored pencils. In 1941, when his studio was underheated, he began a sketchbook of very thorough ink drawings.[72] Most of these were signed and dated. In later years several of them were used as models for the last works he painted on cardboard. Nina Kandinsky described how her husband used to draw in the evening:

> *In the light of an electric lamp, he did only drawings. . . . He had the rare ability to visualize the world of his paintings in his head, with their colors and their shapes, exactly as he carried them out on canvas later. His flashes of inspiration were like high-speed snapshots that appeared to him in a state of illumination, and he tried to get them down on paper immediately, using small quick strokes. At this very first stage in the process he decided on the main colors. Using these sketches, he carried out the original drawings from which he later painted his canvases.*[73]

Close friends—among them Alberto Magnelli—paid tribute to Kandinsky as a master of drawing. In Magnelli's words, they were struck by "how distinct each sign was, how each shape he conceived was perfectly clear; nothing was left to chance, nothing was unforeseen."[74] In each of his final paintings the drawing remained highly visible. The shape of every colored area was very sharply delineated; sometimes he even outlined those areas in black or white.

He moved toward pastel colors, and recommended the use of "mixed" tones, rather than pure colors. "The purples shade off into lilac and the lilacs into purple. But where does the purple end, where does the lilac begin?" By playing on so-called clashes to the point of letting color collapse and decompose, he stood on the very brink of kitsch. His only genuinely theoretical text, "La Valeur d'une oeuvre concrète," published in 1939 in the magazine *XXe Siècle,* reveals some of the guiding principles behind his work of that period: the careful balance between shape and spot, the play of tension-via-color between the large colored surfaces and the tiny dots of color. Although

71. *Il lavoro fascista,* p. 4.
72. *Kandinsky, carnet de dessins, 1941,* Paris, 1972. Text by Gaëtan Picon. The thirty-nine drawings are reproduced in this book, published on the occasion of their exhibition at the Galerie Karl Flinker, Paris; the drawings were sold separately at this time.
73. Nina Kandinsky, p. 191.
74. Alberto Magnelli, "Kandinsky le peintre" in Max Bill, ed., *Wassily Kandinsky,* Paris, 1951, pp. 17-18.

the dots are barely perceptible at first, he depends on them to bring the composition ultimately into balance: "One little spot can be given such a strong accent."

Bruguière paraphrased that idea in a letter he wrote to Kandinsky from Tours, where he had only a few Kandinsky gouaches to keep him company: "An infinitesimal, almost invisible change of just one color can suddenly make the entire work limitlessly irreproachable."[75] Other painters were surprised and perplexed by Kandinsky's unconventional and disconcerting use of color. Magnelli praised him in these terms: "His range of colors is wonderfully varied. He carried out every possible combination without flinching from the most dangerous rapprochements. In this way he was able to convey the greatest tenderness without hesitating."[76]

At the same time as his palette approached Art Nouveau delicacy, Kandinsky reverted to a technique that had won attention for his first entries at the Salon d'Automne at the beginning of the century: black backgrounds. On black paper or paper colored black, he used tempera to deposit a few spots of color—and this was enough to make the whole surface vibrate immediately with phosphorescent spots and filaments—as in *White Line* (cat. no. 10), purchased by the Musée du Jeu de Paume in 1937. Kandinsky was not the only one to use this graphic device. In 1933 Miró painted *Forms on a Black Background* (cat. no. 103).[77] The poet Henri Michaux was beginning his parallel career as calligrapher and produced gouaches and pastels on black backgrounds. One of these, *Prince of the Night* of 1937 (cat. no. 106), is certainly among the most poetic examples of his art.[78]

Kandinsky rarely transposed this technique from works on paper to easel paintings. In his book *On the Spiritual in Art,* he expressed his aversion to black, calling it "eternal silence, without future." He did make considerable use of black in 1922 in his murals for the Juryfreie exhibition in Berlin, but this was an exception, for decorative purposes only. During his Paris period, he produced two paintings that relied solely on the positive-negative interplay of black and white: *Black Forms on White* (cat. no. 45), in 1934, and *Thirty* (cat. no. 68), in 1937. In them Kandinsky verified the effects of the new vocabulary of forms that he was in the process of working out; his axiom was that any shape or pictogram painted black on a white ground looked larger than the same shape or pictogram painted white on black. The only large polychrome work on a flat black ground Kandinsky attempted was *Composition X* (cat. no. 105), an oil painting that looks like a gouache on a monumental scale, in which he overcame his fear of spreading black over a broad area. He even went beyond the prohibition that Malevich had laid down when he decreed that his *Black Square* was the culmination of Constructivism and the utmost limit of easel painting. Kandinsky never again used black in this way on canvas, and black backgrounds were fairly rare among the cardboard paintings he carried out between 1942 and 1944.

Recently, Frank Stella has discerned in the paintings of Kandinsky's Paris period an attempt to go beyond the two-dimensional universe of abstract art. He finds that Kandinsky managed to create a new type of pictorial space without, however, reverting to old-fashioned perspective and three-

75. Letter from Bruguière to Kandinsky dated Jan. 30, 1944. Compare this quotation with the following excerpt from Kandinsky's "L'Art concret," published in *XXe Siècle,* no. 1, Mar. 1938, translated as "Concrete Art" in Lindsay and Vergo II, pp. 816-817: "And how painful it is to see this small point where it does not belong! You have the impression of eating a meringue and of tasting pepper instead. A flower with the odor of rot. . . . Rot—that's the word! Composition becomes decomposition. It's death."

76. Magnelli, "Kandinsky le peintre," p. 17.

77. Reproduced in *Axis,* no. 6, Summer 1936, p. 7.

78. Concerning the fortuitous relationship between Michaux and Kandinsky, see Jean Bouret, "Voyage en grande Garabagne," *Les Lettres françaises,* Dec. 2, 1944.

dimensional illusionism.[79] In about 1934 Kojève had meditated on the same aspect of his uncle's work and compared the spatial effect Kandinsky created before the 1930s with that which gradually emerged thereafter in his paintings. Previously, said Kojève, Kandinsky's painting had been based on a sort of pre-explosive bidimensional unity; the composition was held in place here and there by "protuberances," corners and clamps. The whole thing might explode at any minute—and then no frame or edge would be able to hold anything in. This was the type of spatial effect found in *With the Black Arc* of 1912 (cat. no. 2), whereas after that, Kojève believed, "it was only a coincidence that his new paintings were limited by the dimensions of the paper or canvas; actually, they were as infinite as the world whose aesthetic principles they reflected. Since they are infinite they cannot have a 'center'; or rather—which is the same thing—every point within the painting becomes a 'center.'"[80]

Kandinsky experimented with the traditional painter's device of a painting within a painting. He did this in paintings such as *Complex-Simple* of 1939, which Stella believes shows the artist's studio in very thinly disguised form.[81] Here Kandinsky gives us a new twist on the old theme of the relationship between the painter and his work on the easel, a new version of Vermeer's *The Painter in His Studio*. Kandinsky also goes beyond the two-dimensional space ordinarily expressed on canvas by combining several registers, either of roughly similar dimensions—as in *Thirty*, where he relies on pictograms to convey his effect—or of widely varied sizes—as in *Parties diverses (Various Parts)*, 1940 (cat. no. 118). The latter is like a piece of inlaid work, but he does more than merely assemble separate elements; he takes advantage of the transparency of some of the pieces he has drawn in—those in the panel on the left, especially—has them overlap onto other panels, and by superimposing them so playfully gives tremendous cohesion to his final composition.

New Shapes

The essential feature of Kandinsky's Paris period is the novelty of his shapes. Jean Cassou coined a new word for him: he said Kandinsky "degeometrizes." The basic geometric figures—circle, square, triangle—undergo changes: they become rectangles; the rectangles then turn into trapezoids, as in *Blue World*, 1934 (cat. no. 25); the circles flatten out into ovals. The only fundamental feature of Euclidean geometry that Kandinsky kept was the grid, which is practical for dividing up compositions, as exemplified in *Each for Himself* or *Thirty* (cat. nos. 22, 68; see also figs. 14-17). Minimalistic variations such as those Mondrian wrought on lines and planes did not interest Kandinsky in the least. It was the amorphous, the unexpected that tempted him.

Salvador Dali's first limp paintings caught his attention when they were published in Surrealist reviews; Kandinsky was in Dessau and Berlin at the time. Reproductions of Dali's compositions were among the panoply of pictures that Kandinsky cut out, glued onto cardboard and labeled for use in

79. Stella, "Complexité simple," pp. 84-90.

80. Kandinsky had wanted G. di San Lazzaro to publish Kojève's views in *XXe Siècle* as early as 1938; in fact, they were published only in partial form as Alexandre Kojève, "Pourquoi concret" in "Centenaire de Kandinsky," *XXe Siècle*, vol. XXVII, Dec. 1966, pp. 63-66.

81. Stella, "Complexité simple," p. 88.

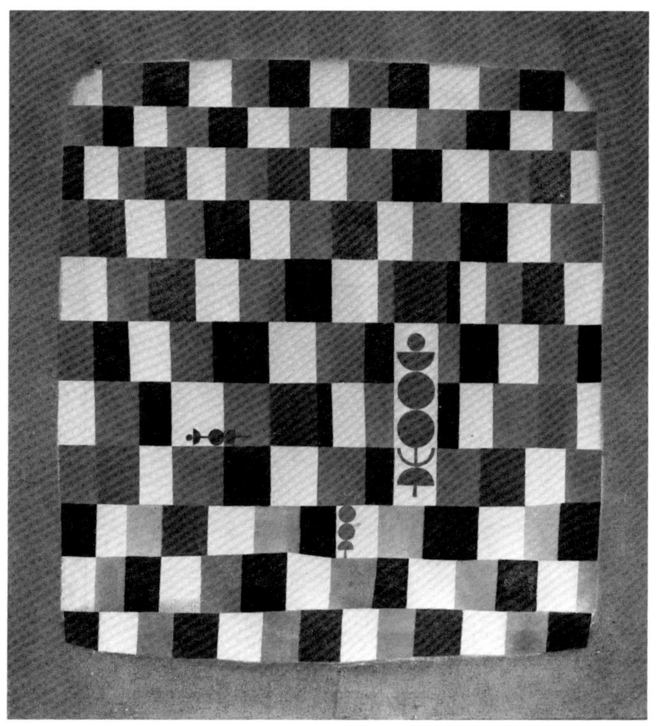

fig. 14
Paul Klee
Überschach. 1937
Oil on canvas
Collection Kunsthaus Zürich

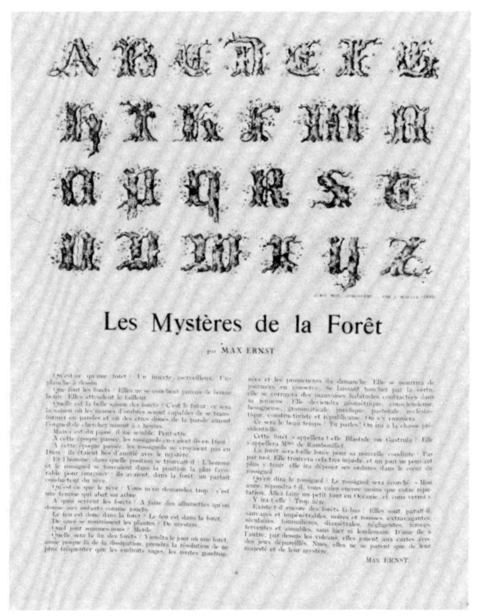

Les Mystères de la Forêt

par MAX ERNST

fig. 15
Max Ernst, "Les Mystères de la forêt" in *Minotaure,* vol. 1, no. 5, May 12, 1934, p. 6

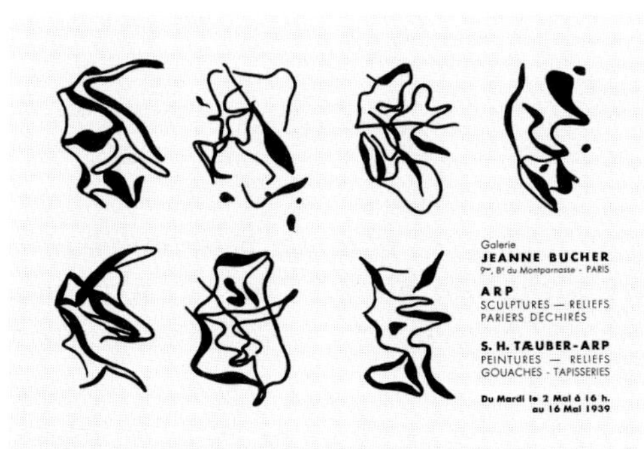

fig. 16
Invitation to exhibition at Galerie Jeanne Bucher, Paris, 1939, with pen and ink drawing by Hans Arp
Collection Fondation Arp, Clamart

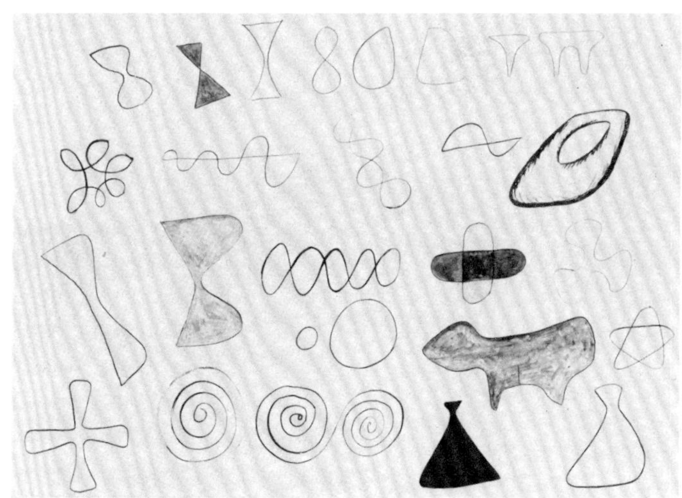

fig. 17
Alexander Calder
Drawing. 1940
Wash on paper
Formerly Collection Willard Gallery, New York

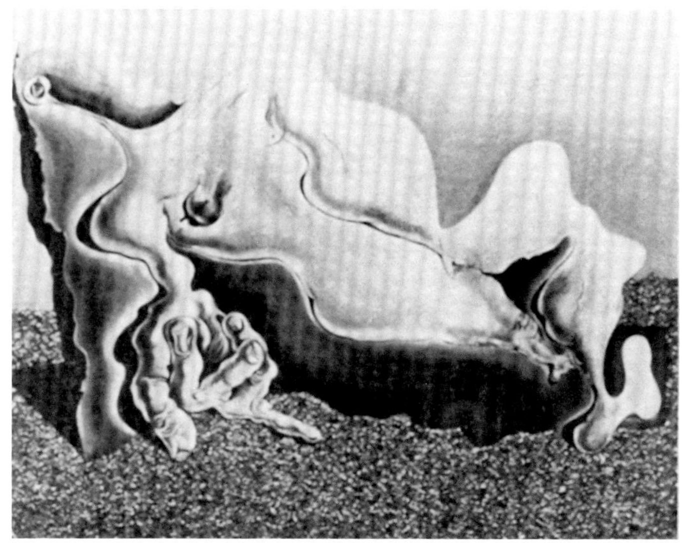

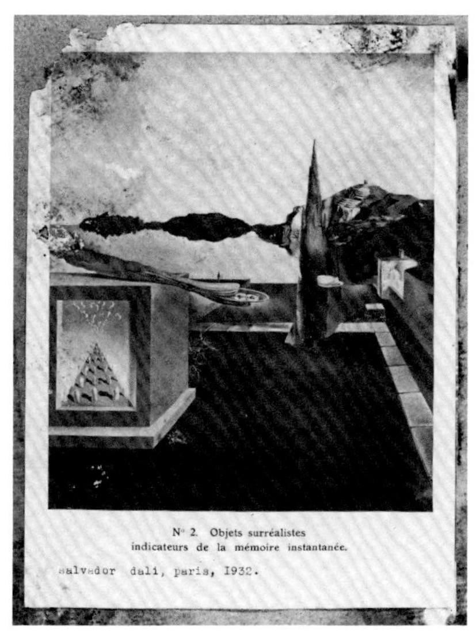

fig. 18
Salvador Dali
Baigneuse. 1928
Oil on panel
Whereabouts unknown

fig. 19
Kandinsky's clipping of work by Salvador Dali for pedagogical documentation
Collection Musée National d'Art Moderne, Centre Georges Pompidou, Paris, Kandinsky Bequest

illustrating his last courses at the Bauhaus (figs. 18, 19). The white corpuscles in Dali's 1929 *Accommodations of Desire* are closely akin to the nine amniotic pouches of *Each for Himself,* which Kandinsky painted five years later.[82] Or again, we could compare the large white jagged-edged mass that inhabits Dali's *Enigma of Desire* of 1929 with Kandinsky's *Black Forms on White* of 1934 (cat. no. 45). It is also instructive to compare the same Kandinsky painting with the cutout wood reliefs that Arp was producing during this period (see cat. nos. 44, 49). For Kandinsky's painted black or white shapes, like Arp's wooden elements of the same colors, are afloat in an undetermined white space. During Kandinsky's visit to Paris in 1933, when he went to Arp's studio in nearby Meudon, he was happy to be able to resume a conversation he had begun with the Alsatian artist-poet in Munich in 1912. Once a nomadic Dadaist, Arp had settled down and experienced a startling conversion: he began to do a series of plaster sculptures that Zervos revealed to the world in *Cahiers d'Art* (fig. 20).[83] In these sculptures Arp was working on forms in gestation, just as his poetry was rooted in the idea of natural growth.

Kandinsky began to investigate the same subject. He cut out pictures from scientific journals—microscopic cross-sections, embryos, extinct animals or animals of very ancient origin such as turtles.[84] This collection was analogous to the one the painter Ozenfant put together to illustrate his ideas on aesthetics, published as a book entitled *Art.*[85] What Kandinsky saw and admired in the curving tip of a fern stem loaded with spores was the astonishing complexity of the forms found in nature. "There is no such thing as a straight line in nature," Delacroix had proclaimed, and Kandinsky took this aphorism to heart. He examined close-ups of insects and tried to determine the precise laws that determined the forms of their integuments. Through the publications of the Muséum National d'Histoire Naturelle, Kandinsky broke out of the straitjacket geometry had placed on him and reintroduced nature into his plastic investigations.

82. *Accommodations des désirs* was reproduced in *La Révolution Surréaliste,* no. 12, Dec. 15, 1929, p. 18.
83. Two reproductions appeared in *Cahiers d'Art,* 8e année, no. 5-6, 1933, p. [236] with the caption: "A sculpture by Arp that shows us what new direction his work has taken since last summer."
84. Kandinsky cut pictures from other kinds of publications as well. In 1932, for example, he asked Zervos to send him a copy of a specific issue of *Cahiers d'Art* so that he could make clippings from it. Some of these clippings were found in the cellar of his apartment house in Neuilly. Mingled among them were exercises by his Bauhaus pupils; these were restored and some were included in the *Kandinsky: Russische Zeit und Bauhausjahre 1915-1933* exhibition of 1984 at the Bauhaus-Archiv, Berlin.
85. Amédée Ozenfant, *Art,* Paris, 1928.

fig. 20
Hans Arp
Concretion. ca. 1933
Whereabouts unknown
Reproduced in *Cahiers d'Art,* 1933

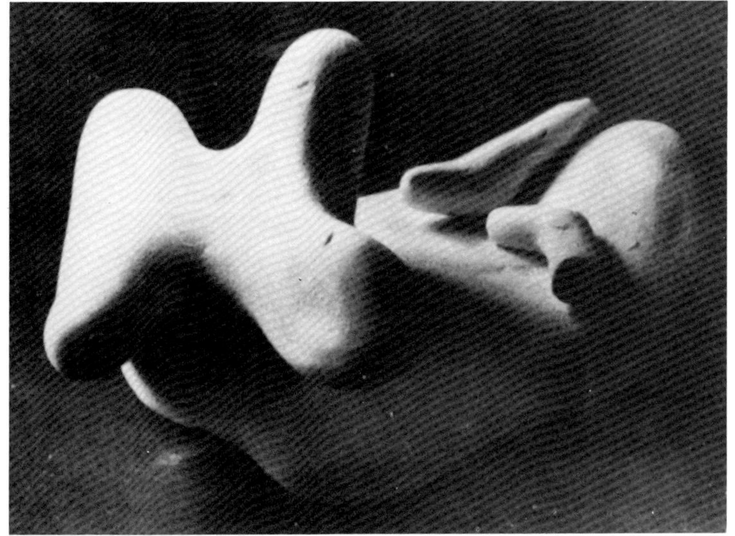

The spirit of the times was marked by a turning toward the cosmos—including comets trailing long tails—and the amorphous. In his most recent work Klee, like Kandinsky, seemed to take his inspiration from "Wertheimer's patterns as *Urformen,* or primordial forms. . . ." growth of forms, metamorphosis of plants.[86] Photographers dwelled on Art Nouveau motifs, and *Minotaure* published close-ups of the cast-iron entrances which Hector Guimard created for the Paris Metro.[87] Dali praised turn-of-the-century creations that had been despised at the time of their execution. *Minotaure* devoted several pages of its luxurious paper to reproductions of Dali's involuntary sculptures: "the shapes that toothpaste takes as it accidentally spills and sprawls become a delicate, ornamental stereotype."

In his biased note on Kandinsky, Zervos decreed, paradoxically, that the poetic Kandinskyesque curving line originated in "a cold cigarette butt lost in an ashtray."[88] The wreath of smoke rising from the cigarette was a caricature of Kandinsky, of course (he was often photographed holding a cigarette, but it was also the evanescent ever-changing curving line that typified his works of the Paris period.[89] It is not just coincidence that his most accomplished work of this period is entitled *Courbe dominante (Dominant Curve)* (cat. no. 6).

86. Marianne L. Teuber, "*Blue Night* by Paul Klee" in *Vision and Artifact,* Mary Henle, ed., New York, 1976, p. 145.
87. *Minotaure,* no. 3-4, 1933, p. 75.
88. Zervos, "Notes sur Kandinsky," p. 153.
89. Vassily Kandinsky, "Toile vide, etc.," *Cahiers d'Art,* 10e année, no. 5-6, 1935, p. 117, translated as "Empty Canvas" in Lindsay and Vergo II, pp. 780-783: "I look through my window. Several chimney stacks of lifeless factories rise silently. They are inflexible. All of a sudden smoke rises from a single chimney. The wind catches it and it instantly changes color. The whole world has changed."

Titles from the Paris Period

As soon as he settled in Paris, Kandinsky gave a French title to every one of his works, regardless of whether it was a painting or a gouache. It was not until 1940 that he stopped assigning titles to his works on paper. Like Klee, he seems to have waited until each work was fully completed before finding a title for it.

Kandinsky seems to have wanted to place his personal seal, so to speak, on each of his works, to say very clearly, this painting is by me, Kandinsky

—as in the case of *Violet dominant (Dominant Violet), Trois Ovales (Three Ovals), Rigide et courbé (Rigid and Bent), Complexité simple (Complex-Simple).* Each title acts as a second monogram. A title is that part of language which is attached to a painting once it is finished, after all is done, and which will forever after come before it. The title turns the painting into a product; the title is the label on it. The act of inscribing a new title in the Handlist is a rite of commemoration, a celebration, a consecration. The painting has been baptized—and always in the language of the country in which he painted it. The names Kandinsky gave his paintings are as Kandinskyesque as *La Mariée mise à nu . . . (The Bride Stripped Bare . . .)* was Duchampesque or *Le Bel Oiseau déchiffrant l'inconnu au couple d'amoureux (The Beautiful Bird Revealing the Unknown to a Pair of Lovers)* was Miróesque. What exactly does this linguistic paternity consist of? Did the titles Kandinsky used for his Paris paintings differ fundamentally from the German titles of the Bauhaus period?

Almost every one of his titles is made up of two words. In French, the ultimate Kandinsky title would be a noun followed by an adjective. Sometimes he added a definite or indefinite article. Sometimes he used three words, but almost never more, and sometimes just one.

Unlike Duchamp's titles, Kandinsky's are never whimsical, never syntactical oddities. They are plain, serious and simple; they keep their promise. In *La Figure blanche (White Figure)* we do see a white shape. In *Deux Points verts (Two Green Points)* we can look for green points—and find them. Whereas Max Ernst and the Surrealists used their titles to add to the poetry of their works, Kandinsky did not indulge in farce and witticism. His straightforward titles become mathematically precise when he adds—as he often does—a numerical adjective to replace either the article or another adjective—as in *Deux Lignes (Two Lines), Trois Ovales (Three Ovals), Trois Etoiles (Three Stars),* and so on. If we count, we find exactly what he announces.

The adjectives often indicate color: *L'Accent rouge (Red Accent), Accent vert (Green Accent), La Figure blanche, Pointes noires (Black Points).* The colors are those of a simple palette—blue, purple, orange, green, brown, black, white, yellow and a great deal of red during the Paris period. They are different from the *rot, grün* or *bräunlich* of the Bauhaus period, which are broken and become violet and orange in Paris. The fact that the colors are mixed, or broken, by juxtaposition, is suggested by such adjectives as *rayé* (striped) or *bigarré* (variegated).

The title calls attention to the forms within the painting. They are always flat shapes—*cercles* (circles), *carrés* (squares), *taches* (spots), *fils* (threads), *rubans* (ribbons), *lignes* (lines), *zigzags.* The features singled out in the title are not always the most important ones in the painting. In *Deux Points verts,* the dots (which are not quite green, in fact, because the lower parts of them are mixed with brown paint) are tiny but so exceptionally bright that they grab our attention. The same thing happens in *Cercle et carré (Circle and Square).* Both of those elements are smaller than the other shapes in the painting but colored brilliant emerald green and orange. The title is a wink in the viewer's direction.

Sometimes the title allows us to perceive a concealed structure. In *Quatre Figures sur trois carrés (Four Figures on Three Squares),* the three squares virtually disappear behind the four cumbersome and complicated figures in the foreground, and would be invisible if the title did not make us see them. In other cases, the title may point out how the space within the painting is allocated: *Sept (Seven)* is indeed divided into seven parts, six strips and a square; in *Cinq Parties (Five Parts)* the canvas is divided into five parts.

Some titles may prevent us from seeing a painting the "wrong" way, as in those psychological tests where one person may make out a profile among the dots and another will discern a different shape. In *Fils fins (Thin Threads),* were it not for the title, we would have no reason to spot the threads rather than the triangular spaces outlined in white or black.

By comparing the titles from the German period with those from the French period, we can see that two themes disappeared. In Germany during the 1920s Kandinsky was still under the spell of the Symbolists' correspondences between the senses, and often included the world of sound in his titles: *Klänge (Sounds)* and *Drei Klänge (Three Sounds)* are examples. Later such allusions disappeared, along with titles that seemed to suggest that the painting depicted a mood or a state of mind. The Paris period does not include many equivalents to the numerous *Peaceful, Obstinate, Joyous, Affirmative, Serene* and *Inflexible* works of earlier days. The Paris titles make little reference to the natural world; Kandinsky's cosmic universe is reduced to a handful of sentimental phrases such as *Monde bleu (Blue World), Bleu de ciel (Sky Blue), Crépuscule (Twilight),* then *Ténèbres (Darkness).* (These last two may reflect the prevailing mood during the Occupation.)

Kandinsky did continue to use paradoxical titles in Paris, a practice he had begun in Berlin. During both periods he was fond of opposites and contradictions—incompatible feelings, contrasting colors or antonyms—expressed in two words side by side, with or without hyphen or conjunction. His titles ranged from such classic oxymorons as *Complexité simple (Complex-Simple), Stabilité animée (Animated Stability), Tension tranquille (Light Tension)* and so on, to simple antithetical combinations. During his German period, Kandinsky had called his paintings *Pointed and Round, Upside Down, Loose-Tight, Dark-Light, Flat-Deep, Serious Joke.* In France he continued in this vein, using such titles as *Rigide et courbé (Rigid and Bent), Division-Unité (Division-Unity).* The antithesis is sometimes conveyed in two separate paintings, as in *Chacun pour soi (Each for Himself)* and *Ensemble.* Does this type of title or of pairs of titles express a pictorial conflict? Was it really impossible for Kandinsky to choose between a given thing and its opposite? Or was he granting himself the greatest freedom of all, the freedom to contradict?

Other penchants become clear as well—a taste for movement, a desire for the lightness of levitation. First there were *Stabilité animée* and the *Fixé (Fixed)* works; then came the titles that defy gravity—*Poids monté (Raised Weight), Vers le haut (Upward), Vers le bleu (Toward Blue);* the playful acrobatics of *Ascension légère (Light Ascent), L'Elan, Voltige (Balancing Act), La Flèche (The Arrow), Montée gracieuse (Graceful Ascent).* The sprightly, poetic quality of these brief, airy titles is always anchored in the pictures themselves, whereas the titles Miró or Tanguy assigned to their works were poetic in an extravagant and narrative way—each title was a story in itself. Kandinsky appreciated Arp's poetry but did not borrow any of the clouds, trees, roots and fruits that fill Arp's titles.

Return to Poetry

This does not mean that Kandinsky was not affected by Miró's poetic *Hirondelle d'amour*; he simply kept poems distinct from paintings. Nor was he interested in illustrating other people's poems, as Arp and Ernst did. He did execute some drypoint frontispieces for volumes of poems by René Char and Tristan Tzara, but they were afterthoughts, added at the publisher's instigation to increase the commercial appeal of each volume (see cat. nos. 31, 36).[90]

Kandinsky enjoyed poetry; he had written some—*Klänge (Sounds)*—in earlier years, and between 1936 and 1938 he took steps to have some of those poems translated from German into Spanish and French. He even wrote some poems in French; we do not know if they were commissioned by art-review editors or whether he was trying to fit into the scale of values in Paris where, at that time, poets still ruled supreme over art criticism. He was certainly motivated also by a sincere desire to find a means, through poetry, to bridge the fatal gap between words and the plastic arts. Perhaps one way to achieve better understanding of Kandinsky's pictorial works from the Paris years would be to read his poems. But there are too few of them. What Eduardo Westerdahl published in *Gaceta de arte* and Eugène Jolas included in *Transition* were translations by Louis Fernandez and Arp, respectively, of a few fragments from *Klänge*.[91] Nevertheless, they took on the value of manifestos. Kandinsky upheld a painter's right to know how to use words: "For many years I have been writing 'prose poems' from time to time," he said in a text which he himself identified on the manuscript as "Reminiscences" but which San Lazzaro published in *XXe Siècle* as "My Woodcuts."[92] In that text Kandinsky reiterated some of the ideas he had expressed in 1930 when Pierre Flouquet interviewed him for his *Journal des poètes*. "Every true painting partakes of poetry, for poetry is not just a matter of words. It is achieved equally well by organizing colors into a certain form, a composition. . . . The source of both these 'languages' is the same. They have in common intuition, and the soul."[93]

The poems Kandinsky wrote in French embody a sense of absurdity and drollery. Like *Klänge*, they are a painter's poems; terms relating to color predominate. His syntax is modest, his vocabulary simple; almost all of his sentences have the same construction but they avoid monotony. It is visual poetry, and the images follow a strange sequence. As in *Klänge*, a narrator anxiously asks questions and no answer is forthcoming. These queries and the succession of elements, animals and human characters that appear and disappear cause a feeling of uneasiness. The people and the things in this poetry of disturbance are not what they are expected to be, do not do what they are expected to do. "You speak and I do not hear you," says one of the

90. René Char, *Le Marteau sans maitre*, Paris, 1934; Tristan Tzara, *La Main passe*, Paris, 1935.

91. In a letter to Kandinsky dated May 23, 1936, Fernandez wrote: "Arp and I translated your poem, and I sent it to Westerdahl." Poems in German by Kandinsky, including "Blick und Blitz," "Ergo," "S," "Erinnerungen," "Anders" and "Immer Zusammen," were published in *Transition*, no. 27, Apr.-May 1938, pp. 104-109.

92. Vassily Kandinsky, "Mes Gravures sur bois," *XXe Siècle*, vol. 1, July 1938, p. 31.

93. "Quel rôle joue l'esprit poétique dans votre création picturale?" *Journal des poètes*, Oct. 10, 1932, Brussels.

poems. Should we take this to be a distress signal from the exiled painter? Knowing the very strong tendency of the German or German-speaking artists to associate poetry and painting, Zervos created a magnificent name for their type of painting, in the context of the Munich conference of 1938. In his *Histoire de l'art contemporain,* published in 1938, he called it "rebellious poetry."[94] What a pity he was the only one to use that term!

Abandonment of Theory

At about this time, Kandinsky wrote a few articles on art in which reason yields to feeling. He expressed his distaste for theory and for attempts to theorize, and urged a return to simplicity.[95] The critics spoke nonsense, so far as he was concerned; the Constructivists indulged in excessive rhetoric. Personally, he would confine his guiding principles to two or three associations of ideas, two or three analogical images that should suffice to justify his pictorial work. His underlying assumption—a revival of romanticism—constituted a reversal of what had been, after all, the avant-garde positions he had upheld in his teaching at the Bauhaus. Now that he had no more pedagogical duties, he was less systematic, less convinced. He simply wrote a few allusive, analogical pages—meant to be used by the art reviews as prefaces or articles—in which he stood by the abstract movements still active in free Europe, his own work setting the example. His writings were actually very repetitious: what he wrote for London, for instance, he had already written for Copenhagen. These fragmentary texts have not yet been gathered together completely, but we do know that they have in common an appeal to turn back the clock. He referred to his first essay, *On the Spiritual in Art,* the ups and downs of whose translation into Italian he was following at that time.

Kandinsky turned a new gaze on his oeuvre of the already remote period of Munich and the *Blaue Reiter*. Probably the mere fact of growing older led him to look back, but he also felt compelled to do so for this reason: he wanted to prove that his abstract pictures did not date from the 1930s but indeed originated in 1911, without placing his seal of approval on the preference the art collectors showed for the Munich period over his later work. These two attitudes may seem contradictory but they stem from a twofold misunderstanding. Few people in Paris in the late 1930s had adequate knowledge to arrive at a thorough understanding of the development of German art; many assumed in all good faith that since no one had talked much about the nonobjective style until approximately 1930, it must therefore have originated at that time. But the museum officials abroad took the opposite stand: knowing what the *Blaue Reiter* had produced, they refused to pay any attention to the evolution of Kandinsky's work since he had settled in Paris.

Alfred Barr, in his monumental *Cubism and Abstract Art,* attributed very little importance to Kandinsky and the invention of abstract art; instead, he championed Cubism in the United States.[96] Gallatin, the art collector who was benefactor and director of the Museum of Living Art in New York,

94. Zervos included in the category of *la poésie rebelle* a number of Surrealists who had broken with German orthodoxy, as well as German refugees and Spanish exiles: Max Ernst, Miró, André Masson, Yves Tanguy, Dali, René Magritte, Arp, Man Ray, Alberto Giacometti. Arp, for his part, ran a short-lived publishing house for German poetry called *Verlag poesie,* located at 19, rue Raffet, Paris 16e. On its schedule were: Arp, *Konfiguration,* Ivan Goll, Hugo Ball, Jakob Van Hoddis, Carl Einstein.

95. Kandinsky, "La Valeur d'une oeuvre concrète," Lindsay and Vergo II, p. 828: "Reason overestimated today, would destroy the only 'unreasonable' domain left to our poor contemporary mankind."

96. Alfred H. Barr, Jr., *Cubism and Abstract Art,* exh. cat., New York, 1936, p. 64: "At any rate Kandinsky's art between 1906-1910 was *Fauve* in character and under the strong influence of Gauguin and Van Gogh, but with an arbitrariness of color and a deformation of 'nature' which surpassed even Matisse. After 1910 his paintings grew more and more abstract, although recognizable objects did not disappear entirely from all his paintings until about 1914."

upheld Mondrian's abstraction exclusively. To get rid of the Kandinsky problem, he bought one of his drawings of 1910—and no more.[97] At The Tate Gallery, the director, John Rothenstein, and the trustees refused the generous offer of a recent Kandinsky by Peggy Guggenheim's sister Hazel and arranged to have it replaced by a work from 1910, a sketch for *Composition IV* unfortunately nicknamed "Cossacks."[98] Kandinsky even had trouble convincing the committee that organized the *Twentieth Century German Art* exhibition at Burlington House in 1938 to replace the earlier works they had selected by more recent paintings.[99]

In Paris, conversely, Kandinsky himself chose some of the Munich paintings he still owned for exhibitions of an official nature. Since he could not show *Composition IV* of 1911 at the exhibition that Dézarrois organized at the Jeu de Paume in 1937, Kandinsky presented *With the Black Arc* of 1912 (cat. no. 2) in the center of the wall space allocated to him (see cat. no. 1). He chose it again for the semiofficial *Salon des Réalités Nouvelles* at the Galerie Charpentier.[100] When the Kunsthalle in Bern organized a major retrospective of his work in 1937, he unearthed his second version of *Old Town* of 1902.[101] From that point on, he overlooked his Bauhaus period and exhibited older works alongside his more recent ones. In 1939, for instance, at the Galerie Jeanne Bucher, he showed watercolors dating from 1910 to 1920 together with gouaches done between 1937 and 1939. Does this necessarily give a retro flavor to his Paris period?

Fitting into Paris

Kandinsky had chosen Paris rather than any other possible place for his exile because he thought that the French capital still set the tone for artistic activity the world over.[102] There were many flourishing galleries in Paris, he believed, and artists streamed into Paris from throughout the world to find confirmation of their talent. Apparently Kandinsky did not take Zervos seriously when he warned him, between 1931 and 1933, that because of the Depression galleries were closing, collectors were selling, the better art reviews were going out of existence.

The official art magazines—*L'Amour de l'Art,* the weekly *Beaux-Arts*—favored a return to figurative, traditional painting.[103] They gave artificial luster to the French Academy and offshoots of it such as the Prix de Rome. In 1937 the subject assigned to the painters competing for the Prix de Rome was "evocation of a pastoral scene"; the sculptors were ordered to deal with an even more conventional subject, "an unclothed Christian waiting to be martyred in the circus at Rome, in the reign of Nero." As spokesman for this semiofficial school of art criticism, Waldemar George inveigled himself into writing aesthetic-political essays that hewed to the fascist line, such as "L'Humanisme et l'idée de patrie, Valeurs françaises, Perspectives fascistes, Le Dilemme allemand, Métamorphoses juives, L'URSS et la culture" (Humanism and the Notion of Fatherland, French Values, the Fascist Outlook, the German Dilemma, Jewish Metamorphoses, Culture and the Soviet Union), published in 1936 in a volume that was indicative of the prevailing climate.

97. *A.E. Gallatin Collection: "Museum of Living Art,"* coll. cat., Philadelphia, 1954, no. 78, Composition 1910 (not reproduced).

98. This decision was made on Dec. 5, 1938.

99. Letter from Peggy Guggenheim to Kandinsky dated July 26, 1938: "Madame Burchard [the organizer of the exhibition] is willing to replace two of your early paintings by two more recent ones, provided Herbert Read, who is in charge of this section, agrees . . . . the committee believes that its choice of earlier paintings was justified."

100. In three successive exhibitions, groups of nonobjective works were shown at the Galerie Charpentier by Yvanhoé Rambosson and Fredo Sidès, the official organizers of the Salon, and Nelly van Doesburg, unofficial organizer. Kandinsky was included in the second exhibition; his works were shown in the same exhibition as those of Bauer, Theo van Doesburg, František Kupka, Mondrian, Pevsner, Georges Vantongerloo and Freundlich.

101. Kunsthalle Bern, *Wassily Kandinsky: Französische Meister der Gegenwart,* Feb. 21-Mar. 29, 1937.

102. In a letter to Grohmann dated Dec. 4, 1933, Kandinsky informed him that he and Nina had finally chosen Paris, which was the art center of the world and offered the greatest opportunities to make a living by selling one's paintings.

103. *L'Amour de l'Art* was a monthly, headed at this time by René Huyghe and Germain Bazin, both of whom pursued brilliant careers at the same time at the Louvre. *Beaux-Arts* was a weekly sponsored and financed by the art dealer Georges Wildenstein; its Editor-in-Chief was Cogniat.

104. Letter from Hélion to Gallatin, dated Oct. 4, 1934. The letters to Gallatin cited in these notes are preserved at The New York Historical Society.

105. Dufy, Roger de la Fresnaye, Othon Friesz, Henri Le Fauconnier, Maurice Utrillo and Maurice de Vlaminck were included together with Kandinsky in *Französische Meister der Gegenwart* at the Kunsthalle Bern. On the influence of André Derain on the artists of the 1930s, see the author's "*Beaux-Arts* en travers de la peinture de 1930 à 1939, ou une décennie perdue," *Les Cahiers du Musée National d'Art Moderne,* no. 7-8, 1981, pp. 386-407.

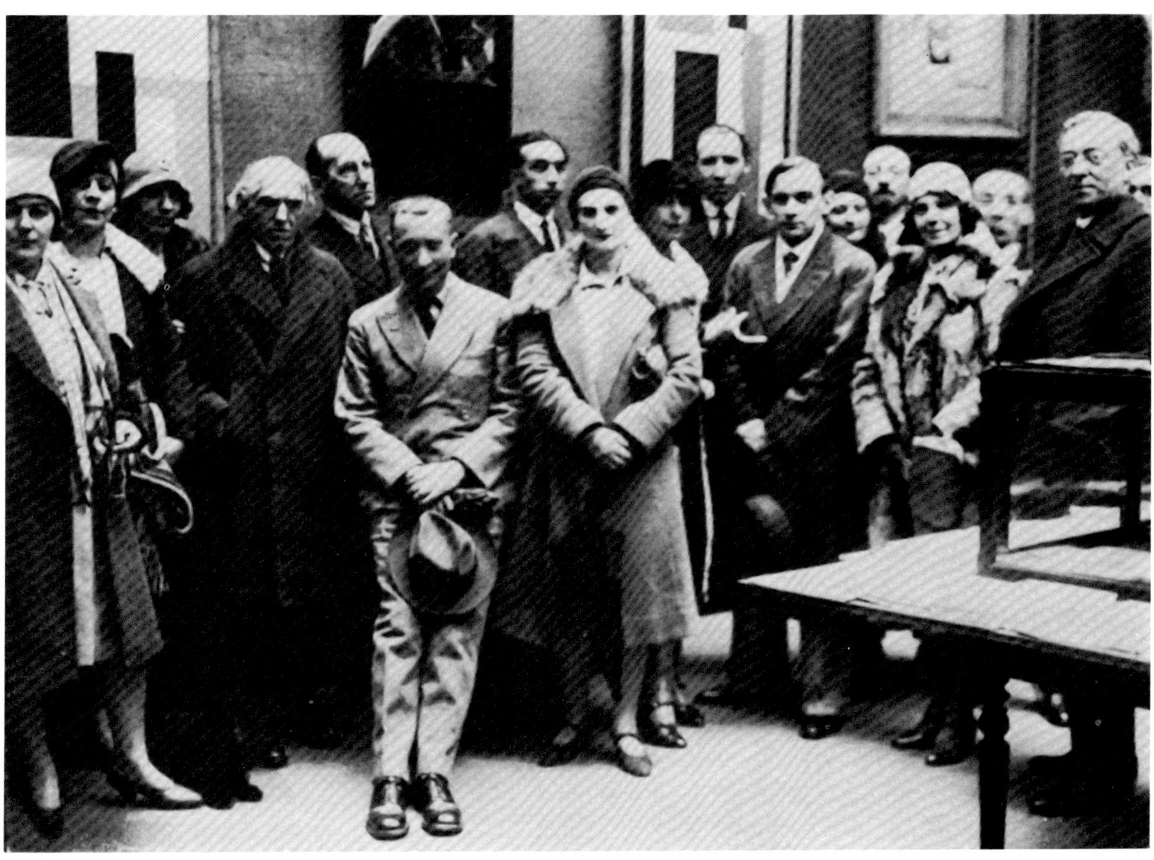

fig. 21
Members and friends of *Cercle et Carré* group, Paris, 1930, l. to r.: Francisca Clausen, Florence Henri, Manolita Torres-García, Joaquín Torres-García, Piet Mondrian, Hans Arp, Pedro Daura, Marcella Cahn, Sophie Taeuber-Arp, Michel Seuphor, Friedrich Vordemberge-Gildewart, Vera Idelson, Luigi Russolo, Nina Kandinsky, Georges Vantongerloo, Kandinsky, Jean Gorin
Collection Musée National d'Art Moderne, Centre Georges Pompidou, Paris, Kandinsky Bequest

Hélion clearsightedly warned Gallatin in 1934: "Mediocrity is triumphant. Everything goes down except enthusiasm in a few studios."[104]

Luckily, Kandinsky frequented those "few studios"; he had always had a gift for choosing the right friends. He overlooked the artificial prestige of the dying Paris school whose most illustrious figures were Maurice Utrillo and Moise Kisling, overlooked Maurice de Vlaminck's pronouncements in favor of traditional and figurative painting, overlooked the unjustified halo awarded André Derain.[105] He said not a word about the Balthus exhibition organized by Pierre Loeb in 1934 at the Galerie Pierre. He left *le bon ton* to André Lhote; and the French expressionism of Marcel Gromaire, Georges Rouault and André Dunoyer de Segonzac did not interest Kandinsky. Likewise the younger generation, laboring under the false ideal of the reactionary *Forces nouvelles* movement was of no concern to him, nor were the politically committed painting and the return to figurative work of the Communist painters. In 1934 Kandinsky chose to notice only Arp's first sculptures, Léger's figurative but nonacademic drawings, the evolution in Giacometti's work: everything that was anticonformist in Paris.[106]

The newly established association *Abstraction-Création* was prepared to welcome him, of course. It had grown out of the ruins of *Cercle et carré,* a fleeting movement (grouped around one art review and an exhibition) in which Kandinsky had taken part in 1930, by accident (fig. 21). *Abstraction-Création* adopted the *Cercle et carré* program and continued to struggle

106. Léger's drawings were shown at the Galerie Vignon, Paris, Apr. 16-28, 1934. Concerning Léger's work of this period, see *Fernand Léger, la poésie de l'objet 1928-1934,* exh. cat., Paris, 1981.

against the "Surrealist depravation."[107] *Abstraction-Création* was an ill-defined, catch-all movement devoted to an overly-negative cause, "non-figuration." As with all such groups, inclusion in it was selective and required a recommendation from one of its members. It was Gleizes who invited Kandinsky and Albers to join *Abstraction-Création* in 1933.[108]

Kandinsky never took part in it fully; both he and Arp found it too narrow-minded. The questionnaire that the group's organizers asked its members to fill out will give us some idea: "How do you think trees have influenced your work? Is a locomotive a work of art?" For a while Arp was the soul of the movement but its intransigeance led him to resign.[109] In her memoirs, Nina Kandinsky takes pleasure in recalling the time when one of the group's most important members came to visit Kandinsky in his studio in Neuilly. "I will never forget Piet Mondrian's visit to our apartment. It was on a glorious spring day. The chestnut trees in front of our building were in blossom and Kandinsky had placed the little tea-table in such a way that Mondrian, from where he was seated, could look out on all of their flowering splendor."[110] Mondrian of course insisted on taking a different seat, so as to turn his back on nature.[111]

Kandinsky and Mondrian were obviously incompatible. In 1931, after reading Mondrian's answer to the survey organized by *Cahiers d'Art* under the overall title "Reflections on Abstract Art," Kandinsky wrote to Zervos, "Mondrian's answer is very interesting but I find him a little narrow-minded in thinking that a given form in art could be eternal. But he is very intelligent."[112] The Kandinskys paid a courtesy call to Mondrian's studio on the rue du Départ; it merely confirmed Kandinsky's opinion. Nina Kandinsky recalls, "One day we went to see him in his studio near the Montparnasse railway station. We were very surprised by the way his studio looked inside. The walls and the furniture were of exactly the same colors as Mondrian used in his paintings. Once we had left and were outdoors again, Kandinsky said, in the most astounded way, 'I really don't understand how he can paint amid such a uniformity of color.'" Yet, despite Kandinsky's astonishment, only Mondrian influenced the young abstract artists of the time (fig. 22).[113] Hélion says so explicitly.[114] Although they respected Kandinsky himself, they were more surprised than convinced by his latest paintings.

Kandinsky held a biased and pejorative view of the movement that had marked artistic life in France at the beginning of the twentieth century. He could not identify himself with the Parisian trend toward abstract painting that stemmed from Neo-Plasticism; as far as he was concerned, it was a consequence of Cubism. The 1930s in Paris were indeed a period of rediscovery and glorification of Cubism. It was felt that Cubism had to be assimilated as one of the basic elements of French culture, and there were several steps in the assimilation process: first, shows organized at the Galerie d'Art Braun & Cie; then semiofficial exhibitions at the new and important Galerie des Beaux-Arts in 1935; then, in an eleventh-hour victory, the "historic" Cubists were included in the official selection of works shown at *Les Maîtres de l'art indépendant,* a large-scale contemporary art exhibition held as part of the *Exposition Internationale.*[115] The assimilation was successful, even though

107. Raynal reviewed the *Cercle et Carré* exhibition in *L'Intransigeant,* Apr. 29, 1930, p. 7: "As a reaction against what its apostles call the Surrealist depravation, the Cercle et Carré group is striving to reactivate the theme of artistic hygiene and 'purity'. . . ." Along the same lines, when she decided to create the art review *Axis,* in a letter to Kandinsky dated Sept. 26, 1934, Myfanwy Evans wrote: "I'm going to start an English magazine on abstract art, but abstract only, not Surrealism."

108. In a letter to Kandinsky dated Jan. 24, 1933, Gleizes asked him to join the *Abstraction-Création* movement, to send photographs of two of his works and to write an article on "The Relationship Between Painting and Music."

109. Open letter of resignation from Fernandez, Hélion, Arp and Sophie Taeuber-Arp to Freundlich dated June 2, 1934: ". . . We are giving you notice that yesterday we sent to Herbin our letter of resignation as members of *Abstraction-Création,* because we do not agree with him on either the way he works in a committee or the line he wants the association to follow. . . ." The complete letter, as well as other documents concerning *Abstraction-Création,* is published in Gladys C. Fabre, *Abstraction-Création 1931-1936,* exh. cat., Münster and Paris, 1978.

110. Nina Kandinsky, p. 202.

111. Mondrian often behaved in an abrupt and sometimes peculiar way. For instance, in a letter to Gallatin dated May 1, 1936, Hélion wrote concerning a group presentation at the Galerie Pierre: "Mondrian, invited, could not show, having no picture ready."

112. Letter from Kandinsky to Zervos dated Apr. 24, 1931. In his answer, Mondrian carefully gave a wide berth to Cubism and its supporters, who rejected any notion of abstraction. "It is indeed true that the body of Cubist work is not such as can be continued, or developed, that it is perfect in itself. But it is not true that Cubism as a mode of plastic expression cannot be perfected or continued." "De l'Art Abstrait: Réponse de Piet Mondrian," *Cahiers d'Art,* 6e année, no. 1, 1931, p. 41.

113. Mondrian was singled out for negative attention by the Surrealists and the defenders of Cubism. Maurice Raynal wrote, in *La Bête noire,* no. 4, July 1936: "They [young artists] stand at the entrance to a dangerous dead

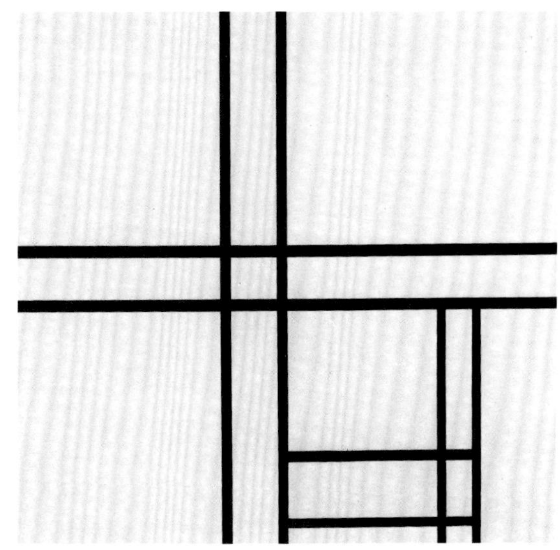

fig. 22
Piet Mondrian
Composition with Black Lines. 1934
Oil on canvas
Anonymous Loan, Dallas Museum of Art

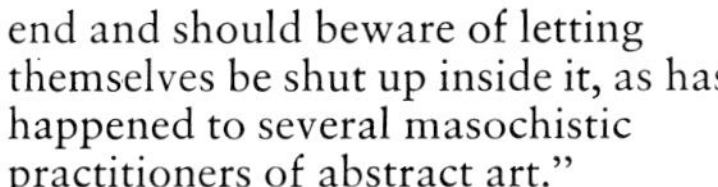

no Cubist works as such were included in the collections brought together by the new Musée National d'Art Moderne until after the end of World War II. The assimilation came about amid a certain amount of confusion, since at the time there were no elementary data available on which to base a comparative history of contemporary art. Kandinsky was annoyed by the critics' attempts to pigeonhole his origins as Cubist. The confusion was due in part to the mistaken notions perpetuated by the grand historical synthesis that *L'Amour de l'Art* undertook to compile in 1935.[116] The officials in charge of running France's museums tried to outline the great movements in modern art, and this synthesis was the vulgate, the truth as they saw it. They knew nothing about Germany.[117]

Kandinsky, for his part, was not very familiar with Cubism. In *On the Spiritual in Art,* he had written a few brief and inaccurate formulae on Cubism:

> *An attempt was made to constitute the picture upon an ideal plane, which thus had to be in front of the material surface of the canvas. In this way, composition with flat triangles became composition with triangles that had turned plastic, three-dimensional, i.e., pyramids (so-called "Cubism"). Here also, however, inertia very quickly set in . . . . Cubism, for example, as a transitional form reveals how often natural forms must be forcibly subordinated to constructive ends, and the unnecessary hindrances these forms constitute in such cases.*[118]

He felt that Cubism had exhausted itself very quickly because it had not achieved complete abstraction of natural forms. To Kandinsky, Cubism was at most an interesting moment of transition, a way-station.[119]

In 1929 Kandinsky plunged into the thick of the art world in Paris again by corresponding with Zervos, when he was asked to answer a survey about the relationship between two dates, 1830 and 1930; the questions were put

end and should beware of letting themselves be shut up inside it, as has happened to several masochistic practitioners of abstract art."

114. Information from interview by the author, May 1984.

115. Paris, Petit Palais, *Les Maîtres de l'art indépendant, 1895-1937,* June-Oct. 1937, organized by Raymond Escholier.

116. René Huyghe, "L'Allemagne et l'Europe centrale," *L'Amour de l'Art,* no. VII, Sept. 1934, p. 419: ". . . Non-figurative art. In 1911 the *Blaue Reiter* was organized in Munich and included Franz Marc, Macke and Kandinsky. Before the movement broke up during the war, it was joined by Klee and Campendonk. It was actually a second type of expressionism, influenced by the Cubist attempt to substitute pure geometrical combinations for representation, even deformed representation, of reality. In 1910 a Cubist exhibition had in fact taken place in Munich itself . . . . Under the impetus of French Cubism but with an altogether different meaning, German abstract art completed the ruin and disintegration of the visible world which expressionism had begun."

117. *Ibid.,* p. 420. "Kandinsky was born in Moscow and did not really evolve his abstract art until the period 1914-1921, which he spent in Russia. His use of color is based on that sense of harmonics—vivid as rustic joy, keen, warm and resonant—that we find in Russian popular art, and in the work of Chagall."

118. Lindsay and Vergo II, pp. 195, 208.

119. In his answer to the *Cahiers d'Art* questionnaire (see note 109), Arp took the same position: "I can understand why a Cubist painting is called abstract, because the parts that make up the object which served as model for the painting have been removed."

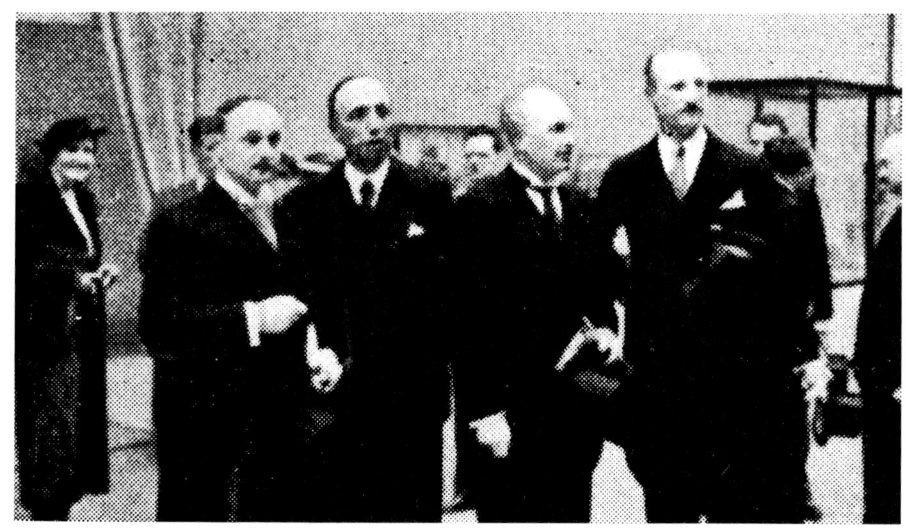

fig. 23
André Dézarrois, second from left, with Mrs. Hermann Hubacher; Hermann Hubacher, sculptor; Louis Hautecoeur, Director, Musée du Luxembourg, Paris; Mr. Blondel, French chargé d'affaires in Rome, at opening ceremony, Swiss Pavilion, *Venice Biennale,* 1938
Collection Musée National d'Art Moderne, Centre Georges Pompidou, Paris, Kandinsky Bequest

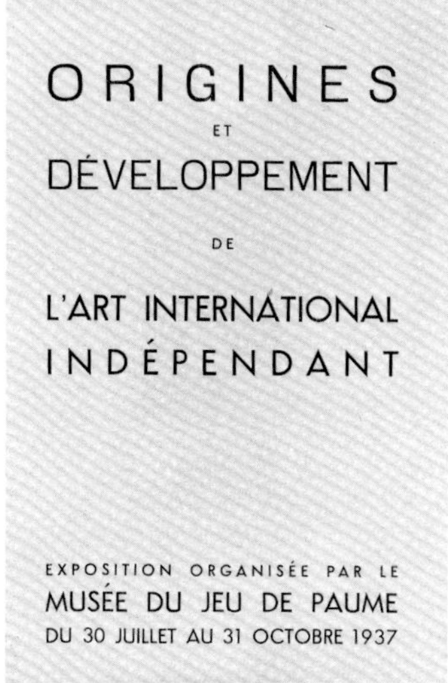

ORIGINES
ET
DÉVELOPPEMENT
DE
L'ART INTERNATIONAL
INDÉPENDANT

EXPOSITION ORGANISÉE PAR LE
MUSÉE DU JEU DE PAUME
DU 30 JUILLET AU 31 OCTOBRE 1937

fig. 24
Catalogue for *Origines et développement de l'art international indépendant,* Musée du Jeu de Paume, Paris, 1937
Collection Musée National d'Art Moderne, Centre Georges Pompidou, Paris, Kandinsky Bequest

by Maurice Raynal and E. Tériade, both of them critics on the daily paper *L'Intransigeant,* and both of them supporters of Cubism. Kandinsky's answer joined together different tendencies, an indication that his ideas on Cubism were unclear. "In Cubism and in absolute and abstract painting I see a first attempt to bring two enemies—classic form and romantic form—together to make a single content."[120]

In a note he wrote in 1935 for *Cahiers d'Art,* it is curious to see how, for thematic reasons, he effected a rapprochement between Cubism and his own guiding principle of synthesis in the arts: "It is no mere coincidence that the Cubist painters repeatedly used musical instruments and objects related to music—a guitar, a mandolin, a piano, notes, etc. Their choice was undoubtedly unconscious; it was dictated by the close relationship between music and painting."[121] But in a letter Nina wrote to John Evans, a very wealthy potential patron of the arts, Kandinsky had her say very bluntly that "Cubism started at the same time [as abstract art]. It is the last note of the 19th century, its methods are destructive. Abstract art destroys nothing and only searches for positive creation, for our day and for the future. It is an art which is pure, healthy and young."[122]

Who was prepared to listen to such language? Certainly not one curator of one French museum. In 1937 Kandinsky had occasion to work with Dézarrois, curator at the Musée du Jeu de Paume (fig. 23).[123] The idea was to organize, in only a few weeks, an exhibition that would run concurrently with the official contemporary art show being held at the Petit Palais—and which refused to accept entries from any of the painters who had recently settled in Paris, that is, all of the abstract and Surrealist painters (fig. 24).[124] Kandinsky fought on behalf of the abstract painters; he submitted lists of names and naturally he helped to write the text on art theory for the show's modest catalogue (fig. 25). Though more prudent than ever, he offered

120. "Enquête 1830-1930," *L'Intransigeant,* Dec. 2, 1929, p. 5.

121. "W. Kandinsky," *Cahiers d'Art,* 10e année, no. 1-4, 1935, pp. 53-56.

122. A copy of this letter, signed by Nina Kandinsky, is preserved in the Kandinsky Archive.

123. Letter from Dézarrois to the French Director General of Fine Arts, dated Feb. 24, 1937, preserved in the Archives Nationales, Paris: "I have already had the honor of calling your attention to the works which Kandinsky, the American Cubist painter, exhibited at the galerie Buchet [*sic*] at the end of the year."

124. This exhibition, *Origines et développement de l'art international indépendant,* was held at the Musée du Jeu de Paume, July 26-Oct. 31, 1937.

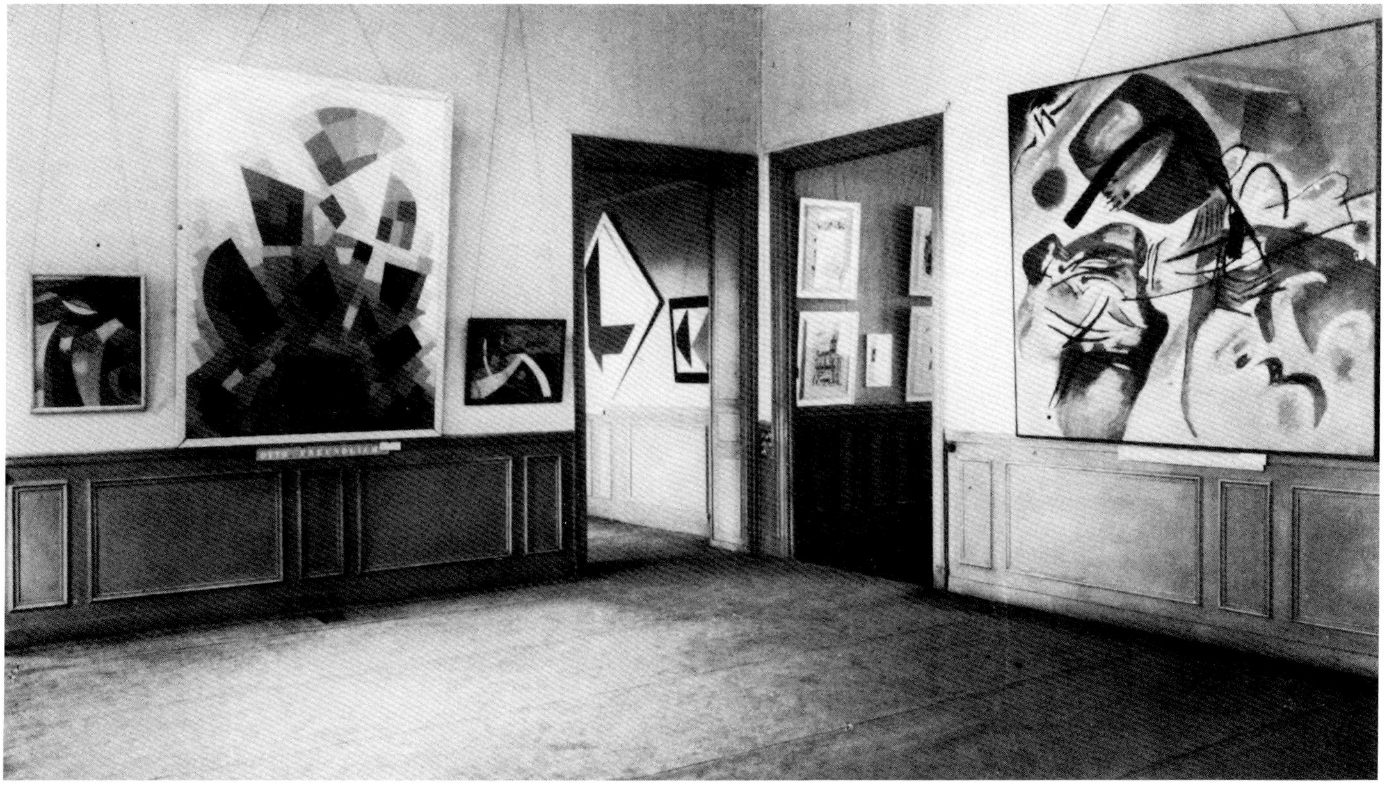

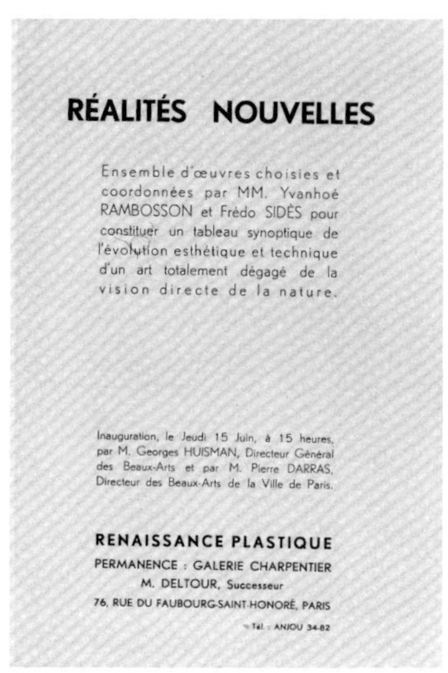

RÉALITÉS NOUVELLES

Ensemble d'œuvres choisies et coordonnées par MM. Yvanhoé RAMBOSSON et Frédo SIDÈS pour constituer un tableau synoptique de l'évolution esthétique et technique d'un art totalement dégagé de la vision directe de la nature.

Inauguration, le Jeudi 15 Juin, à 15 heures, par M. Georges HUISMAN, Directeur Général des Beaux-Arts et par M. Pierre DARRAS, Directeur des Beaux-Arts de la Ville de Paris.

RENAISSANCE PLASTIQUE

PERMANENCE : GALERIE CHARPENTIER

M. DELTOUR, Successeur

76, RUE DU FAUBOURG-SAINT-HONORÉ, PARIS

Tél. : ANJOU 34-82

fig. 25
Installation view and catalogue, *Réalités Nouvelles,* Galerie Charpentier, Paris, 1939
Collection Musée National d'Art Moderne, Centre Georges Pompidou, Paris, Kandinsky Bequest

abundant explanations, for Dézarrois had a tendency to accept everything and mix everything together in a way that was favorable to Cubism. On May 10, 1937, Kandinsky wrote to him:

> *The only point on which I have any doubt as to accuracy is the difference between two movements, Cubism and Abstract Art (which I prefer to call Concrete Art); both of them stemmed from Cézanne* [this is a concession on Kandinsky's part] *but later they developed independently from one another. Both movements came into the world at almost the same time: 1911. Cubism is something like a brother to abstract art but by no means its father.*

In his catalogue, which was very brief, Dézarrois situated abstract art far behind Cubism and Surrealism. Worse still, the paintings by Kandinsky included in it were not even dated. So on July 31 Kandinsky wrote another letter—of protest this time—to the obstinate curator.

> *You remember when we were sitting at the entrance to your museum. I told you that "among other sources" for my "abstract form" was Cézanne's work, but that my work had never had anything to do with Cubism . . . . I was especially struck by Matisse's paintings in 1905-06.* [Kandinsky preferred to say he was close to Fauvism.] *I still remember very clearly a "decomposed" carafe he did, with the stopper painted quite*

far from where "it should be" that is, in the neck of the carafe. In that painting by Matisse, the "natural relationships" were destroyed. [He notes this so as all the better to refute any Cubist influence whatsoever.] *At the same time I had found the courage to do my first abstract painting, without ever having seen a Cubist painting. It was in 1912 that for the first time I saw a photograph of a Picasso* (Woman with Guitar) *and I reproduced it in my book "Der blaue Reiter." In the same book there was a reproduction of my large "abstract" canvas entitled* Composition V, *that I had painted in 1911.*

But in Paris, in 1937, who had ever seen the almanac of the *Blaue Reiter*? Even Herbert Read, in his 1934 book *Art Now,* overlooked that movement completely—he did not mention it once. It was of vital importance for Kandinsky to convince the public that he had painted abstract canvases as early as 1911. But Dézarrois turned a deaf ear. He did not even allow Kandinsky to show at the Jeu de Paume his *Composition IV* of 1911, which Dézarrois considered still figurative.

In another attempt to prove his all-important point, Kandinsky insisted that *La Marianne,* a daily paper that was sometimes receptive to nonconformist painting, reproduce his *With the Black Arc* of 1912 (cat. no. 2), rather than some other painting. Kandinsky made the same statement to the journalist Paul Chadourne as he had to Dézarrois. "Allow me to point out the vital difference between my 'non-figurative' form and the other 'abstract' forms such as 'Constructivism,' 'Neo-Plasticism,' etc., whose roots go back to Cubism. Cubism never had any influence over the way my painting developed. My 'sources' are Cézanne's painting, instead, and later 'Fauvism,' especially Matisse."[125]

As concerned as Kandinsky was to disassociate himself from Cubism, he was equally eager to keep his distance from another category in which the critics tended to put him, Constructivism. Kazimir Malevich's name was not very familiar at the time. Not many people were even certain whether he was alive.[126] But several artists, Domela in particular, were eager to make works from the Constructivist period known in the magazine *Plastique*.[127] Thus, Kandinsky had to defend himself against the pernicious tendency to assimilate him with the Constructivists. (For a while he had even been confused with Chagall.) Kandinsky took up the matter in his written lecture to Dézarrois on modern painting. "This abstract (or concrete) art I am talking about points in two directions or, as we might say, to a sort of subsection under the name Constructivism (the two Russians, Malevich and Tatlin, are examples). The Constructivists generally say they originated in Cubism; then they took Cubism so far that they excluded all 'sentiment' or 'intuition' from it, and they try to arrive at art solely by means of 'reason' and mathematical calculation."[128]

He continues the discussion when writing to Herbert Read. "The difference between abstract art (in general) and Constructivism (one part of abstract art) is obvious. My point of view is that Constructivism is one of the means by which to paint a painting. A painting has to be constructed. But

125. Letter from Kandinsky to Chadourne dated Apr. 1, 1937.

126. Letter from James Johnson Sweeney to Kandinsky dated Dec. 30, 1935: "Another point . . . I seem vaguely to remember that on my visit to you, you mentioned the death of the painter Malewitch. Perhaps I was mistaken in this. If my recollection is not at fault, would it be too much to ask of you to write me a few details concerning Malewitch's death—where he died and what date . . . ."

127. César Domela, "Malewitsch in memoriam," *Plastique,* no. 1, Spring 1937, p. 5.

128. Letter from Kandinsky to Dézarrois dated May 10, 1937.

that does not necessarily mean that a painting that has been constructed is art. It is a somewhat complicated business, yet at the same time it is very simple. The path I chose was different: naturalism, expressionism, abstract art."[129]

Such agitation over a matter of dates seems pointless to us today because we now have more ample knowledge of Kandinsky's oeuvre thanks to: the revelations afforded by the Gabriele Münter- und Johannes Eichner-Stiftung after it was incorporated into the Städtische Galerie im Lenbachhaus in Munich in 1957; the reappearance of paintings in the museums of Soviet Russia; and the transformation of the Solomon R. Guggenheim collection into a permanent museum. What Kandinsky was defending in the 1930s seems obvious to us today, and we are sorry to see how much energy he expended on the struggle to establish his identity. It is no less true, however, that the *monstres sacrés* of Cubism were acutely aware of their historical importance and lorded it over Paris, from which they were never forced into exile. They looked down to some extent on this Germanified Russian who claimed to have invented a new approach to painting all by himself. Braque's glory was great and growing greater. The ex-Cubist received nothing but compliments on his recent works from everyone in Kandinsky's entourage. Even Kandinsky's own nephew Kojève wrote him in Berlin in 1930: "I've been to see the Braque show twice. I really like Braque's paintings, especially the largest ones."[130] Kandinsky learned to be more circumspect about Braque, now that he had reverted to what the public liked. In 1943 he wrote to Bruguière: "The large Braque room at the Salon d'Automne had nothing new to offer. Nowadays Braque is considered the greatest French painter, and all they talk about is true French painting—a very patriotic spirit!"[131]

As for Picasso, he and Kandinsky never visited each other's studios and never ran into each other. Picasso had been reigning supreme over Paris for years. His *papiers collés* were rediscovered and his retrospective at the Galeries Georges Petit in 1932 was an event. Through certain friends they had in common, such as Julio González, it sometimes came about that Kandinsky and Picasso took part in the same group shows. A Picasso and a Kandinsky were reproduced on the same page in the *Abstraction-Création* magazine. Each of them submitted a work to a show organized by Castelucho- Diana, the art-supplier on the boulevard Montparnasse.[132] Both were represented at the Club des Architectes at the 1937 *Exposition Internationale*. They both showed in Dézarrois's exhibition at the Jeu de Paume. But that was all. Yet they had two things in common: both owned works by the Douanier Rousseau, and both remained in Paris during the German Occupation. Kandinsky did not argue with Picasso's supremacy. In 1930, when Kojève went to see the exhibition of Picasso's series of large nudes on the beach, and sent some acid comments on them to his uncle, Kandinsky gently reprimanded him. "Like you, I have the feeling Picasso is just 'having fun,' but he is a great master, and we have to forgive him for his mischievous jokes."[133]

Kandinsky liked Léger much better.[134] When Kandinsky launched a campaign to save the Bauhaus in Berlin, Léger was one of the few artists in Paris to respond—by sending a small painting as a lottery prize. Léger and Zervos

129. Letter from Kandinsky to Read dated Apr. 2, 1938. Copy preserved in the Kandinsky Archive, MNAM.

130. Letter from Kojève to Kandinsky dated May 29, 1930.

131. Letter from Kandinsky to Bruguière dated Dec. 1, 1943.

132. The informal exhibition was held June 14-29, 1935, and included works by B. G. Benno, Fernandez, González, Hélion, Henri Laurens, Léger, Lipchitz and Magnelli in addition to Kandinsky and Picasso.

133. Letter from Kandinsky to Kojève dated June 26, 1930.

134. In a letter to Grohmann dated June 30, 1934, Kandinsky wrote that he was about to visit Léger in half an hour. In a letter to Grohmann the next day Kandinsky wrote that everything went very well at Léger's. Léger made a strong impression on him and he felt that Léger was certainly a "great, hearty fellow" with strong, healthy roots.

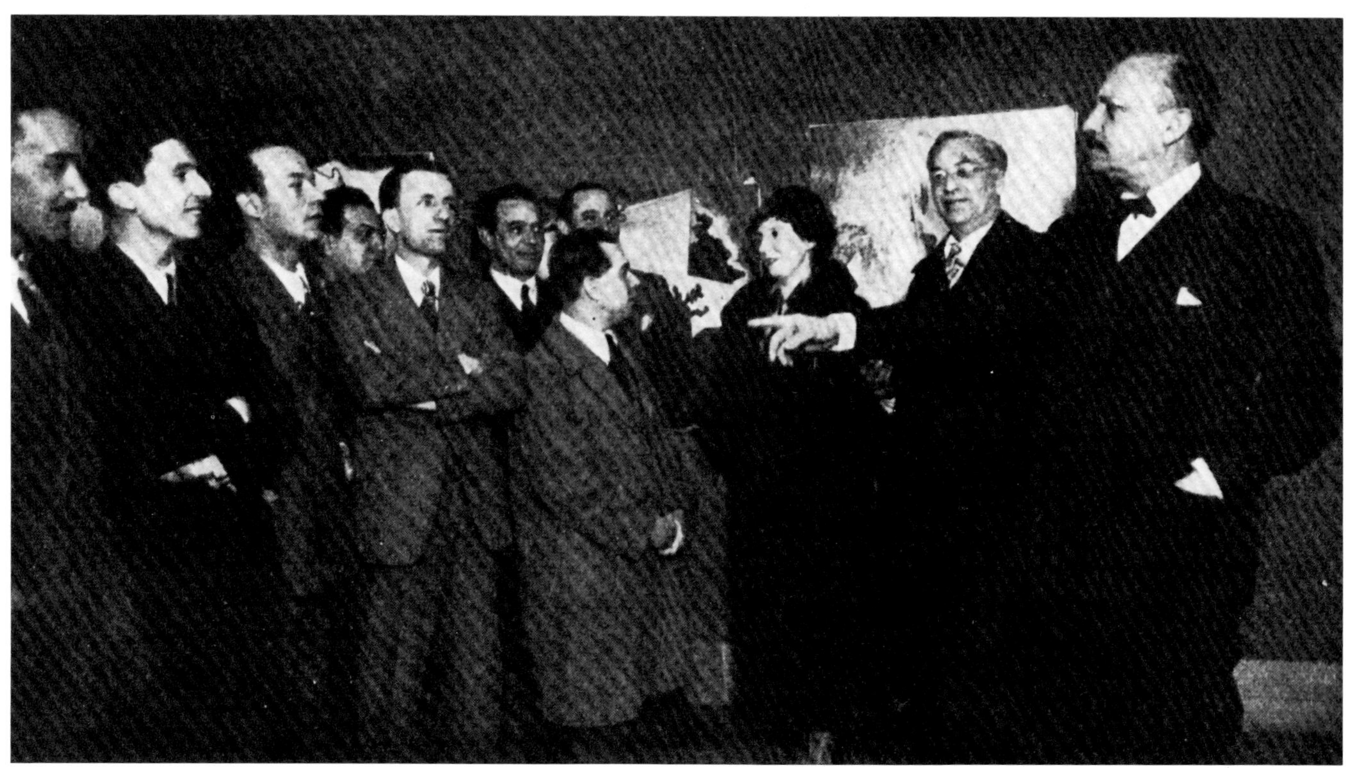

fig. 26
Marinetti and the Kandinskys at Galerie Bernheim-Jeune, Paris, 1935, with Futurists, l. to r.: Fillia, Filippo De Filippis, Pippo Oriani, Nino Rosso, Giuseppe Rosso and Franco Costa

Collection Musée National d'Art Moderne, Centre Georges Pompidou, Paris, Kandinsky Bequest

were close friends, and this made it easier for Kandinsky and Léger to get along; together they gave their support to a series of lectures delivered in Paris by the Italian Futurist Filippo Tommaso Marinetti.[135] But what especially appealed to Kandinsky were Léger's frank way of speaking and his stature as an artist. Léger's work itself, authentic though it was, did not belong to Kandinsky's universe. Léger did not actually paint much during this period; he traveled back and forth three times between the United States and Europe, did a great deal of drawing, was involved in social and political discussions and was interested in mural art.

Because Kandinsky unconditionally supported all of the verbose lectures delivered by the Italian Futurists, who were themselves embroiled in the fascist propaganda machine, many poets and artists suspected him of harboring reactionary sympathies.[136] There are several reasons why Kandinsky gave Marinetti such a hearty welcome (fig. 26). It was partly based on fidelity to artistic affinities that had become apparent before World War I, affinities the Surrealists knew nothing about and therefore could not take into account. Moreover, through Marinetti, Kandinsky doubtless also was hoping to keep open the possibility of organizing some shows of his work in Italy.[137] And finally, Kandinsky and the Italian Futurists thought alike on several points

135. Kandinsky wrote about these lectures in a letter to Albers dated May 24, 1935.

136. Letter from Giuseppe Ghiringhelli to Kandinsky dated June 19, 1934: "You may indeed say that our gallery is a fascist gallery! . . . Our modernity is absolutely and typically fascist." Kandinsky quoted this in a letter to Grohmann dated June 30, 1934. Ghiringhelli ran the Galleria del Milione in Milan. In 1934 he organized a Kandinsky exhibition and a show of engravings by Albers, the catalogue for which has a short introductory text by Kandinsky which is not included in the collections of his complete writings; see *Il Milione: Bolletino della Galleria del Milione,* no. 34, Dec. 23, 1934, p. 3. An informal group show at del Milione in 1938 included works by Arp, Domela, Kandinsky, Magnelli, Kurt Seligmann, Taeuber-Arp and Paule Vézelay; see *Il Milione: Bolletino della Galleria del Milione,* no. 58, Mar. 5, 1938.

of ideology (fascism, after all, claimed to save mankind from the more materialistic doctrines) and aesthetics; the Futurists' aeropainting, being dynamic and optimistic, was somewhat similar to Kandinsky's own work from the Paris period.[138] So it is not surprising that Kandinsky recommended one of the Italian Futurists for inclusion in Dézarrois's Jeu de Paume exhibition: "We must have an Italian Futurist, and I recommend Prampolini, whose work I'm sure you must be familiar with. A serious and gifted artist."[139] Kandinsky continued to befriend the Futurists even though they supported Italy's colonial war. He admired the orderliness that prevailed in Italy when he vacationed in Leghorn in 1936.[140] Not until 1939 and 1940, when his Italian translator di Cesarò urged him to take refuge in Italy, did Kandinsky declare himself clearly in favor of France—where he had just been naturalized (fig. 27).[141]

Kandinsky's strong Futurist sympathies quickly soured his relationship with the Surrealists, despite the enthusiastic reception they had given him when he first settled in Neuilly. The polemical essayists in the Surrealist and Communist magazines ridiculed the Futurists. René Crevel, for instance, vituperated against Marinetti and the Italian Futurist academicians; in 1935 he topped off with an aluminum hat an imaginary and gaudy uniform he thought appropriate for them.[142] He lashed out at Enrico Prampolini, who laid himself open to criticism by giving such paradoxical titles as *Believe, Obey, Combat* and *Book and Rifle* to paintings he did for fascist youth centers. The Kandinskys' apolitical attitude and their very bourgeois lifestyle in Paris kept Breton's faithful followers at a distance for some years.

Yet the very complete collections of such reviews as *La Révolution Surréaliste* and *Le Surréalisme au Service de la Révolution* in Kandinsky's library would seem to prove that Kandinsky kept abreast of the movement while living in Dessau. And, on the part of the Surrealists themselves, Breton actively supported Kandinsky's first exhibitions in Paris, and bought two watercolors from the small Kandinsky show at the Galerie Zak in 1929.[143] Here again, Zervos acted as middleman. He was determined to bring Kandinsky and the Surrealists together at all costs. In 1932 he wrote Kandinsky that he intended:

> *. . . to have six volumes printed, one for each of the best poets living today: André Breton, Eluard, Tristan Tzara, Péret, Arp and Hugnet . . . . It will be a 50-page volume, with three etchings. When Eluard himself saw the etching you had done for it, he asked me if he could count on you to illustrate his volume. Eluard is the best poet we have today. Personally, I really must urge you very strongly to work with the poets I have chosen . . . . The illustrators we have selected, aside from yourself, should be Klee, Miró, Arp, Dali and Masson.*

And Kandinsky was just about to start illustrating Eluard's poems, which he liked very much, when Zervos announced that he had to abandon the project for lack of a sponsor. In 1933, on Breton's advice, Char asked Kandinsky to send him an etching for an edition of Char's *Le Marteau sans maître* (cat. nos. 31, 32).

fig. 27
First Italian translation, by G. A. Colonna di Cesarò, of Kandinsky's *Concerning the Spiritual in Art,* Rome, 1940
Collection Musée National d'Art Moderne, Centre Georges Pompidou, Paris, Kandinsky Bequest

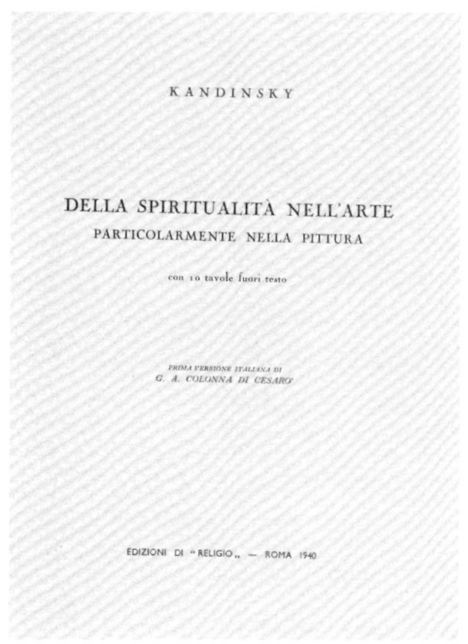

KANDINSKY

DELLA SPIRITUALITÀ NELL'ARTE
PARTICOLARMENTE NELLA PITTURA

con 10 tavole fuori testo

PRIMA VERSIONE ITALIANA DI
G. A. COLONNA DI CESARÒ

EDIZIONI DI "RELIGIO" — ROMA 1940

137. In a letter to Grohmann dated Dec. 2, 1935, Kandinsky said he hoped to go to Rome, where the fascists had guaranteed that they would organize an exhibition—until the war with Ethiopia broke out.

138. Letter from Kandinsky to Grohmann dated May 11, 1938. Marinetti lectured with great success at the Ecole du Louvre, on the subjects of Futurism and aeropainting. He visited Kandinsky together with Dézarrois, who gave him a lecture on American painting.

139. Letter from Kandinsky to Dézarrois dated May 10, 1937. Prampolini, who lived in Paris in 1935, participated in *L'Art italien XIXe et XXe siècles* held at the Musée du Jeu de Paume from May-July 1935. He showed no. 102, *Apparition des êtres aérodynamiques,* no. 103, *Simultanéité des éléments aériens* and no. 104, *L'Automatisme quotidien.*

140. Letter from Kandinsky to Grohmann dated Sept. 19, 1938.

141. Twenty-seven letters to Kandinsky from di Cesarò, dated 1927-40 are preserved in the Kandinsky Archive.

142. René Crevel, "Discours au peintre," *Commune,* no. 23, June 1935, pp. 1135–1141.

143. Nina Kandinsky, p. 184.

The Surrealists appreciated Kandinsky's work and asked him to show some of it in their selection at the sixth Salon des Surindépendants.[144] Arp complimented him on what he saw there. "November 12, 1933 . . . your paintings hang beautifully. You lead the Surrealist procession. In addition to the watercolors, there are also two small oils. Unfortunately, there is no large painting."[145] Having participated in this Salon, he was immediately assimilated with the Surrealists, and in 1934 when Cassou, who reported on artistic events in Paris, was asked by the magazine *L'Amour de l'Art* to write a general review of Surrealism, he noted, "Situated alongside this movement are a group of German artists and the Germanified Russian, Kandinsky."[146]

While it is true that Kandinsky's conservative politics disappointed his potential friends, it is equally true that the Surrealists themselves did not live up to everything he had been led to expect by reading their magazines. He suffered from a delusion, and it led to misunderstanding. Kandinsky considered the Surrealist movement more literary than pictorial and he adopted a wait-and-see attitude. In 1929, answering a survey on neoromanticism conducted by *L'Intransigeant,* he dealt cautiously with Surrealism."An important postwar development is Surrealism, which tries to create a new relationship with nature; the *Surrealists* may look upon abstract forms as cold . . . . It seems that the Surrealists prefer a more romantic treatment."[147]

By 1936 Kandinsky felt even more reserved about the Surrealists and, in his written lecture to Dézarrois, he carefully distinguished between himself and them. "The Surrealist movement is much younger [than abstract painting], but it is quite well-known even so in widely differing countries and possesses a considerable literature." Although Kandinsky did not participate in the great Surrealist retrospectives—in London in 1936, then at the Galerie des Beaux-Arts in Paris in 1938—he lent reproductions of his works to two Danish Surrealist-oriented magazines, *Konkretion* and *Linien,* and wrote articles for them. The comic-opera war between the "*Abstraits*" and the "*Surréalistes*" in Paris either did not exist or changed its rules from time to time.[148] Moreover Kandinsky was slightly disappointed by the Surrealists' rigorous orthodoxy and their preference for libidinous themes. He wrote to Grohmann, saying he found the earlier Dadaists more authentic than the Surrealists, who needed to be titillated like a bunch of old men.[149] The notion of "inner dictation" or "inner necessity" so dear to Kandinsky had nothing to do with the Surrealists' automatic writing, nor were his terms "irrational" or "nonrational" equivalent to their use of the word "unconscious."[150]

Nonetheless, relations between Kandinsky and the Surrealists were not at a standstill; one part of the Surrealist group was relatively close to Kandinsky in his preoccupation with the exclusively plastic aspect of art. A new schism had come about in the Surrealists' ranks as the result of two developments: the Stalinist purges in the Soviet Union and the hard-line Communists' absolute insistence on figurative art. Louis Aragon hewed to the rigorous line laid down by the French Communist party, while Breton went over to the Trotskyite dissidents. The plastic artists backed away from a movement that had been split open by too many literary and political quarrels. Writing to Gallatin in 1936, Hélion rightly noted that the Surrealists' shows

144. Paris, *Association Artistique Les Surindépendants,* Oct. 27-Nov. 27, 1933, organized by René Mendès-France.

145. Letter from Arp to Kandinsky dated Nov. 12, 1933. This letter, which was written in German, is published in full in French translation in *Hans/Jean Arp: le temps des papiers déchirés,* exh. cat., Paris, 1983, p. 36.

146. Jean Cassou, "Dada et le surréalisme," *L'Amour de l'Art,* no. 3, Mar. 1934, pp. 337-344.

147. *L'Intransigeant,* Dec. 2, 1929, p. 5.

148. In a lecture delivered on Apr. 30, 1936, as "La Situation actuelle de la peinture" in *Renouveau esthétique,* Anatole Jakovski noted: "The present situation is one of stagnation, which is worsened by a great many intestine quarrels. A sign of the times: Mr. André Breton, leader of the Surrealist party, who delivered a lecture last year in Prague, is indignant about the fact that in many countries abstract works have filtered through and mingle freely with orthodox Surrealist works. In order to prevent further occurrences of what he considers a regrettable mismatch, he suggests placing a special stamp on the Surrealist works, of the sort that might be used to certify, 'This is a Paramount film.'"

149. Letter from Kandinsky to Grohmann dated Jan. 28, 1936, and Nina Kandinsky, p. 196.

150. Letter from Kandinsky to Albers dated May 24, 1935.

151. Letter from Hélion to Gallatin dated Apr. 24, 1936.

152. Letter from Kandinsky to Thiemann dated Mar. 14, 1938. In a letter to Grohmann dated Jan. 28, 1936, Kandinsky wrote that the Surrealists did not even want to look at Albers's recent engravings; the only exceptions the Surrealists made, he said, were for Arp and himself.

153. See *L'Intransigeant,* Apr. 26, 1930: "The *Revue de l'art concret* has published its introductory issue: Carlsund, Doesburg, Hélion, Tutundjan and Wantz . . . ." In that issue the signatories proclaimed as the second maxim of *Art Concret* that "a work of art must be entirely conceived and shaped by the mind before it is carried out. It must not receive any formal 'information' either from nature, from sensitivity or from sentimentality." Since in their work Arp and Kandinsky flatly contradicted these principles, both painters completely distorted van Doesburg's flimsy definition of *Art Concret.*

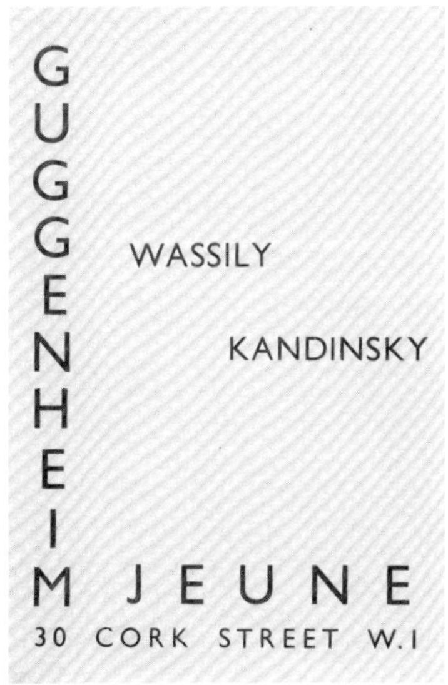

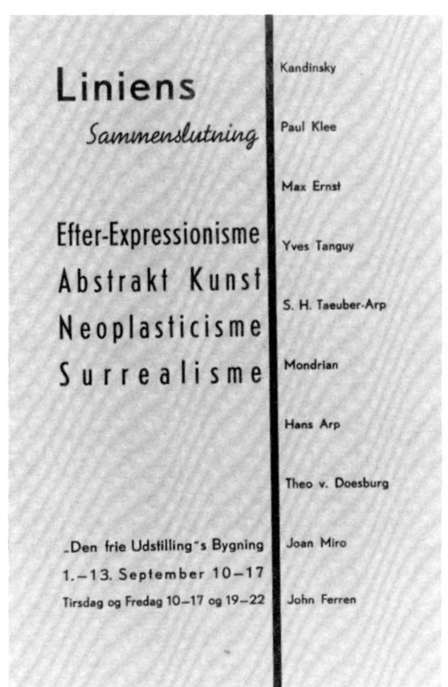

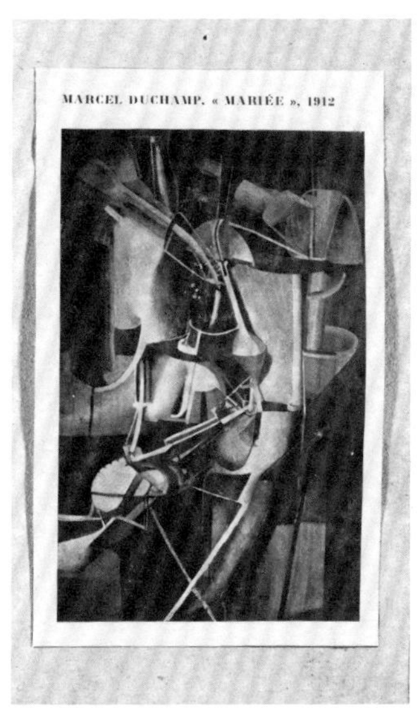

fig. 28
Catalogue for Kandinsky exhibition at Guggenheim Jeune, London, 1938
Collection Musée National d'Art Moderne, Centre Georges Pompidou, Paris, Kandinsky Bequest

fig. 29
Catalogue for *Liniens,* organized by Ejler Bille, Bjerke Petersen and Richard Mortensen of periodical *Linien,* Denmark, 1937
Collection Musée National d'Art Moderne, Centre Georges Pompidou, Paris, Kandinsky Bequest

fig. 30
Kandinsky's clipping of work by Marcel Duchamp for pedagogical documentation
Collection Musée National d'Art Moderne, Centre Georges Pompidou, Paris, Kandinsky Bequest

brought together works by artists who had all just left the movement or were about to leave it. "In London a big Surrealist show will gather people having left the group, such as Giacometti and practically Miró and Arp."[151] This development helped to bring the *Abstraits* and the *Surréalistes* together in magazines that had sworn to exclude the Surrealists' theories. In this way, first *Axis,* then *Plastique,* reconciled figures who had seemed estranged.

Pierre Loeb's gallery and the Galerie Jeanne Bucher were havens of peace and reconciliation, as witness this letter from Breton to Kandinsky, possibly written in 1936, more likely in 1939. "I haven't had the time to tell you what a strong spell the works I saw chez Madame Bucher cast over me. They are made of the essence of all the times we have been happy and will be happy again." Kandinsky, meanwhile, had learned to look distrustfully on the fickle Surrealists. To Thiemann, a former Bauhaus student who had remained in Germany, he wrote, "I will refrain from speaking badly of the Surrealists. A. Breton (the Führer of the movement) wrote a very good article on my painting in my English catalogue, which I am enclosing. [This was the catalogue of the show Peggy Guggenheim organized in London in 1938 (fig. 28).] Generally speaking, the Surrealists are against abstract art; the only exceptions they make are Arp and myself."[152] In 1940 the Surrealists —poets, painters and dealers—left Paris and went either to the United States or into the French *maquis.*

Since Kandinsky was not satisfied by either blinkered abstraction or coarse Surrealism, he looked for a third option, a synthesis that would reconcile the qualities of both (fig. 29). He proposed Concrete Art, a composite term that was not new. Van Doesburg, the most violently opinionated of the abstract painters, had suggested it in 1930.[153] Gradually Arp and Kandinsky had altered its meaning by reviving the alogic that had been the strong point of Dadaism.[154] In his written lecture on art history to Dézarrois, Kandinsky had delivered a veritable eulogy for Dadaism (fig. 30).[155]

154. Kandinsky also altered for his own purposes the word "alogic," which had been applied to Malevich's work between 1912 and 1914.

155. Letter from Kandinsky to Dézarrois dated May 10, 1937.

I have the impression I did not see Dada on your list, yet Dada was undoubtedly the starting point of Surrealism. Perhaps unwittingly, the Dadaists fought against logic by replacing it with "alogic." This fact is of the greatest importance in art history because art has never been "logical" and the laws that govern art are often very different from those that govern mathematics. In my opinion, the most important Dada artists were Arp and Duchamp (the theoretician was Hugo Ball). Arp should be classified now as a "concrete sculptor."[156]

Did Zervos have a premonition when he applied the word "concrete" to Kandinsky's work shortly after the artist moved to Paris? In his article of 1934, Zervos remarked how "the spectacle of nature directly influenced Kandinsky's work and always prevented him from going astray into abstraction without a concrete basis."[157]

Despite several articles he published in the new art review *XXe Siècle*, Kandinsky was always vague about what the term "concrete" covered;[158] and Arp, the poet, did not clarify the issue. From now on, Arp declared, he intended to produce only "paintings and sculptures of nature which would no longer be abstract but rather, creations as sensual and concrete as a leaf or a stone."[159] In attempting to justify his change in terminology, Kandinsky confined his explanations to rather Franciscan aphorisms. In the short preface he wrote for the *Abstract and Concrete Art* exhibition held in London in 1939 and organized jointly by Peggy Guggenheim and the Galerie de Beaune in Paris, Kandinsky was simplicity itself.[160] "One must never set up philosophical 'barriers' between a work and what is inside of it. In short, one must be naive." And indeed, he ended his plea somewhat naively with a paraphrase of the Scriptures. "You will recall who said, 'Be simple, like unto the little children.'"

The notion of concrete art did not survive the second half of the 1940s. It did set the tone for three or four *Konkrete Kunst* exhibitions at the Kunsthalle Basel in 1944 and an *Art Concret* show at the Galerie René Drouin in Paris in 1945.[161] Then, over Arp's protests, it was torn apart by the art critics—both the defenders of nonfigurative art, such as Léon Degand, and its detractors.[162]

The simplicity Kandinsky referred to in writing about concrete art pervaded the spirit of the times; spontaneous, naive art was all the rage in Paris. Jeanne Bucher, while continuing to defend Kandinsky and Arp, launched two naive painters, André Bauchant and Auguste Déchelette.[163] Andry-Farcy, curator of the Musée de Peinture et de Sculpture de Grenoble, organized official shows devoted entirely to the naive school, where painting "came from the heart" and triumphed over pure reason.[164] Wilhelm Uhde, who had been one of the first collectors of Cubist art and had "invented" the Douanier Rousseau, set the tone and legitimized the new fad that was sweeping Paris, and Paris only. The time would come when people would praise to the skies drawings by madmen and children.

Kandinsky had no taste for naive art or amateur painters. He had kept a few children's drawings he had used to illustrate his courses at the Bauhaus,

156. In a letter to Grohmann dated Jan. 28, 1936, Kandinsky reported that Dadaism was becoming fashionable again in Paris. Kandinsky's judgement was probably based on the fact that various articles on the movement entitled "L'Esprit Dada dans la Peinture," by Georges Hugnet had appeared in *Cahiers d'Art*: "I. Zürich & New York," 7e année, no. 1-2, 1932, pp. 57-65; "II. Berlin (1918-1922)," 7e année, no. 6-7, 1932, pp. 281-[285]; "III. Cologne et Hanovre," 7e année, no. 8-10, 1932, pp. 358-364; "(Fin)," 11e année, no. 8-10, 1936, pp. 267-[272].

157. Zervos, "Notes sur Kandinsky," p. 154.

158. For example, "L'Art concret," *XXe Siècle*, 1938. In this article, Kandinsky specified that concrete art was thriving, especially in the free countries.

159. Letters of protest from Arp and Jean Gorin to *Arts*, published July 6, 1945, p. 2.

160. *London Bulletin*, no. 14, May 1939, p. 2. The text was published in French because this issue of the Bulletin served as the catalogue for the exhibition when it was presented in Paris. See *XXe Siècle*, no. 1, 1939: "Guggenheim-Jeune is presenting an abstract art show in Paris and London: May 23-June 14 at the Galerie de Beaune, 25, rue de Beaune, in Paris, and May 10-31 [*sic*] at the main gallery in London."

161. Kunsthalle Basel, *Konkrete Kunst*, May 18-Apr. 16, 1944; Paris, Galerie René Drouin, *Art concret*, June 15-July 13, 1945.

162. Léon Degand, "Le Sens des mots" in *Les Lettres françaises*, June 23, 1945, p. 4.

163. In a letter to Grohmann dated June 25, 1943, Kandinsky wrote that the next day he would attend the opening of the Bauchant show at the Galerie Jeanne Bucher.

164. Paris, Salle Royale, *Les Maîtres populaires de la réalité*, 1937, for example. Kandinsky lent Rousseau's *Paysage aux poules blanches* (cat. no. 21) to this exhibition.

and he still retained a deep feeling for folk art. He went to see the Russian art exhibition at the Jeu de Paume because it included a section on folk art, and he liked to look at the toys displayed in the windows of the Printemps department store at Christmas time. But he did not reduce Rousseau's genius to the level of naive painting.

Like Pierre Loeb, Kandinsky made a distinction between the Douanier Rousseau and the other naive painters, and indeed used the Douanier and his work to support his statements in favor of Concrete Art. "We cannot but wholeheartedly love the pure faith of Henri Rousseau, who was entirely persuaded that he painted according to the dictates of his dead wife. Artists know well this mysterious voice which guides their brush and measures the design and the color."[165] Rousseau was doubtless the only French painter he could refer to for purposes of justifying his theory of "inner necessity," and his was probably the only painting that did not disappoint Kandinsky. He held onto his two Rousseaus even during the dark days of the Occupation.[166] When financial problems became pressing, he did consider, briefly, selling *The Painter and His Model* (cat. no. 173), and offered it to Andry-Farcy, who might have bought it for the museum in Grenoble.[167] He also talked of selling it to Grohmann. But nothing came of either plan, and both this Douanier Rousseau and the other one, *The Poultry Yard* (cat. no. 172)—which had been included in the *Blaue Reiter* show in Munich—were ultimately included in Nina Kandinsky's bequest to the Musée National d'Art Moderne in Paris. By a remarkable coincidence, just as Kandinsky was exhibiting in the last one-man show held during his lifetime, at the Galerie l'Esquisse in 1944, the Musée de la Ville de Paris reopened for the first time after the liberation of Paris with a Douanier Rousseau retrospective.[168] At the time Kandinsky died, the Douanier's native city, Laval, decided to bring home the gentle Rousseau's body. So it was that both painters' names happened to appear together in the art sections of the newspapers during this liberation period. *La France au Combat,* on January 11, 1945, headlined, "Vasily Kandinsky Has Died at the Age of 78 . . . . The Gentle Rousseau Will Rest Near the Children."

Paul Klee was another painter who had inhabited Kandinsky's universe throughout the eleven years he lived in Neuilly-sur-Seine. During the years Kandinsky and Klee spent together in Weimar and Dessau, they exchanged their works, and Kandinsky owned a number of gouaches and paintings by Klee. Were they hung on his living room walls, like the Rousseaus? Nobody knows. Kandinsky and Klee had last seen each other in 1933 (Kandinsky had written a touching farewell article in the Bauhaus newspaper[169]) and had had few opportunities to meet again. In 1937, when Kandinsky went to Bern for his retrospective, he met Klee there. Klee was already very ill, and they never saw each other again. They rarely wrote one another, and left it to their wives to keep in touch. Klee's last message is particularly moving and testifies to their profound friendship. Because it was written during that prewar waiting period known as *"la drôle de guerre,"* it was in French, as the French censors would not allow correspondence in any other language (cat. no. 213).

165. Kandinsky, "La Valeur d'une oeuvre concrète," Lindsay and Vergo II, p. 825.

166. These paintings are reproduced and identified as belonging to Kandinsky in *Cahiers d'Art,* 9e année, no. 9-10, 1934, p. [269]: "Two unpublished paintings by Henri Rousseau belonging to Mr. W. Kandinsky." The publication of the paintings here completes the cataloguing of the Douanier's work begun by Zervos in his *Rousseau,* Paris, 1927.

167. Letter from Andry-Farcy to Kandinsky dated Sept. 1943.

168. *Exposition du centenaire de Rousseau,* Dec. 22, 1944-Jan. 21, 1945. Catalogue by Anatole Jakovski, preface by Paul Eluard.

169. *Bauhaus Zeitschrift für Gestaltung,* Dec. 3, 1931, p. [2].

170. Nina Kandinsky, p. 229.

171. Four works by Klee, *Château des croyants, Sans titre, Paroles parcimonieuses de l'avare, Dix-sept égarés,* were reproduced in *La Révolution Surréaliste,* no. 3, Apr. 15, 1925, pp. 5, 13, 21, 27.

172. Paris, Galerie Simon, Jan. 24-Feb. 5, 1938; Galerie Balay-Carré, July 1938.

173. Paris, Galerie Georges Bernheim, *Paul Klee,* Feb. 1-15, 1929. Catalogue with text "Merci Paul Klee" by René Crevel.

174. Letter from Kojève to Kandinsky dated Feb. 3, 1929.

175. Loeb, *Voyages,* p. 135.

176. See Anthony Blunt, "The 'Realism' Quarrel," *Left Review,* vol. III, Apr. 1937, pp. 169-171.

177. Letter from Read to Kandinsky dated Mar. 25, 1938.

178. Louis Aragon, "Expositions: La Peinture au Tournant (I)" *Commune,* 2e année, June 1935, pp. 1181-1182, 1185-1189.

179. Letter from Kandinsky to Taeuber-Arp dated May 9, 1942. In this letter Kandinsky wrote about the preface for *10 Origin,* Zürich, 1942.

180. Kandinsky's only mistake in this connection was to have placed too much trust in the art critic Jakovski. Although Jakovski wrote articles in 1934 and 1935 in support of the abstract artists Kandinsky, Hélion and Giacometti, he later stopped defending them and specialized in the promotion of naive art, which was much more lucrative at that time.

181. In a letter to Grohmann dated Feb. 11, 1935, Kandinsky eagerly inquired whether Grohmann had received *Axis* and *Gaceta de arte.*

182. Letter from Kandinsky to Read dated Apr. 2, 1938. In a letter to Klee dated Jan. 9, 1938, Kandinsky wrote that Tériade wanted to publish two lithographs by Klee in *Verve,* one concerned with the moon and the other with the stars. Ultimately, Masson executed works on these themes for the magazine. *Plastique* was a slim review published by Domela, Arp and most importantly Taeuber-Arp and financed partly by Gallatin and the painter G.L.K. Morris. Five issues appeared between 1937 and 1939. *Plastique* was the first instrument of liaison between the abstract artists of Paris and the *American Abstract Artists.* Concerning *Transition,* see Dougald MacMillan, *Transition: the History of a Literary Era, 1927-1938,* London, 1975. Kandinsky executed

Bern, Kisterweg 6
December 30, 1939
My dear friend and young comrade—I say young because sometimes I don't quite remember exactly—my important encounter with you does not only date from yesterday—and yet sometimes it seems to me as if it was only yesterday. We certainly haven't wasted our time, either of us. Your letter of December 12 gave me such pleasure; I could feel your heart beating—such a generous heart! Thank you!

Kandinsky was profoundly shaken by his old friend's death in 1940. He learned of it while in Cauterets, a small spa in the Hautes Pyrénées region of southwestern France, where he had to stay for three months because of the exodus from Paris.[170] In Paris, at any rate, Kandinsky had to compete with Klee whether he liked it or not. Klee was the better known of the two when Kandinsky moved to Neuilly.[171] Kahnweiler was willing to handle Klee's work but refused to accept Kandinsky's. Two different galleries, Kahnweiler's Galerie Simon, as well as Balay-Carré, held shows in Klee's honor in 1938, and both were wildly successful.[172] Klee's name had been known, after all, since 1926, when the first exhibition of his work was held in Paris. In 1929, a second show, organized at Georges Bernheim, accompanied by a catalogue with a preface by René Crevel, had introduced the public to Klee's marvelous little works that were neither abstract nor Surrealist.[173] When Kojève saw the Klee show, he somewhat naively asked his uncle, "How do you situate yourself in relation to Klee?"[174] And Kandinsky must have been at a loss to answer him. Loeb, in his *Voyages à travers la peinture,* hardly mentioned Kandinsky and had nothing but good things to say about Klee.

> *Among the painters and the poets who use this new language to some extent, we should note Kandinsky, who, along with Mondrian, created nonobjective art; Miró, who began by analyzing synthesis and carrying it to its utmost limits, and is now crawling through prehistoric caves and dodging entirely away to another planet; whereas Klee (who was omitted, for reasons I cannot understand, from* Le Surréalisme et la peinture) *brings us into a marvelous world of enchantment with his astonishingly varied watercolors, as lightly woven and as amazingly sturdy as spiderwebs.*[175]

Did Klee's death have a liberating effect on Kandinsky? Certainly, in the last few years of his life, Kandinsky, like Klee, gave himself over to unbridled fantasy and penetrated into the world of enchantment. He reexperienced the frantic appetite for work that Klee expressed in his last paintings and, like him, produced small formats only.

Until the very end of his life, Kandinsky's festival of color and form contrasted with the flat, unleavened realism advocated by—paradoxically—both the conformist aesthetics of the bourgeoisie and the leftist ideologies. What with academic reactionism on the right and "proletarian realism" on the left, little scope remained for an art that had risen above day-to-day

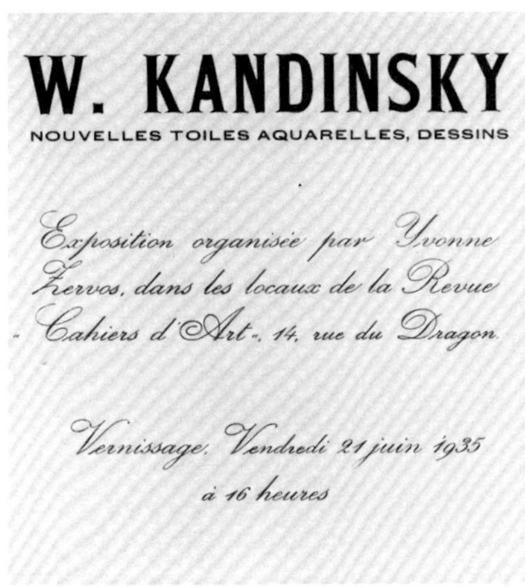

fig. 31
Invitation to second Kandinsky exhibition at Galerie des "Cahiers d'Art," Paris, 1935
Collection Musée National d'Art Moderne, Centre Georges Pompidou, Paris, Kandinsky Bequest

triviality.[176] Herbert Read warned Kandinsky of the damage wrought by the bleak new trend. "There seems to be a reaction against any kind of 'abstract' art just now—the reactionaries never did like it, but even the revolutionaries turn against it in favour of a dreary 'socialist realism.' "[177]

This was a period of dramatic changes. Aragon was the apostle of a reversion to the human element, as opposed to abstraction. In 1935, writing about an exhibition held at the Maison de la Culture in Paris, he stressed the abrupt transformation in Giacometti's work. The sculptor had left Surrealism behind and come back to the human figure. "The two heads that Giacometti calls *Les deux opprimés* are only an inadequate reflection of what he is seeking. He says now that all of his earlier work was an attempt to flee reality and speaks disdainfully of a sort of mysticism that had slipped into his work. His drawings have already revealed his hatred of the society in which he lives."[178]

Accordingly, the last writings that Kandinsky published have to be read in context, a polemical context. His "few magical and tranquil words" are meant to ward off the incessant attacks on even so much as the possibility of abstract art.[179] With the discerning judgement that governed all his life, Kandinsky wrote and illustrated only for the most independent magazines, those that were most receptive to the imminent potentialities of plastic art and whose typography was outstanding.[180] He identified himself with their struggle and strove actively to enhance their circulation.[181] Enthusiastically, he listed them for Herbert Read and was thrilled to think that such magazines could still exist. "Have you received the last issue of *Verve*? It's very handsome. *XXe Siècle* was more modest but very precious too. We now have 3 (three!) art reviews in Paris. No, I beg your pardon, four. I forgot *Cahiers d'Art*. Ah, pardon me, once again, five if we think of *Plastique*. And there is even a sixth one, not quite Parisian and not quite a review of the plastic arts, but a sort of 'American cousin,' so to speak, but born in Paris. It is called *Transition*, and it is very important."[182]

This letter, written in 1938, shows what vitality Kandinsky still had at seventy-two. Unable to find an important dealer who would free him from financial worries, Kandinsky militated through the small galleries that had not built up clienteles; there, he exhibited along with much younger artists and was willing to take his turn between two painters who were showing for the first time. In 1934 and 1935 he showed his recent works at the new Galerie des "Cahiers d'Art," run by Yvonne Zervos (fig. 31).[183] It was not a real gallery, and this letter from Hélion to Gallatin shows that its vocation was uncertain. "March 26, 1934. [Zervos] has transformed his office rue du Dragon into a two-floors gallery very good-looking indeed. The first show opened last week is devoted to modern architecture. The following will be for the new Mirós. Third one might be for the young abstract painting." (This was right after the Kandinsky show.) One year later Hélion was disenchanted. "February 22, 1935. The *cahier d'art* have a mediocre show of young architects and modern furniture. . . . Never a season so poor in shows. *Cahier d'Art* . . . appear but twice a year. Zervos is now selling furnitures in his gallery, which gives an infortunate [*sic*] mercenary feeling to the visitor."[184]

the drawings for the cover of *Transition*, no. 27, Apr.-May 1938 (cat. no. 41), the issue in which some of his German poems appear (see note 91). In a letter to Grohmann dated Apr. 11, 1938, and a letter to Jolas dated Dec. 26, 1937, Kandinsky mentioned this issue.

183. Christian and Yvonne Zervos introduced the Kandinskys to Paris. Kandinsky mentioned them often in his letters to Grohmann, see particularly the letter dated Jan. 7, 1934. In 1937 they fell out over the conception of the exhibition *Origines et développement de l'art international indépendant* (see note 124) and because, in Kandinsky's view, Zervos thereafter did not strongly support abstract art. Their quarrel was confirmed by Kandinsky's letter to Zervos dated June 1, 1937, and by Zervos's very negative review of *Origines et développement* in *Cahiers d'Art*, 12e année, no. 4-5, 1937, pp. 162-164, for example: "Influenced by Cézanne and Matisse, Kandinsky had (in 1911) decomposed the representation of objects and made them into mere pretexts for the development of shapes and colors. Picabia had laid down (in 1909) the first bases of the art which is wrongly called abstract."

184. Letter from Hélion to Gallatin dated Mar. 26, 1934.

fig. 32
Guest book from group show at Galerie Jeanne Bucher, Paris, 1944
Courtesy Galerie Jeanne Bucher, Paris

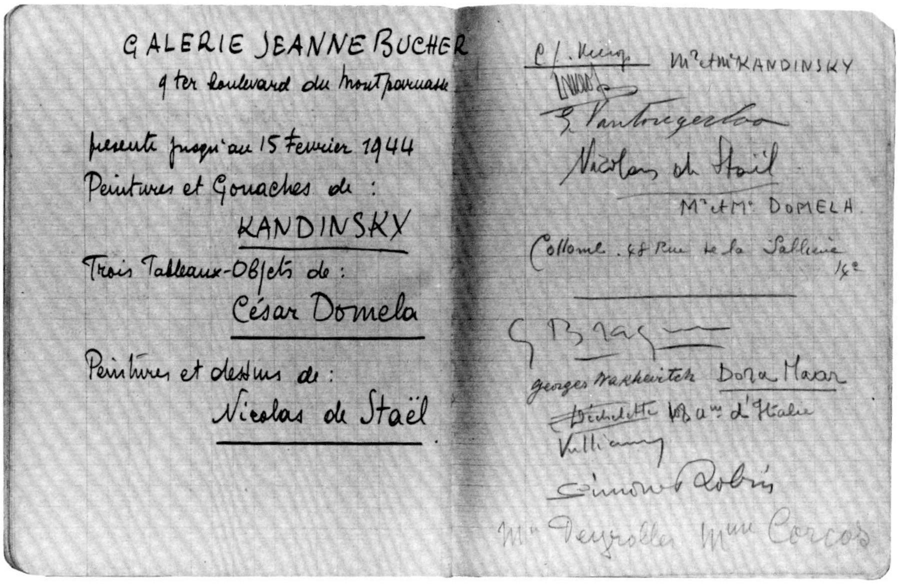

Was that why in 1938 Kandinsky began showing in the gallery that Jeanne Bucher had just opened on the boulevard Montparnasse?[185] It was a modest but authentic gallery, which issued publications and had genuine influence over developments in the Paris art world. Kandinsky exhibited alongside Domela and Nicolas de Staël (fig. 32). He had three one-man shows, including one in 1942, during the German Occupation, when abstract art was completely dissident (fig. 33). It was Jeanne Bucher who introduced Kandinsky to Dézarrois in 1936, and it was she who kept him supplied with tobacco during the years it was rationed or unavailable. Kandinsky and Jeanne Bucher held each other in mutual esteem, which, although neither of them indulged in sentimental effusiveness, matured into sincere friendship in the final years, when both of them suffered from isolation.

For Kandinsky, although careful in his choice of visitors, liked to be in contact with young artists, and his correspondence with the Alberses allowed him to keep up to date on what was going on at Black Mountain ("Only the Alberses write happy letters.");[186] that with Hannes Beckmann on events in Prague; with Grohmann and Thiemann, on developments in Germany. Among his visitors were Ben Nicholson and Barbara Hepworth, Hélion, Ejler Bille, Pevsner, Hartung, Fernandez and Domela.[187] He gave lavish advice by correspondence to Richard Mortensen and others.[188] Hartung later recalled his visit to Kandinsky's before the war. Kandinsky was part of the Paris art world and had a definite influence over it. Hélion, for instance, outlined to Gallatin which studios he should include in his schedule of visits in 1938. "June 10, 1938 . . . Hartung's drawings and small pictures and Magnelli's collages . . . . we have been much impressed by the three last constructions by Pevsner, the new Mondrians, and the recent Kandinsky's. The latter is certainly in one of his best periods and has done very remarkable gouaches that would really make a visit to his Neuilly studio worthwhile."

185. Kandinsky had contacted Jeanne Bucher in 1932, but the Depression had forced her to close her gallery for a time. She organized three one-man exhibitions of Kandinsky's work: *Kandinsky* (recent paintings, and watercolors and graphics from 1910-35), Dec. 3-19, 1936; *Kandinsky* (watercolors and gouaches from 1910-20 and 1937-39), June 2-17, 1939; *Wassily Kandinsky* (recent paintings and watercolors), July 21-Aug. 4, 1942. See review of the latter exhibition by G. di San Lazzaro, "Au point du jour—le tableau retourné," *L'Italie Nouvelle,* no. 255, July 25, 1942, p. 1. Jeanne Bucher introduced Kandinsky to Noëlle Lecoutoure and Marcel Panier, who organized the last Kandinsky exhibition held during his lifetime: Paris, Galerie l'Esquisse, *Etapes de l'oeuvre de Wassily Kandinsky,* Nov. 7-Dec. 7, 1944.

186. Letter from Kandinsky to Klee dated Dec. 16, 1934.

187. His visitors also included former Bauhaus pupils, such as Florence Henri, who had turned to photography and design in Paris.

188. For example, letter from Kandinsky to Mortensen dated Feb. 12, 1939. Letter preserved in the Kandinsky Archive, MNAM.

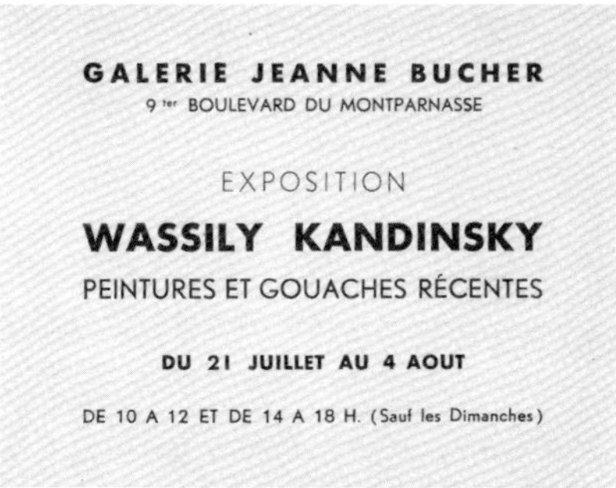

fig. 33
Invitation to final Kandinsky exhibition at Galerie Jeanne Bucher, Paris, 1942
Collection Musée National d'Art Moderne, Centre Georges Pompidou, Paris, Kandinsky Bequest

Kandinsky in turn visited the younger artists in their studios and was receptive to their search for expression. The days of great friendships were over; he was too old to find a new Franz Marc or a new Paul Klee. But he was close to Miró, "the little man who always paints large canvases, is a real little volcano who really projects his paintings."[189] Their correspondence is insignificant—chiefly concerned with hotel reservations for a vacation—but later Miró did recall having exchanged a painting with Kandinsky.[190] Kandinsky paid him an even greater tribute at the end of 1943—public transport was virtually nonexistent at the time—when he went to the trouble of going all the way to the Galerie Jeanne Bucher to see the Miró exhibition there. On December 1, 1943, Kandinsky wrote to Bruguière, who had asked what was happening in Paris: "All I've seen is the Miró show at Jeanne Bucher, where there were some fine pictures in Miró's style."[191]

Hans Arp and his wife Sophie Taeuber-Arp are often mentioned in Kandinsky's correspondence.[192] The last text Kandinsky wrote was in Taeuber-Arp's memory. Arp held Kandinsky in similar esteem. In describing his first visit to Kandinsky, in 1912, Arp was probably actually recalling the tone of their conversation decades later in Neuilly-sur-Seine. "What Kandinsky had to say was tender, rich, vivacious and humorous. Inside his studio, words, form and color merged together and were transformed into fabulous unheard of worlds such as no one has ever seen. And by listening carefully I could hear, behind the roar and tumult of those worlds, the tintinnabulation of those brilliant, gaudy, onion-domed Russian cities."[193]

Magnelli was the last artist to call on Kandinsky, who exchanged a lovely canvas from 1929, *Loose Connection,* for a schoolboy's slate Magnelli had painted in 1937 (cat. no. 135).[194] Although illness had made Kandinsky very weak, he showered encouragement and optimism on the younger painter. For Magnelli was just back from the country, where he had been forced to hide, and was disheartened by so many years without painting and by the difficulties of producing abstract work in a Paris that was still occupied. When Kandinsky died on December 13, 1944, *On the Spiritual in Art* had not yet been translated into French. But he left behind Arp, Miró and Magnelli as a trio of spiritual heirs.[195]

189. Letter from Kandinsky to Grohmann dated Dec. 2, 1935.
190. Joan Miró, *Ceci est la couleur de mes rêves. Entretiens avec Georges Raillard,* Paris, 1977, p. 68.
191. *Peintures, gouaches et dessins de Joan Miró,* Oct. 19-Nov. 15, 1943.
192. For example, letter in support of Arp from Kandinsky to André de Ridder dated Nov. 2, 1933; letter from Kandinsky to Grohmann dated Mar. 15, 1934; letter from Kandinsky to Klee dated Oct. 21, 1939.
193. Jean Arp, "Kandinsky le poète," in Max Bill, ed., *Wassily Kandinsky,* Paris, 1951, p. 89.
194. Alberto Magnelli, "Une foi profonde," *XXe Siècle,* no. XXVII, Dec. 1966, pp. 91-92.
195. Barr presented the reverse of this view, attributing the formal changes in Kandinsky's work to the influence of Miró and Arp, without, however, attempting to support his assertions, in *Cubism and Abstract Art,* p. 68: "Subsequently his work became more drily geometrical but in the last few years he has turned to more organic forms, perhaps under the influence of the younger Parisians Miró and Arp, to whom he pointed the way twenty years before." Kandinsky was very upset by the scornful treatment he was given throughout this catalogue, and wrote a long letter of protest to Barr dated July 16, 1936.

Epilogue

Moving from one quotation to another, we have covered the eleven years that Kandinsky lived in Paris, from 1933 to 1944, the last eleven years of his life. Through these excerpts, these verbal snapshots, we have brought a number of unaccustomed authorities into the Kandinskian pantheon. We have seen various movements go by, groups fall apart and regroupings take place, while individuals remain. Our purpose, in this brief introduction to a period that remains enigmatic in Kandinsky's career, has been to remove certain labels and sometimes replace them by others, to avoid paraphrases when the original text is richer and more colorful than any anachronistic monologue we might invent, and to subject to the corrosive effects of this reconstituted dialogue the outmoded stereotypes upon which the history of art sometimes relies.

In 1913 Munich and the Berlin of *Der Sturm* were not ready to welcome the newness of brilliantly colored but subjectless painting, and they hurled abuse at "the Russian" who wanted to inflict it on them. Similarly, in the 1930s, Paris did not understand how this "former brute" could give himself over to decadent "softness," and the critics smiled mockingly at his "effeminate" works—seeming to consider Kandinsky a new Hercules obliged by Omphale to sit at her feet and spin, or a new Samson weakened by Delilah.

Kandinsky immediately understood the distance between his adoptive city and his new manner of painting. In an article he wrote in memory of his friend Franz Marc, for *Cahiers d'Art,* we find these disillusioned lines: "The times were difficult but heroic. We went ahead with our painting. The public spat on it. Today we go ahead with our painting and the public says, 'That's pretty.' This is a change but it does not mean that the times have become any easier for artists."[196]

Translated by Eleanor Levieux

196. W. Kandinsky, "Franz Marc," *Cahiers d'Art,* 11e année, no. 8-10, 1936, p. 274.

KANDINSKY AND SCIENCE: THE INTRODUCTION OF BIOLOGICAL IMAGES IN THE PARIS PERIOD

Vivian Endicott Barnett

After Kandinsky settled in Paris and began to paint again in 1934, his work manifested stylistic and iconographic changes. The artist was then sixty-seven years old; he stayed in France for almost eleven years, until his death there in 1944. During this last decade Kandinsky completed one hundred and forty-four oil paintings and more than two hundred and fifty watercolors and gouaches in addition to producing several hundred drawings. This substantial body of late work possesses a unity that sets it apart from what he had done between 1897 and 1933, although it can be related to his earlier work. The question of what is new and what is already familiar in Kandinsky's Paris pictures is complex and difficult to analyze. However, this is one of the essential questions posed by his late work. The visual evidence of Kandinsky's paintings and works on paper undeniably reveals that new motifs are introduced into his art in 1934. Moreover, it is generally agreed that during the Paris period Kandinsky's colors changed: he selected new hues, favored pastels rather than primaries and achieved original and intricate color harmonies. In the summer of 1934, at the time of Kandinsky's first exhibition at the Galerie des "Cahiers d'Art" in Paris, Christian Zervos wrote: "The influence of nature on his work has never been so perceptible as in the canvases painted in Paris. The atmosphere, light, airiness and sky of the Ile-de-France completely transforms the expressiveness of his work."[1]

Other significant changes took place when Kandinsky resumed work in Paris early in 1934. He returned to painting large canvases, he began to add sand to discrete areas of his paintings and he incorporated biomorphic—even biological—forms into his art. However, these features had been tentatively introduced before or—in the case of the large size of his pictures—had once been prevalent in Kandinsky's work. Thus, it becomes exceedingly difficult to differentiate between innovation and the culmination of earlier tendencies.

Certain biographical facts about the artist clarify and qualify the changes that attended Kandinsky's relocation to Paris. This was the second time he was forced to leave Germany because of political events. Moreover, Kandinsky and his wife, Nina, had left their native Russia in December 1921 and during the intervening years had lived in Weimar, Dessau and Berlin. Although he did not move to France until the very end of 1933, the transition from the Bauhaus in Germany to Paris took place gradually from 1928 to 1934.[2] He took annual trips there during this time, and his work was exhibited at the Galerie Zak in January 1929, at the Galerie de France in March 1930, in the *Cercle et Carré* group show at the Galerie 23 in the spring of 1930

I am grateful to Christian Derouet for generously permitting me to study Kandinsky's drawings, papers and books at the Musée National d'Art Moderne, Centre Georges Pompidou, in Paris, and to Jessica Boissel for assisting with my research there. I have relied upon several people for their scientific knowledge and I would like to thank them for their essential help: Dr. Michael Bedford, Harold and Percy Uris Professor of Reproductive Biology, Cornell University Medical College; Dr. Arthur Karlin, Professor of Biochemistry and Neurology, College of Physicians and Surgeons of Columbia University; Dr. Niles Eldredge, Chairman of Department of Invertebrates, American Museum of Natural History; Dr. Peter H. Barnett, Associate Professor of Philosophy, John Jay College, The City University of New York; and Eric Wahl. The Annex of The New York Public Library and the Bibliothèque Centrale of the Muséum National d'Histoire Naturelle in Paris have provided essential sources of information.

1. Christian Zervos, "Notes sur Kandinsky," *Cahiers d'Art*, 9e année, no. 5-8, 1934, p. 154. Author's translation.
2. Many years earlier, in 1906-07, Kandinsky had lived in Sèvres outside Paris with Gabriele Münter.

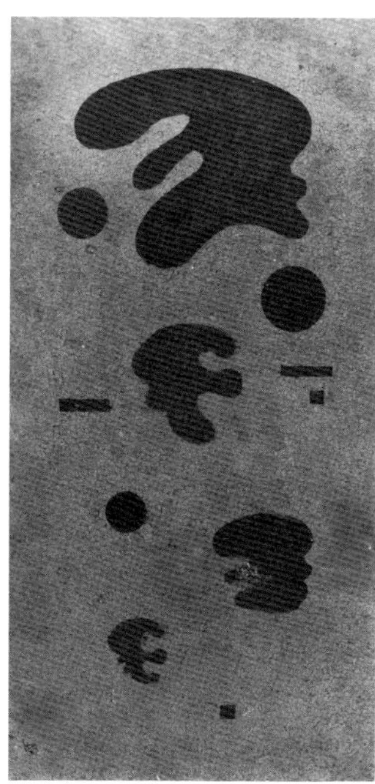

fig. 1
Vasily Kandinsky
Start. 1934
Private Collection, Basel

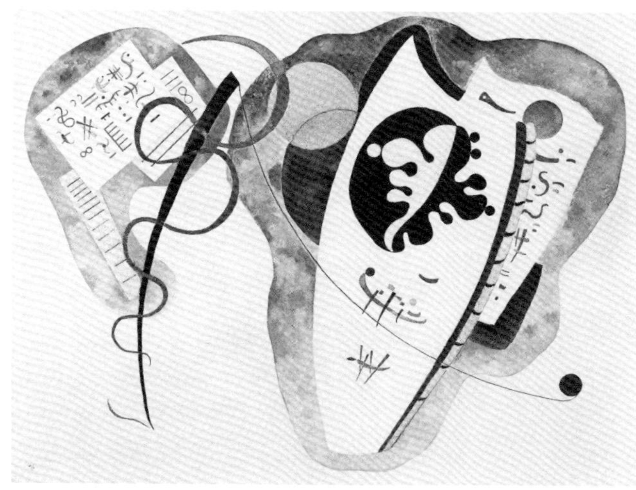

fig. 2
Vasily Kandinsky
Two Surroundings. 1934
Collection Stedelijk Museum, Amsterdam

and at the Surrealist exhibition of the *Association Artistique Les Surindépendants* in late October and November of 1933. Following the closing of the Bauhaus in Berlin in July 1933, Vasily and Nina Kandinsky vacationed at Les Sablettes near Toulon in France in late August and September and spent most of October in Paris. At the end of the month they returned to Berlin and remained there until December 16, 1933.[3] After spending five days in Switzerland they arrived in Paris on December 21, 1933, and were installed in a new apartment in Neuilly-sur-Seine by the beginning of 1934.[4] Not surprisingly there is a hiatus in Kandinsky's work between August 1933, when he painted *Development in Brown* in Berlin, and February 1934, when he resumed work in Paris and titled his first picture *Start* (fig. 1).

When Kandinsky began to paint again in 1934, he introduced certain specific and original motifs into his work. By analyzing the images in his pictures, it is possible to determine when new motifs entered his pictorial vocabulary and which forms persist from previous periods. For example, *Graceful Ascent* of March 1934 (cat. no. 21) retains the geometric and curvilinear imagery as well as the strict hierarchical grid-like structure of his Bauhaus work. However, the pastel hues and delicate nuances of value signal the lightness and sweetness of color he created during the Paris period. Likewise, imagery from earlier periods appears in *Two Surroundings* of November 1934 (fig. 2), which displays the whiplash line and the suggestion of rowers in a boat first seen in Kandinsky's painting before World War I, when he lived in Munich, as well as the overlapping circles and rows of calligraphic marks familiar from his work done when he was at the Bauhaus in Dessau.[5] However, the addition of fine-grained sand to specific zones of the canvas that occurs here is unique to Kandinsky's work of 1934-35, although in previous years he had occasionally experimented with sprinkling sand on his paintings. Similarly, the distinctive black and white curved form at the right enters Kandinsky's pictorial vocabulary in 1934.

The new motifs the artist introduced in 1934 must be singled out and identified. These forms derive from the world of biology—especially zoology

3. Information from correspondence with Will Grohmann—especially Kandinsky's letters dated Oct. 8, 31 and Dec. 20, 1933—and Kandinsky's letter to Josef Albers dated Jan. 9, 1934. The letters to Grohmann cited in the text belong to the Archiv Will Grohmann, Staatsgalerie Stuttgart, and those to Albers belong to the Josef Albers Papers preserved in the Manuscript and Archive Department of the Sterling Memorial Library, Yale University, New Haven.
4. Information from Kandinsky's letters to Galka Scheyer dated Dec. 20, 1933, and Jan. 5, 1934, and his letter to Will Grohmann dated Jan. 7, 1934. The letters to Scheyer cited in the text are preserved in the Blue Four Galka Scheyer Collection of the Norton Simon Museum of Art, Pasadena.
5. For example, *Lines of Marks (Zeichenreihen)* of July 1931 (Collection Kunstmuseum Basel; HL watercolors 442).

and embryology—and from the work of other artists with which Kandinsky was familiar. In 1934 there is a remarkable incidence in his painting of images of amoebas, embryos, larvae and marine invertebrates, as well as leaf forms and punctuation marks. By focusing on the period from 1934 through 1937, the new imagery of Kandinsky's late work will be defined and interpreted. Once established, his new iconography is continued and elaborated upon throughout his Paris work. Not only paintings but also watercolors and drawings will be analyzed in basically chronological order.[6] This essay will emphasize innovation rather than the sense of continuity that permeates Kandinsky's art.[7] Works that incorporate new imagery will be discussed and, whenever possible, the new motifs will be related to specific sources.

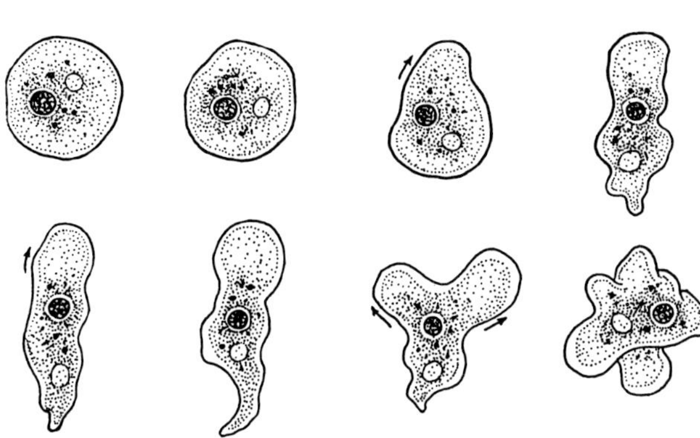

fig. 3
Shapes of an amoeba from Henry A. Barrows, *General Biology*, 1935, p. 98, after Verworn

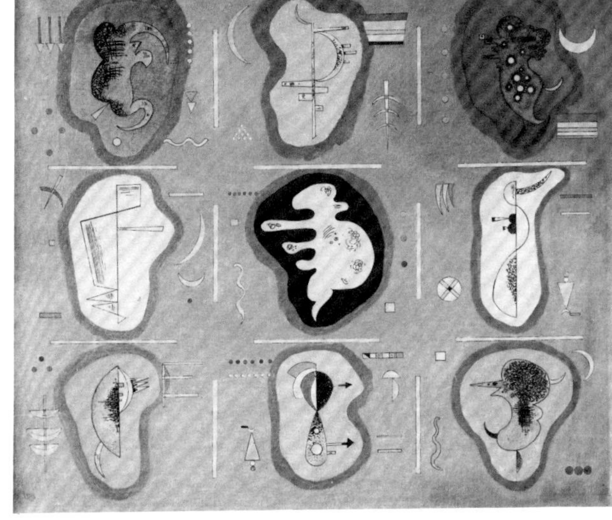

fig. 4
Vasily Kandinsky
Each for Himself. 1934
Private Collection

Although the title *Start*, which Kandinsky gave the first painting he did in Paris, would appear to be an English word, "start" was an international term commonly used in sports.[8] "Start" vividly conveys the fast beginning associated with a race or takeoff. With reference to Kandinsky's resumption of painting after a lengthy hiatus, it seems somewhat ironic but clearly expresses an optimistic beginning. Executed in tempera over plaster on a small board, this picture presents dark blue, green and purple elements against a light blue background. The artist contrasts circular, square and rectangular forms with four distinctly amoeboid shapes whose amorphousness is immediately remarkable and innovative. In fact, Kandinsky introduced images of amoebas (fig. 3)—a simple unicellular form of life—into his paintings in 1934. It is especially significant that this most elemental stage of life is depicted in a work of art titled *Start*. The concurrence of image and meaning cannot be accidental.

He elaborates upon the simple amoeboid form in the canvas *Each for Himself* of April 1934 (fig. 4; cat. no. 22). The central white figure and, to an even greater degree, the watercolor study for it (cat. no. 23), resemble an

6. Kandinsky kept a *Hauskatalog* or Handlist in which he recorded his paintings and specified their titles, exact dates, media, dimensions and exhibition histories. Each entry was numbered and accompanied by a small sketch. In addition, after 1922, Kandinsky maintained a separate Handlist for watercolors and gouaches.
7. The author emphasizes continuity and the unity of Kandinsky's pictorial modes in her book *Kandinsky at the Guggenheim*, New York, 1983.
8. Hugo Moser, *Deutsche Sprachgeschichte*, Stuttgart, 1955, p. 177.

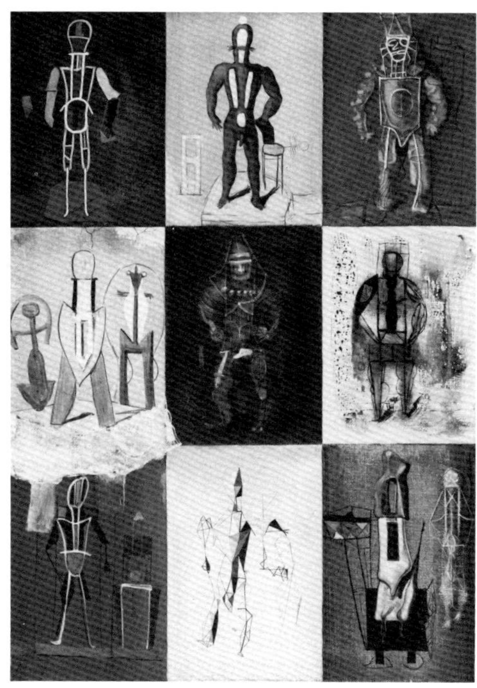

fig. 5
Victor Brauner
Petite morphologie. 1934
Menil Foundation

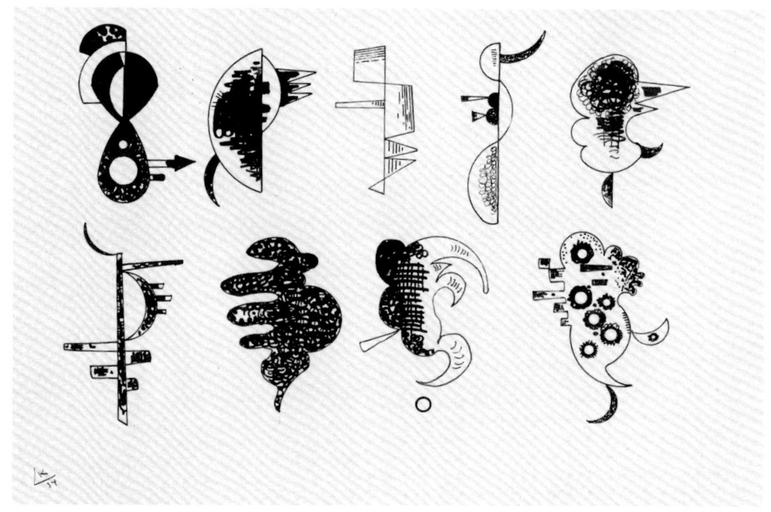

fig. 6
Vasily Kandinsky
Drawing for *Each for Himself.* 1934
Formerly Galerie Karl Flinker, Paris

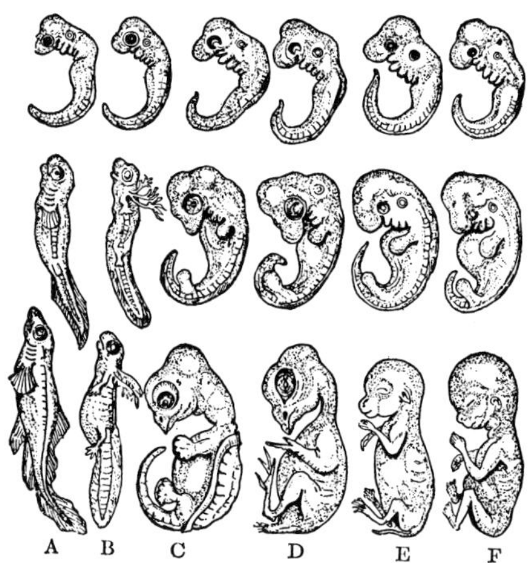

fig. 7
Progressive stages in the development of vertebrate embryos from Barrows, 1935, p. 499, after Darwin

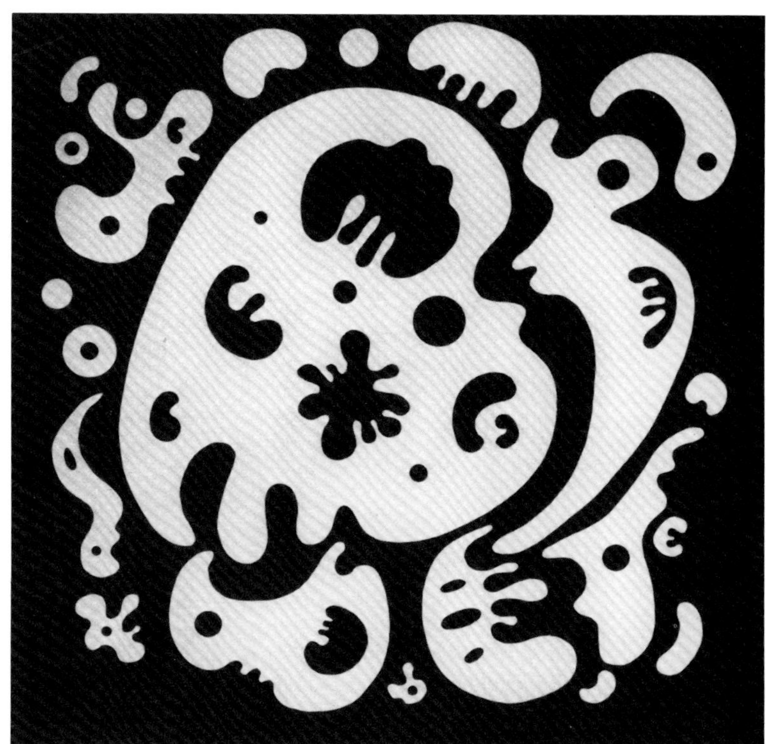

fig. 8
Vasily Kandinsky
Black Forms on White. 1934
Collection Association-Fondation Christian et Yvonne Zervos, Vézelay

amoeba in overall shape (including pseudopods) and in internal details such as vacuoles. Likewise, the figure in the upper right corner possesses decidedly cellular characteristics and vaguely embryonic qualities (fig. 7). Each figure is enclosed in a womb-like shape; in particular, the one at the lower right corner looks like a uterus. Although two of the nine images are amoeboid, others bear striking similarities to drawings by Pablo Picasso and Julio González. For example, the sculptural form in the middle of the top row resembles González's coeval drawings and sculptures, *Woman Combing Her Hair, Woman with a Mirror* and *Maternity*.[9] The figure with female attributes on the right in the middle row brings to mind Picasso's drawings from *Une Anatomie*, which were published in *Minotaure* in February 1933.[10]

Not only are the figures in *Each for Himself* innovative but also the format of the picture is completely new in Kandinsky's work. By organizing three registers of three figures each in compartmentalized zones, Kandinsky presents the mathematical format that recurs in *Thirty* of 1937, *Fifteen* of 1938 (cat. nos. 68, 67), and *4 x 5 = 20* of 1943 (HL 725). The simplicity and rigid geometry of the pictorial organization suggests Piet Mondrian's canvases.[11] However, the closest parallel can be found in a coeval painting by Victor Brauner, *Petite morphologie* (fig. 5), where nine figures are arranged in three rows. Moreover, the Surrealist overtones of several of Kandinsky's motifs indicate Brauner as a possible source of inspiration. Brauner had lived in Paris since 1930; his work was shown together with that of Kandinsky in the autumn of 1933 in the Surrealist exhibition organized by the *Association Artistique Les Surindépendants*.[12]

fig. 9
Hans Arp
Drawing from "L'Air est une Racine" in *Le Surréalisme au Service de la Révolution*, 1933, p. 33
Collection The Museum of Modern Art Library, New York

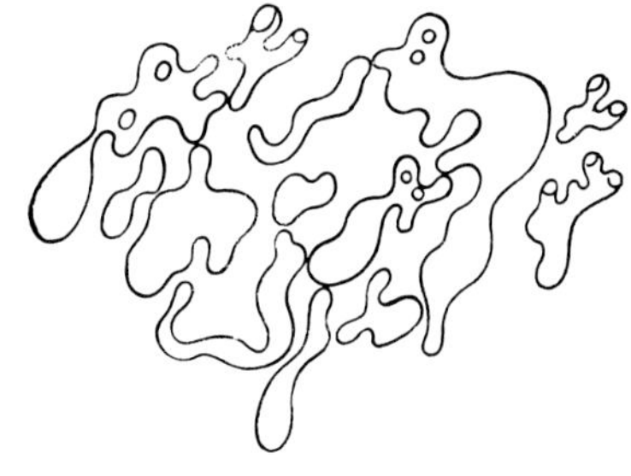

Before he painted *Each for Himself*, Kandinsky executed an ink drawing (fig. 6) in which the nine figures are depicted in a different sequence. In the final version two shapes have been reversed and each of the nine figures has been suspended within its womb-like space. In the painting horizontal and vertical bars separate the zones, and arrows, curving worm-like forms and small geometric details have been added to articulate the nine compartments. Kandinsky's painting *Figure in Red* of December 1930 (HL 535) foreshadows the Surrealist figures in *Each for Himself*. However, both the format and the elaboration of these forms in *Each for Himself* appear for the first time in the 1934 painting.

In *Black Forms on White* (fig. 8; cat. no. 45), which was also painted in April, the black amoeboid shapes shown on a white ground in the center suggest a macrophage. In addition, various forms of primitive life are indicated by the white shapes on black ground in the peripheral zones. Contemporary illustrations of both amoeboid and embryonic forms (figs. 3, 7) prove the relevance of biological knowledge to Kandinsky's painting. *Black Forms on White* also contains forms suggestive of elements in blood: two white circles with centers at the left edge can be identified as red cells, the two small amoeboid shapes at the top can be associated with white cells, and the small curved elements at the upper left and lower right corners look like platelets.[13]

The difficulty and the complexity of problems encountered in interpreting Kandinsky's pictures become apparent when *Black Forms on White* is compared with a drawing by Hans Arp (fig. 9) that was published in *Le Sur-*

9. Margit Rowell, *Julio González*, exh. cat., New York, 1983, cat. nos. 141, 142, 144-149 and Josephine Withers, *Julio González: Sculpture in Iron*, New York, 1978, pl. 66.
10. *Minotaure*, no. 1, Feb. 1933, pp. 33-37.
11. See the view of Mondrian's atelier in *Cahiers d'Art*, 6e année, no. 1, 1931, p. 43. Also *Composition B with Red* and *Composition with Red and Black* of 1936 in Michel Seuphor, *Piet Mondrian: Life and Work*, New York, 1956, cc 376, 377.
12. Dominique Bozo, *Victor Brauner*, exh. cat., Paris, 1972, n.p.
13. I am indebted to Dr. Michael Bedford for these observations made in conversation with the author, July 2, 1984.

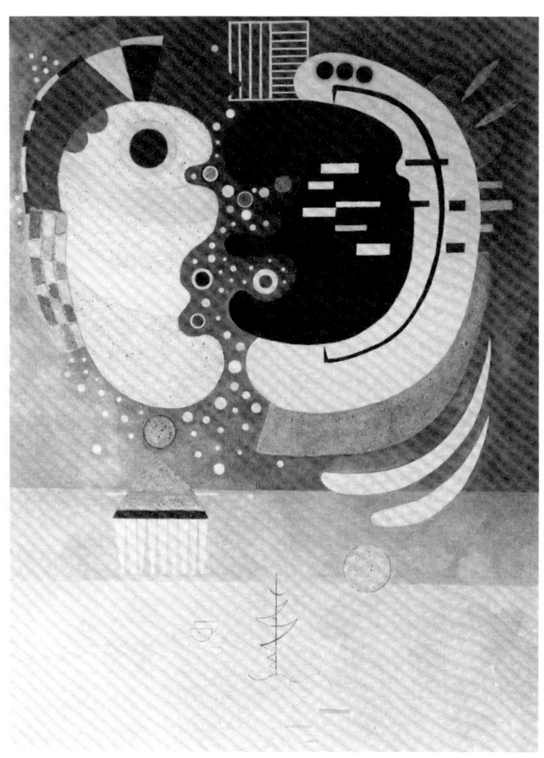

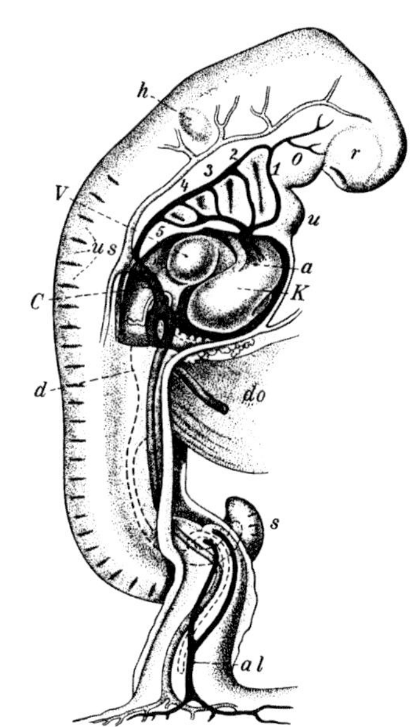

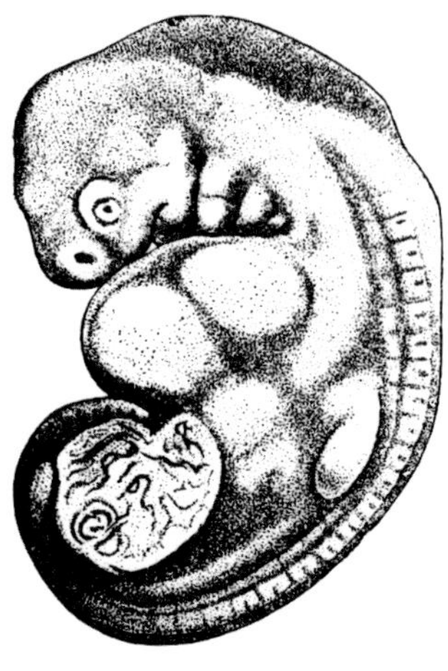

fig. 11
Human embryo from *Abstammungslehre: Systematik, Paläontologie und Biogeographie,* 1914, p. 61

fig. 12
Human embryo from *Zellen-und Gewebelehre: Morphologie und Entwicklungsgeschichte. II. Zoologischer Teil,* 1913, p. 388

fig. 10
Vasily Kandinsky
Between Two. 1934
Private Collection

réalisme au Service de la Révolution in 1933.[14] The curving forms, the large figure with eyes at the right and the overall configuration are amazingly similar in Arp's drawing and this painting of 1934. Did Kandinsky and Arp share common interests in specific biological forms and in natural growth? How was Kandinsky influenced by Surrealism? To what extent did he seek inspiration from science in general and zoology and embryology in particular?

In May 1934 Kandinsky completed the large painting *Between Two* (fig. 10). Here two curving forms face each other; they are defined as sand-covered areas on the canvas and are set off from the red background.[15] The figure on the left bears an overwhelming resemblance to an embryo. The large eye and lateral articulation as well as the definition of specific areas leave no doubt as to the identity of the image and certainly demand explanation. Moreover, the curved form on the right also seems embryonic, its curved internal rod resembles a notochord and the adjacent black area can be interpreted as a yolk sac.[16]

In the artist's library, which is preserved in the Kandinsky Archive at the Musée National d'Art Moderne, Centre Georges Pompidou in Paris, is the encyclopedia *Die Kultur der Gegenwart,* to which Kandinsky referred in his illustrations from the mid-1920s for the book *Point and Line to Plane (Punkt und Linie zu Fläche).* The many volumes of this encyclopedia were published in Leipzig and Berlin during the teens. Diagrams of human embryos from two of the volumes in this series provide specific images known to the artist (figs. 11, 12). In addition, the circles on the red background that sur-

14. "L'Air est une Racine," *Le Surréalisme au Service de la Révolution,* no. 6, May 15, 1933, p. 33.
15. "Centenaire de Kandinsky," *XXe Siècle,* no. 27, Dec. 1966, p. 81, color repr.
16. Observations made in conversation with the author by Dr. Arthur Karlin, May 4, 1984, and by Dr. Michael Bedford, July 2, 1984.
17. See Kenneth C. Lindsay and Peter Vergo, eds., *Kandinsky: Complete Writings on Art,* Boston, 1982, vol. II, p. 630.
18. I would like to thank Dr. Niles Eldredge for bringing this to my attention in conversation, June 4, 1984.

round the embryonic form in *Between Two* resemble the blood cells illustrated in the encyclopedia volume that covers zoology on the page opposite a diagram Kandinsky copied for *Point and Line to Plane* (fig. 13).[17] Even his title, *Entre deux,* alludes to the fact that a new life begins from the union between two people.

The next painting listed after *Between Two* in Kandinsky's Handlist of oil paintings is *Blue World* (fig. 14; cat. no. 25) which also dates from May 1934. Although the imagery of *Blue World* is more fanciful and imaginative than that of the preceding work, various embryological and larval forms can be identified. The most obvious embryo is situated to the right of center on an ochre sand-covered rectangle. In addition, the figure at the upper left resembles a fish embryo (fig. 15) and the curved large-bellied shape on the salmon-colored rectangular zone at the lower right suggests a salamander embryo (fig. 16). Adjacent to the latter in Kandinsky's painting are multicolored, segmented creatures that seem to be insects.[18] Moreover, the large blue worm-form in the middle of *Blue World* looks like a nematode (fig. 17).

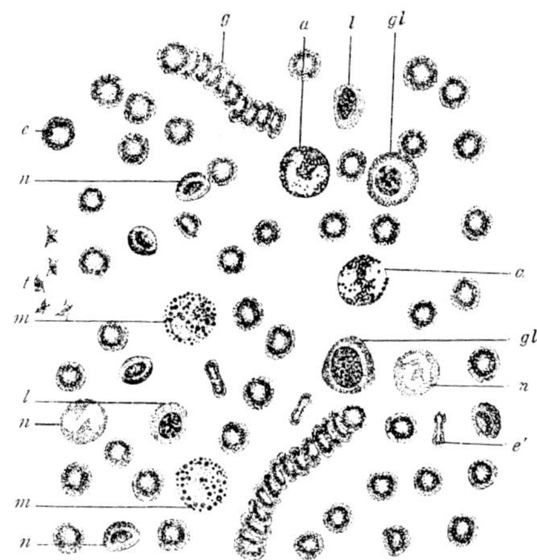

fig. 13
Blood cells from *Zoologischer Teil,* 1913, p. 74

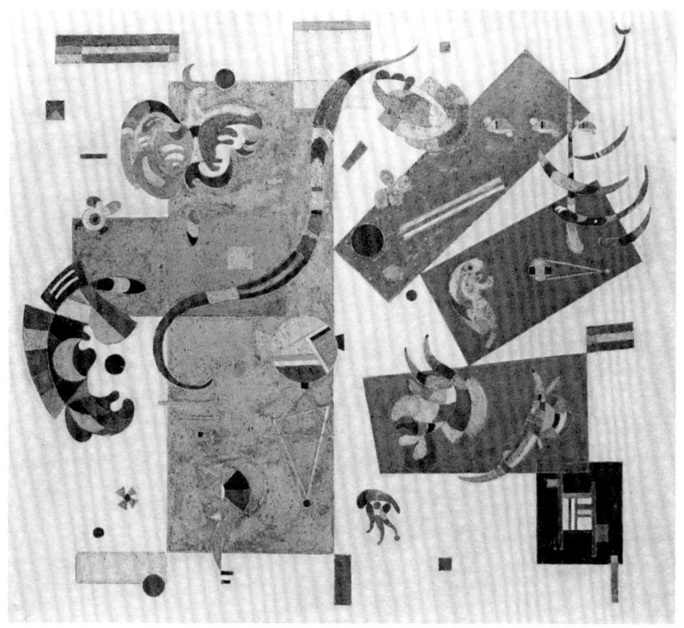

fig. 14
Vasily Kandinsky
Blue World. 1934
Collection Solomon R. Guggenheim Museum, New York

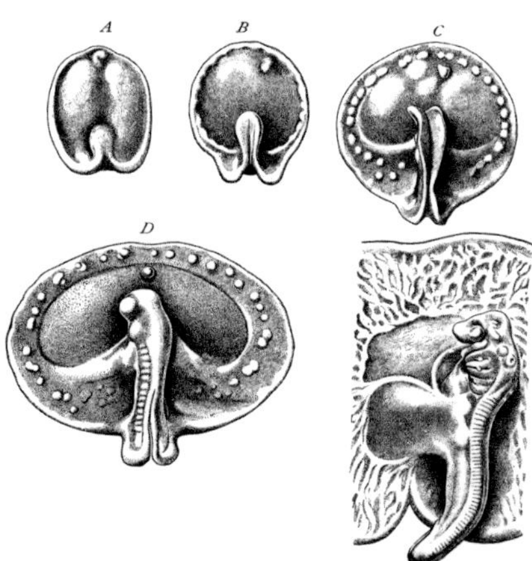

fig. 15
Fish embryo from *Zoologischer Teil,* 1913, p. 358

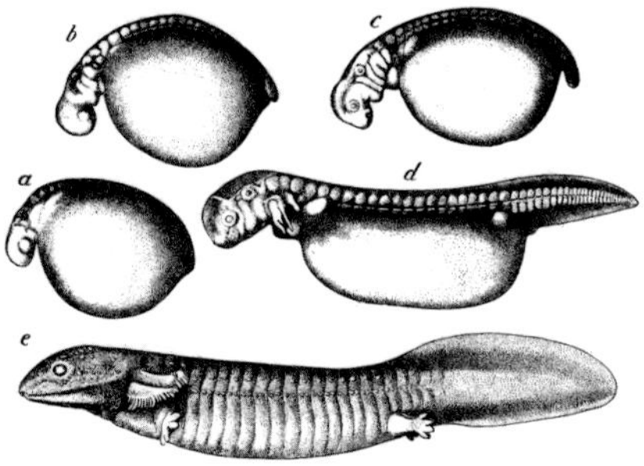

fig. 16
Salamander embryo from *Zoologischer Teil,* 1913, p. 346

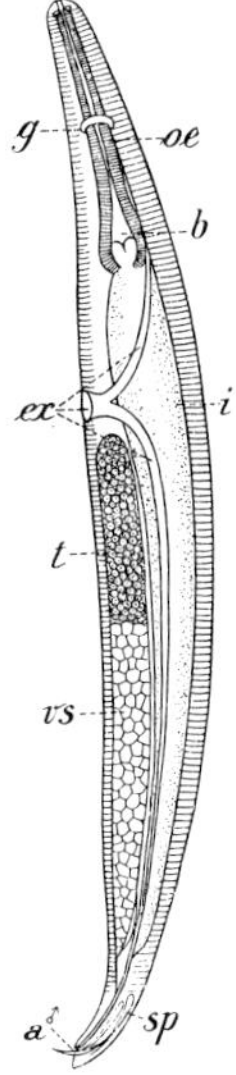

fig. 17
Nematode from *Zoologischer Teil,* 1913, p. 232

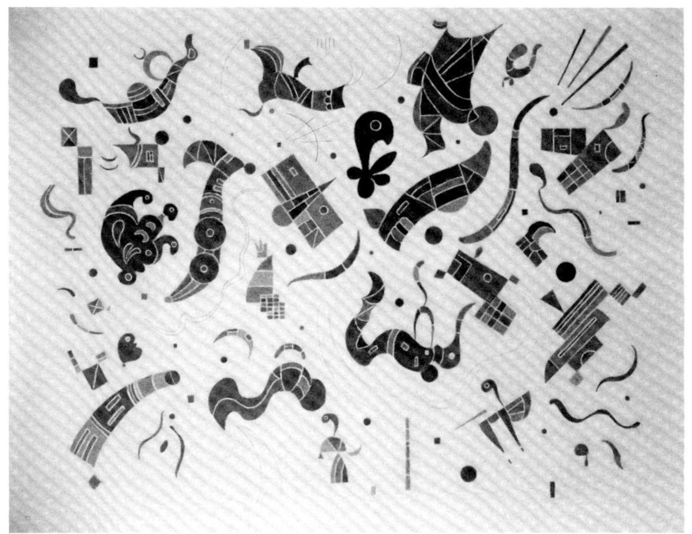

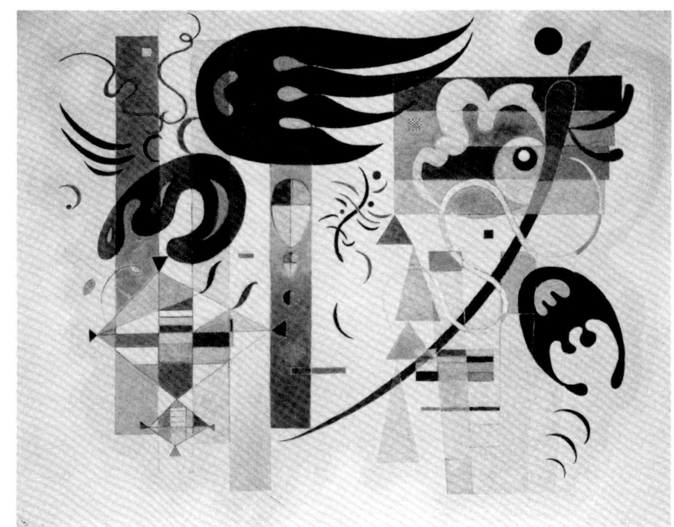

fig. 18
Vasily Kandinsky
Relations. 1934
Collection Mr. and Mrs. David Lloyd Kreeger

fig. 19
Vasily Kandinsky
Dominant Violet. 1934
Collection Mark Goodson, New York

The volume of Kandinsky's encyclopedia devoted to zoology contains all of the scientific diagrams cited in the discussion of *Blue World* as well as related illustrations of insect embryos.[19] All subsequent figures of scientific material reproduced from *Die Kultur der Gegenwart* appeared in volumes of the encyclopedia that belonged to the artist.

All of Kandinsky's canvases discussed above were exhibited at the Zervos's Galerie des "Cahiers d'Art" at 14, rue du Dragon in Paris from May 23 to June 9, 1934. They were included in a small one-man show that took place after Joan Miró's exhibition there and before Max Ernst's.[20] Kandinsky and Christian Zervos first met in 1927;[21] Zervos published Will Grohmann's monograph on Kandinsky in 1931 and the following year the artist contributed an article to Zervos's publication, *Cahiers d'Art.* The first exhibition of Kandinsky's Paris pictures appears to have gone unnoticed by the French press, except for Zervos's article in *Cahiers d'Art.*[22]

After this exhibition, during the summer of 1934, Kandinsky executed *Relations* and *Dominant Violet* (figs. 18, 19; cat. nos. 28, 27). In both he has accentuated precise, pictorial elements by applying fine-textured sand to the canvas and painting over it. The imagery in these pictures derives from the world of nature and relies upon curving lines and whiplash lines. In *Relations* the forms resemble snakes, spermatozoa, worms and parasites (for example, in the lower left corner) as well as birds. *Dominant Violet* prominently displays a large curving red shape on the right that looks like a nematode (fig. 17). However, the picture's connotations are predominantly those of the deep sea; the large, billowing forms look like medusas, jellyfish and related marine invertebrates. Moreover, the shape at the lower right corner distinctly looks like cross-sections of medusas.

Kandinsky's predilection for abstractions that originate in natural forms and his fanciful and imaginative stylization of natural forms bring to mind the well-known volumes by Ernst Heinrich Haeckel, *Kunstformen der Natur,*

19. *Zellen-und Gewebelehre: Morphologie und Entwicklungsgeschichte. II. Zoologischer Teil,* Berlin and Leipzig, 1913, pp. 258, 269.
20. *Cahiers d'Art,* 9e année, no. 1-4, 1934, opposite p. 11. See also Kandinsky's letter to Albers dated June 19, 1934.
21. Information supplied by Christian Derouet; their earliest correspondence dates from Dec. 1927.
22. There was no mention in *L'Intransigeant* although Miró's exhibition at the same gallery was reviewed in the May 17 issue. It is possible to determine which paintings were exhibited from the Handlist, which corresponds for the most part with the pictures reproduced in *Cahiers d'Art,* no. 5-8, 1934, pp. 149-157.

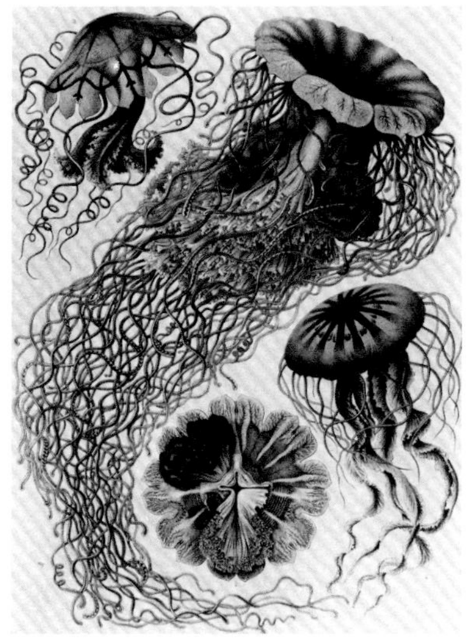

fig. 20
Medusas from Ernst Haeckel, *Kunstformen der Natur,* 1904, pl. 8

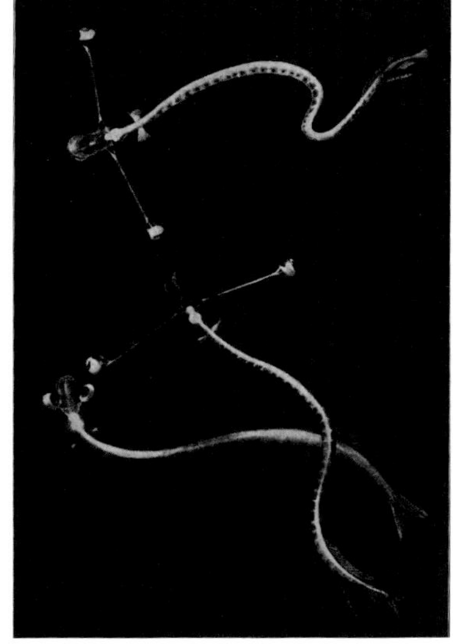

fig. 21
Deep-sea fish from *Die Koralle,* 1931, p. 495

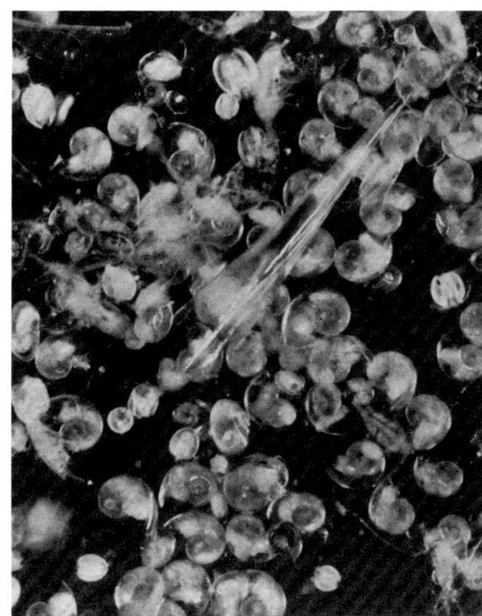

fig. 22
Plankton from *Die Koralle,* 1931, p. 496

which were published in 1904. Although Haeckel's beautifully colored illustrations belong to an Art Nouveau aesthetic, many reproductions can be linked with Kandinsky's work:[23] for example, one of the many renditions of medusas (fig. 20) can be related to *Dominant Violet.* Another plate from *Kunstformen der Natur* that depicts microscopic marine-life (radiolaria) was reproduced in *Cahiers d'Art* early in 1934 and undoubtedly was known to Kandinsky.[24] The images in *Dominant Violet* and other paintings from 1934 to 1935 attest to Kandinsky's awareness of deep-sea life. Proof of his interest can be found in the papers he saved. Among many clippings Kandinsky took from magazines and newspapers is part of an article from *Die Koralle* by G. von Borkow called "Life Under Pressure: The Unveiled Life."[25] Two illustrations from this article are particularly relevant to *Dominant Violet:* the firola or deep-sea snail resembles the undulating pink form at the upper right and the deep-sea fish (fig. 21) corresponds to many curvilinear elements. Kandinsky's preoccupation with curved lines and his detailed analysis of them in *Point and Line to Plane* clearly indicate that he would have been fascinated by the bright and undulating lines of the deep-sea fish.

A greatly enlarged photograph of plankton (fig. 22) from von Borkow's article on deep-sea life has relevance to *Division-Unity* (cat. no. 47), among other pictures. Plankton, brine shrimp, snails and larval stages of marine life become small, curving motifs that are evocatively and amusingly rendered in Kandinsky's work. Traces of these natural forms can be perceived in *Composition IX, Multiple Forms,* both of 1936, *Sky Blue* of 1940 (cat. nos. 7, 60, 116) and *Sweet Trifles* of 1937 (fig. 42).

23. Ernst Haeckel, *Kunstformen der Natur,* Leipzig, 1904, pls. 4, 8, 18, 30, 47, 84, 94.
24. Pl. 31 was reproduced in *Cahiers d'Art,* 9e année, no. 1-4, 1934, p. 100.
25. G. von Borkow, "Leben unter Hochdruck: Die entschleierte Welt der Tiefsee," *Die Koralle,* Jg. 6, Heft 11, Feb. 1931, pp. 495-499. Kandinsky also cut out from the same issue the article "Die Zunge ist ja so interessant!" by L. Schwarzfuss with photographs of cats' tongues seen under magnification.

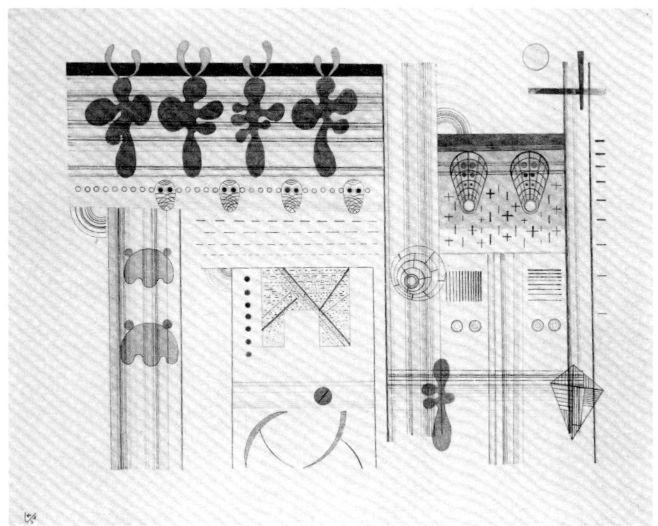

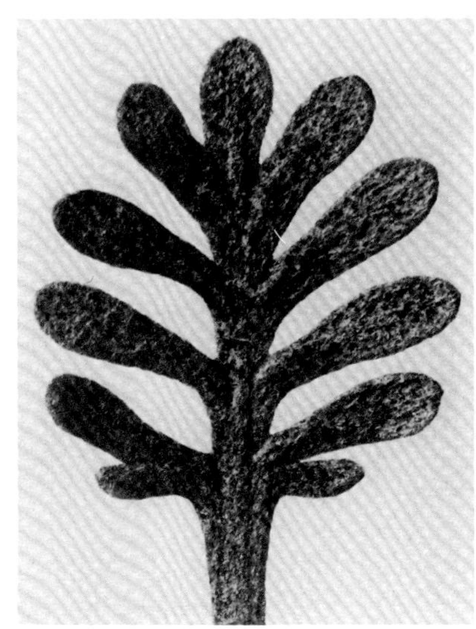

fig. 23
Vasily Kandinsky
Fragile-Fixed. 1934
Formerly Galerie Maeght, Paris

fig. 24
Leaf from Karl Blossfeldt, *Urformen der Kunst,* 1929, pl. 37

In the painting *Fragile-Fixed* of September 1934 (fig. 23), a specific leaf-shape enters Kandinsky's vocabulary. It recurs in modified form in *Balancing Act* of February 1935 (HL 612) and again in *Brown with Supplement* of March of the same year (cat. no. 53). Here the bright green leaves recall the prominent and remarkably similar leaves in Picasso's work: the 1929 sculpture that was reproduced in *Minotaure* in 1933; the 1931 still life illustrated the same year in *Cahiers d'Art*; and *The Lamp* of June 1931, which was exhibited at the Galeries Georges Petit in Paris in 1932.[26] Although Matisse's leaves have been singled out as the point of reference, they postdate the appearance of leaf-forms in Kandinsky's work.[27] The large scale and stylized outline of Kandinsky's leaves point to still another source known to him: namely Karl Blossfeldt's *Urformen der Kunst* which was published in Berlin in 1929. Two copies of the book exist in the artist's library at the Musée National d'Art Moderne. Blossfeldt's photographs consist primarily of flowers and leaves magnified to such a degree that they become abstractions (fig. 24). In June 1929 three such photographs were reproduced in *Documents*.[28] Blossfeldt's significance as a photographer, like Haeckel's as an illustrator, lay in his discovery of art in nature.

The last painting Kandinsky did in 1934 exemplifies the richness of his imagery and the invention of his pictorial forms. *Striped* (cat. no. 29) unites alternating black and white vertical bands, whiplash lines and biological forms with similar configurations (snakes, worms and nematodes), and it juxtaposes birds at the upper left with an exclamation point at the upper right. In the central segment, a red circle at the top contrasts with a star-shaped biomorphic form below. In a preparatory drawing (fig. 25), the distinctive structure of this multitentacled form emphasizes the central nucleus and accentuates the many entwining legs—characteristics of an echinoid, a

26. "L'Atelier de sculpture," *Minotaure,* no. 1, 1933, p. 20 and Christian Zervos, *Pablo Picasso,* Paris, 1955, vol. VII, nos. 326, 347, 377.
27. See Will Grohmann, *Kandinsky: Life and Work,* New York, 1958, p. 228.
28. *Documents,* no. 3, June 1929, pp. 165, 167, 168.

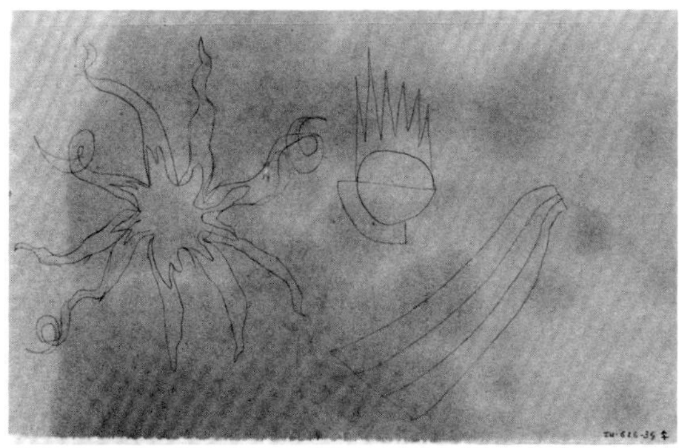

fig. 25
Vasily Kandinsky
Drawing for *Striped*
Collection Musée National d'Art Moderne, Centre Georges Pompidou, Paris, Kandinsky Bequest

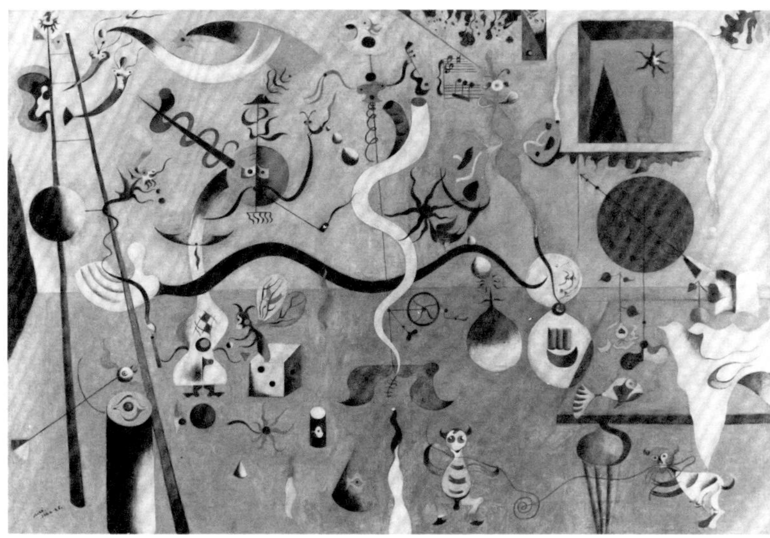

fig. 27
Joan Miró
Carnival of Harlequin. 1924-25
Collection Albright-Knox Art Gallery, Buffalo, New York, Room of Contemporary Art Fund, 1940

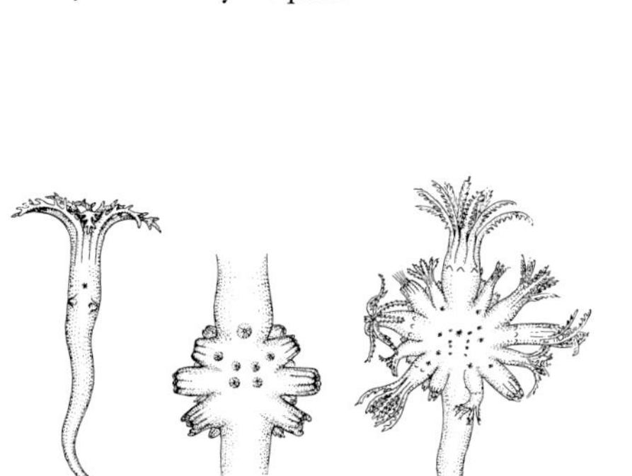

fig. 26
Sea polyps from *Allgemeine Biologie,* 1915, p. 411

species related to the common five-legged starfish. The depiction of a stage in the growth of sea polyps in the biology volume of Kandinsky's encyclopedia (fig. 26) recalls the star shape in *Striped.* In the canvas the distinctions between nucleus and tentacles are preserved and the colorful dots in the center correspond to those in the diagram.

The affinities between Kandinsky's imagery and forms in nature do not, however, preclude references to paintings by other artists. The tentacled, many-legged form articulated most clearly in Kandinsky's drawing brings to mind Miró's familiar sign for female genitalia. In writing about his picture *Carnival of Harlequin* of 1924-25 (fig. 27), Miró refers specifically to the female sex organ in the form of a spider; he depicts it three times within the painting.[29] Moreover, in both Kandinsky's and Miró's paintings there are ladders at the upper left and white teardrop shapes adjacent to eyes at the lower left. Comparison of *Striped* and *Carnival of Harlequin* reveals not only similarities in specific motifs but also in overall composition. Soon after his arrival in Paris, Kandinsky met Miró and he surely saw the Surrealist's work in exhibitions—such as that at the Galerie des "Cahiers d'Art" in May 1934—as well as in periodicals. In fact, *Carnival of Harlequin* and *The Tilled Field* (fig. 45) were among several influential pictures by Miró that were illustrated in the first issue of *Cahiers d'Art* in 1934 (no. 1-4), which immediately preceded the issue with Zervos's article devoted to Kandinsky's first Paris pictures. The motifs in such paintings by Kandinsky as *Delicate Accents* of 1935 (HL 624), *Black Points* (HL 637) and *Accompanied Center* of 1937 (cat. no. 86) attest to his familiarity with Miró's work.[30]

29. Steven A. Nash, *Albright-Knox Art Gallery: Painting and Sculpture from Antiquity to 1942,* New York, 1979, pp. 415-417.
30. See Stanley William Hayter, "The Language of Kandinsky," *Magazine of Art,* vol. 38, May 1945, pp. 178-179, for a comparison of *The Carnival of Harlequin* and *Accompanied Center.*

fig. 28
Paul Klee
Gartentor M. 1932
Öffentliche Kunstsammlung, Kunstmuseum Basel

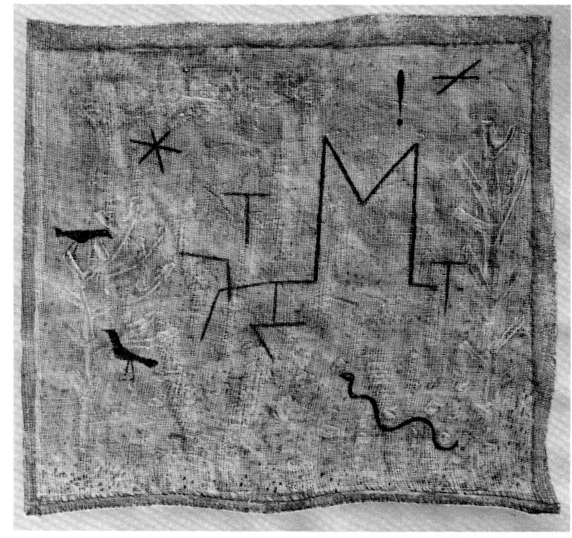

During 1934 certain specific signs entered Kandinsky's pictorial vocabulary. The exclamation point makes its first appearance in *Striped,* and a single quotation mark or inverted comma can be discerned at the left edge in *Dominant Violet* and at the bottom center in *Striped.* The latter motif is isolated and accentuated in *Green Accent* of 1935 (cat. no. 51) and totally dominates *Circuit* of 1939 (cat. no. 114). The exclamation point recurs in *Rigid and Bent* of 1935 (HL 625) and *Sweet Trifles* of 1937 (fig. 42). These signs had appeared in many works by Miró: for example, an exclamation point can be found in *Le Renversement* of 1924 which belonged to Katherine S. Dreier.[31] However, Kandinsky's primary source of inspiration was undoubtedly Paul Klee. Pictorial signs such as arrows, exclamation points and apostrophes as well as numbers and words functioned as integral parts of Klee's compositions.[32] Kandinsky and Klee were close friends who met first in Munich in 1911 and who worked together at the Bauhaus. In fact, Klee and Kandinsky lived in a Master's double house in Dessau from June 1926 until early 1933 and, even after they left Germany, stayed in contact. Kandinsky knew Klee's work intimately and would have understood the incorporation of punctuation marks in his art. Exclamation points can be found in Klee's pictures in the late teens and early twenties, and they become especially prevalent in 1932 (for example, fig. 28).[33] Kandinsky was surely familiar with two of Klee's paintings that include exclamation points: *Around the Fish* of 1926 (Collection The Museum of Modern Art, New York), which was reproduced in Grohmann's monograph on Klee in 1929, as well as his *Departure of the Ghost* of 1931 (Collection Mr. and Mrs. Burton Tremaine, Meriden, Connecticut), which was illustrated in the 1934 issue of *Cahiers d'Art* that also contained Zervos's article on Kandinsky. In addition, commas are prominently placed in Klee's paintings such as *Stadt R* of 1919 (Collection Städtische Galerie im Lenbachhaus, Munich) and *Initial Landschaft* of 1932 (Private Collection).

31. See Robert L. Herbert, Eleanor S. Apter and Elise K. Kenney, eds., *The Société Anonyme and the Dreier Bequest at Yale University: A Catalogue Raisonné,* New Haven, 1984, pp. 462-463. It is possible that Kandinsky had seen Miró's picture reproduced in the 1926 catalogue of the Société Anonyme exhibition at the Brooklyn Museum since he knew Katherine Dreier and corresponded with her often.
32. See Rosalind E. Krauss, "Magnetic Fields: The Structure," in *Joan Miró: Magnetic Fields,* exh. cat., New York, 1972, p. 29.
33. Klee Oeuvre Catalogue, nos. 75, 166, 168, 175, 213, 240.

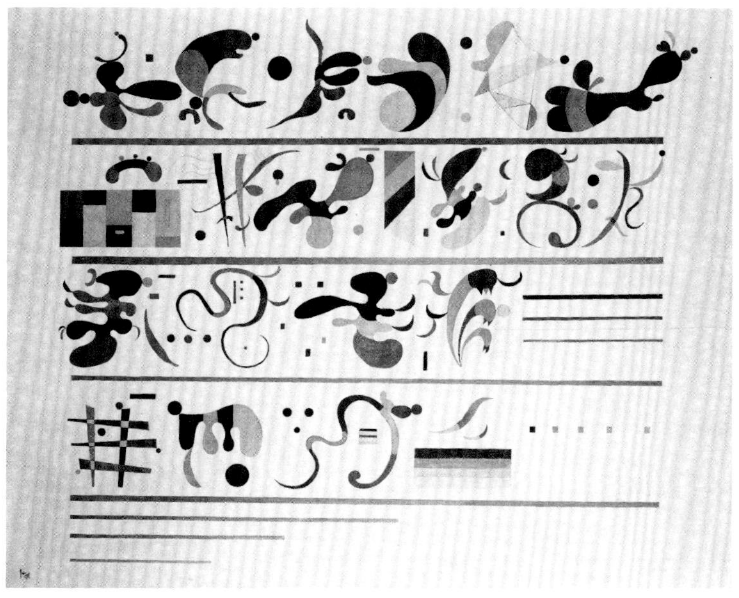

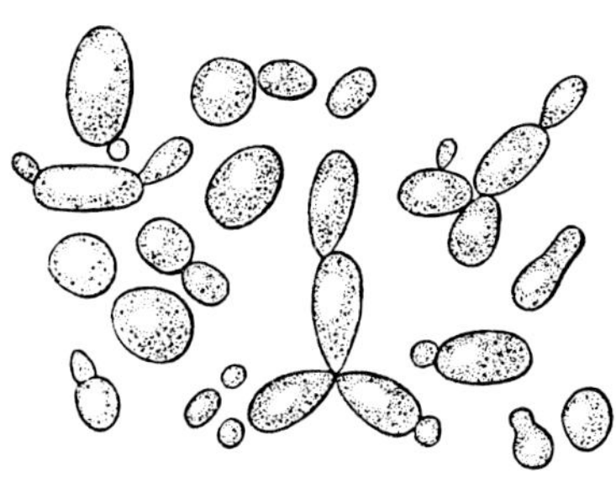

fig. 30
Saccharomyces fungus from *Zellen-und Gewebelehre: Morphologie und Entwicklungsgeschichte. I. Botanischer Teil*, 1913, p. 74

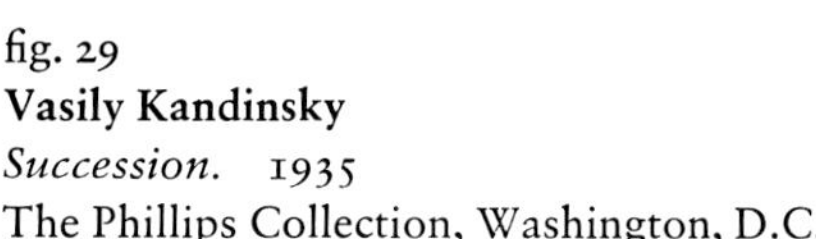

fig. 29
Vasily Kandinsky
Succession. 1935
The Phillips Collection, Washington, D.C.

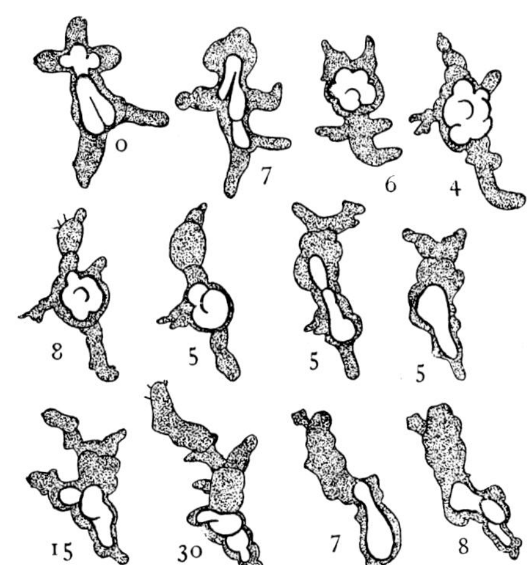

fig. 31
Cells of salamander larvae from *Zoologischer Teil*, 1913, p. 55

In comparison with the remarkable innovations made in Kandinsky's work from 1934, the introduction of new motifs subsided during 1935-36. At this time the artist developed and elaborated upon the imagery he had recently invented. Paintings such as *Accompanied Contrast* and *Two Green Points* (cat. nos. 48, 54) retain images prevalent during the early 1930s, while the style of others shares similarities with the geometric idiom associated with the Bauhaus period in general: for example, *Two Circles* (HL 614) and *Points* (HL 621). In terms of specific images reflecting an awareness of natural sciences and biomorphic forms, several pictures provide relevant motifs. *Succession* (fig. 29; cat. no. 57), which was painted in April 1935, consists of four horizontal registers that contain brightly colored, curving shapes. This format is familiar from the Bauhaus period, specifically from the watercolor *Lines of Marks* of 1931 (HL 442). Although the 1935 canvas and the earlier work on paper share the same composition, the imagery of the Paris picture represents a significant departure from that of his Bauhaus work. The thrust of the curving shapes and the distinctive placement of small circles balanced on these forms in the painting recall an illustration of saccharomyces fungus in Kandinsky's encyclopedia (fig. 30). A diagram of cells from salamander larvae (fig. 31) in another volume of this encyclopedia can also be associated with the dynamic forms in *Succession.* Not only the individual shapes but also their schematic articulation is similar in Kandinsky's painting and the scientific diagrams.

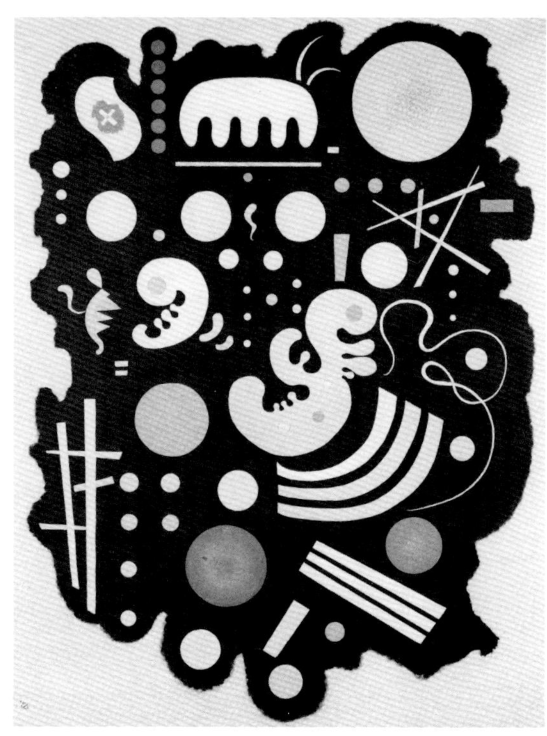

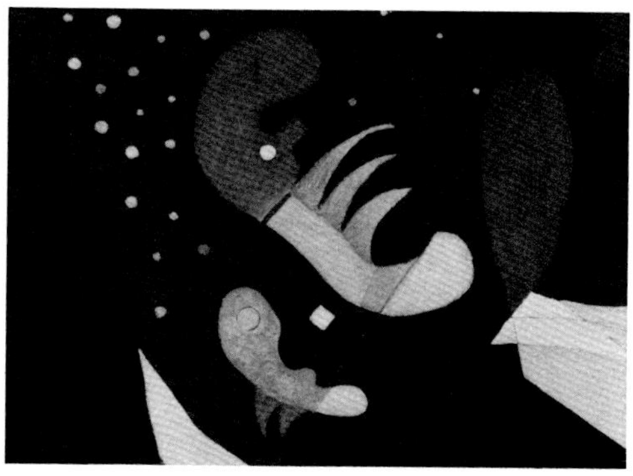

fig. 33
Vasily Kandinsky
Detail of *Composition IX*. 1936
Collection Musée National d'Art Moderne, Centre Georges Pompidou, Paris

fig. 32
Vasily Kandinsky
Variegated Black. 1935
Formerly Galerie Maeght, Paris

Several paintings from 1935-36 depict embryos. In *Variegated Black* of October 1935 (fig. 32) three embryonic forms are recognizable: an early stage at the left edge, an adjacent, more clearly identifiable one painted white with a pink eye and a bright green imaginative variant on the right. In Kandinsky's major canvas *Composition IX* (cat. no. 7), which was completed by February 1936, an obviously embryonic shape at the upper left is represented together with a yolk sac. Even the pink and white vertical zones can be read as the placental barrier that separates the fetal side from the maternal side. In the central portion of *Composition IX* there is ambiguity in the form that resembles both an embryo and a brine shrimp or crayfish (fig. 33).[34] Elsewhere in the painting embryonic images also merge with allusions to brine shrimp and plankton (see fig. 22). An exactly coeval picture, *Multiple Forms* (cat. no. 60), manifests similar embryonic and crustacean images. Comparison of the canvas with a preparatory drawing reveals significant differences between the preliminary and final versions. The embryonic form at the upper right has not been explicitly defined in the sketch for *Multiple Forms* (fig. 34); however, the fish at the upper left has been omitted in the final version. This depiction of a fish resembles the angler fish in Kandinsky's clipping from von Borkow's article in *Die Koralle*. The image at the lower corner of *Multiple Forms* is clearly that of a fish. In *Rigid and Bent* of December 1935, Kandinsky includes a marine creature—probably a sea horse—painted green and raised in slight relief because sand was added to the pigment.

34. See *Zoologischer Teil*, p. 249.

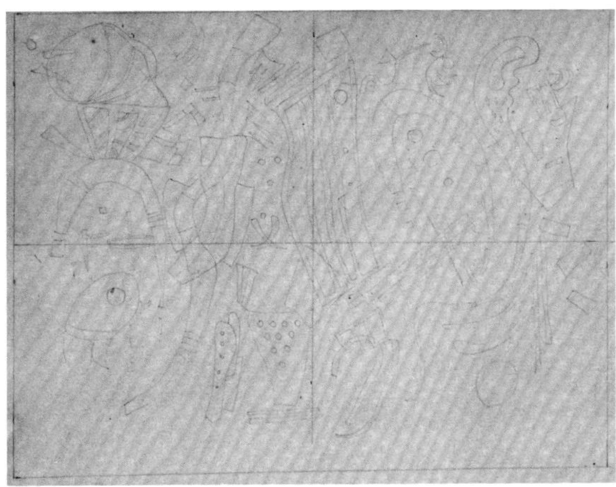

fig. 34
Vasily Kandinsky
Drawing for *Multiple Forms*. 1936
Collection Musée National d'Art Moderne, Centre Georges Pompidou, Paris, Kandinsky Bequest

fig. 35
Vasily Kandinsky
Green Figure. 1936
Collection Musée National d'Art Moderne, Centre Georges Pompidou, Paris, Kandinsky Bequest

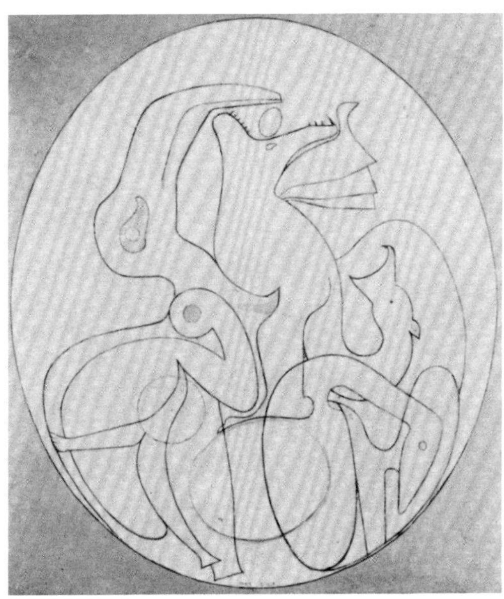

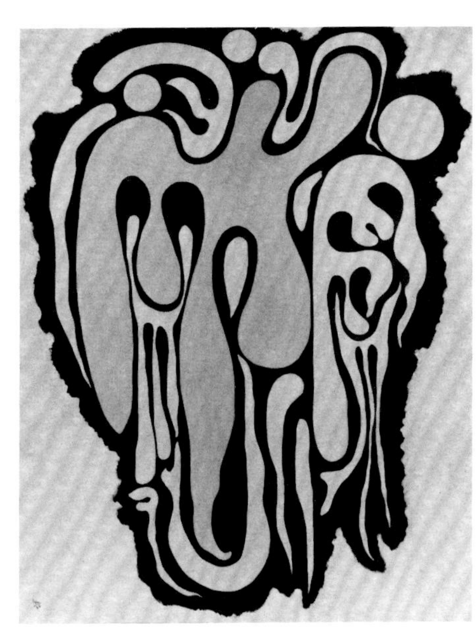

fig. 36
Max Ernst
The Interior of Sight: The Egg
published in *Cahiers d'Art*, 1933

It is difficult to identify any specific biological sources for *Green Figure* of March 1936 (fig. 35; cat. no. 62), although it brings to mind cross-sections of organisms. The greenish-tan figure suggests parallels with the work of Max Ernst and Picasso. In 1929 Ernst painted several versions of *The Interior of Sight: The Egg* where bird forms are contained within an oval, and in 1935 he did a series on the *Garden of the Hesperides* which also relates to *Green Figure*.[35] The organic contortions of Kandinsky's figure as well as the way it is separated by a "sac" from the surrounding pinkish tan background may refer to the first version of Ernst's *The Interior of Sight: The Egg*, which was reproduced in *Cahiers d'Art* in 1933 (fig. 36). Several of Picasso's paintings of acrobats were published in *Documents* in 1930: these abstracted figures have elongated and distorted limbs similar to the shapes in *Green Figure*, and in some works the colors feature gray-tan and green (see cat. no. 63).[36] Despite vague biomorphic associations, *Green Figure* appears to be an amalgam of figures that were familiar to Kandinsky from other artists' work.

35. See Werner Spies with Sigrid and Günter Metken, *Max Ernst: Werke 1929-38*, Houston and Cologne, 1979, nos. 1564-1567, 1574-1579, 2200-2202.
36. See Zervos, VII, nos. 307-310 and Michel Leiris, "Toiles récentes de Picasso," *Documents*, 2e année, no. 2, 1930.

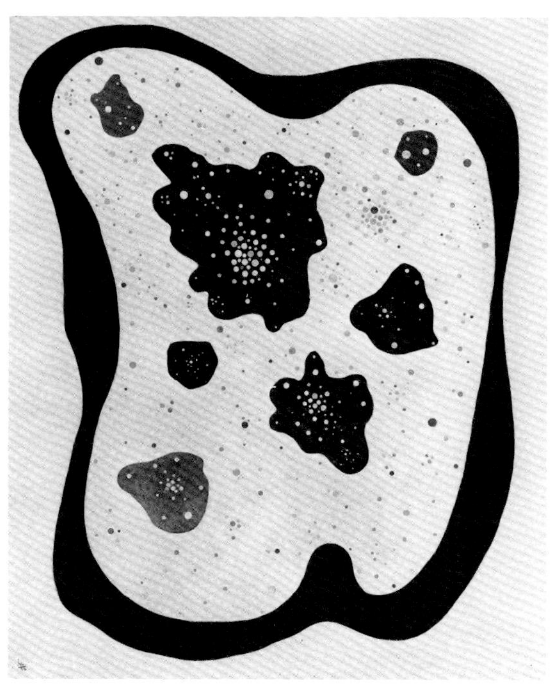

fig. 37
Vasily Kandinsky
Environment. 1936
Collection Solomon R. Guggenheim Museum, New York

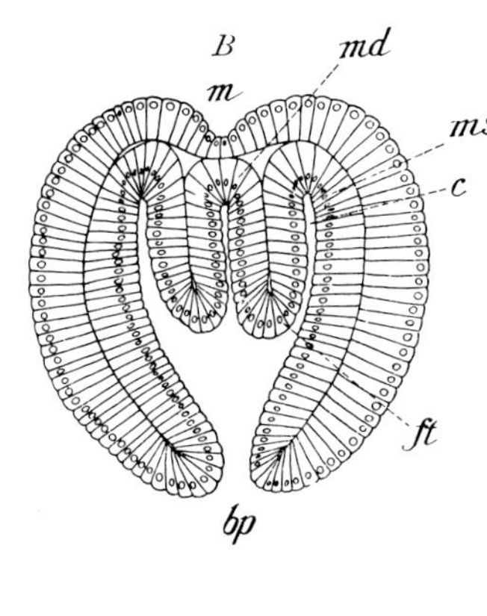

fig. 39
Stages in the development of a worm from *Zoologischer Teil,* 1913, p. 217

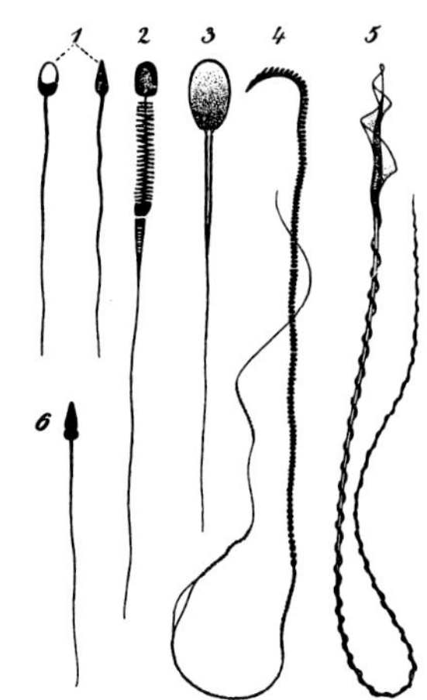

fig. 40
Human and animal sperm from *Zoologischer Teil,* 1913, p. 56

In complete contrast stands another painting by Kandinsky, *Environment* from October 1936 (fig. 37). Here the artist has depicted in greatly enlarged scale an amoeba. The cell wall is clearly defined; many small multicolored circles represent the cytoplasm and several colored zones correspond to vacuoles and a nucleus. Moreover, Kandinsky's painting closely resembles an illustration in his encyclopedia (fig. 38). Of all Kandinsky's works where biological references can be discerned, *Environment* is probably the most direct and obvious.

Within the checkerboard format of *Thirty* (cat. no. 68) calligraphic and geometric patterns are placed over thirty alternately black and white squares. Kandinsky defines the images with wit and lively energy: an amoeba (second row and second from the left), a curving white form with six pendules (fourth row and fourth from the left) that resembles a developmental stage of a worm (fig. 39) and several varieties of sperm (top row at far left and fourth row at far left) that recur in many pictures and correspond to scientific illustrations (fig. 40). In general, the motifs are already familiar from Kandinsky's work. In *Thirty* the strict and exacting format of compartments has even greater meaning than the individual elements in its clear relation to scientific texts and diagrams (for example, fig. 41).

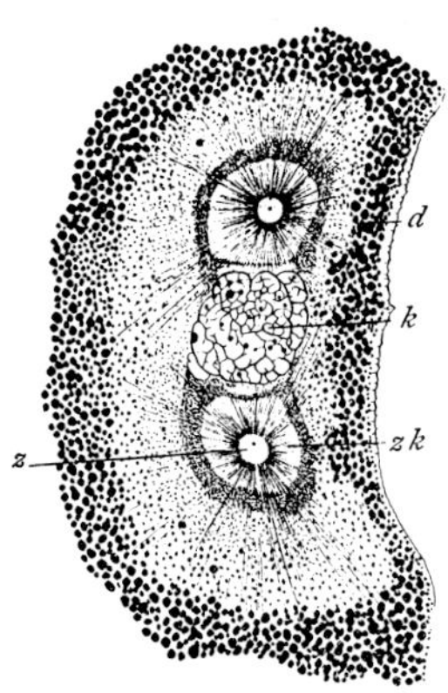

fig. 38
Cell of worm egg from *Zoologischer Teil,* 1913, p. 49

Another canvas from 1937, *Sweet Trifles* (fig. 42), is based on rigid bilateral compartmentalization. Within the boxes Kandinsky juxtaposes geometric patterns with biomorphic forms. He places an exclamation point over an earthworm balancing on an imaginatively colored caterpillar and positions an arrow next to a bright blue amphibian perching on a slug. The playfulness and humor of the picture are conveyed by its title, *Bagatelles douces,* and by the exclamation point. On the left side the articulation of many forms sug-

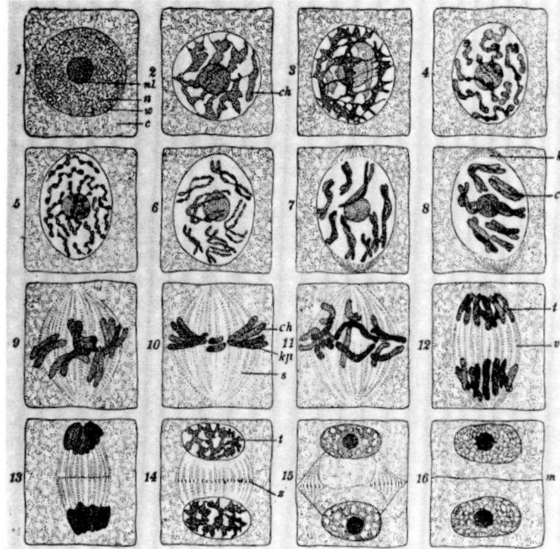

fig. 41
Diagram of plant cells from *Botanischer Teil,* 1913, p. 53

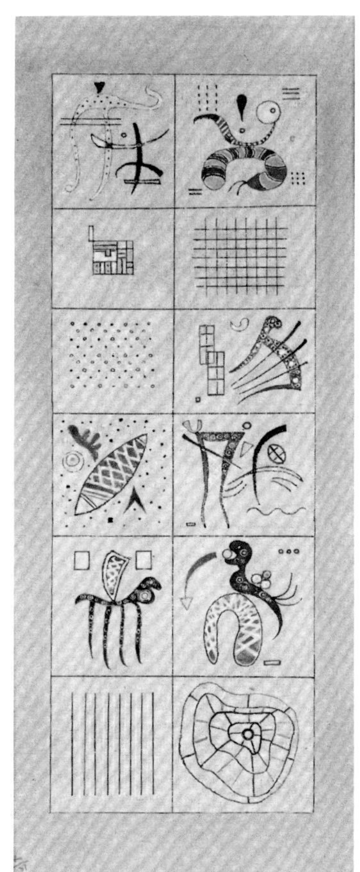

fig. 42
Vasily Kandinsky
Sweet Trifles. 1937
Collection Musée National d'Art Moderne, Centre Georges Pompidou, Paris, Kandinsky Bequest

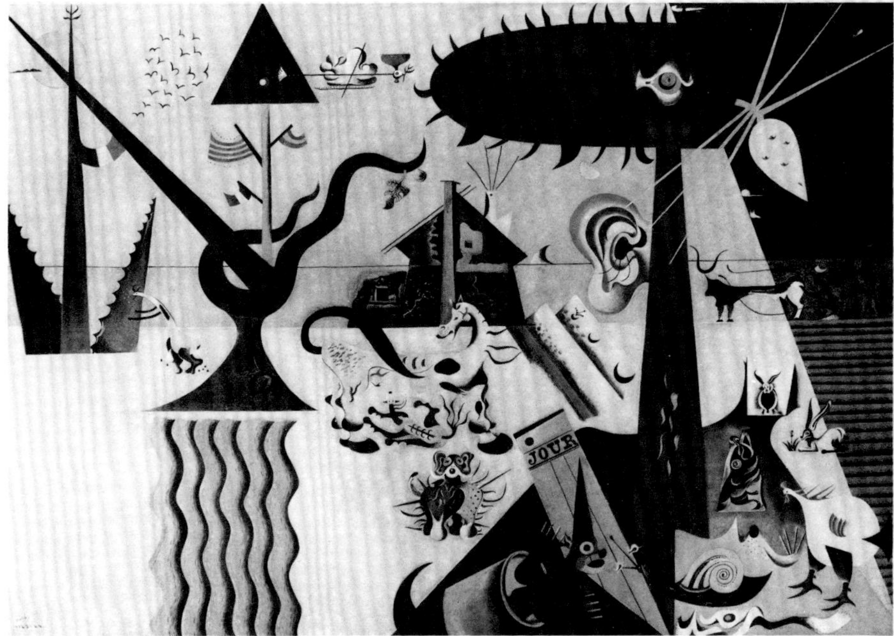

fig. 45
Joan Miró
The Tilled Field. 1923-24
Collection Solomon R. Guggenheim Museum, New York

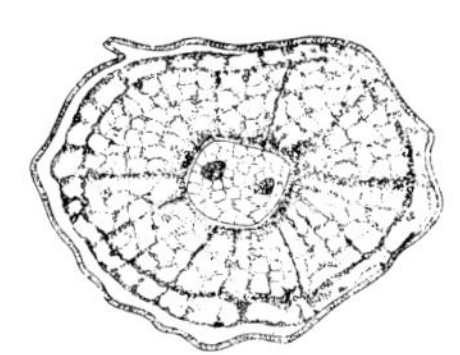

fig. 43
Nucleus of an echinoderm from *Zoologischer Teil,* 1913, p. 28

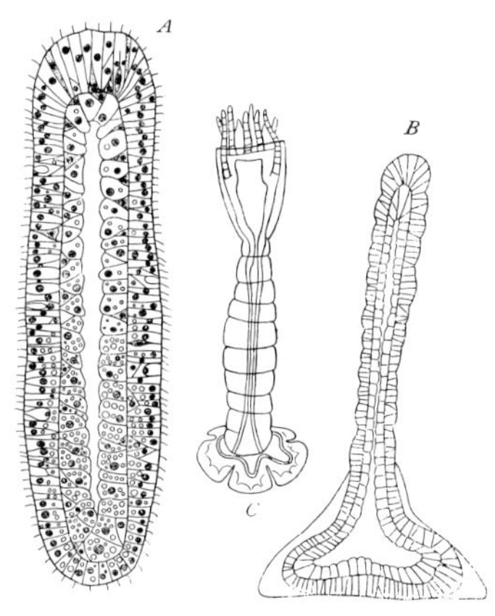

fig. 44
Stages in the development of a hydra from *Zoologischer Teil,* 1913, p. 197

gests cellular matter; moreover, in the lower right corner the multicellular form distinctly resembles an illustration of the nucleus of an echinoderm in the zoology volume of *Die Kultur der Gegenwart* (fig. 43).

Likewise, *Accompanied Center* (cat. no. 86) contains a clearly biological reference at the upper right: the horizontal, wavy, segmented shape looks like cross-sections of hydras that are illustrated in his encyclopedia (fig. 44). *Accompanied Center* is filled with an abundance of images evocative of marine life: sea worms, hydras, diatoms, five larval forms suspended from a horizontal line at the lower right and scaly, spiny orange patterns in the center. In addition—and on a different level—Kandinsky's painting resembles Miró's *The Tilled Field* (fig. 45) in the wavy lines at the lower left, the prominent eye

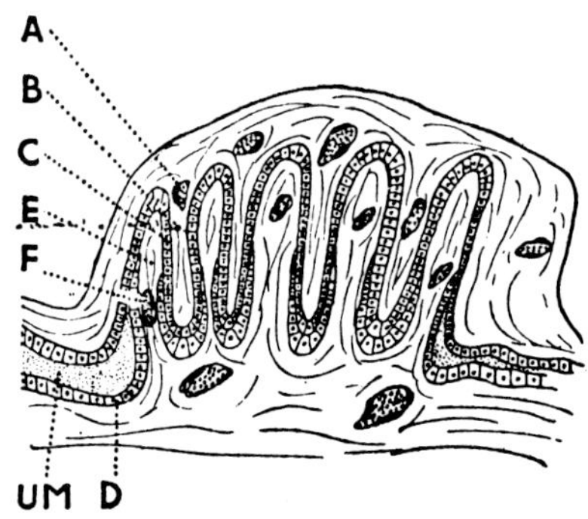

fig. 46
Placental tissue from H. C. Waddington, *How Animals Develop,* 1936, p. 107

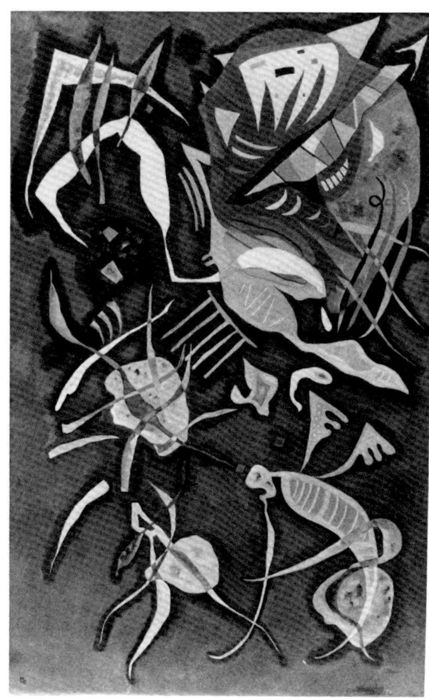

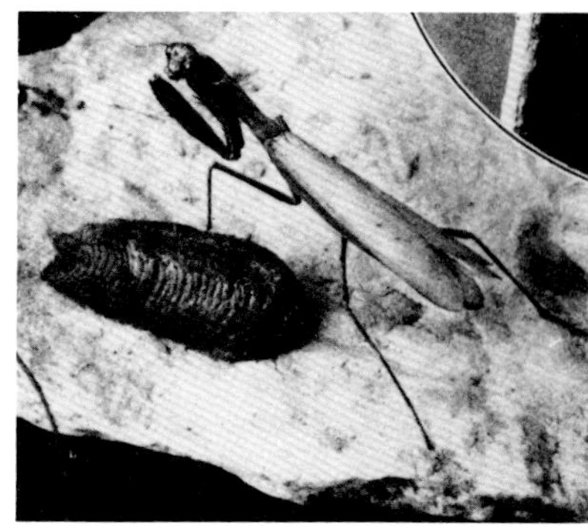

fig. 48
Praying mantis laying her eggs

fig. 47
Vasily Kandinsky
Grouping. 1937
Collection Moderna Museet, Stockholm

at the upper right, the inclusion of flags and in the spikey black points outlining shapes. Although it is doubtful that Kandinsky could have seen Miró's painting in an exhibition, he would have found it reproduced on page thirty in the first issue of *Cahiers d'Art* in 1934.

During the summer of 1937 Kandinsky painted *Capricious Forms* (cat. no. 89), in which the imagery is emphatically biological. Yellow, pink, tan and green shapes look like sections of soft tissue. Specifically, the forms at bottom center and in the middle at the left edge are clearly recognizable as embryonic; others resemble contemporary illustrations of placental tissue (fig. 46). In a sketchbook containing many preparatory drawings, Kandinsky made a study with colored pencils for *Capricious Forms* which includes a greater variety of hues than the final version and shows an overall pink tonality.[37] In the canvas red and green circles accentuate the shapes as well as the detailed red, blue and green linear patterns that articulate distinct layers of tissue.

The next painting recorded in Kandinsky's Handlist is *Grouping* (fig. 47), which was painted in September and October 1937. Two preparatory drawings as well as the final painted version reflect an insect world. Insect legs and bodies are suggested throughout, and a well-defined winged creature occupies the lower right corner. Basically mosquito-like, this creature also bears a certain resemblance to a photographic illustration of a praying mantis laying her eggs that Kandinsky clipped from an unidentified German magazine (fig. 48).[38] Among the artist's papers preserved in the Kandinsky Archive are other reproductions, in color, of insects that Kandinsky cut out and mounted on cardboard.[39] Insects were symbolic and highly suggestive images

37. Musée National d'Art Moderne, Centre Georges Pompidou, Paris, Kandinsky Bequest AM 1981.65.678
38. The caption reads *"Gottesanbeterin liegt ihre Eier,"* and it was taken from p. 117.
39. These are of watercolor illustrations by E. v. Bruckhausen and are from pp. 764 and 765 of an unidentified publication.

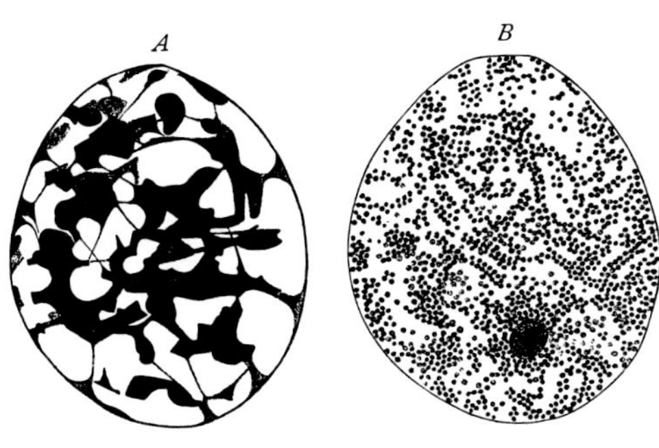

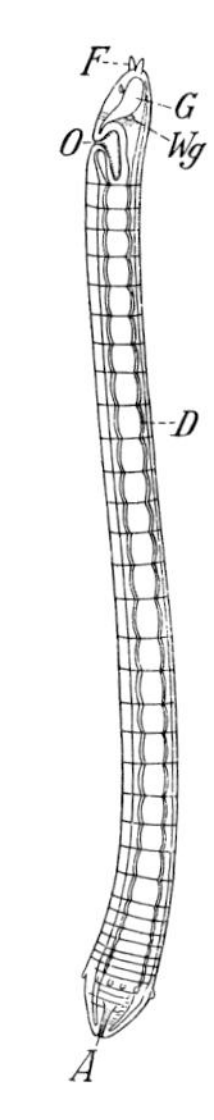

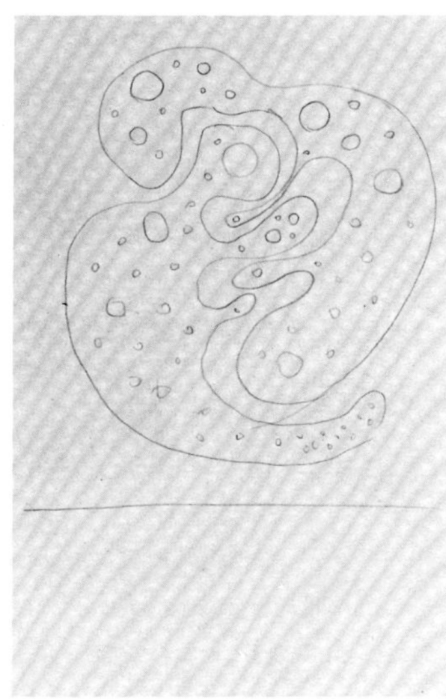

fig. 49
Salamander cell from *Allgemeine Biologie,* 1915, p. 231

fig. 50
Annelid from *Zoologischer Teil,* 1913, p. 234

fig. 51
Vasily Kandinsky
Untitled drawing
Collection Musée National d'Art Moderne, Centre Georges Pompidou, Paris, Kandinsky Bequest

within Surrealist art. In 1934 André Masson painted *Betrothal of Insects* and *Summer Divertissement,* which depict praying mantises: these pictures must be seen in relation to Kandinsky's 1937 canvas.[40]

In April 1938 Kandinsky completed two oil paintings in which there are clear biological references. *Ordered Arrangement (Many-Colored Ensemble)* (cat. no. 92) contains within an oval center a plethora of small circles that have cellular associations (fig. 49). In addition, there are shapes resembling nematode and annelid worms (fig. 50), a pink bird at the left and an embryonic form at the right. It was probably in relation to this embryo that Kandinsky made two small sketches (one of which is reproduced as fig. 51). To an even greater degree than in the painting *Ordered Arrangement (Many-Colored Ensemble),* the biological origins of the imagery are evident in these drawings. More stylized variations on this embryonic form persist in his work throughout the late 1930s and early 1940s. In *Penetrating Green* from April 1938 (cat. no. 93) a red sperm is immediately recognizable and is prominently placed in the middle of the composition within a vertical receptacle on a green ground. Two large shapes that vaguely resemble sperm fill the lateral zones. Even Kandinsky's title is expressive of the imagery and leaves little doubt about the meaning.

By 1938 Kandinsky's images become more fanciful, stylized and even decorative. For example, *Sky Blue* of March 1940 (cat. no. 116) retains biomorphic forms familiar from the first years in Paris, but these are transformed into stylizations of the motifs. For the most part, Kandinsky's paintings, watercolors and drawings from 1938 and after no longer manifest the overtly zoological and embryological motifs that characterize his work from 1934 to 1937. There are, however, vestiges of biological entities as well as specific biomorphic images. In general, Kandinsky does not depict embryonic forms after 1938; however, the exceptions—*Intimate Celebration* of 1942 and *Brown Impetus* of 1943 (cat. nos. 144, 155)—refer back to *Blue World* (cat. no. 25)

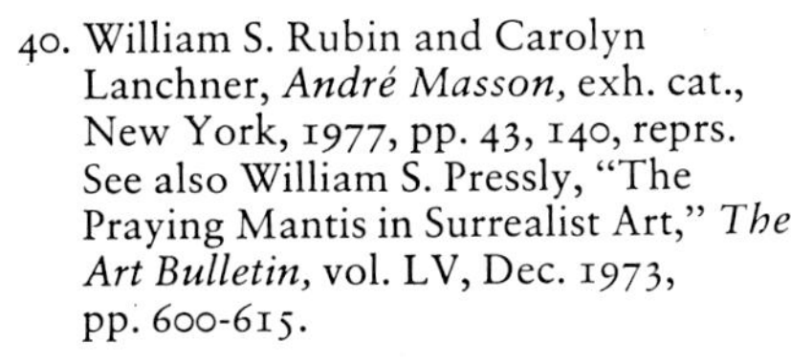

40. William S. Rubin and Carolyn Lanchner, *André Masson,* exh. cat., New York, 1977, pp. 43, 140, reprs. See also William S. Pressly, "The Praying Mantis in Surrealist Art," *The Art Bulletin,* vol. LV, Dec. 1973, pp. 600-615.

and *Variegated Black* (fig. 32). Another painting from 1943, *Circle and Square* (cat. no. 156) shows four figures with clear sexual references; the representation of phallic images is indisputable. Although Kandinsky's title, *Circle and Square (Cercle et carré),* alludes to the magazine and exhibitions organized by the group of that name, it cannot disguise the nature of his imagery.

In addition to the visual evidence which has been described at length, there is substantial physical evidence of other kinds and significant documentary proof to link images in Kandinsky's art with scientific illustrations in his encyclopedia. In preparation for *Point and Line to Plane,* which was published in 1926, he executed a pencil drawing (fig. 52). The inscription provides the source, because in it Kandinsky copied the caption, *"Lockeres Bindegewebe von der Ratte,"* and also specified the title, *"D. Kult. d. Gegenw.,"* the volume, *"Abteilung IV²,"* and page number.[41] It is this volume on zoology that contains by far the largest number of illustrations corresponding to images in Kandinsky's work. In addition to the obvious reference in *Point and Line to Plane,* the artist left traces in his own copy of this encyclopedia volume. Next to page five, where an amoeba is illustrated (fig. 53), there is a small piece of paper with Kandinsky's handwriting, and facing page 234, where an annelid is reproduced (fig. 50), his calling card is inserted as a marker.[42] In the other volume of Abteilung IV², whose subject is botany, Kandinsky put slips of paper between pages 138 and 139 as well as 154 and 155, and wrote on each *"Kreis"* or circle. The illustration on page 138 depicts the cross-section of a plant stem with many rings of quite uniform circles, while that on page 139 (fig. 54) contains rounded shapes with much greater variety in size and configuration. In view of Kandinsky's love for the circle as a formal element as well as the symbolic significance of the motif in his work from about 1922 to 1930,[43] it is not surprising that he would respond to obviously circular forms in his encyclopedia. What is interesting is the way he sees the abstract forms of art in nature.

In the volume on general biology, the invitation card to the opening of Kandinsky's exhibition of watercolors and drawings at the Galerie Ferdinand Möller on January 30, 1932, is placed between pages 218 and 219. In addition, inserted in the section on botany in the volumes on physiology and ecology are an invitation to an opening for the *Kreise der Freunde des Bauhauses* on January 15, 1932, and an invitation to a Lyonel Feininger exhibition organized by this group in January 1932. The fact that all three markers date from January 1932 proves that Kandinsky was using his encyclopedia at that time. During the 1920s volumes of the same encyclopedia were influential for Paul Klee.[44] Moreover, other artists at the Bauhaus were aware of various volumes on science in this series. However, the impact of its biological illustrations—principally from the volume on zoology—becomes apparent in Kandinsky's work only after he moved to Paris.

Likewise, there is evidence that Kandinsky cut the photographic reproductions now preserved among his papers out of magazines and newspapers during the early 1930s, while he was still at the Bauhaus.[45] The article on

41. See also *Physiologie und Okologie: I. Botanischer Teil,* 1917, p. 165, which is reproduced as fig. 73 in *Point and Line to Plane.*
42. The author studied the encyclopedia volumes in Apr. 1984 at the Centre Georges Pompidou.
43. See Grohmann, pp. 187-188 and Barnett, 1983, pp. 43-44.
44. Sarah Lynn Henry, "Form-Creating Energies: Paul Klee and Physics," *Arts,* vol. 52, Sept. 1977, pp. 119, 121. However, according to Felix Klee in conversation with the author, July 19, 1984, the encyclopedia series is not included among the books that belonged to Paul Klee that are now in his possession.
45. I am indebted to Christian Derouet for this information and also for bringing the clippings to my attention.
46. Wassily Kandinsky, *Tutti gli scritti: Punto e linea nel piano, Articoli teorici, I corsi inediti al Bauhaus,* Philippe Sers, ed., Milan, 1973, p. 283.
47. *Ibid.,* pp. 284, 289, 290.

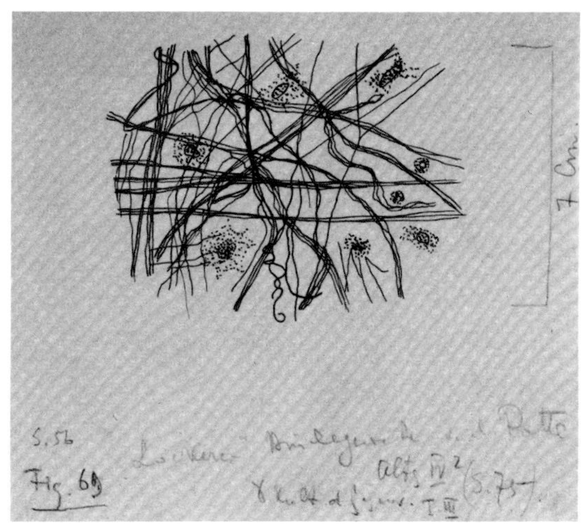

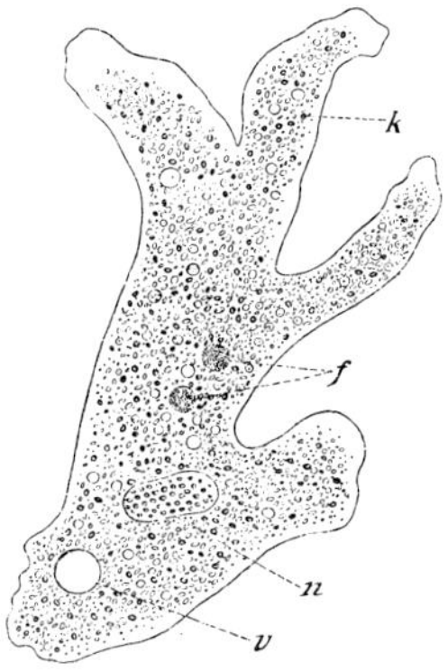

fig. 53
Amoeba from *Zoologischer Teil,* 1913, p. 5

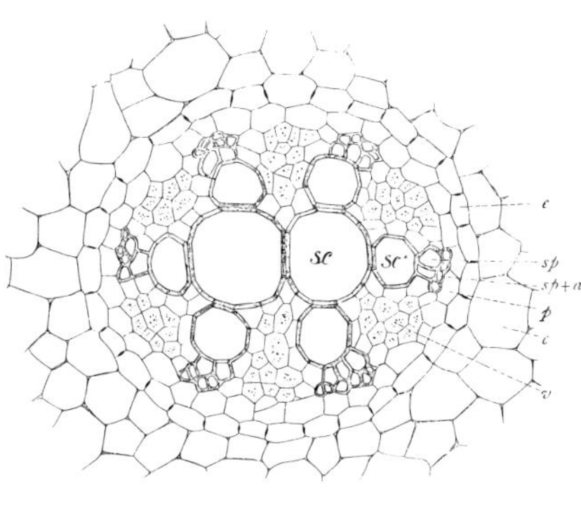

fig. 54
Cross-section of plant stem from *Botanischer Teil,* 1913, p. 139

fig. 52
Vasily Kandinsky
Drawing for *Point and Line to Plane* after *Zoologischer Teil*
Collection Musée National d'Art Moderne, Centre Georges Pompidou, Paris, Kandinsky Bequest

deep-sea life in *Die Koralle* (figs. 21, 22) appeared in February 1931. Virtually all the press cuttings have captions in German, thus indicating a date prior to 1934. Although most of the specific publications remain unknown pending further research, many of the images are of animals, airplanes, people from primitive cultures, objects shown under high magnification and subjects generally characterized as technology and nature. In his Bauhaus teaching notes for the second, or summer, semester of 1931, Kandinsky compared art, science, technology and nature.[46] His list of images to show includes a Mercedes-Benz car, a Junkers airplane, an aerial view and a giraffe: a photograph or magazine illustration of each still exists among the artist's papers. Another very significant clipping (fig. 55) shows diatoms arranged within a rigid, bilateral format that resembles the pictorial organization of *Sweet Trifles* (fig. 42). Diatoms—unicellular algae or microscopic plankton found in both fresh and salt water—are recognizable in several of Kandinsky's paintings from the Paris years.

Thus, Kandinsky's interest in scientific and natural phenomena is demonstrated by his treatise *Point and Line to Plane* and by his pedagogical material for the Bauhaus courses. Likewise, his familiarity with volumes of his encyclopedia, *Die Kultur der Gegenwart,* is confirmed by these sources.[47] However, the artist only introduced biological motifs into his work after he moved to Paris. It is relevant, at this point, to consider what natural history and scientific resources were available there in 1934. Although there is no proof that Kandinsky ever visited the Muséum National d'Histoire Naturelle in Paris, its extensive and impressive collections, which were permanently on view in galleries adjacent to the Jardin des Plantes, would have been accessible and instructive. Photographs dating from 1932 to 1935 in the Muséum Archives document the Galerie de Zoologie and the Galerie d'Anatomie Comparée de Paléontologie et d'Anthropologie. The former contained

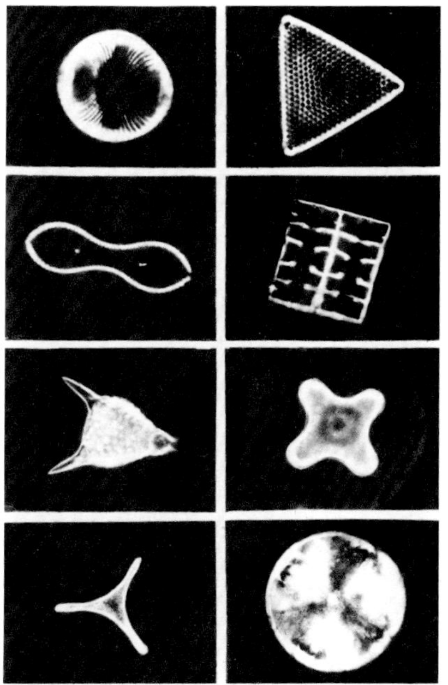

fig. 55
Diatoms

vast numbers of cases filled with all varieties of fish, starfish, crustacea, shells and insects.[48] Immediately upon entering the latter, one finds thousands of fetal specimens in glass jars. Comprising many species and organized according to the embryological development of organs and central systems, this permanent exhibition makes an overwhelming and unforgettable impression on the viewer. The collection of comparative anatomy was founded by Georges Cuvier.[49] It cannot be coincidental that in one of Kandinsky's encyclopedia volumes, there are obvious signs of perusal (coffee stains) as well as a marker for the pages relevant to Cuvier.[50] The Zoology Gallery and the Comparative Anatomy Gallery at the Muséum were established in the late nineteenth century and to this day retain virtually their original appearance. It should be mentioned that, in contrast, the Musée d'Ethnographie at the Muséum National d'Histoire Naturelle was closed in August 1935 and reopened at a new location at the present Trocadéro on the occasion of the *Exposition Internationale des Arts et Techniques* in 1937.

During the mid-1930s many artists took an active interest in various scientific disciplines and incorporated related images and concepts in their work. Marcel Duchamp, Miró, Ernst and Klee as well as Kandinsky demonstrated an awareness of and responsiveness to science. Many images in Miró's pictures clearly derive from biological species and refer to natural phenomena. Miró uses technological motifs such as machines and utilitarian objects as a springboard for other paintings: his large abstract *Painting* of June 1933 (Collection The Museum of Modern Art, New York) is based on a collage of woodworking tools.[51] Ernst found inspiration in scientific illustrations throughout his career. In 1934 he painted *Blind Swimmer (The Effect of Touch)* (formerly Collection Julien Levy), which is an amalgam of two photographs demonstrating air flow that were published in *La Nature* magazine in September 1901.[52] His coeval painting titled *Blind Swimmer* (Collection The Museum of Modern Art, New York) is based on a diagram showing the effects of magnetism. Both canvases were reproduced in the issue of *Cahiers d'Art* in 1934 that included Kandinsky's recent pictures, and Ernst's work was exhibited at Zervos's gallery in June of that year. Moreover, Ernst's 1934 mural for the Corso Bar in Zürich relies upon an illustration from *Flore des serres et des jardins* of 1847. In canvases as well as collages, Ernst presents images from nineteenth- and early twentieth-century scientific illustration and photography.

Early in 1934 in Paris Kandinsky surely became aware of a general interest in science there and he must have perceived even more acutely the current predilection for Surrealist art. The previous autumn Kandinsky had exhibited with the Surrealists in the annual show organized by the *Association Artistique Les Surindépendants* and, in this regard, Arp had written to him: "your paintings hang beautifully. you lead the Surrealist procession."[53] Kandinsky had known Arp since 1911 and had participated in Dada activities at the Galerie Dada and Cabaret Voltaire in Zürich in 1916. By the 1930s there was no longer a Surrealist movement in Paris, since various members of the group were by then pursuing different directions. However, Kandinsky encountered several individuals who had been associated with the Surrealist

48. The Galerie de Zoologie has been closed to the public for years, but M. Laissus and Mme Rufino kindly allowed me to see the displays in the galleries, which have all remained intact.
49. Karl Baedeker, *Paris and Its Environs*, Paris, 1937, p. 353.
50. *Abstammungslehre: Systematik, Paläontologie, Biogeographie*, Leipzig and Berlin, 1914, pp. 322-323, marker pp. 352-353.
51. William Rubin, *Miró in the Collection of The Museum of Modern Art*, New York, 1973, pp. 58-62, 124.
52. Charlotte Stokes, "The Scientific Methods of Max Ernst: His Use of Scientific Subjects from *La Nature*," *Art Bulletin*, vol. 62, Sept. 1980, pp. 454-465; Aaron Scharf, "Max Ernst, Etienne-Jules Marey and the Poetry of Scientific Illustration," in *One Hundred Years of Photographic History*, Van Deren Coke, ed., Albuquerque, 1975, pp. 118-126 and Werner Spies, *Max Ernst—Loplop: The Artist in the Third Person*, New York, 1983, pp. 91-95.
53. Letter from Arp to Kandinsky dated Nov. 12, 1933, preserved in the Kandinsky Archive, Musée National d'Art Moderne, Centre Georges Pompidou, Paris.

fig. 56
Hans Arp
Two Heads. 1929
Collection The Museum of Modern Art, New York. Purchase

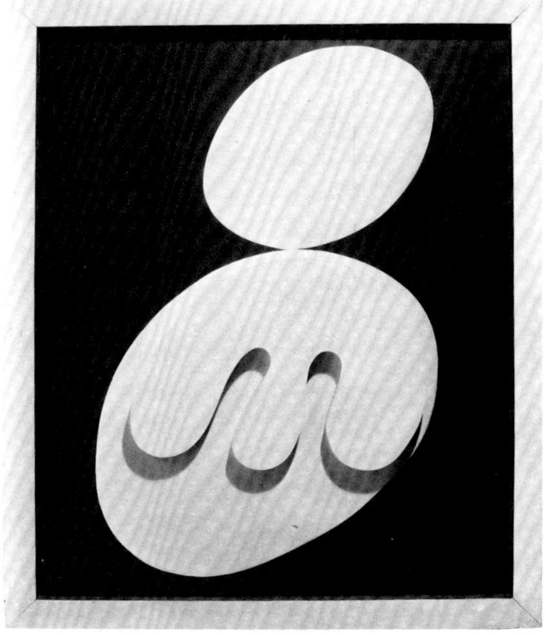

group soon after his arrival: he saw Arp and met Miró in March and he had contact with Ernst and Man Ray in June. Kandinsky's paintings such as *Striped* and *Accompanied Center* (cat. nos. 29, 86) relate to both biological forms and Surrealist imagery in the work of Miró. To an even greater degree, a correspondence is visible between Kandinsky's pictures and Arp's work, where organic shapes with their sense of vitality and growth are particularly evocative. Images similar to the freestanding biomorphic forms familiar from Arp's sculptures—*Torso* of 1931 and *Human Concretion* of 1934—can be detected in Kandinsky's canvases *Composition IX* of 1936 and *Various Actions* of 1941 (cat. nos. 7, 123). Arp's relief *Two Heads* of 1929 (fig. 56) closely resembles specific rounded forms in Kandinsky's painting *Dominant Violet* (fig. 19; cat. no. 27), as well as the encyclopedia illustration depicting the stages in the development of a worm (fig. 39). The congruence of biological forms and Surrealist motifs is striking—and refers to the work of Arp. In fact, the influence of Surrealism in general and Arp and Miró in particular probably inspired Kandinsky to introduce biological images into his work in 1934.

Although the influence of Arp and Miró upon his Paris period appears undeniable, Kandinsky reacted strongly when, in 1936, Alfred Barr stated in the *Cubism and Abstract Art* catalogue that "in the last few years he has turned to more organic forms, perhaps under the influence of the younger Parisians, Miró and Arp, to whom he pointed the way twenty years before.[54] Kandinsky wrote to Galka Scheyer:

> *The last straw, however, is the conjecture that my Parisian painting may have been influenced by Arp or Miró. With equal justification Barr could have named Corot instead of Arp and Velázquez instead of Miró. One*

54. Alfred H. Barr, Jr., *Cubism and Abstract Art*, exh. cat., New York, 1936, p. 68.

learns from everyone—even from the weak (as one should not!). Miró once told me he would be forever grateful for the "liberation." I often hear such things from younger artists who have no reason to flatter me. Actually these "influences" are not essential to form, which historians seldom recognize. The adoption of form is decadence. I am grateful to Barr, however, because he doesn't trace my painting from Cubism.[55]

Kandinsky's art differs from the work of the Surrealists in several essential ways: it does not delve into the unconscious and it does not concern itself with either mythology or dreams. In his pictures there is no evidence of the influence of Freud and psychoanalysis. Kandinsky never experimented with automatism and did not use accident as a creative method. His work lacks both found objects and collages. Moreover, Kandinsky did not share the Communist political orientation of many Surrealists. Although Kandinsky's correspondence reflects a quite vehement opposition to Surrealism, his published writings are more restrained. In his 1937 essay "Assimilation of Art," written for an issue of *Linien* that included work by several artists with strong Surrealist associations, he alludes only obliquely to the style. Here he reveals a relatively moderate position toward forms in nature:

Therefore, I do not become shocked when a form that resembles a "form in nature" insinuates itself secretively into my other forms. I just let it stay there and I will not erase it. Who knows, maybe all our "abstract" forms are "forms in nature," but . . . "objects of use?"
These art forms and forms in nature (without purpose) have an even clearer sound that we must absolutely listen to.[56]

While Kandinsky's writings are critical of Surrealism, they say surprisingly little about biological sciences—especially embryology and zoology.[57] The few references in *Point and Line to Plane* and in his Bauhaus teaching notes have already been cited. In the latter he discusses zoology and equates unicellular organisms (protozoa) with organisms capable of polymorphic development, and thus of becoming "a sum"; and he speaks of protozoa as "original beings."[58] In August 1935 Kandinsky wrote a short text for the Danish periodical *Konkretion,* in which he referred to his earlier published writings and stated that:

this experience of the "hidden soul" in all the things, seen either by the unaided eye or through microscopes or binoculars, is what I call the "internal eye." This eye penetrates the hard shell, the external "form," goes deep into the object and lets us feel with all our senses its internal "pulse."[59]

Since an explanation or documentation of the embryological and zoological forms in Kandinsky's paintings is absent from his writings, interpretations and meanings proposed for them remain hypothetical. The very fact that embryos are depicted so frequently in Kandinsky's work in 1934 and subsequent years raises questions about his personal life. Early in 1917 the artist, then

55. Letter from Kandinsky to Galka Scheyer dated May 29, 1936. Author's translation.

56. Lindsay and Vergo II, p. 803.

57. For example, an early reference to "grown men and embryos" in his discussion of ornamentation in *On The Spiritual in Art* does not have meaning with regard to science (Lindsay and Vergo I, p. 199).

58. *Scritti,* p. 290.

59. Lindsay and Vergo II, p. 779.

fifty-one years old, married Nina Andreevskaia, who was very much younger than he. According to all the information known about them and according to their friends, the Kandinskys had no children. Recently, after Nina Kandinsky's death, it has emerged that they had a son called Volodia who was born in September 1917 and died in June 1920.[60] This fact remained a complete secret during Vasily's and Nina's lifetimes. Although there is no evidence that events in Kandinsky's life influenced his art, the subconscious effects of personal experiences may have emerged many years after their occurrence. When he was old and relatively isolated in Paris, Kandinsky's awareness of his childlessness may have become increasingly acute. Can we deny the relevance of the artist's personal life when his paintings reflect it?

Approached from an entirely different point of view, Kandinsky's paintings of the Paris period suggest a specific biological and philosophical concept.[61] His apparently conscious effort to create biomorphic forms that simultaneously resemble embryos and marine invertebrates can be related to the "principle of recapitulation," the rule or heuristic maxim that the development of the embryo of each organism passes rapidly through phases resembling its evolutionary ancestors. Thus, it is commonly observed that the human fetus successively takes on fish-like, amphibian, reptilian and bird-like characteristics before developing distinctly mammalian features. Furthermore, the human embryo shares these stages, which occur during the first several weeks of development, with all mammal embryos. The diagram of comparative embryological development (fig. 7) was made after Darwin and supports his theory by showing that successive evolutionary specializations are superimposed on existing structures, and that the earlier stages are vestigially retained.

There are a number of hypothetical reasons why Kandinsky would have been interested in, even intrigued with, the principle of recapitulation, which was extremely popular from 1870 to 1910.[62] While the principle that ontogeny (embryonic development) repeats phylogeny (successive evolution of major zoological groups) antedates Darwinian evolution theory by several decades, the most fruitful application of the principle was as an indirect proof of evolution itself. The person who attempted this proof was Ernst Heinrich Haeckel, who was one of Darwin's most prominent early supporters. Haeckel used the principle to make major advances in linking comparative anatomy to embryology in his area of greatest expertise, marine invertebrates. He also used the principle to postulate the "missing link," Pithecanthropus, between man and ape. In his fieldwork Haeckel focused on marine invertebrates—radiolaria, hydras and medusas—the very images prevalent in Kandinsky's Paris pictures. An accomplished draftsman, he was responsible for the illustrations as well as the text in *Kunstformen der Natur* (see fig. 20). However, he was most famous for his theoretical work in embryology.[63] Around the turn of the century his fame was such that Kandinsky must have been familiar with his work.[64]

Second, Kandinsky would have been interested in the phylogeny/ontogeny recapitulation principle because of its resemblance to an ancient, spiritually oriented philosophical theme which inverts its order; namely, the

60. I am indebted to Karl Flinker for this information conveyed in correspondence with the author, Apr. 29, 1983.
61. I am most grateful to Peter H. Barnett for his assistance, especially on the history of science and philosophy.
62. Ernst Mayr, *The Growth of Biological Thought,* Cambridge, Mass., 1982, pp. 471-474.
63. Eric Wahl brought these interrelationships to my attention and assisted me with many research questions.
64. Haeckel (1834-1919) is referred to frequently in several volumes of *Die Kultur der Gegenwart: Allgemeine Biologie, Anthropologie* and *Naturphilosophie.* Two important books on him were published in 1934: Gerhard Heberer, *Ernst Haeckel und seine wissenschaftliche Bedeutung. Zum Gedächtnis der 100. Wiederkehr seines Geburtstages,* Tübingen, and Heinrich Schmidt, *Ernst Haeckel: Denkmal eines grossen Lebens,* Jena.

intellectual or spiritual development of humanity from prehistoric times corresponds to the intellectual and spiritual growth of each individual. Georg Wilhelm Friedrich Hegel's *Phenomenology of Mind* and *Philosophy of History* are founded on this principle and it is prevalent in the work of a variety of nineteenth-century thinkers such as Ralph Waldo Emerson and Herbert Spencer.

Finally, Kandinsky is known to have been familiar with theosophy and its literature.[65] There is evidence in the writings of H.P. Blavatsky, the founder of the movement, that she and other theosophists were both acutely aware of and ambivalent toward mid-nineteenth century developments in natural history and embryology.[66] Although Blavatsky abhorred the materialistic interpretation Haeckel and Thomas Henry Huxley gave to the recapitulation principle, she cited parallels to it in ancient cabalistic and Vedantic writings. The theosophists believed that man's spirit governed the whole evolutionary process and that humanity developed from amorphous egg-like creatures through a hermaphrodite stage before becoming sexually differentiated. Thus, the theosophists came to agree with the most advanced biologists that all life proceeds from a single original germ. However, for theosophists this germ is not protoplasm but the spirit. Rudolf Steiner lectured extensively on Haeckel and his theories of evolution in relation to theosophy in 1905-06 and his text "Haeckel, die Welträtsel und die Theosophie" was first published in *Lucifer Gnosis,* no. 31, in 1905.[67] Steiner's writings on the subject date from as early as 1899 and his vital interest in Haeckel's ideas continued throughout his life. By 1913, when Steiner organized the Anthroposophical Society, the relevant texts had been published in many editions in German and they would later be translated into Russian, French and English.[68]

In terms of Kandinsky's painting, embryological imagery can be interpreted on multiple levels. First, the embryonic forms are not immediately recognizable: art historians, critics and viewers in general have been slow to identify even the part of nature from which he derived his motifs.[69] As in the paintings Kandinsky executed in Munich before World War I, the images are hidden and abstracted from reality. When natural forms are shown under great magnification or excerpted from their contexts, their identities are disguised. However, a leaf is still a leaf even though it no longer looks like one. Second, an embryo is not recognizable as an adult member of its species yet it contains implicitly everything that it will become. The genetic makeup of each embryo will determine its psychological as well as physical being. Moreover, the embryo is a generalized image. At an early stage it is neither ostensibly human nor individual: it is already an abstraction.

In a note to *Point and Line to Plane,* Kandinsky explicitly connects embryonic and evolutionary development to abstract art.

> *Abstract art, despite its emancipation, is subject here also to "natural laws," and is obliged to proceed in the same way that nature did previously, when it started in a modest way with protoplasm and cells, progressing very gradually to increasingly complex organisms. Today, abstract art creates also primary or more or less primary art-organisms,*

65. See Rose-Carol Washton Long, *Kandinsky: The Development of an Abstract Style,* Oxford, 1980, ch. 2, Sixten Ringbom, *The Sounding Cosmos: A Study in the Spiritualism of Kandinsky and the Genesis of Abstract Painting,* Åbo, 1970, and Sixten Ringbom, "Kandinsky und das Okkulte" in *Kandinsky und München,* exh. cat., Munich, 1982, pp. 85-101.
66. I would like to thank Cynthia Goodman for her insights and Nancy Spector for her assistance with research on this subject.
67. This issue of *Lucifer Gnosis* is not preserved in either the Gabriele Münter- und Johannes Eichner-Stiftung, Städtische Galerie im Lenbachhaus in Munich or in the Kandinsky Archive, Musée National d'Art Moderne, Paris. The latter possesses only one copy of *Lucifer Gnosis* (no. 14 from July 1904). However, Kandinsky's knowledge of several texts in *Lucifer Gnosis* (nos. 8, 10-11, 18-19, 30-34) has been proven by Sixten Ringbom ("Die Steiner Annotationen Kandinskys" in *Kandinsky und München,* exh. cat., Munich, 1982, pp. 102-105).
68. In the Archiv und Bibliothek of the Goetheanum in Dornach, Switzerland, the author consulted "Haeckel und seine Gegner," "Ernst Haeckel und die Welträtsel," "Die Kämpfe um Haeckels' 'Welträtsel,' " "Die Kultur der Gegenwart im Spiegel der Theosophie" and "Haeckel, die Welträtsel und die Theosophie." The best published source is Johannes Hemleben, *Rudolf Steiner und Ernst Haeckel,* Stuttgart, 1965.
69. For general references in art-historical literature, see Rose-Carol Washton, *Kandinsky: Parisian Period 1934-1944,* exh. cat., New York, 1969, pp. 16-17 and "Vasily Kandinsky: A Space Odyssey," *Art News,* vol. LXVIII, Oct. 1969, p. 49 as well as Hans Konrad Roethel, *Kandinsky,* New York, 1979, p. 42.

whose further development the artist today can predict only in uncertain outline, and which entice, excite him, but also calm him when he stares into the prospect of the future that faces him. Let me observe here that those who doubt the future of abstract art are, to choose an example, as if reckoning with the stage of development reached by amphibians, which are far removed from fully developed vertebrates and represent not the final result of creation, but rather the "beginning."[70]

Kandinsky's images of amoebas, embryos and marine invertebrates convey a spiritual meaning of beginning, regeneration and a common origin of all life. Because of his spiritual beliefs and his ideas on abstract art, Kandinsky would have responded to the meanings of rebirth and renewal inherent in the new imagery of his Paris pictures.

70. Lindsay and Vergo II, p. 628.

CATALOGUE

English titles precede the original-language titles, which appear in parentheses.

When Kandinsky gave his paintings or watercolors a number in his Handlist (HL) or watercolors Handlist (HL watercolors), this is cited after the title and date.

Dimensions are given in inches and centimeters; height precedes width precedes depth.

*Indicates not in exhibition.
†Indicates not illustrated.

I. KANDINSKY AND THE MUSEES NATIONAUX IN FRANCE

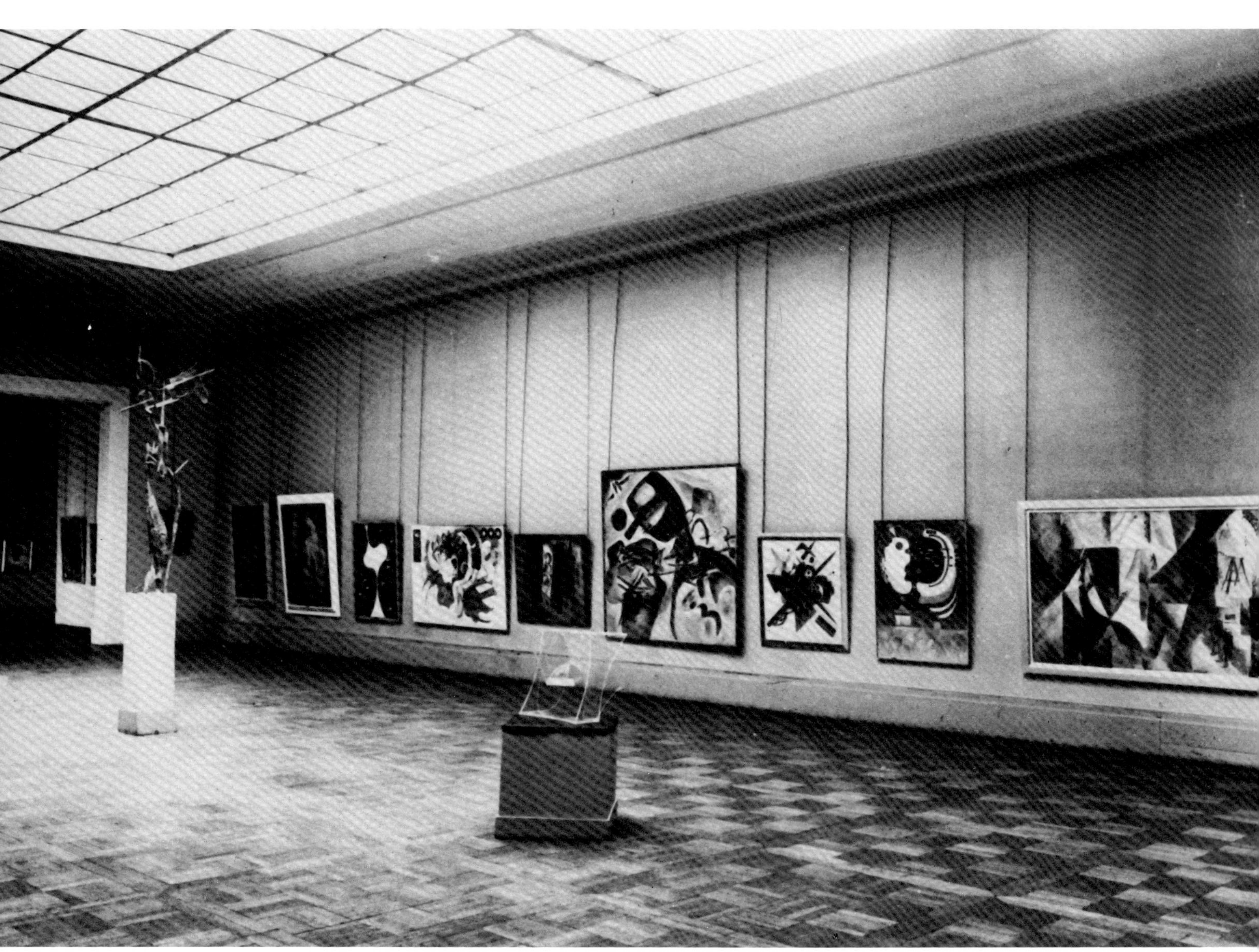

1 *View of Exhibition "Origines et développement de l'art international indépendant," Paris, Jeu de Paume, July 30–October 31, 1937.* 1937
Photograph
Collection Musée National d'Art Moderne, Centre Georges Pompidou, Paris

Vasily Kandinsky
2 *With the Black Arc (Mit schwarzem Bogen).* Fall 1912
(HL 154)
Oil on canvas, 74⅜ x 78" (189 x 198 cm.)
Collection Musée National d'Art Moderne, Centre Georges Pompidou, Paris, Gift of Mme Nina Kandinsky

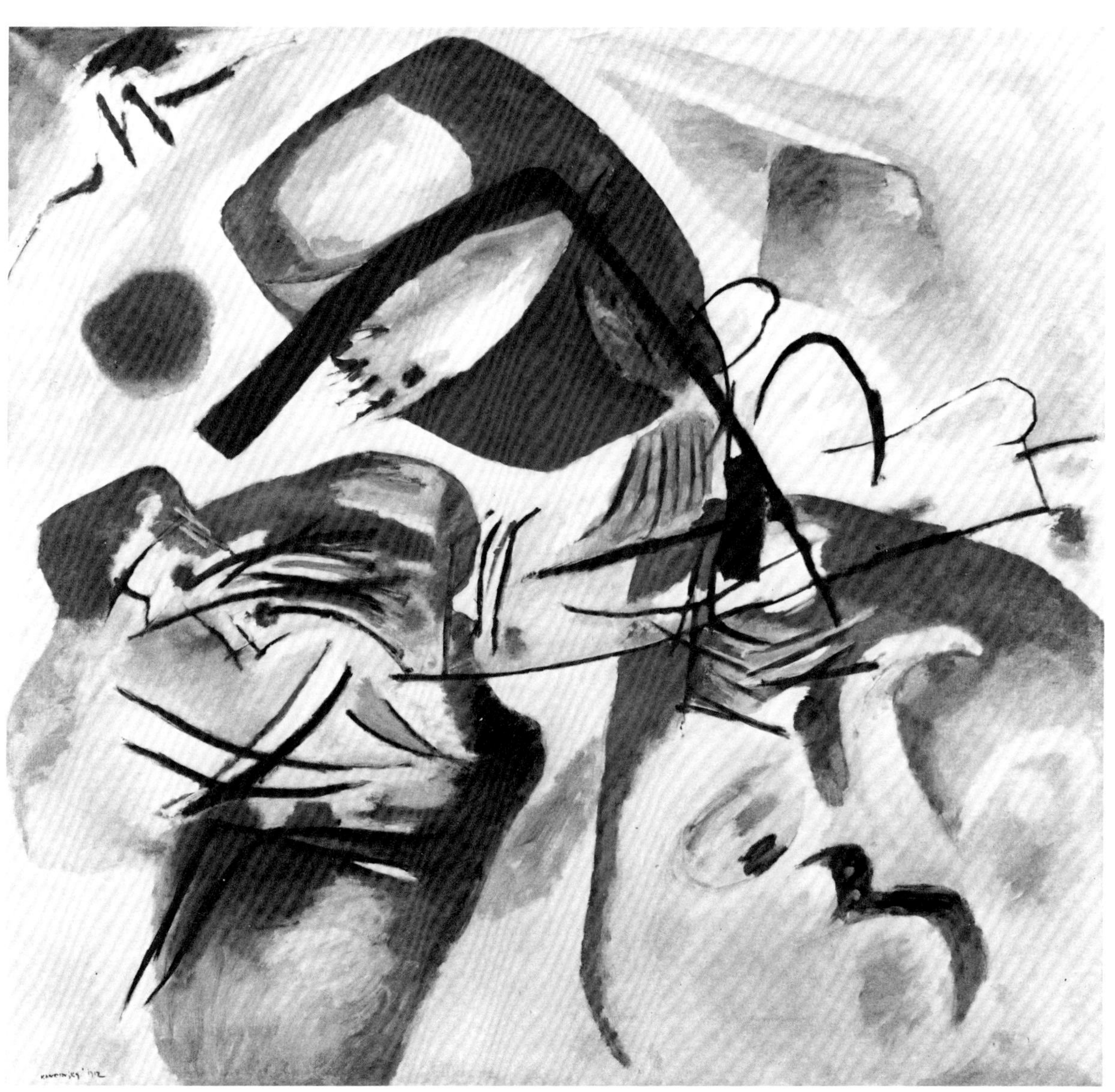

Vasily Kandinsky

3 *On White (Auf Weiss).* February–April 1923
(HL 253)
Oil on canvas, 41⅜ x 38 9/16″
(105 x 98 cm.)
Collection Musée National d'Art Moderne, Centre Georges Pompidou, Paris, Gift of Mme Nina Kandinsky

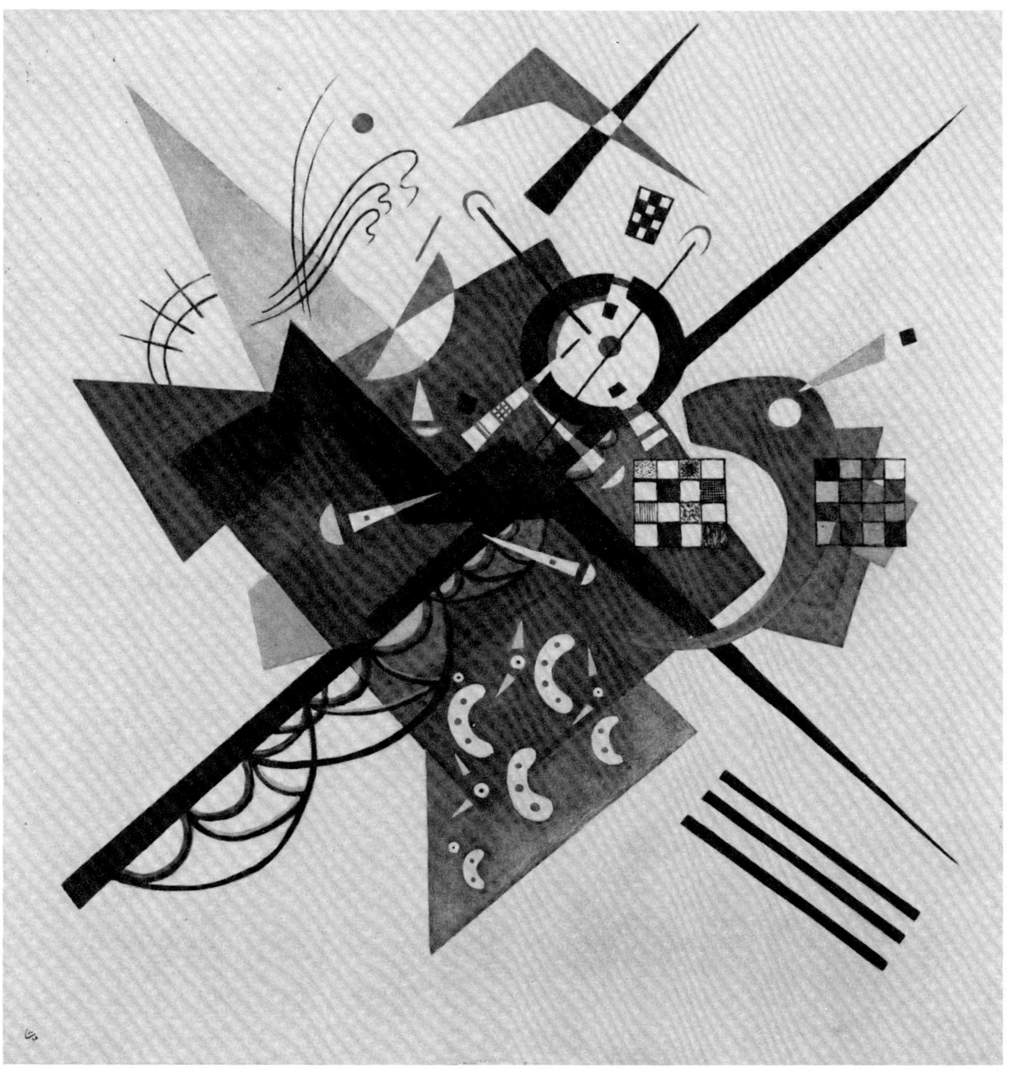

Vasily Kandinsky

4 *Development in Brown (Entwicklung in Braun).* August 1933

(HL 594)

Oil on canvas, 41⅜ x 47¼″ (105 x 120 cm.)

Collection Musée National d'Art Moderne, Centre Georges Pompidou, Paris

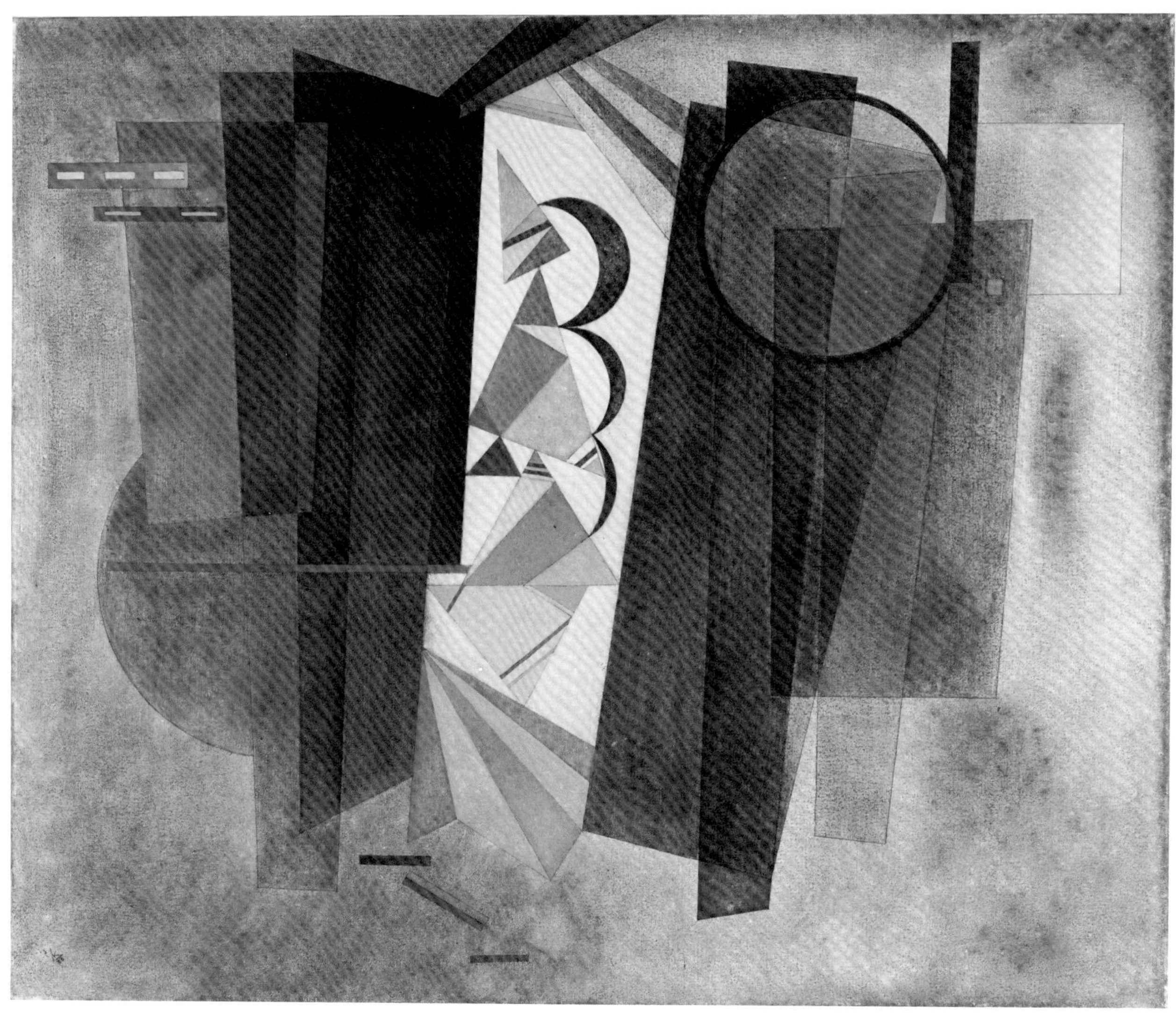

Vasily Kandinsky

*5 *Between Two (Entre deux).* May 1934
(HL 601)
Mixed media on canvas, 51 3/16 x 38 3/16"
(130 x 97 cm.)
Private Collection

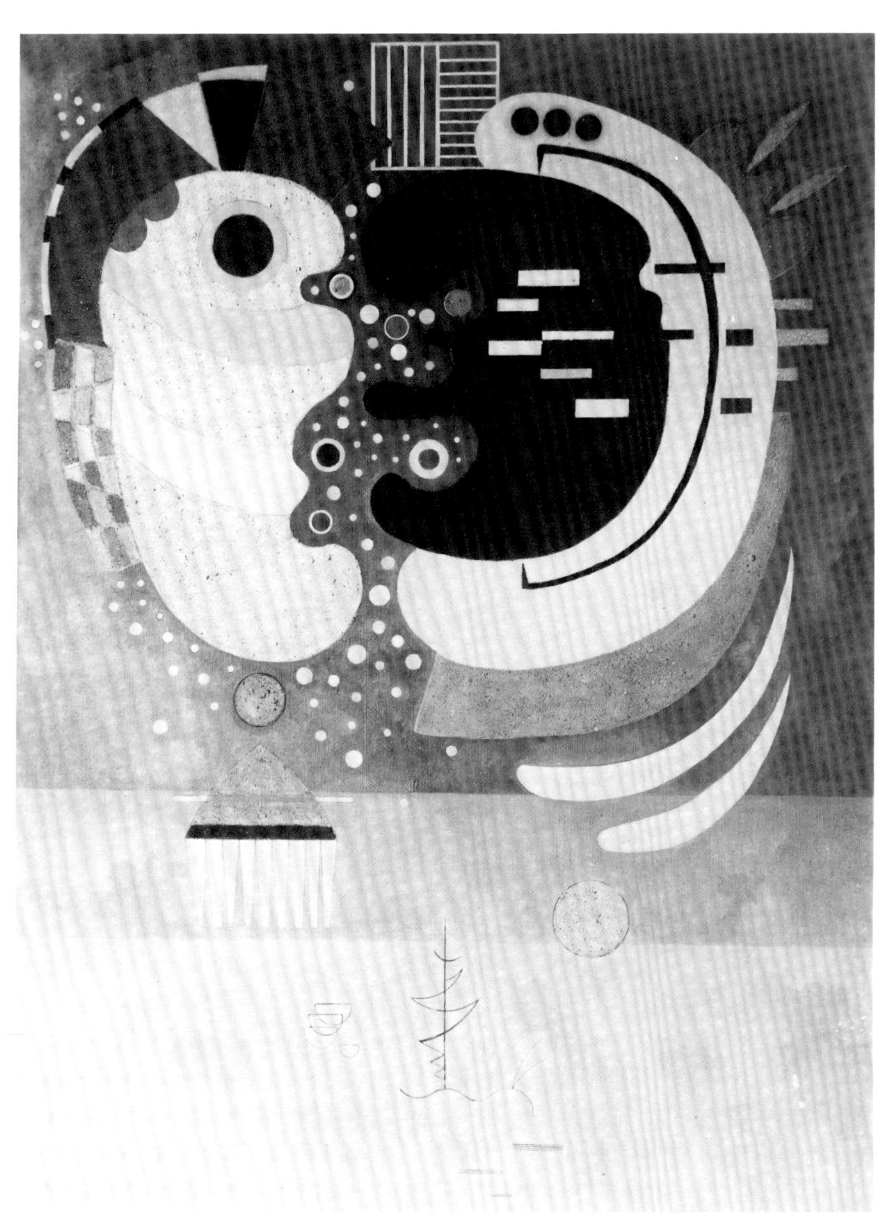

Vasily Kandinsky

6 *Dominant Curve (Courbe dominante).*
April 1936
(HL 631)
Oil on canvas, 50⅞ x 76½″
(129.4 x 194.2 cm.)
Collection Solomon R. Guggenheim
Museum, New York

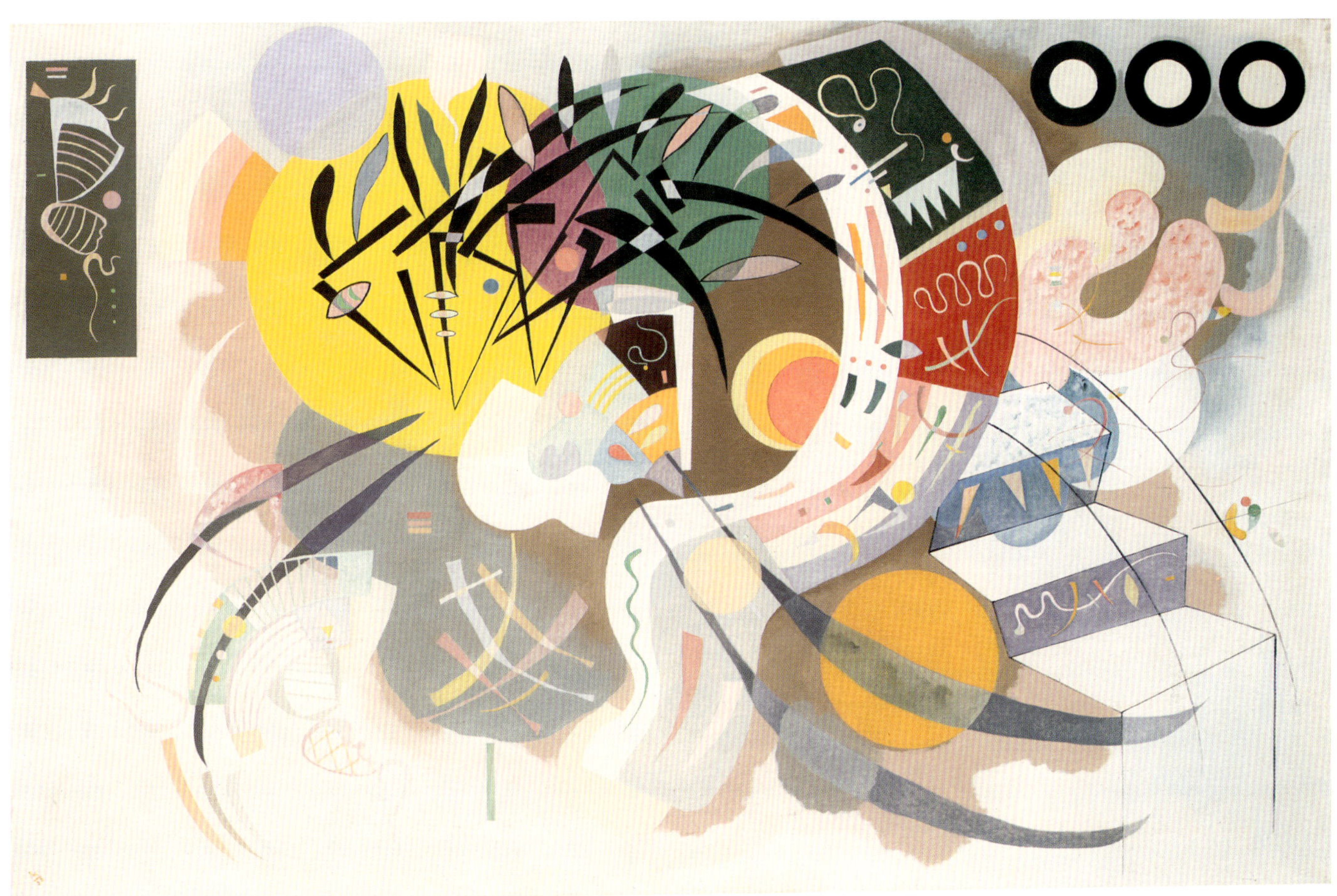

Vasily Kandinsky

7 *Composition IX*. February 1936
(HL 626)
Oil on canvas, $44\frac{11}{16}$ x $76\frac{3}{4}$″
(113.5 x 195 cm.)
Collection Musée National d'Art Moderne,
Centre Georges Pompidou, Paris

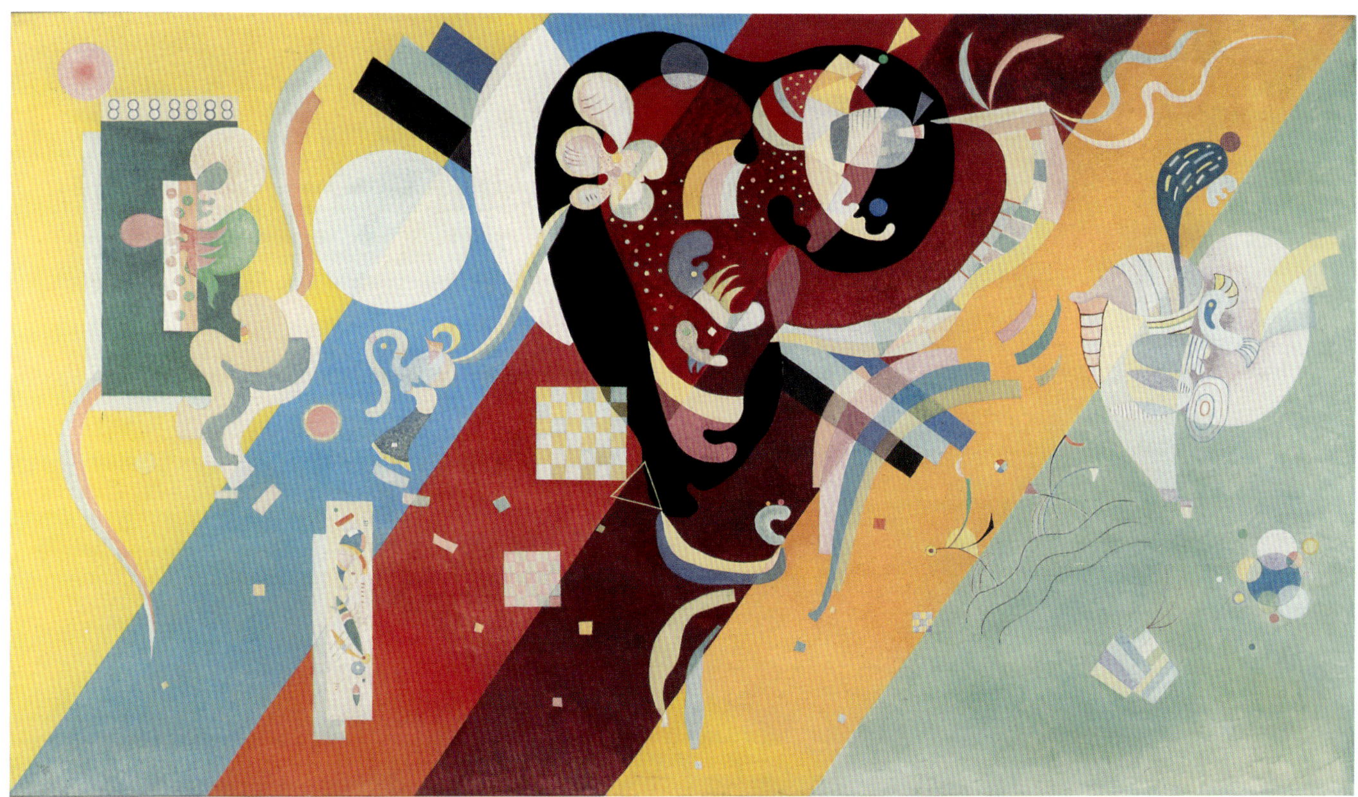

Vasily Kandinsky

8 *Drawing of Frame for "Composition IX" (Cadre pour "Composition IX").* April 16, 1939

Pencil on paper, $3\frac{3}{4}$ x 5″ (9.5 x 12.8 cm.)

Collection Musée National d'Art Moderne, Centre Georges Pompidou, Paris, Kandinsky Bequest

Vasily Kandinsky

9 *Study for "Composition IX" (Etude pour la "Composition IX").* 1936

Pencil and India ink on paper, $12\frac{13}{16}$ x $19\frac{15}{16}$″ (32.5 x 50.6 cm.)

Collection Musée National d'Art Moderne, Centre Georges Pompidou, Paris, Kandinsky Bequest

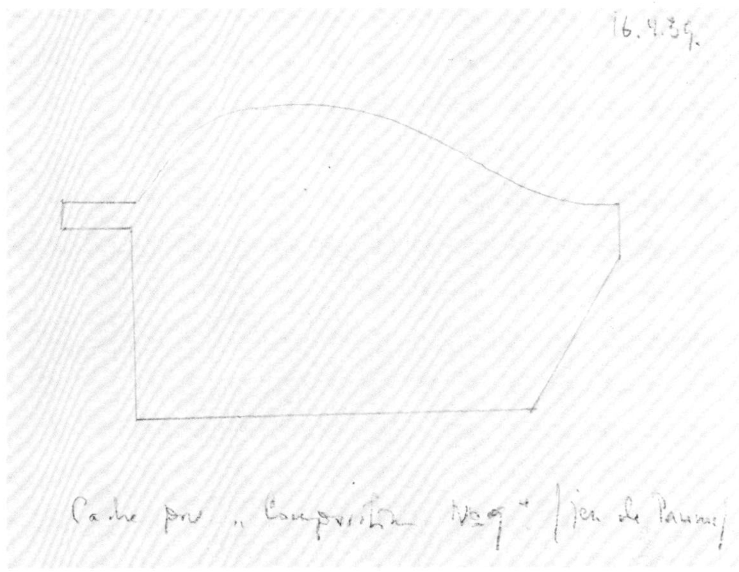

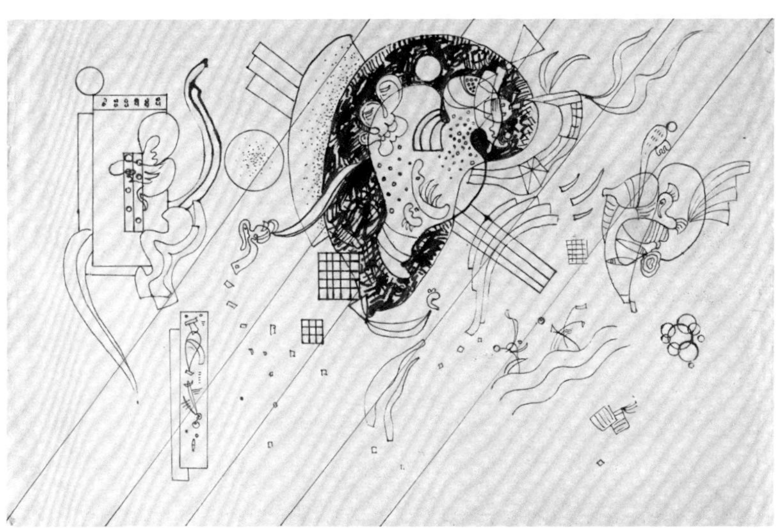

Vasily Kandinsky

10 *White Line (La Ligne blanche).* June 1936
(HL watercolors 571)
Gouache and tempera on black paper mounted on cardboard, 19⅝ x 15¼″ (49.9 x 38.7 cm.)
Collection Musée National d'Art Moderne, Centre Georges Pompidou, Paris

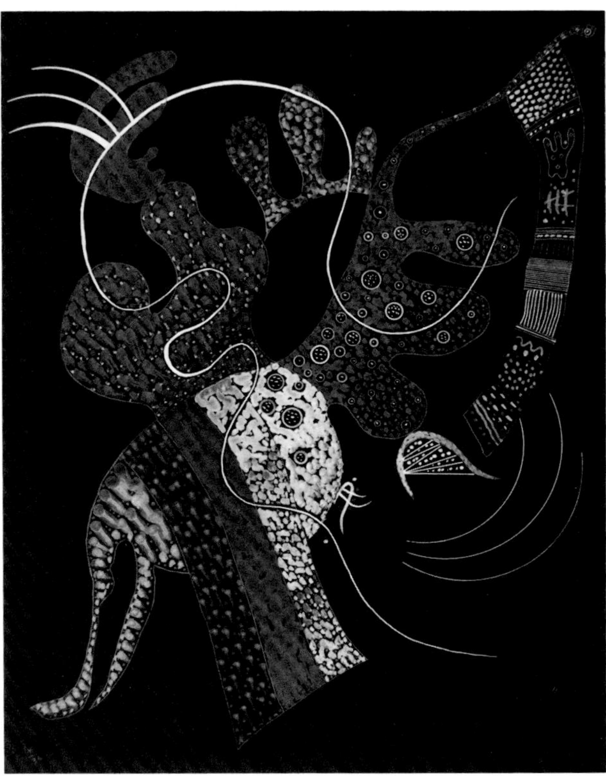

11 *Letter from André Dézarrois, Musée du Jeu de Paume, to Kandinsky.* July 9, 1937
Typescript on paper, 10 13/16 x 7⅞″ (27.5 x 20 cm.)
Collection Musée National du Louvre, Paris

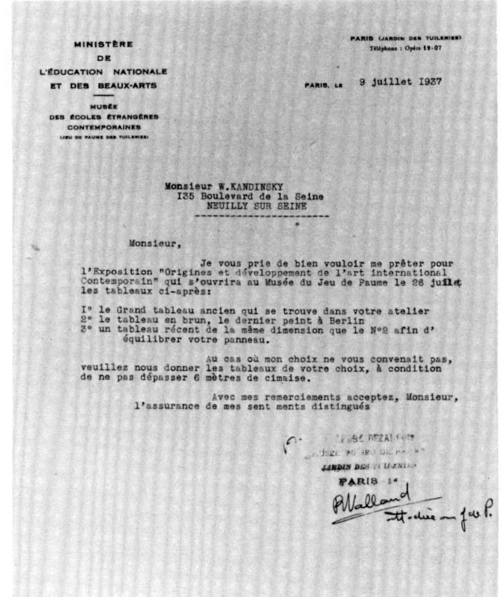

MINISTÈRE
DE
L'ÉDUCATION NATIONALE
ET DES BEAUX-ARTS

MUSÉE
DES ÉCOLES ÉTRANGÈRES
CONTEMPORAINES
(JEU DE PAUME DES TUILERIES)

PARIS (JARDIN DES TUILERIES)
Téléphone : Opéra 12-07

PARIS, LE 9 juillet 1937

Monsieur W.KANDINSKY
135 Boulevard de la Seine
NEUILLY SUR SEINE

Monsieur,

Je vous prie de bien vouloir me prêter pour l'Exposition "Origines et développement de l'art international Contemporain" qui s'ouvrira au Musée du Jeu de Paume le 26 juillet les tableaux ci-après:

1° le Grand tableau ancien qui se trouve dans votre atelier
2° le tableau en brun, le dernier peint à Berlin
3° un tableau récent de la même dimension que le N°2 afin d'équilibrer votre panneau.

Au cas où mon choix ne vous convenait pas, veuillez nous donner les tableaux de votre choix, à condition de ne pas dépasser 6 mètres de cimaise.

Avec mes remerciements acceptez, Monsieur, l'assurance de mes sent ments distingués

JARDIN DES TUILERIES
PARIS 1er

P.Walland

12 a-b *Letter from Kandinsky to André Dézarrois, Musée du Jeu de Paume, and Enclosed List of Loans for Exhibition at Musée du Jeu de Paume.* July 15, 1937

Letter, typescript on paper, $10\frac{13}{16}$ x $7\frac{7}{8}$" (27.5 x 20 cm.); enclosure, typescript on paper, $10\frac{13}{16}$ x $7\frac{7}{8}$" (27.5 x 20 cm.)

Collection Musée National du Louvre, Paris

13 *Enclosure from Letter from Kandinsky to André Dézarrois.* 1937

Ink on paper, $7\frac{7}{8}$ x $5\frac{3}{16}$" (20 x 13 cm.)

Collection Musée National du Louvre, Paris

14 *Enclosure from Letter from Kandinsky to André Dézarrois.* 1937

Ink on paper, $7\frac{7}{8}$ x $5\frac{3}{16}$" (20 x 13 cm.)

Collection Musée National du Louvre, Paris

K A N D I N S K Y

Neuilly s/S., 135 Bd de la Seine.

le 15 Juillet 19[37]

Monsieur DEZARROIS, Directeur du Musée de "Jeu de Paume", Paris.

Monsieur,

J'ai fait tout mon possible de me contenter de huit mt. de sim[aise] et enfin j'ai reussi de présenter 4 périodes de mon développement. Malheureusement j'ai été forcé de supprimer la "racine" de ma forme "non-figurative", c'est-à-dire une toile de 1911 ("Composition No 4"), où se laissent voir encore des restes des "objets" d'une manière assez claire. Mais je me subordonne aux "conditions données".

Voilà les périodes présentés:

"L'arc noir" 1912....... période dit "lyrique"
(une de mes premières toiles "non-fig.")
"Sur blanc" 1923 ..... " " "froid"
"Développement en brun" 1933 ..... " " "surfaces approfondies"
"Entre deux" 1934 et
"Courbe dominante" 1936 .... " " "synthétique"

Ces dernières deux toiles sont des exemples de ma production parisienne.

Je me permets de vous bien prier de faire accrocher mes toiles en ordre indéqué par moi sur la liste adjointe - une chose vraiment très importante pour ma peinture. Je vous serais très reconnaissant.

Je vous remercie très cordialement de m'avoir donnée la possibilité de montrer pour la première fois le développement de mon art au public parisien, et je vous prie bien, Monsieur, d'agréer l'expression de mes sentiments les plus respectueux et distingués.

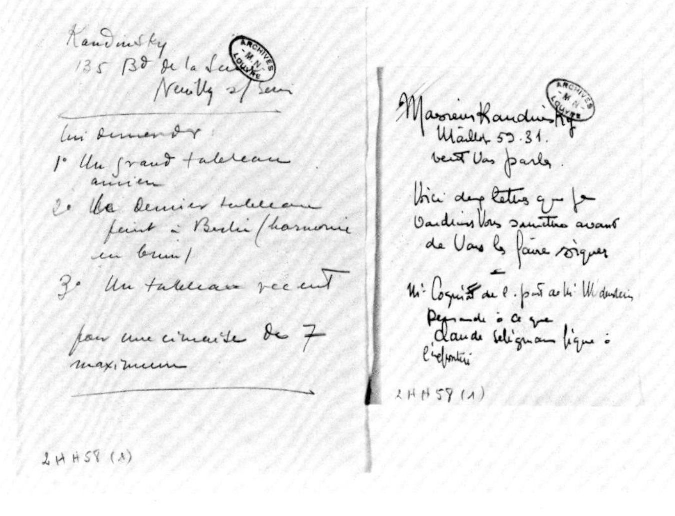

Kandinsky
135 Bd de la Seine
Neuilly s/ Seine

lui demander
1° Un grand tableau ancien
2° Un dernier tableau peint à Berlin (harmonie en brun)
3° Un tableau récent

pour une cimaise de 7 maximum

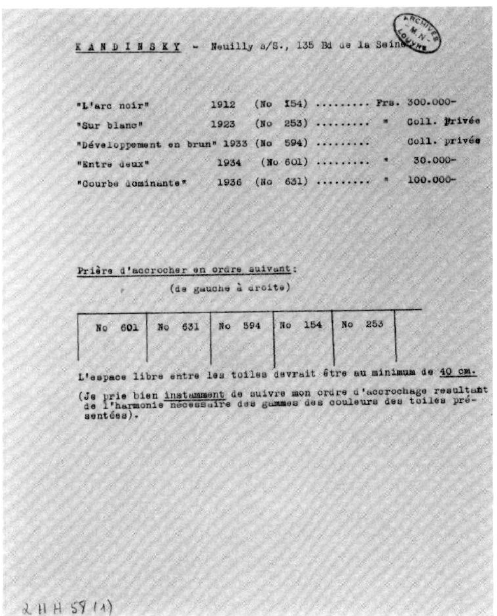

K A N D I N S K Y - Neuilly s/S., 135 Bd de la Seine

"L'arc noir"	1912	(No 154)	....	Frs. 300.000-
"Sur blanc"	1923	(No 253)	....	" Coll. privée
"Développement en brun"	1933	(No 594)	....	Coll. privée
"Entre deux"	1934	(No 601)	....	" 30.000-
"Courbe dominante"	1936	(No 631)	....	" 100.000-

Prière d'accrocher en ordre suivant:
(de gauche à droite)

No 601	No 631	No 594	No 154	No 253

L'espace libre entre les toiles devrait être au minimum de 40 cm.

(Je prie bien instamment de suivre mon ordre d'accrochage resultant de l'harmonie nécessaire des gammes des couleurs des toiles présentées).

M. Magnelli
20 Villa Seurat
Paris 14e

lui demander
deux tableaux récents
pour une cimaise de 5 mètres maximum.

II. KANDINSKY'S SURROUNDINGS IN NEUILLY-SUR-SEINE

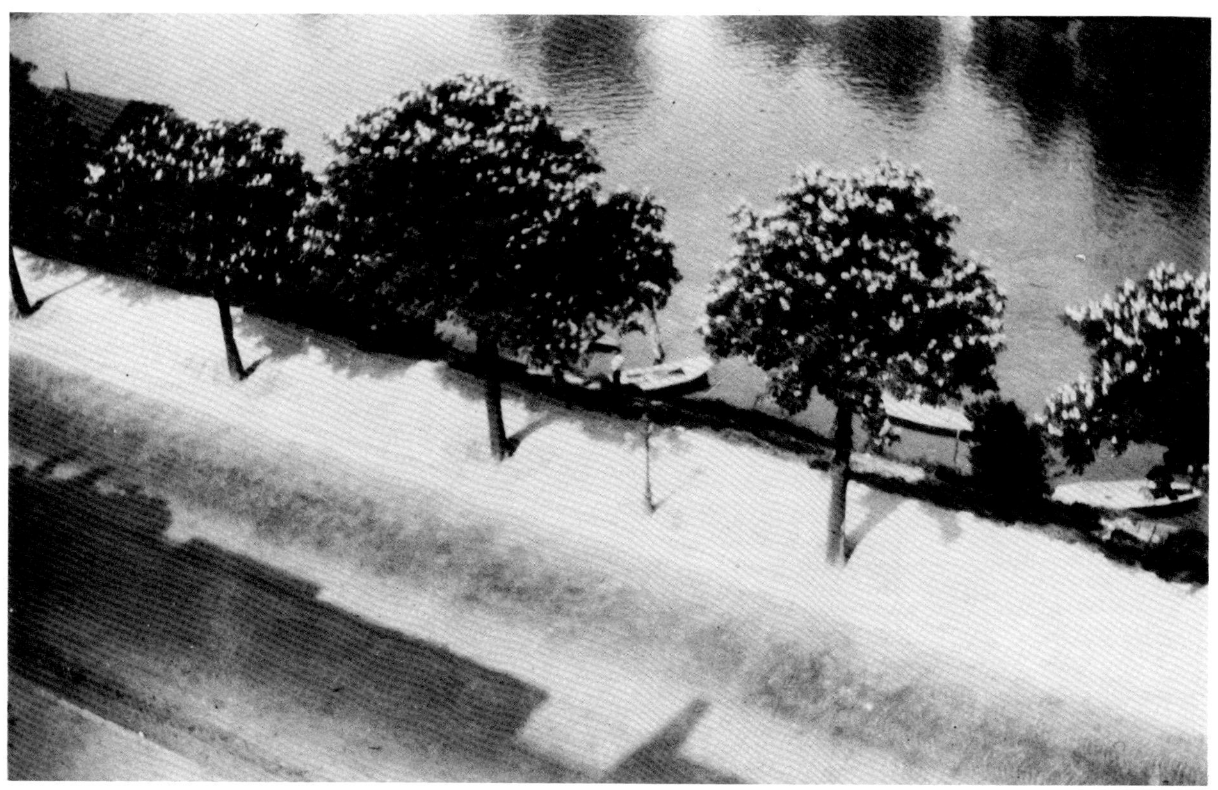

15 *View of Neuilly-sur-Seine.* n.d.
Photograph
Collection Musée National d'Art Moderne, Centre Georges Pompidou, Paris, Kandinsky Bequest

16 *View of Neuilly-sur-Seine.* n.d.
Photograph
Collection Musée National d'Art Moderne, Centre Georges Pompidou, Paris, Kandinsky Bequest

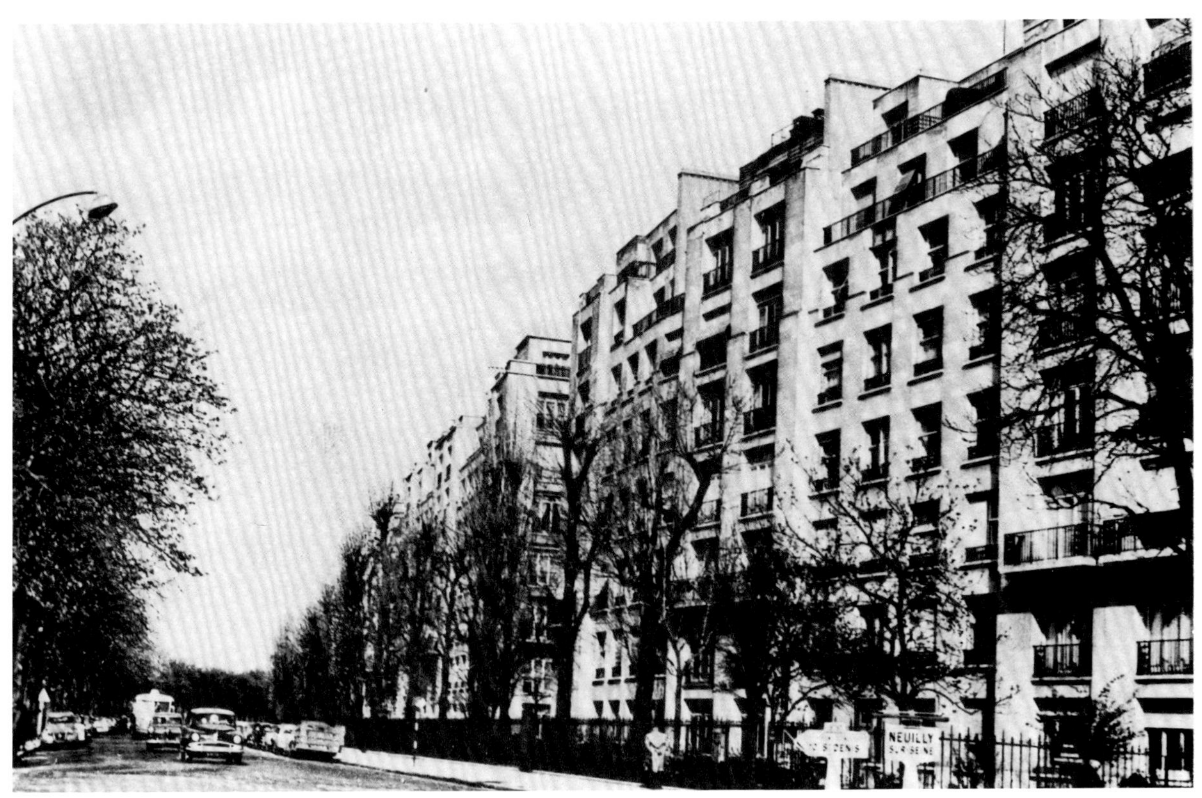

17 *View of Neuilly-sur-Seine.* n.d.
Photograph
Collection Musée National d'Art Moderne,
Centre Georges Pompidou, Paris,
Kandinsky Bequest

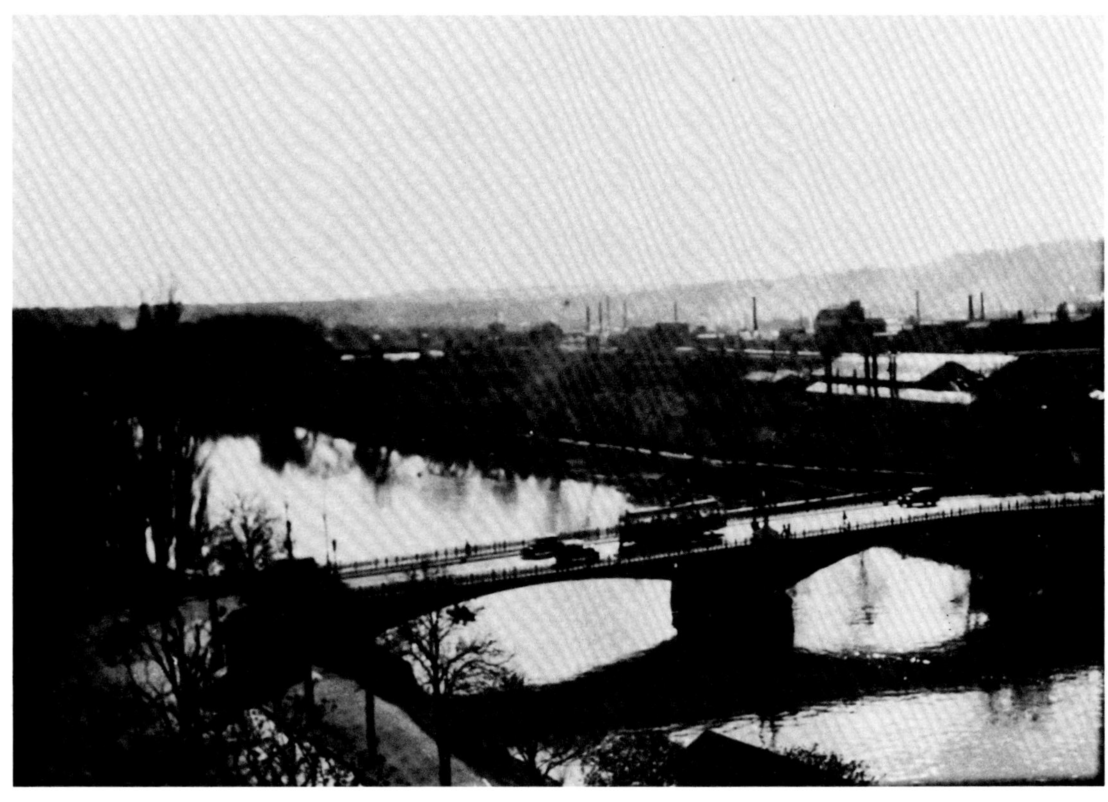

18 *View of Bois de Boulogne and Rose Garden of Bagatelle, Neuilly-sur-Seine.* n.d.
Postcard
Collection Musée National d'Art Moderne, Centre Georges Pompidou, Paris, Kandinsky Bequest

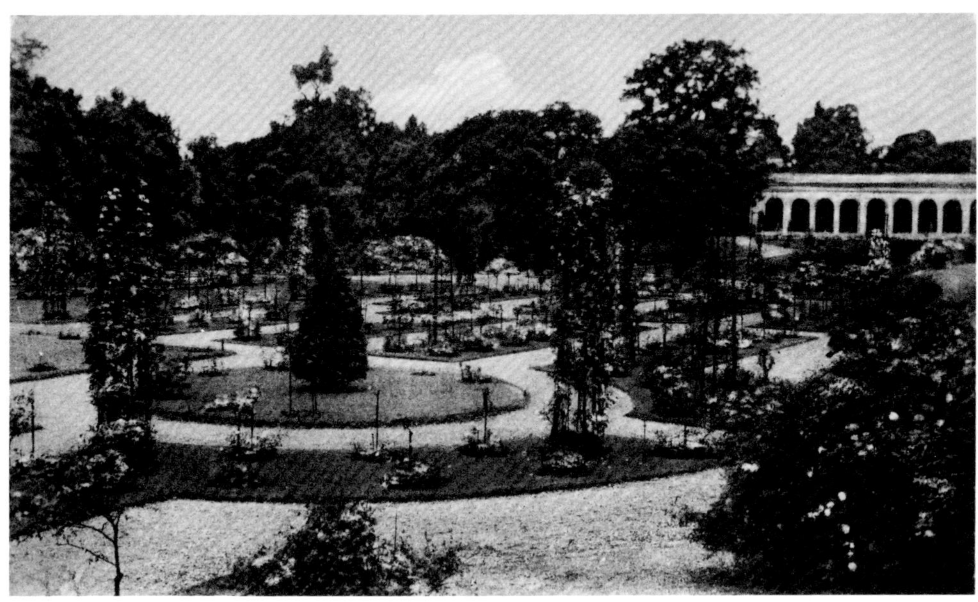

Joseph Breitenbach

19 *View from Kandinsky's Apartment in Neuilly-sur-Seine.* 1938

Photograph

Collection Musée National d'Art Moderne, Centre Georges Pompidou, Paris, Kandinsky Bequest

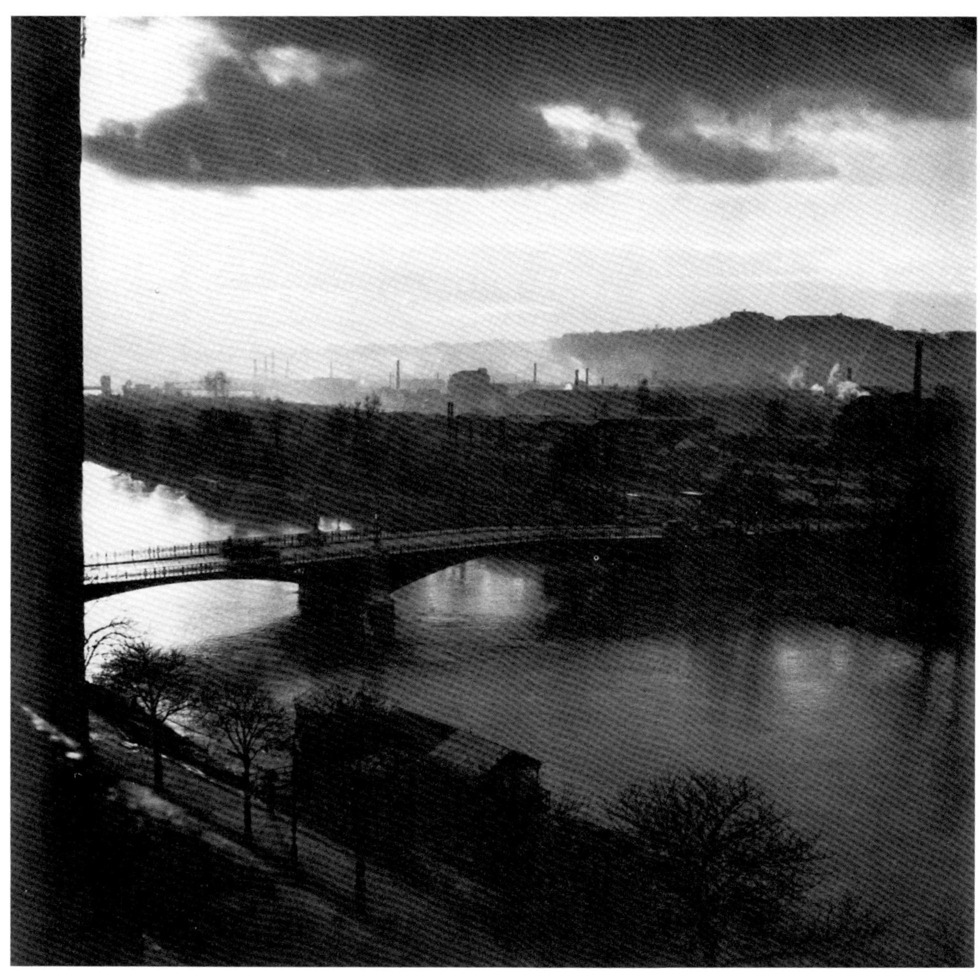

Joseph Breitenbach

20 *View from Kandinsky's Apartment in Neuilly-sur-Seine.* 1938

Photograph

Collection Musée National d'Art Moderne, Centre Georges Pompidou, Paris, Kandinsky Bequest

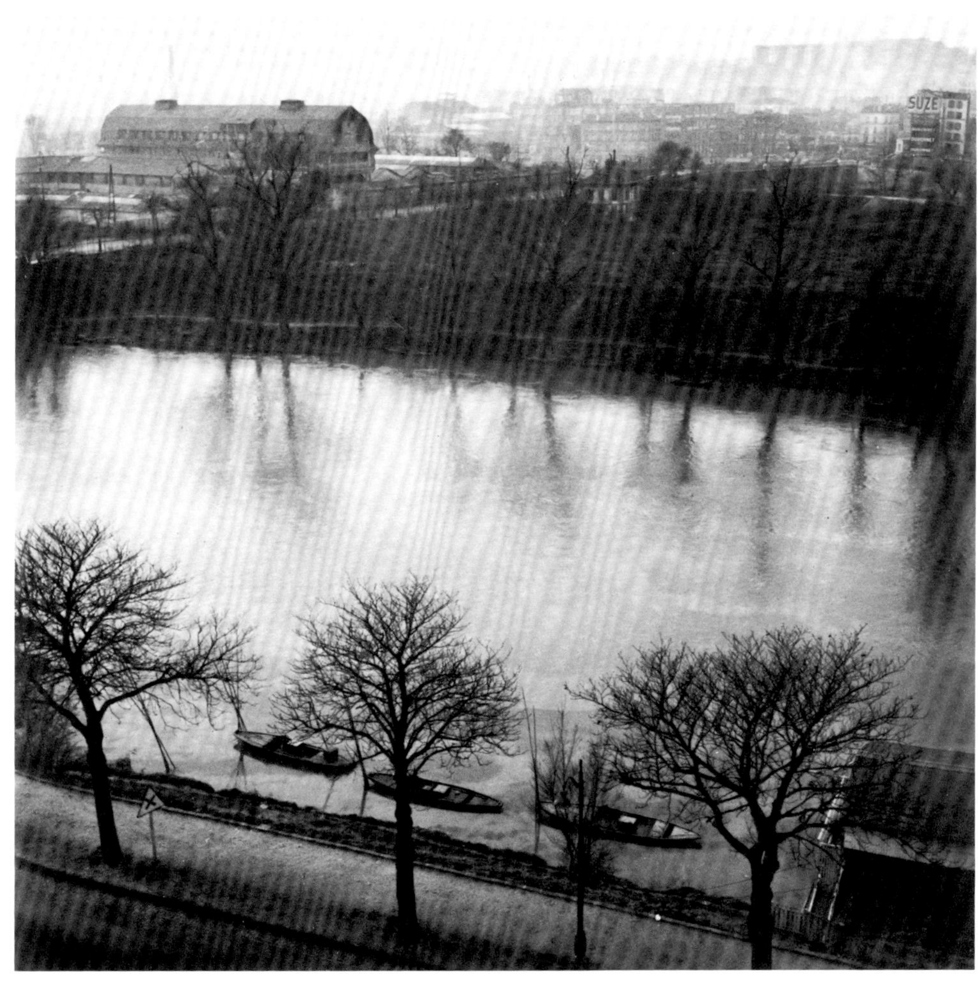

III. KANDINSKY'S FIRST PAINTINGS EXECUTED IN PARIS, 1934-1939

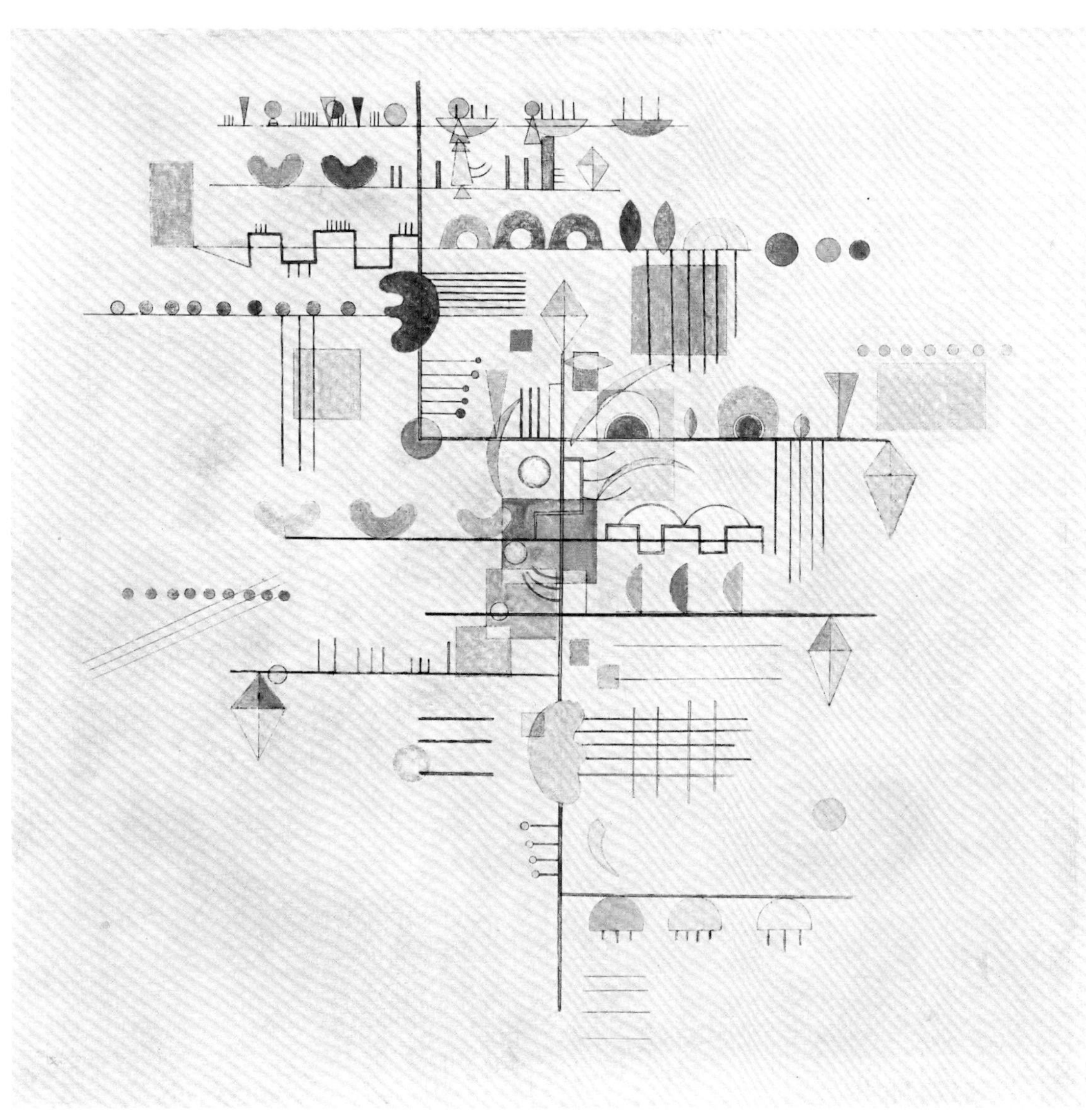

Vasily Kandinsky
21 *Graceful Ascent (Montée gracieuse).* March 1934
(HL 596)
Oil on canvas, 31⅝ x 31¾″ (80.4 x 80.7 cm.)
Collection Solomon R. Guggenheim Museum, New York

Vasily Kandinsky
22 *Each for Himself (Chacun pour soi).* April 1934
(HL 598)
Oil and tempera on canvas, 23⅝ x 28″ (60 x 71 cm.)
Private Collection

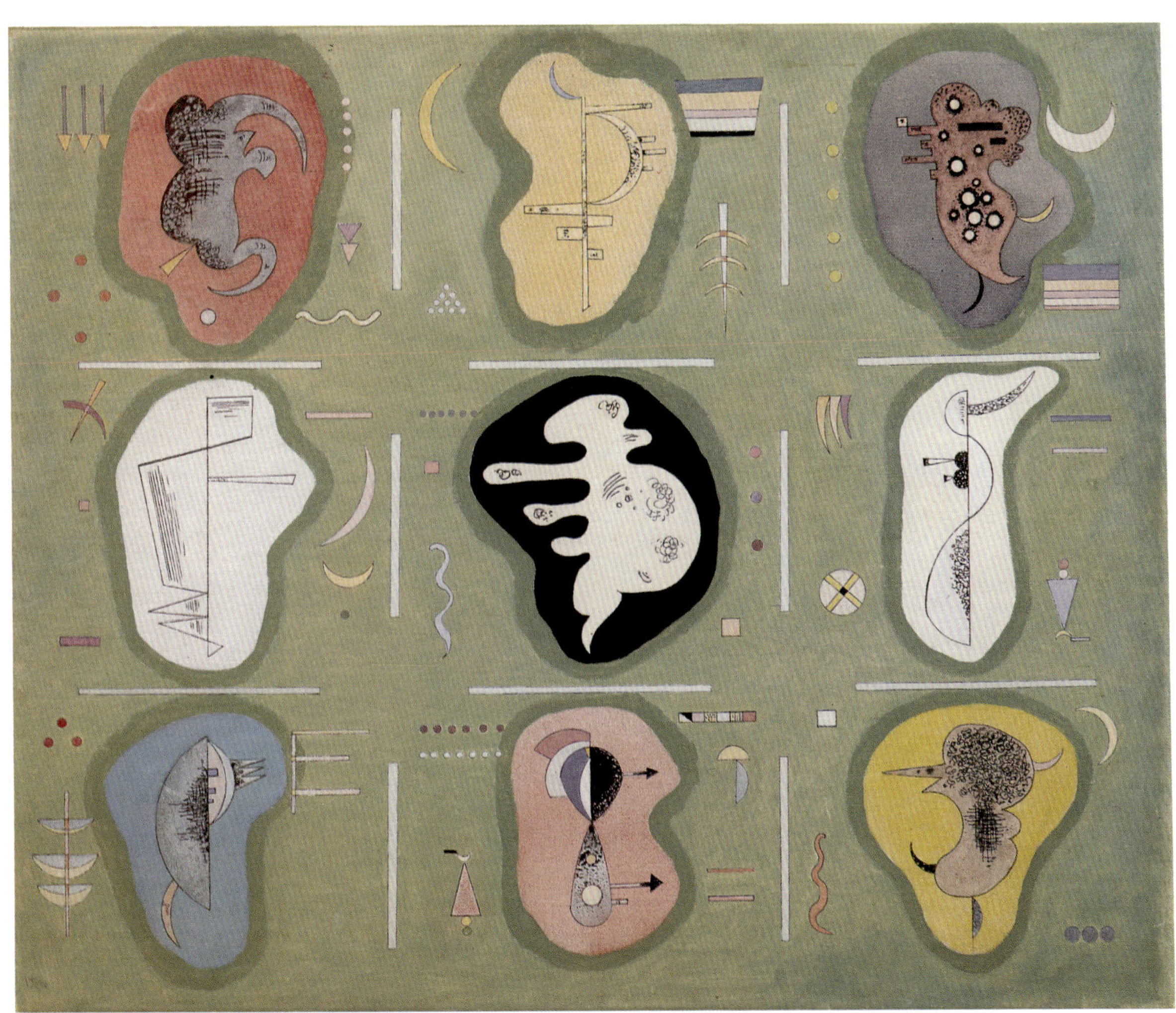

Vasily Kandinsky

23 *Study for "Each for Himself" (Etude en aquarelle pour "Chacun pour soi").* March 1934

(HL watercolors 522b)

Watercolor and India ink on paper, 12½ x 9⅝" (31.6 x 24.4 cm.)

Collection Musée National d'Art Moderne, Centre Georges Pompidou, Paris, Kandinsky Bequest

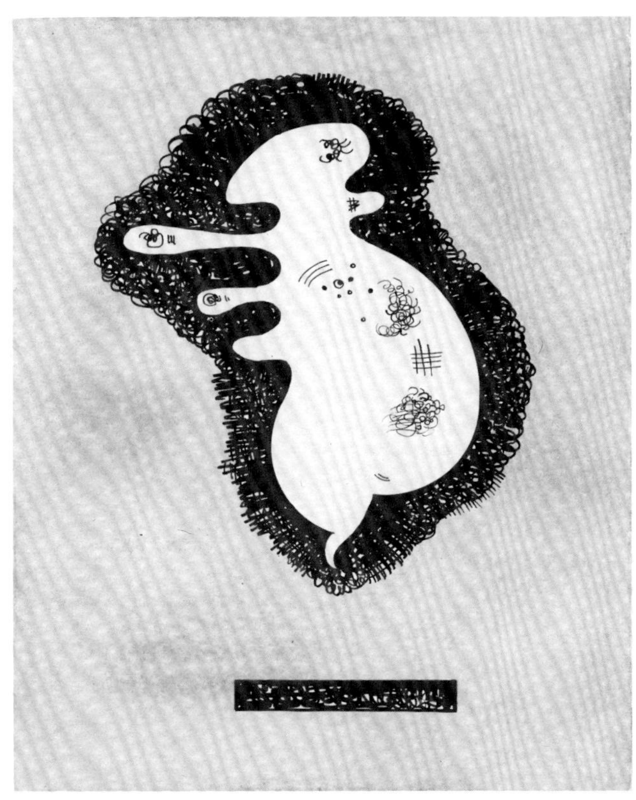

Vasily Kandinsky

24 *Ensemble.* April 1934
(HL 599)
Oil and watercolor on canvas,
23⅝ x 27½" (60 x 70 cm.)
Lent by Davlyn Gallery, New York

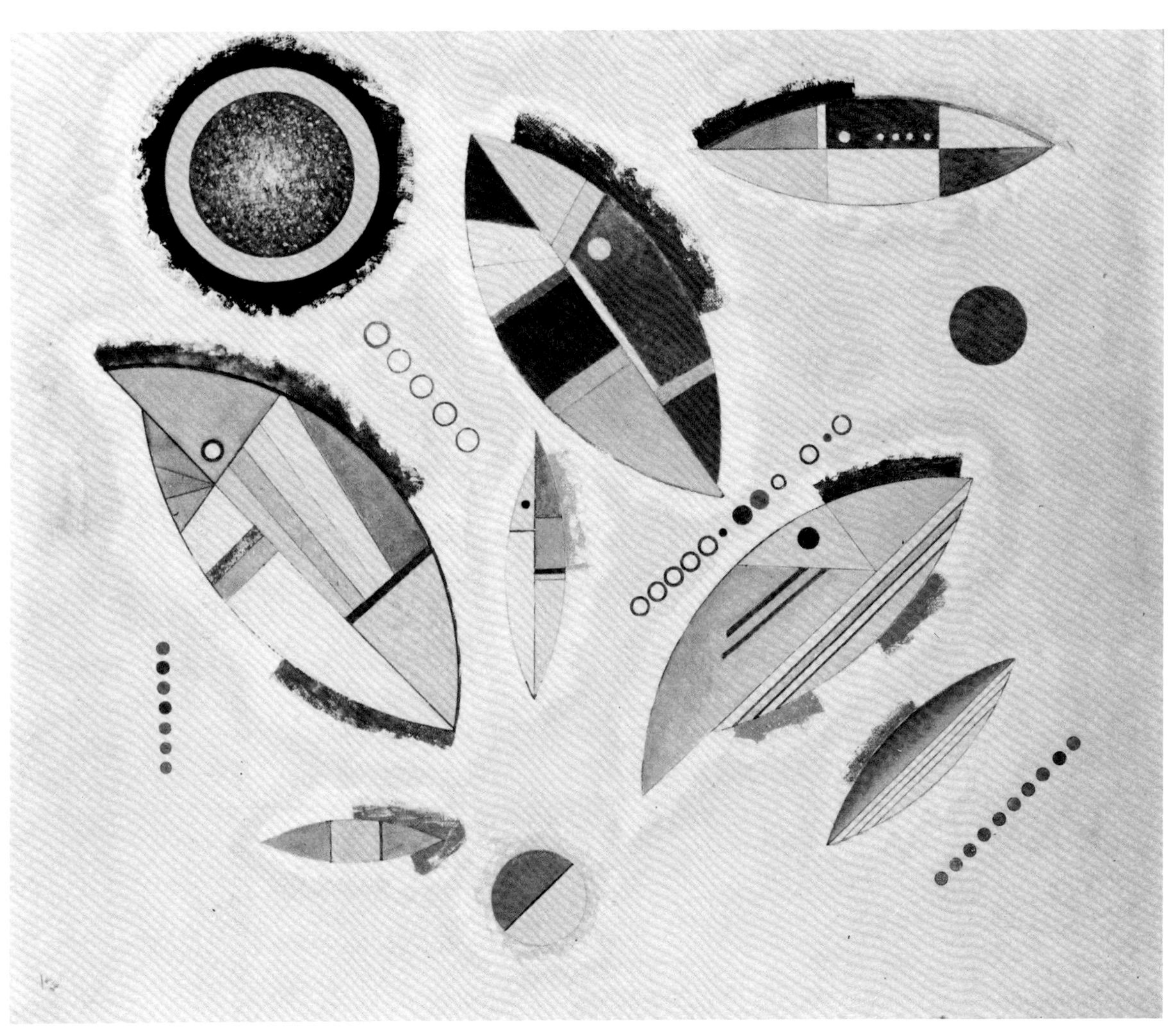

Vasily Kandinsky

25 *Blue World (Monde bleu).* May 1934
(HL 602)
Oil with sand on canvas, 43½ x 47⅜"
(110.6 x 120.2 cm.)
Collection Solomon R. Guggenheim
Museum, New York

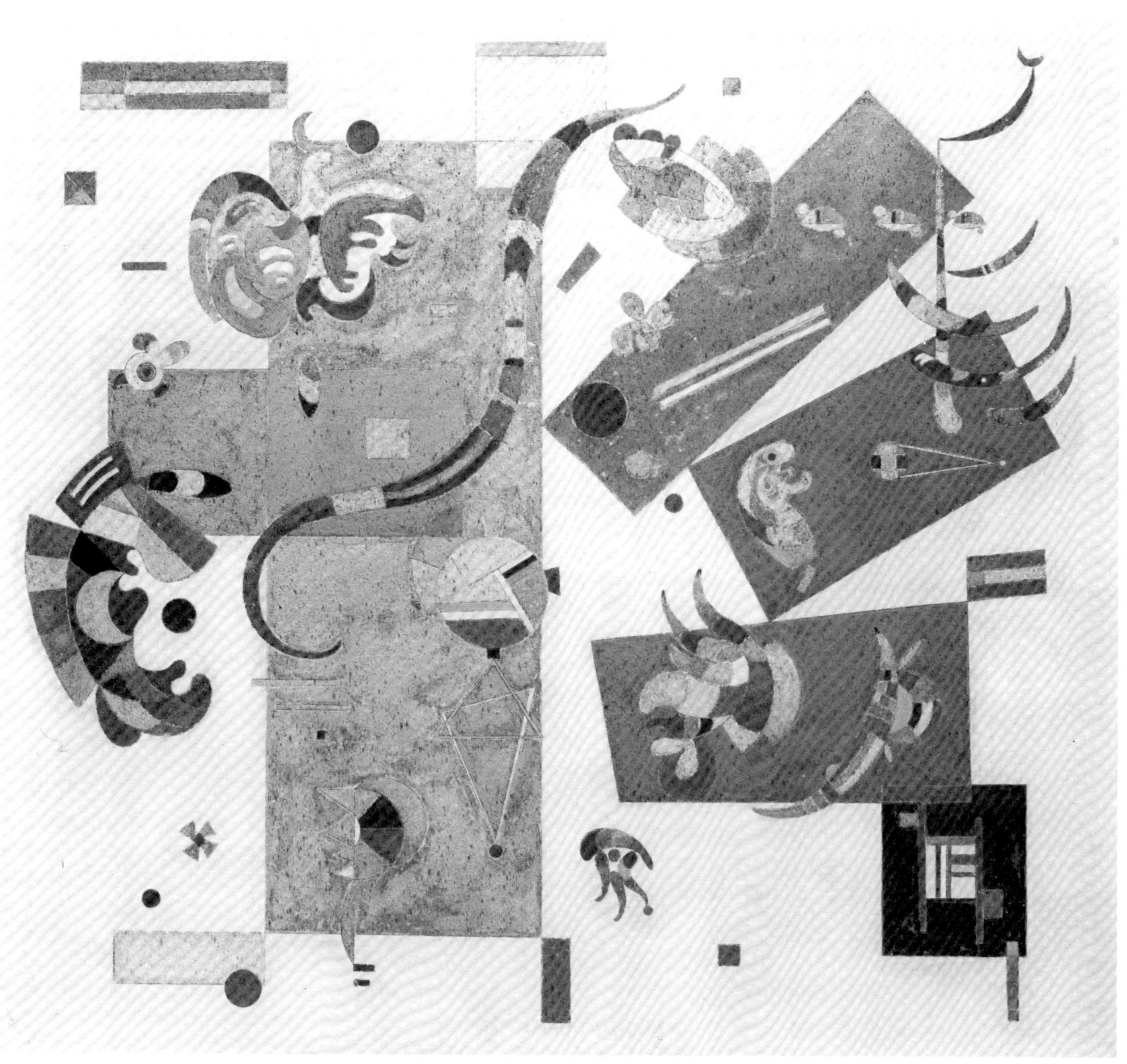

Vasily Kandinsky

26 *Study for "Blue World" (Etude pour "Monde bleu").* 1934

Pencil on paper, $5\frac{7}{16} \times 5\frac{15}{16}''$ (14.1 x 15 cm.)

Collection Musée National d'Art Moderne, Centre Georges Pompidou, Paris, Kandinsky Bequest

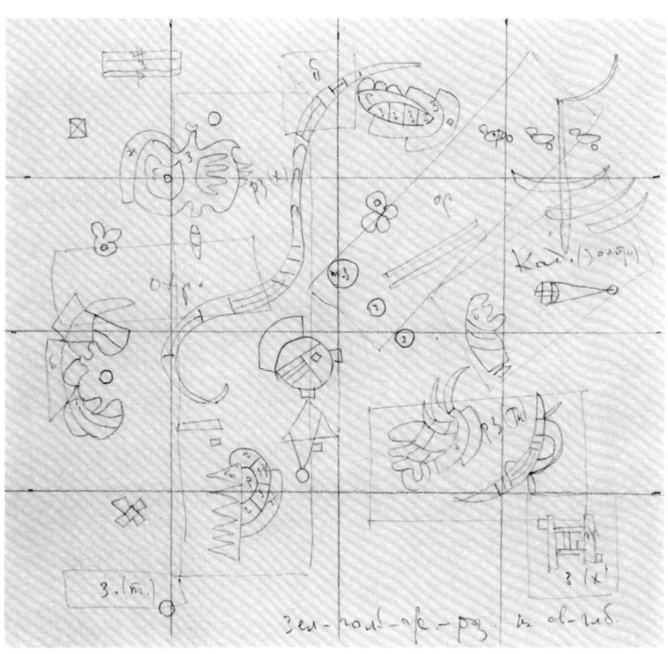

Vasily Kandinsky
27 *Dominant Violet (Violet dominant).*
June 1934
(HL 603)
Oil with sand on canvas, 51 3/16 x 63 3/4"
(130 x 162 cm.)
Collection Mark Goodson, New York

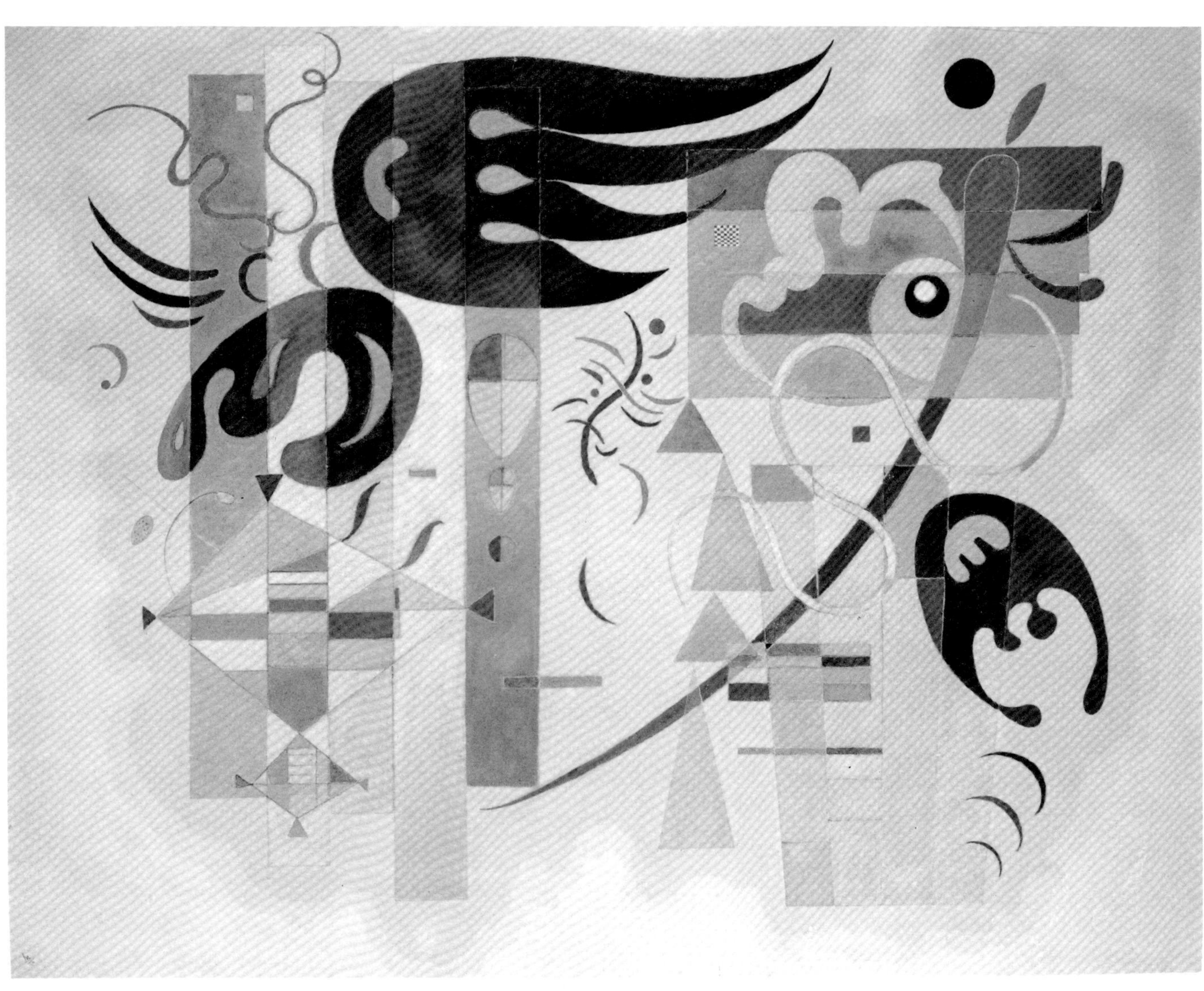

Vasily Kandinsky

*28 *Relations.* July 1934
(HL 604)
Oil with sand on canvas, 35 1/16 x 45 11/16"
(89 x 116 cm.)
Collection Mr. and Mrs. David Lloyd Kreeger

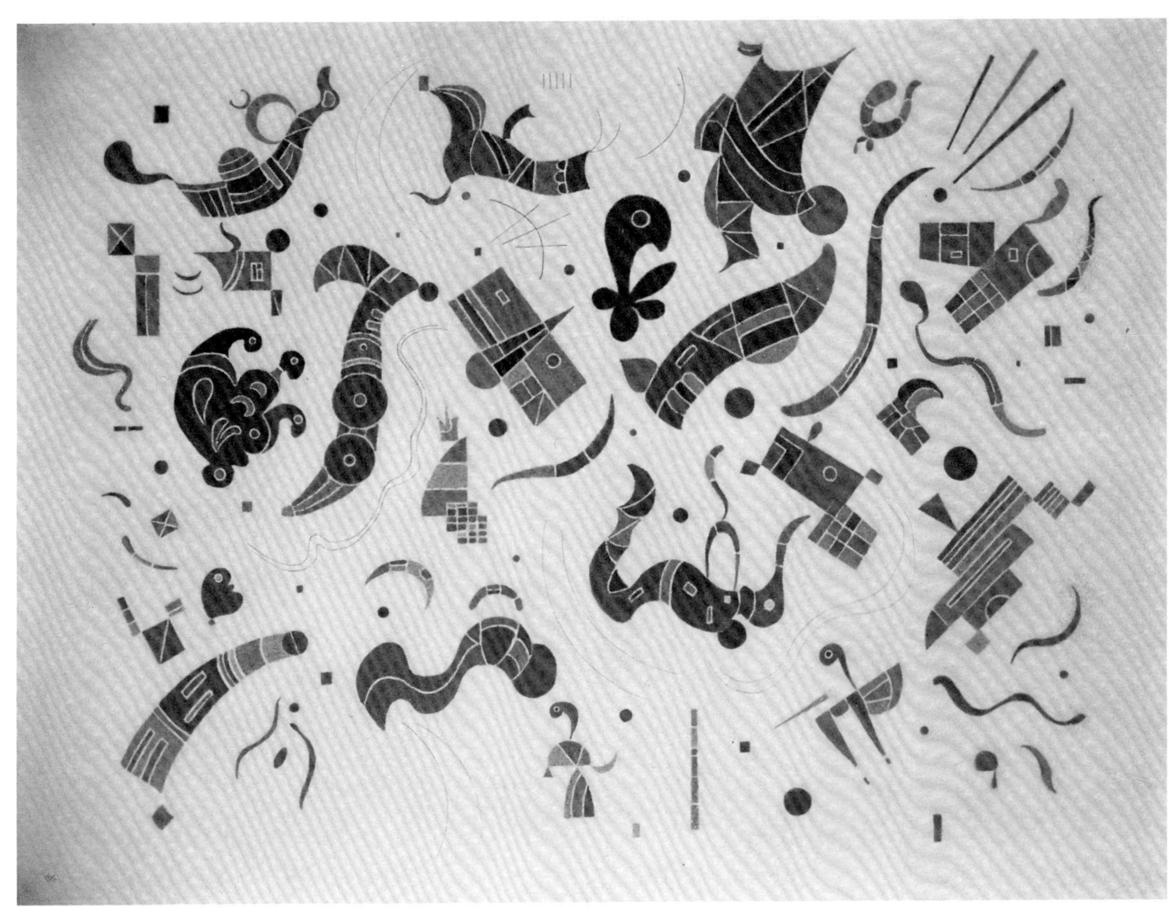

Vasily Kandinsky

29 *Striped (Rayé).* November 1934
(HL 609)
Oil with sand on canvas, 31⅞ x 39⅜″
(81 x 100 cm.)
Collection Solomon R. Guggenheim Museum, New York

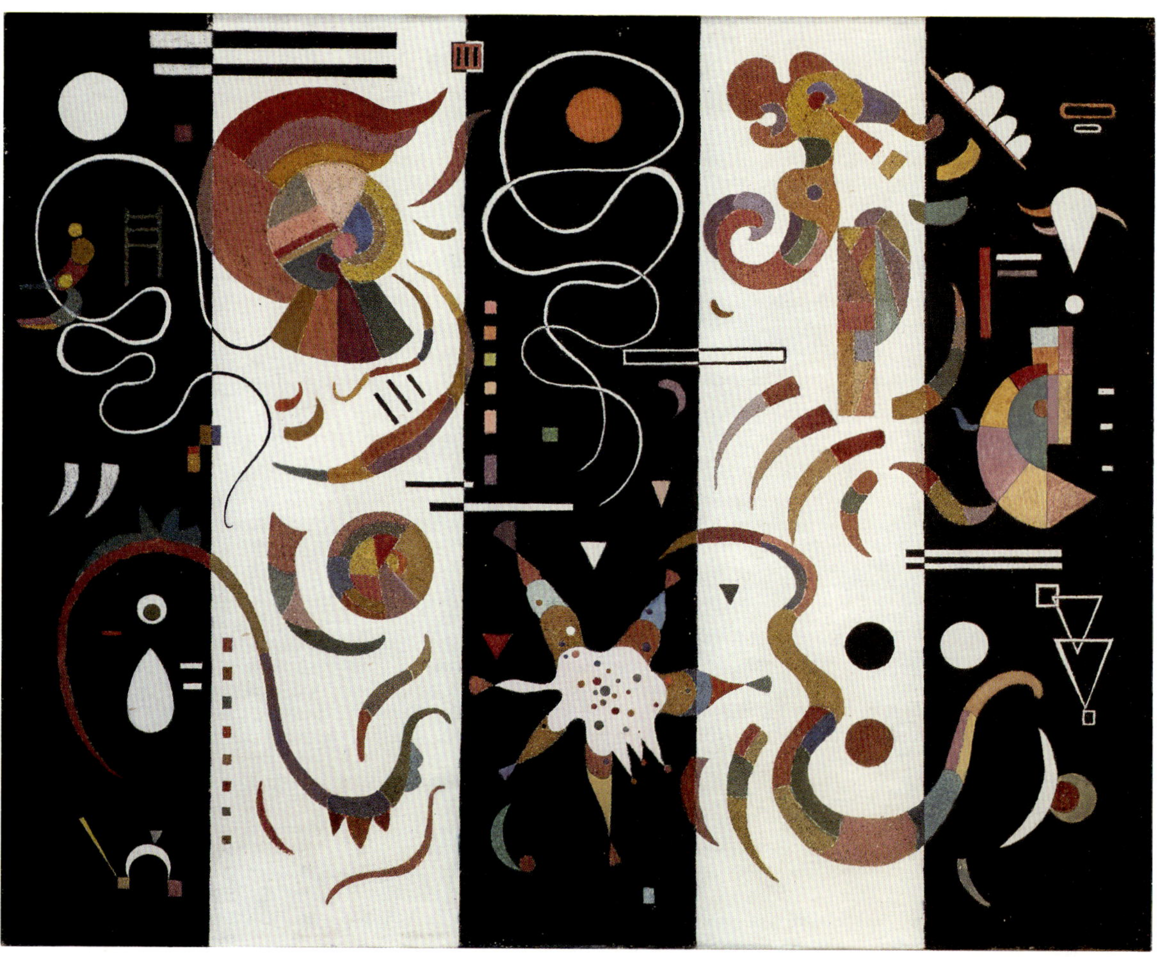

Willi Baumeister

30 *Standing Figure with Red Field (Stehende Figur mit rotem Feld).* 1933

Oil with sand on canvas, 31⅞ x 26$\frac{9}{16}$" (81 x 65 cm.)

Collection Archiv Baumeister, Stuttgart

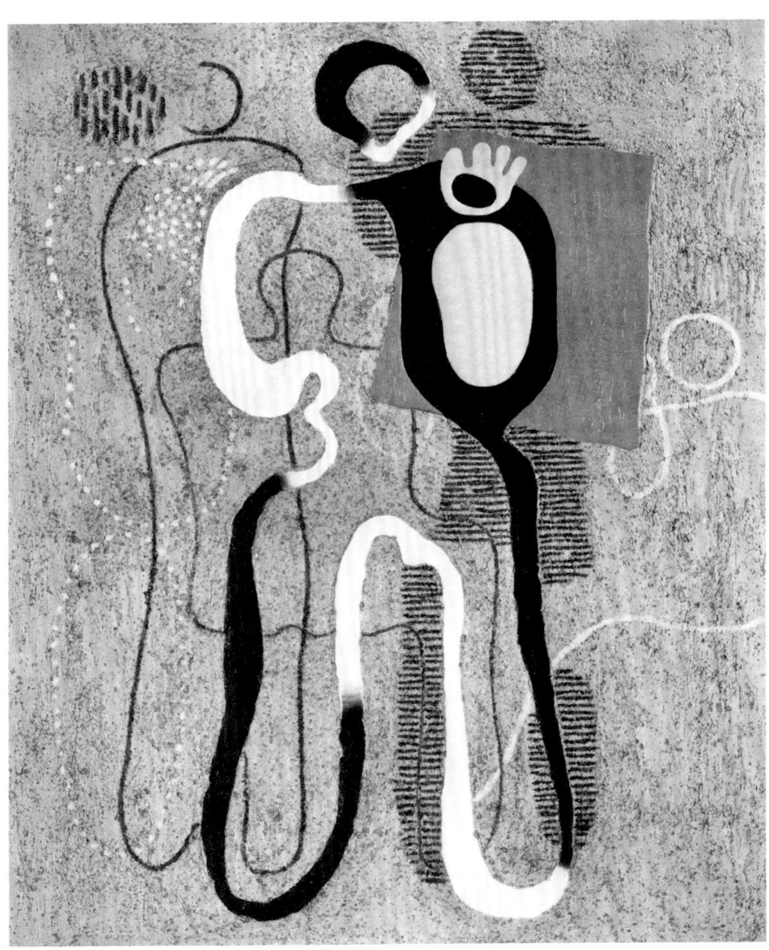

Vasily Kandinsky

31 *Etching for René Char's "Le Marteau sans maître."* 1934

Drypoint on paper, $5\frac{1}{2}$ x $3\frac{15}{16}$" (13.9 x 9.9 cm.)

Collection Musée National d'Art Moderne, Centre Georges Pompidou, Paris, Kandinsky Bequest

René Char

32 *Le Marteau sans maître.* Paris, Editions Surréalistes, 1934

Inscribed by the author to Kandinsky

Book, $7\frac{1}{2}$ x $5\frac{1}{2}$" (18.9 x 13.9 cm.)

Collection Musée National d'Art Moderne, Centre Georges Pompidou, Paris, Kandinsky Bequest

†33 *Letter from René Char to Kandinsky.* November 26, 1933

Ink on paper, $10\frac{5}{8}$ x $8\frac{1}{4}$" (27 x 21 cm.)

Collection Musée National d'Art Moderne, Centre Georges Pompidou, Paris, Kandinsky Bequest

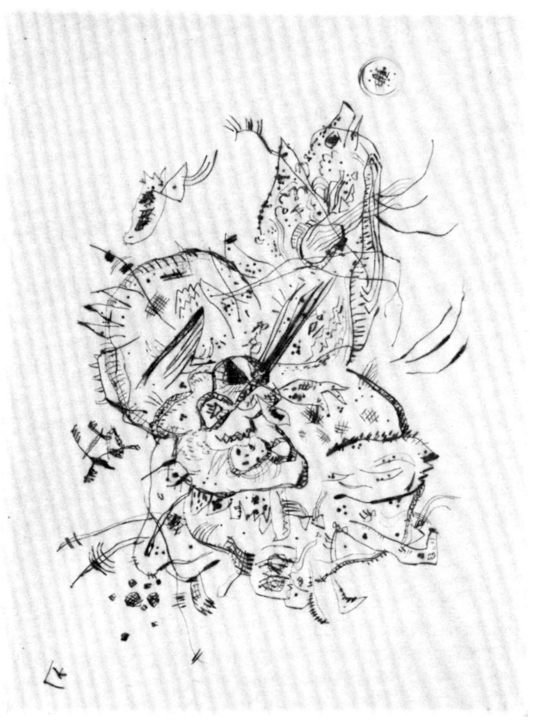

à Kandinsky
Peintre du merveilleux
Incandescent
de tout coeur
son reconnaissant
René Char

LE MARTEAU SANS MAITRE

34 *Letter from René Char to Kandinsky.* December 12, 1933
Ink on paper, $9\frac{7}{8} \times 8\frac{1}{16}''$ (25 x 20.5 cm.)
Collection Musée National d'Art Moderne, Centre Georges Pompidou, Paris, Kandinsky Bequest

René Char

35 *Migration.* n.d.
Poem, ink on paper, $9\frac{3}{4} \times 8''$ (24.8 x 20.3 cm.)
Collection Musée National d'Art Moderne, Centre Georges Pompidou, Paris, Kandinsky Bequest

RENÉ CHAR
9, RUE VICTOR-CONSIDÉRANT
PARIS-XIVe

12 Déc. 33

Cher Monsieur.

Arrivé à l'instant votre petite merveille. Je ne veux pas attendre davantage pour vous remercier de votre hâte, de votre gentillesse, de votre adaptation exemplaire.

Le livre "Le marteau sans maître" est en chantier. Je vous enverrai les premiers états, à moins que vous ne soyez à cette date parmi nous, ce que je souhaite bien vivement.

Bref, de toutes façons à bientôt et encore merci n'est-ce pas.

Bien cordialement à vous

René Char

Fonds KANDINSKY

MIGRATION

Le poids du raisin modifie la position des feuilles. La montagne avait un peu glissé sans dégager d'époque. Toutefois à travers les ossuaires argileux, la foulée des bêtes excrémentielles en marche vers le convulsif ambre jaune. En relation avec l'inertie.

La sécurité est un parfum. L'homme morne et emblématique vit toujours en prison, mais sa prison se trouve à présent en liberté. Le mouvement et le sentiment ont réintégré la fronde mathématicienne. La fabuleuse simulatrice, celle qui s'ensevelit en marchant, qui remporta dans la nuit tragique de la préhistoire les quatre doigts tabous de la main fantôme, a rejoint ses quartiers d'étude, à la zone des clairvoyances. Dans le salon manqué, sur les grands carreaux hostiles, le dormeur et l'aimée, trop impopulaires pour ne pas être réels, accouplent interminablement leurs bouches ruisselantes de salive.

René Char

Fonds KANDINSKY

Vasily Kandinsky

36 *Etching for Tristan Tzara's "La Main passe."* 1935

Drypoint on paper, 6 3/16 x 4 3/4"
(15.7 x 12 cm.)

Collection Musée National d'Art Moderne, Centre Georges Pompidou, Paris, Kandinsky Bequest

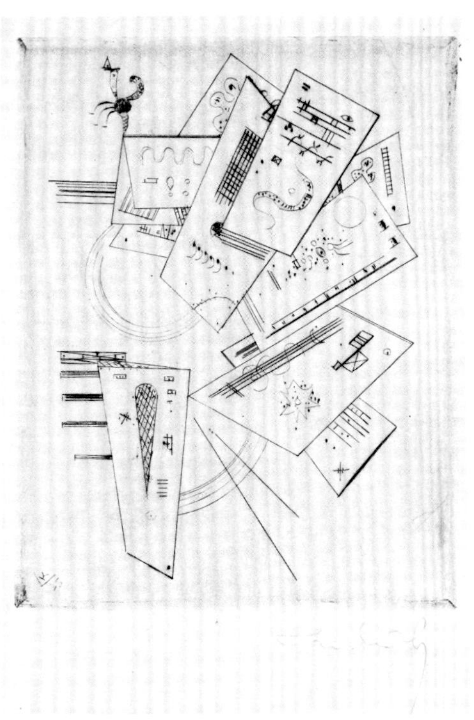

Vasily Kandinsky

37 *Study for a Woodcut (Etude pour une gravure sur bois).* ca. 1935

Pencil on paper, 8¼ x 10$\frac{5}{16}$″ (20.9 x 26.9 cm.)

Collection Musée National d'Art Moderne, Centre Georges Pompidou, Paris, Kandinsky Bequest

Vasily Kandinsky

38 *Woodblock for a Print (Bois pour une gravure).* ca. 1935

Carved wood, 9⅛ x 10$\frac{11}{16}$″ (23.1 x 27.1 cm.)

Collection Musée National d'Art Moderne, Centre Georges Pompidou, Paris, Kandinsky Bequest

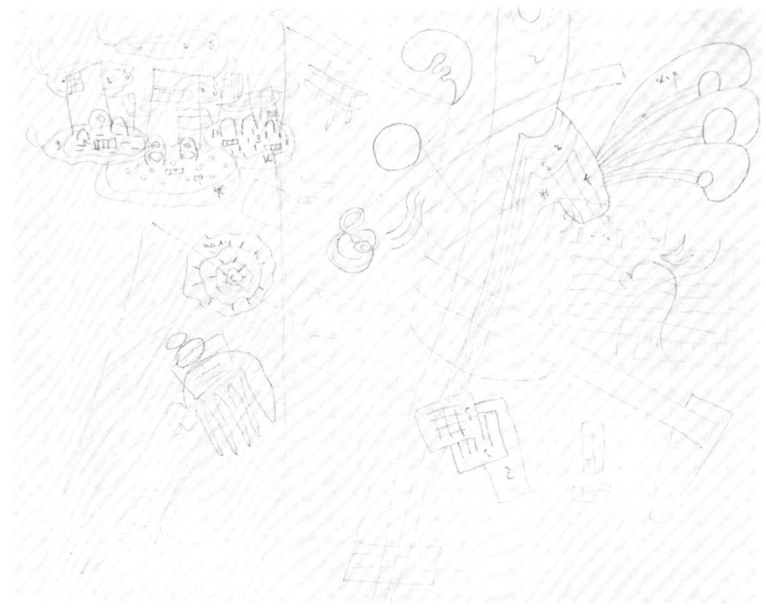

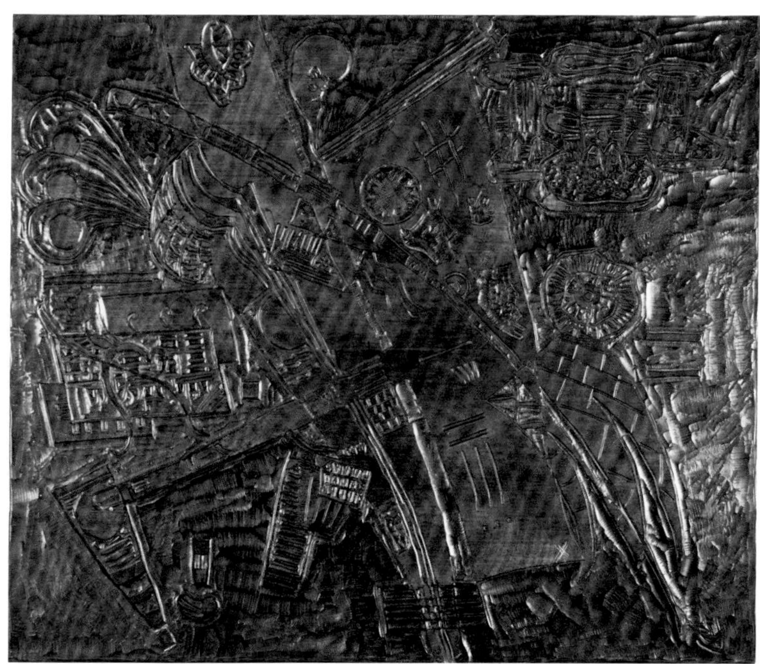

Vasily Kandinsky

39 *Synthesis (Sintesi).* 1935
Silkscreen on paper, 19¾ x 25⅜″
(50 x 65.4 cm.)
Collection Musée National d'Art Moderne, Centre Georges Pompidou, Paris, Kandinsky Bequest

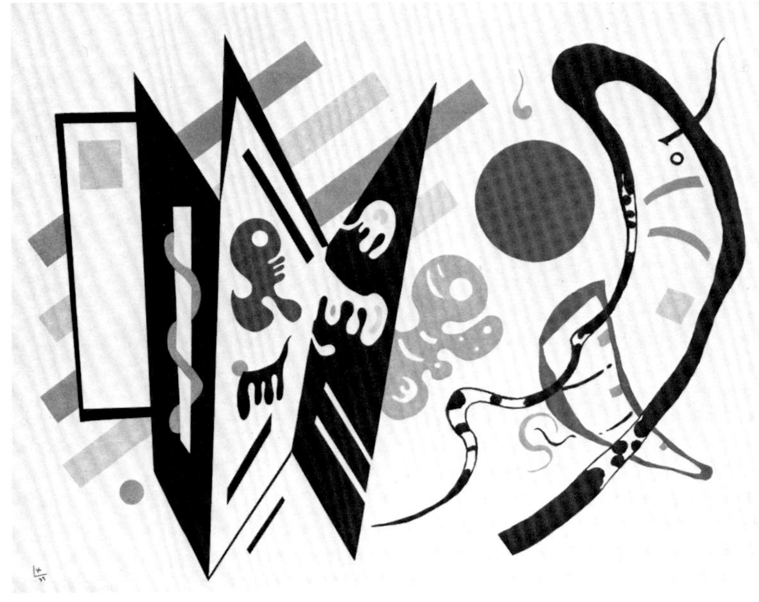

Vasily Kandinsky

40 *Woodcut for "XXe Siècle" (Gravure sur bois pour "XXe Siècle").* 1939
Color woodcut on paper, 9⅝ x 12½″
(24.5 x 31.9 cm.)
Collection Solomon R. Guggenheim Museum, New York

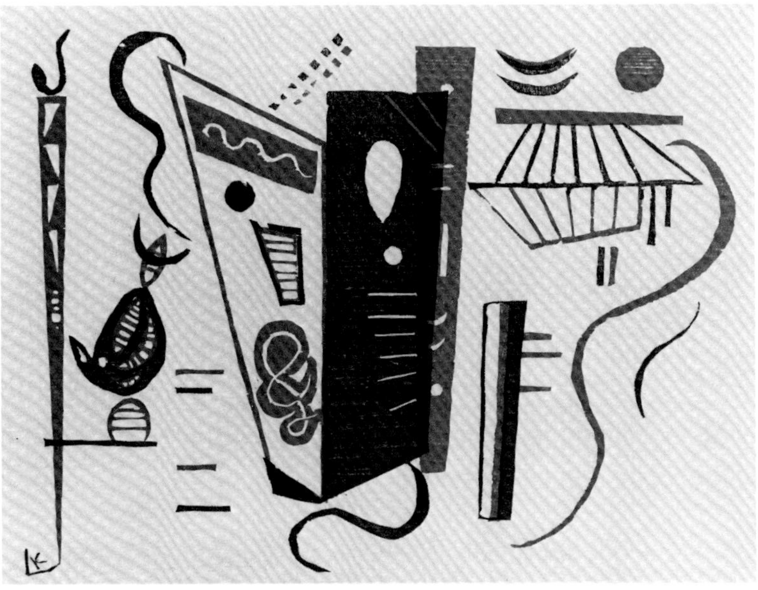

41 *Transition.* No. 27, April–May 1938
Cover design by Vasily Kandinsky
Screenprint on paper, 7⅞ x 5¼″
(20 x 13.3 cm.)
Collection Musée National d'Art Moderne, Centre Georges Pompidou, Paris, Kandinsky Bequest

Vasily Kandinsky

42 *Etching for Stephen Spender's "Fraternity" (Gravure pour "Fraternity" de Stephen Spender).* 1939
Drypoint on paper, 5 x 3³⁄₁₆″
(12.8 x 8.1 cm.)
Collection Musée National d'Art Moderne, Centre Georges Pompidou, Paris, Kandinsky Bequest

Stephen Spender

†43 *Fraternity.* Paris, Atelier 17, 1939
Book, 8¹³⁄₁₆ x 6½″ (22.4 x 16.5 cm.)
Collection Musée National d'Art Moderne, Centre Georges Pompidou, Paris, Kandinsky Bequest

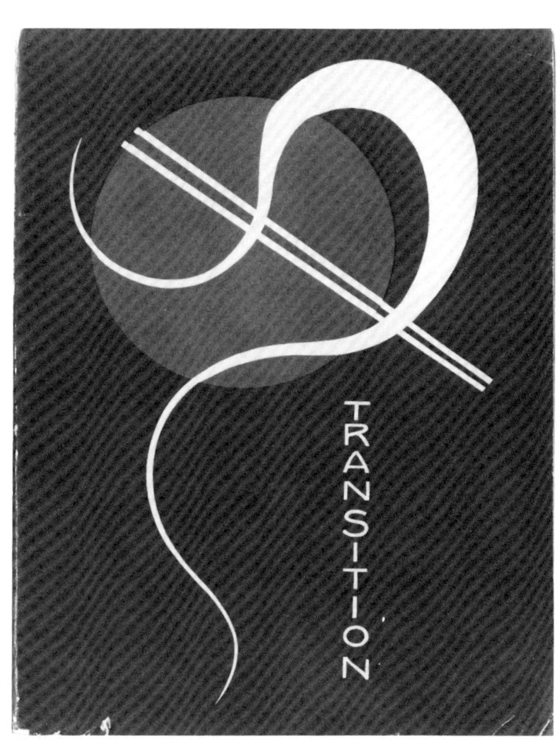

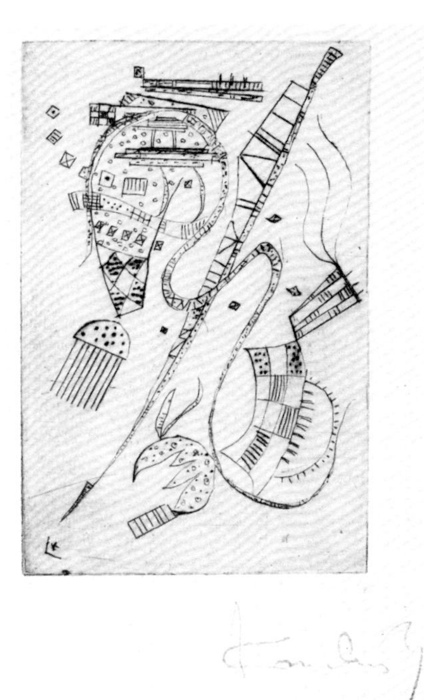

Hans Arp

44 *Configuration.* 1930
Carved and painted wood, 27½ x 33½″ (69.9 x 85.1 cm.)
Philadelphia Museum of Art, The A.E. Gallatin Collection

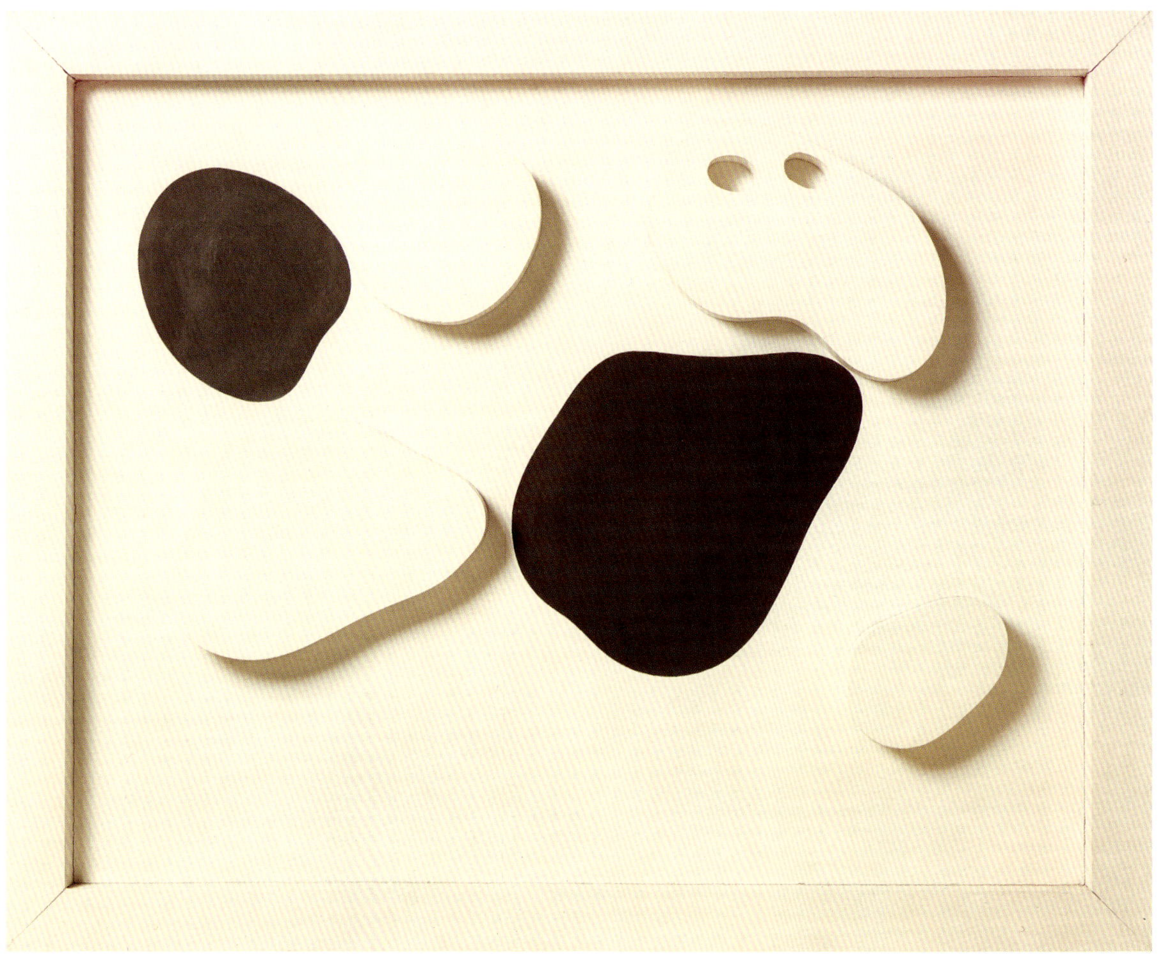

Vasily Kandinsky

45 *Black Forms on White (Formes noires sur blanc).* April 1934

(HL 600)

Oil on canvas, 27½ x 27½" (70 x 70 cm.)

Collection Association-Fondation Christian et Yvonne Zervos, Vézelay

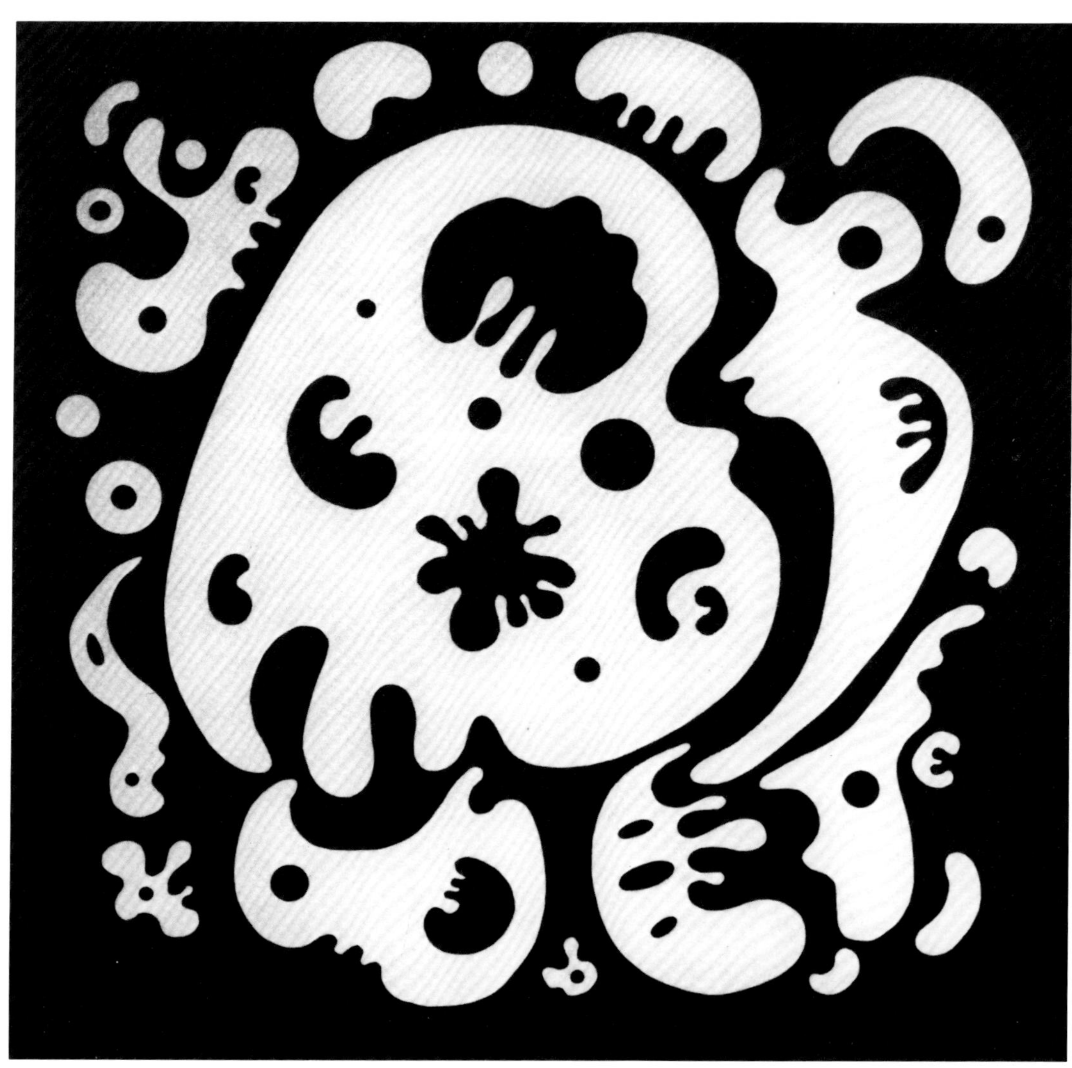

Ben Nicholson

46 *1936 (white relief).* 1936
Oil on carved board, $26\frac{1}{2}$ x $36\frac{1}{2}$"
(67.5 x 93 cm.)
Collection Lillian H. Florsheim
Foundation for Fine Arts

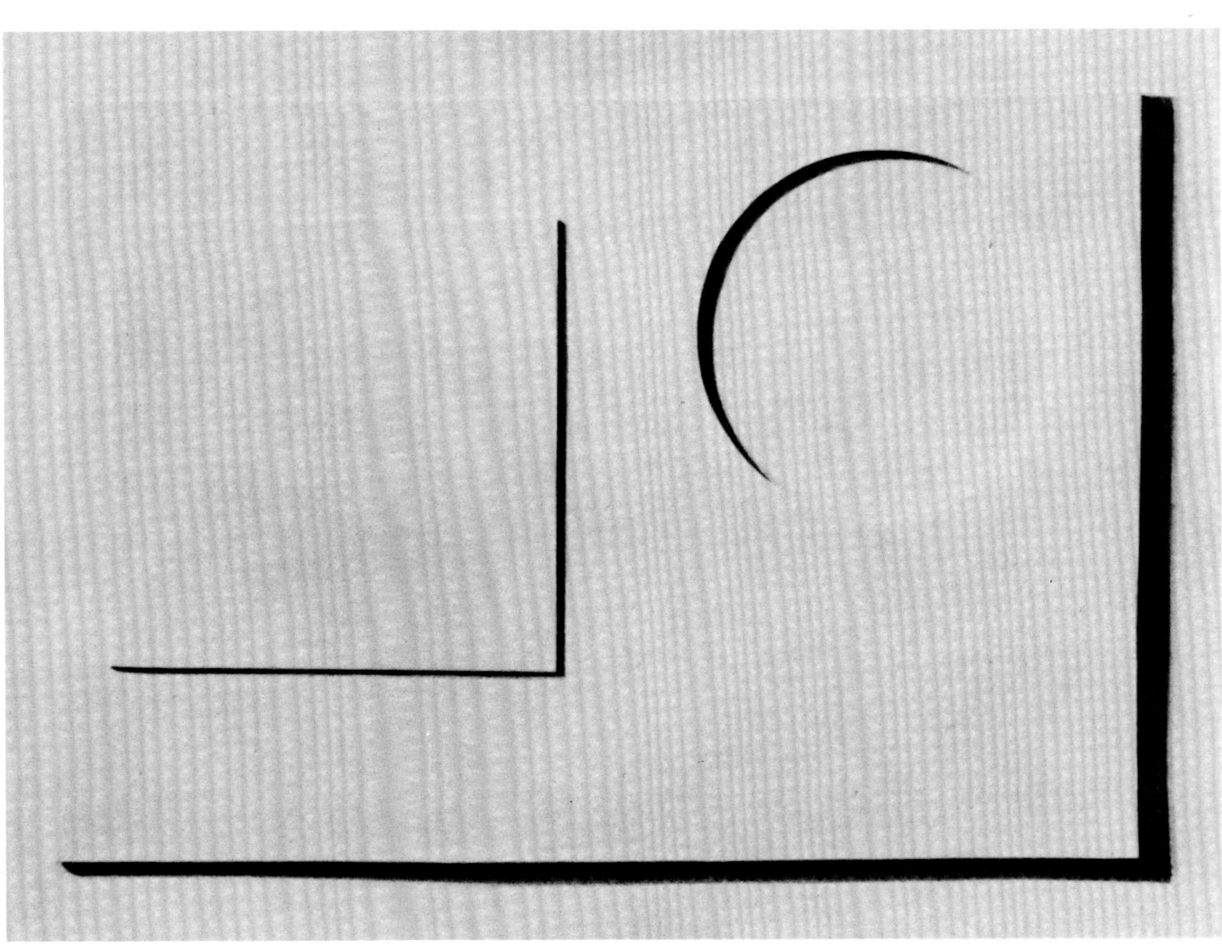

Vasily Kandinsky

47 *Division–Unity (Division–Unité).*
October 1934
(HL 606)
Oil with sand on canvas, 28⅛ x 28⅛″
(71.5 x 71.5 cm.)
Collection The Museum of Modern
Art, Seibu Takanawa

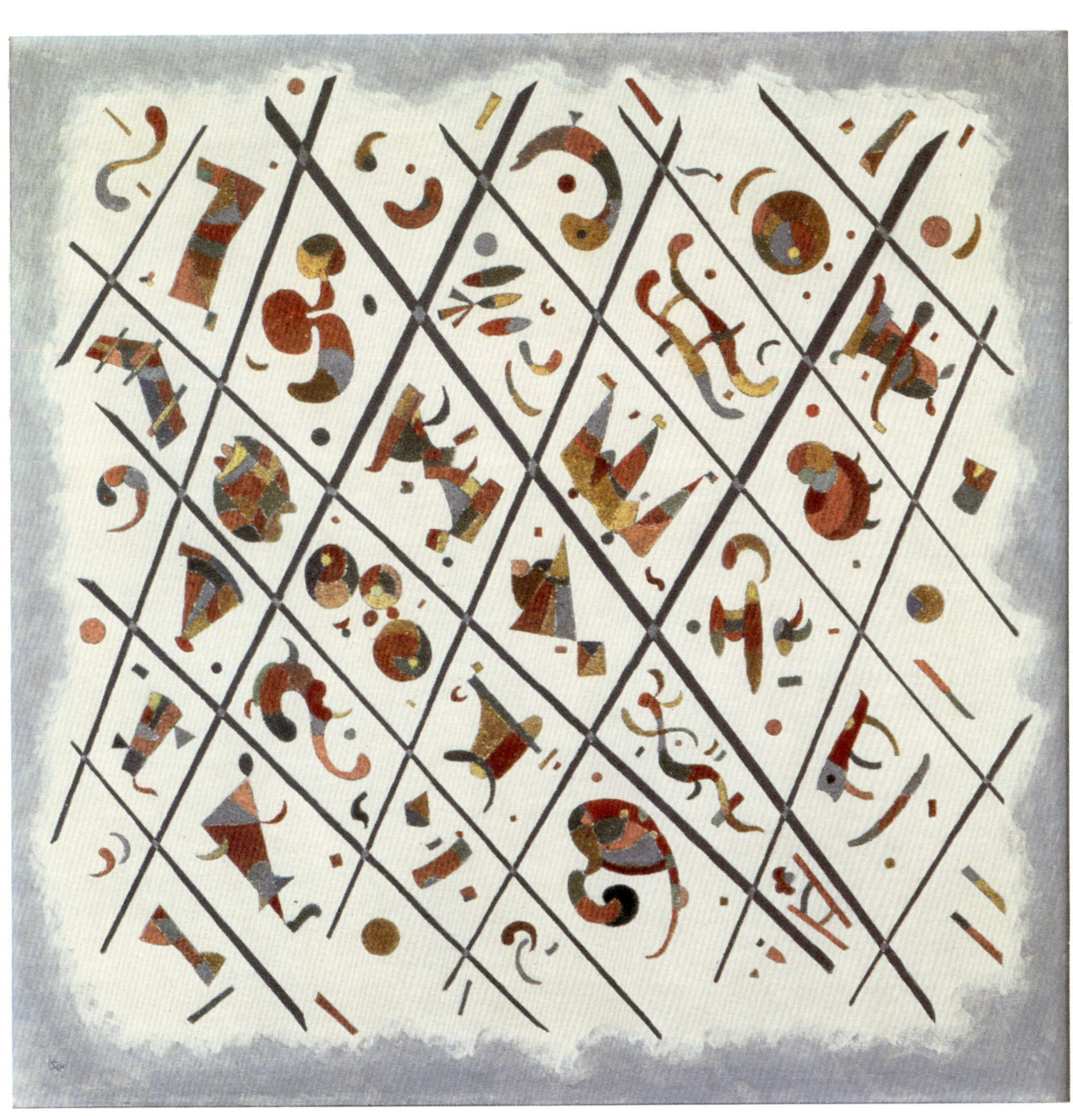

Vasily Kandinsky

48 *Accompanied Contrast (Contraste accompagné).* March 1935

(HL 613)

Oil with sand on canvas, 38¼ x 63⅞″ (97.1 x 162.1 cm.)

Collection Solomon R. Guggenheim Museum, New York, Gift, Solomon R. Guggenheim, 1937

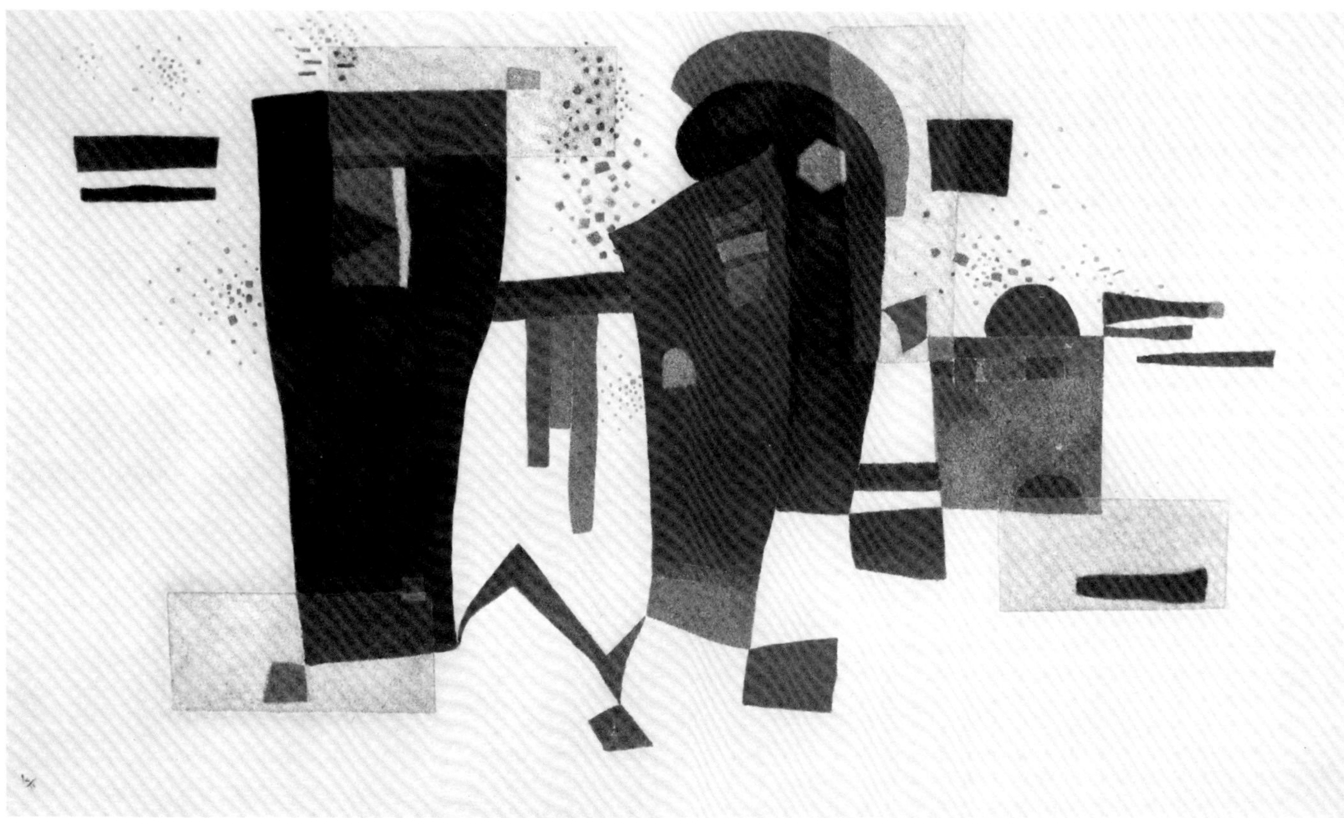

Hans Arp

49 *Objects Placed According to the Laws of Chance (Objets placés d'après les lois du hasard).* 1933

Carved and painted wood, $22\frac{1}{8} \times 27\frac{1}{2}$" (55 x 70 cm.)

Private Collection, Paris

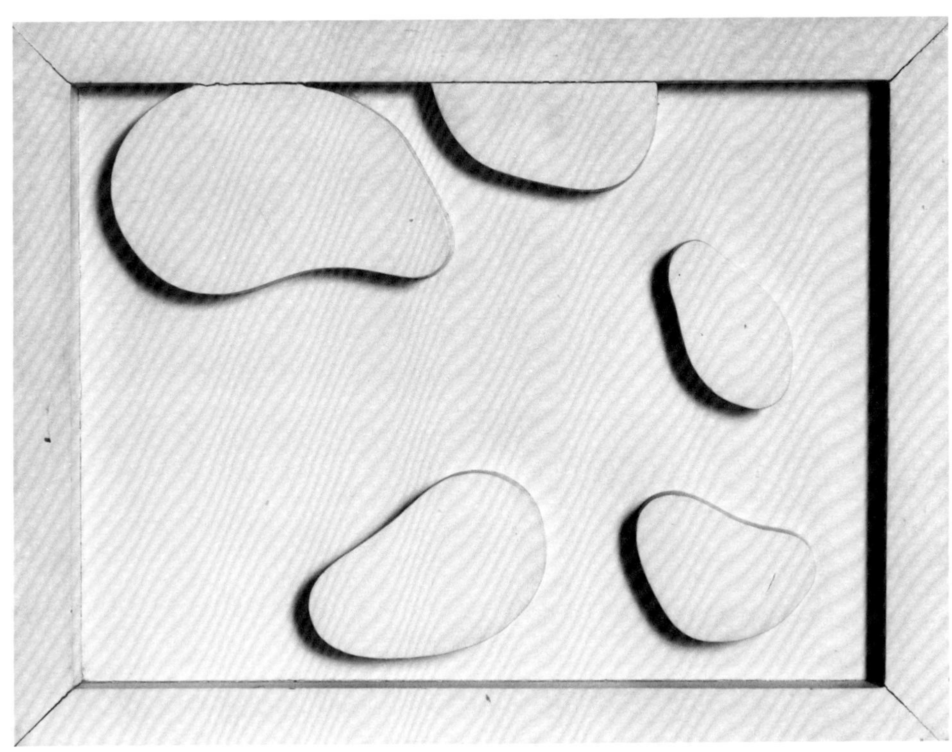

Piet Mondrian

50 *Composition with Blue (Composition avec bleu).* 1937

Oil on canvas, 31½ x 30⅜" (80 x 77 cm.)

Collection Haags Gemeentemuseum, The Hague, The Netherlands

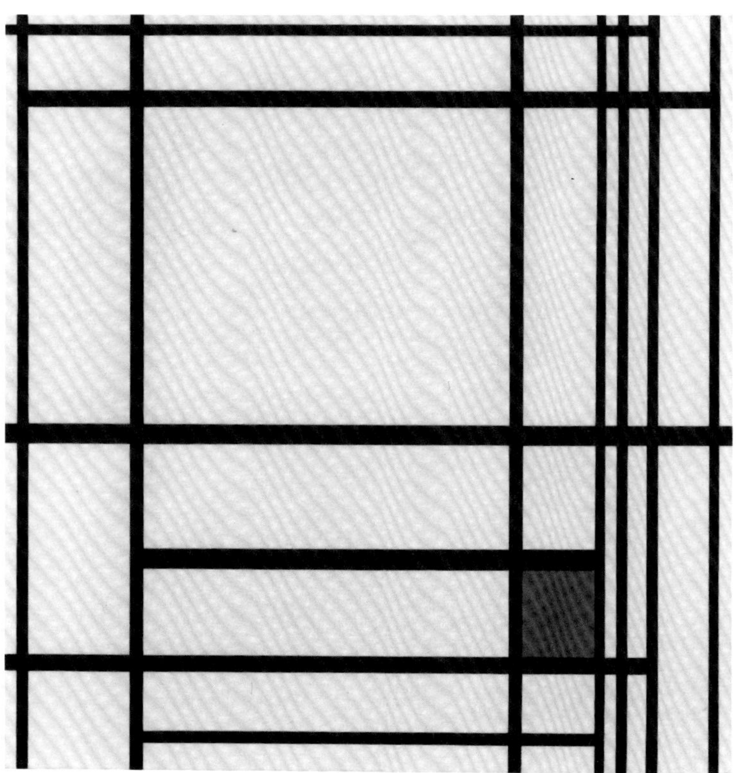

Vasily Kandinsky

51 *Green Accent (Accent vert).*
November 1935

(HL 623)

Tempera and oil on canvas, 32 x 39 3/8″ (81.1 x 100.2 cm.)

Collection Solomon R. Guggenheim Museum, New York, Gift, Solomon R. Guggenheim, 1937

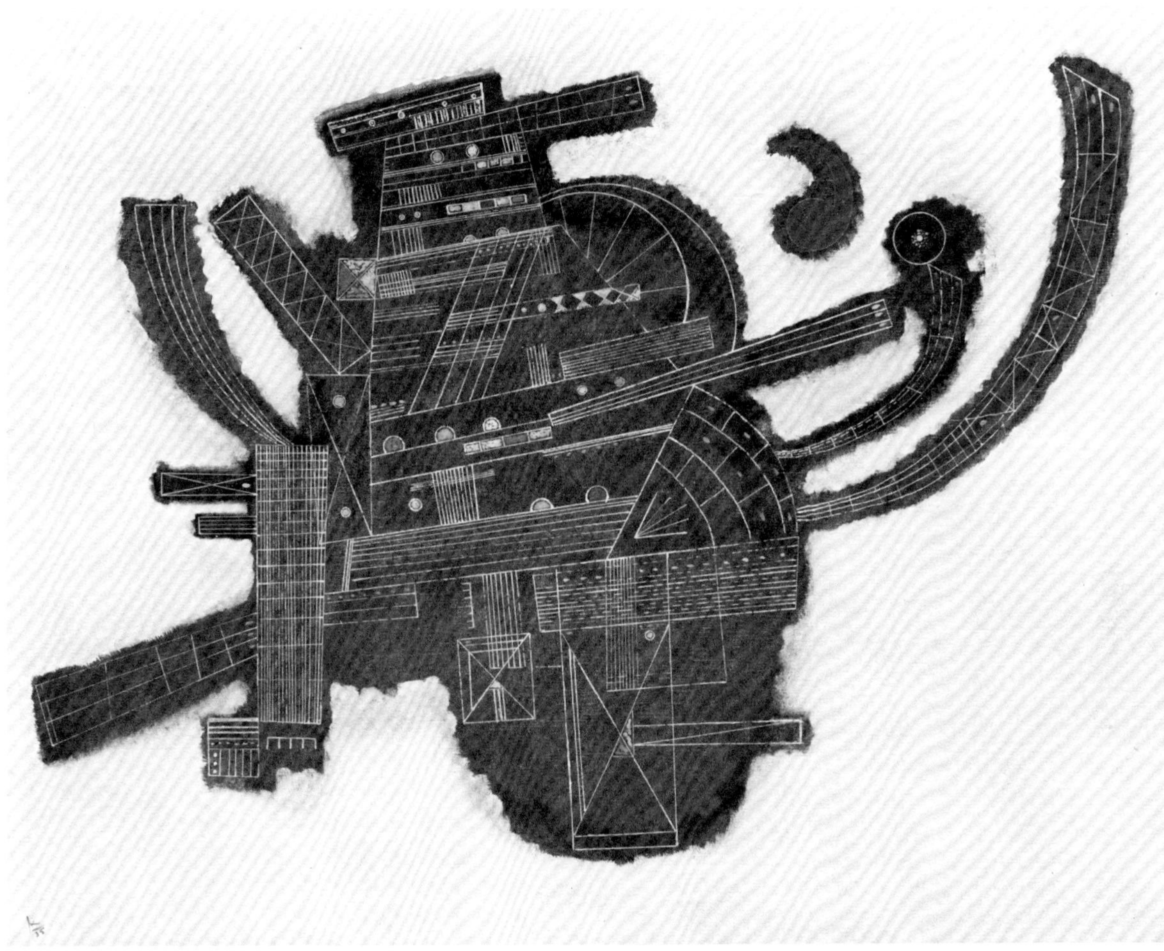

Josef Albers

52 *Heraldic.* 1935
Oil on aluminum, 16¾ x 16″
(42.5 x 40.7 cm.)
Collection Anni Albers and the
Josef Albers Foundation

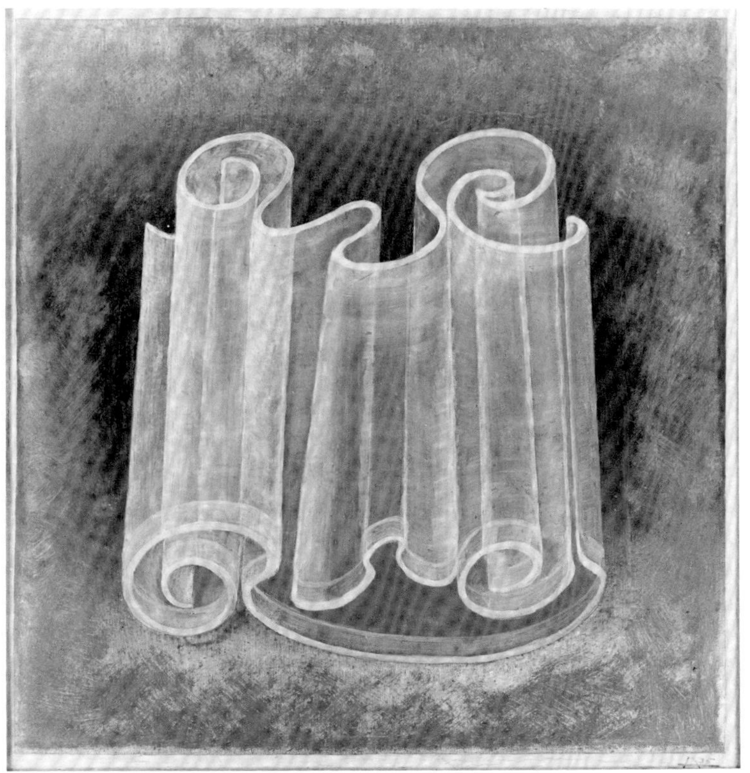

Vasily Kandinsky

53 *Brown with Supplement (Brun supplémenté).* March 1935

(HL 615)

Oil on canvas, 31⅞ x 39⅜" (81 x 100 cm.)

Collection Museum Boymans-van Beuningen, Rotterdam

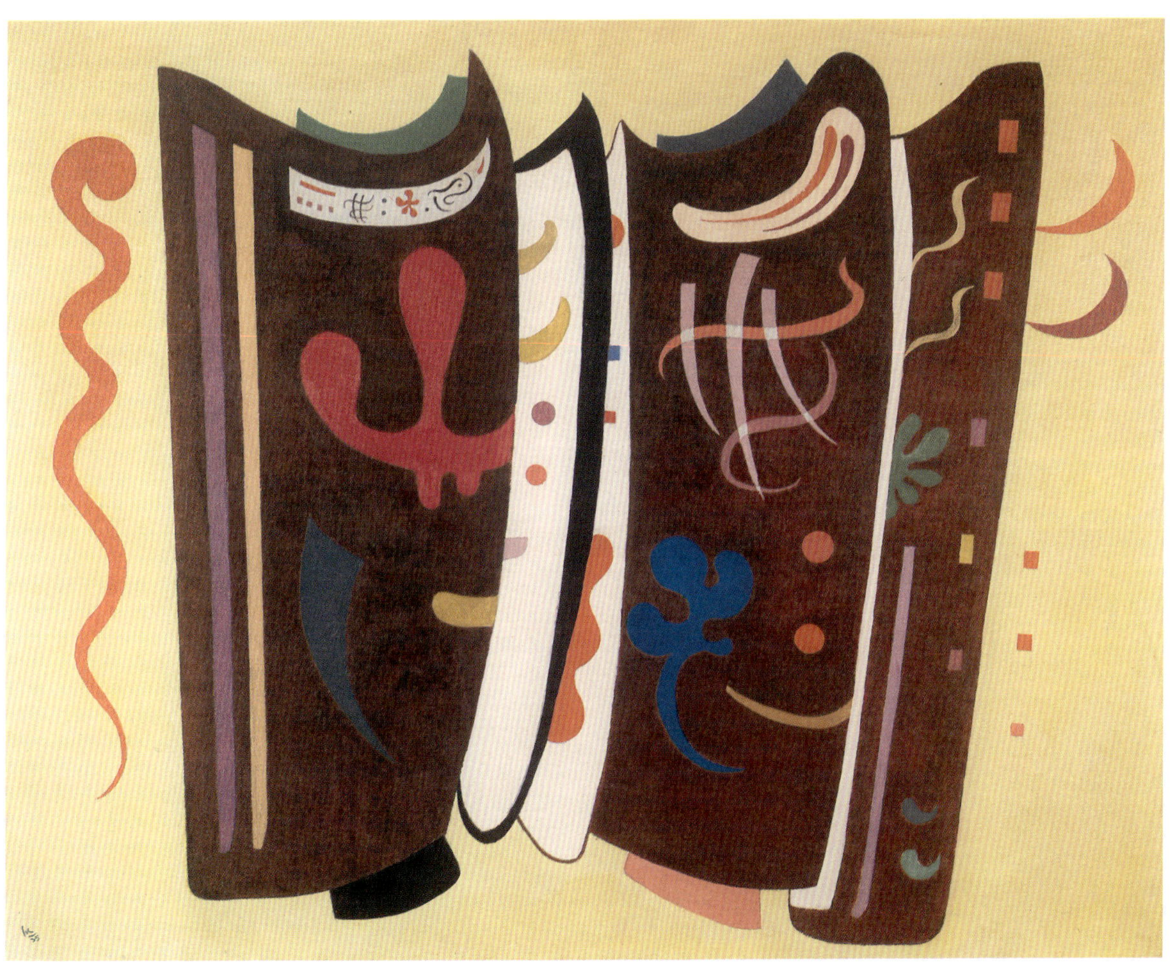

Vasily Kandinsky

54 *Two Green Points (Deux Points verts).*
April 1935
(HL 616)
Oil with sand on canvas,
44⅞ x 63 13/16" (114 x 162 cm.)
Collection Musée National d'Art Moderne,
Centre Georges Pompidou, Paris,
Gift of Mme Nina Kandinsky

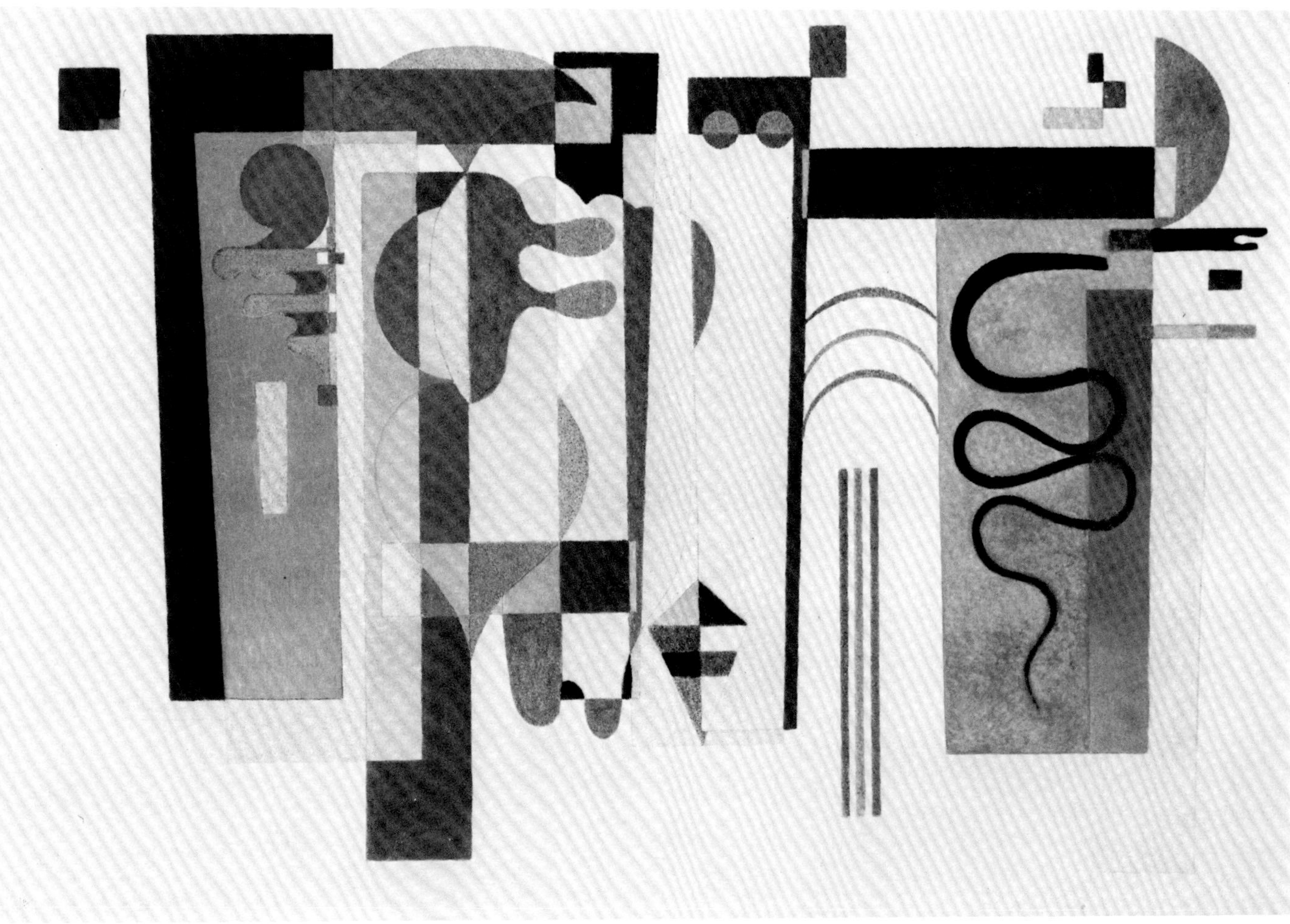

Vasily Kandinsky

55 *Reunited Surfaces (Study for Painting No. 616) (Surfaces réunies [Projet pour toile no. 616]).* August 1934

(HL watercolors 535)

Watercolor on paper, 11 1/16 x 16 1/2" (28.2 x 42 cm.)

Collection Musée National d'Art Moderne, Centre Georges Pompidou, Paris, Gift of Mme Nina Kandinsky

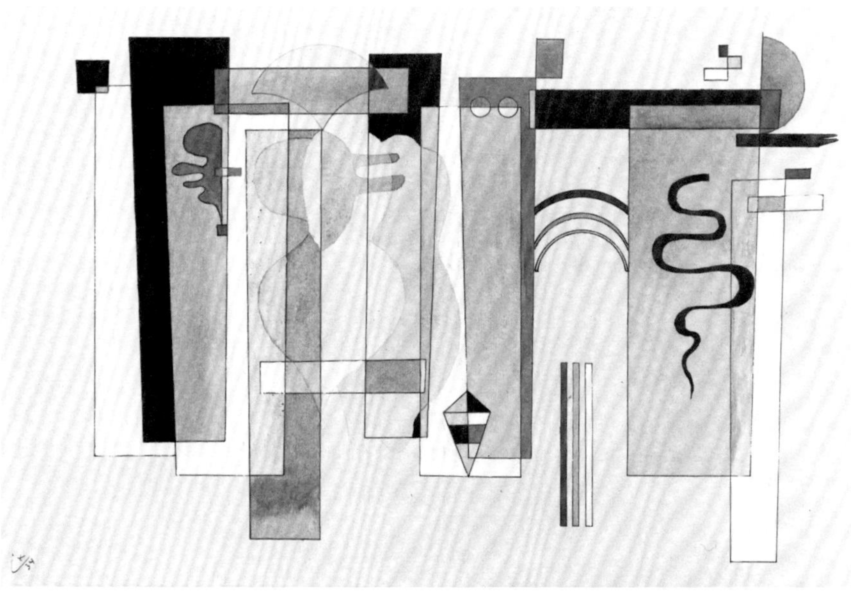

Vasily Kandinsky

56 *Line (Ligne).* November 1934
(HL watercolors 537)
Watercolor and India ink on paper mounted on paper, 21 x 8″ (52.7 x 20.3 cm.)
Collection Musée National d'Art Moderne, Centre Georges Pompidou, Paris, Kandinsky Bequest

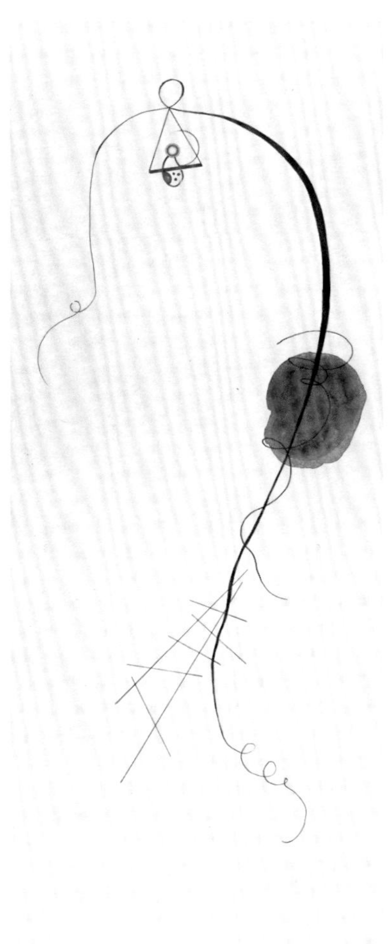

Vasily Kandinsky
57 *Succession.* April 1935
(HL 617)
Oil on canvas, 32 x 39½″ (81 x 100 cm.)
The Phillips Collection, Washington, D.C.

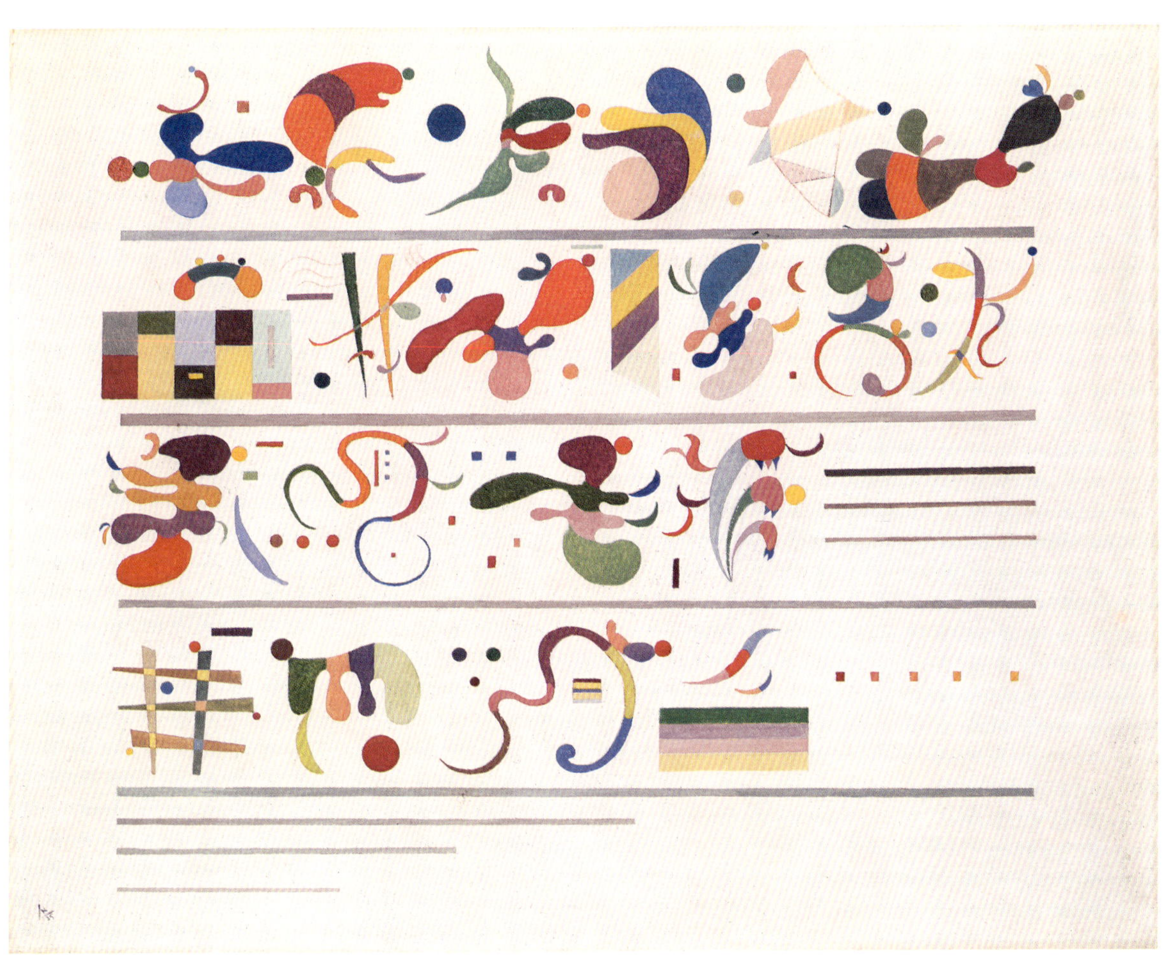

Vasily Kandinsky

58 *Floating (Volant).* June 1936
(HL watercolors 566)
Gouache and pencil on black paper,
12¼ x 19¾" (31 x 50.2 cm.)
Collection Solomon R. Guggenheim
Museum, New York

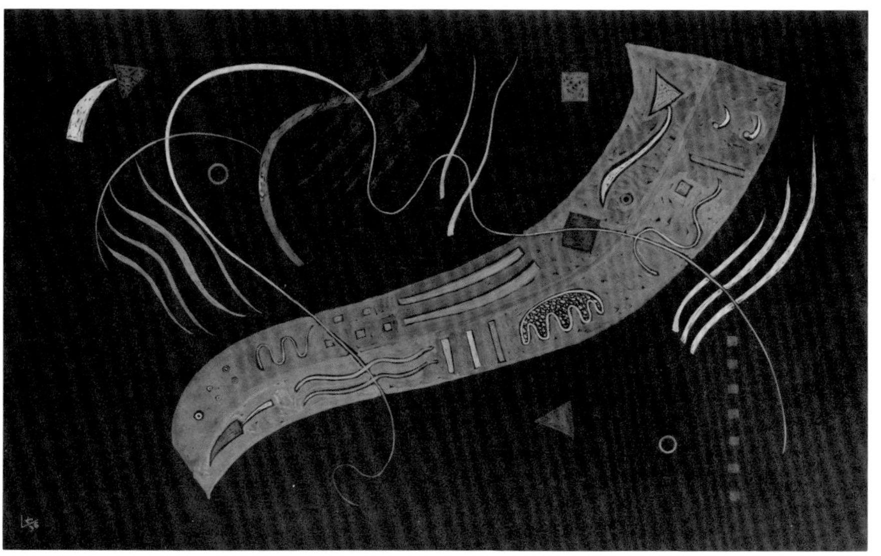

Joan Miró

59 *Drawing Enclosed with a Letter from Miró to Kandinsky.* n.d.

Pencil on paper, 10 11/16 x 8 5/16" (27.1 x 21 cm.)

Collection Musée National d'Art Moderne, Centre Georges Pompidou, Paris, Kandinsky Bequest

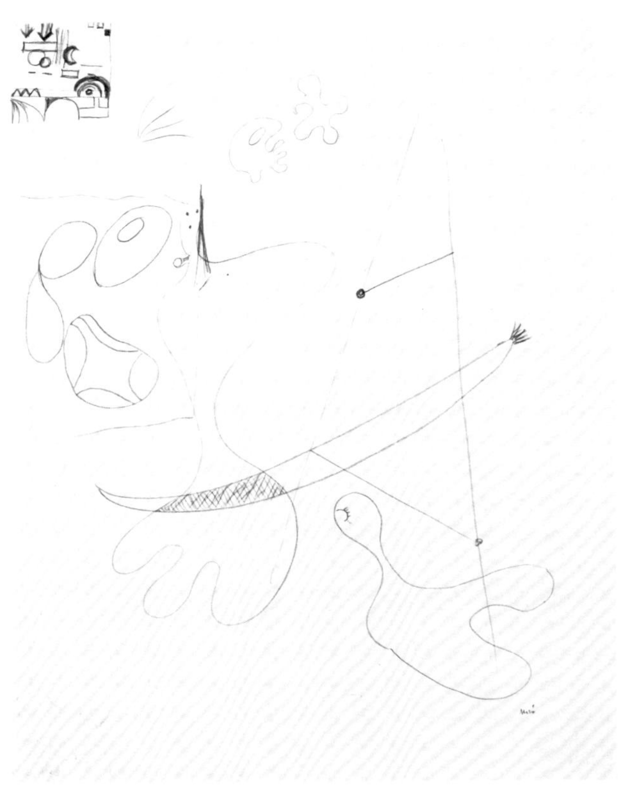

Vasily Kandinsky

60 *Multiple Forms (Formes multiples).* February 1936
(HL 627)
Oil on canvas, 38 3/16 x 51 3/8"
(97 x 130.5 cm.)
Lent by Galerie Rosengart, Lucerne

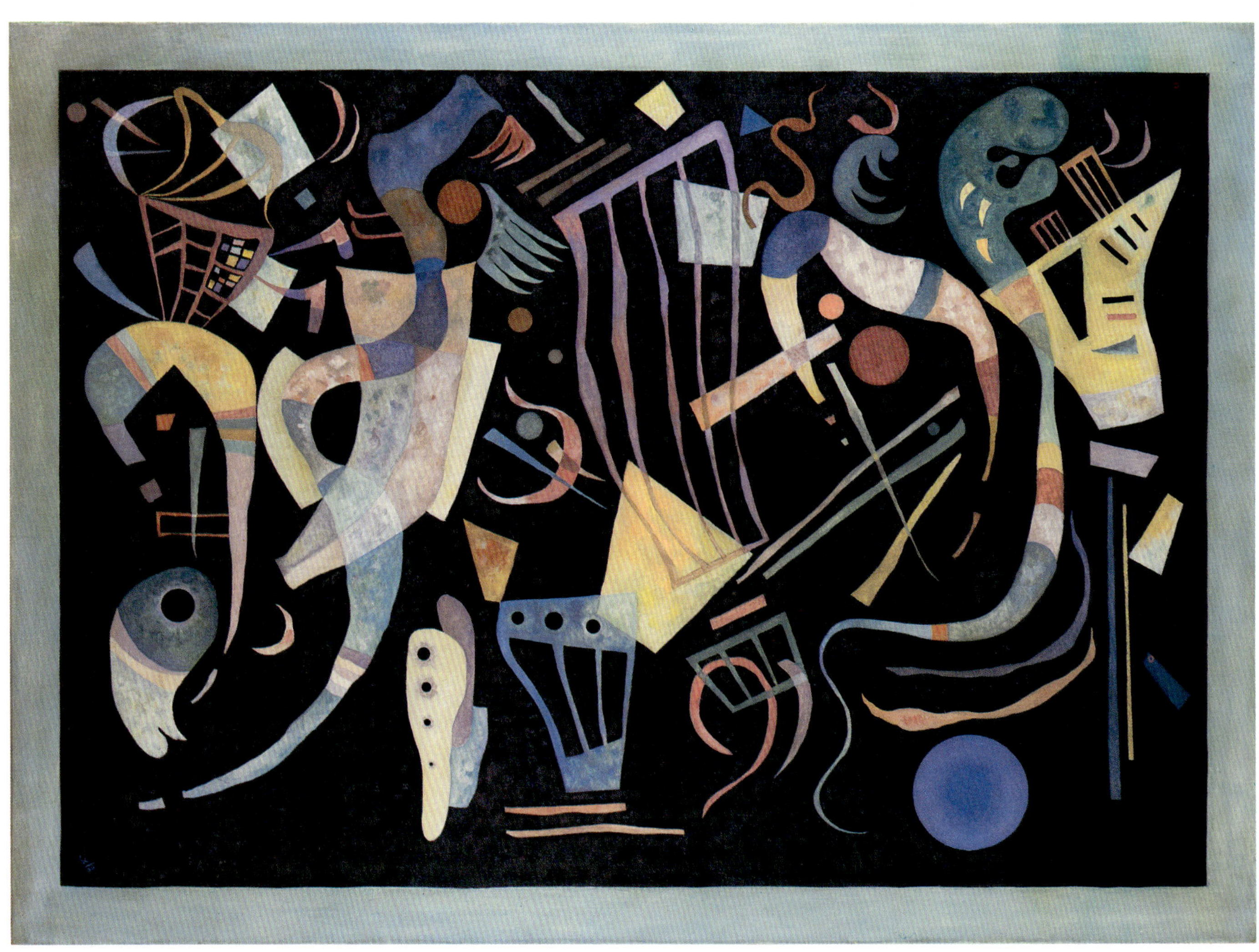

Joan Miró

61 *The Ladder for Escape (L'Echelle de l'évasion).* 1940

Gouache, watercolor, brush and ink on paper, 15¾ x 18¾" (40 x 47.6 cm.)

Collection The Museum of Modern Art, New York, Bequest of Helen Acheson

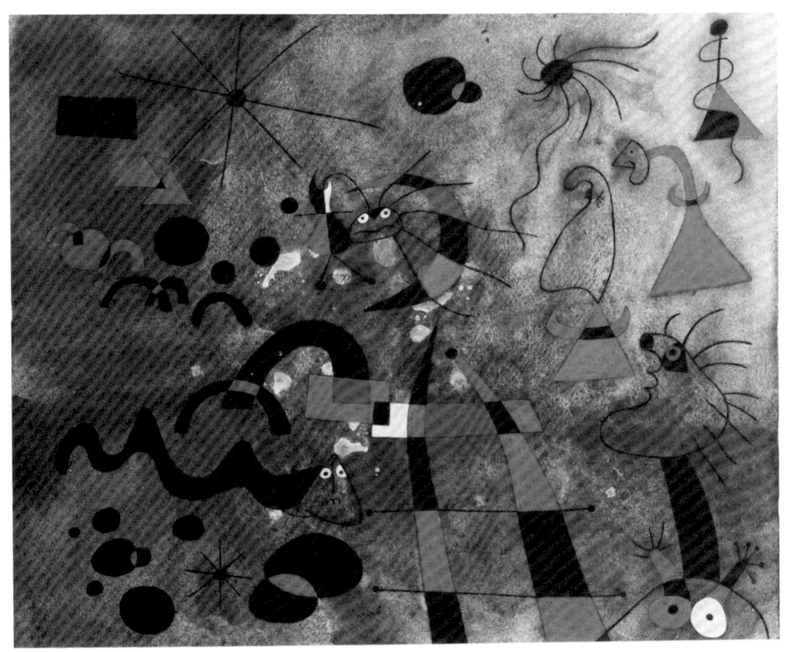

Vasily Kandinsky

62 *Green Figure (Figure verte).* March 1936
(HL 628)
Oil on canvas, 46¼ x 35⅛"
(117.5 x 89.3 cm.)
Collection Musée National d'Art Moderne, Centre Georges Pompidou, Paris, Kandinsky Bequest

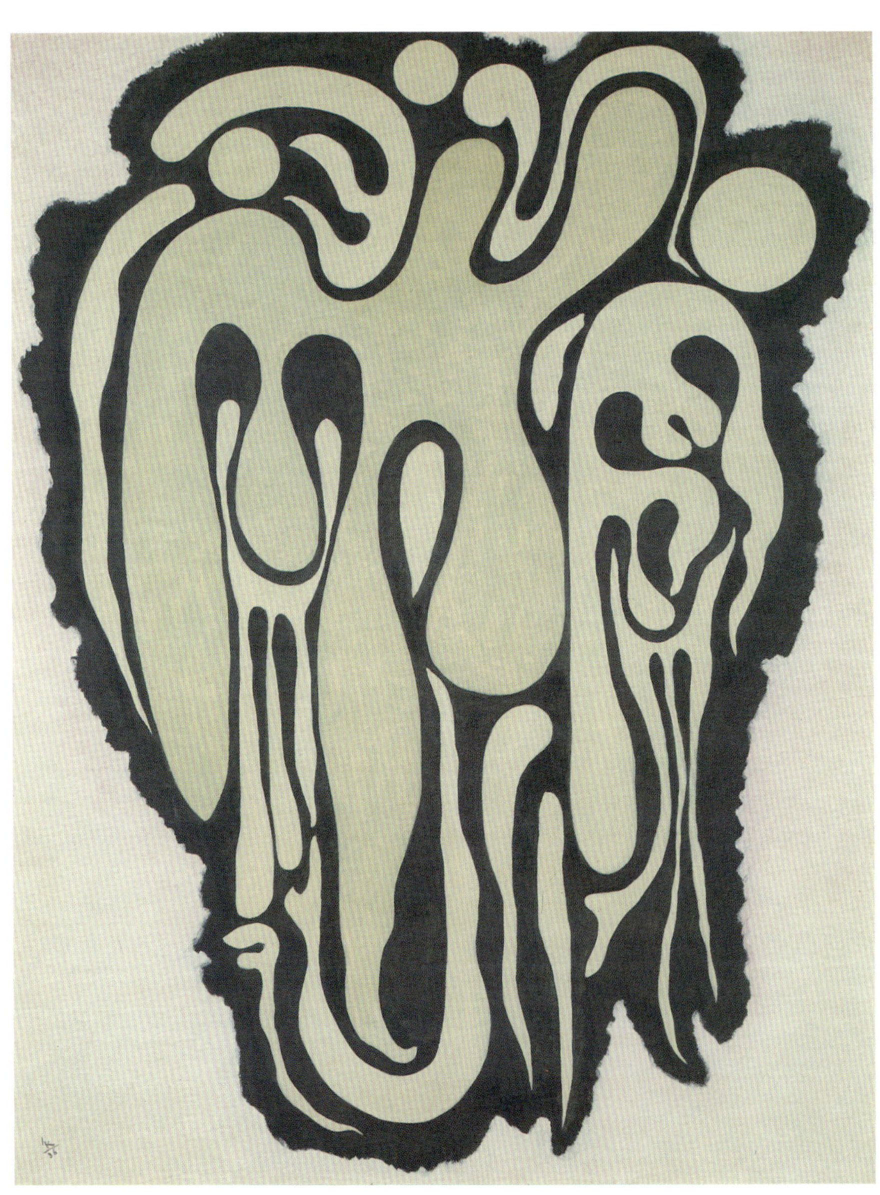

Pablo Picasso

63 *Acrobat Woman (Femme acrobate).*
January 19, 1930
Oil on plywood, 25 3/16 x 19 5/16"
(64 x 49 cm.)
Collection Marina Picasso

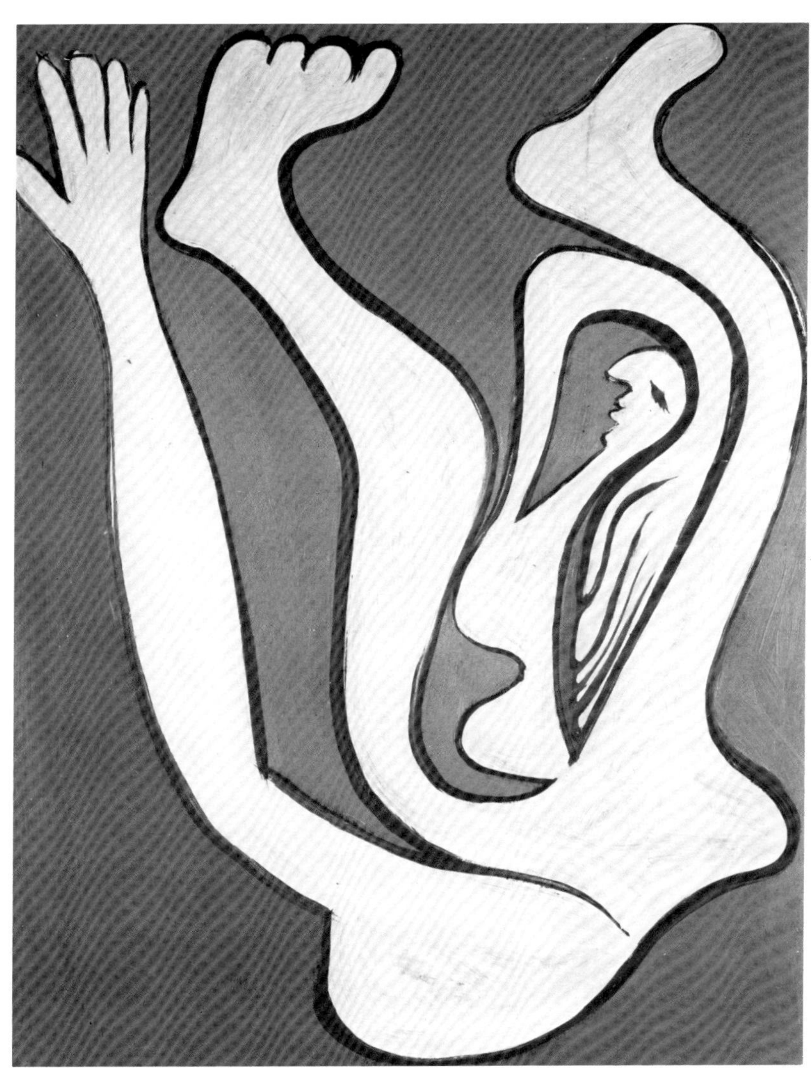

Hans Arp

64 *Composition.* 1937
Collage of torn paper with India ink and pencil on paper, 13¼ x 11½″ (33.6 x 29.3 cm.)
Philadelphia Museum of Art, The A. E. Gallatin Collection

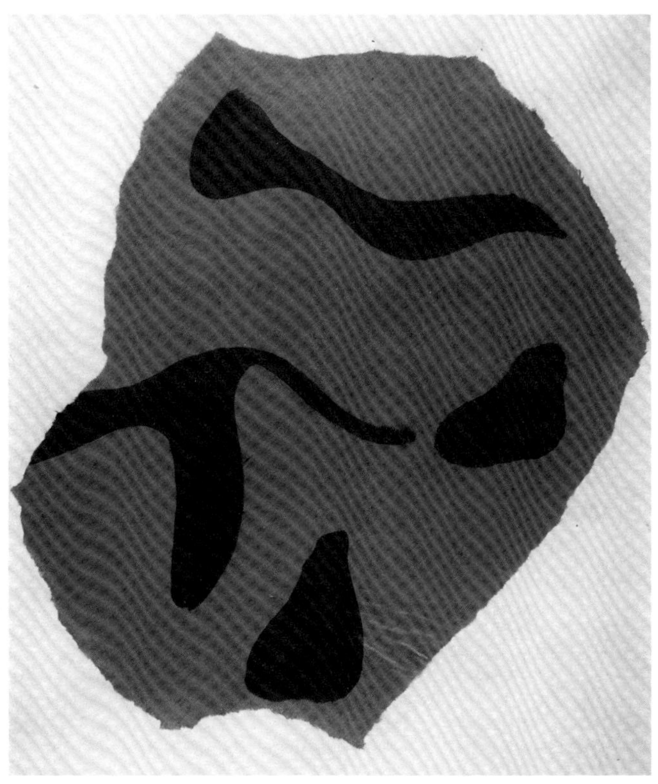

Paul Klee

65 *How Everything Grows (Was alles wächst).* 1932

Watercolor on paper, $18^{15}/_{16}$ x $12^{1}/_{4}$" (47.9 x 31.5 cm.)

Collection Kunstmuseum Bern, Paul Klee-Stiftung

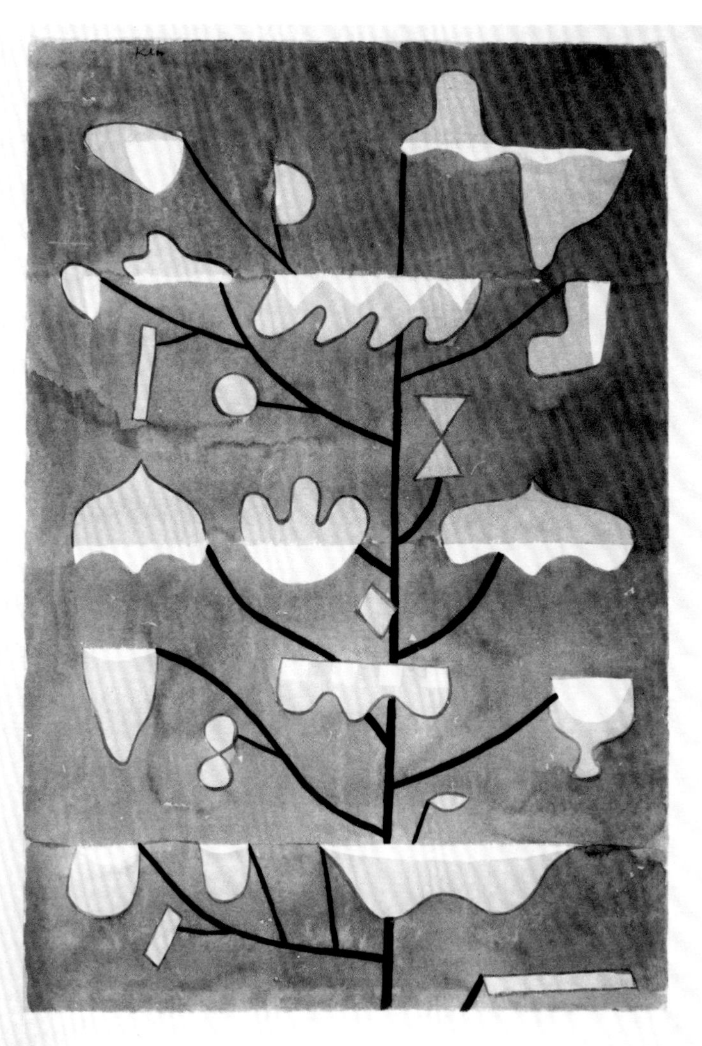

COMPARTMENTALIZATION: PROBLEMS OF FORM AND CONSTRUCTION

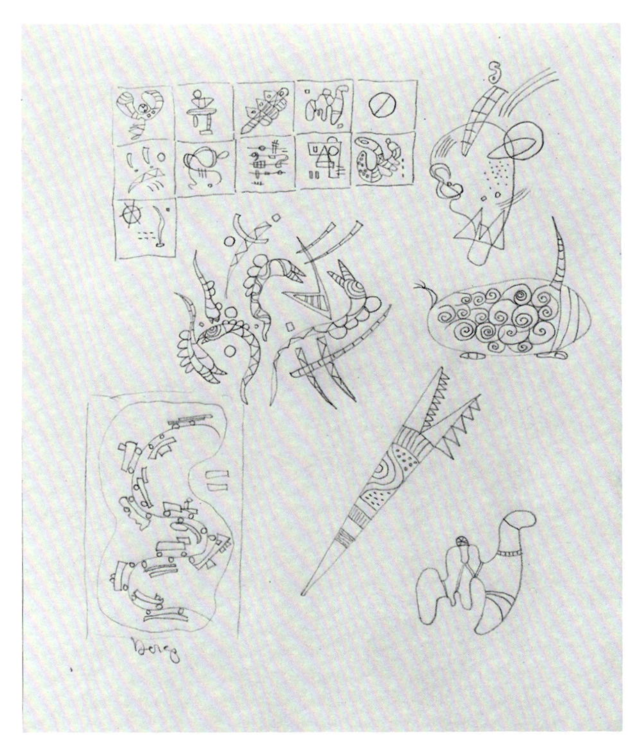

Vasily Kandinsky

66 *Study for "Fifteen" (Etude pour "Quinze").* 1938
Sketchbook page, pencil on paper, 13 1/16 x 10 11/16" (33.1 x 27.1 cm.)
Collection Musée National d'Art Moderne, Centre Georges Pompidou, Paris, Kandinsky Bequest

Vasily Kandinsky

67 *Fifteen (Quinze).* April 1938
(HL watercolors 589)
Tempera with gouache on black paper mounted on board, 13 5/8 x 19 3/4" (34.5 x 50 cm.)
Collection Kunstmuseum Bern

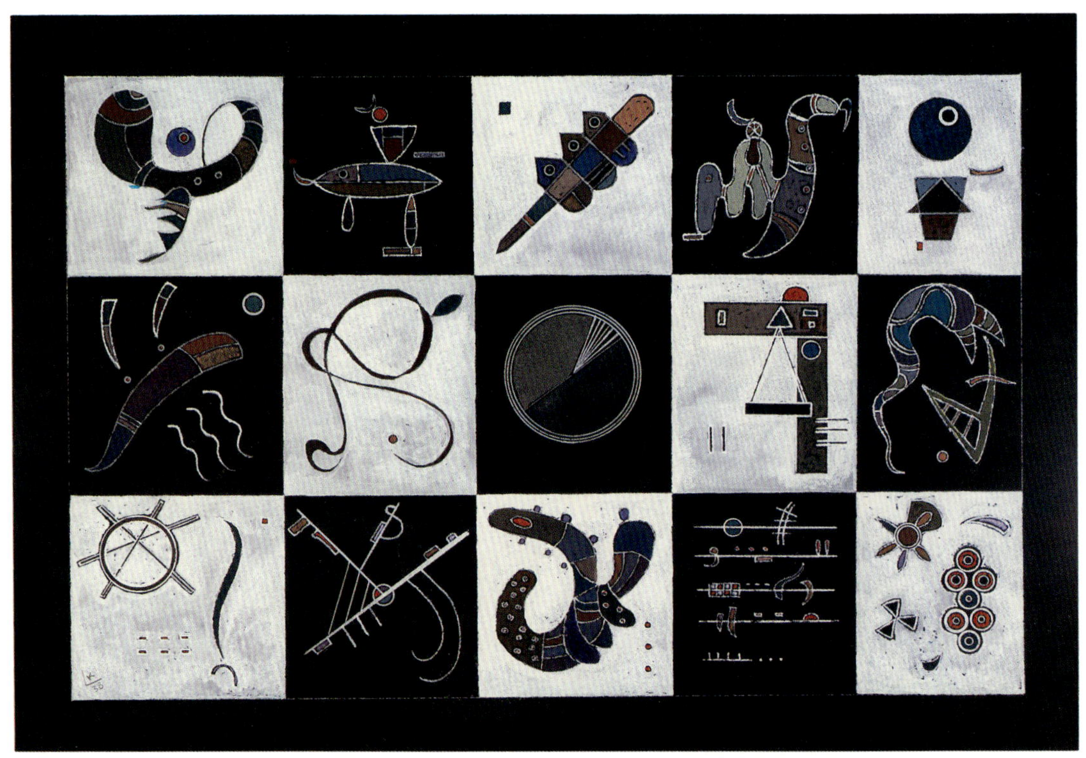

Vasily Kandinsky

68 *Thirty (Trente).* December 1936–January 1937
(HL 636)
Oil on canvas, 31⅞ x 39⅜" (81 x 100 cm.)
Collection Musée National d'Art Moderne, Centre Georges Pompidou, Paris, Gift of Mme Nina Kandinsky

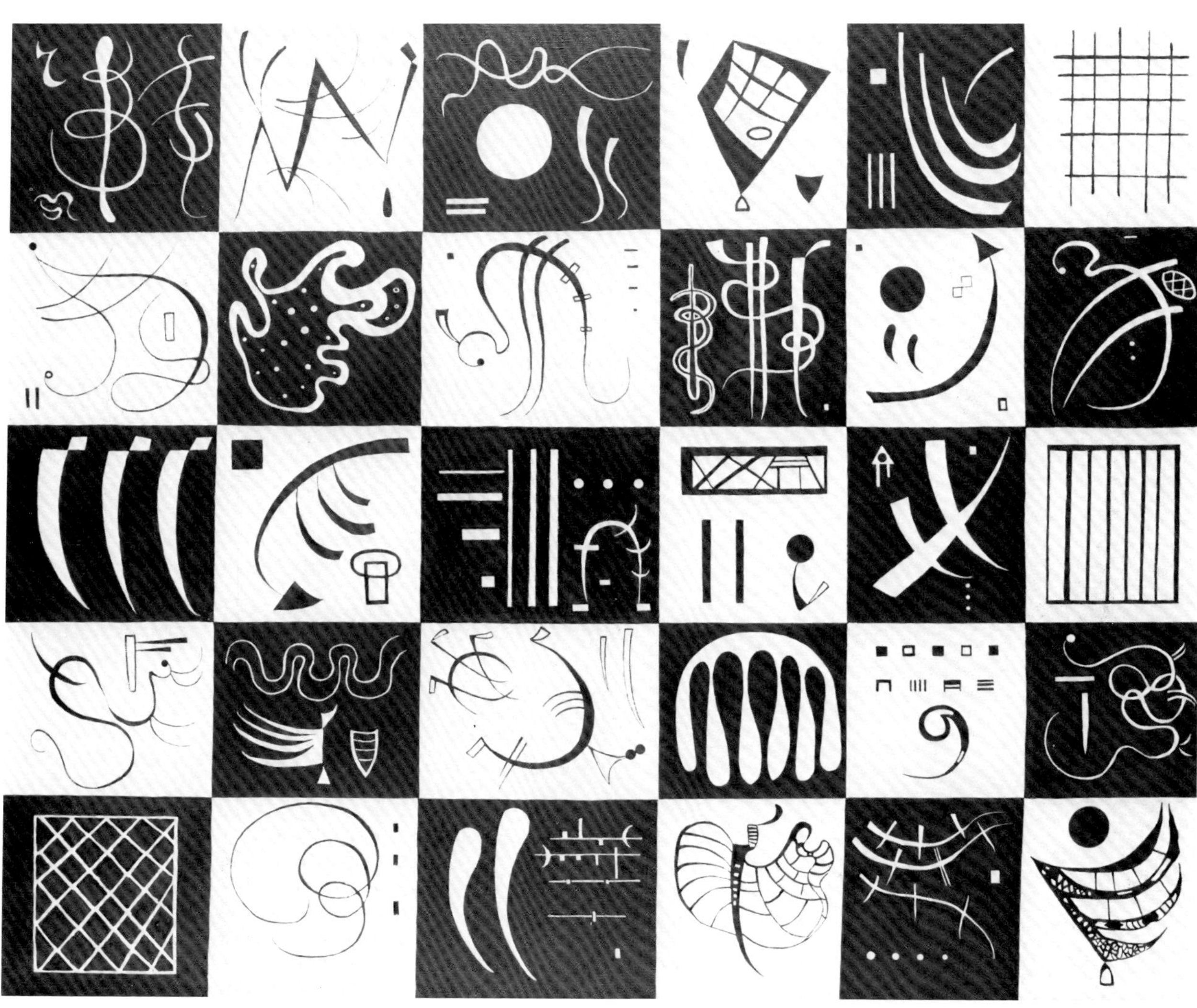

František Kupka
69 *Abstraction.* ca. 1930
Gouache on paper, 11 x 10⅝″
(28 x 27 cm.)
Collection Musée National d'Art Moderne,
Centre Georges Pompidou, Paris

František Kupka
70 *Abstraction.* ca. 1930
Gouache on paper, 11 x 11″ (28 x 28 cm.)
Collection Musée National d'Art Moderne,
Centre Georges Pompidou, Paris

František Kupka
71 *Black and White Abstraction (Abstraction noir et blanc).* ca. 1930
Ink on paper, 11¼ x 11¼″
(28.5 x 28.5 cm.)
Collection Musée National d'Art Moderne,
Centre Georges Pompidou, Paris

František Kupka
72 *Black and White Abstraction (Abstraction noir et blanc).* ca. 1930
Gouache on paper, 11 x 11″ (28 x 28 cm.)
Collection Musée National d'Art Moderne,
Centre Georges Pompidou, Paris

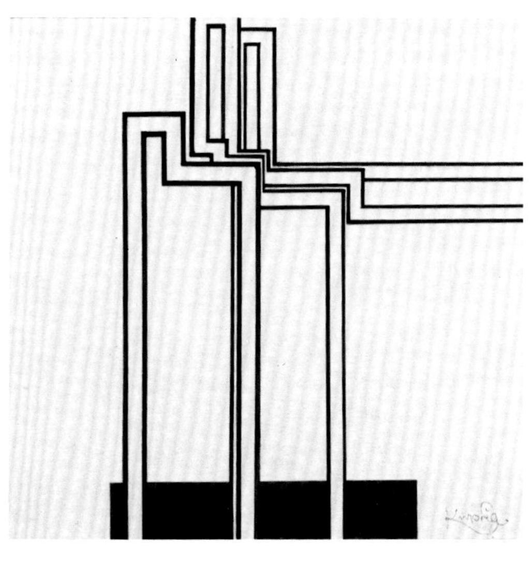

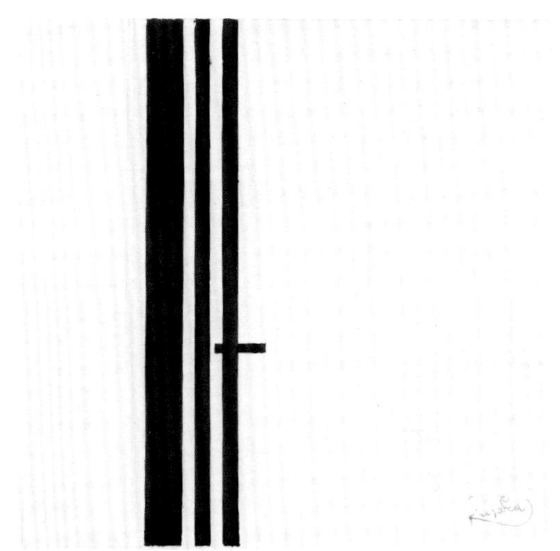

František Kupka

73 *Black and White Abstraction (Abstraction noir et blanc).* ca. 1930
Gouache on paper, 11 x 11″ (28 x 28 cm.)
Collection Musée National d'Art Moderne, Centre Georges Pompidou, Paris

František Kupka

74 *Black and White Abstraction (Abstraction noir et blanc).* ca. 1930
Gouache on paper, 11 x 11″ (28 x 28 cm.)
Collection Musée National d'Art Moderne, Centre Georges Pompidou, Paris

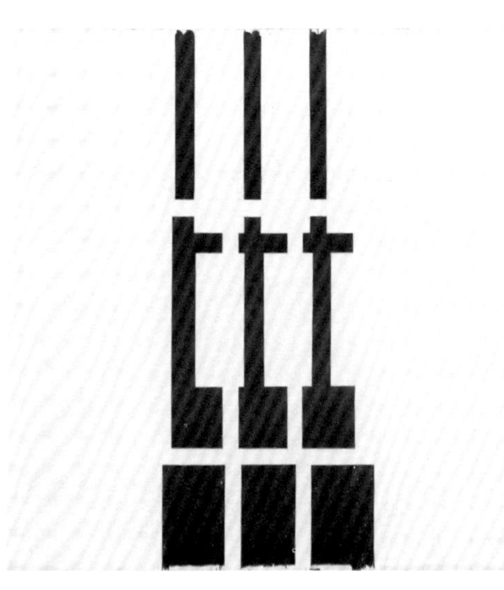

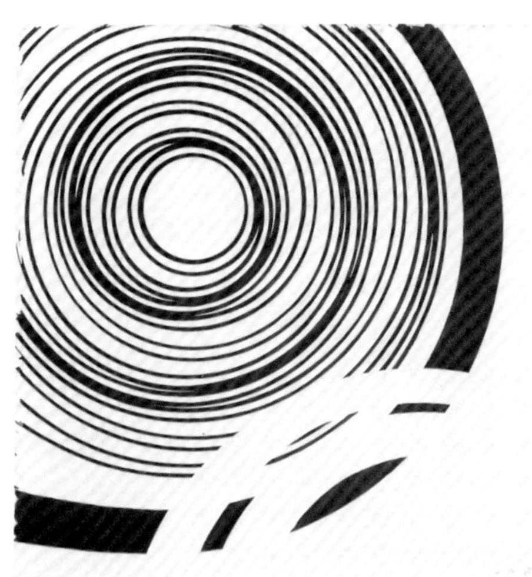

František Kupka

75 *Black and White Abstraction (Abstraction noir et blanc).* ca. 1930
Gouache on paper, 11 x 11″ (28 x 28 cm.)
Collection Musée National d'Art Moderne, Centre Georges Pompidou, Paris

František Kupka

76 *Black and White Abstraction (Abstraction noir et blanc).* ca. 1930
Gouache on paper, 11 x 11″ (28 x 28 cm.)
Collection Musée National d'Art Moderne, Centre Georges Pompidou, Paris

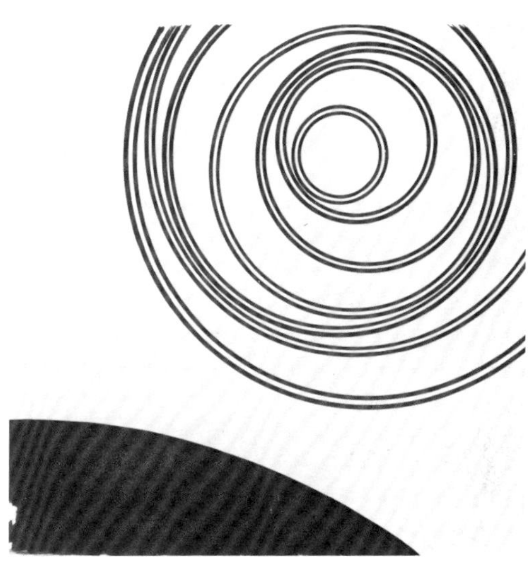

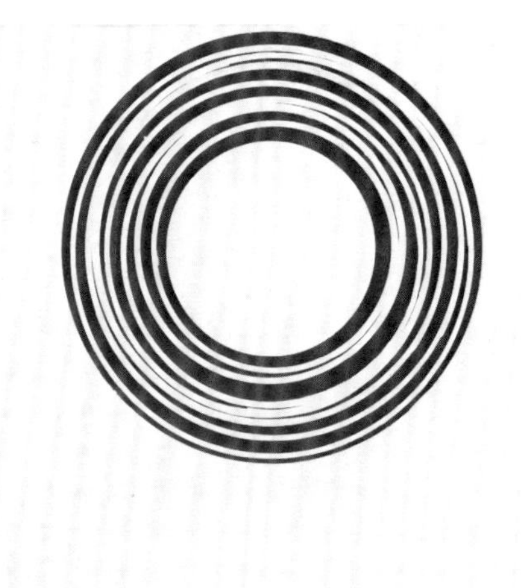

František Kupka

77 *Black and White Abstraction (Abstraction noir et blanc).* ca. 1930
Gouache on paper, 11 x 11" (28 x 28 cm.)
Collection Musée National d'Art Moderne, Centre Georges Pompidou, Paris

František Kupka

78 *Black and White Abstraction (Abstraction noir et blanc).* ca. 1930
Gouache on paper, 11 x 11" (28 x 28 cm.)
Collection Musée National d'Art Moderne, Centre Georges Pompidou, Paris

František Kupka

79 *Black and White Abstraction (Abstraction noir et blanc).* ca. 1930
Gouache on paper, 11 x 11" (28 x 28 cm.)
Collection Musée National d'Art Moderne, Centre Georges Pompidou, Paris

František Kupka

80 *Black and White Abstraction (Abstraction noir et blanc).* ca. 1930
Gouache on paper, 11 x 11" (28 x 28 cm.)
Collection Musée National d'Art Moderne, Centre Georges Pompidou, Paris

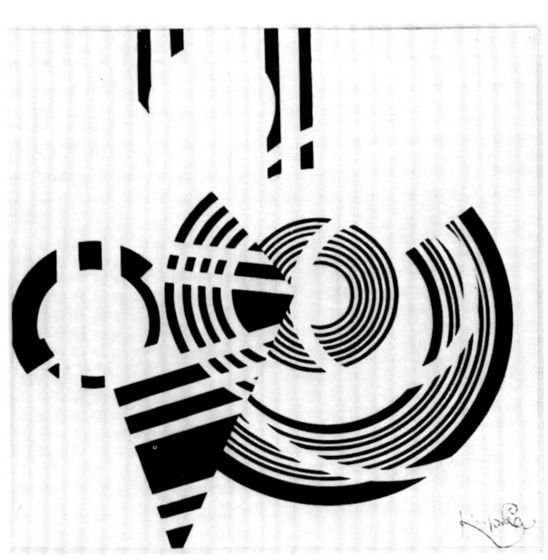

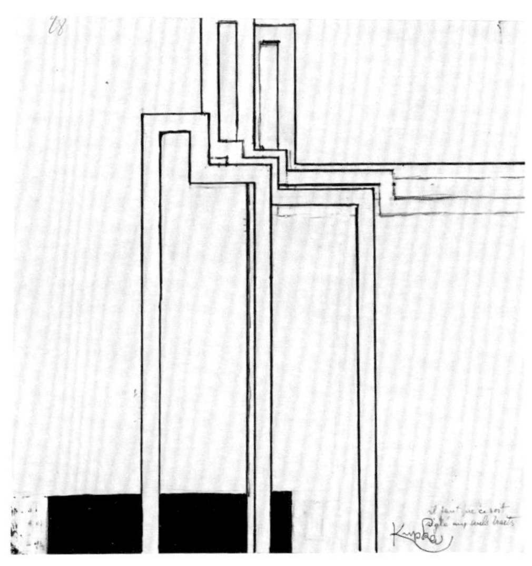

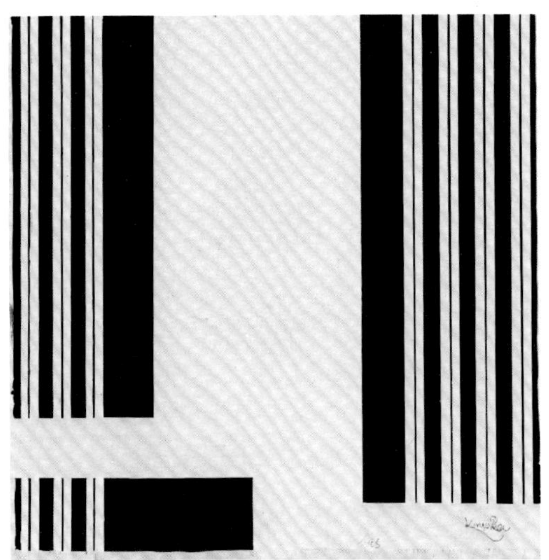

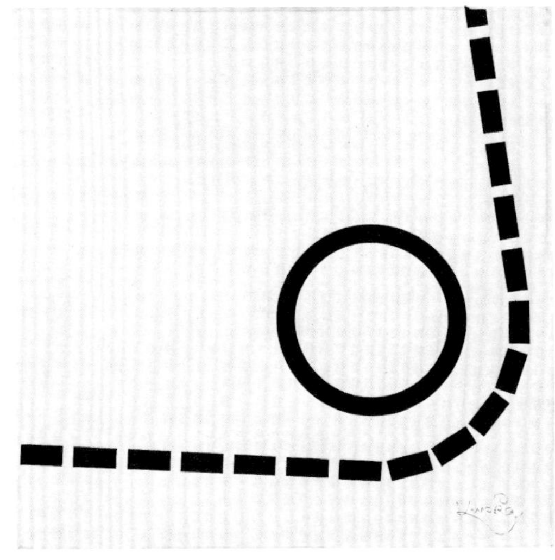

Pablo Picasso

81 a-b *The Dream and Lie of Franco (Songe et mensonge de Franco).* 1937

Etching and aquatint on paper, two parts, sight, each 14 x 17$^{15}/_{16}$" (35.5 x 45.5 cm.)

Peggy Guggenheim Collection, Venice

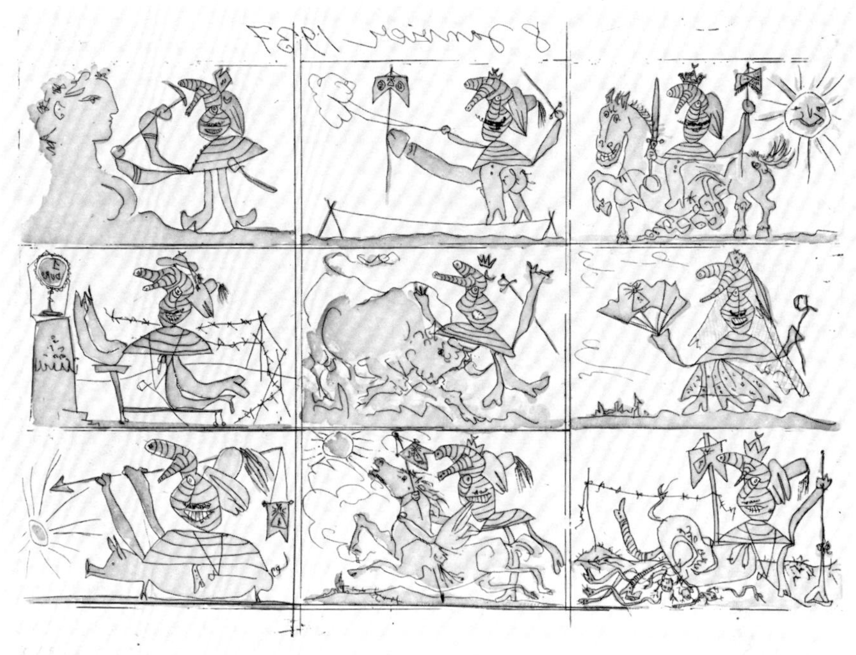

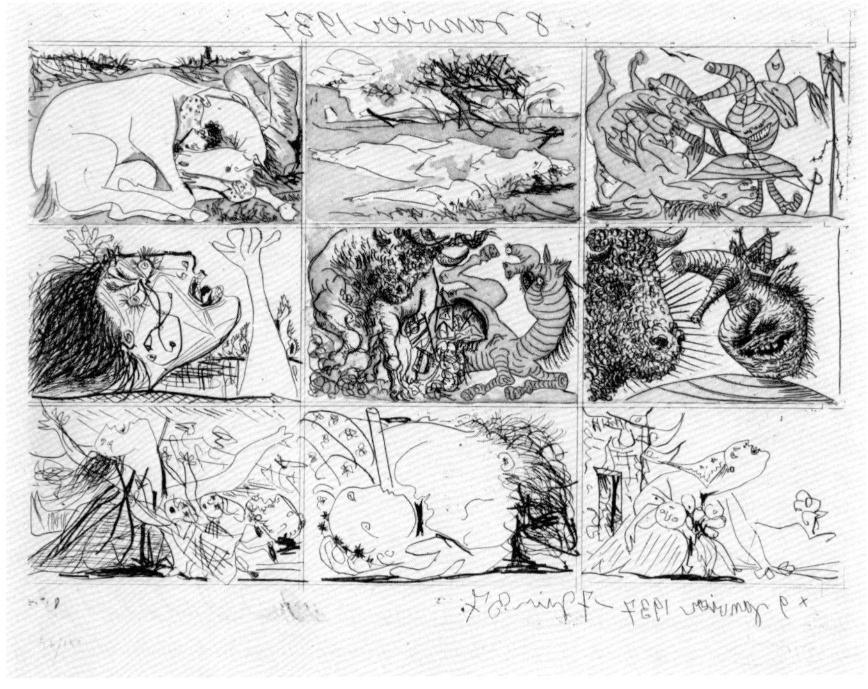

Hans Arp and Sophie Taeuber-Arp

83 *Landmark (Jalon).* 1938
Wood, 23⅝ x 9⅞ x 14³⁄₁₆″
(60 x 25 x 36 cm.)
Collection Fondation Arp, Clamart

Hans Arp

82 *Pagoda Fruit on Dish (Configuration) (Fruit de pagode sur coupe [Configuration]).*
1934
Cast cement, fruit, 9 x 14⁹⁄₁₆ x 11″
(23 x 37 x 28 cm.); dish, 5½ x 15¾ x 11¾″
(14 x 40 x 29 cm.)
Private Collection, Paris

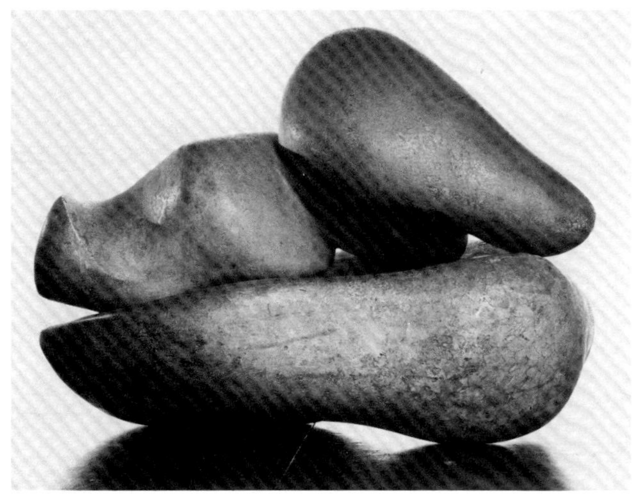

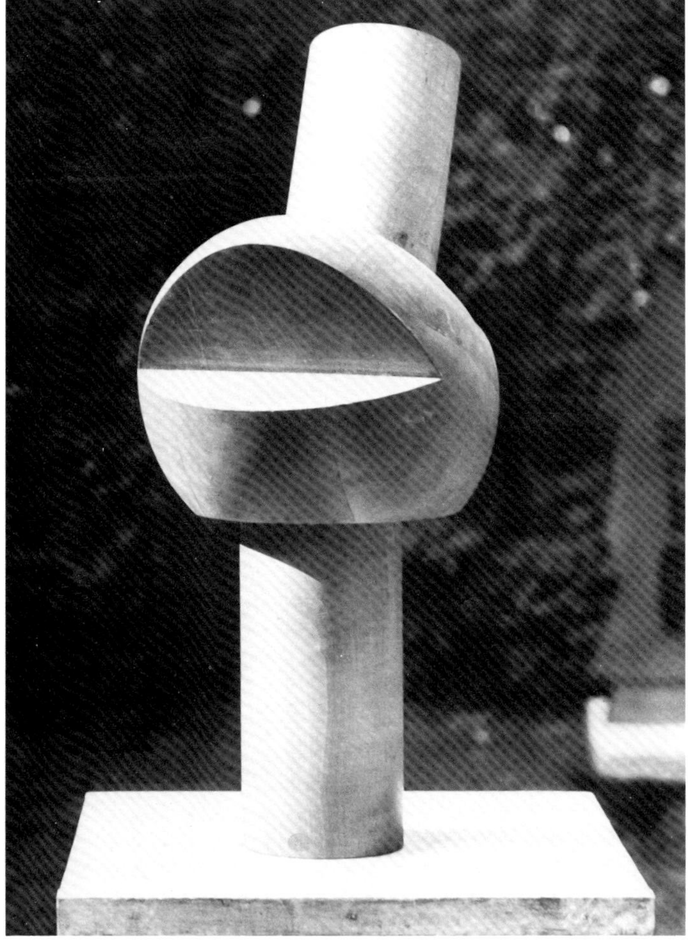

Julio González

84 *Head. The Snail (Tête. L'Escargot).* ca. 1935
Wrought iron, 17¾ x 15¼″ (45.1 x 38.7 cm.)
Collection The Museum of Modern Art, New York. Purchase

Alberto Giacometti

85 *Drawing for "The Palace at 4 A.M." (Dessin pour "Le Palais à quatre heures du matin").* 1932
Pen and ink on paper, 7 9/16 x 9 9/16″ (19.2 x 24.2 cm.)
Collection Kupferstichkabinett, Kunstmuseum Basel, K. A. Burckhardt-Koechlin Bequest

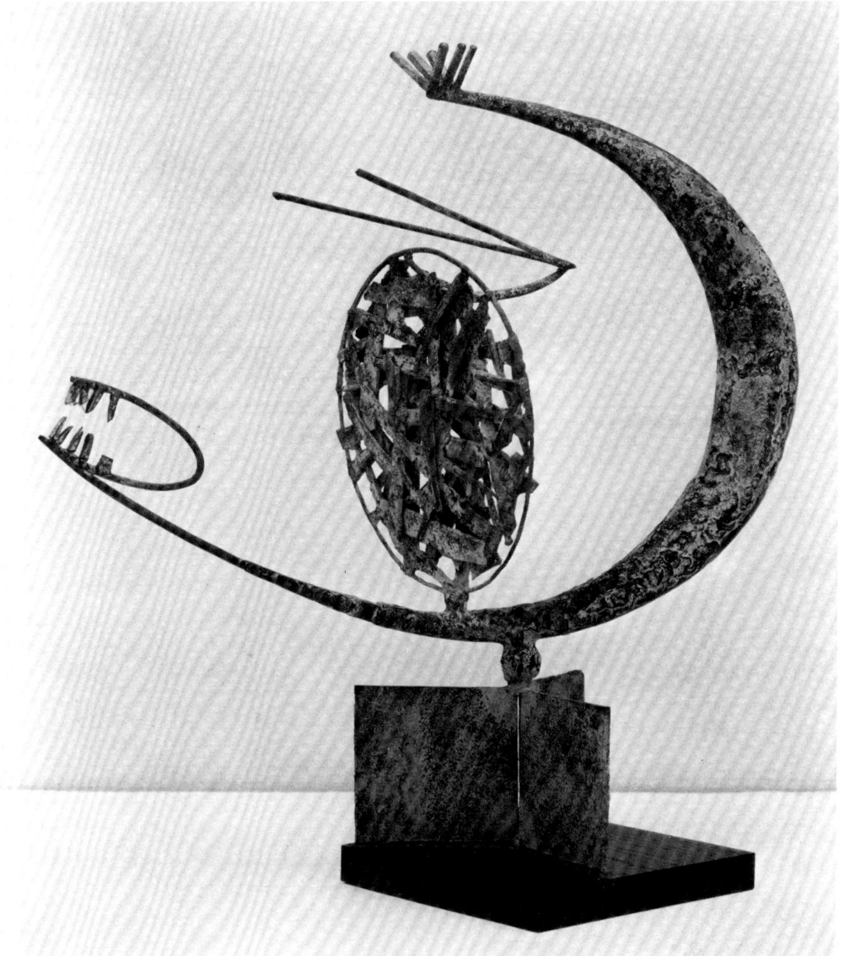

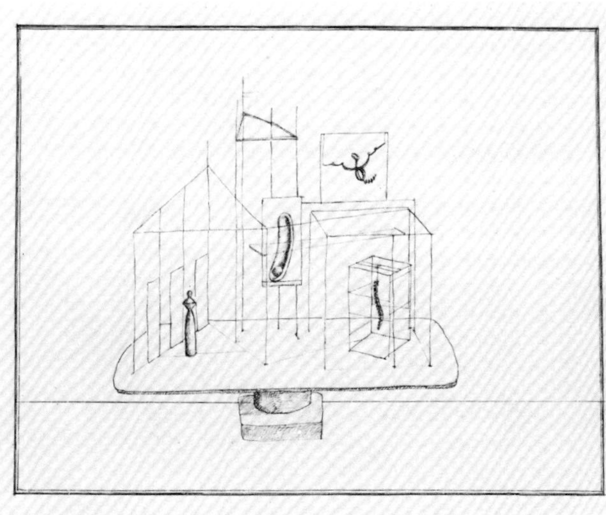

Vasily Kandinsky
86 *Accompanied Center (Milieu accompagné).* May 1937
(HL 641)
Oil on canvas, 44⅞ x 57½"
(114 x 146 cm.)
Collection Mr. and Mrs. Adrien Maeght

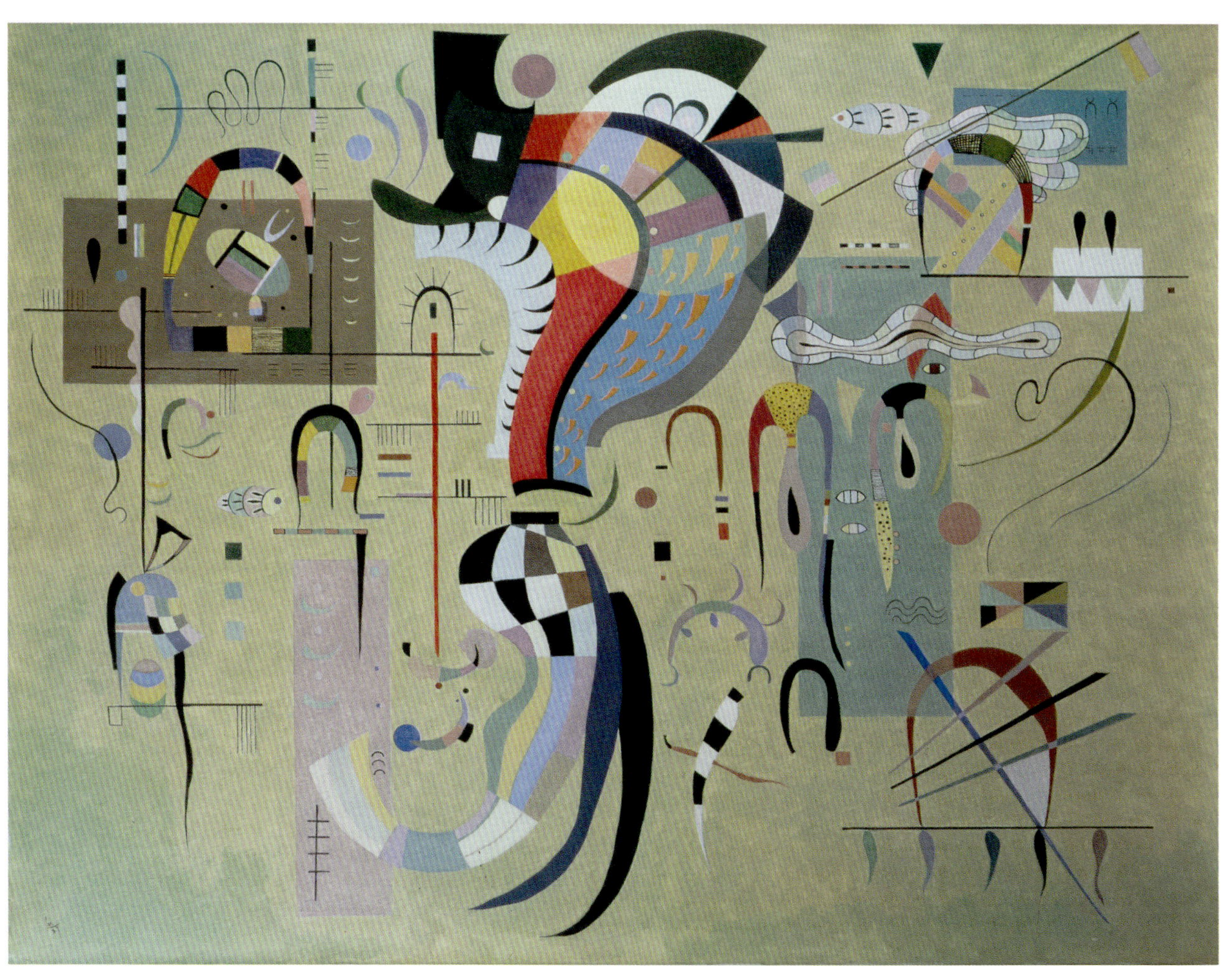

Vasily Kandinsky

87 *Study for "Accompanied Center" (Etude pour "Milieu accompagné").* 1937

Pencil on paper, 6 3/8 x 8 5/8″
(16.2 x 21.8 cm.)

Collection Musée National d'Art Moderne, Centre Georges Pompidou, Paris, Kandinsky Bequest

Vasily Kandinsky

88 *Study for "Accompanied Center" (Etude et mise au carreau de "Milieu accompagné").* 1937

Pencil on paper, 9 7/16 x 12 7/16″
(23.9 x 31.5 cm.)

Collection Musée National d'Art Moderne, Centre Georges Pompidou, Paris, Kandinsky Bequest

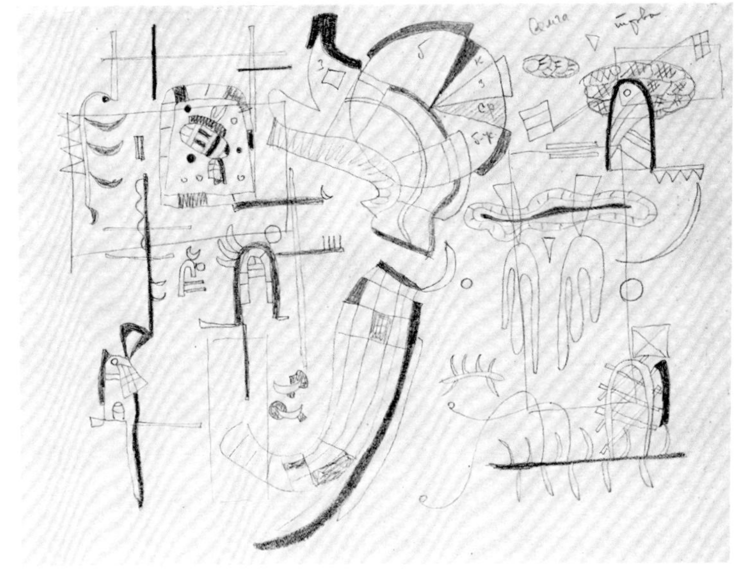

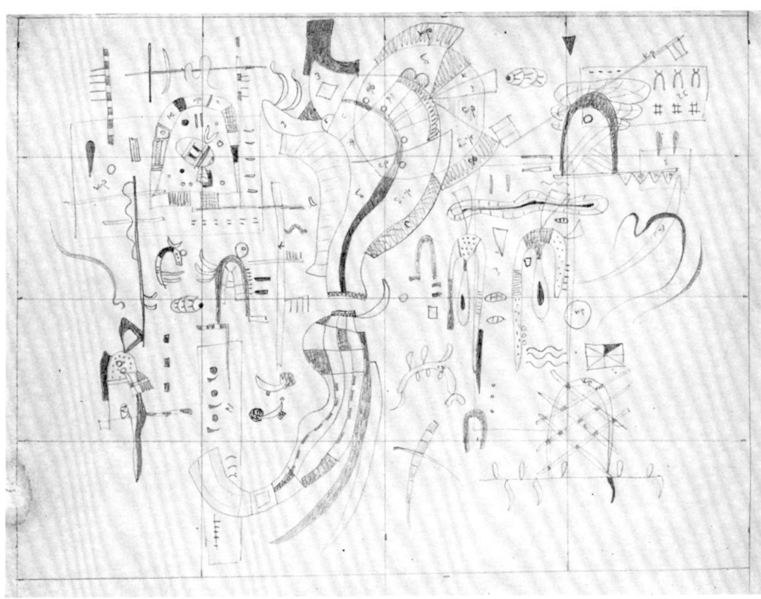

Vasily Kandinsky

89 *Capricious Forms (Formes capricieuses).*
July 1937
(HL 643)
Oil on canvas, 35 x 45¾″
(88.9 x 116.3 cm.)
Collection Solomon R. Guggenheim Museum, New York

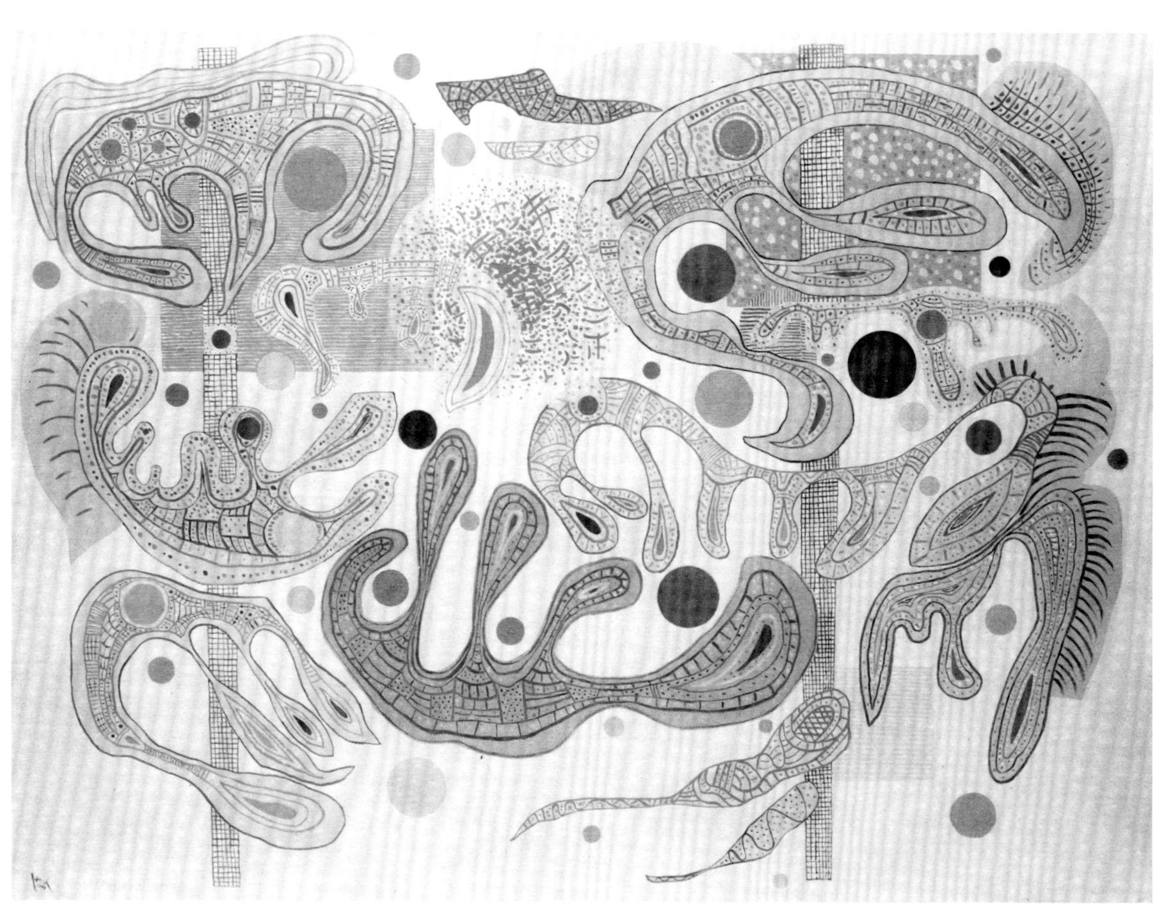

Vasily Kandinsky

*90 *Study for "Capricious Forms" (Etude pour "Formes capricieuses").* 1937
Sketchbook page, colored pencils on paper, $10^{11}/_{16}$ x $13^{1}/_{16}$" (27.1 x 33.1 cm.)
Collection Musée National d'Art Moderne, Centre Georges Pompidou, Paris, Kandinsky Bequest

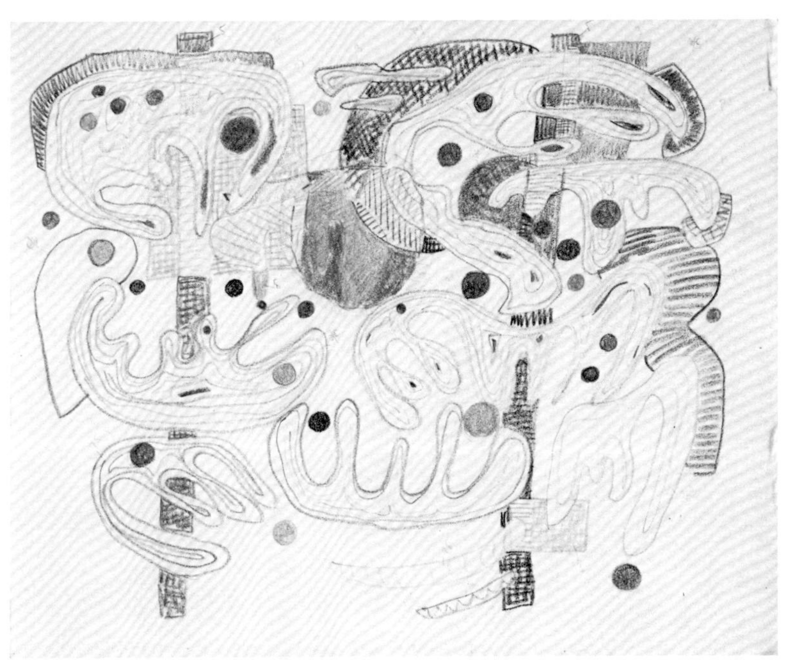

Vasily Kandinsky

91 *Animated Stability (Stabilité animée).*
December 1937
(HL 646)
Mixed media on canvas, 45¾ x 35″
(116 x 89 cm.)
Lent by Davlyn Gallery, New York

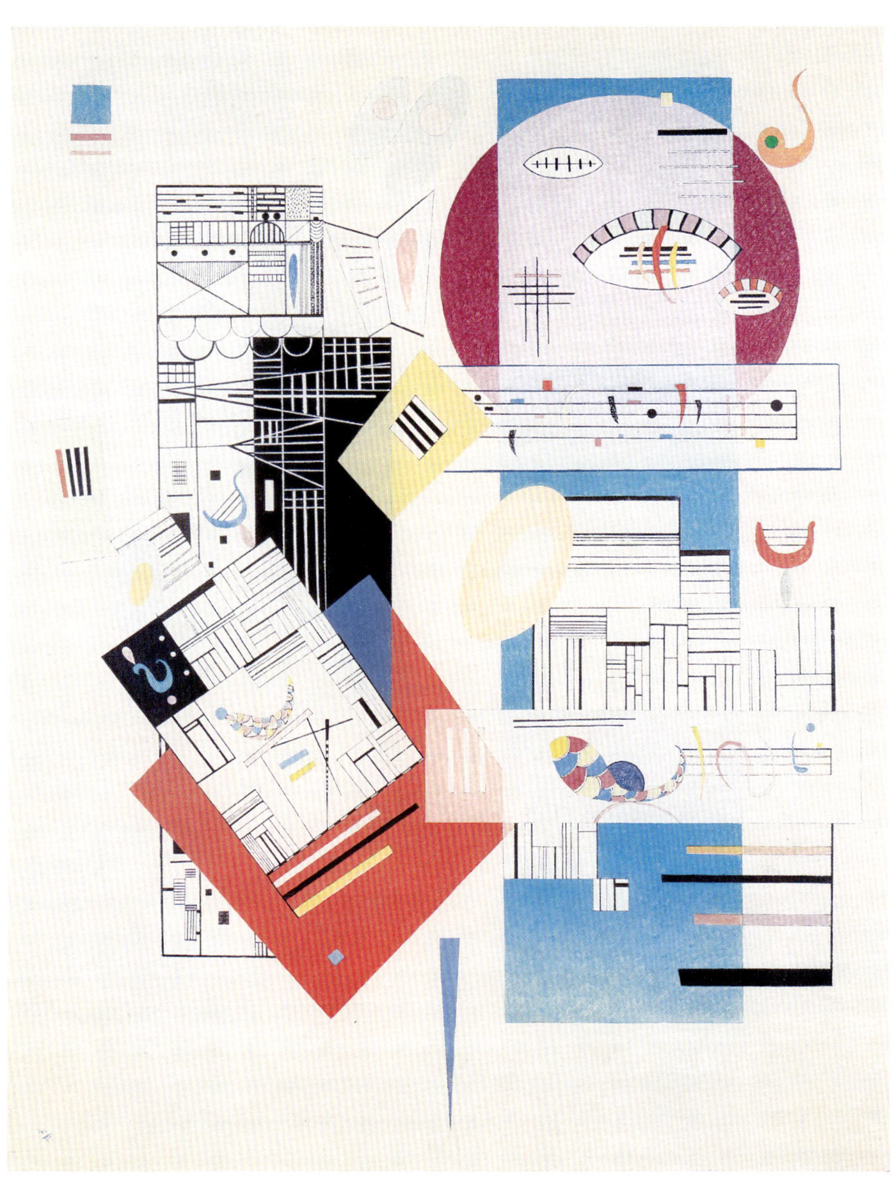

Vasily Kandinsky

92 *Ordered Arrangement (Many-Colored Ensemble) (Entassement reglé [Ensemble multicolore]).* February–April 1938

(HL 650)

Oil and enamel on canvas, $45^{11}/_{16}$ x $35^{1}/_{16}$" (116 x 89 cm.)

Collection Musée National d'Art Moderne, Centre Georges Pompidou, Paris, Gift of Mme Nina Kandinsky

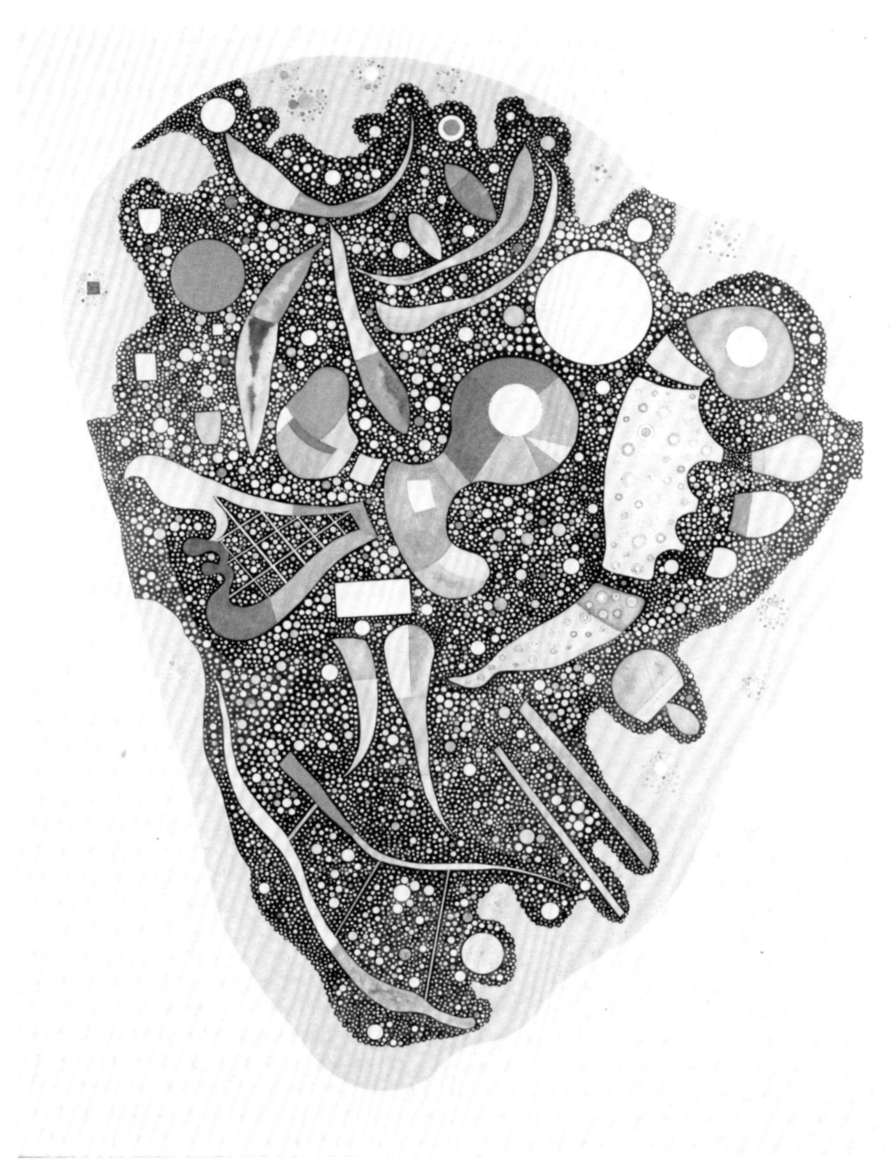

Vasily Kandinsky

93 *Penetrating Green (Le Vert pénétrant).* April 1938

(HL 651)

Oil on canvas, 29½ x 49¼"
(75 x 125.1 cm.)

Collection The Baltimore Museum of Art,
Bequest of Saidie A. May

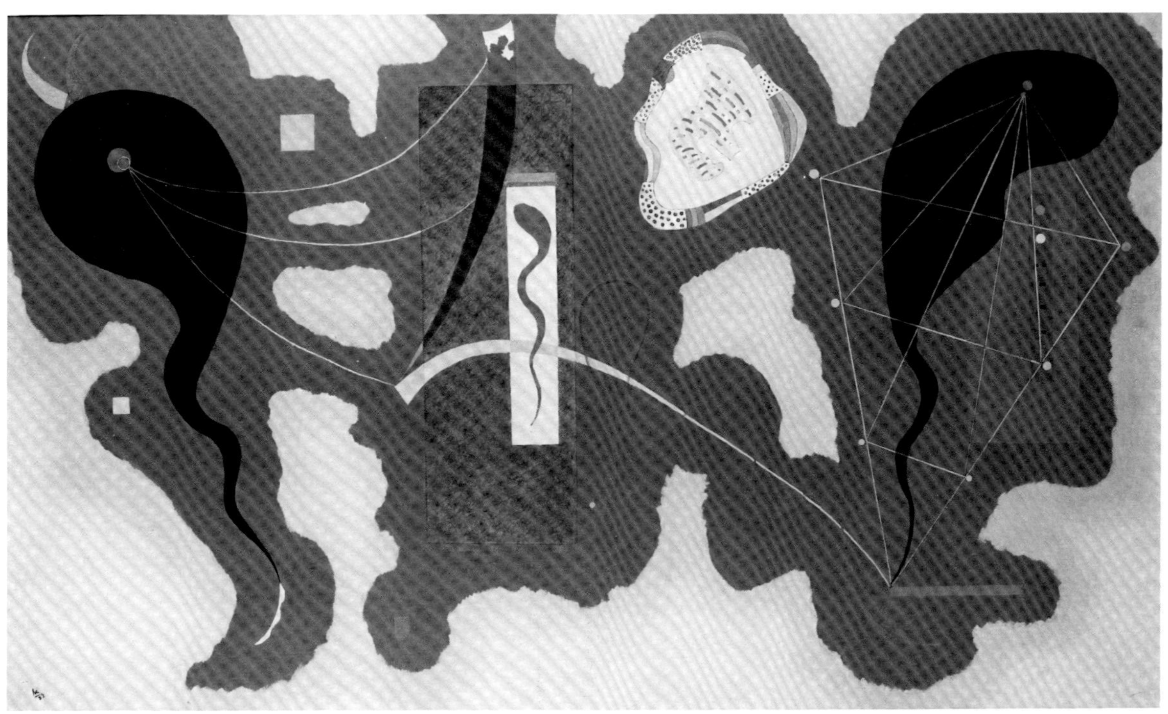

Vasily Kandinsky

94 *Yellow Painting (La Toile jaune).* July 1938

(HL 653)

Oil and enamel on canvas, $45\frac{7}{8}$ x 35″ (116.4 x 88.8 cm.)

Collection Solomon R. Guggenheim Museum, New York

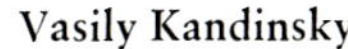

Vasily Kandinsky

*95 *Study for "Yellow Painting" (Etude pour "La Toile jaune").* 1938

Sketchbook page, India ink and watercolor on paper, 13 x $10\frac{5}{8}$″ (33 x 27 cm.)

Collection Musée National d'Art Moderne, Centre Georges Pompidou, Paris, Kandinsky Bequest

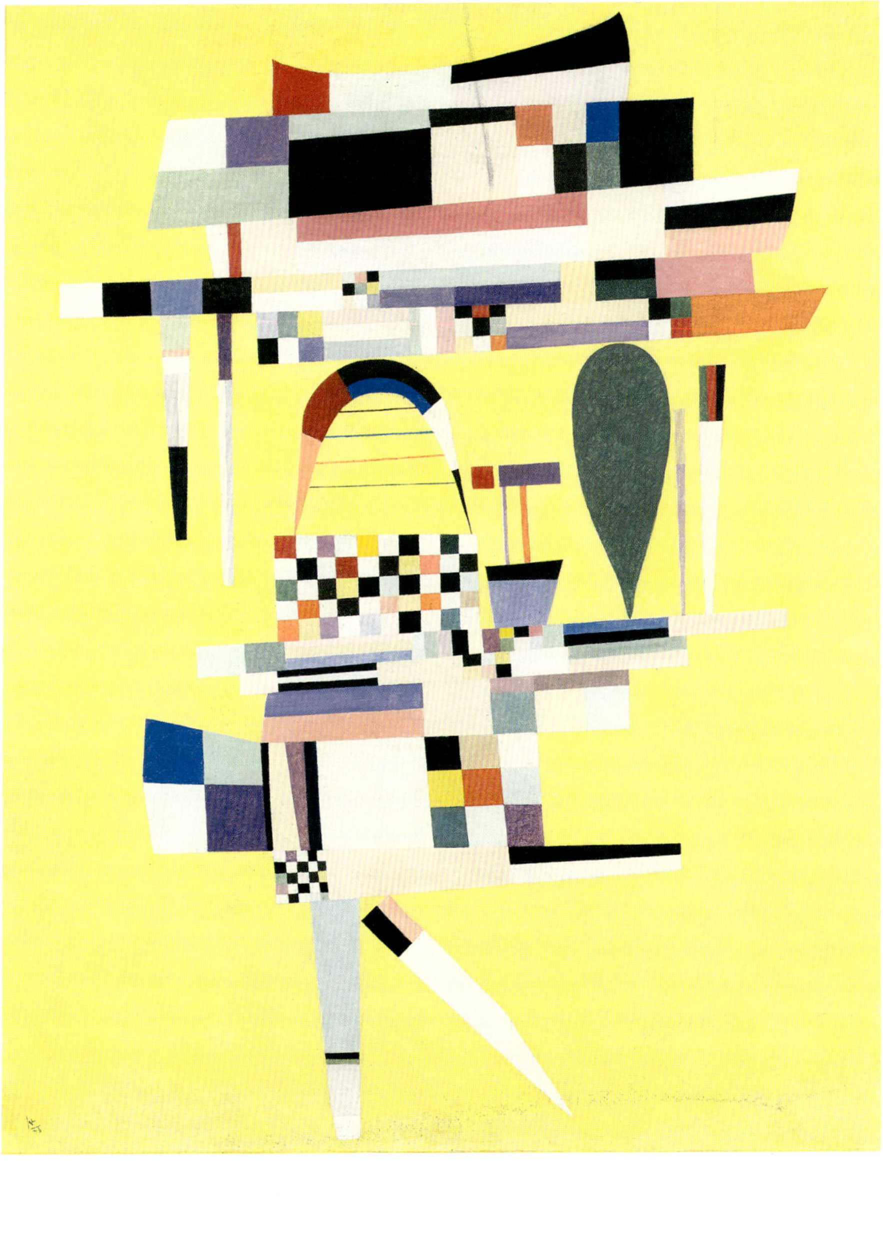

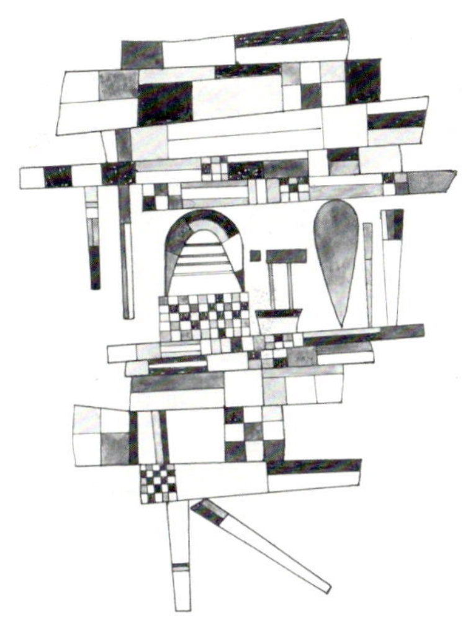

IV. PHOTOGRAPHS OF KANDINSKY

Man Ray
96 *Portrait of Kandinsky.* ca. 1934
Photograph
Collection Musée National d'Art Moderne, Centre Georges Pompidou, Paris, Kandinsky Bequest

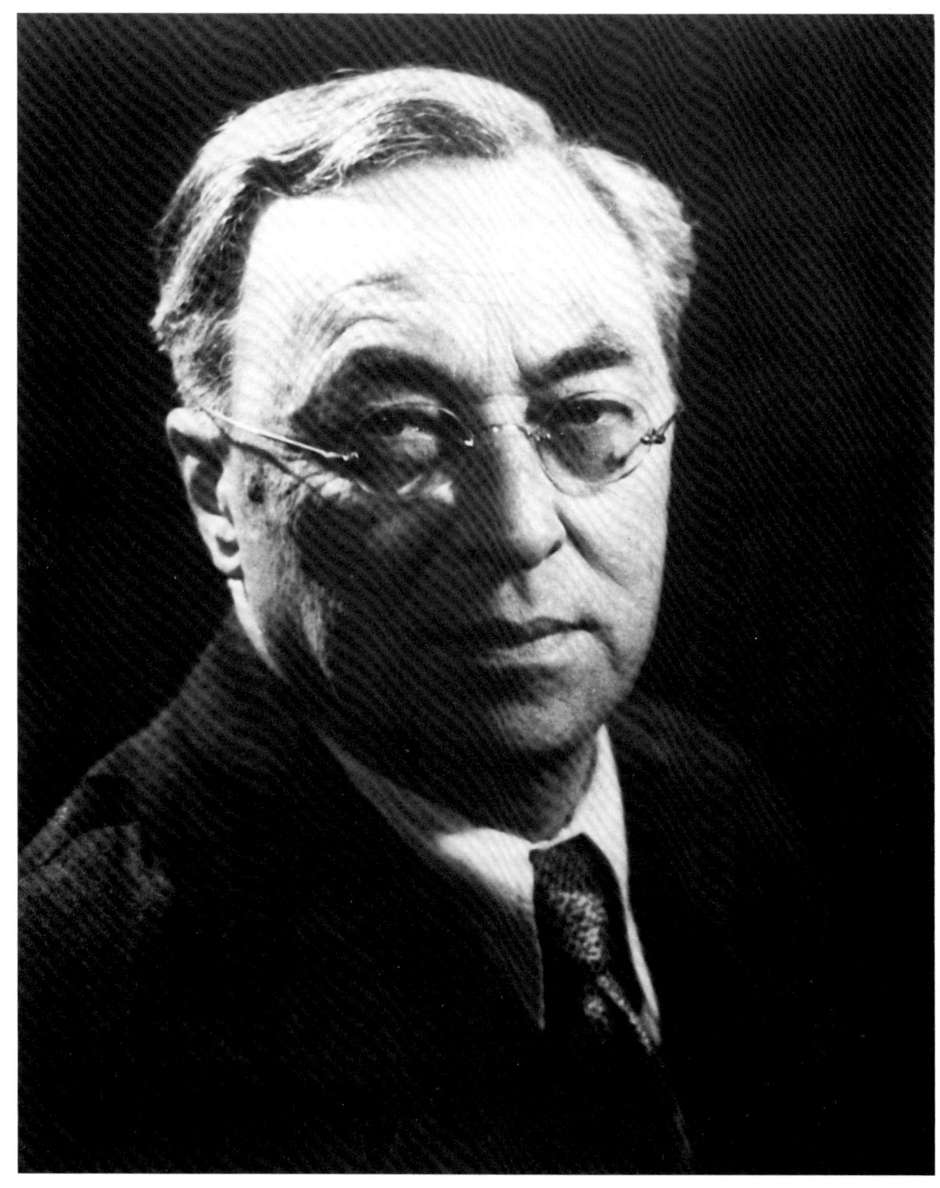

Florence Henri
97 *Portrait of Kandinsky.* 1935
Photograph
Collection Musée National d'Art Moderne, Centre Georges Pompidou, Paris, Kandinsky Bequest

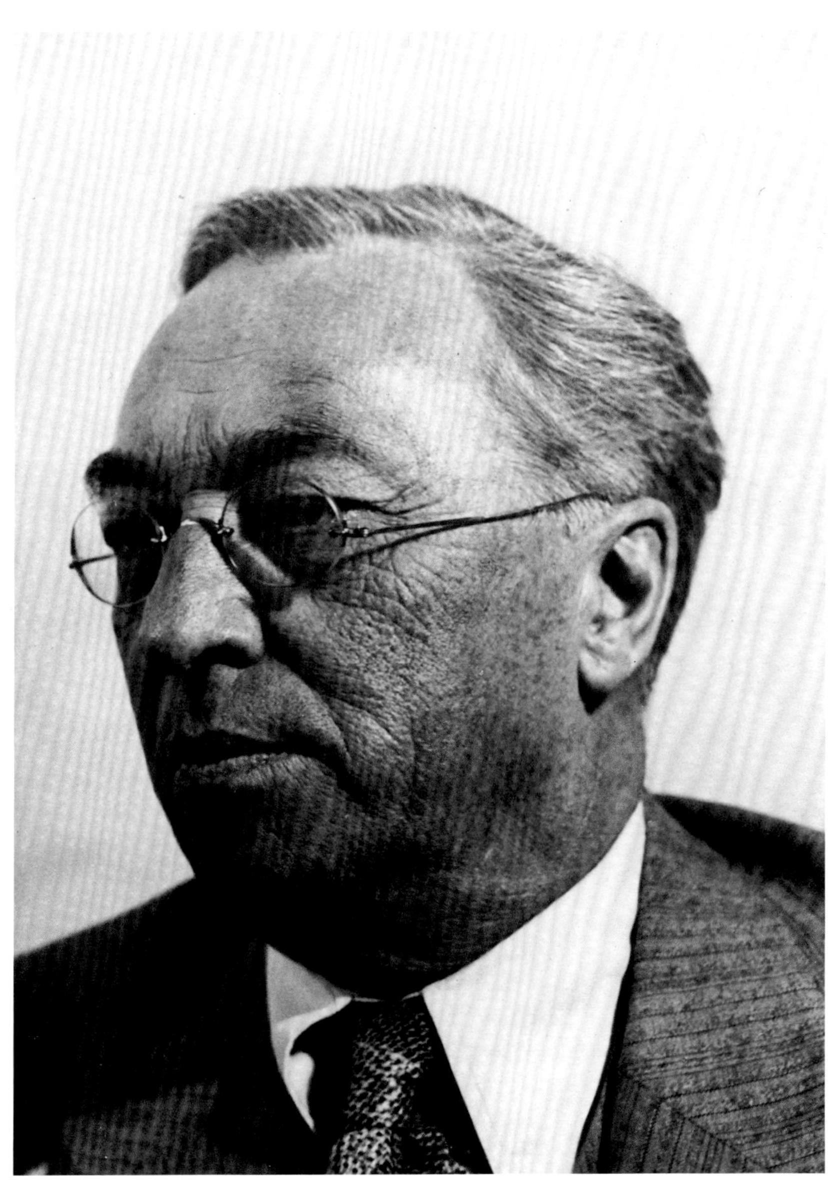

Lipnitzki

98 *Kandinsky in His Studio in Neuilly-sur-Seine.* ca. 1937

Photograph

Collection Musée National d'Art Moderne, Centre Georges Pompidou, Paris, Kandinsky Bequest

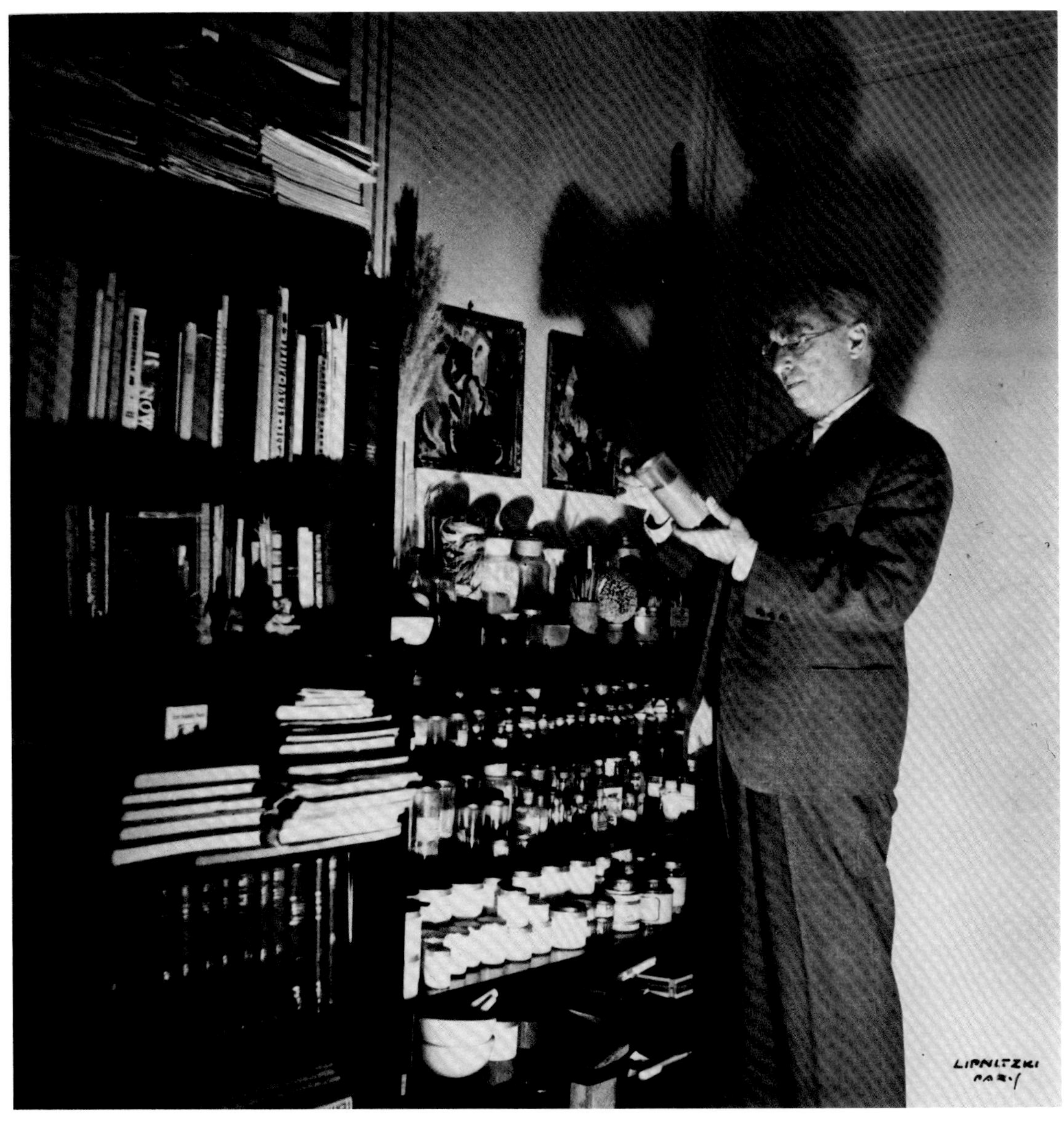

Lipnitzki

99 *Kandinsky in His Studio in Neuilly-sur-Seine.* ca. 1937

Photograph

Collection Musée National d'Art Moderne, Centre Georges Pompidou, Paris, Kandinsky Bequest

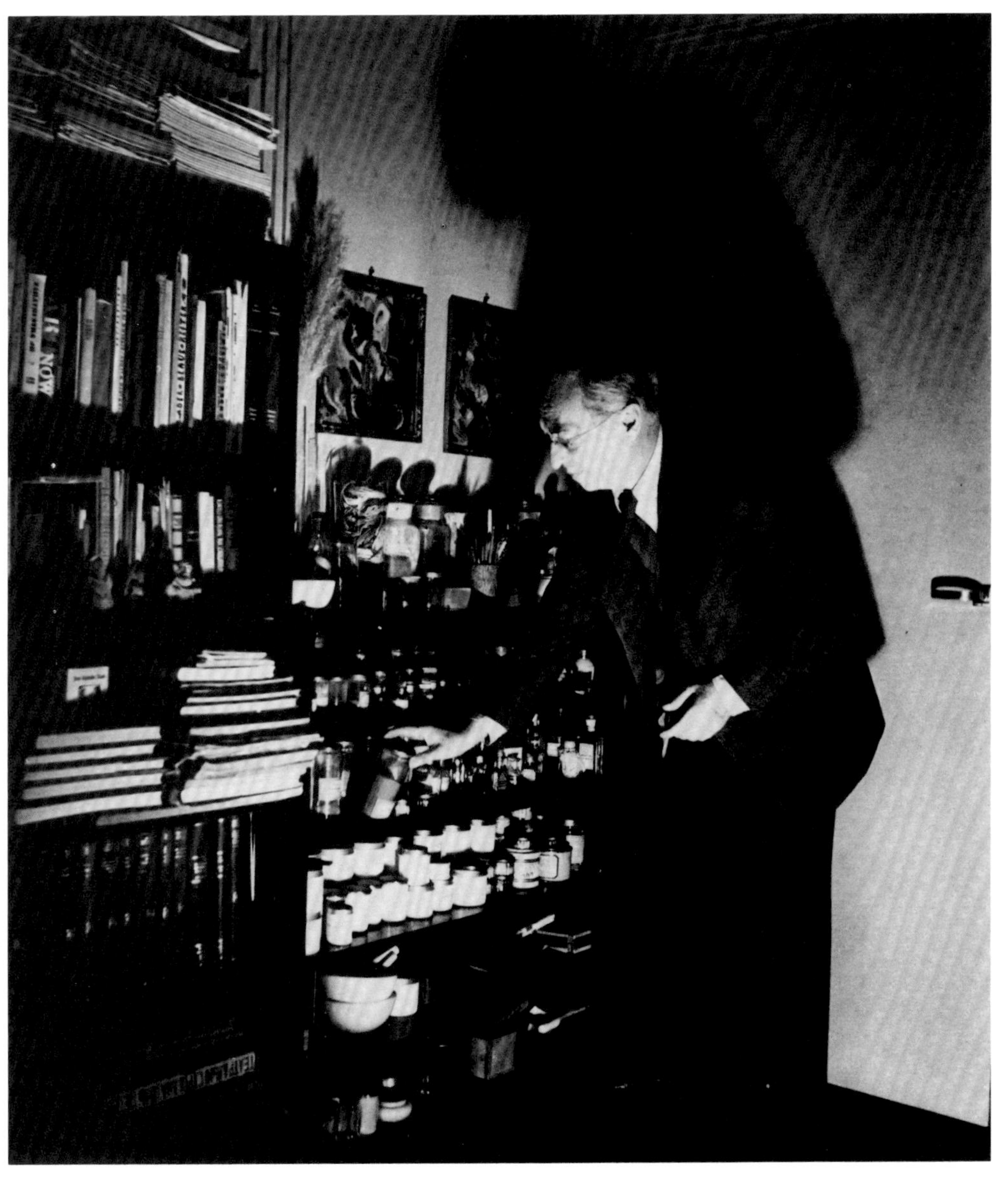

Lipnitzki

100 *Kandinsky in His Studio in Neuilly-sur-Seine.* ca. 1937

Photograph

Collection Musée National d'Art Moderne, Centre Georges Pompidou, Paris, Kandinsky Bequest

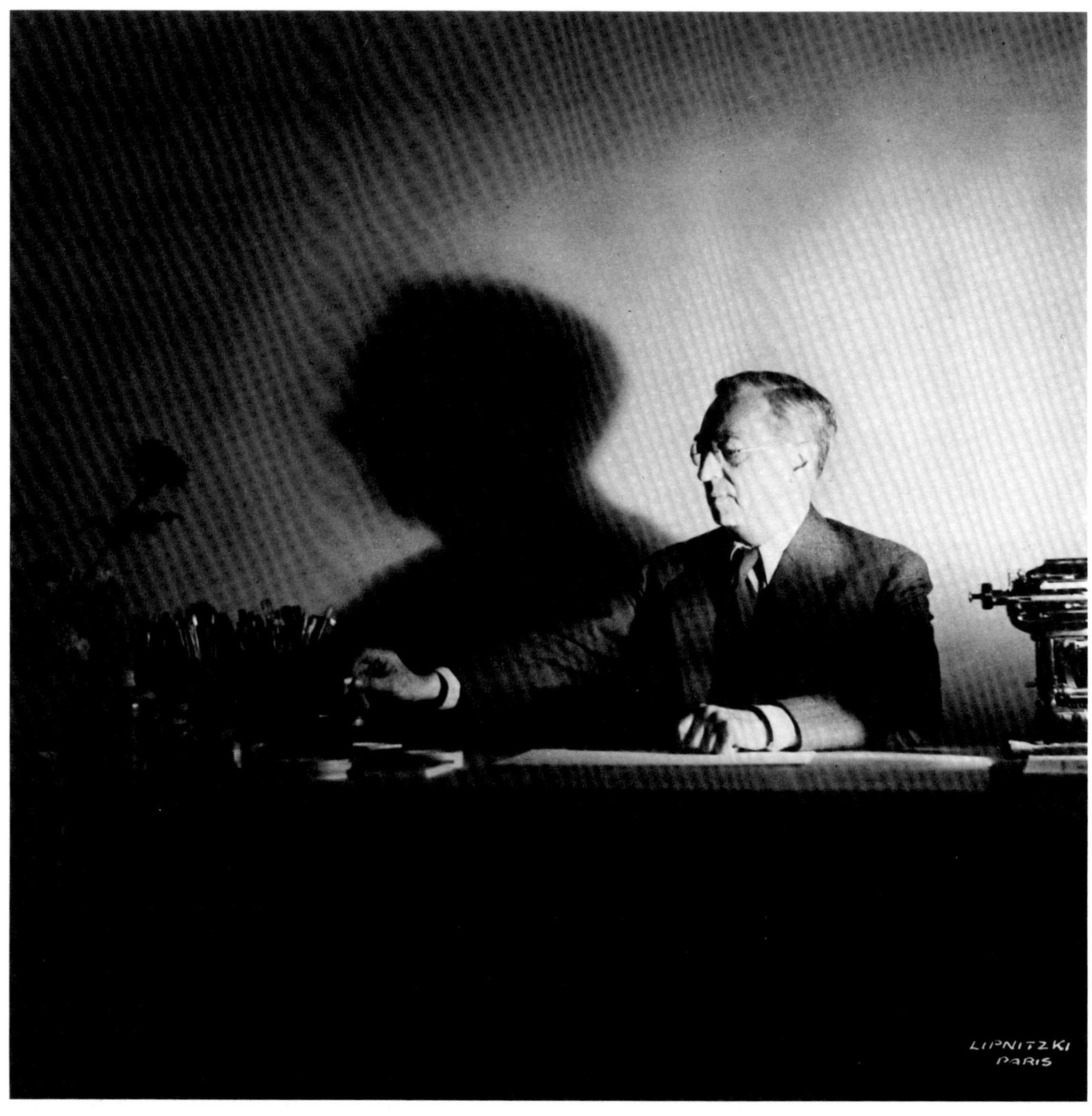

Joseph Breitenbach

101 *Portrait of Kandinsky.* Paris, 1938
Photograph
Collection Musée National d'Art Moderne, Centre Georges Pompidou, Paris, Kandinsky Bequest

Hannes Beckmann

102 *Portrait of Kandinsky.* ca. 1938
Photograph
Collection Musée National d'Art Moderne, Centre Georges Pompidou, Paris, Kandinsky Bequest

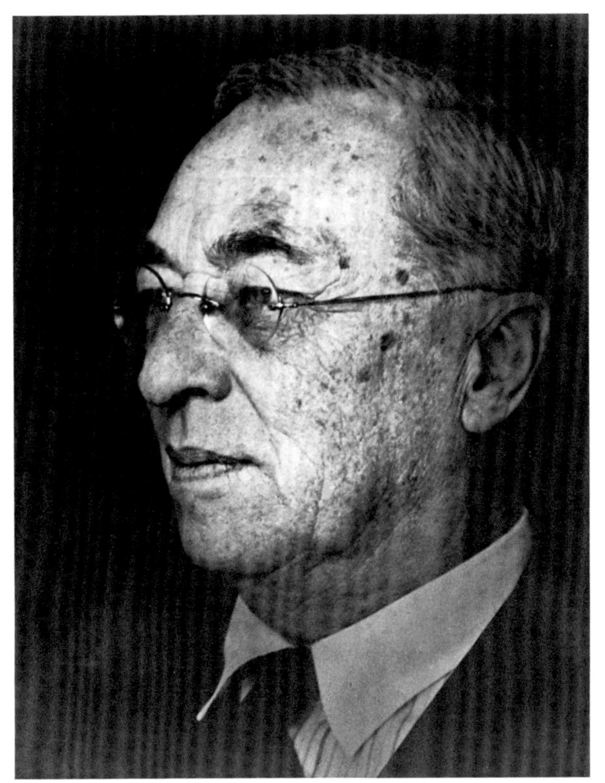

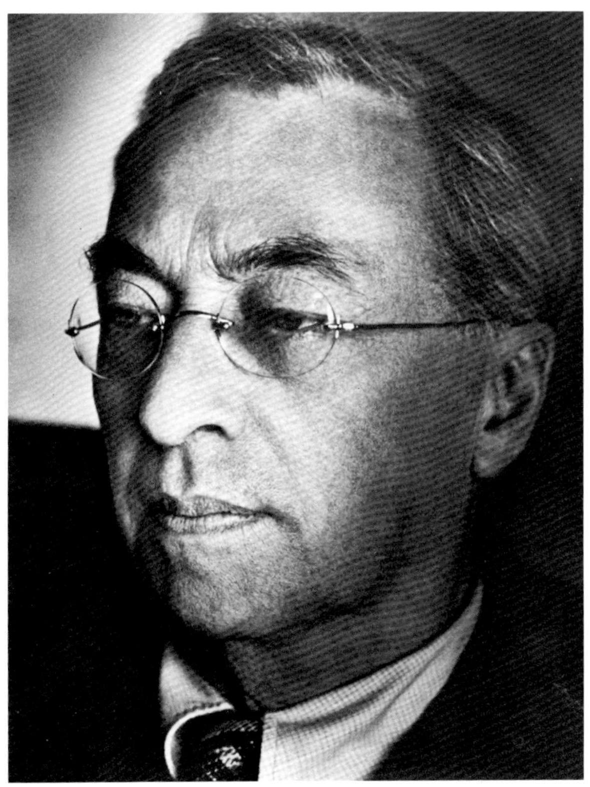

V. KANDINSKY'S PAINTING DURING THE WAR, 1939-1944

BLACK BACKGROUNDS

Joan Miró

103 *Forms on a Black Background (Formes sur fond noir).* 1933
Oil on canvas, 41 1/8 x 29 5/16"
(104.5 x 74.5 cm.)
Collection Mr. and Mrs. Adrien Maeght

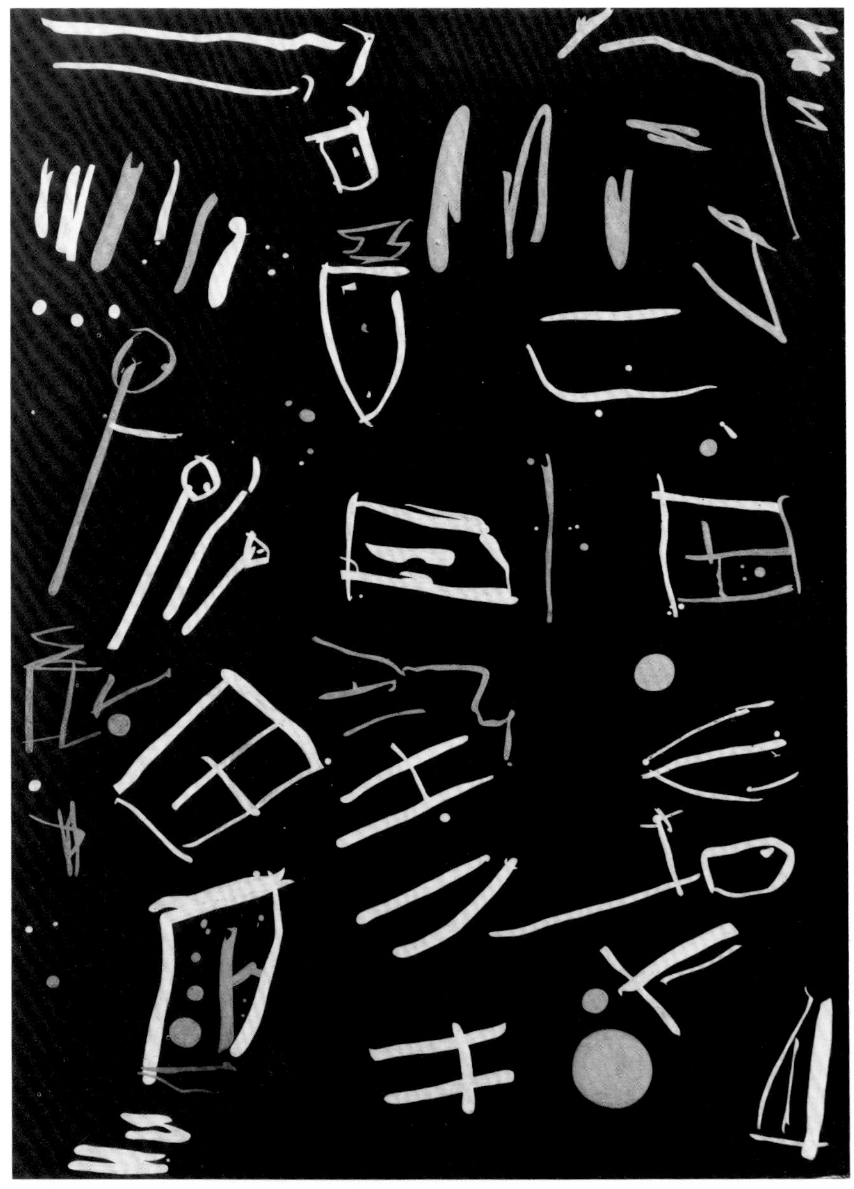

Paul Klee

104 *Untitled (Still Life) (Ohne Titel [Stilleben]).*
1940
Oil on canvas, 39⅞ x 31¾"
(100 x 80.5 cm.)
Private Collection, Switzerland

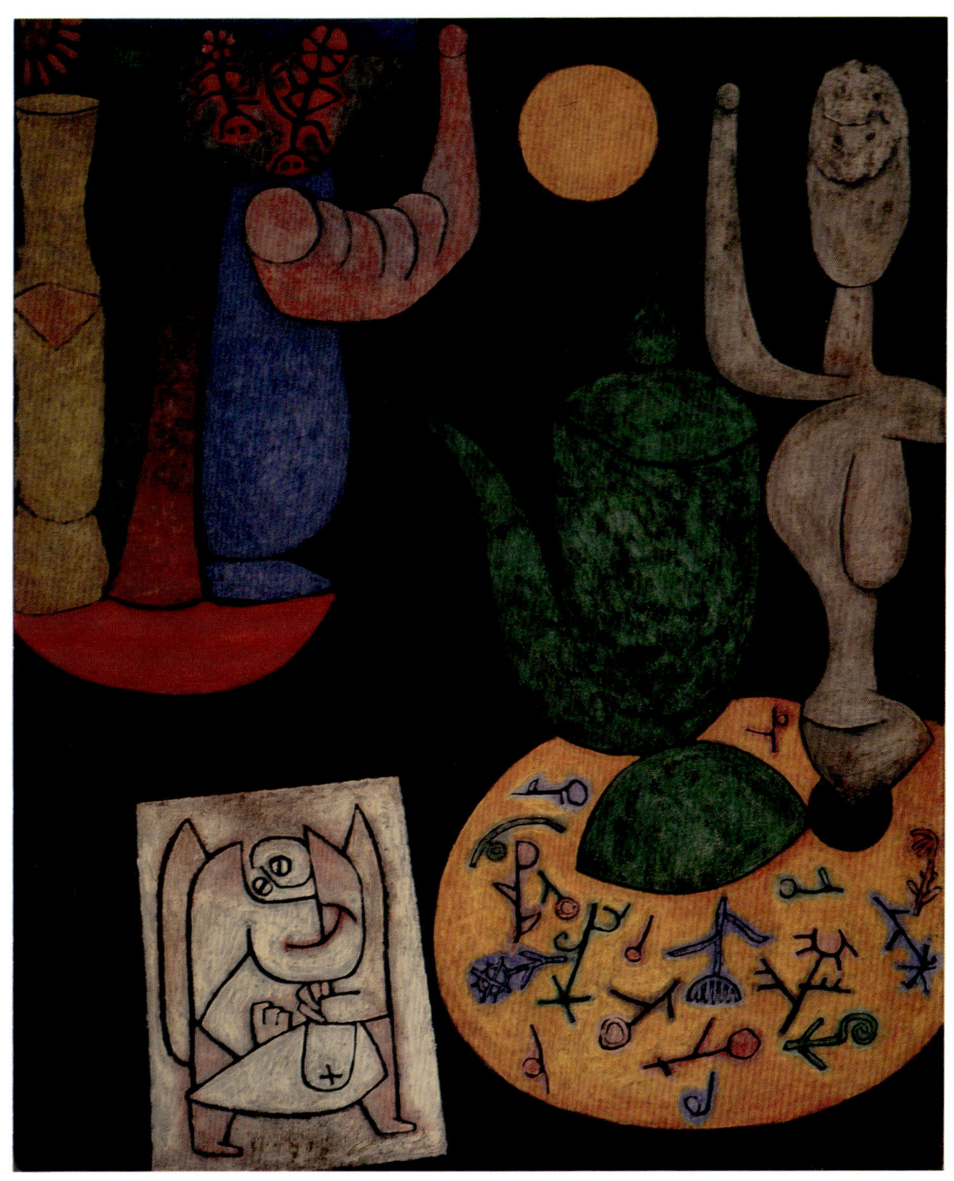

Vasily Kandinsky

105 *Composition X.* December 1938–
January 1939
(HL 655)
Oil on canvas, 51 3/16 x 76 3/4"
(130 x 195 cm.)
Kunstsammlung Nordrhein-Westfalen,
Düsseldorf

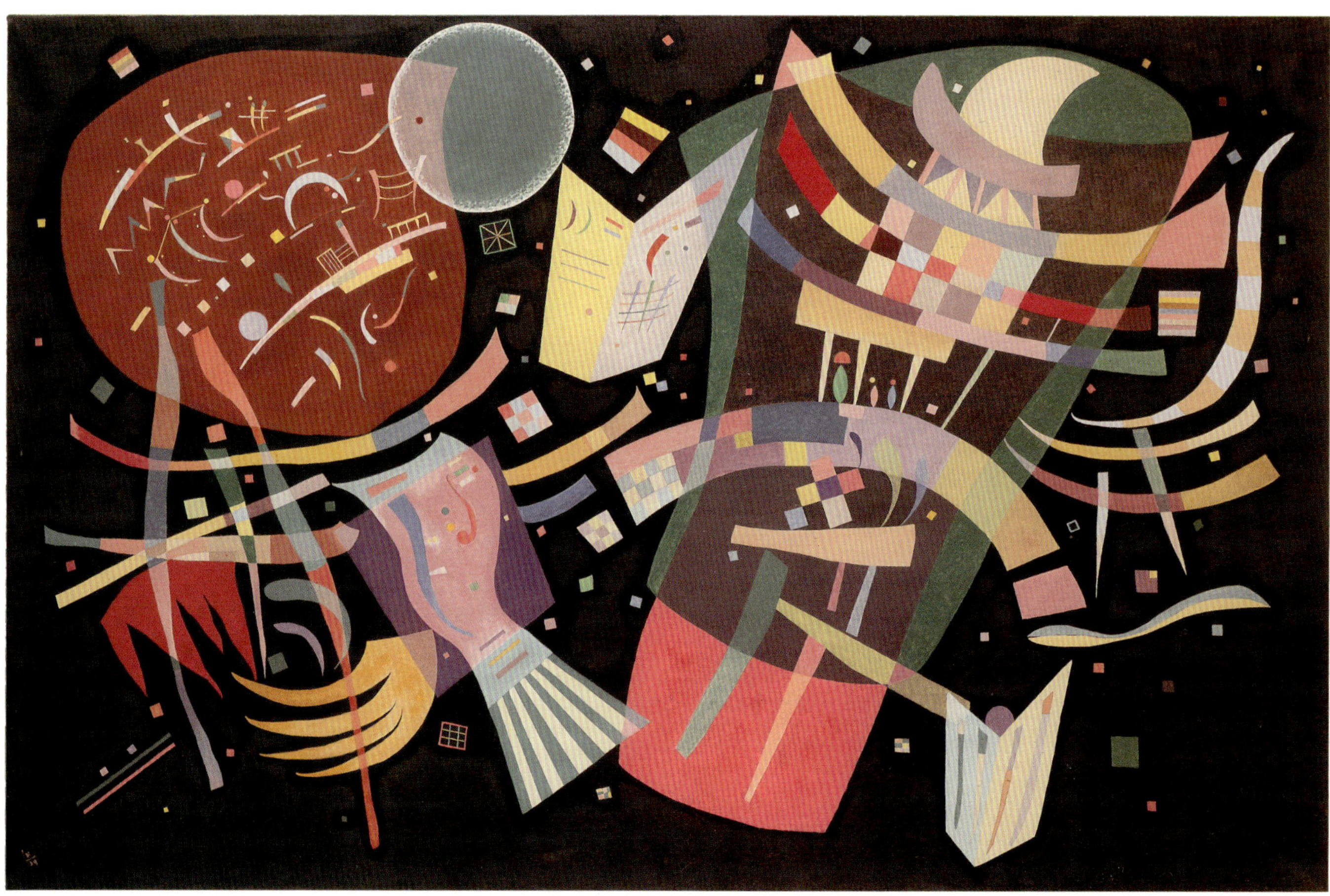

Henri Michaux

106 *Prince of the Night (Le Prince de la nuit).* 1937
Gouache on paper, 12¾ x 9⅝″ (32.3 x 24.5 cm.)
Collection Musée National d'Art Moderne, Centre Georges Pompidou, Paris

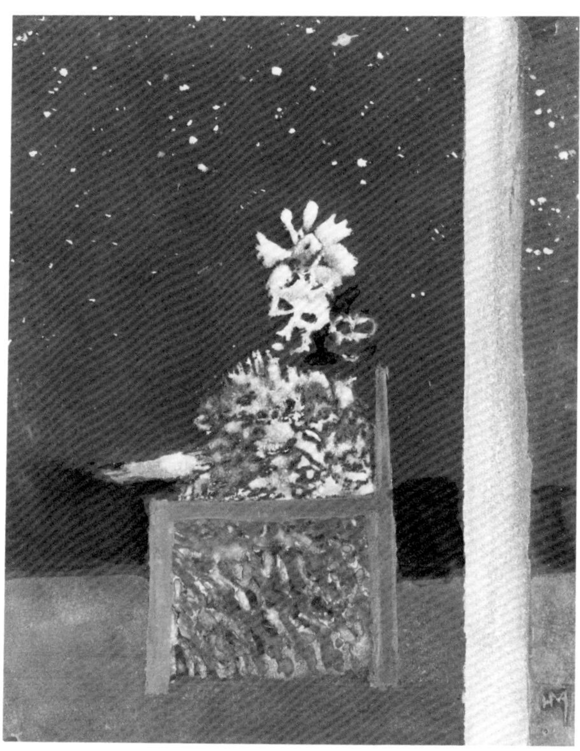

Vasily Kandinsky

107 *Points (Pointes).* May 1939
(HL watercolors 624)
Gouache and watercolor on black paper mounted on paper, 19½ x 13⅝"
(49.5 x 34.5 cm.)
Collection Musée National d'Art Moderne, Centre Georges Pompidou, Paris, Kandinsky Bequest

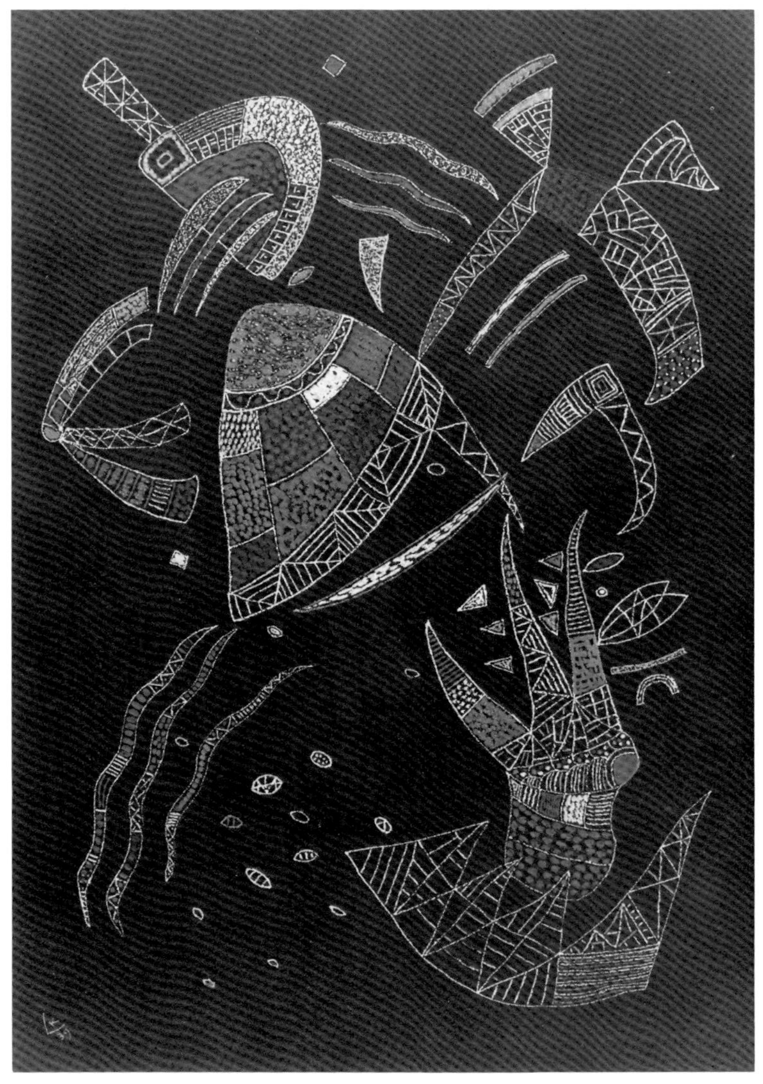

Vasily Kandinsky

108 *Untitled (Sans titre).* 1940
(HL watercolors 639)
Gouache on black paper, 19⅝ x 13¾"
(49.8 x 35 cm.)
Solomon R. Guggenheim Museum, Hilla Rebay Collection

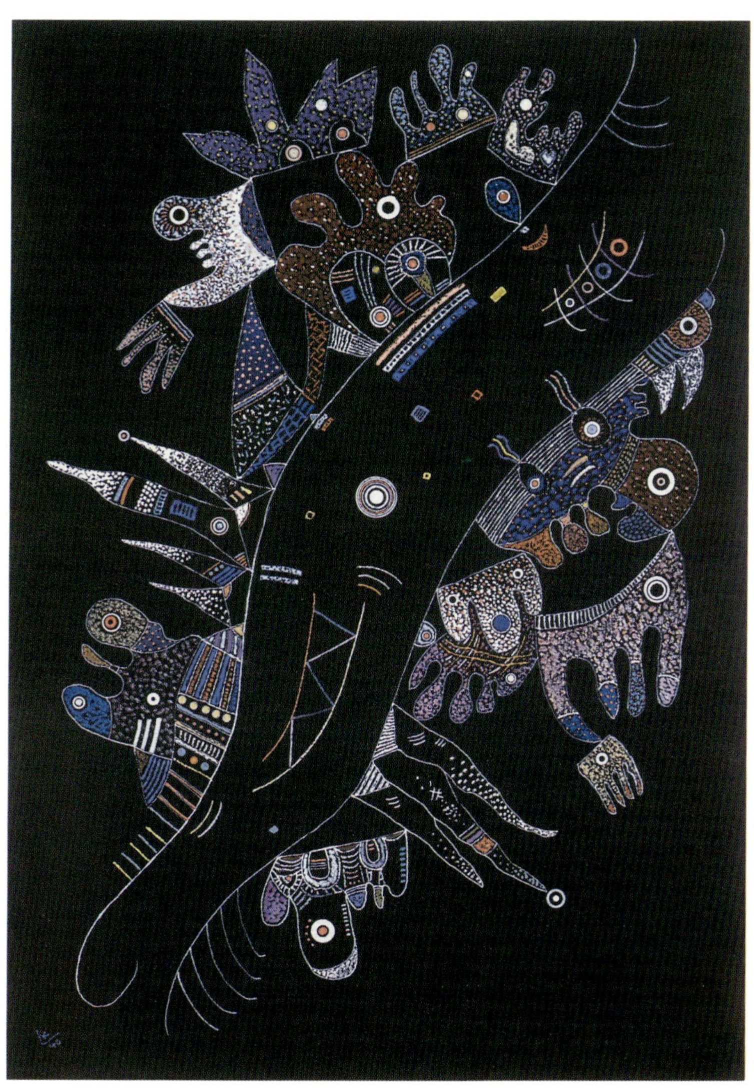

Vasily Kandinsky

109 *Untitled (Sans titre).* 1940
(HL watercolors 689)
Gouache on paper, 19½ x 12$\frac{9}{16}$″
(49.5 x 32 cm.)
Collection Musée National d'Art Moderne,
Centre Georges Pompidou, Paris,
Gift of Mme Nina Kandinsky

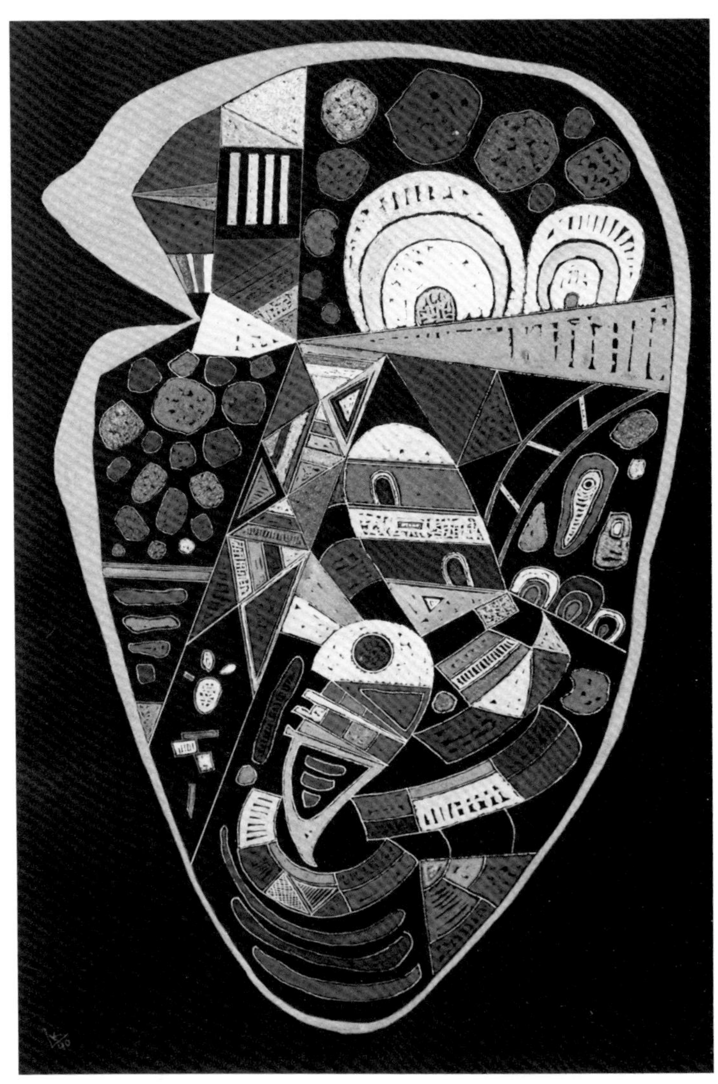

Vasily Kandinsky

110 *Toward Blue (Vers le bleu).*
February 1939
(HL 656)
Oil and enamel on canvas, 25⅝ x 31⅞"
(65 x 81 cm.)
Collection Musée National d'Art Moderne,
Centre Georges Pompidou, Paris,
Kandinsky Bequest

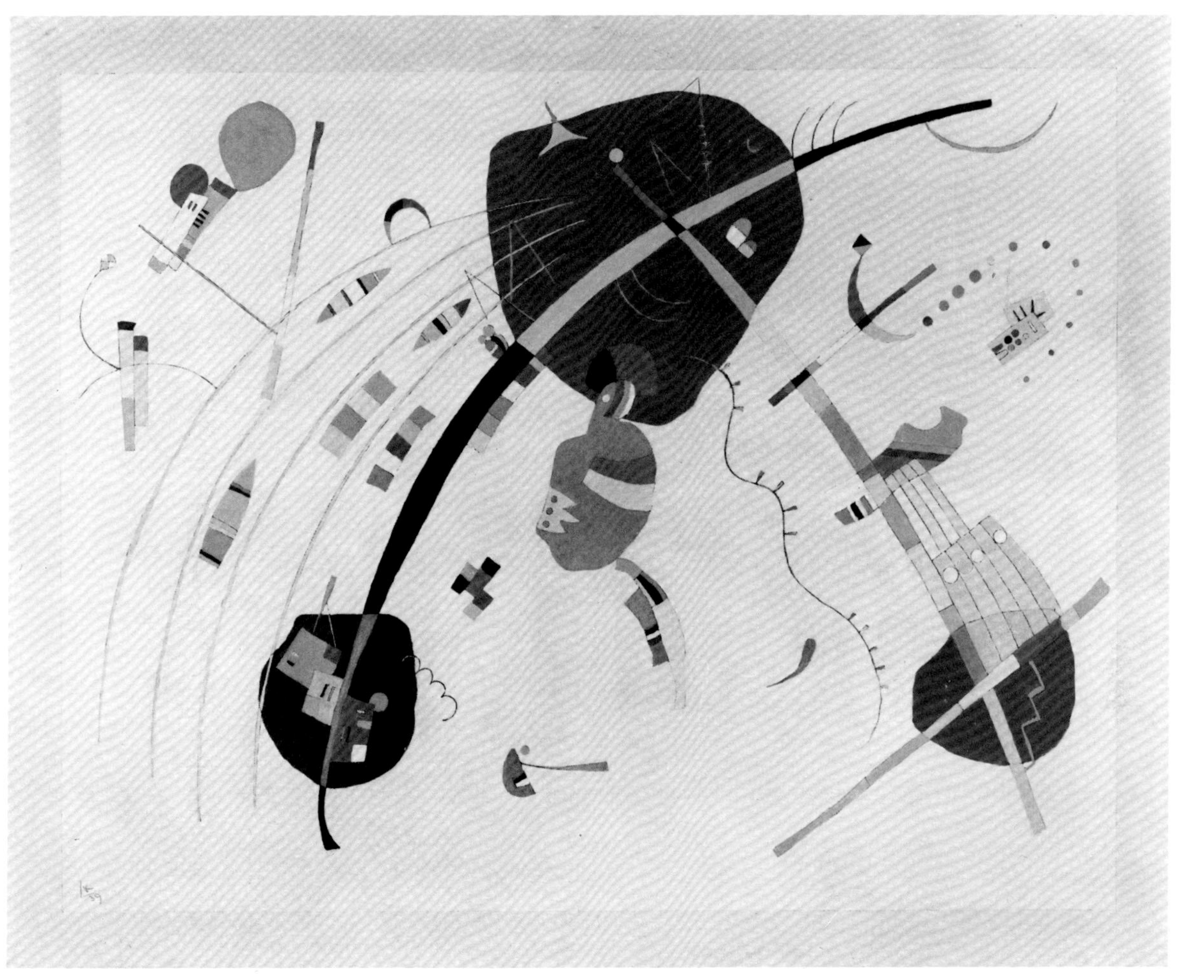

Vasily Kandinsky

111 *Study for "Toward Blue" (Etude pour "Vers le bleu").* 1939

Pencil and grease pencil on paper, 8 1/16 x 11 1/2" (20.4 x 29.3 cm.)

Collection Musée National d'Art Moderne, Centre Georges Pompidou, Paris, Kandinsky Bequest

Vasily Kandinsky

112 *Study for "Toward Blue" (Etude pour "Vers le bleu").* 1939

Watercolor and India ink on cardboard, 10 3/4 x 15 1/4" (27.2 x 38.6 cm.)

Collection Musée National d'Art Moderne, Centre Georges Pompidou, Paris, Kandinsky Bequest

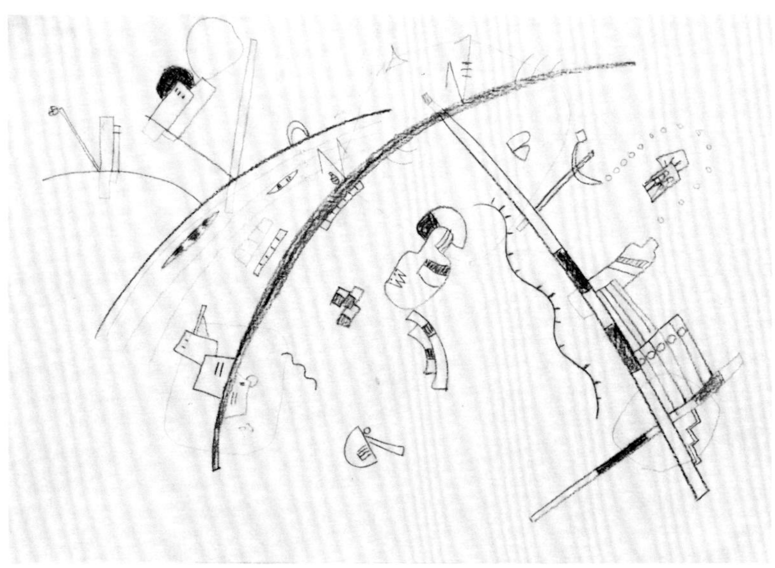

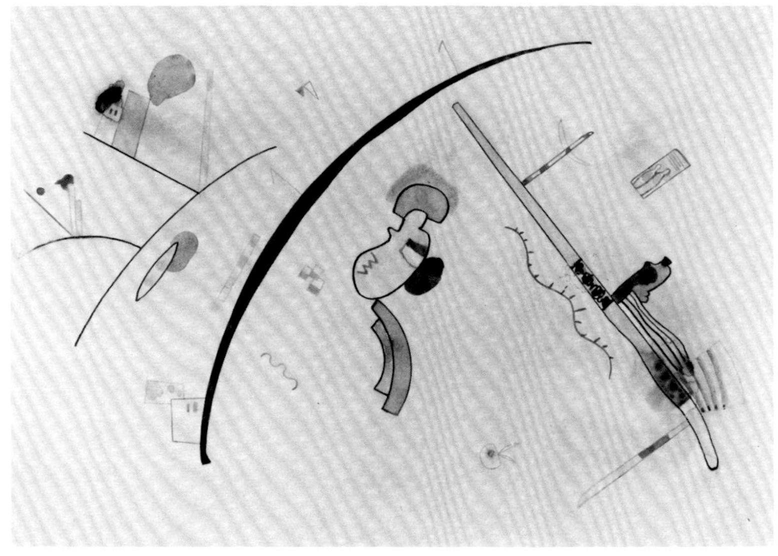

Vasily Kandinsky

113 *Untitled (Sans titre).* 1940

(HL watercolors 656)

Watercolor on white paper mounted on cardboard, 19 3/16 x 12 5/16" (48.7 x 31.2 cm.)

Collection Musée National d'Art Moderne, Centre Georges Pompidou, Paris, Gift of Mme Nina Kandinsky

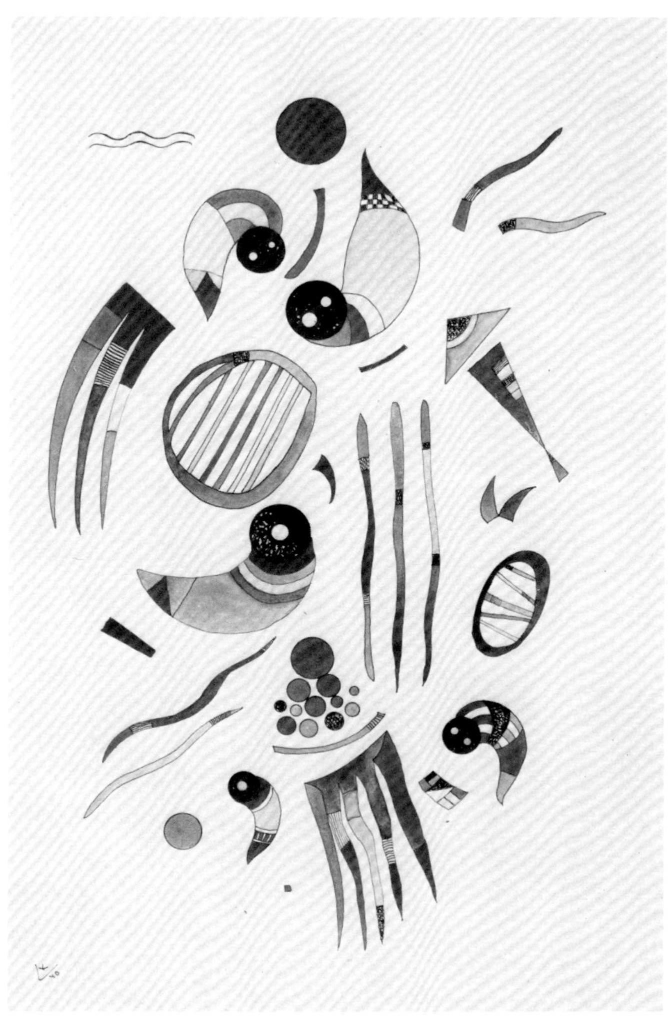

Vasily Kandinsky
114 *Circuit.* June 1939
(HL 663)
Oil on canvas, 36⅝ x 28⅞" (93 x 73 cm.)
Private Collection

Vasily Kandinsky
115 *Study for "Circuit" (Etude pour "Circuit").* 1939
Pencil on paper, 8⅝ x 6¼" (21.9 x 16 cm.)
Collection Musée National d'Art Moderne, Centre Georges Pompidou, Paris, Kandinsky Bequest

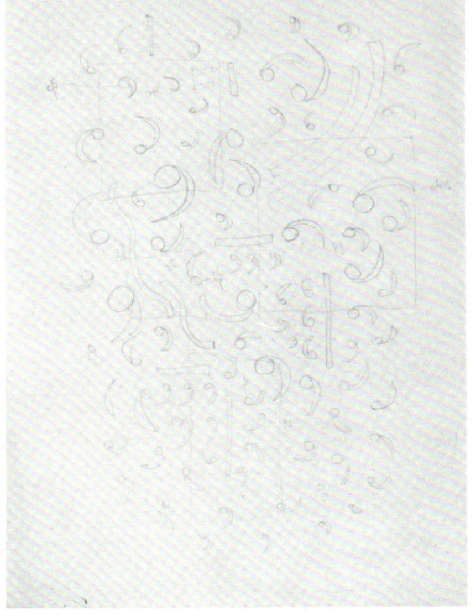

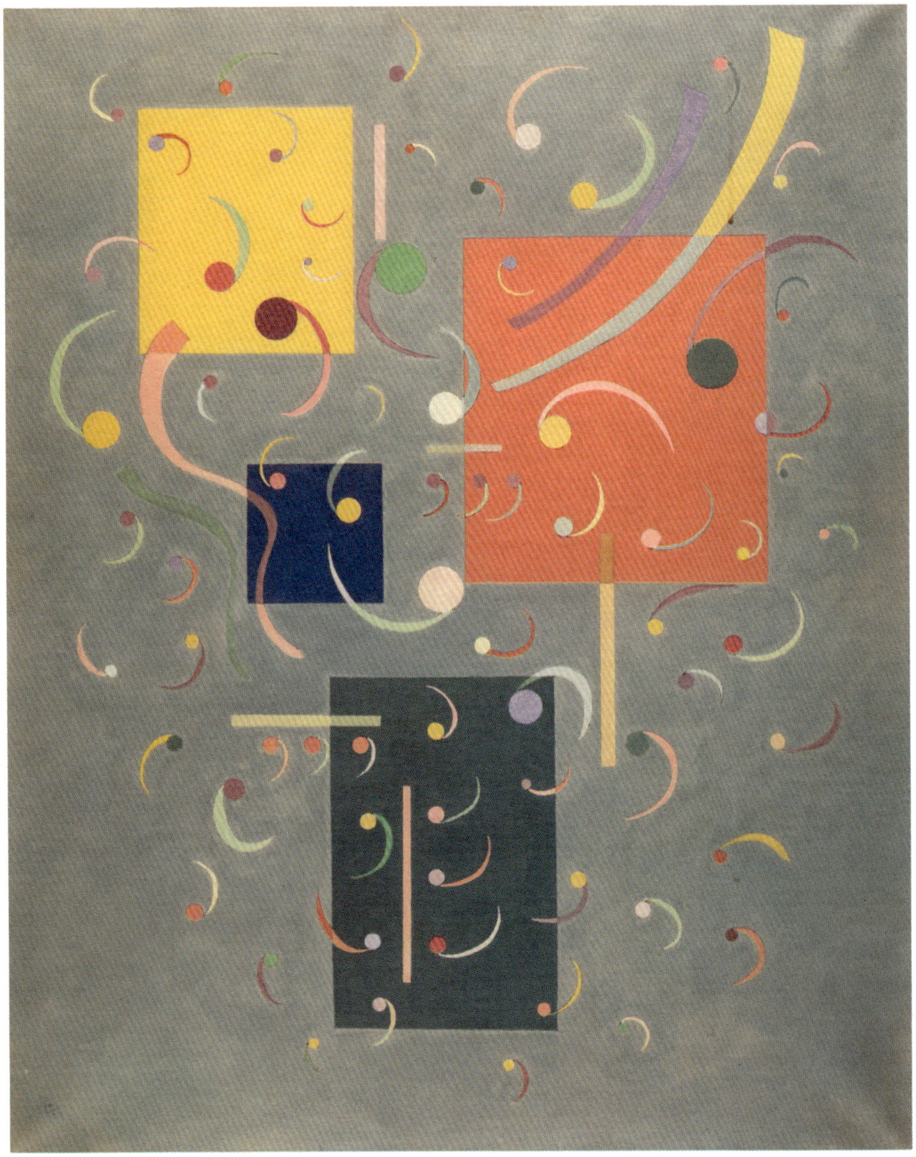

Vasily Kandinsky

116 *Sky Blue (Bleu de ciel).* March 1940
(HL 673)
Oil on canvas, 39⅜ x 28¾" (100 x 73 cm.)
Collection Musée National d'Art Moderne, Centre Georges Pompidou, Paris, Gift of Mme Nina Kandinsky

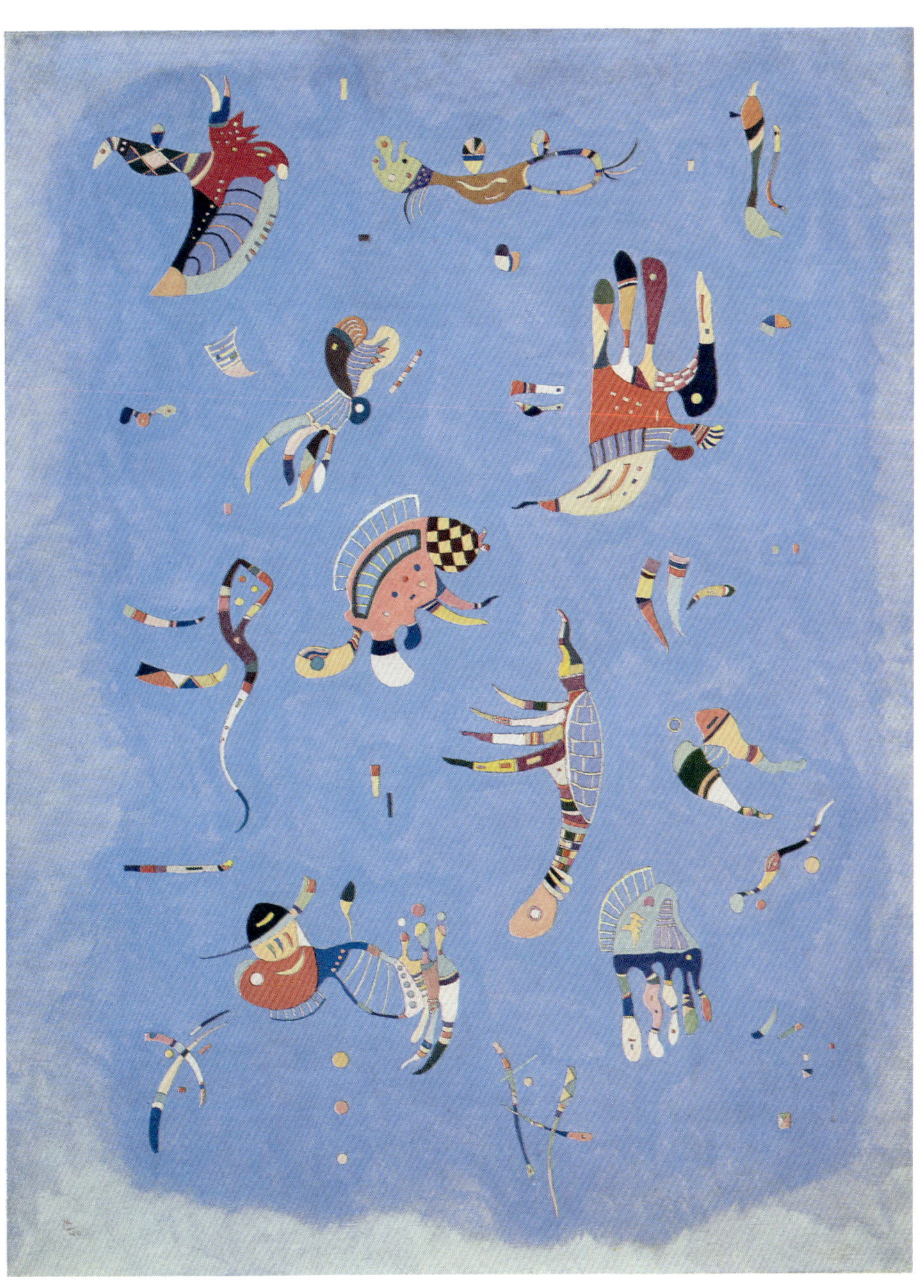

Vasily Kandinsky

117 *The Whole (L'Ensemble).* January–February 1940
(HL 671)
Oil on canvas, 31⅞ x 45⅝" (81 x 116 cm.)
Collection Lawrence D. Saidenberg, New York

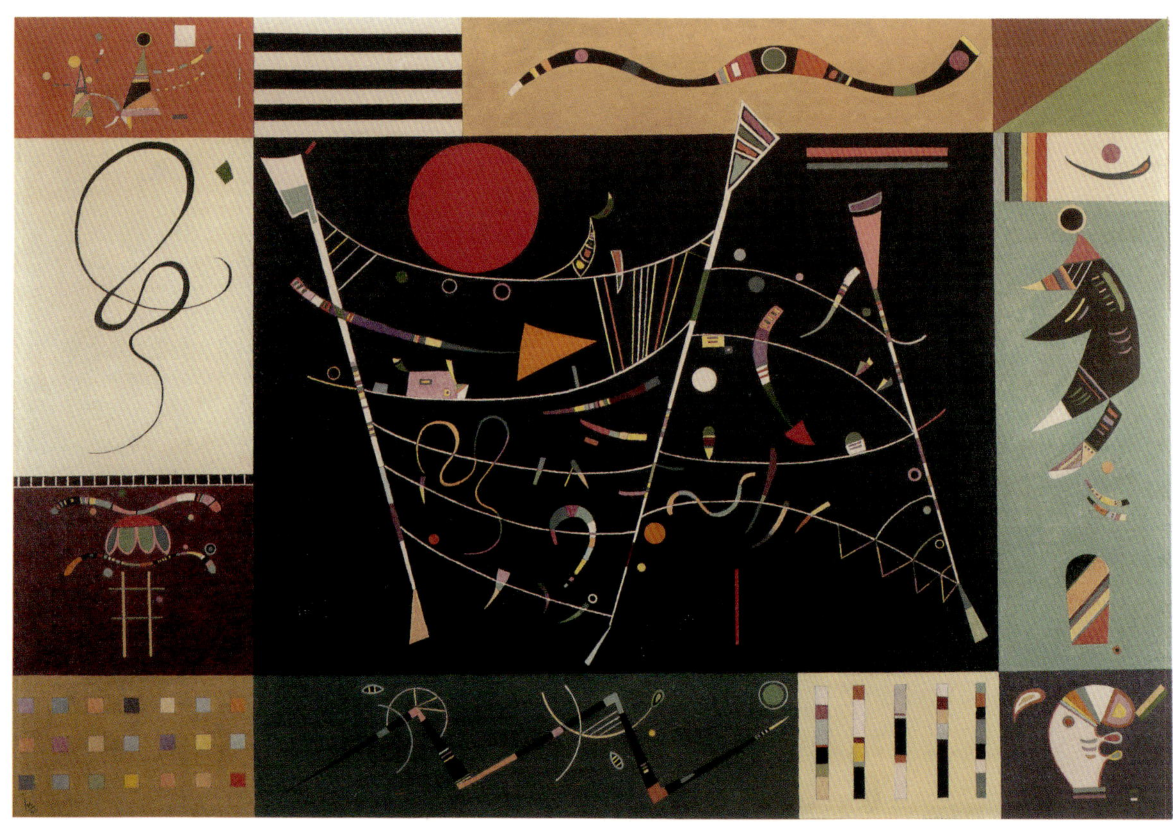

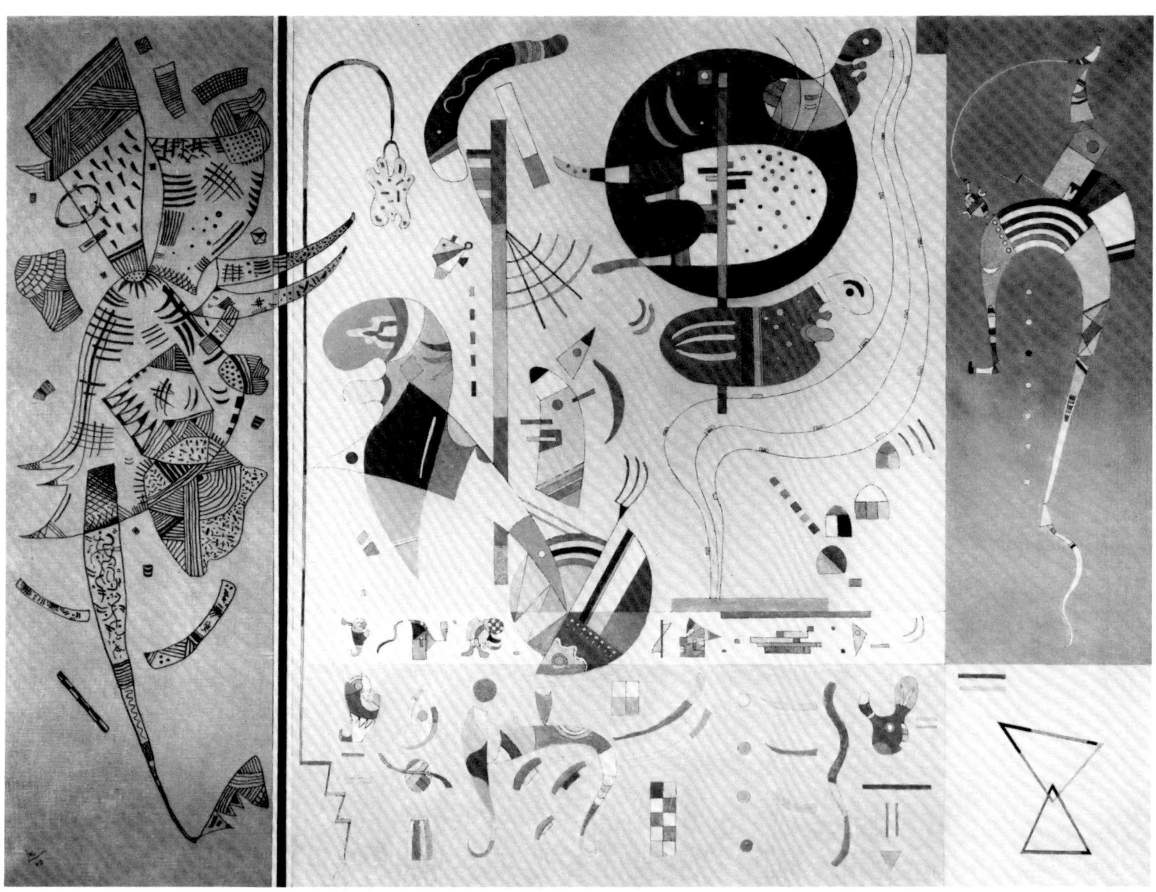

Vasily Kandinsky

118 *Various Parts (Parties diverses).* February 1940
(HL 672)
Oil on canvas, 35 x 45 11/16" (89 x 116 cm.)
Städtische Galerie im Lenbachhaus, Munich, Extended loan of the Gabriele Münter- und Johannes Eichner-Stiftung, Munich

Vasily Kandinsky

119 *Study for "Various Parts" (Etude pour "Parties diverses").* 1940
India ink on paper, 6 7/8 x 9 1/16"
(17.8 x 23 cm.)
Collection Musée National d'Art Moderne, Centre Georges Pompidou, Paris, Kandinsky Bequest

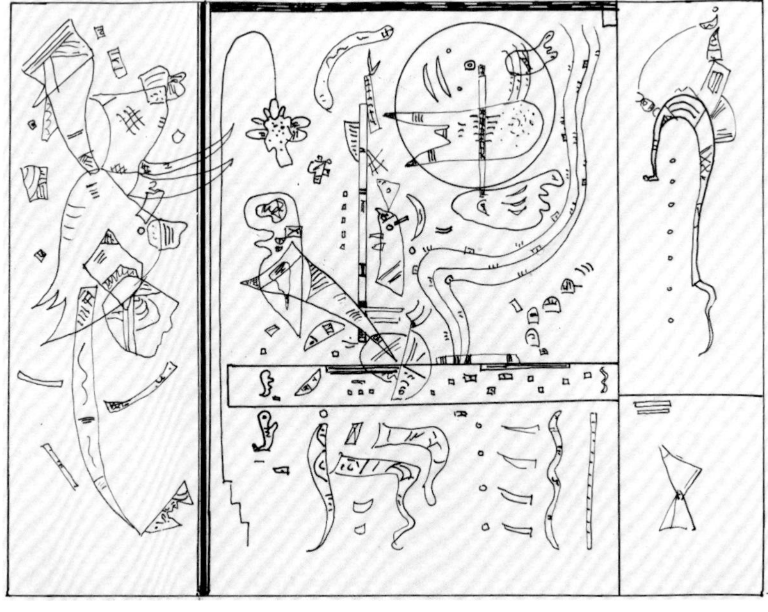

Vasily Kandinsky

120 *Around the Circle (Autour du cercle).* May–August 1940

(HL 677)

Oil on enamel on canvas, 38⅛ x 57½″ (96.8 x 146 cm.)

Collection Solomon R. Guggenheim Museum, New York

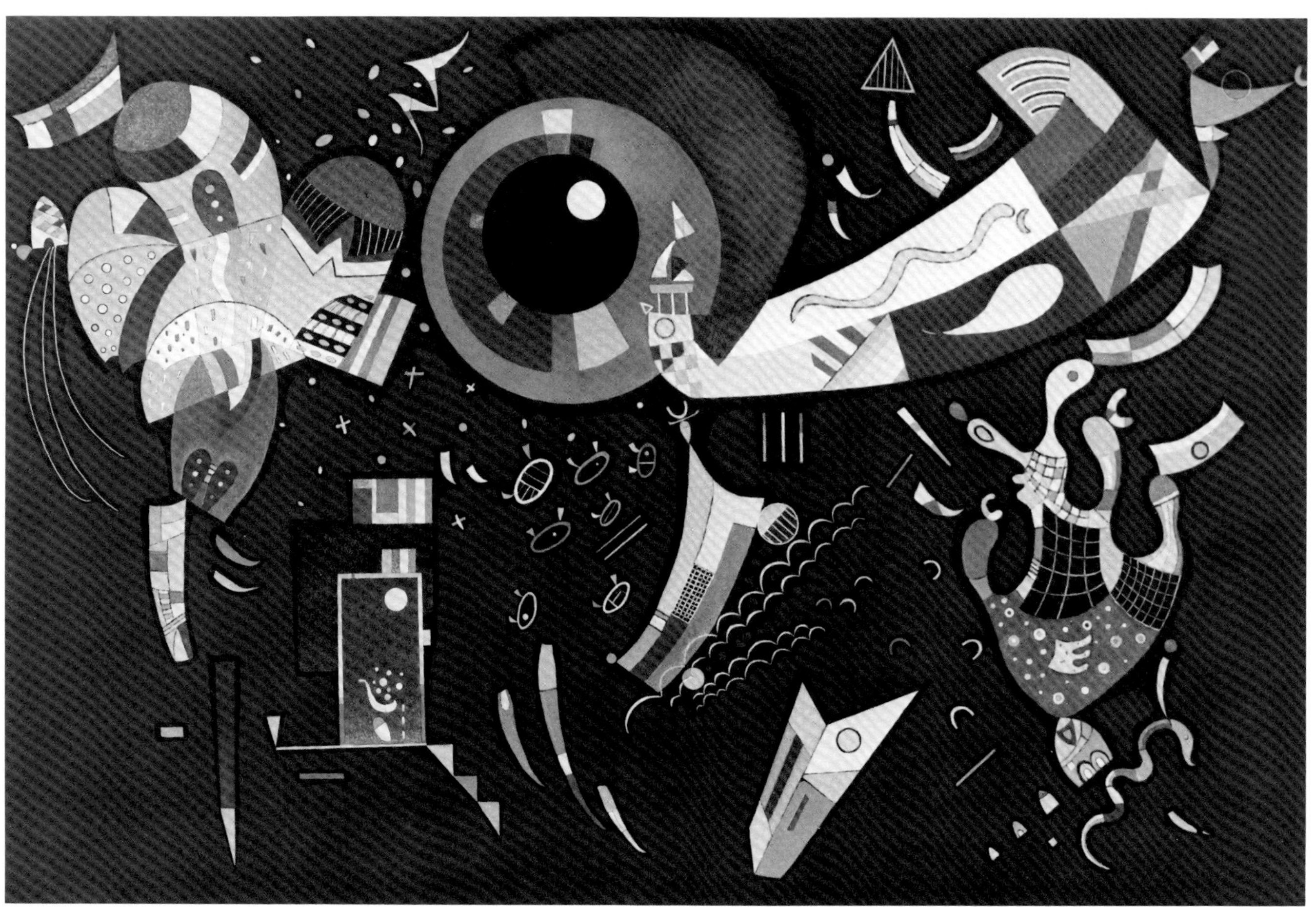

Vasily Kandinsky

121 *Study for "Around the Circle" (Etude pour "Autour du cercle").* ca. 1940

Pencil on paper, 6⁵⁄₁₆ x 8¹¹⁄₁₆″ (16.1 x 22 cm.)

Collection Musée National d'Art Moderne, Centre Georges Pompidou, Paris, Kandinsky Bequest

Vasily Kandinsky

122 *Study for "Around the Circle" (Etude pour "Autour du cercle").* 1940

India ink on paper, 9⅜ x 12⅜″ (23.8 x 31.4 cm.)

Collection Musée National d'Art Moderne, Centre Georges Pompidou, Paris, Kandinsky Bequest

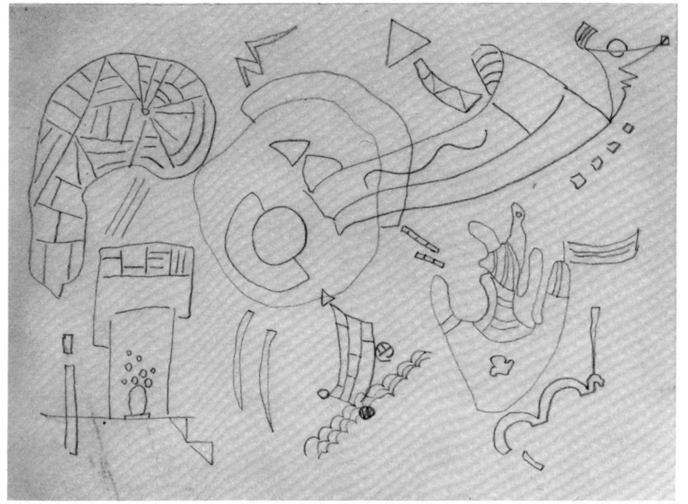

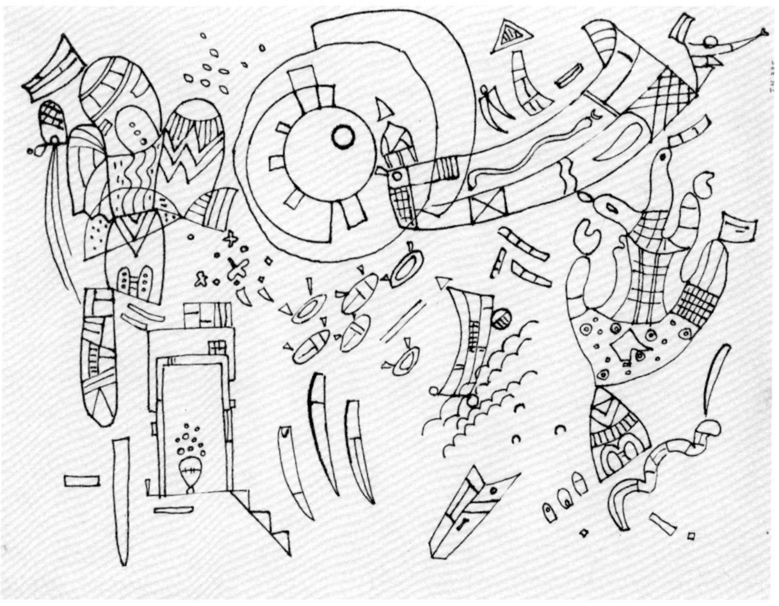

Vasily Kandinsky

123 *Various Actions (Actions variées).*
August–September 1941
(HL 683)
Oil and enamel on canvas, 35⅛ x 45¾"
(89.2 x 116.1 cm.)
Collection Solomon R. Guggenheim Museum, New York

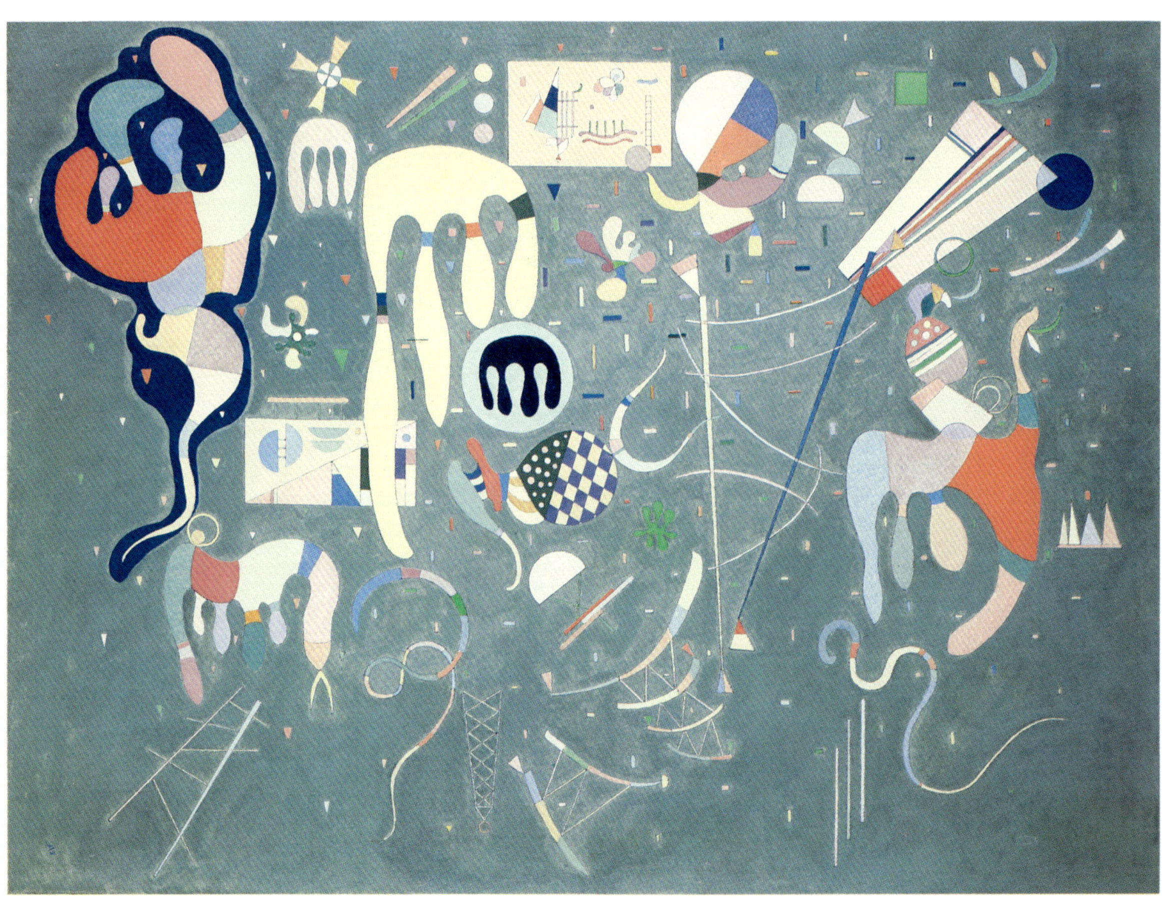

Vasily Kandinsky

124 *Study for "Various Actions" (Etude pour "Actions variées").* 1940–41

Pencil on paper, 8 3/16 x 10 1/16" (20.8 x 25.5 cm.)

Collection Musée National d'Art Moderne, Centre Georges Pompidou, Paris, Kandinsky Bequest

Vasily Kandinsky

125 *Study for "Various Actions" (Etude pour "Actions variées").* 1940–41

Pencil on paper, 8 1/4 x 10 5/8" (20.9 x 26.9 cm.)

Collection Musée National d'Art Moderne, Centre Georges Pompidou, Paris, Kandinsky Bequest

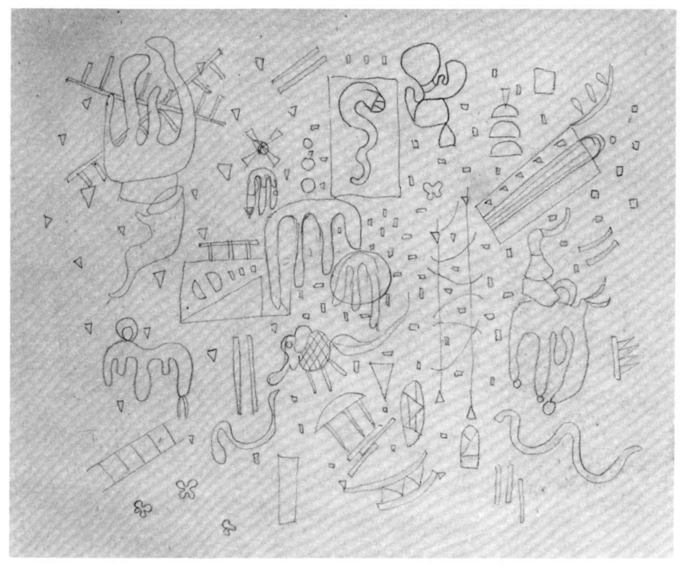

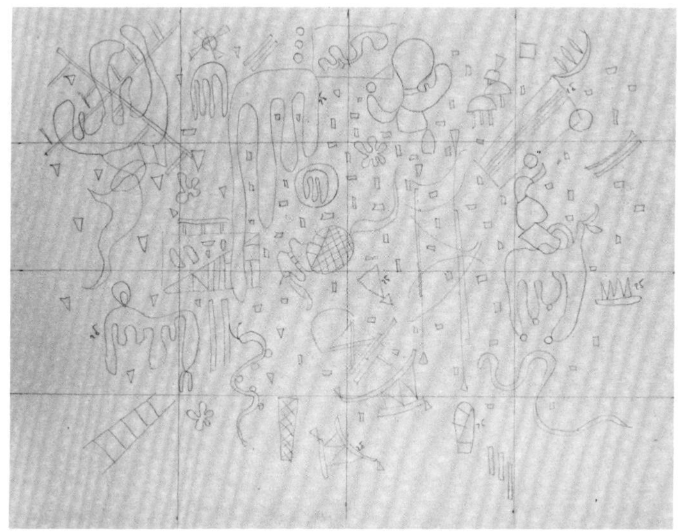

Vasily Kandinsky

126 *Balancing (Balancement).* January 1942
(HL 686)
Oil on canvas, $35\frac{1}{16} \times 46\frac{1}{16}''$
(89 x 117 cm.)
Collection Mr. and Mrs. Adrien Maeght

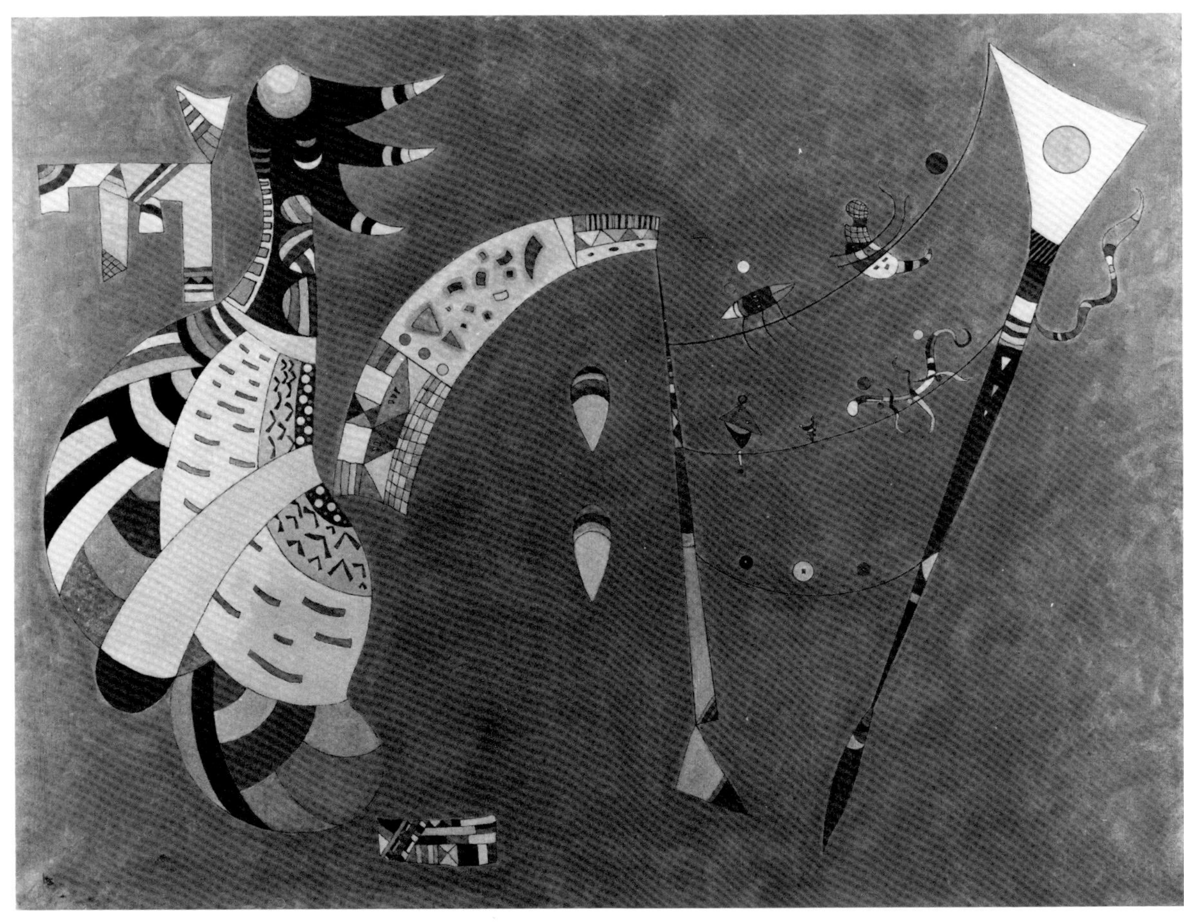

Vasily Kandinsky

127 *Reciprocal Accord (Accord réciproque).*
January–February 1942
(HL 687)
Oil and enamel on canvas, 44⅞ x 57½″
(114 x 146 cm.)
Collection Musée National d'Art Moderne,
Centre Georges Pompidou, Paris,
Gift of Mme Nina Kandinsky

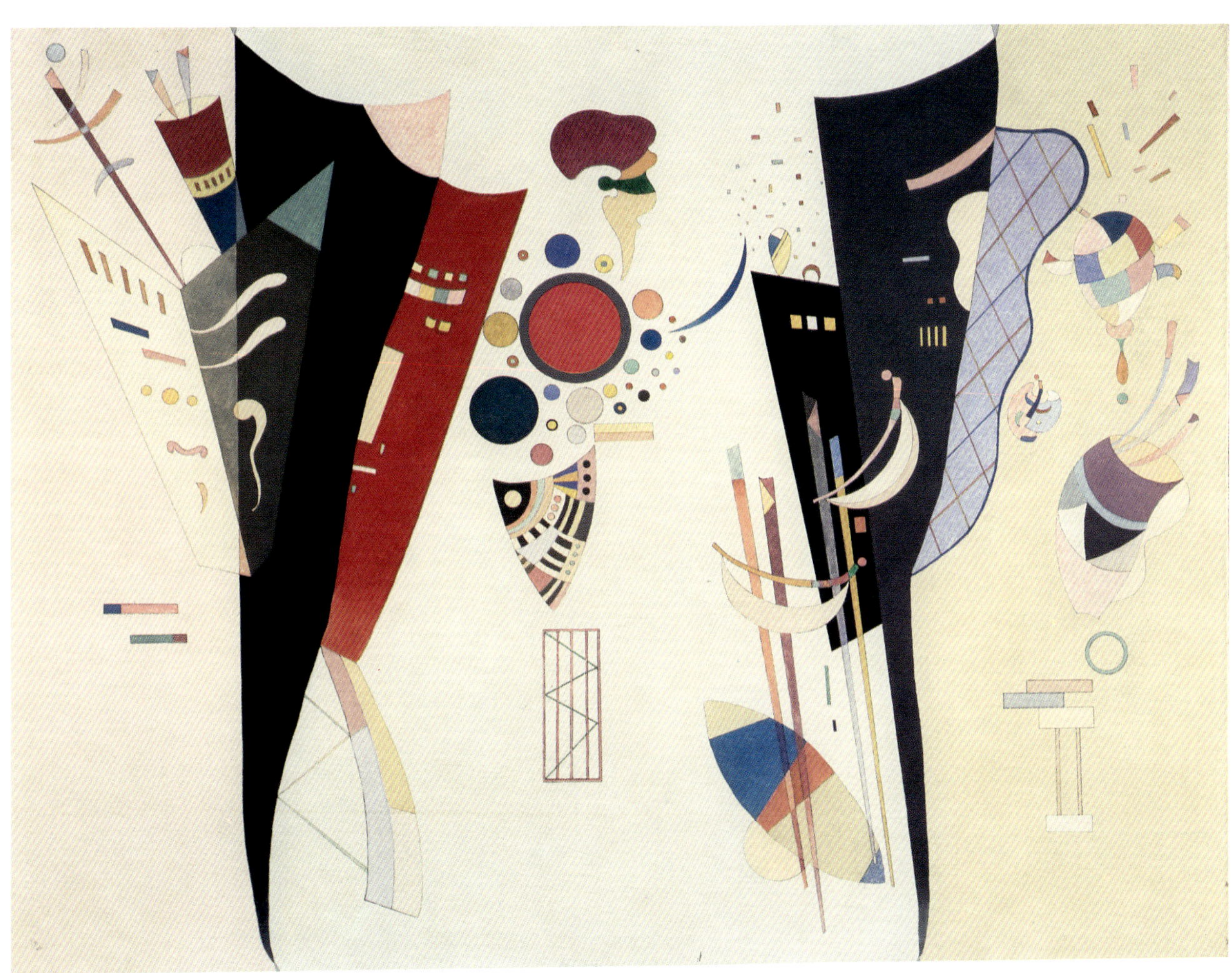

Vasily Kandinsky

128 *Study for "Reciprocal Accord" (Etude pour "Accord réciproque").* 1942

India ink on paper, 8 3/16 x 10 1/4″ (20.8 x 26.1 cm.)

Collection Musée National d'Art Moderne, Centre Georges Pompidou, Paris, Kandinsky Bequest

Vasily Kandinsky

129 *Study for "Reciprocal Accord" (Etude pour "Accord réciproque").* 1942

India ink on paper, 8 3/16 x 10 5/8″ (20.8 x 27 cm.)

Collection Musée National d'Art Moderne, Centre Georges Pompidou, Paris, Kandinsky Bequest

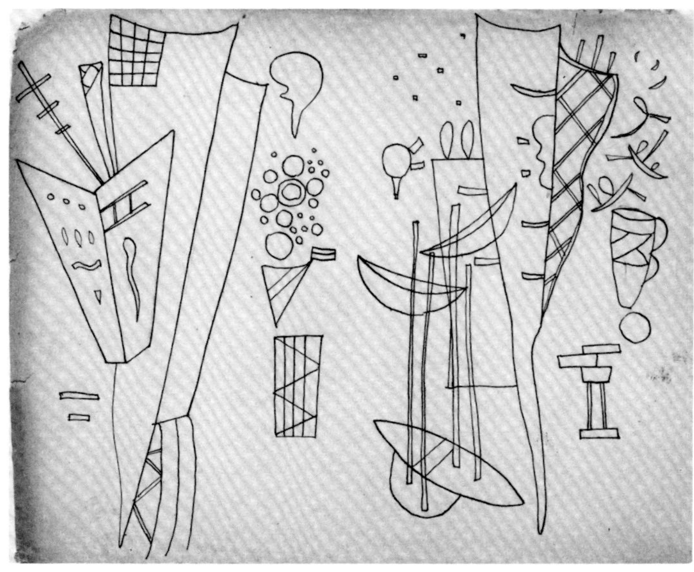

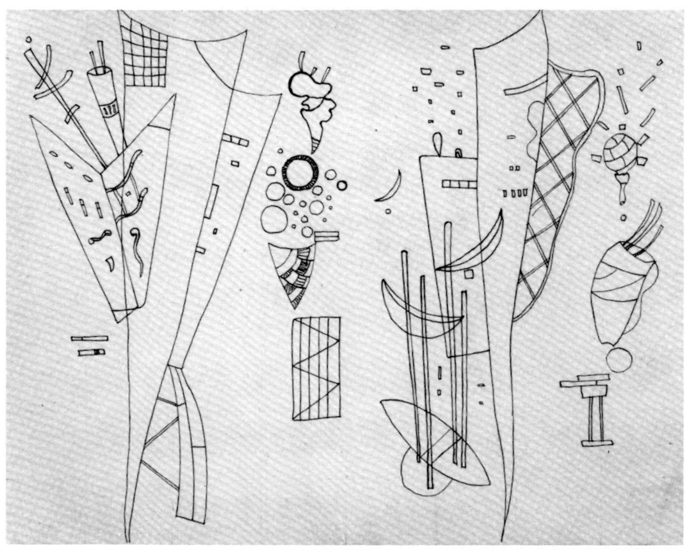

Vasily Kandinsky

130 *Delicate Tensions (Tensions délicates).*
June–July 1942
(HL 690)
Oil on canvas, 31⅞ x 39⅜″
(81 x 100 cm.)
Collection Mr. and Mrs. Adrien Maeght

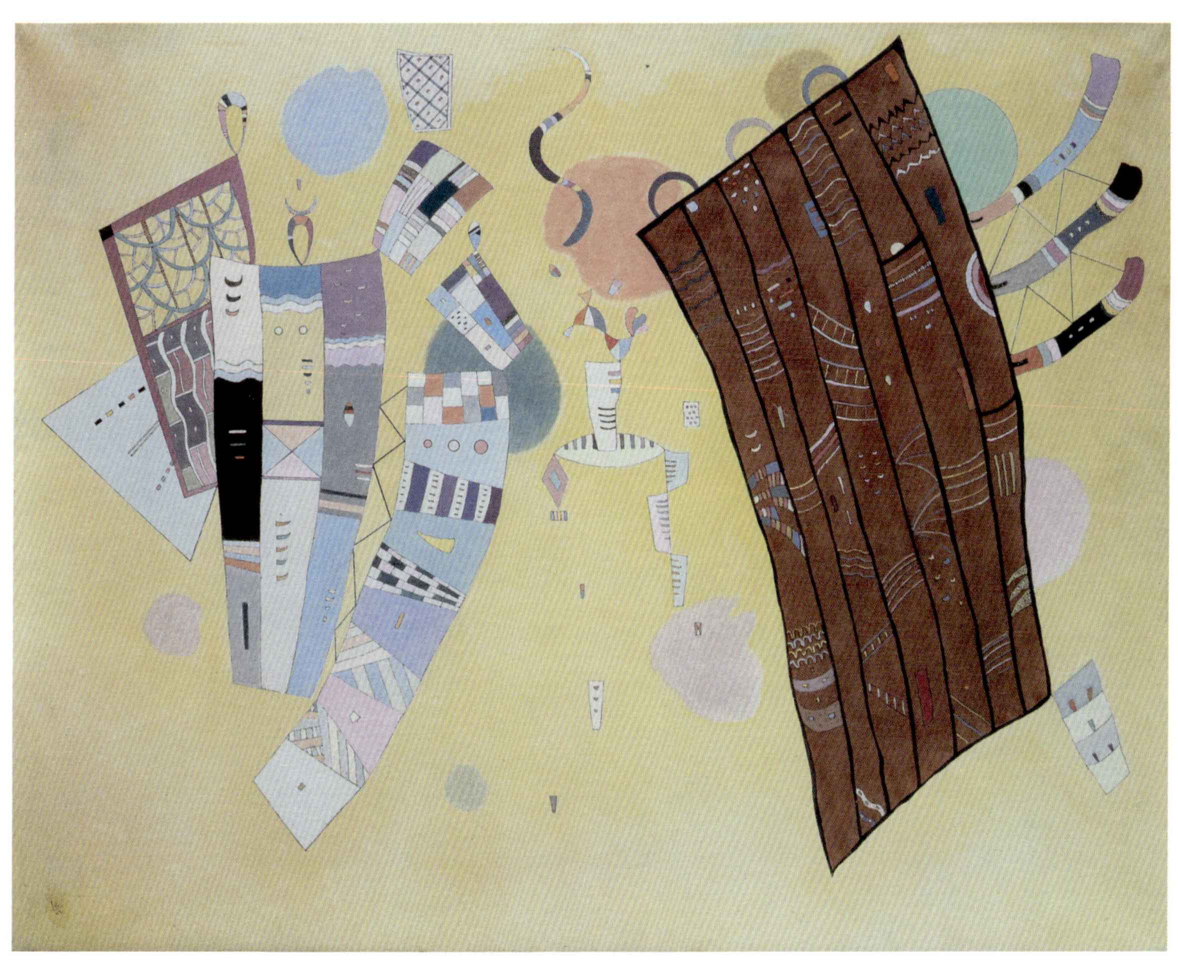

Joan Miró

131 *Awakening at Dawn (Le Réveil au petit jour).* January 27, 1941
Gouache on paper, 18 x 15"
(45.7 x 38.1 cm.)
The Colin Collection, New York

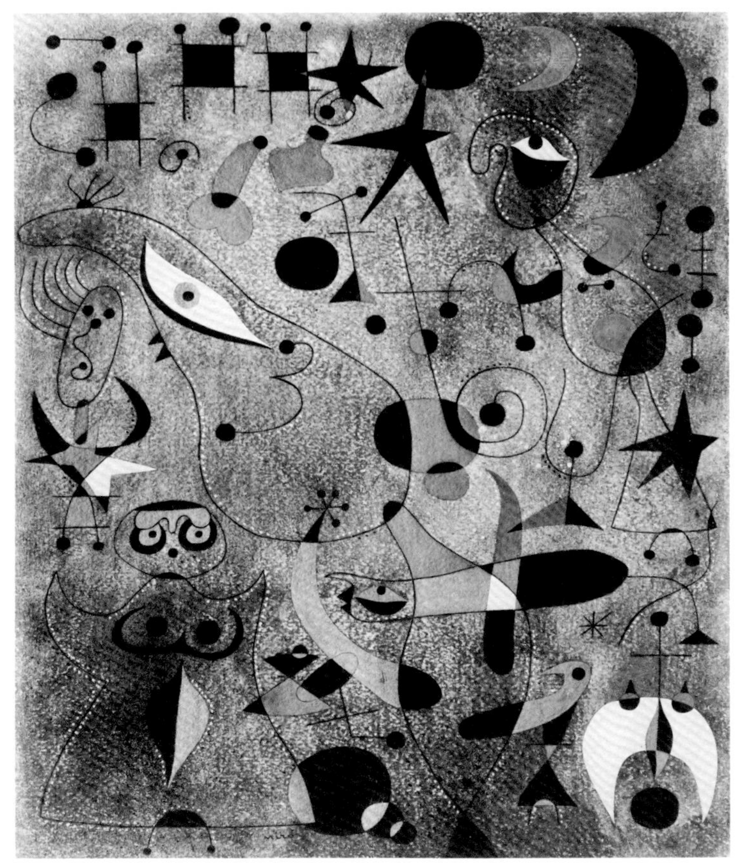

Hans Arp

132 *Crumpled Paper (Runic Signs) (Papier froissé [Signes runiques]).* 1941–42
Ink on paper, 24¾ x 18⅞" (63 x 48 cm.)
Collection Alberto and Susi Magnelli

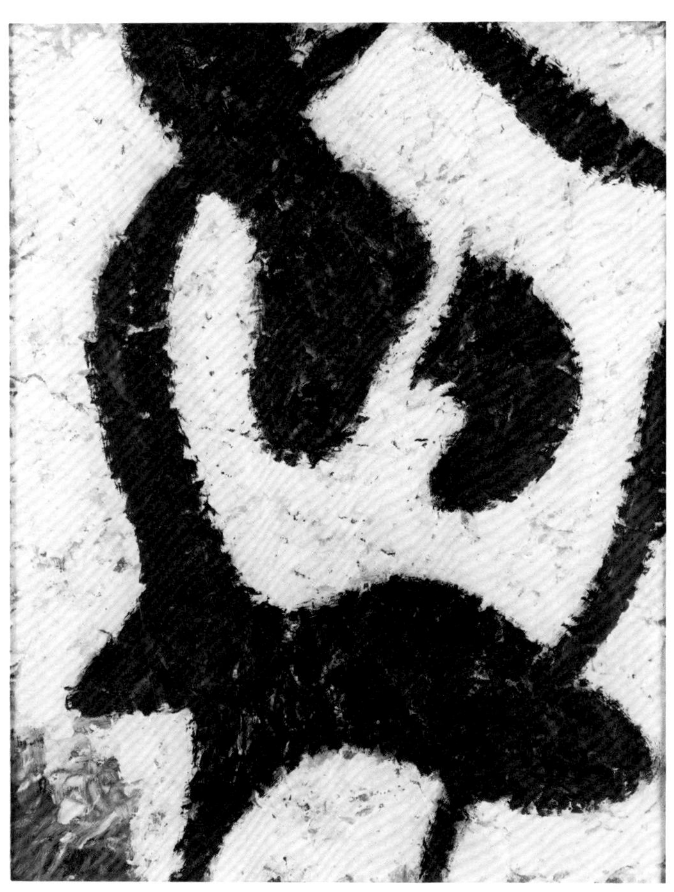

Hans Reichel

133 a-l *Sketchbook from Gurs (Cahier de Gurs).* 1941–42

Notebook of 12 pages with 24 watercolors on paper, 16⅛ x 11$^{13}/_{16}$″ (41 x 30 cm.)

Collection Madame Schimek-Reichel, Paris

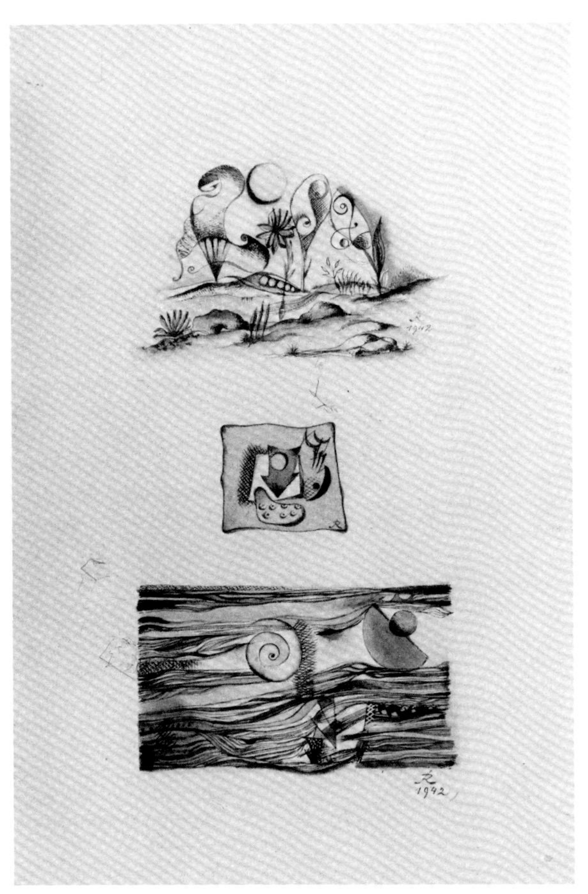

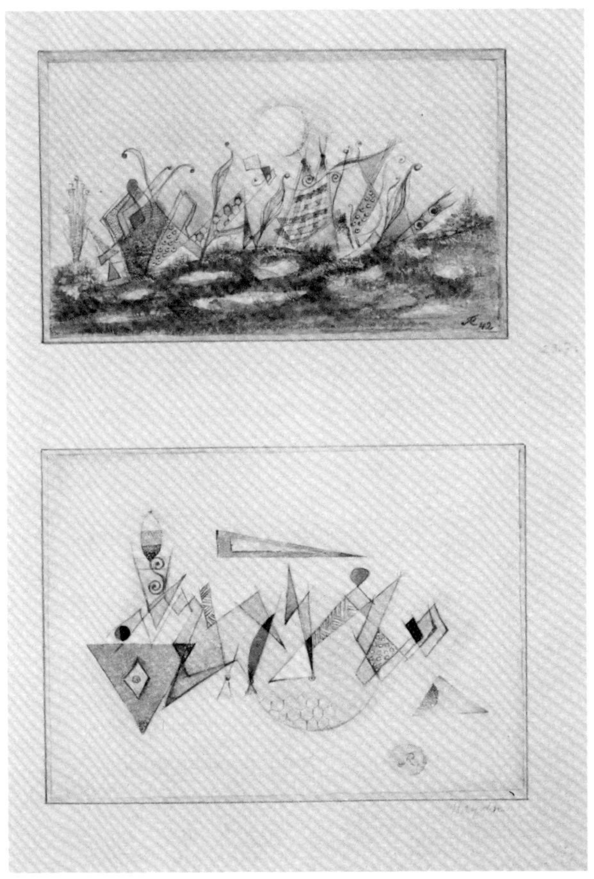

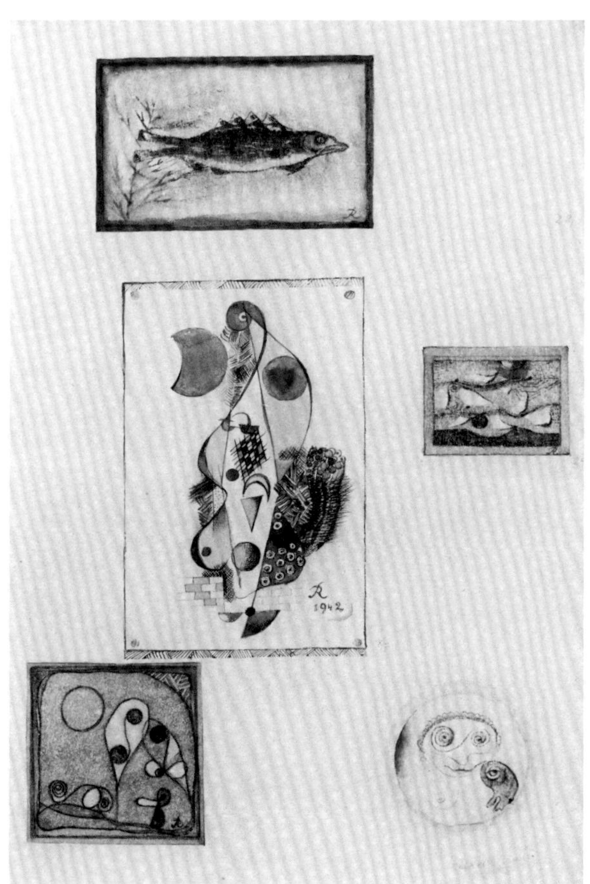

Alberto Magnelli

134 *Untitled (Sans titre).* 1942
Gouache on paper, 10⅝ x 8¼″
(27 x 21 cm.)
Collection Musée National d'Art Moderne,
Centre Georges Pompidou, Paris,
Kandinsky Bequest

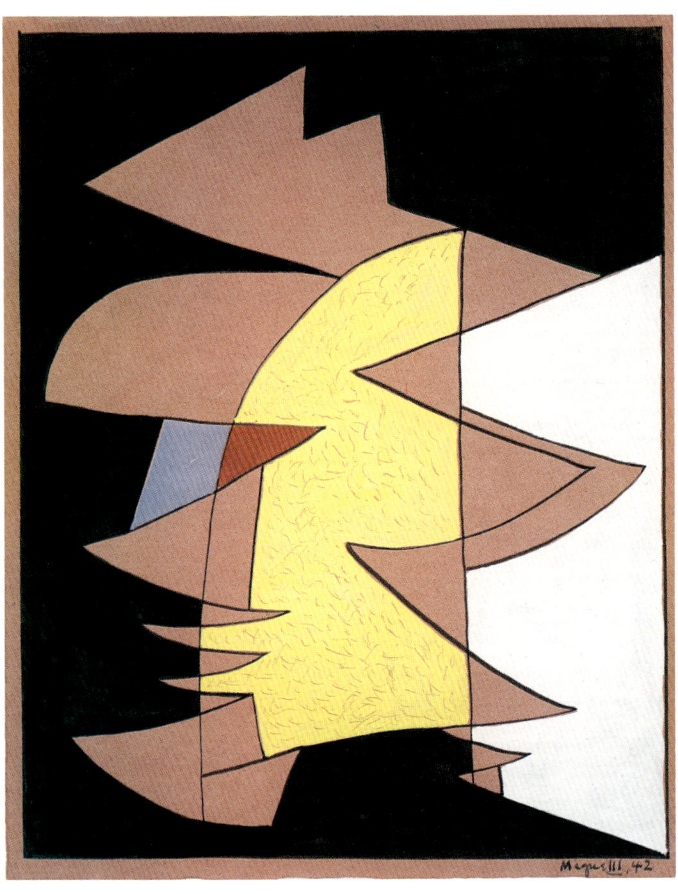

Alberto Magnelli

135 *Student's Slate (Ardoise d'écolier).* 1937

Gouache on slate, 5⅞ x 9¹⁄₁₆″ (14.9 x 23 cm.)

Collection Musée National d'Art Moderne, Centre Georges Pompidou, Paris, Kandinsky Bequest

Vasily Kandinsky

136 *Sketch for a Textile (Esquisse pour un tissu).* 1943

Gouache on paper, 13½ x 13″ (34.4 x 33 cm.)

Lent by Galerie Beyeler, Basel

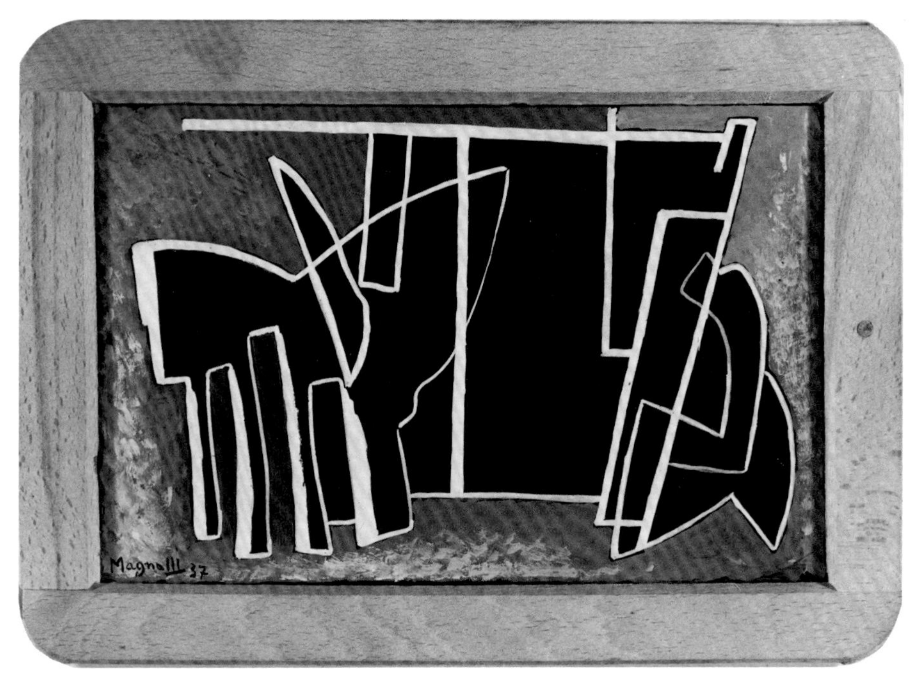

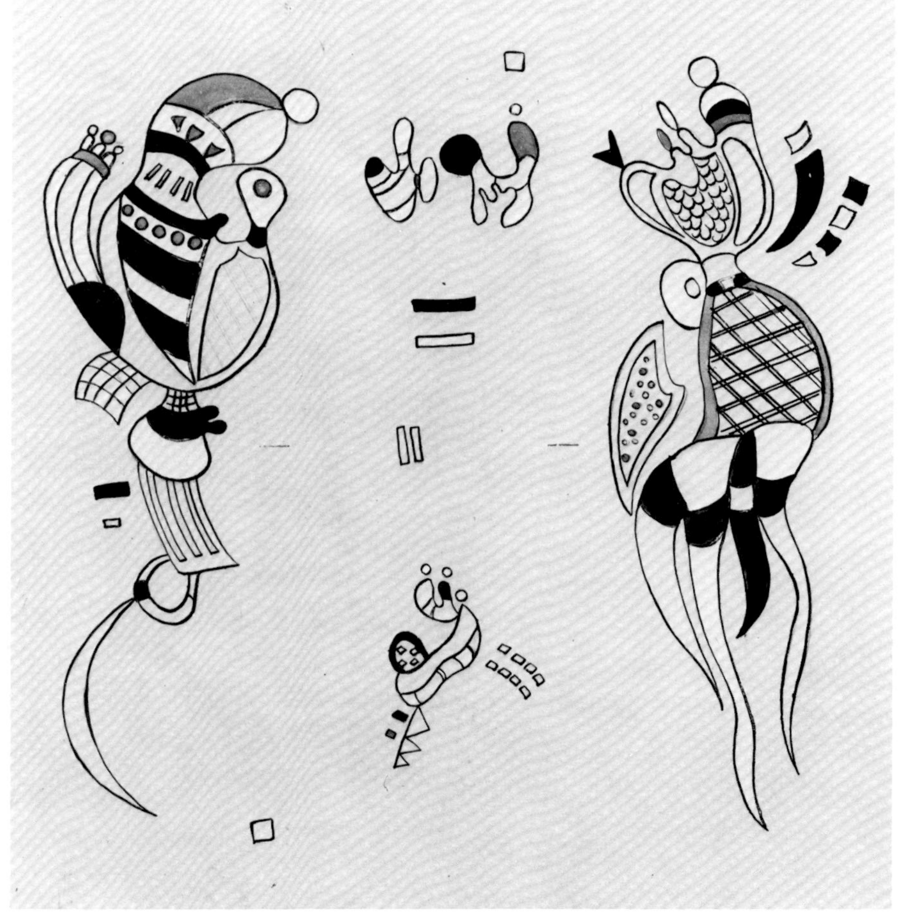

Vasily Kandinsky

137 *Study for a Textile Design (Etude pour l'impression des étoffes).* ca. 1944
Watercolor and ink on brown paper, 41⁹⁄₁₆ x 18½" (105.5 x 47 cm.)
Collection Musée National d'Art Moderne, Centre Georges Pompidou, Paris, Kandinsky Bequest

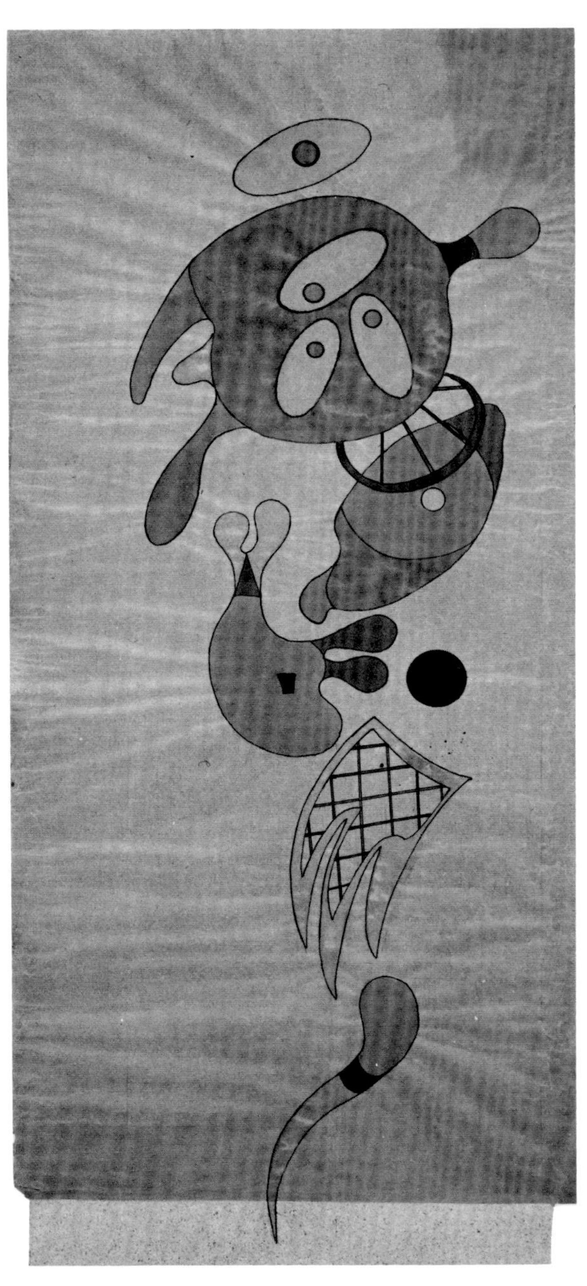

Vasily Kandinsky

138 *Study for a Textile Design (Etude pour l'impression des étoffes).* ca. 1944

Watercolor and ink on brown paper, 39⅜ x 14⁹⁄₁₆" (100 x 37 cm.)

Collection Musée National d'Art Moderne, Centre Georges Pompidou, Paris, Kandinsky Bequest

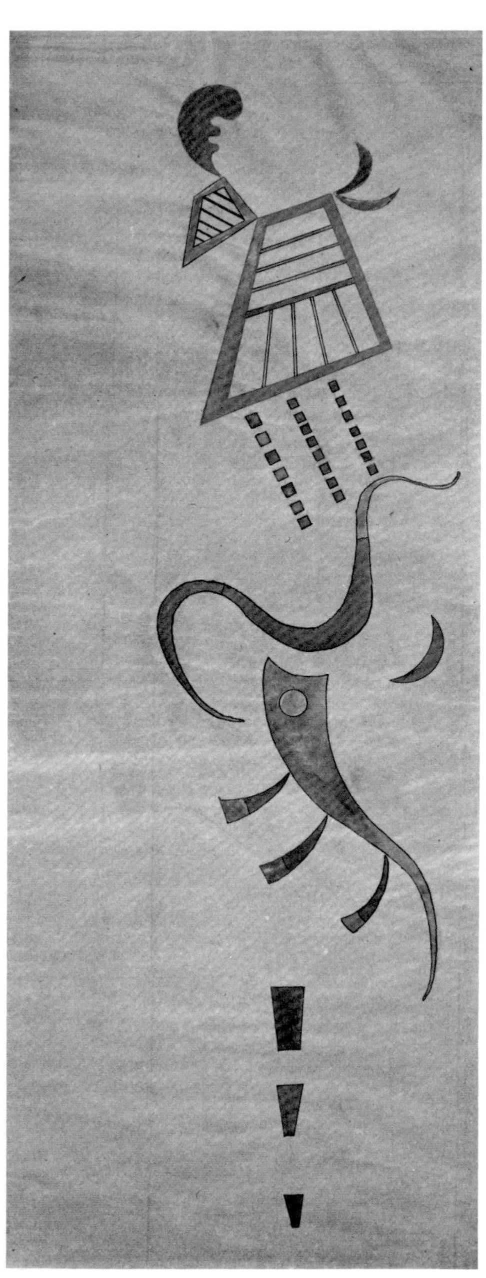

Vasily Kandinsky

139 *A Fluttering Figure (Une Figure flottante).* July 1942
(HL 691)
Oil on mahogany, $10\frac{1}{4} \times 7\frac{7}{8}''$ (26 x 20 cm.)
Collection Musée National d'Art Moderne, Centre Georges Pompidou, Paris, Kandinsky Bequest

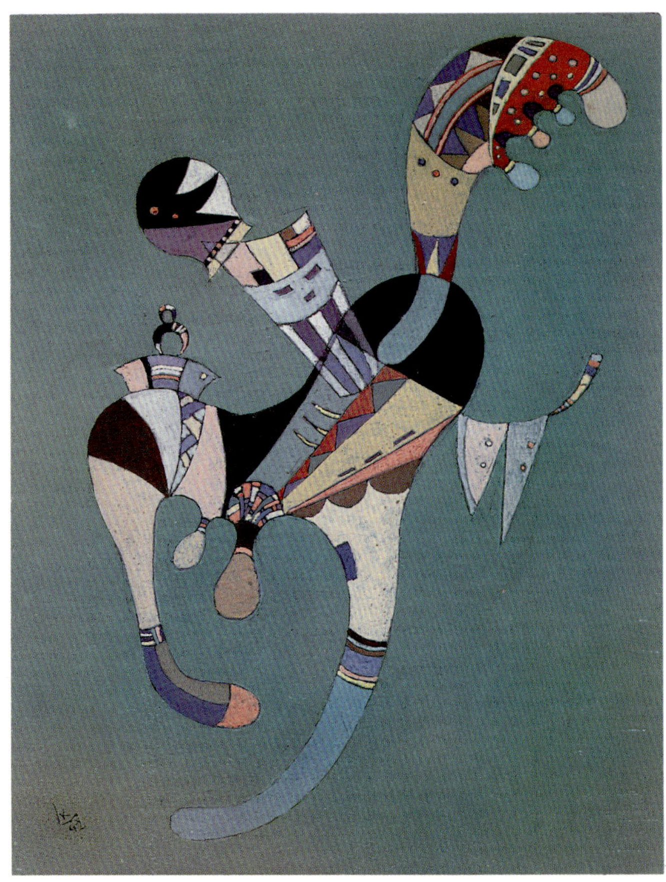

Vasily Kandinsky

140 *Vertical Accents (Accents verticaux).*
July 1942
(HL 692)
Oil on wood panel, 12⅝ x 16½"
(32.1 x 42 cm.)
Collection Solomon R. Guggenheim Museum, New York

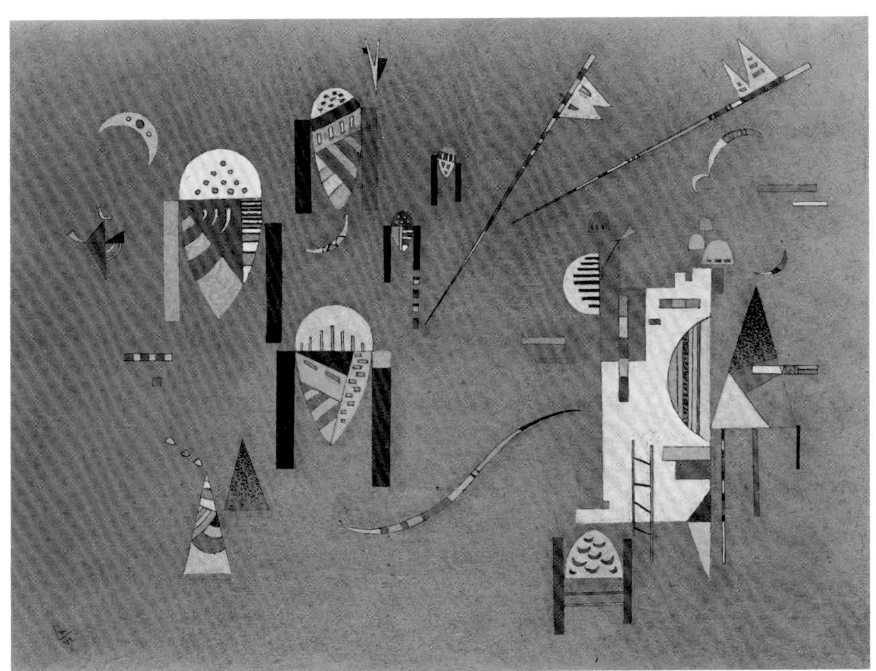

Vasily Kandinsky

141 *Three Between Two (Trois entre deux).*
October 1942
(HL 696)
Oil on board, 19¼ x 19¼″ (49 x 49 cm.)
Collection Arnold A. Saltzman, New York

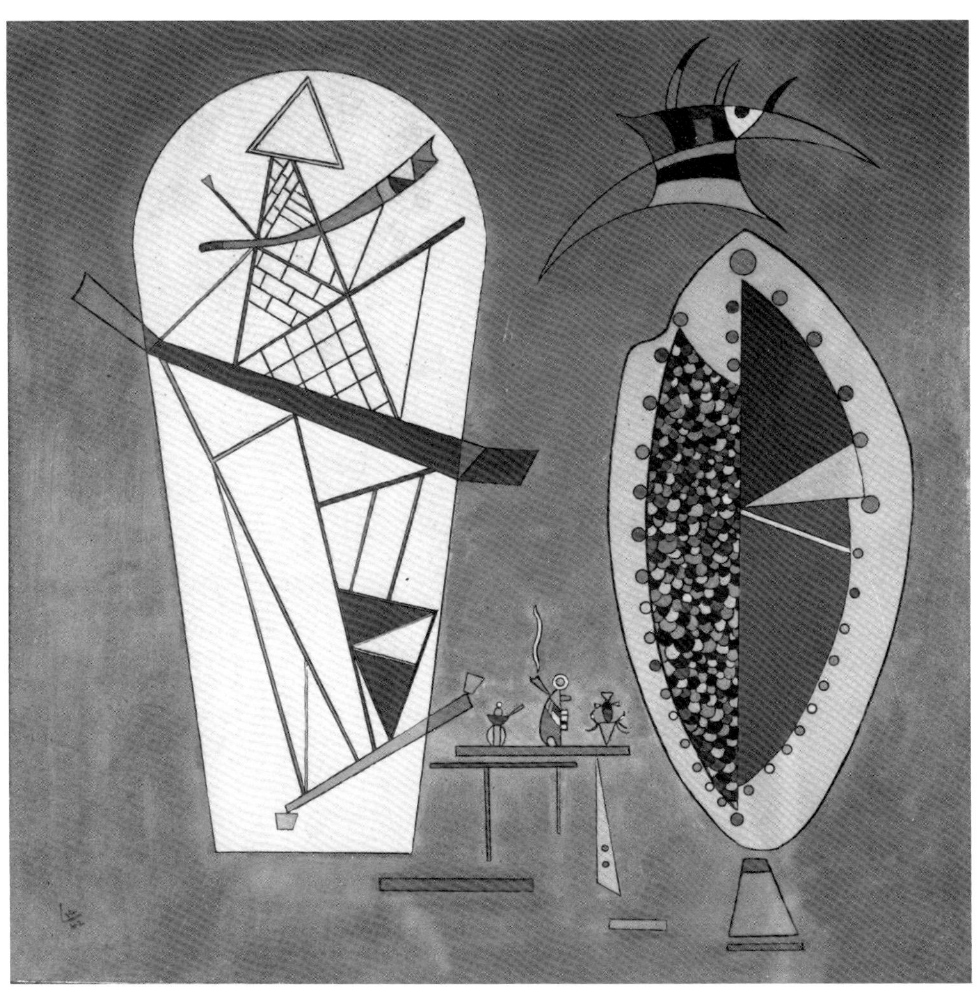

Vasily Kandinsky

142 *Joyful Theme (Thème joyeux).* October 1942

(HL 697)

Oil on paperboard, 19⅛ x 19¼"

(48.7 x 48.9 cm.)

Private Collection

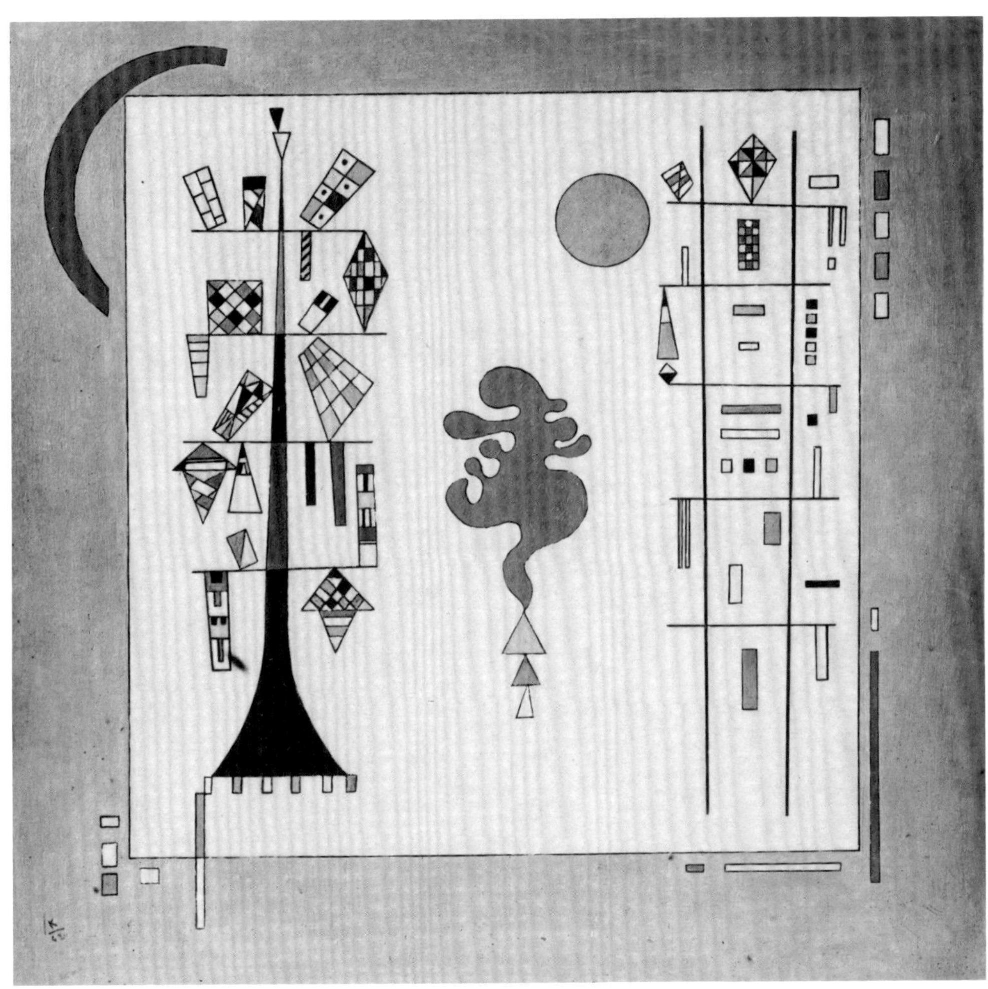

Vasily Kandinsky

143 *Three Ovals (Trois Ovales).* October 1942
(HL 698)
Oil and tempera on cardboard,
19¼ x 19¼" (49 x 49 cm.)
Lent by Davlyn Gallery, New York

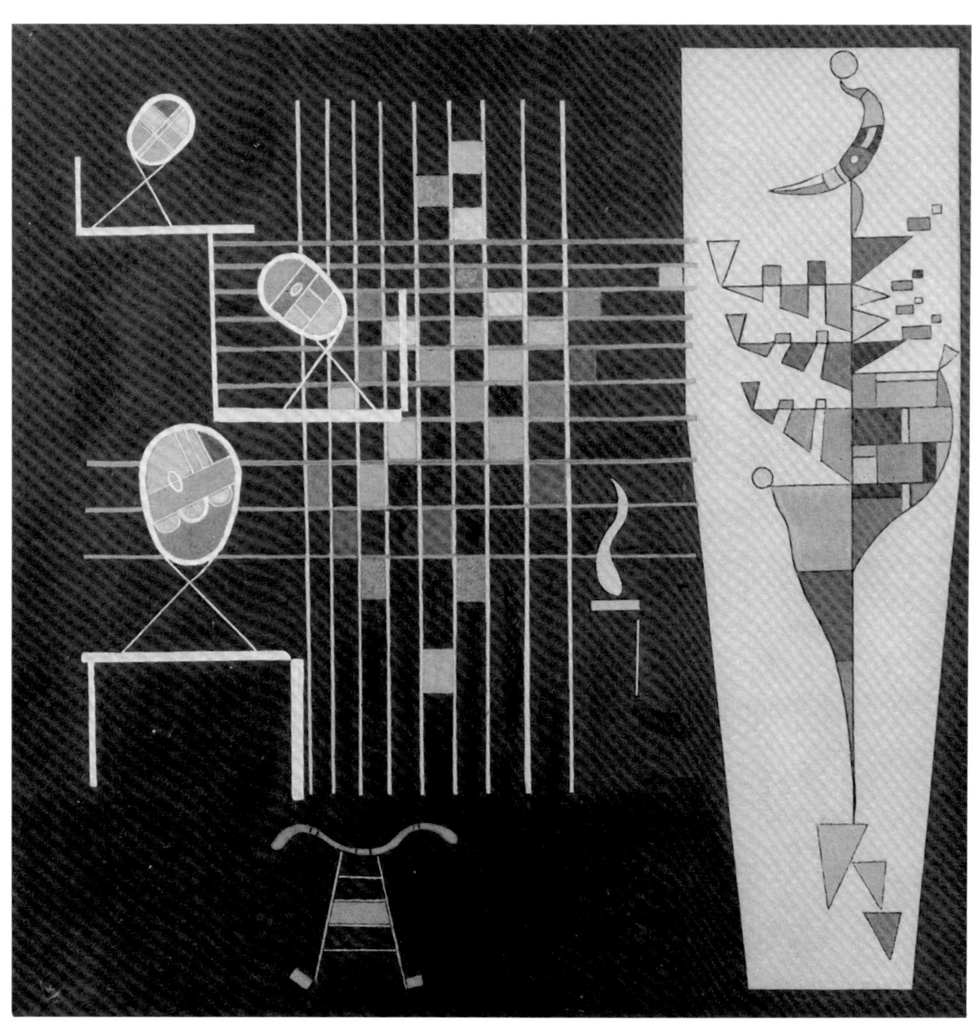

Vasily Kandinsky

144 *An Intimate Celebration (Une Fête intime).* December 1942
(HL 701)
Oil and tempera on cardboard, 19⅜ x 19⁹⁄₁₆″ (49.2 x 49.6 cm.)
Collection Musée National d'Art Moderne, Centre Georges Pompidou, Paris, Kandinsky Bequest

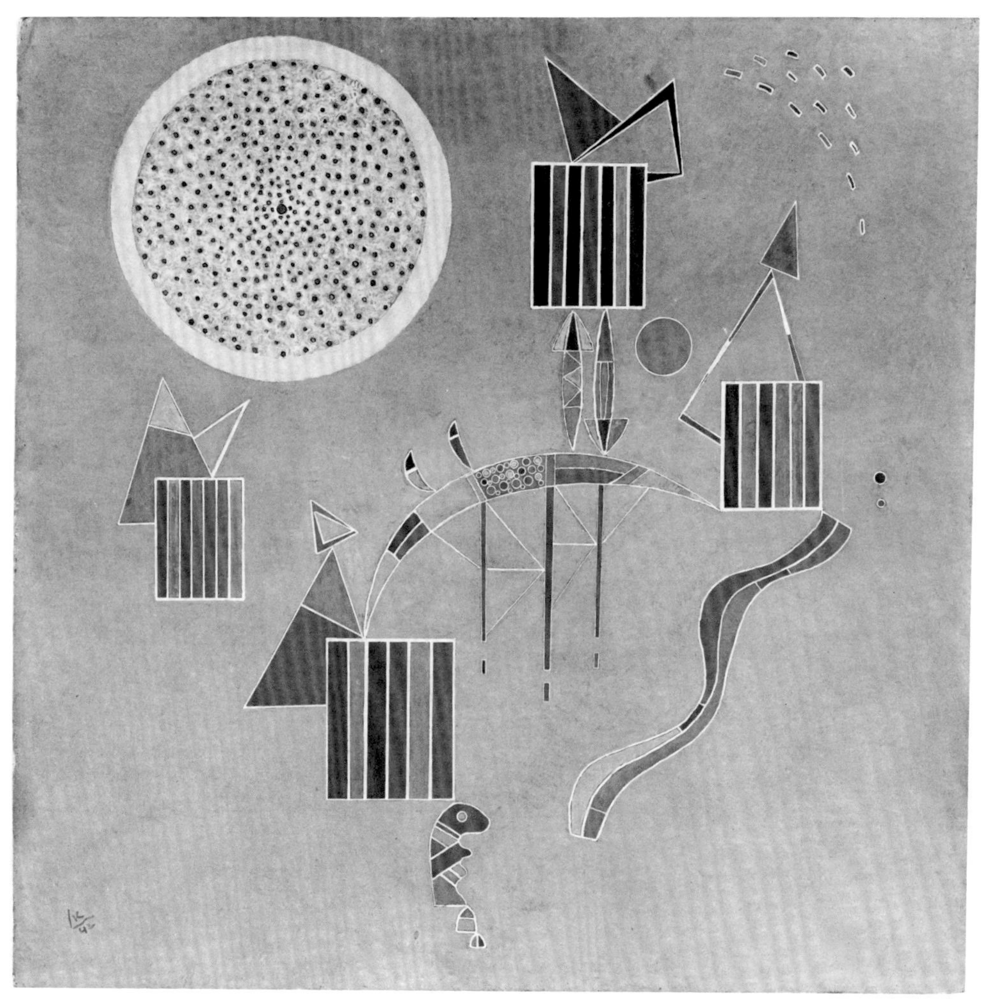

Vasily Kandinsky

145 *Netting (Le Filet).* December 1942
(HL 703)
Tempera on cardboard,
16½ x 22⅞" (42 x 58 cm.)
Collection Musée National d'Art Moderne,
Centre Georges Pompidou, Paris,
Kandinsky Bequest

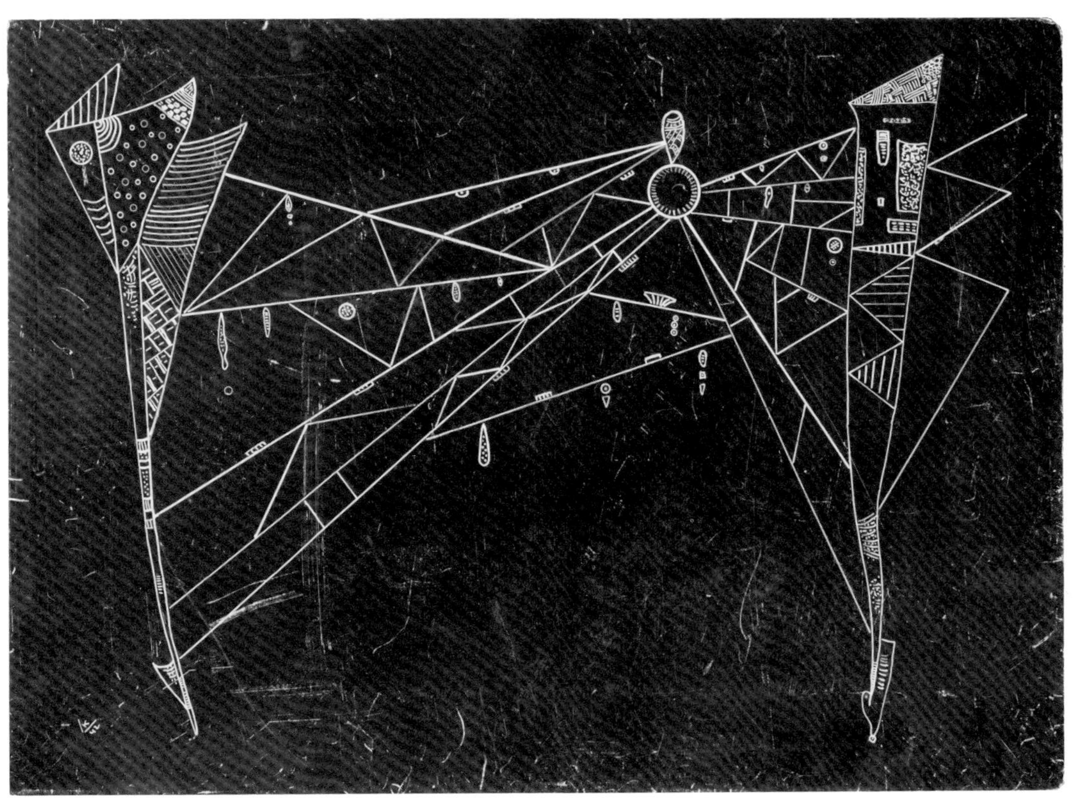

Vasily Kandinsky

146 *Dark Center (Le Milieu sombre).*
January 1943
(HL 704)
Oil on cardboard, 16½ x 22¾″
(42 x 57.8 cm.)
Lent by Galerie Beyeler, Basel

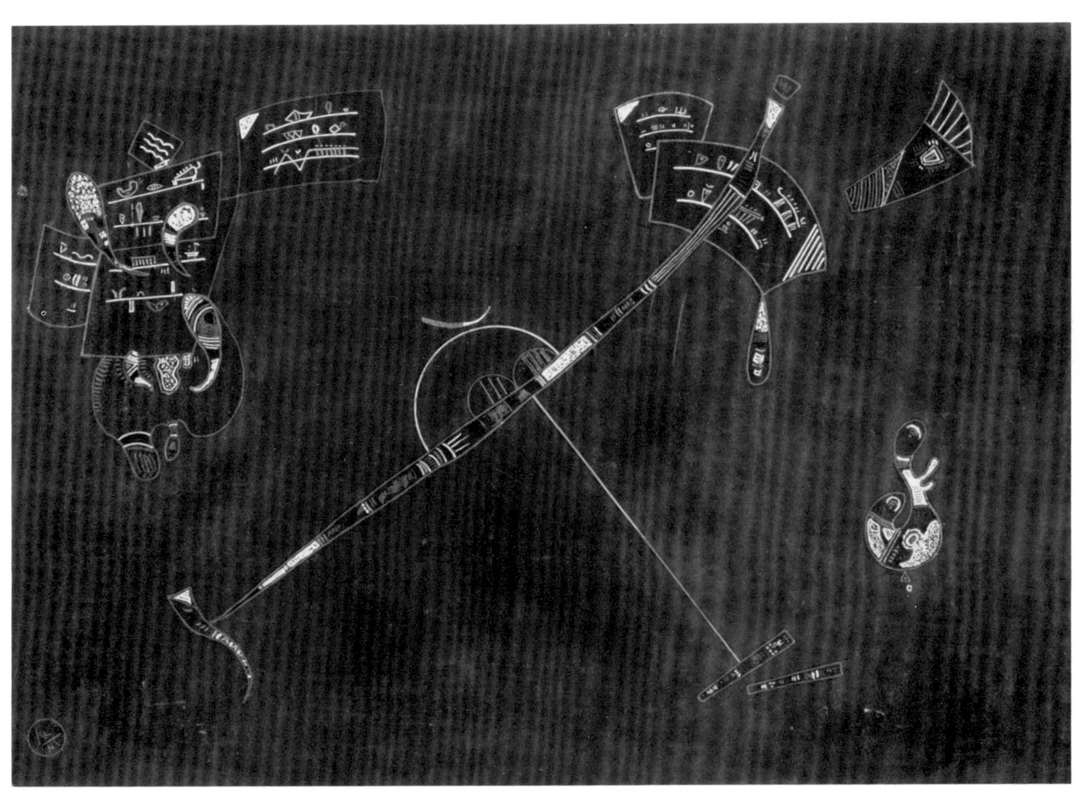

Vasily Kandinsky

147 *White Figure (La Figure blanche).*
January 1943
(HL 705)
Oil on board, 22⅝ x 16½"
(57.3 x 41.8 cm.)
Collection Solomon R. Guggenheim
Museum, New York

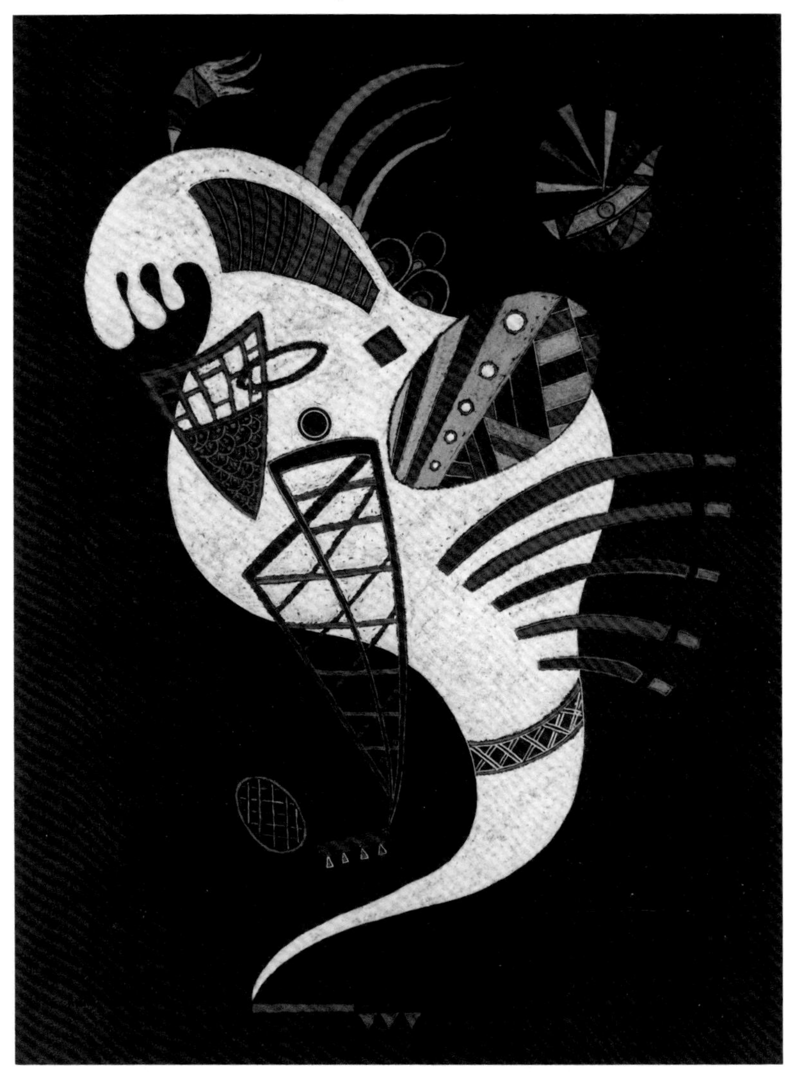

Vasily Kandinsky

148 *Light Ascent (Ascension légère).*
December 1942–January 1943
(HL 706)
Oil on paperboard, 22¼ x 16½″
(58 x 42 cm.)
Collection Mr. and Mrs. Adrien Maeght

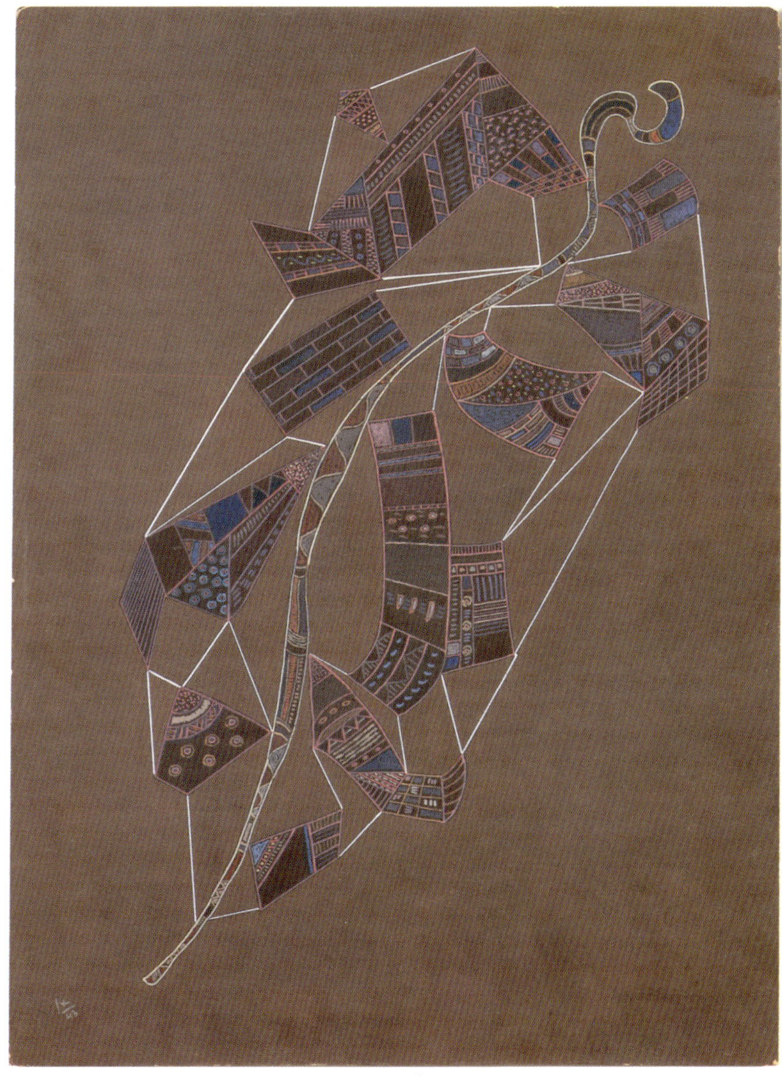

Vasily Kandinsky

149 *Fanlike (En éventail).* February 1943
(HL 707)
Tempera and oil on board, 22¾ x 16⅜"
(58 x 42 cm.)
Latner Family Collection

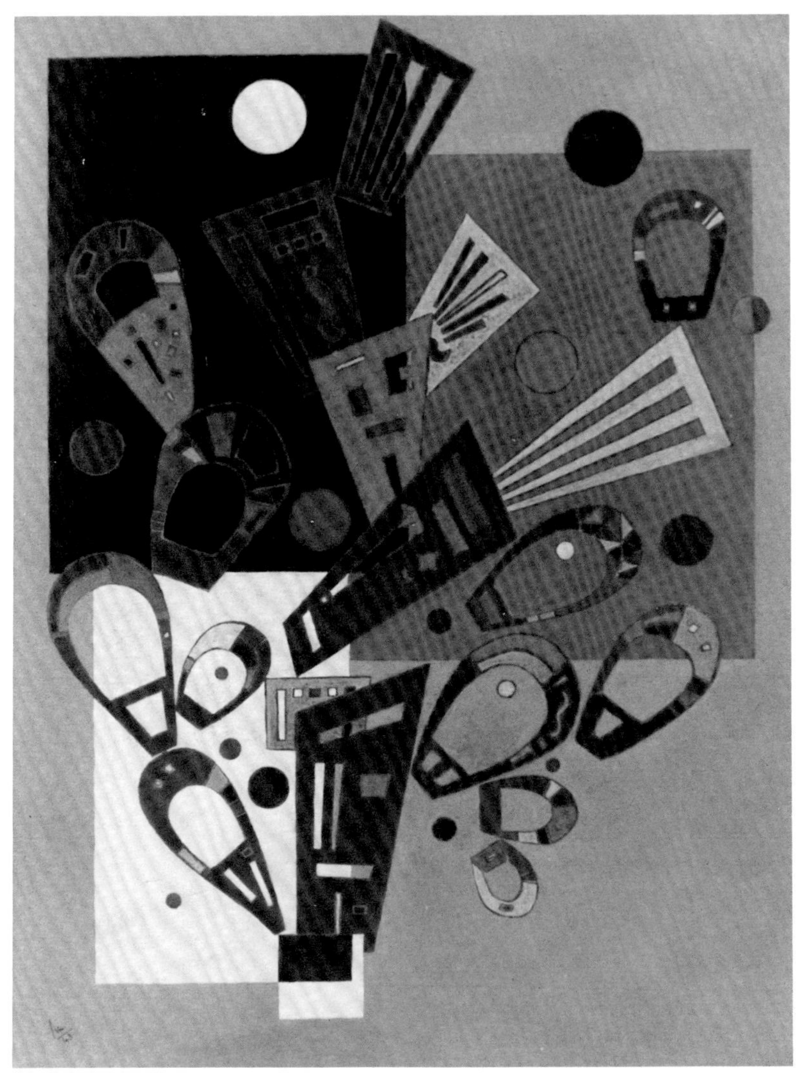

Vasily Kandinsky
150 *Simplicity (Simplicité).* February 1943
(HL 708)
Tempera and oil on cardboard,
$22\frac{7}{8}$ x $17\frac{1}{2}$" (57.7 x 41.5 cm.)
Collection Kunstmuseum Bern

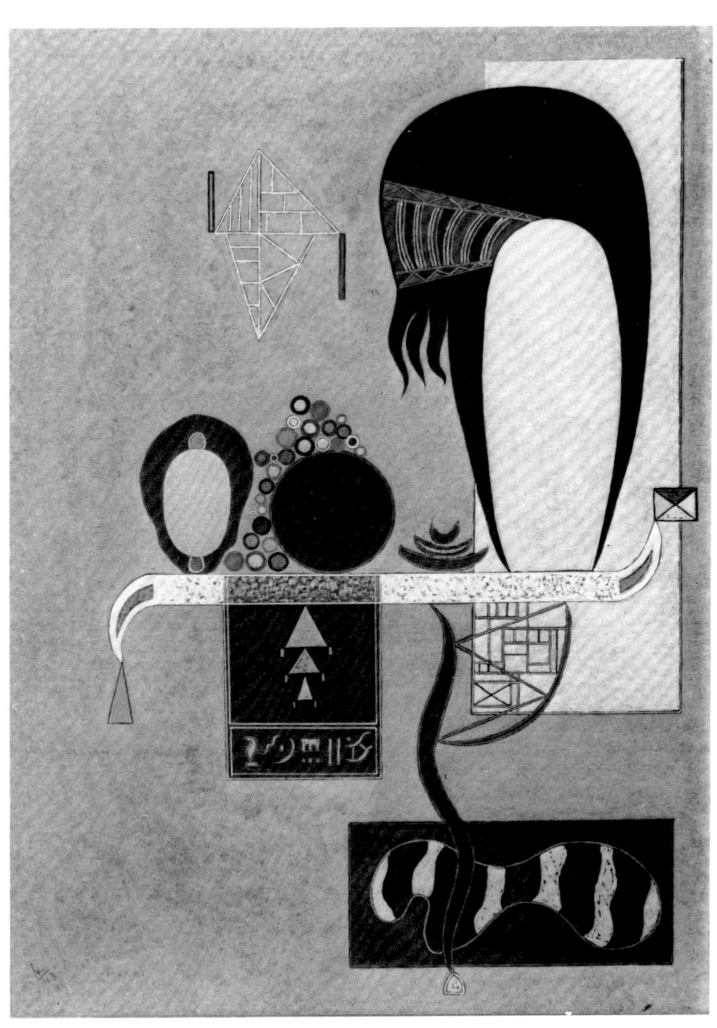

Vasily Kandinsky

151 *Around the Line (Autour de la ligne).*
February 1943
(HL 710)
Oil on cardboard, 16½ x 22⅞″
(42 x 58 cm.)
Thyssen-Bornemisza Collection,
Lugano, Switzerland

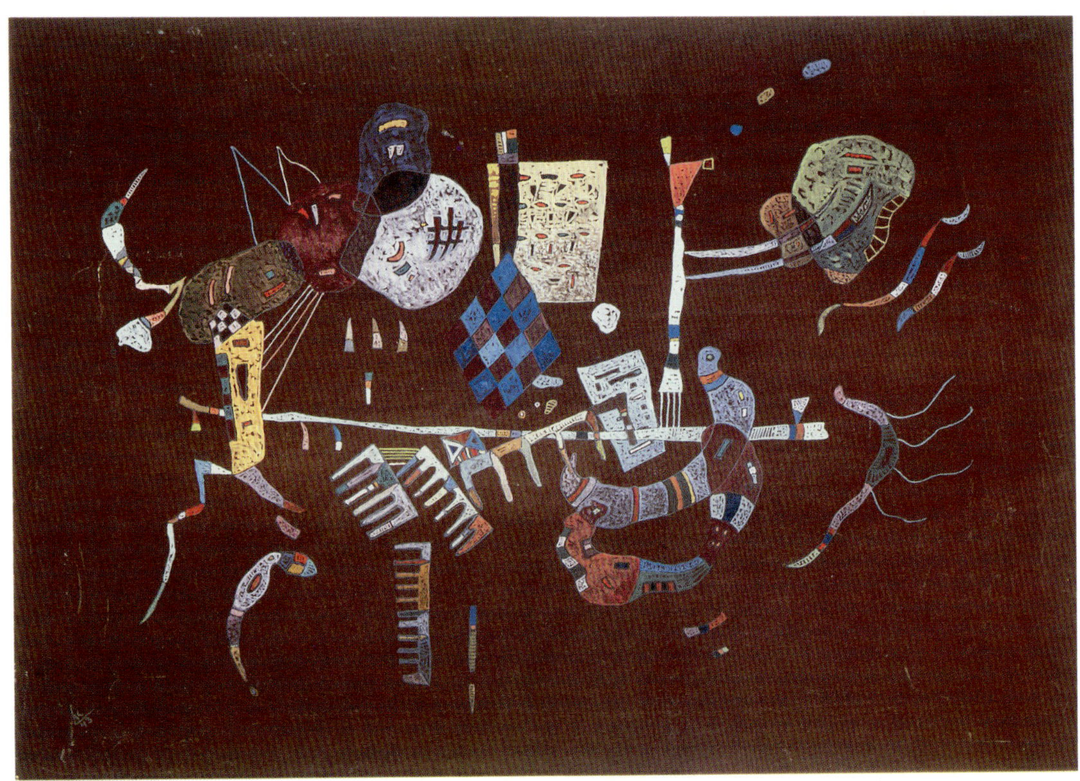

Vasily Kandinsky

152 *The Arrow (La Flèche).* February 1943
(HL 711)
Oil on paperboard, $16\frac{1}{2}$ x $22\frac{13}{16}$"
(42 x 58 cm.)
Öffentliche Kunstsammlung,
Kunstmuseum Basel

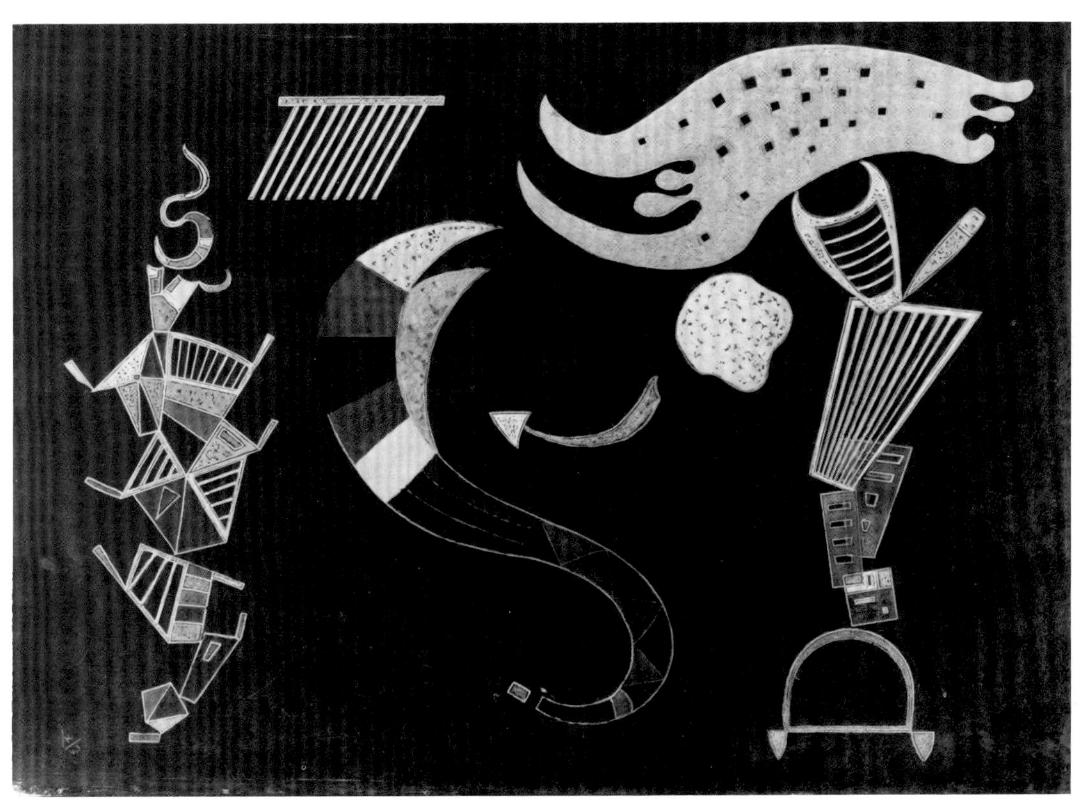

Vasily Kandinsky

153 *The Zigzag (Le Zigzag).* March 1943
(HL 712)
Oil on cardboard, 16½ x 22⅞"
(42 x 58 cm.)
Private Collection

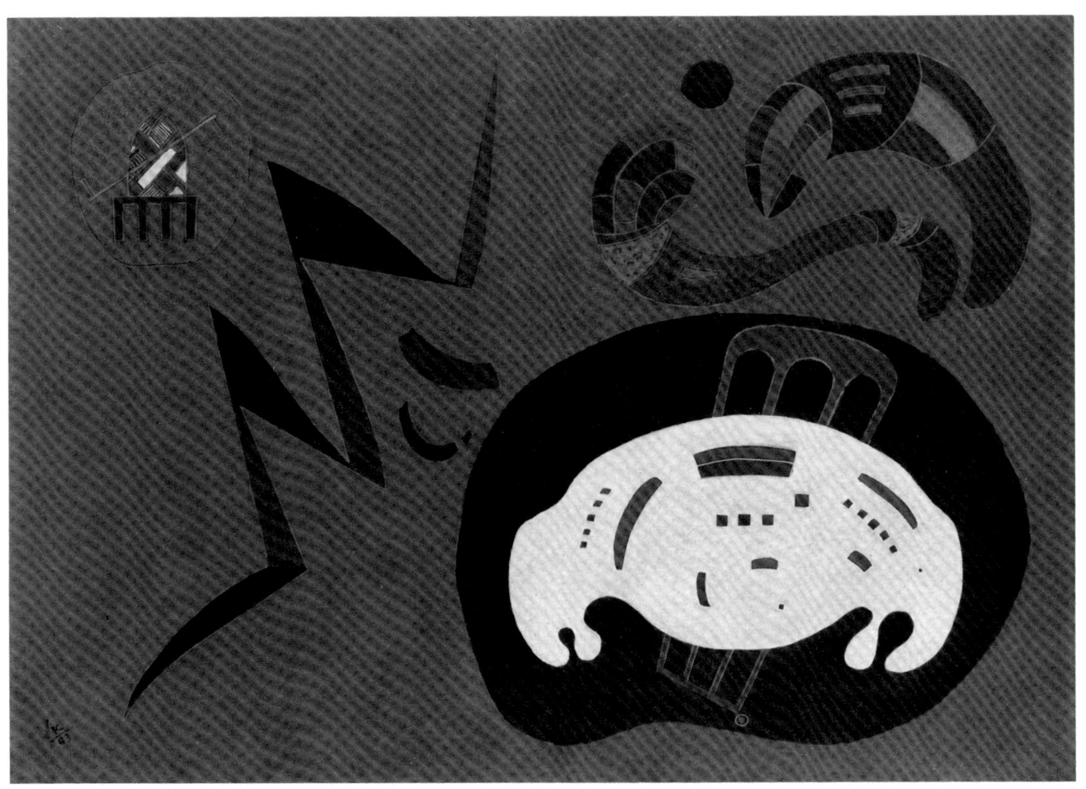

Vasily Kandinsky

154 *Seven (Sept).* March 1943
(HL 714)
Oil on cardboard, $22^{13}/_{16}$ x $16^{1}/_{2}$″
(58 x 42 cm.)
Collection Max Bill, Zürich

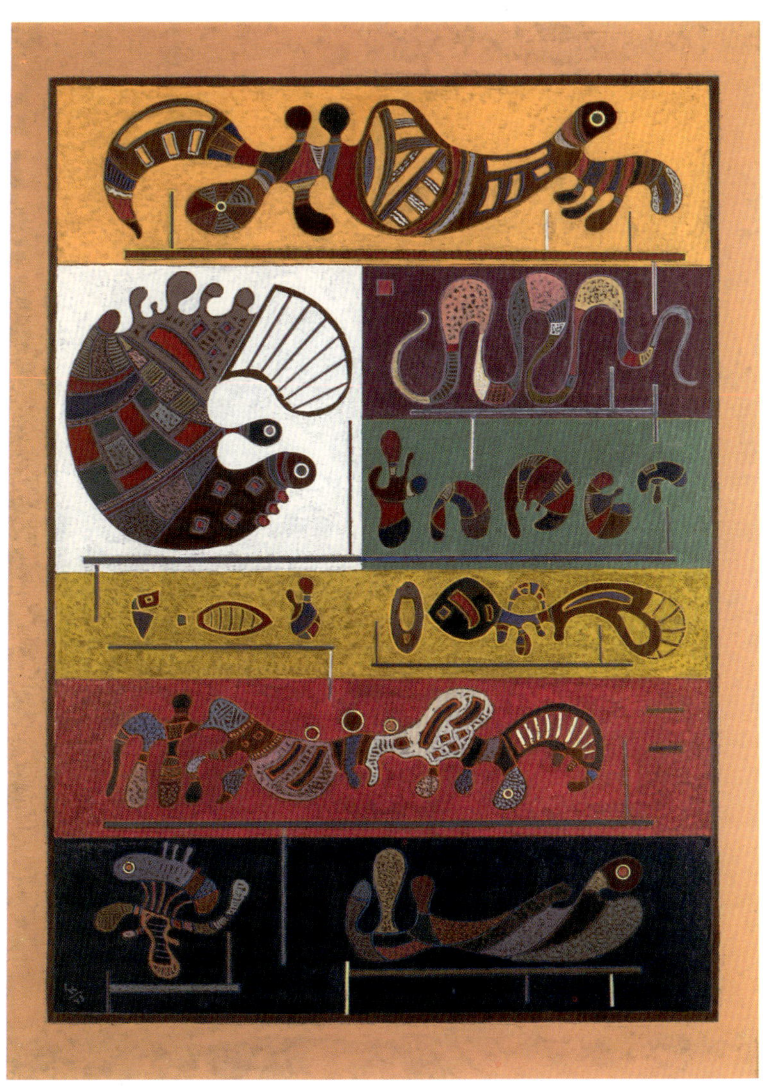

Vasily Kandinsky

155 *Brown Impetus (L'Elan brun).* April 1943
(HL 715)
Oil on wood, $16\frac{1}{2}$ x $22\frac{13}{16}$" (42 x 58 cm.)
Collection Mr. and Mrs. Adrien Maeght

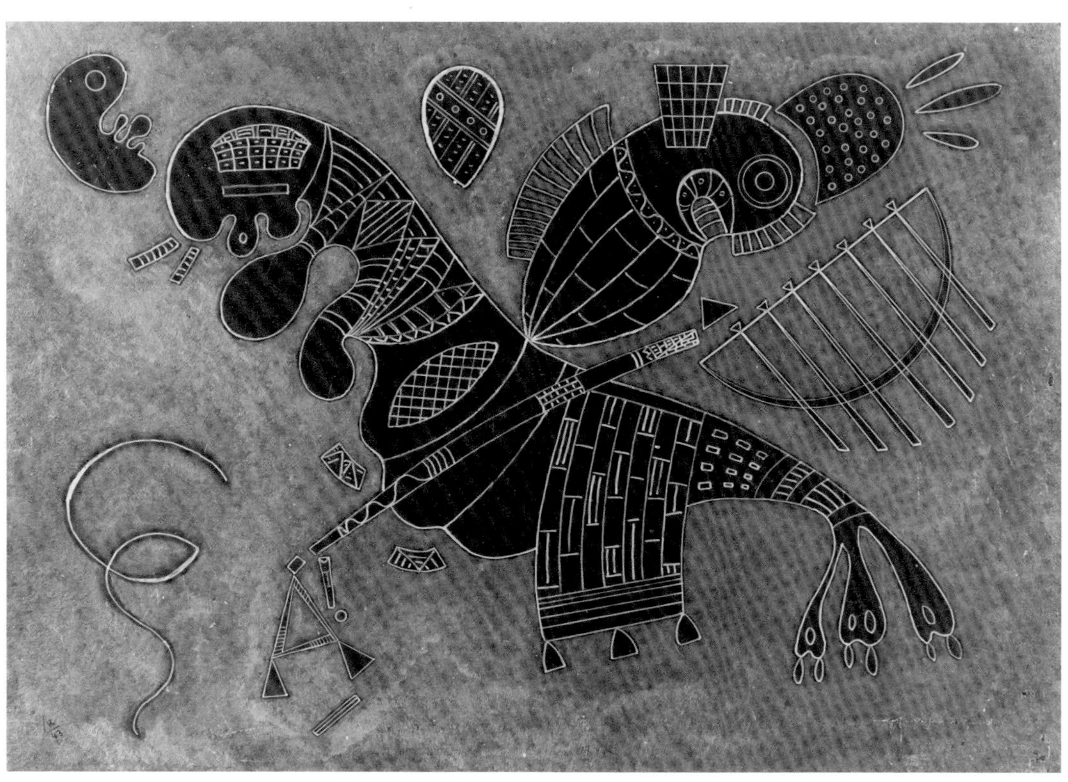

Vasily Kandinsky

156 *Circle and Square (Cercle et carré).*
April 1943
(HL 716)
Oil and tempera on cardboard,
$16\frac{1}{2}$ x $22\frac{13}{16}$" (42 x 58 cm.)
Collection Musée National d'Art Moderne,
Centre Georges Pompidou, Paris,
Kandinsky Bequest

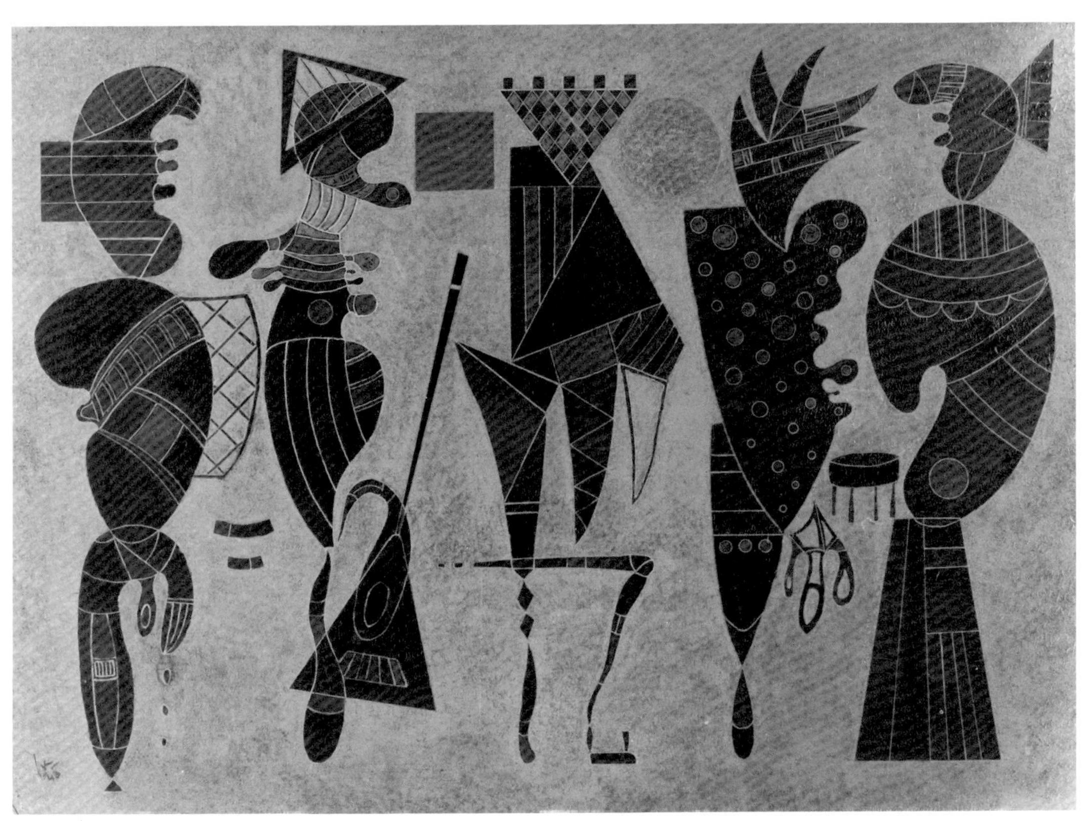

Vasily Kandinsky

157 *Fragments.* May 1943

(HL 718)

Oil and gouache on board, 16½ x 22¾"
(41.9 x 57.7 cm.)

Collection Solomon R. Guggenheim
Museum, New York

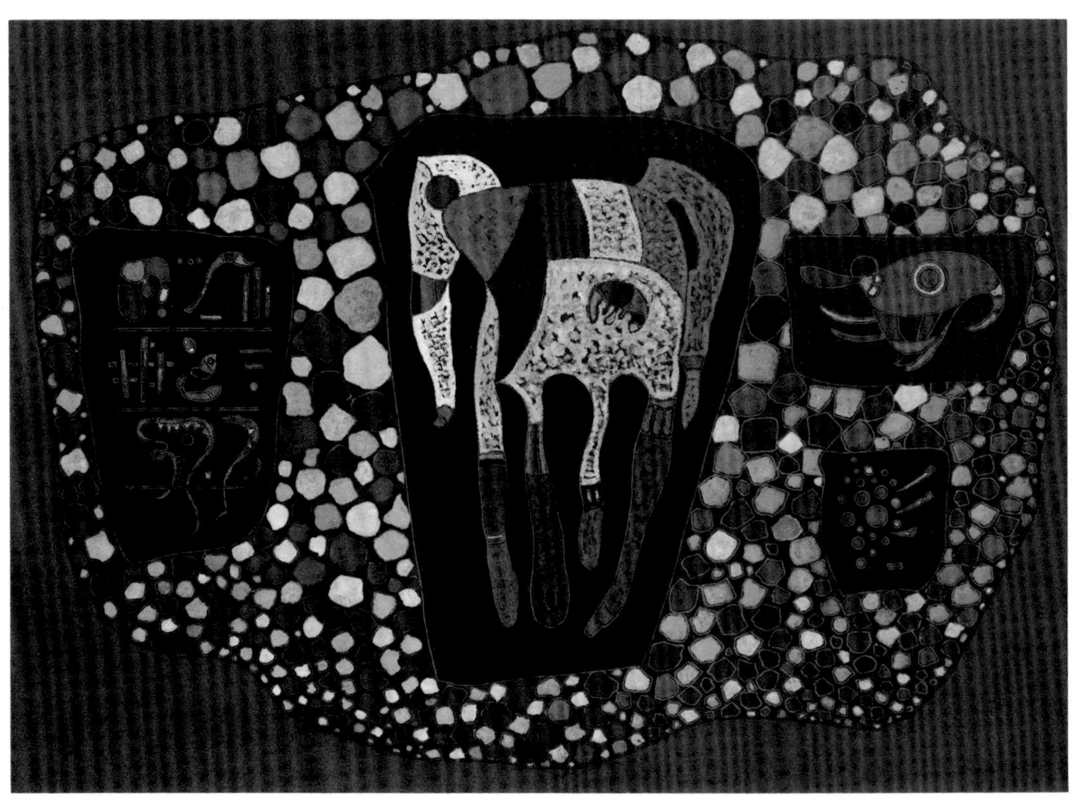

Vasily Kandinsky

158 *Twilight (Crépuscule).* June 1943
(HL 720)
Oil on board, 22¾ x 16½″
(41.8 x 57.6 cm.)
Collection Solomon R. Guggenheim
Museum, New York

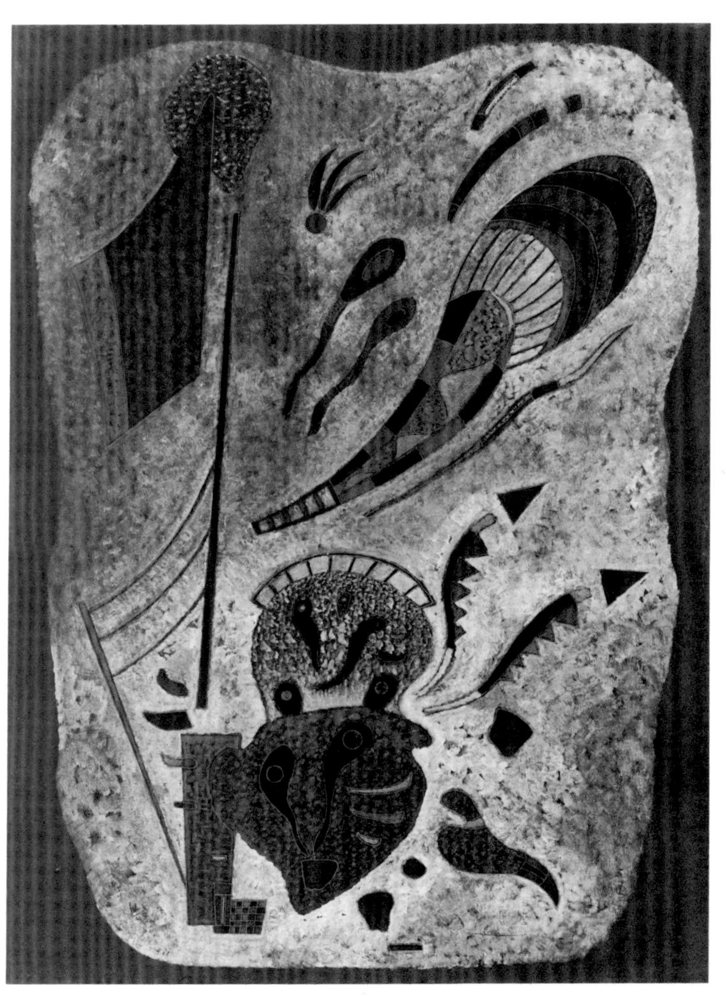

Vasily Kandinsky

159 *Red Accent (L'Accent rouge).* June 1943 (HL 722)

Oil on board mounted on panel, $16\frac{1}{2} \times 22\frac{3}{4}$" (41.8 x 57.9 cm.)

Solomon R. Guggenheim Museum, Hilla Rebay Collection

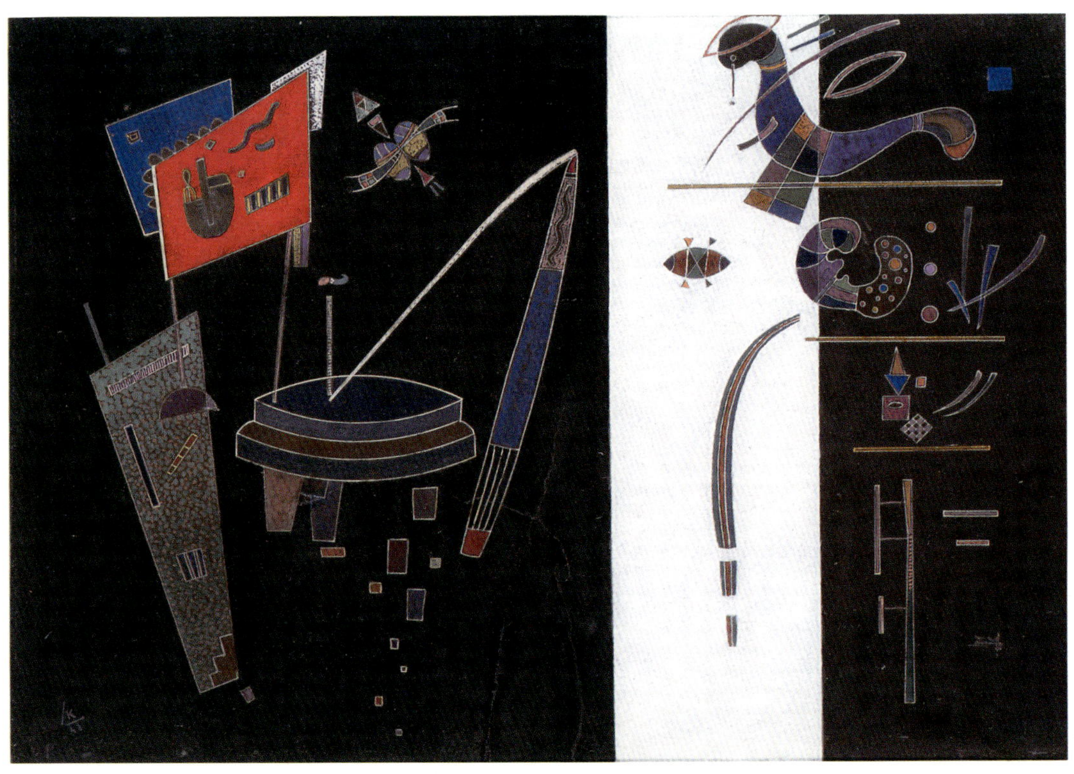

Vasily Kandinsky

160 *The Red Point (La Pointe rouge).*
July 1943
(HL 724)
Oil on paperboard, 16½ x 22$^{13}/_{16}$"
(42 x 58 cm.)
Collection Mr. and Mrs. Adrien Maeght

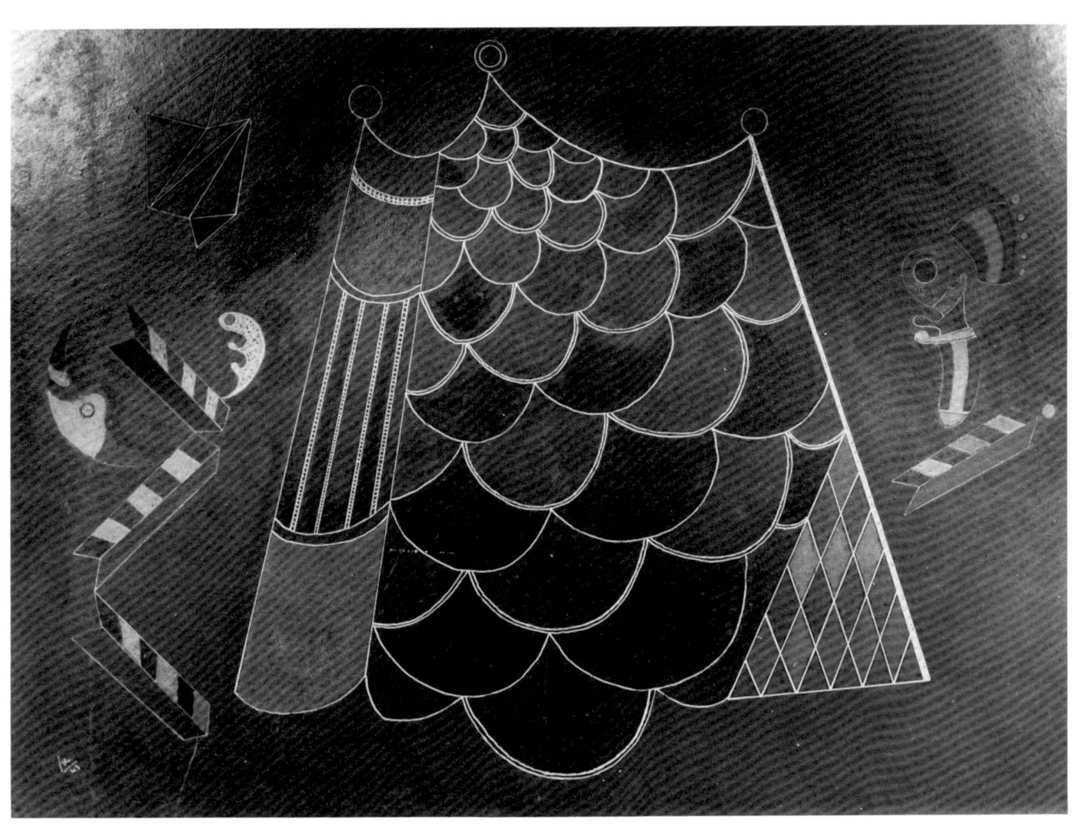

Vasily Kandinsky
161 *A Conglomerate (Un Conglomérat).* October 1943
(HL 728)
Gouache and oil on cardboard, 22 13/16 x 16 1/2" (58 x 42 cm.)
Collection Musée National d'Art Moderne, Centre Georges Pompidou, Paris, Kandinsky Bequest

Vasily Kandinsky
162 *Disquiet (Inquiétude).* November–December 1943
(HL 730)
Oil on cardboard, 16 1/2 x 22 13/16"
(42 x 58 cm.)
Private Collection

Vasily Kandinsky
163 *Ribbon with Squares (Ruban aux carrés).* January 1944
(HL 731)
Gouache and oil on board, 16 1/2 x 22 3/4" (42 x 57.8 cm.)
Collection Solomon R. Guggenheim Museum, New York

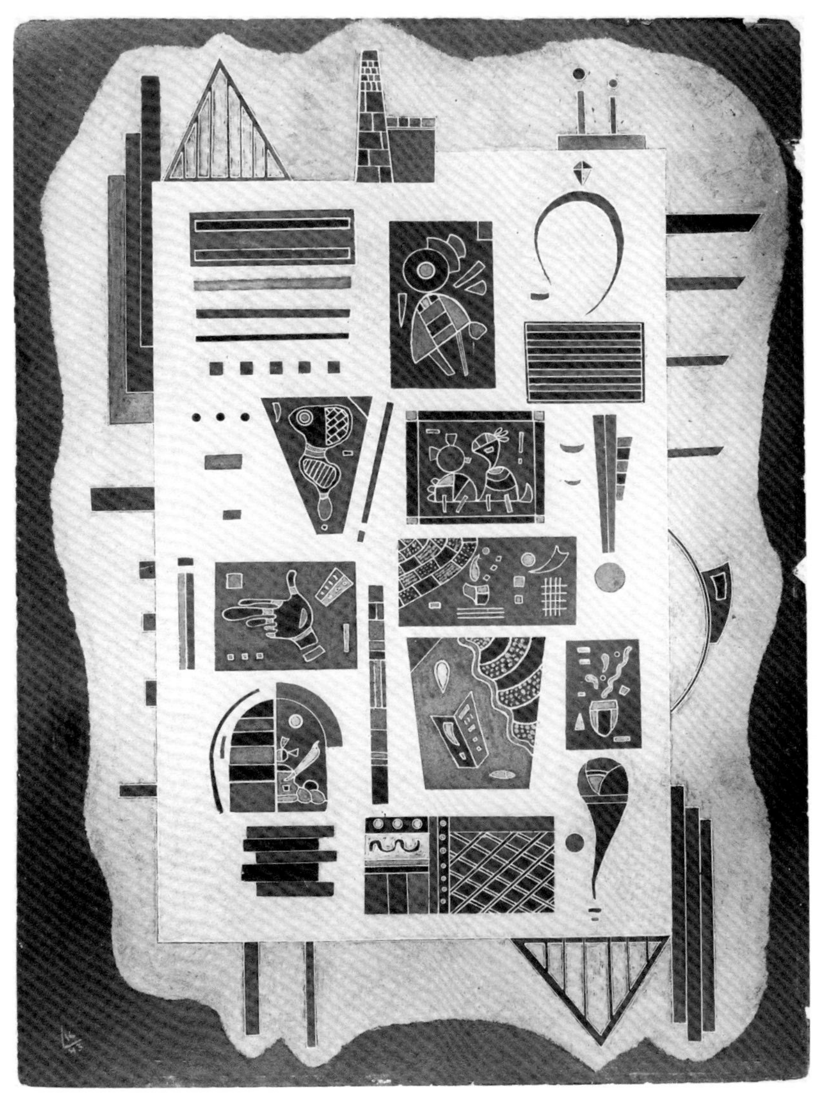

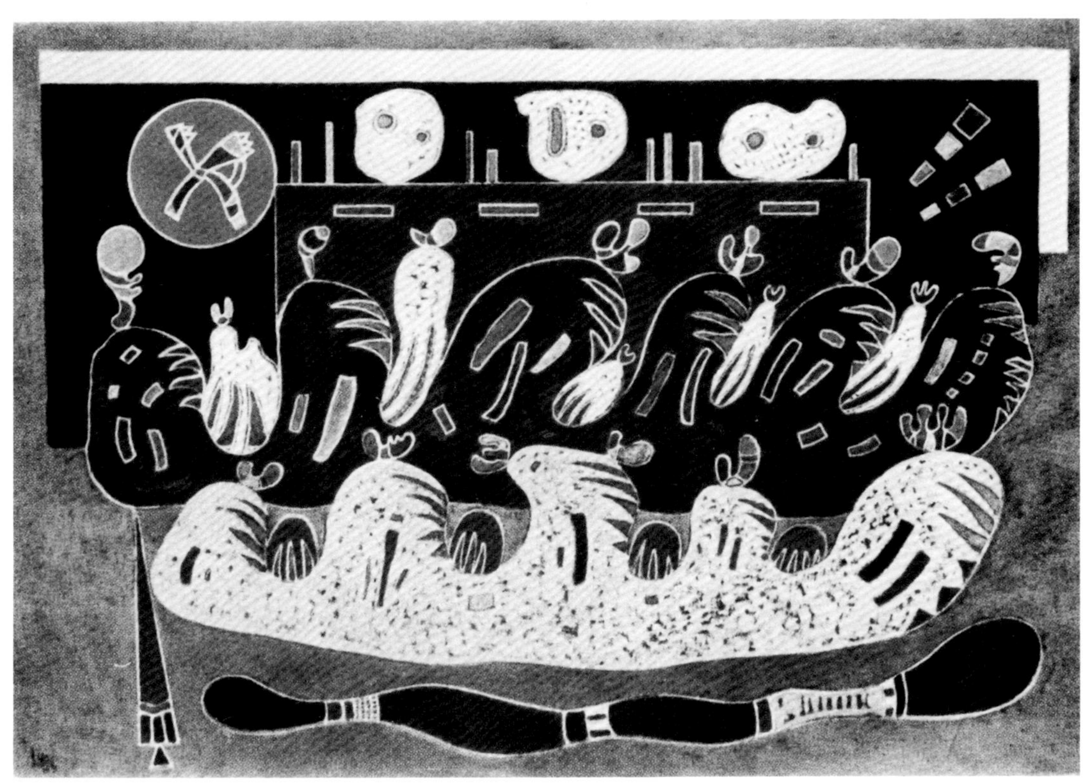

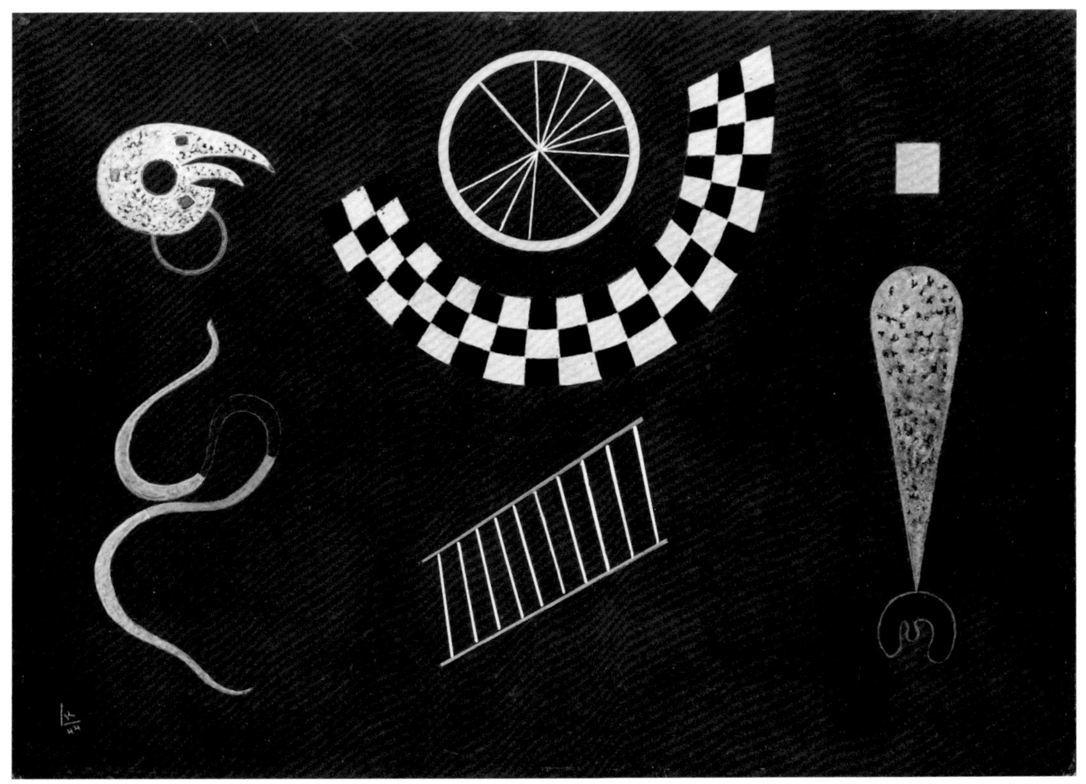

Vasily Kandinsky

164 *Isolation.* January 1944
(HL 733)
Gouache on cardboard, $16\frac{1}{2} \times 22\frac{13}{16}''$
(42 x 58 cm.)
Collection Mr. and Mrs. Adrien Maeght

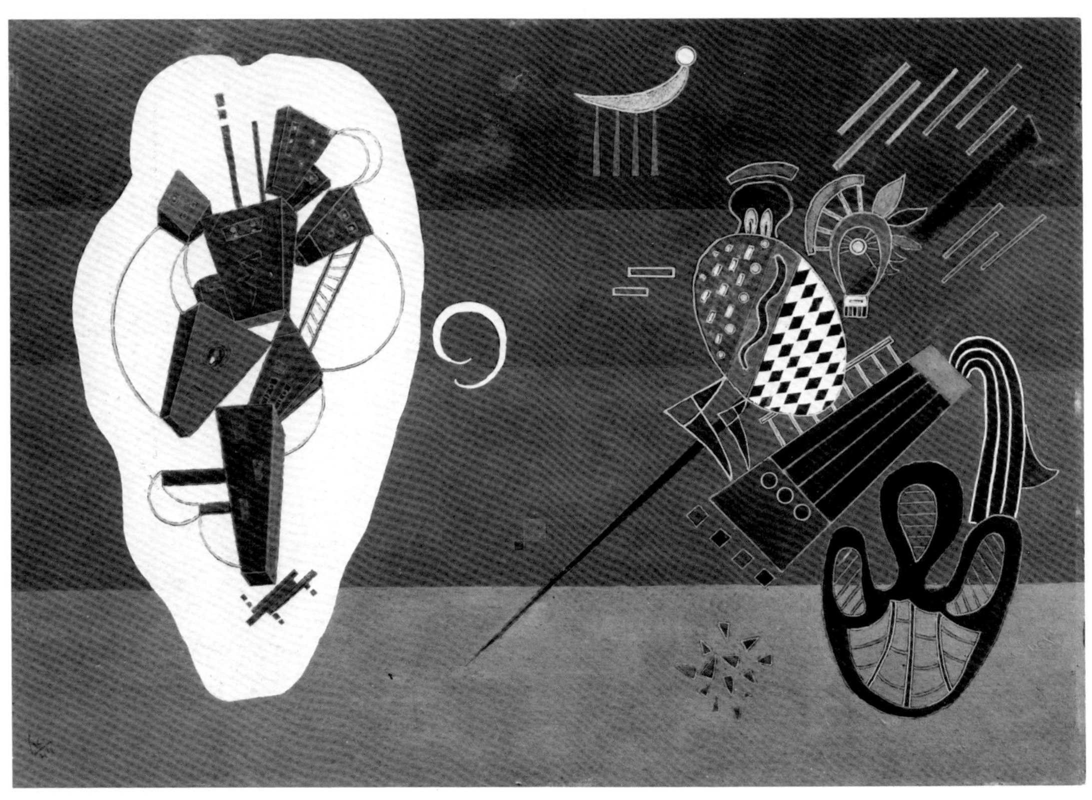

Vasily Kandinsky

165 *The Little Red Circle (Le Petit Rond rouge).* January 1944
(HL 734)
Gouache and oil on cardboard,
$16\frac{1}{2}$ x $22\frac{13}{16}$" (42 x 58 cm.)
Collection Musée National d'Art Moderne,
Centre Georges Pompidou, Paris,
Kandinsky Bequest

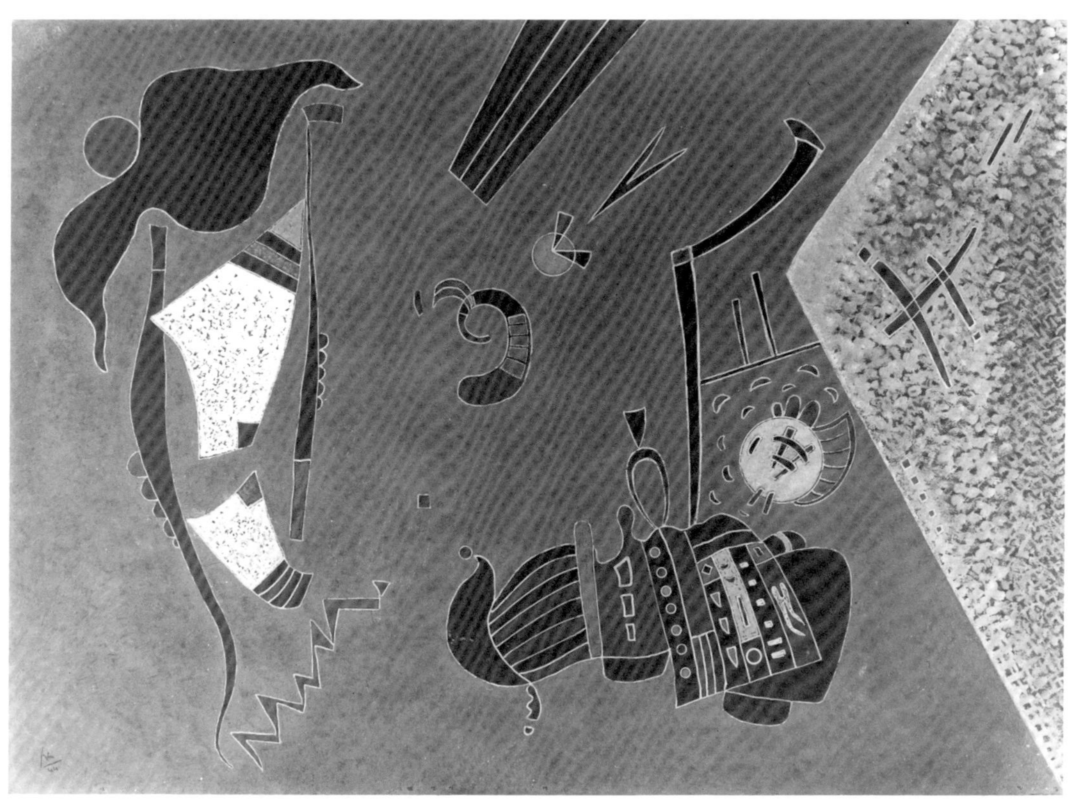

Vasily Kandinsky

166 *Three Black Bands (Trois Bandes noires).*
February 1944
(HL 736)
Oil on paperboard, $18^{1}/_{16}$ x $21^{1}/_{4}$"
(46 x 54 cm.)
Private Collection

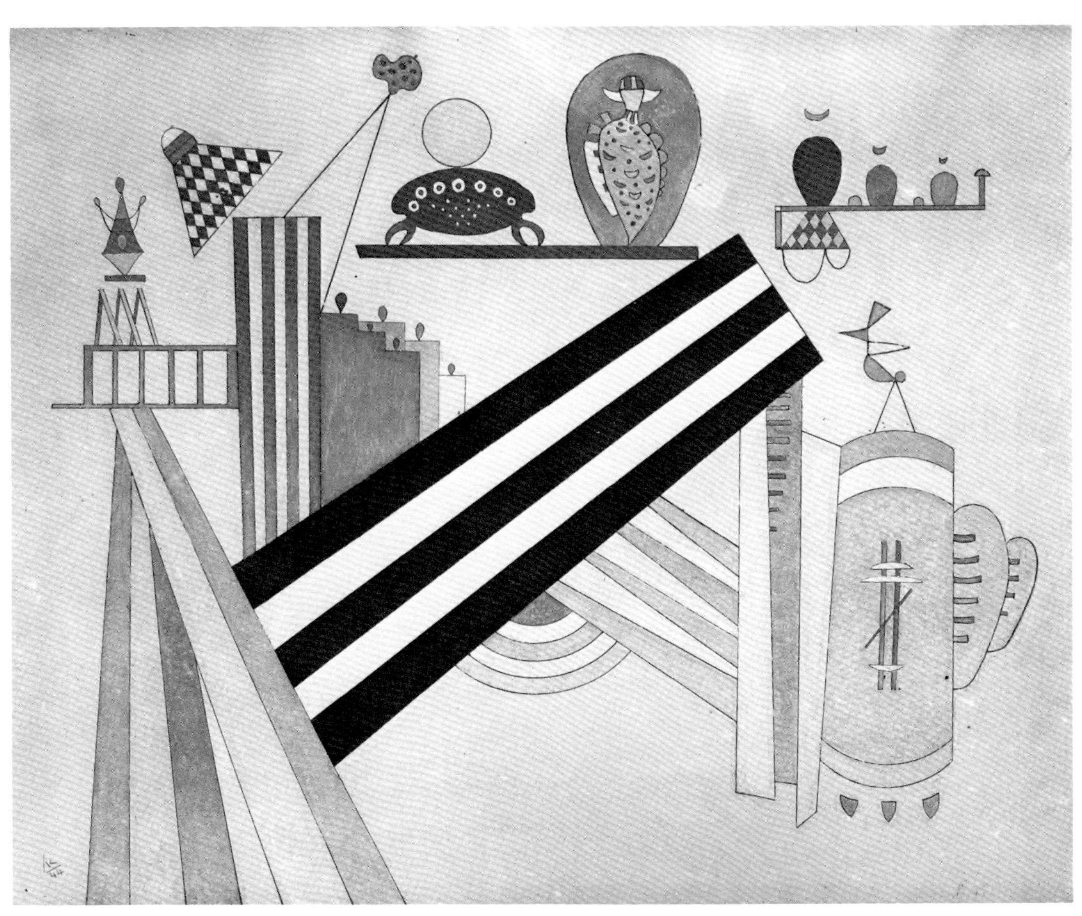

Vasily Kandinsky

167 *The Green Band (Le Lien vert).*
February 1944
(HL 737)
Oil on cardboard, 18⅛ x 21¼″
(46 x 54 cm.)
Private Collection, Milan

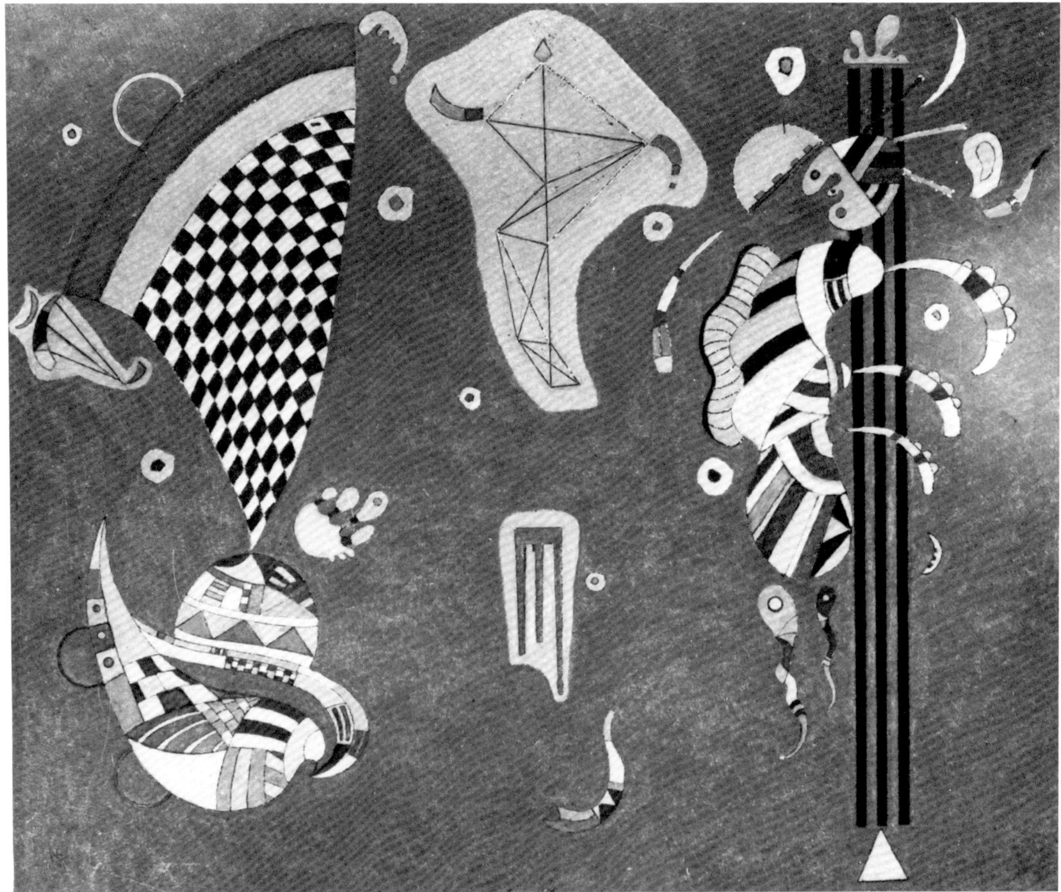

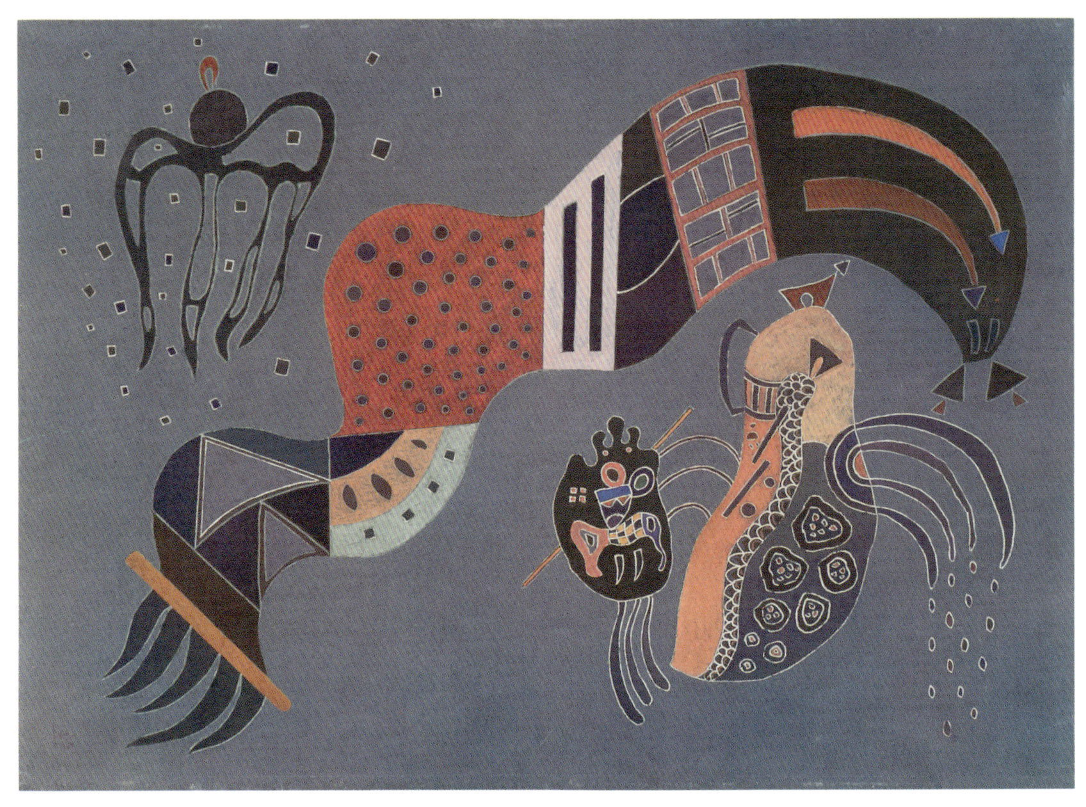

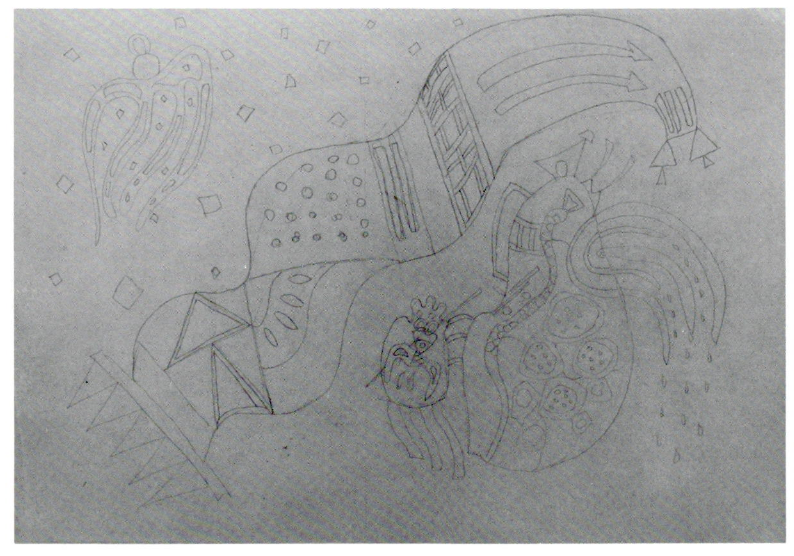

Vasily Kandinsky

168 *Tempered Elan (L'Elan tempéré).* March 1944
(HL 738)
Oil on cardboard, $16\frac{1}{2} \times 22\frac{13}{16}''$ (42 x 58 cm.)
Collection Musée National d'Art Moderne, Centre Georges Pompidou, Paris, Kandinsky Bequest

Vasily Kandinsky

169 *Study for "Tempered Elan" (Etude pour "L'Elan tempéré").* 1944
Pencil on paper, $7\frac{3}{4} \times 11\frac{3}{16}''$ (19.5 x 28.4 cm.)
Collection Musée National d'Art Moderne, Centre Georges Pompidou, Paris, Kandinsky Bequest

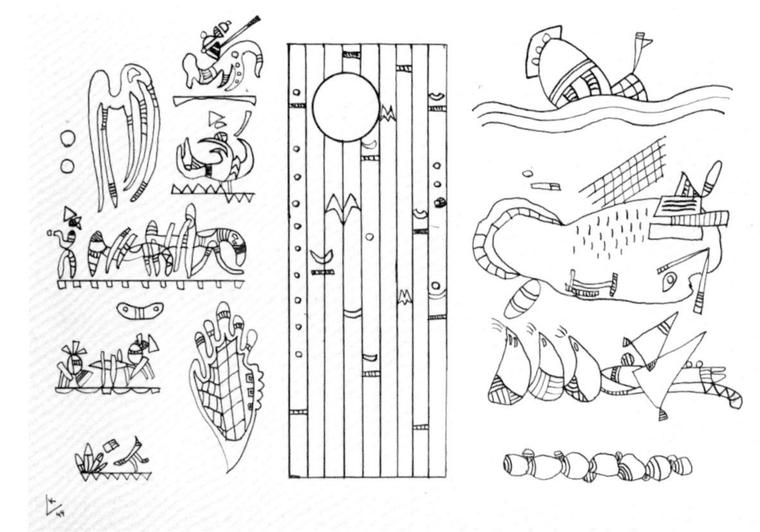

Vasily Kandinsky

170 *Study for an Unexecuted Work (Etude pour un tableau inachevé).* 1944
India ink on paper, $7\frac{5}{8} \times 11\frac{3}{16}''$ (19.4 x 28.4 cm.)
Collection Musée National d'Art Moderne, Centre Georges Pompidou, Paris, Kandinsky Bequest

Vasily Kandinsky

171 *Study on a Drawing Board (Etude sur une planche à dessin).* 1944
Watercolor, India ink and pencil on paper mounted on board, sheet, $11\frac{7}{8} \times 18\frac{1}{8}''$ (30.2 x 46 cm.); board, $17\frac{15}{16} \times 24\frac{13}{16} \times 1\frac{7}{8}''$ (45.5 x 63 x 4.8 cm.)
Collection Musée National d'Art Moderne, Centre Georges Pompidou, Paris, Kandinsky Bequest

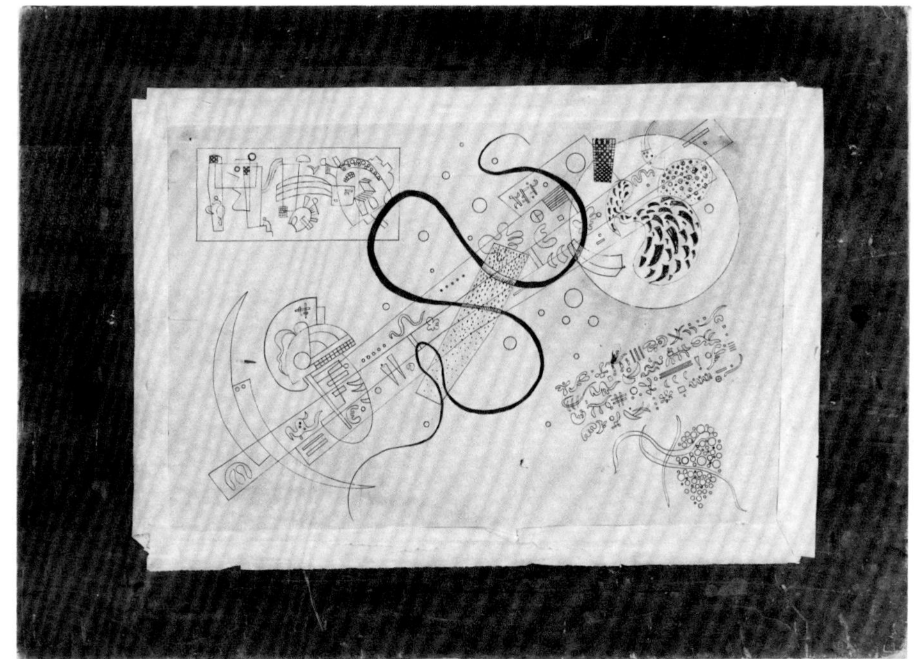

VI. KANDINSKY AND THE PARISIAN MILIEU IN THE 1930s

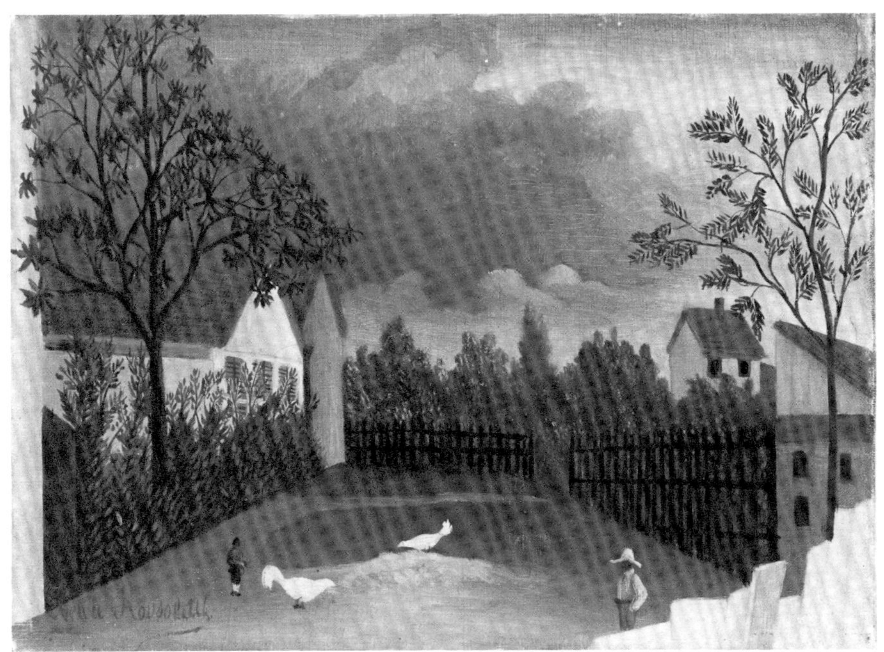

THE PAINTING OF HENRI ROUSSEAU

Henri Rousseau

172 *The Poultry Yard (La Basse-Cour).* 1896–98
Oil on canvas, 9 11/16 x 13″ (24.6 x 32.9 cm.)
Collection Musée National d'Art Moderne, Centre Georges Pompidou, Paris, Kandinsky Bequest

Henri Rousseau

173 *The Painter and His Model (Le Peintre et son modèle).* 1900–05
Oil on canvas, 18 5/16 x 21 7/8″ (46.5 x 55.5 cm.)
Collection Musée National d'Art Moderne, Centre Georges Pompidou, Paris, Kandinsky Bequest

Vasily Kandinsky

174 *Sketch and Passage from a Letter Concerning the Possible Sale of a Painting by the Douanier Rousseau.* ca. 1943
Pencil on paper, 4 3/4 x 5 5/16″ (12.2 x 13.5 cm.)
Collection Musée National d'Art Moderne, Centre Georges Pompidou, Paris, Kandinsky Bequest

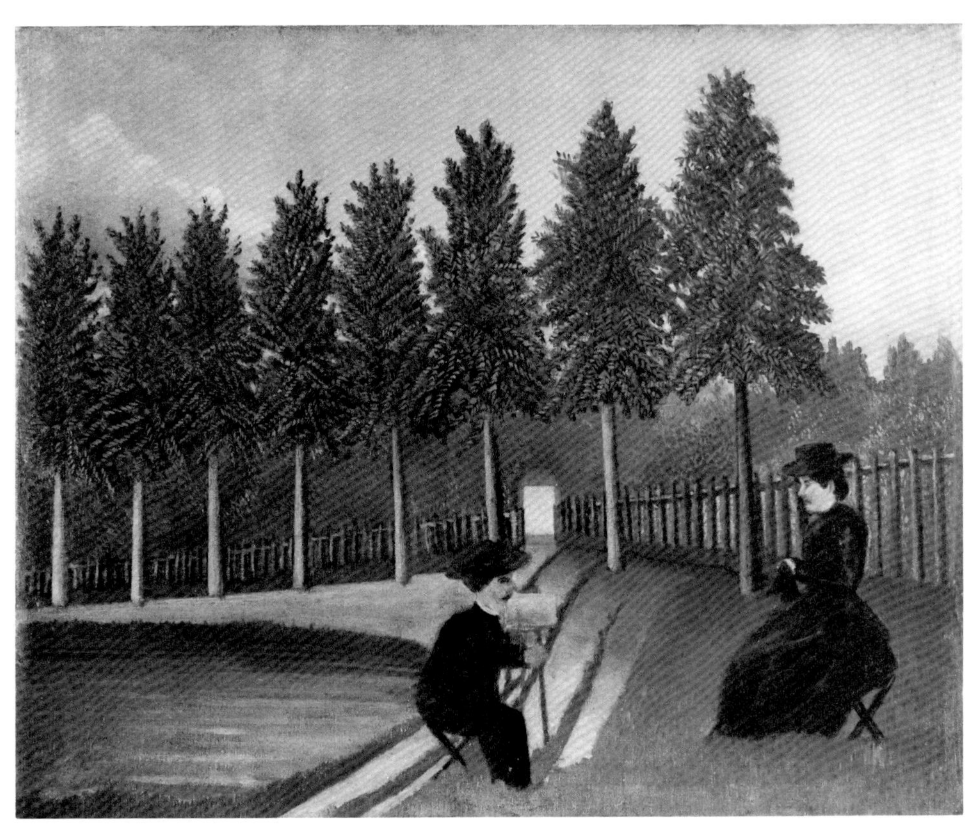

<u>Henri Rousseau</u> – 10 F. (55 × 46)
Sa femme assise (à droite) et lui-même (au centre) devant un petit chevalet. Au fond peupliers.*) Reproduction aux „Cahiers d'art" 1934, No 9–10.
Prix: 500 mille <u>net</u>.

*) et buissons d'automne.

CONTACTS WITH OTHER ARTISTS

175 *24 Essais de Jakovski.* Editions G. Orobitz et Cie, Paris, 1935

Book with 23 etchings by Hans Arp, Alexander Calder, Giorgio de Chirico, Hans Erni, Max Ernst, Louis Fernandez, Alberto Giacometti, Nicolas Ghika, Julio González, Jean Hélion, Vasily Kandinsky, Fernand Léger, Jacques Lipchitz, Alberto Magnelli, Joan Miró, Ben Nicholson, Amédée Ozenfant, Pablo Picasso, Kurt Seligmann, Sophie Taeuber-Arp, Joaquín Torres-García, Gérard Vulliamy, Ossip Zadkine

Etchings on paper, each 13⅜ x 10⅝" (34 x 27 cm.)

a. Collection Fondation Arp, Clamart
b. Collection Kupferstichkabinett, Kunstmuseum Basel

Vasily Kandinsky

176 *Preparatory Drawing for Etching for "24 Essais de Jakovski" (Etude pour gravure pour "24 Essais de Jakovski").* 1934

India ink and pencil on paper, 10½ x 8⅛" (26.6 x 20.7 cm.)

Collection Musée National d'Art Moderne, Centre Georges Pompidou, Paris, Kandinsky Bequest

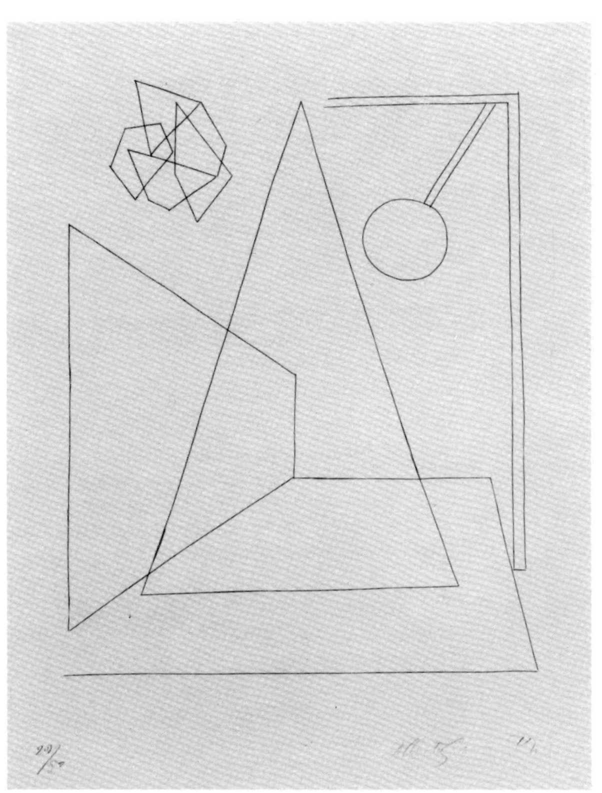

Etching by Giacometti

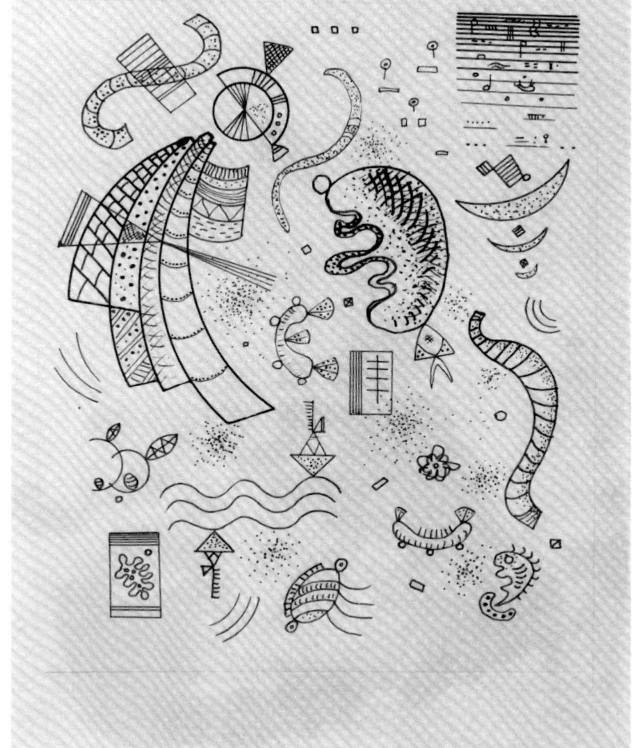

Katherine S. Dreier

177 *Untitled.* 1934

Watercolor and lithograph on paper,
11⅜ x 15¹⁵⁄₁₆" (28.9 x 40.4 cm.)

Collection Musée National d'Art Moderne,
Centre Georges Pompidou, Paris,
Kandinsky Bequest

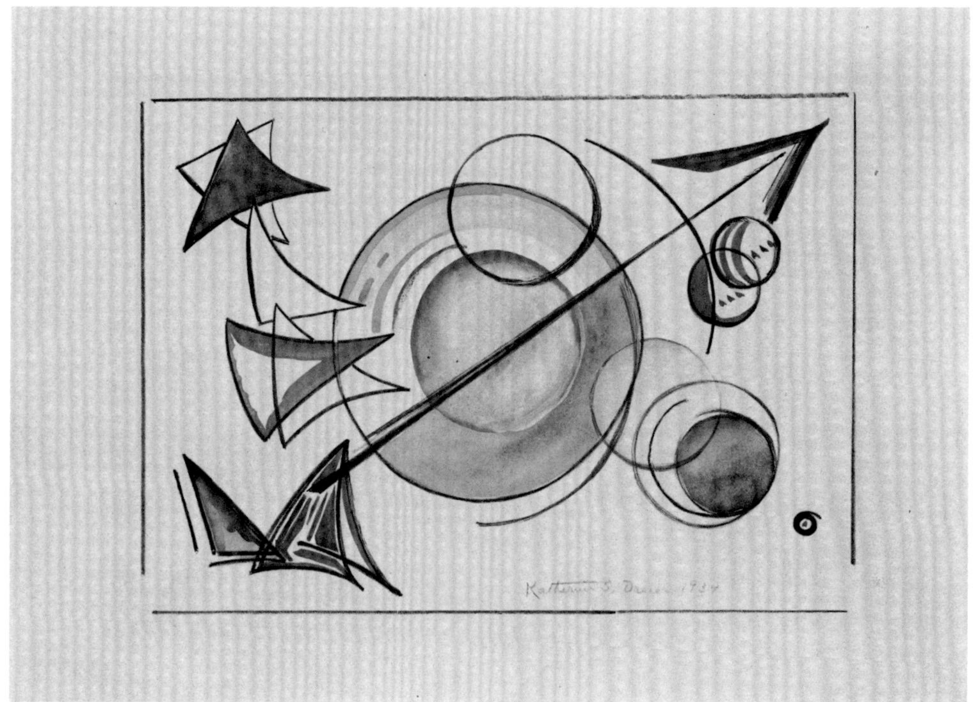

Otto Freundlich

178 *Composition.* December 1935
Gouache on paper, 65 x 55⅛″
(165 x 140 cm.)
Collection Musée National d'Art Moderne,
Centre Georges Pompidou, Paris

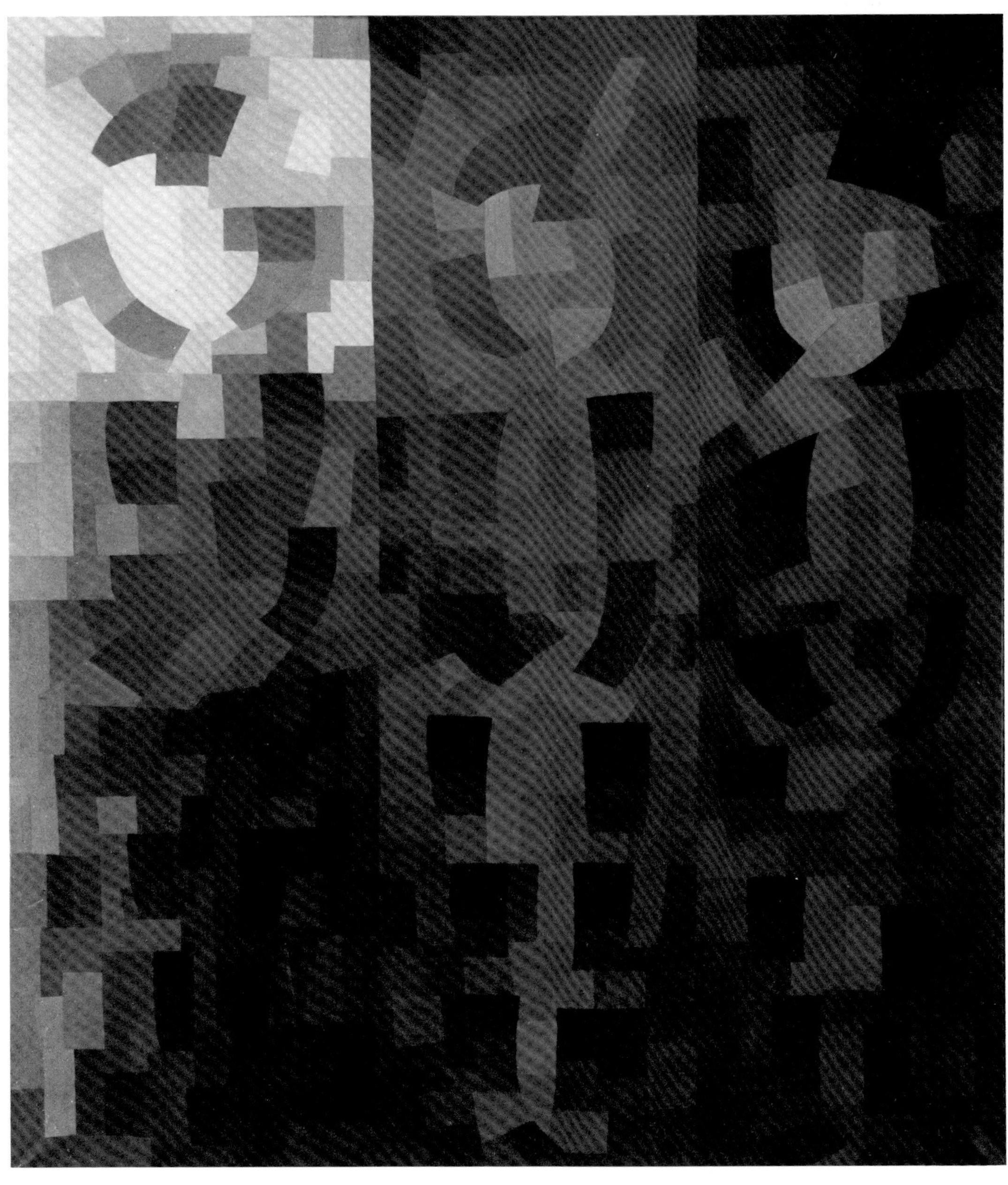

Antoine Pevsner

179 *Construction.* 1932
Bronze and plastic, $22\frac{5}{8}$ x $26\frac{1}{8}$ x $8\frac{3}{4}$"
(57.4 x 66 x 22.2 cm.)
Collection Solomon R. Guggenheim Museum, New York

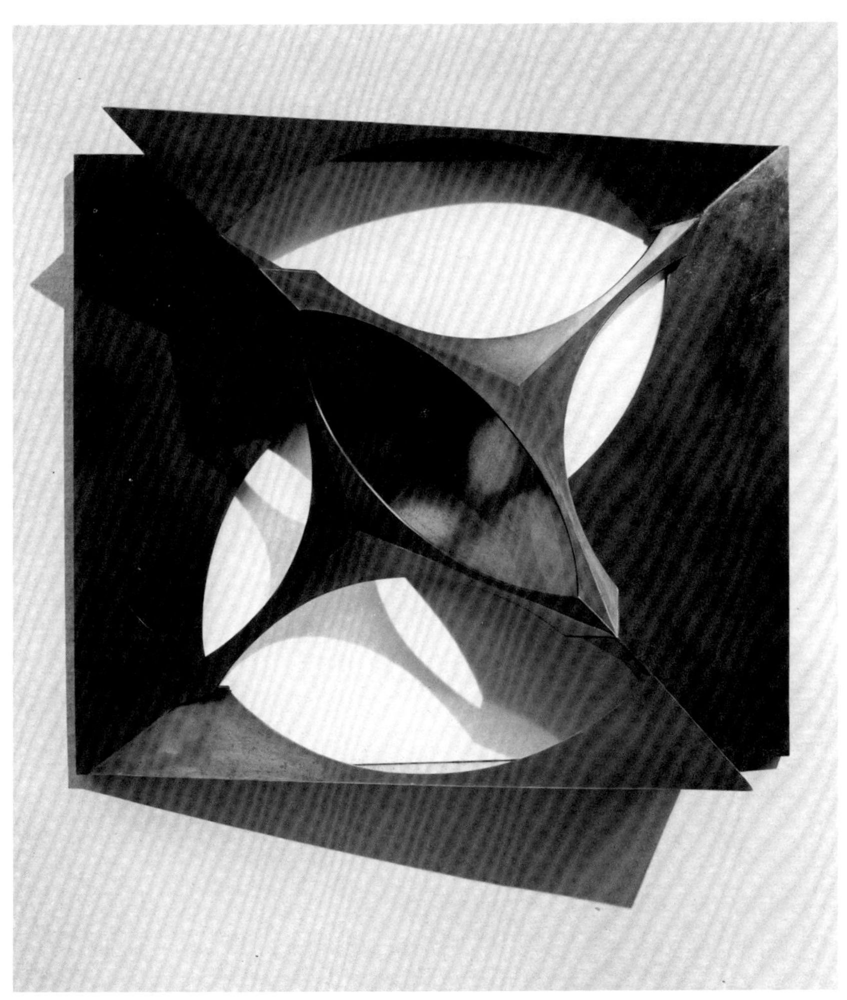

Antoine Pevsner

180 *Construction for an Airport.* 1934–35
Bronze and plastic, 32¼ x 28¼ x 32$^{11}/_{16}$″ (82 x 72 x 83 cm.)
Collection Museum Moderner Kunst, Vienna

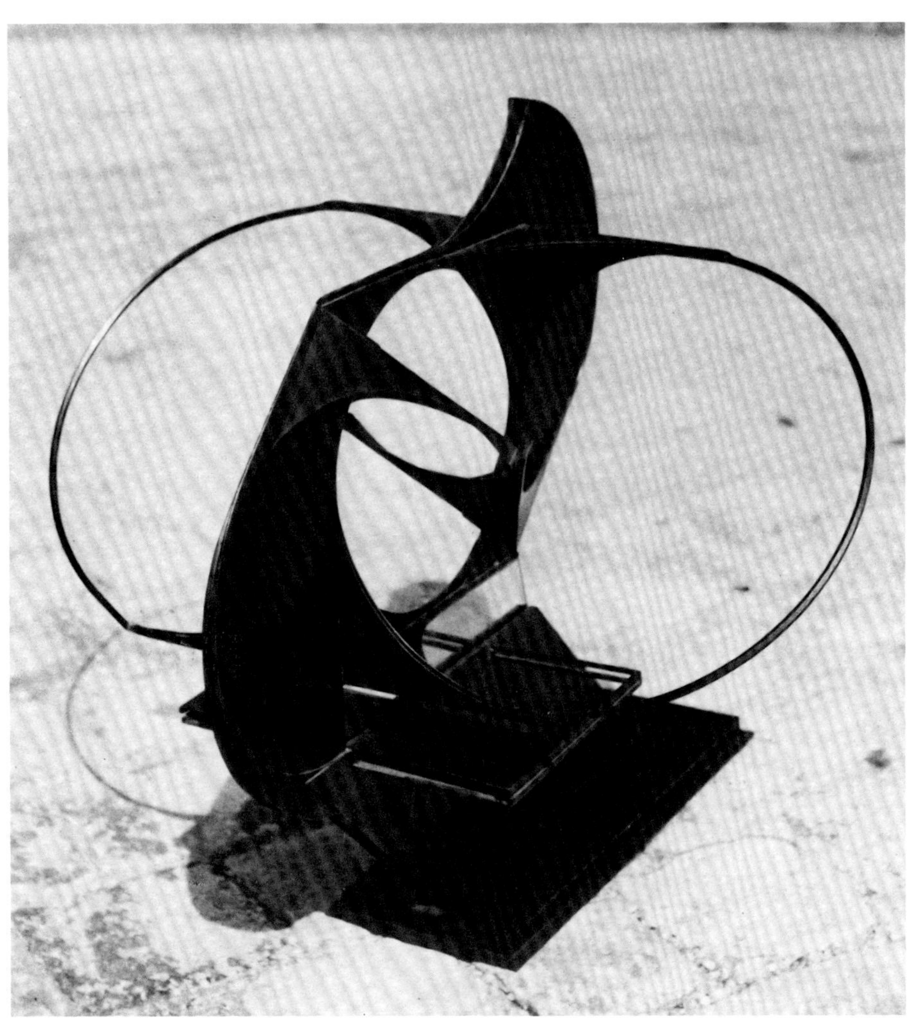

Fernand Léger

181 *The Transport of Forces (Le Transport des forces).* 1937

Gouache on paper, 19⅞ x 41$\frac{5}{16}$" (50.5 x 105 cm.)

Collection Musée National Fernand Léger, Biot

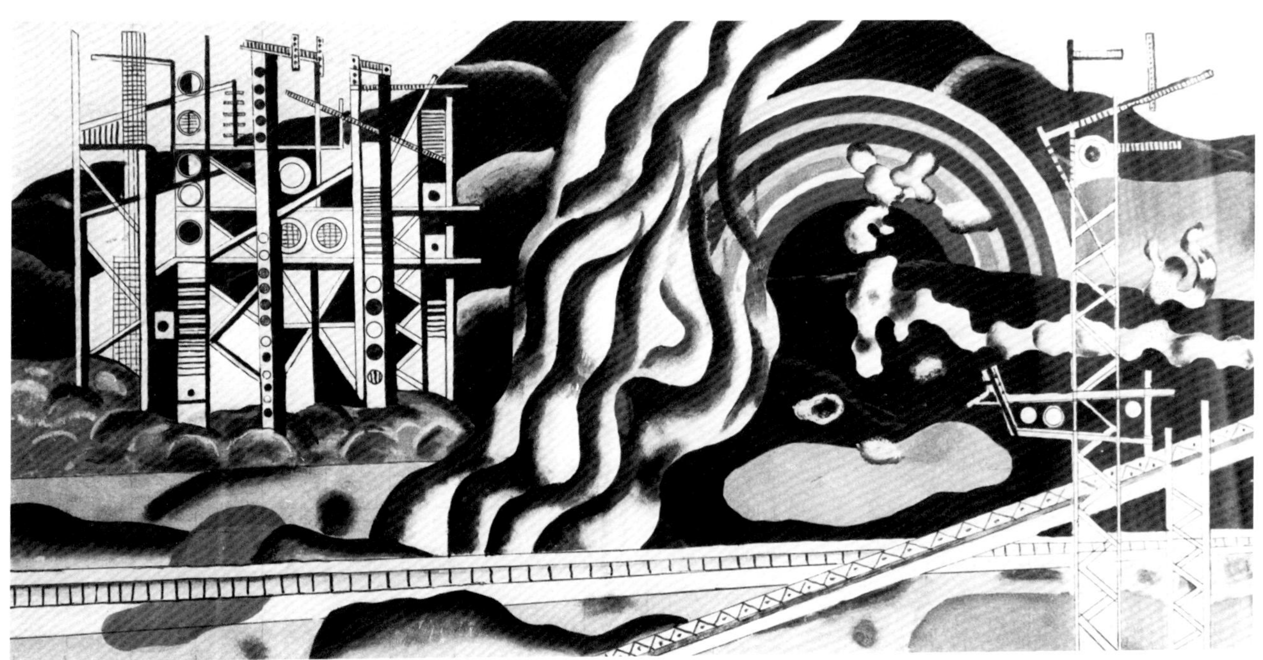

Robert Delaunay

182 *Design for the Mural "Propeller and Rhythm," from the Palais de l'Air, International Exhibition, 1937 (Projet pour le panneau du Palais de l'Air "Hélice et rythme," Exposition Internationale, 1937).*
1937
Watercolor on paper mounted on canvas, 28⅜ x 32¹¹⁄₁₆" (72 x 83 cm.)
Collection Musée National d'Art Moderne, Centre Georges Pompidou, Paris

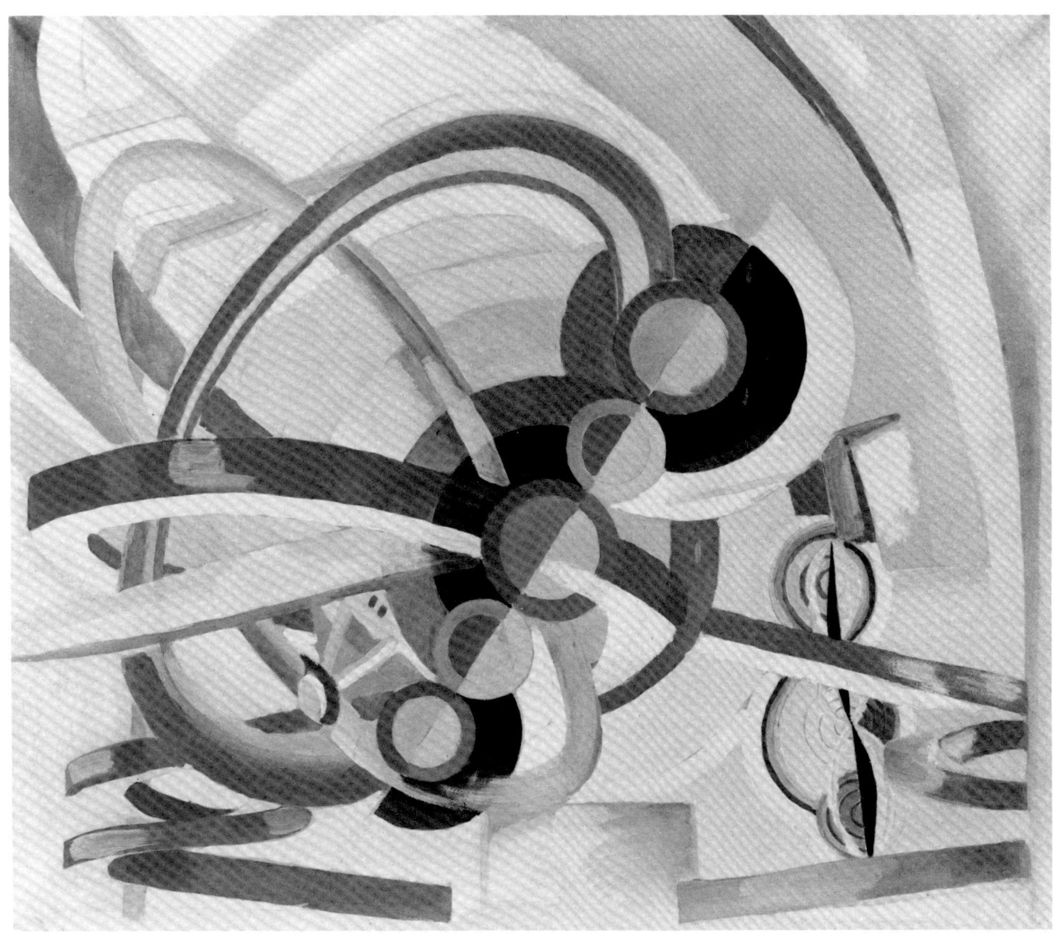

Sonia Delaunay

183 *Colored Rhythm (Rythme coloré).* 1942
Gouache on paper, 25 3/16 x 20 1/8"
(64 x 51 cm.)
Collection Megatrends, Limited

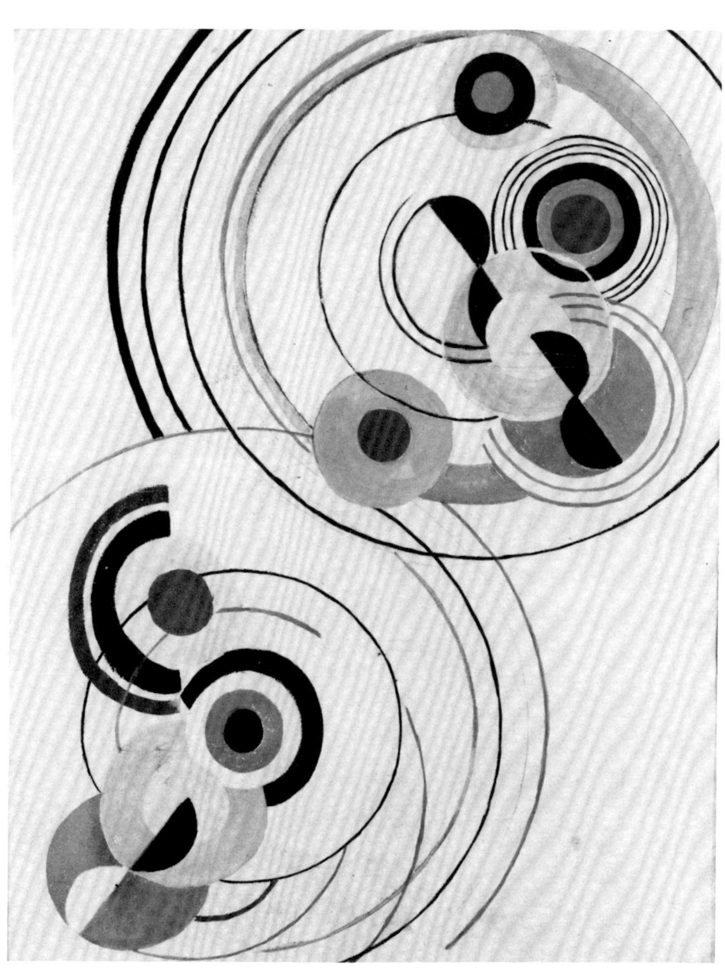

Georges Vantongerloo

184 *Extended, Green Curves (Etendue, courbes vertes).* 1938
Oil on Masonite, 31½ x 25½″
(80 x 64.5 cm.)
Collection Max Bill, Zürich

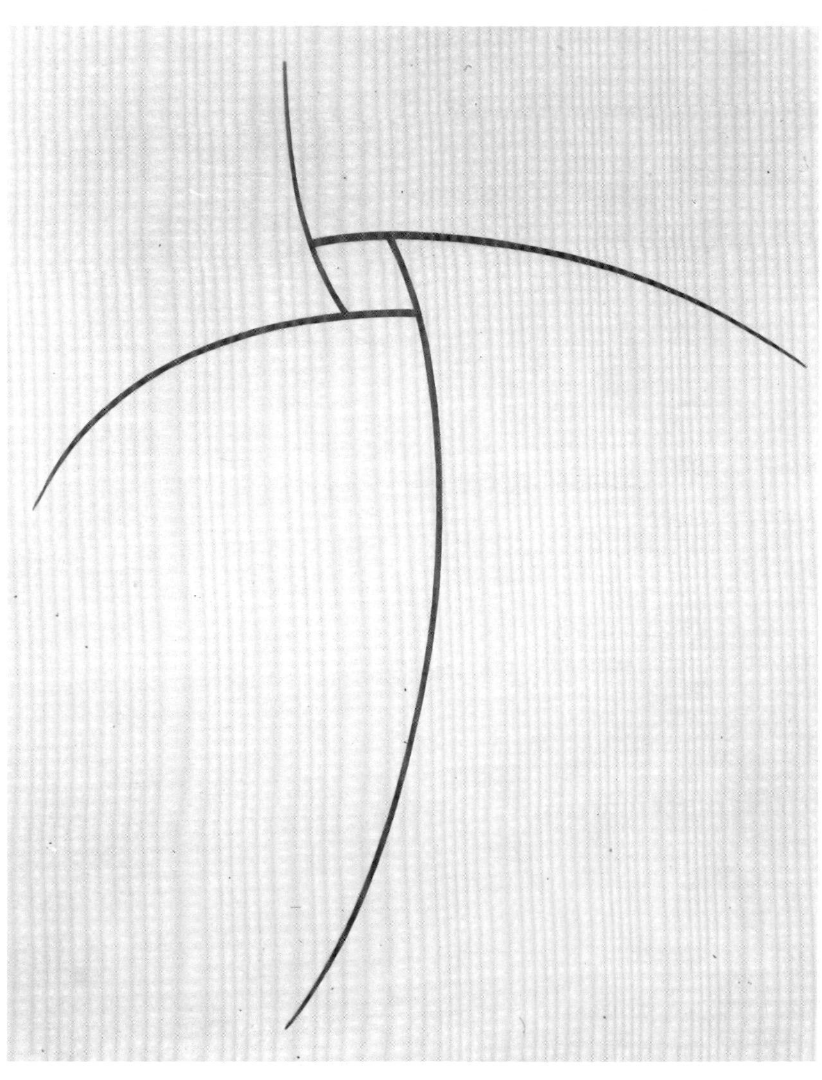

Josef Albers

185 *Prismatic II.* 1936
Oil on Masonite, 18⅝ x 19⅞″
(47.3 x 50.5 cm.)
Collection Anni Albers and the Josef Albers Foundation

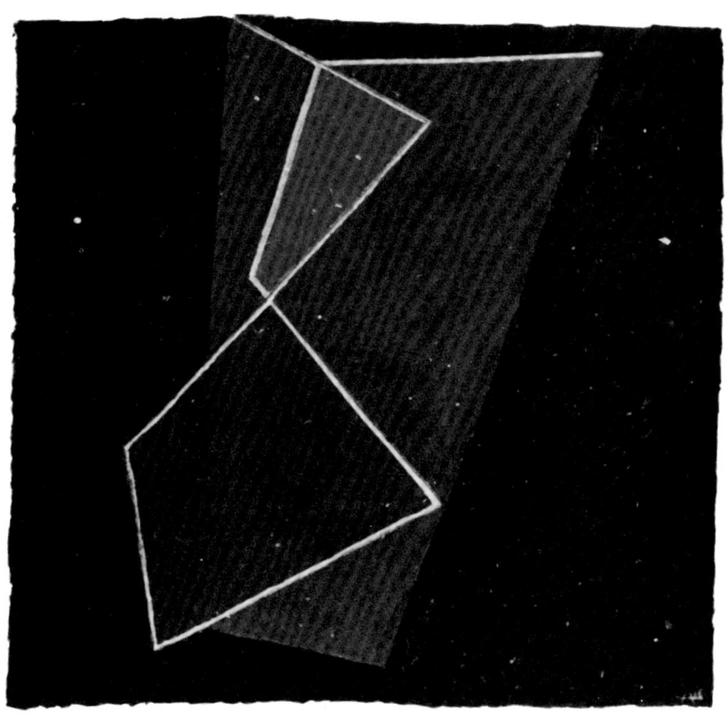

Alberto Magnelli

186 *Bouncing Forms (Formes rebondissantes).*
1937
Oil on canvas, 39⅜ x 49⅛"
(100 x 125 cm.)
Collection Musée de Vallauris, France

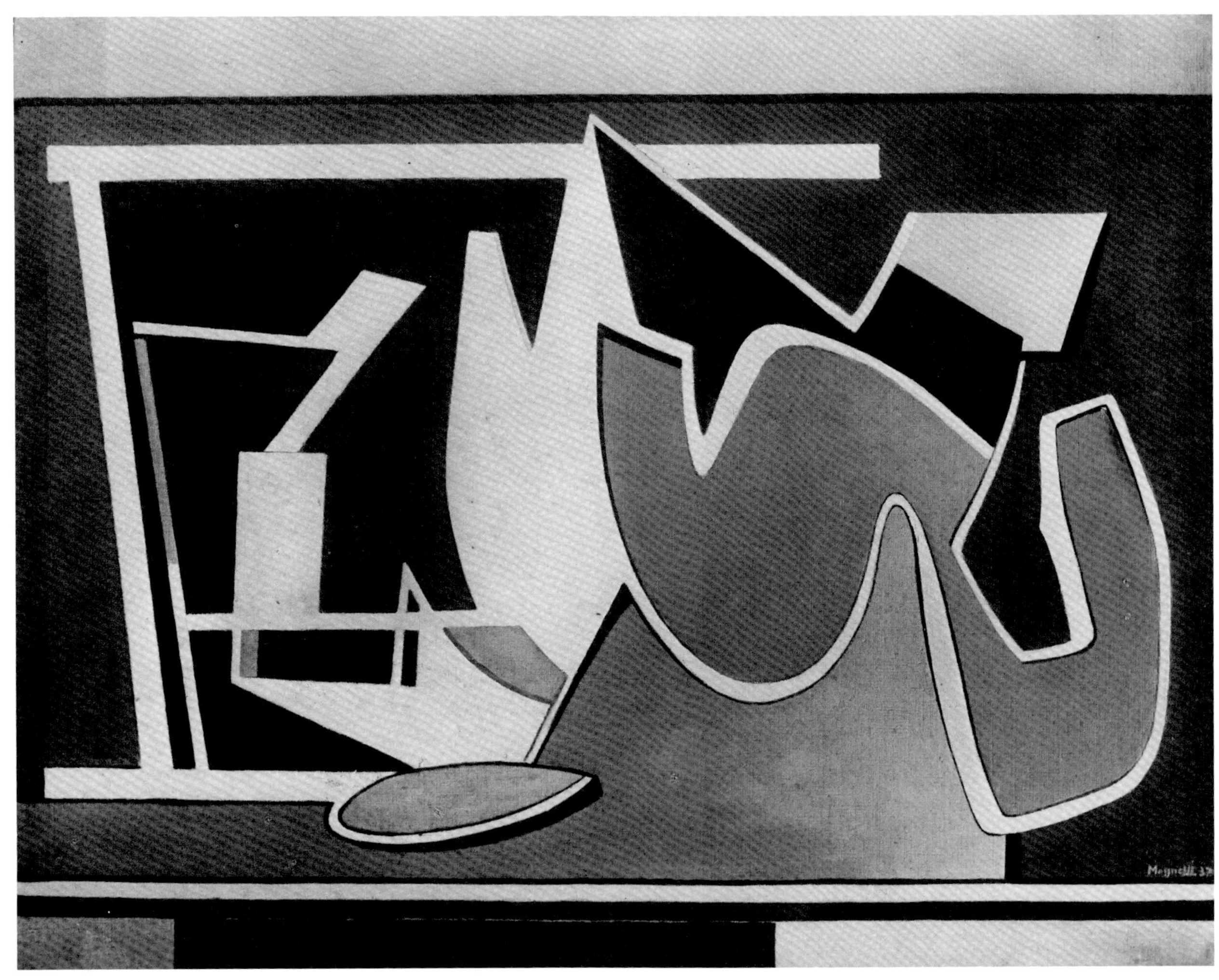

Sophie Taeuber-Arp

187 *Lines of Summer (Lignes d'été).* 1942
Pastel on paper, 19⅛ x 14¾"
(48.5 x 37.5 cm.)
Collection Emanuel Hoffmann-Foundation, Kunstmuseum Basel

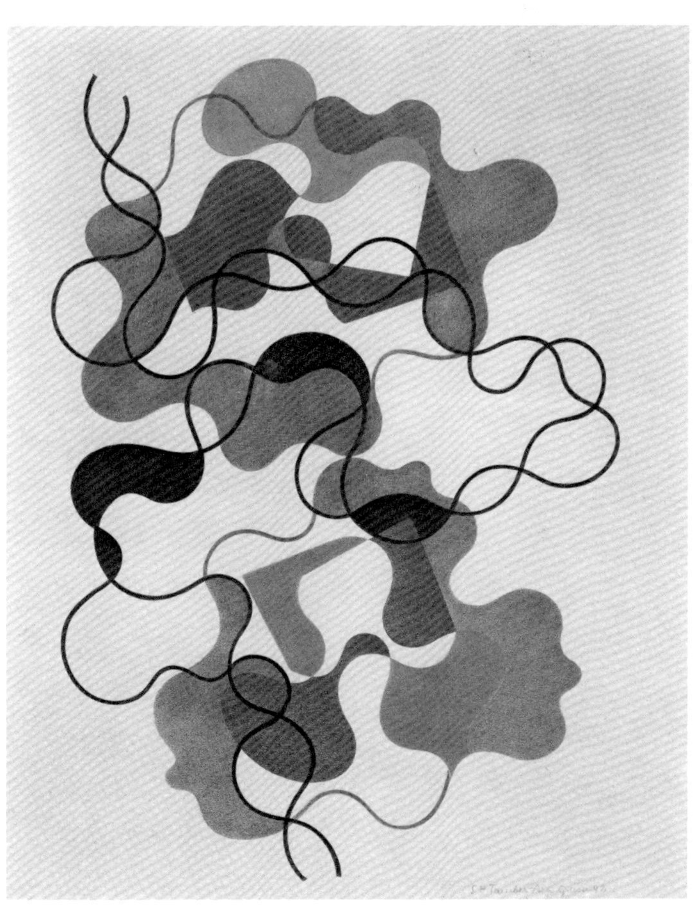

Paule Vézelay

188 *Composition.* 1934
Oil on canvas, 28⁵⁄₁₆ x 13⅜" (72 x 34 cm.)
Collection Association-Fondation
Christian et Yvonne Zervos, Vézelay

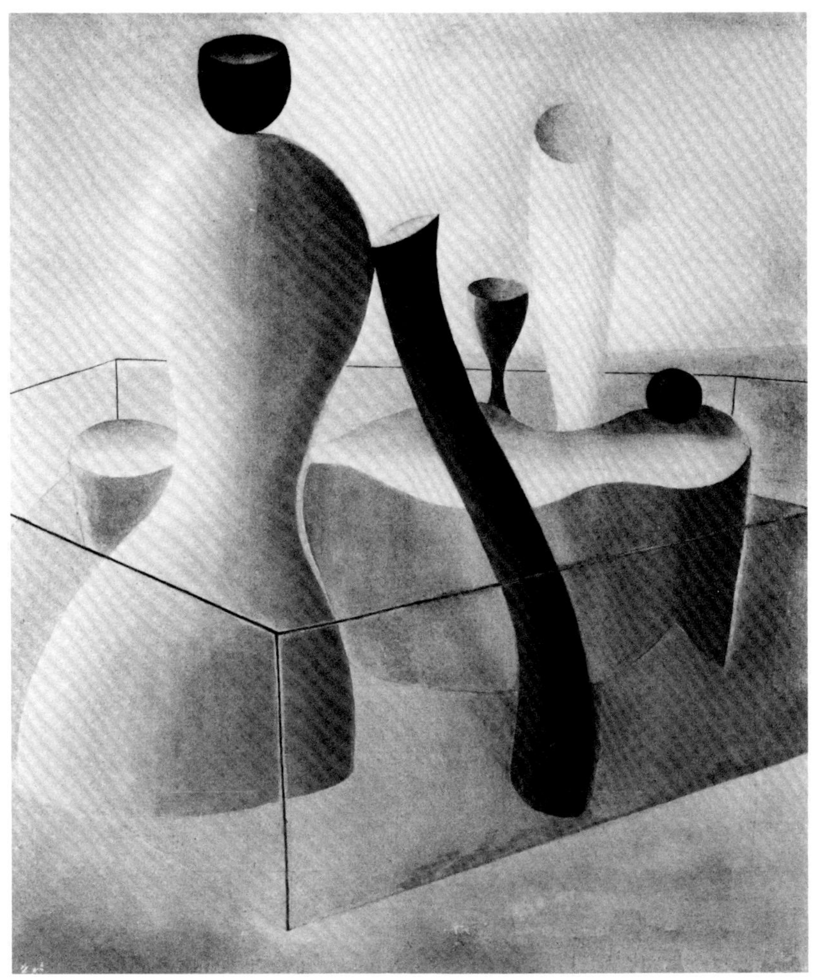

César Domela

189 *Relief No. 15G.* 1942
Plexiglass, ebony, brass and copper on wood, $31\frac{1}{16}$ x $25\frac{1}{8}$ x $1\frac{1}{8}$" (79 x 64 x 3 cm.)
Collection Domela

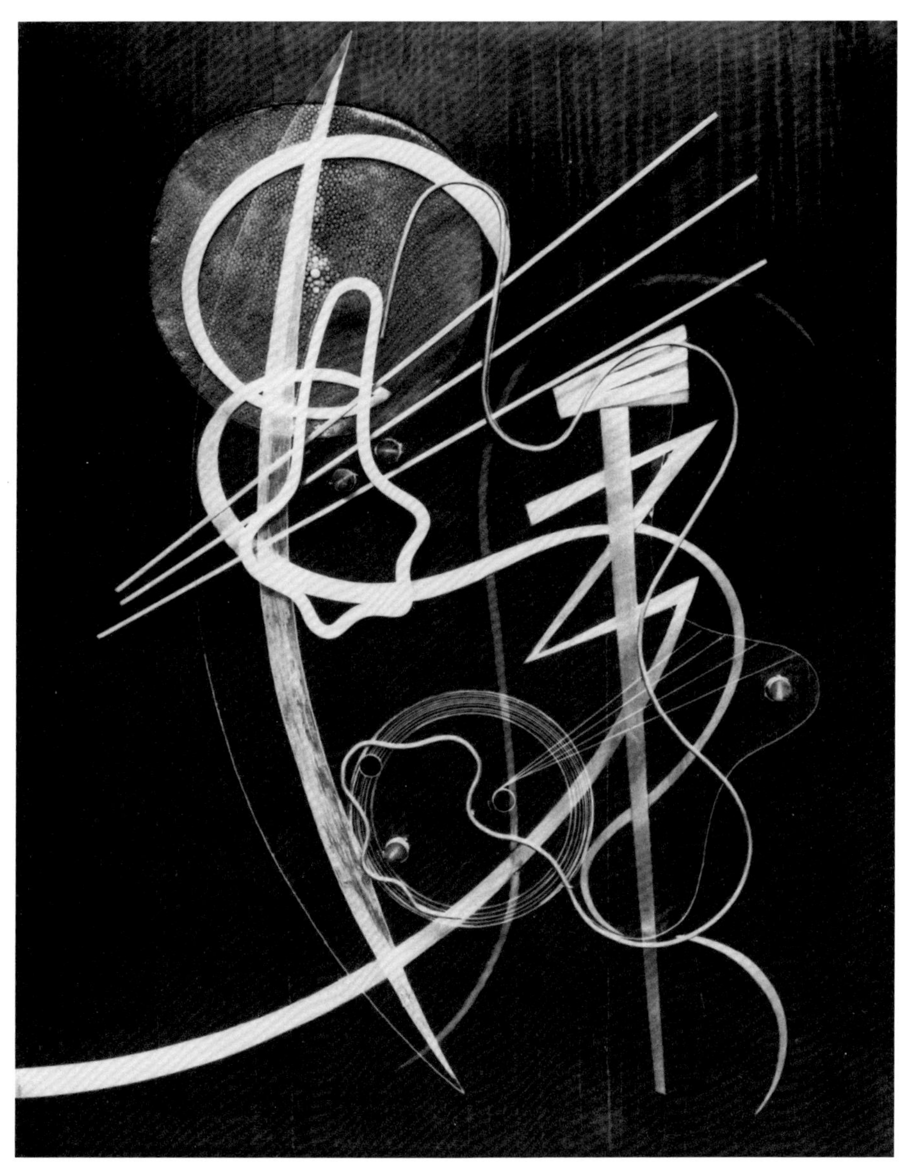

Jean Hélion

190 *Composition.* 1934
Oil on canvas, 51½ x 63¾″
(130.8 x 162 cm.)
Collection Mr. and Mrs. Burton Tremaine,
Meriden, Connecticut

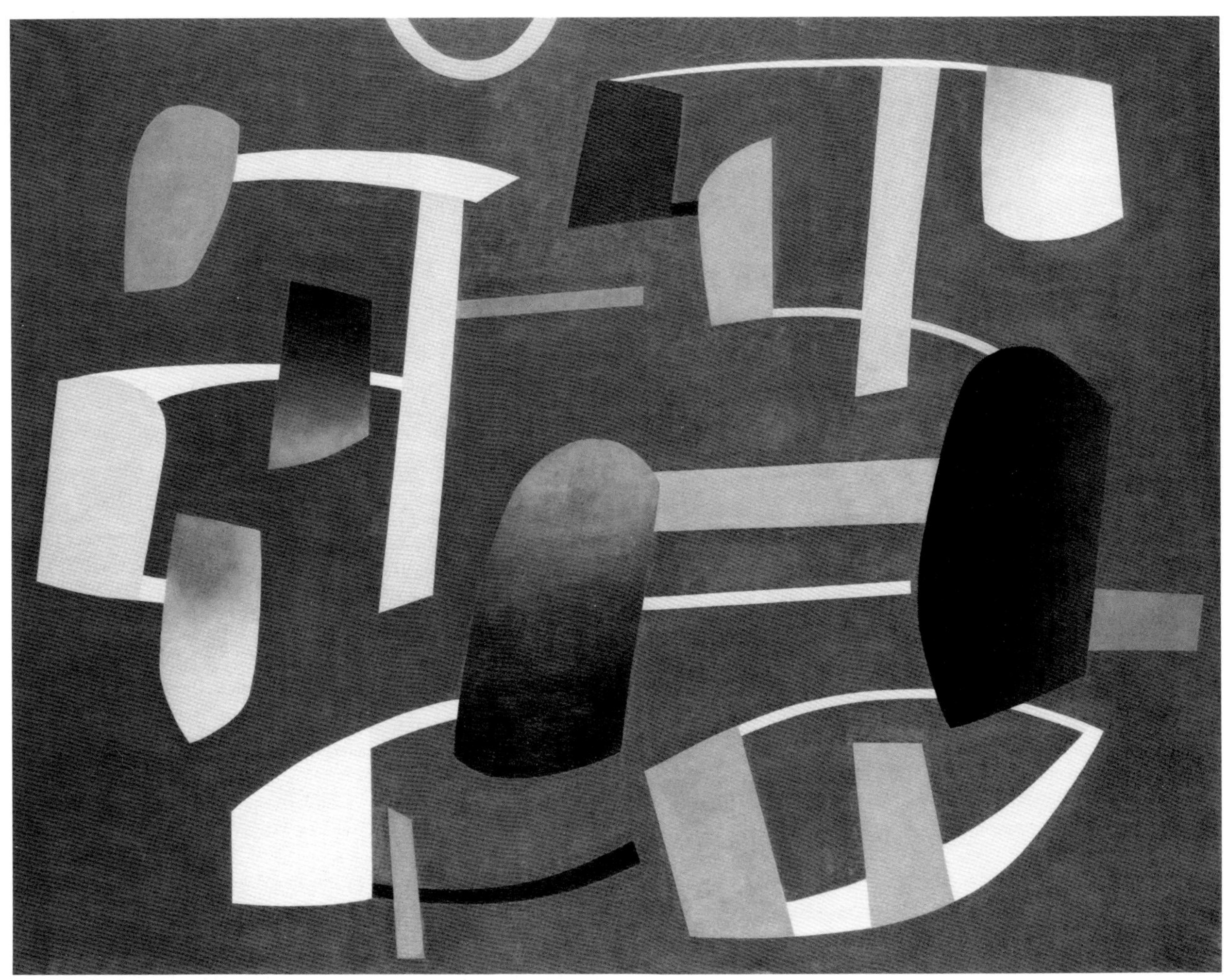

Max Bill

191 *Construction in Brass (Construction en laiton).* 1939
Brass, $55\frac{1}{8} \times 14\frac{1}{8} \times 14\frac{1}{8}$"
(140 x 36 x 36 cm.)
Private Collection, Zumikon

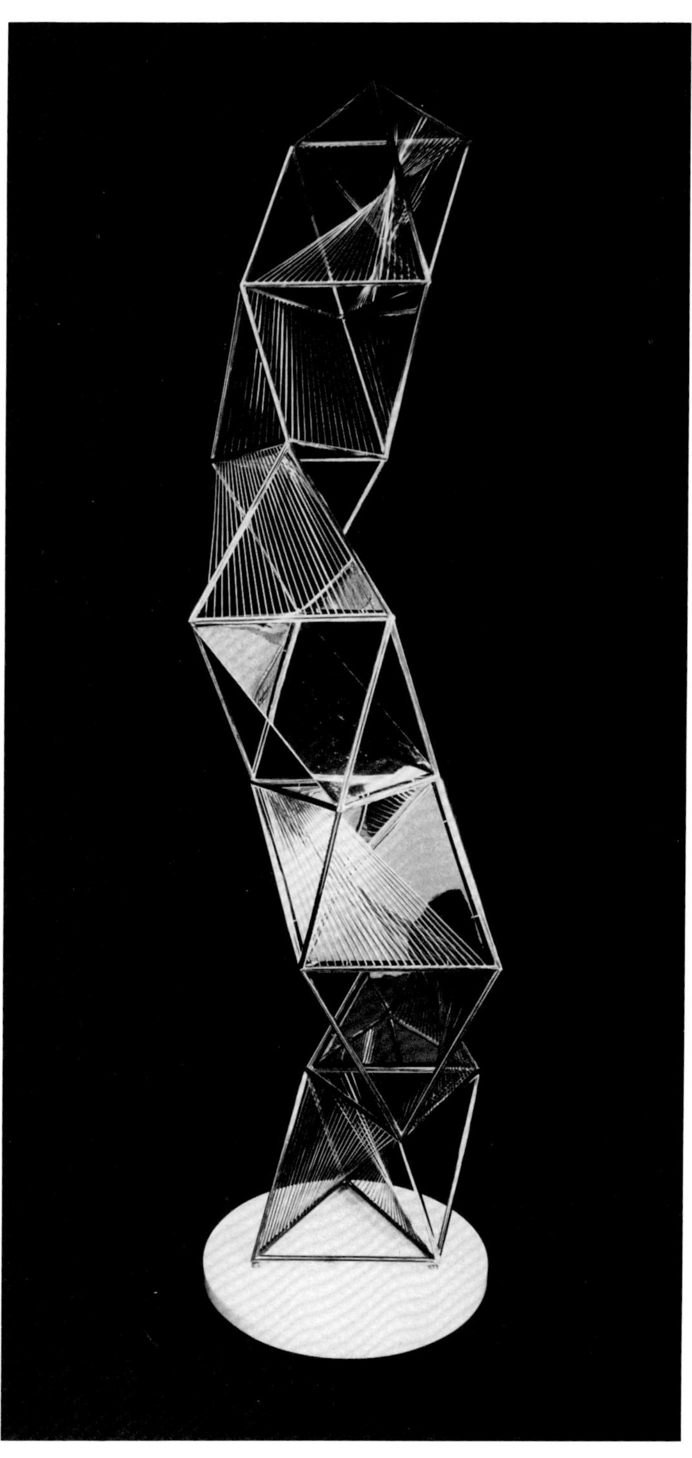

†192 a-j *10 Origin.* Max Bill, ed., Allianz Verlag, Zürich, 1942

Portfolio with 10 etchings by Georges Vantongerloo, Alberto Magnelli, Leo Leuppi, Max Bill, Hans Arp, Sophie Taeuber-Arp, Richard P. Lohse, Sonia Delaunay, César Domela, Vasily Kandinsky

Etchings on paper, each 10$^{13}/_{16}$ x 8$^{1}/_{2}$" (27.5 x 21.5 cm.)

Collection Domela

Vasily Kandinsky

193 *Proof for Woodcut for "10 Origin" (Epreuve pour gravure sur bois pour "10 Origin").* May 16, 1942

Woodcut on paper, 8$^{1}/_{4}$ x 6$^{5}/_{8}$" (21 x 16.8 cm.)

Collection Musée National d'Art Moderne, Centre Georges Pompidou, Paris, Kandinsky Bequest

Alberto Magnelli

194 *Untitled (Sans titre).* 1942

Etching on paper, 10$^{3}/_{4}$ x 8$^{1}/_{4}$" (27.3 x 21 cm.)

Collection Musée National d'Art Moderne, Centre Georges Pompidou, Paris

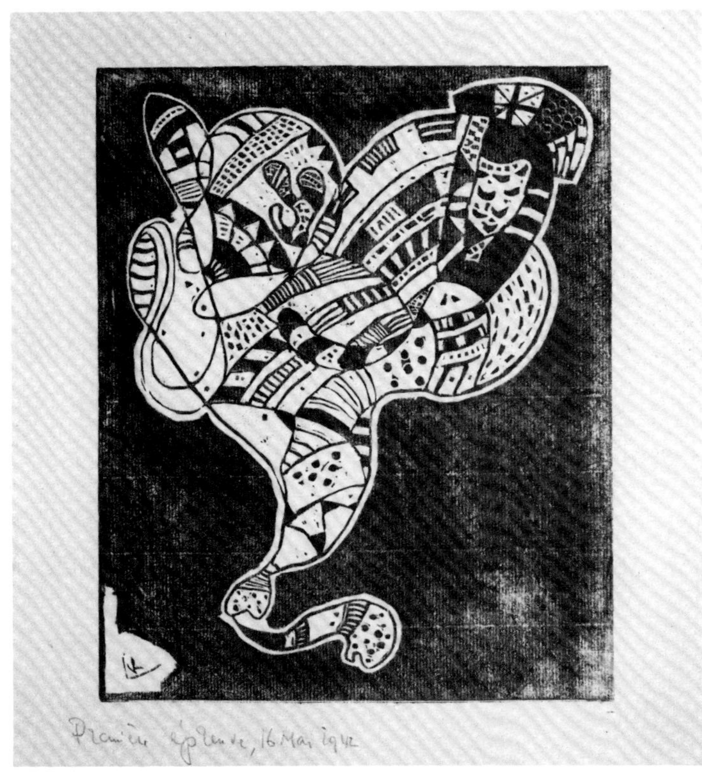

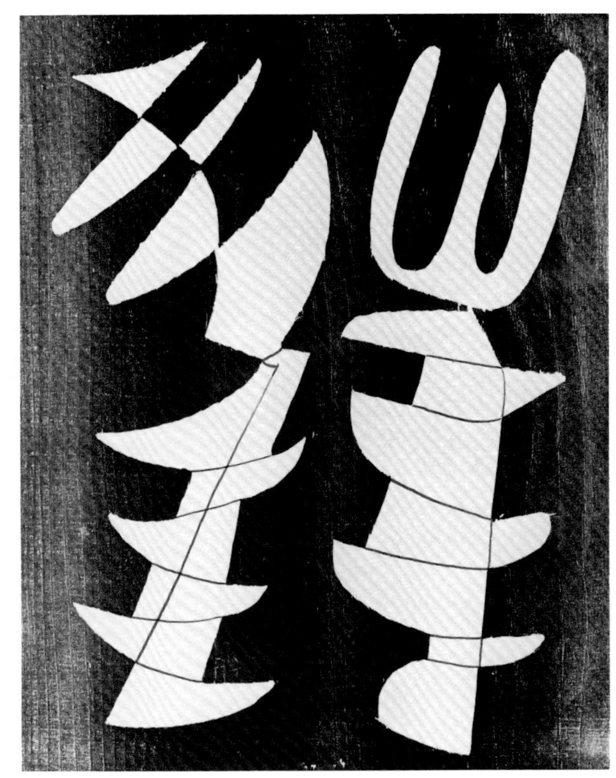

Maria-Helena Vieira da Silva
195 *The Card Game (Le Jeu de cartes).* 1937
Oil on canvas, 28⅝ x 36¼" (73 x 92 cm.)
Lent by Galerie Jeanne Bucher, Paris

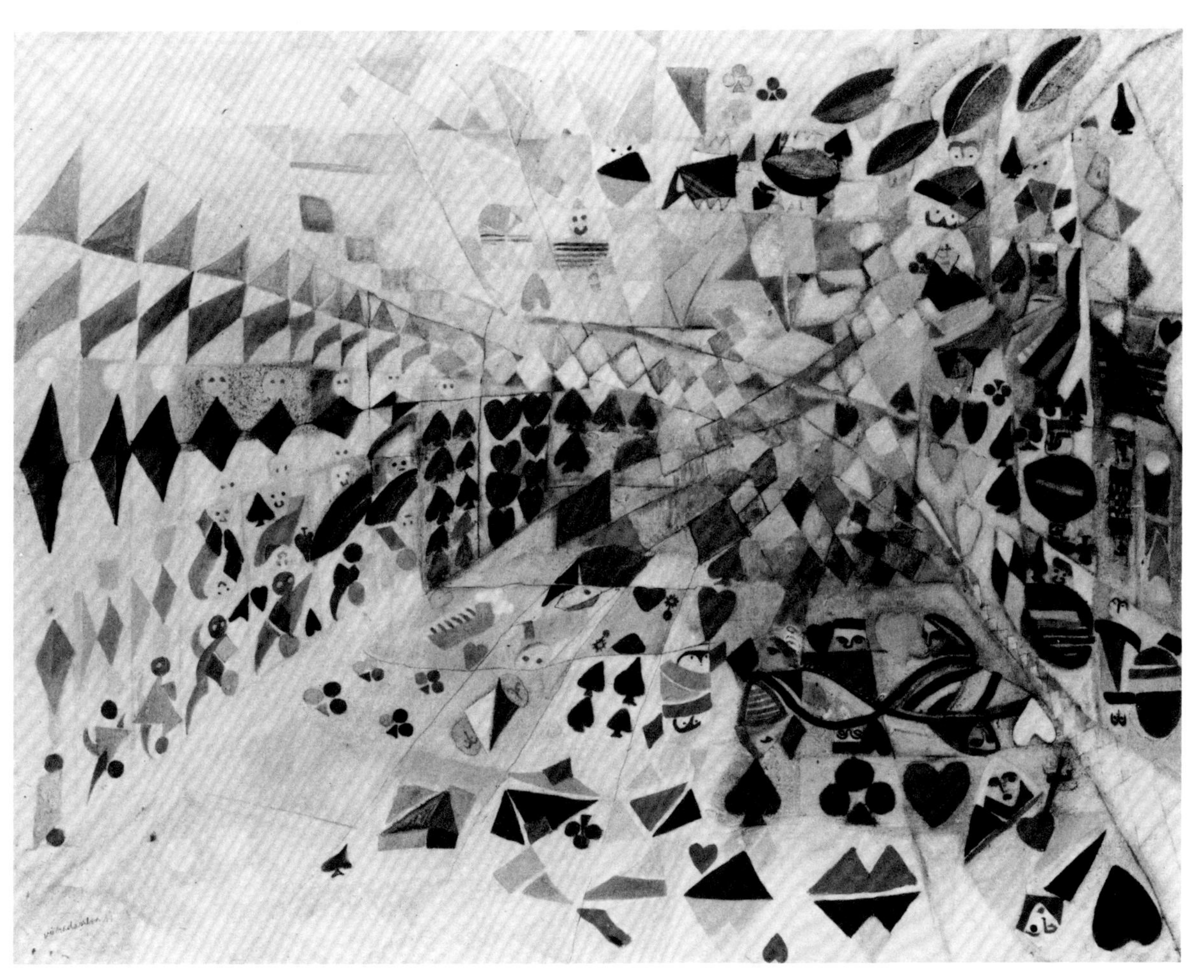

Ejler Bille

196 *Animals in Various Rooms.* 1937
Oil on canvas, 28¾ x 21¼" (73 x 54 cm.)
Collection Esbjerg Kunstforening, Esbjerg, Denmark

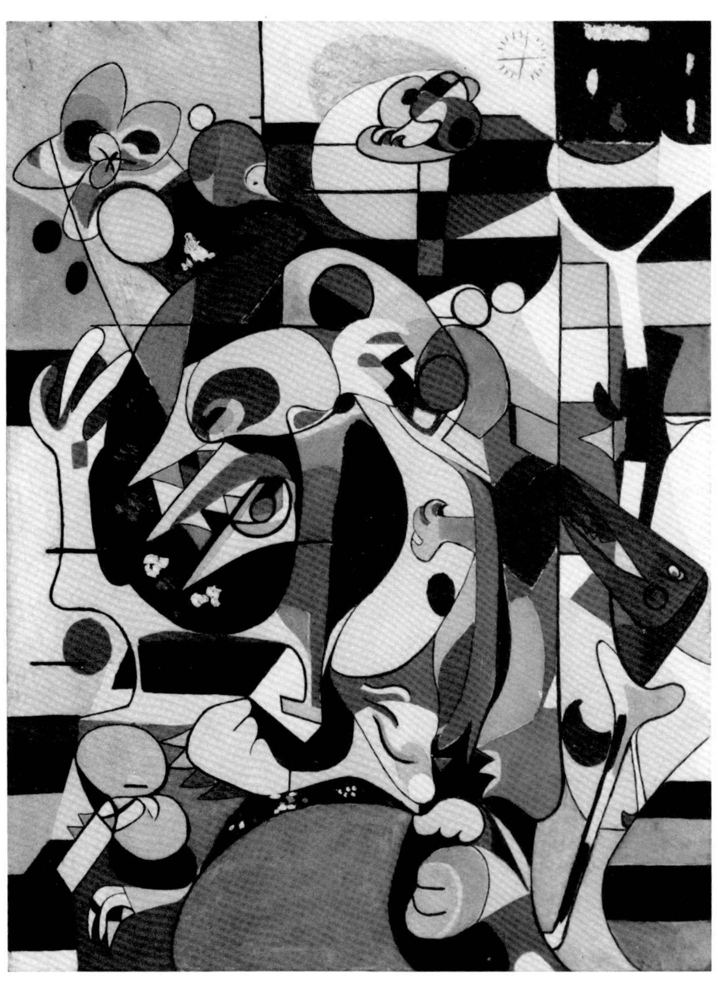

Richard Mortensen

197 *Portrait of a Thistle.* 1938

Oil on canvas, 59 x 43¼″ (150 x 110 cm.)

Collection Statens Museum for Kunst, Copenhagen

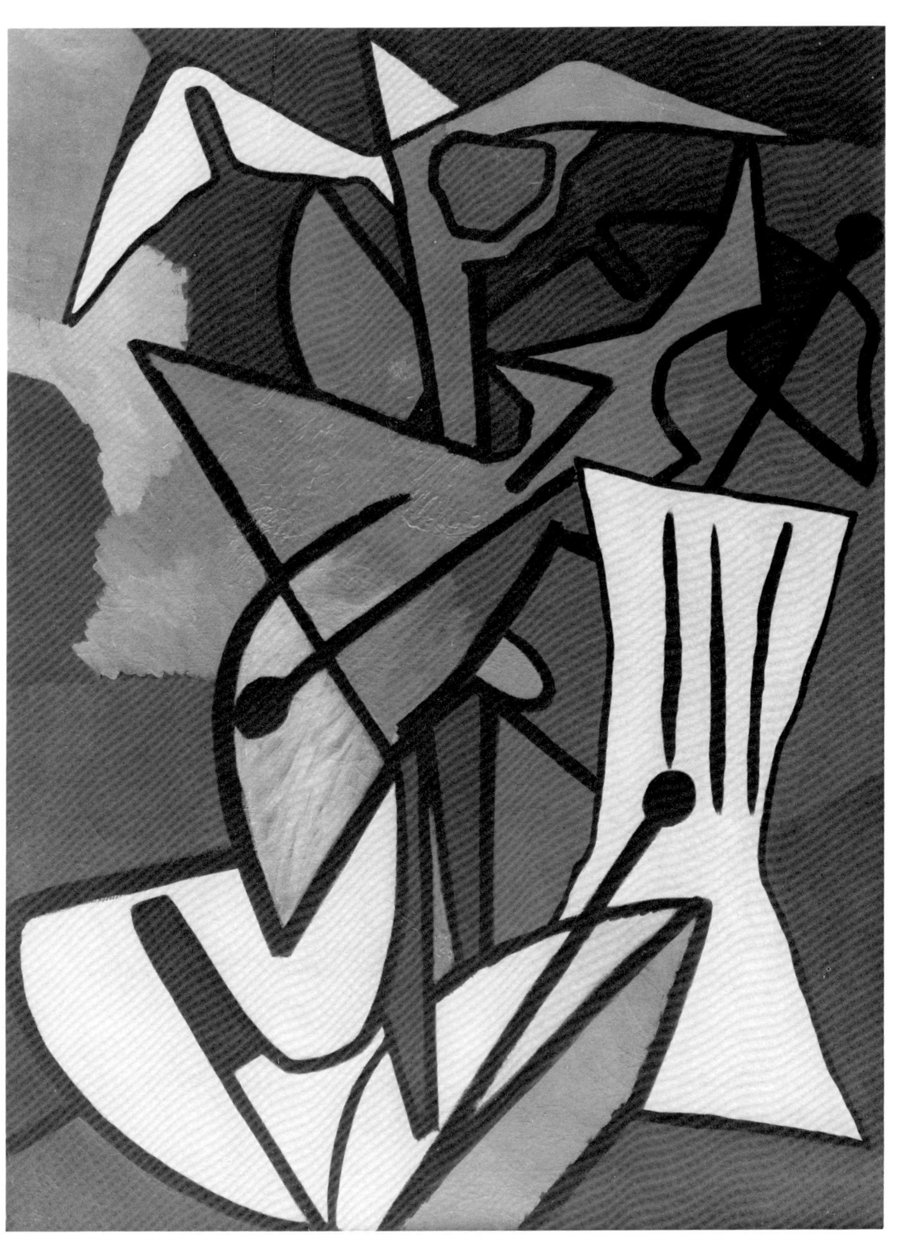

Richard Mortensen

198 *Untitled.* January 27, 1939
India ink on paper, 10¼ x 14⅛″
(25.9 x 35.9 cm.)
Collection Musée National d'Art Moderne,
Centre Georges Pompidou, Paris,
Kandinsky Bequest

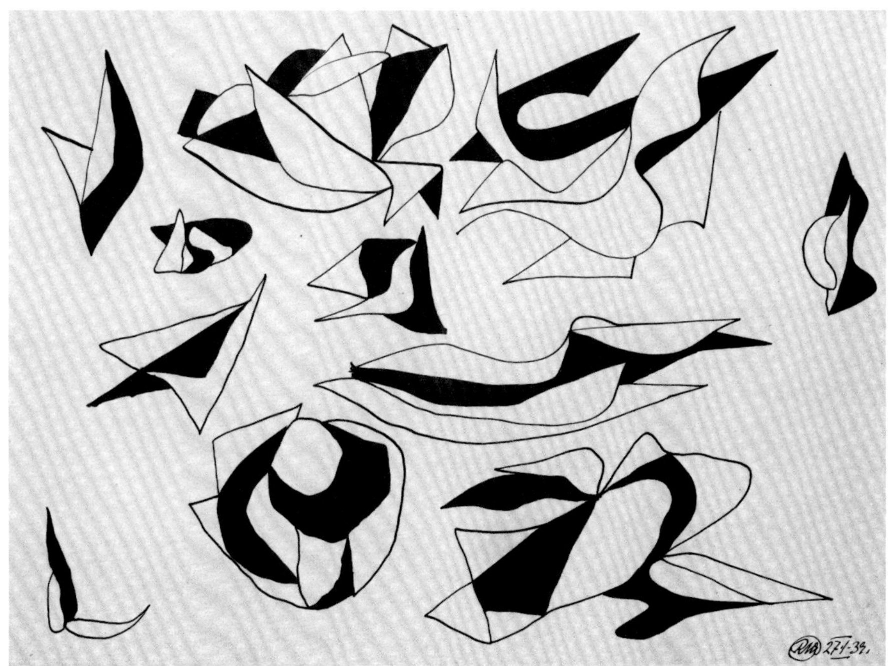

Nicolas de Staël

199 *Composition.* 1944
Oil on canvas, 41⅜ x 27³⁄₁₆″ (105 x 69 cm.)
Private Collection

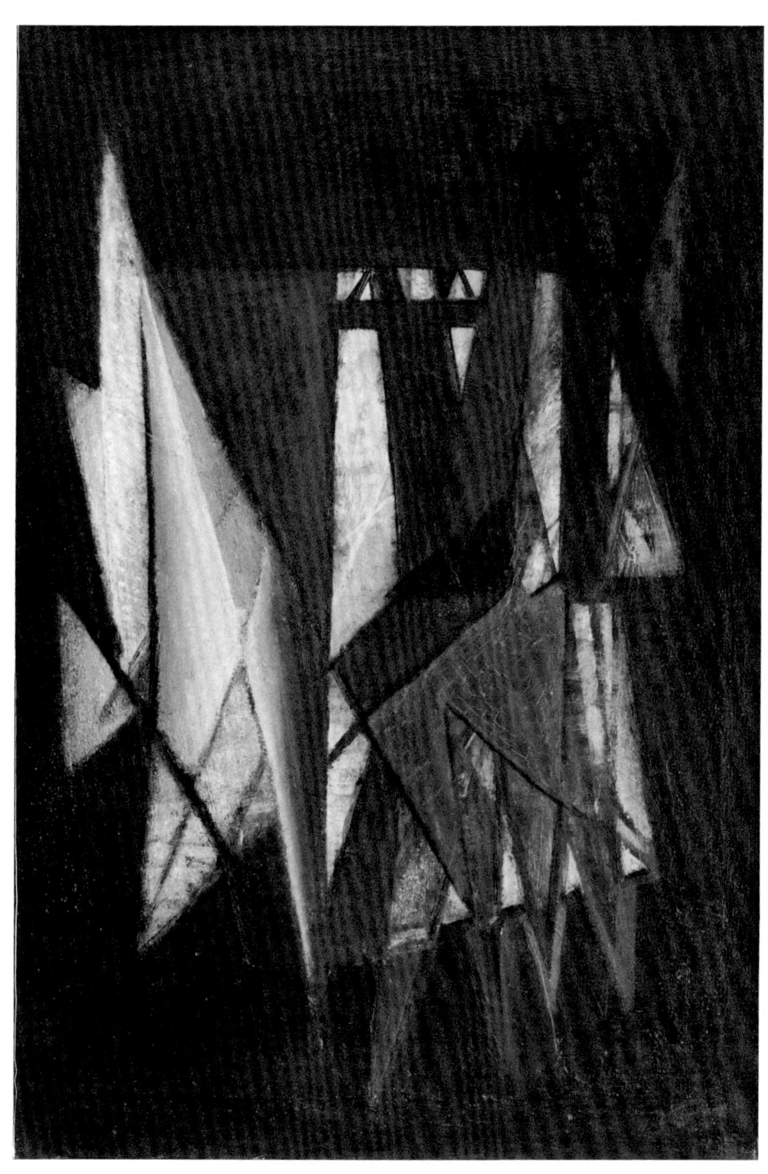

DOCUMENTS

200 *Letter from Kandinsky to Will Grohmann.* December 4, 1933
Staatsgalerie Stuttgart, Archiv Will Grohmann

201 *Letter from Kandinsky to Will Grohmann.* January 7, 1934
Staatsgalerie Stuttgart, Archiv Will Grohmann

202 *Letter from Solomon R. Guggenheim to Kandinsky.* February 7, 1934
Collection Musée National d'Art Moderne, Centre Georges Pompidou, Paris, Kandinsky Bequest

203 *Letter from Anni Albers to Kandinsky.* February 9, 1935
Collection Musée National d'Art Moderne, Centre Georges Pompidou, Paris, Kandinsky Bequest

204 *Postcard from Piet Mondrian to Kandinsky.* April 25, 1935
Collection Musée National d'Art Moderne, Centre Georges Pompidou, Paris, Kandinsky Bequest

205 *Letter from Kandinsky to Katherine S. Dreier.* June 12, 1935
Collection American Literature, The Beinecke Rare Book and Manuscript Library, Yale University

206 *Letter from Joan Miró to Kandinsky.* July 12, 1935
Collection Musée National d'Art Moderne, Centre Georges Pompidou, Paris, Kandinsky Bequest

207 *Postcard from Hans Arp to Kandinsky.* September 18, 1936
Collection Musée National d'Art Moderne, Centre Georges Pompidou, Paris, Kandinsky Bequest

208 *Letter from Hilla Rebay to Kandinsky.* December 9, 1936
Collection Musée National d'Art Moderne, Centre Georges Pompidou, Paris, Kandinsky Bequest

209 *Letter from Kandinsky to Hilla Rebay.* December 16, 1936
The Hilla von Rebay Foundation Archive

210 *Letter from André Dézarrois to Kandinsky.* April 5, 1937
Collection Musée National d'Art Moderne, Centre Georges Pompidou, Paris, Kandinsky Bequest

211 *Letter from Marguerite Guggenheim to Kandinsky.* February 15, 1938
Collection Musée National d'Art Moderne, Centre Georges Pompidou, Paris, Kandinsky Bequest

212 *Letter from Kandinsky to Katherine S. Dreier.* August 5, 1938
Collection American Literature, The Beinecke Rare Book and Manuscript Library, Yale University

213 *Letter from Paul Klee to Kandinsky.* December 30, 1939
Collection Musée National d'Art Moderne, Centre Georges Pompidou, Paris, Kandinsky Bequest

214 *Letter from Varian Fry of the Centre Américain de Secours to Kandinsky.* May 7, 1941
Collection Musée National d'Art Moderne, Centre Georges Pompidou, Paris, Kandinsky Bequest

215 *Postcard from Kandinsky to Hans Arp.* July 28, 1942
Collection Fondation Arp, Clamart

216 *Letter from Alberto Magnelli to Kandinsky.* January 22, 1944
Collection Musée National d'Art Moderne, Centre Georges Pompidou, Paris, Kandinsky Bequest

217 *Letter from Kandinsky to Alberto Magnelli.* January 28, 1944
Collection Bibliothèque Nationale, Paris

218 *Letter from Filippo Tommaso Marinetti to Kandinsky.* n.d.
Collection Musée National d'Art Moderne, Centre Georges Pompidou, Paris, Kandinsky Bequest

219 *Kandinsky,* exhibition catalogue, Galleria del Milione, Milan, April 24–May 9, 1934
Collection Musée National d'Art Moderne, Centre Georges Pompidou, Paris, Kandinsky Bequest

Vasily Kandinsky

220 *Manuscript for "Line and Fish."* March 1935
Collection Musée National d'Art Moderne, Centre Georges Pompidou, Paris, Kandinsky Bequest

221 *Kandinsky,* exhibition catalogue, Galerie des "Cahiers d'Art," Paris, June 21–September 10, 1935
Collection Musée National d'Art Moderne, Centre Georges Pompidou, Paris, Kandinsky Bequest

222 *Kandinsky: toiles récentes, aquarelles, graphiques de 1910–1935,* exhibition catalogue, Galerie Jeanne Bucher, Paris, December 3-19, 1936
The Blue Rider Research Trust

Vasily Kandinsky

223 "Tilegnelse af Kunst" ["Assimilation of Art"], *Linien,* Copenhagen, 1937
Collection Musée National d'Art Moderne, Centre Georges Pompidou, Paris, Kandinsky Bequest

224a-d *Kandinsky's Naturalization Documents.* 1938
Collection Musée National d'Art Moderne, Centre Georges Pompidou, Paris, Kandinsky Bequest

225 *Wassily Kandinsky,* exhibition catalogue, Guggenheim Jeune, London, February 18–March 18, 1939
The Blue Rider Research Trust

Vasily Kandinsky

226 *Manuscript for "Stabilité animée."* March 1938
Collection Musée National d'Art Moderne, Centre Georges Pompidou, Paris, Kandinsky Bequest

227 *Etapes de l'oeuvre de Wassily Kandinsky,* exhibition catalogue, Galerie l'Esquisse, Paris, November 7–December 7, 1944
Collection Musée National d'Art Moderne, Centre Georges Pompidou, Paris, Kandinsky Bequest

CHRONOLOGY

By Vivian Endicott Barnett with Christian Derouet, Susan B. Hirschfeld, Lewis Kachur, Clark V. Poling, Jane Sharp and Susan Alyson Stein.

The following is a modified version of the chronology in *Kandinsky at the Guggenheim,* New York, 1983.

1866
December 4. Vasilii Vasilievich Kandinsky born in Moscow to Vasilii, a tea merchant, and Lidia Tikheeva Kandinsky.

1871
Family moves to Odessa. Parents are divorced.

1876
Attends Gymnasium where he learns to play piano and cello. First of yearly trips, made until 1885, to Moscow with father.

1886
Studies economics and law at University of Moscow.

1889
May 28–June 30. Makes expedition to Vologda province sponsored by Society of Natural Science and Anthropology. Subsequently publishes two articles on tribal religious beliefs and peasant law.
Travels to Paris.

1892
Completes university studies and passes law examination. Marries cousin Ania Shemiakina.
Second trip to Paris.

1893
Writes dissertation "On the Legality of Laborer's Wages." Appointed teaching assistant at Faculty of Law, University of Moscow.

1895
Becomes artistic director of Kušnerev printing firm in Moscow. Designs covers for chocolate boxes.

1896
Sees a *Haystack* by Monet at *French Industrial and Art Exhibition* in Moscow.
Declines lectureship at University of Dorpat; instead moves to Munich to study painting and soon enrolls in art school of Anton Ažbe.

1897
Meets Alexej Jawlensky and Marianne von Werefkin as well as other Russian artists Igor Grabar and Dmitrii Kardovsky, who spend time in Munich and study with Ažbe.

1898–99
Fails entrance examination to Munich Academy; works independently.

1900
Student of Franz von Stuck at Academy in Munich.
Participates in *Moskovskoe tovarishchestvo khudozhnikov (Moscow Association of Artists)* annual; shows with them yearly until 1908.

1901
April. His first art review, "Kritika kritikov" ("Critique of Critics"), published in *Novosti dnia (News of the Day),* Moscow.
May. Cofounds *Phalanx* exhibition society; becomes its president later this year.
August 15–November. First *Phalanx* exhibition. Eleven more are held until 1904.
Fall. Participates in *Exhibition of the Association of South Russian Artists,* Odessa.
Trip to Odessa.
Phalanx art school established; Kandinsky teaches drawing and painting there.

1902
Meets Gabriele Münter, a student in his painting class.
Reviews contemporary art scene in Munich, "Korrespondentsiia iz Miunkhena" ("Correspondence from Munich"), for periodical *Mir Iskusstva (World of Art),* St. Petersburg.
Participates in *Mir Iskusstva* exhibition, St. Petersburg.
Spring. Participates in VI Berlin Secession.
Meets David Burliuk.

1903
Spring. Stops teaching; *Phalanx* school closes.
Late August. Peter Behrens offers Kandinsky position teaching decorative painting at Düsseldorf Kunstgewerbeschule (School of Arts and Crafts). By September declines offer.
Meets Vladimir Izdebsky in Munich.

1904
April. Works on theory of colors.
Summer. Participates in Munich Kunstverein exhibition.
Makes craft designs for *Vereinigung für angewandte Kunst (Society for Applied Art),* Munich.
June. Participates in inaugural exhibition of *Les Tendances Nouvelles,* Paris; beginning of association with this group.
September. Separates from wife.
Fall. Participates in Salon d'Automne, Paris; exhibits there yearly until 1910.
December. Last *Phalanx* exhibition; by year's end association dissolves. Kandinsky's *Stikhi bez slov (Poems without Words),* woodcuts, published by Stroganov, Moscow.
Participates in first exhibition of *New Society of Artists,* St. Petersburg, and *XV Exhibition of the Association of South Russian Artists,* Odessa; shows with latter five times, until 1909.
Receives medal at *Exposition Internationale de Paris.*

1905
Joins *Deutscher Künstlerbund.*
Awarded medal by *XIIe Exposition du Travail,* Paris.
Elected to jury of Salon d'Automne, Paris.

1906
Spring. Participates in XI Berlin Secession.
May 22. Arrives in Paris with Münter. Lives at 12, rue des Ursulines, Paris. At end of June moves to 4, petite rue des Binelles, Sèvres, where he and Münter live for one year.
Joins *Union Internationale des Beaux-Arts et des Lettres,* Paris, the organization that sponsored *Les Tendances Nouvelles* and its exhibitions.
Summer. Participates in *Ausstellung des Deutschen Künstlerbund,* Weimar.
July. Participates in *Exhibition of Signs and Posters* organized by Leonardo da Vinci Society, Moscow.
October–November. Participates in Galerie Wertheim exhibition, Berlin.
December. Participates in XII Berlin Secession.

1906–07
Winter. Participates in *Brücke* exhibition, Dresden.

1907
Spring. Participates in Salon des Indépendants, Paris; exhibits there until 1912.
May. Shows 109 works in *Le Musée du Peuple* exhibition, Angers, sponsored by *Les Tendances Nouvelles.*
Mid-June. Returns to Munich.
Begins *Klänge* woodcuts.
September 1907–April 1908. Lives with Münter in Berlin.
December. Participates in XIV Berlin Secession.

1908
Mid-August–September. First sojourn in Murnau; spends summer with Münter, Jawlensky and Werefkin at Griesbräu Inn.
Meets Thomas de Hartmann; begins collaborative work with him.

1908–09
Winter. Participates in Sergei Makovsky's Salon, St. Petersburg.

1909
January. Cofounds *Neue Künstlervereinigung München (NKVM) (New Artists' Society of Munich)* and is elected its president.
Spring. Begins writing abstract stage compositions *Der gelbe Klang, Grüner Klang* and *Schwarz und Weiss (The Yellow Sound, Green Sound* and *Black and White).*
Summer. His *Zylographies,* woodcuts, published by *Les Tendances Nouvelles* in Paris.
July. Participates in *Allied Artists' Association* annual, Royal Albert Hall, London; shows with them until 1913.
July–August. Münter acquires house in Murnau; she and Kandinsky often stay here until outbreak of World War I.
First *Hinterglasmalereien* (glass paintings).
First Improvisations.
October. Becomes Munich correspondent for journal *Apollon (Apollo),* St. Petersburg; writes reviews, "Pismo iz Miunkhena" ("Letters from Munich"), for one year.
December 1–15. First *NKVM* exhibition, Heinrich Thannhauser's Moderne Galerie, Munich.
December 17, 1909–February 6, 1910. Participates in Izdebsky's first International Salon, Odessa, which travels to Kiev, St. Petersburg and Riga during 1910.
Begins *Klänge* prose poems.

1910
January. Paints first Compositions.
September 1–14. Second *NKVM* exhibition at Thannhauser's Moderne Galerie, Munich.
October–December. Visits Weimar and Berlin en route to Russia. Spends time in St. Petersburg, Moscow and Odessa. In contact with older avant-garde artists Izdebsky, Nikolai Kul'bin and Vladimir Markov.
December. Participates in *Bubnovnyi valet (Jack of Diamonds)* exhibition, Moscow. Shows fifty-four works at Izdebsky's second International Salon, Odessa. Catalogue includes Kandinsky's essay "Soderzhanie i forma" ("Content and Form"). Returns to Munich at end of year. Completes manuscript of *Über das Geistige in der Kunst (On the Spiritual in Art).*

1911
January 2. Hears Arnold Schönberg's music for the first time; he soon initiates correspondence with the composer.
January 10. Resigns *NKVM* presidency.
February 9. His essay "Kuda idet 'novoe' iskusstvo?" ("Whither the 'New' Art?") published in periodical *Odesskie novosti (Odessa News).*
June. Writes to Franz Marc about plans for *Der Blaue Reiter (The Blue Rider)* almanac.
Mid-September. Meets Schönberg.
Fall. Divorce from Ania Shemiakina finalized.
Meets Paul Klee. Correspondence with Robert Delaunay, Natalia Goncharova and Mikhail Larionov.
December 2. Kandinsky, Marc, Münter and Alfred Kubin leave *NKVM* after jury rejects Kandinsky's *Composition V.*
December 18. *Erste Ausstellung der Redaktion der Blaue Reiter (First Exhibition of the Editorial Board of the Blue Rider)* opens at Thannhauser's Moderne Galerie, Munich.
December. *Über das Geistige in der Kunst* published by Piper, Munich.
December 29, 31. Shorter Russian version of *Über das Geistige in der Kunst* read by Kul'bin at *Second All-Russian Congress of Artists,* St. Petersburg.

Writes essay "Über Bühnenkomposition" ("On Stage Composition").

1912

January. Participates in *Jack of Diamonds* exhibition, Moscow.
February 12–April. Second *Blaue Reiter* exhibition held at Galerie Hans Goltz, Munich.
April. Second edition of *Über das Geistige in der Kunst* published by Piper, Munich.
May. *Der Blaue Reiter* almanac published by Piper, Munich.
May 25–September 30. Participates in *Sonderbund Internationale Kunstausstellung,* Cologne.
July 7–31. Participates in *Moderner Bund* exhibition, Zürich.
July. Extracts from *Über das Geistige in der Kunst* published by Alfred Stieglitz in *Camera Work,* New York.
Fall. Third edition of *Über das Geistige in der Kunst* published by Piper, Munich.
October 2–30. First one-man exhibition in Berlin at Galerie Der Sturm; exhibition subsequently tours to other German cities.
October 16–December 13. Travels in Russia, stays in Odessa and Moscow.
November 5–18. One-man exhibition at Gallery Oldenzeel, Rotterdam.
December 10. Kurdibowsky presents Kandinsky's art theories in lecture at meeting of *Society of Painters,* St. Petersburg.
December. Several *Klänge* poems published without Kandinsky's consent in Russian vanguard publication *Poshchechina obshchestvennomu vkusu (A Slap in the Face of Public Taste),* Moscow.
Klänge, prose poems and woodcuts, published by Piper, Munich.

1913

Kandinsky and Marc prepare for second *Der Blaue Reiter* almanac, but volume never appears.
February 17–March 15. Shows one work, *Improvisation 27 (Garden of Love),* at Armory Show, New York, which travels to Chicago and Boston.
Kandinsky, Erich Heckel, Klee, Oskar Kokoschka, Kubin and Marc plan to collaborate on Bible illustrations.
September. Kandinsky's essay "Malerei als reine Kunst" ("Painting as Pure Art") appears in *Der Sturm,* Berlin.
September 20–December 1. Participates in Herwarth Walden's *Erster deutscher Herbstsalon (First German Autumn Salon)* at Galerie Der Sturm, Berlin.
October. Album *Kandinsky, 1901-1913* published by Der Sturm, Berlin, includes "Rückblicke" ("Reminiscences") as well as his descriptions of paintings *Composition IV, Composition VI* and *Painting with White Border.*
November 7–December 8. Participates in *Moderne Kunst Kring (Modern Art Circle),* Stedelijk Museum, Amsterdam.

1914

January 1. One-man show opens at Thannhauser's Moderne Galerie, Munich.
January. Invited to lecture at opening of one-man exhibition at *Kreis für Kunst,* Cologne. Submits manuscript but does not deliver lecture.
March. Second edition of *Der Blaue Reiter* almanac published by Piper, Munich. Hugo Ball plans book on the new theater with participation of Kandinsky, Klee, Marc, de Hartmann and others. War curtails production.
April 23. English edition of *Uber das Geistige in der Kunst* published in London and Boston; shorter Russian version published later in Petrograd.
Kandinsky's letters to Arthur Jerome Eddy published in Eddy's book *Cubists and Post-Impressionists* in Chicago.
May–August 1. For foyer of apartment of Edwin A. Campbell, 635 Park Avenue, New York, executes four panels (now Collection The Museum of Modern Art, New York).
June. Extracts from Kandinsky's "Formen—und Farben Sprache," translated by Edward Wadsworth, appear in *Blast I,* London.
August 3. After outbreak of World War I leaves Munich area with Münter for Switzerland.
August 6–November 16. Sojourn in Goldach on Lake Constance, Switzerland. Begins work on notes that later form the basis for his Bauhaus Book, *Punkt und Linie zu Fläche (Point and Line to Plane),* of 1926.
Writes stage composition *Violetter Vorhang (Violet Curtain).*
December. Returns to Russia, traveling through Zürich and across Balkans. Arrives in Moscow after one-week stay in Odessa; resides at 1 Dolgii Street until December 1921.

1915

Executes no oil paintings this year.
Alexander Rodchenko and Varvara Stepanova live temporarily in Kandinsky's apartment.
March. David Burliuk rents studio next to Kandinsky's.
April. Participates in *Vystavka zhivopisi 1915 god (Exhibition of Painting: 1915),* Moscow, with Natan Altman, David and Vladimir Burliuk, Goncharova, Larionov and others.
May. Spends three weeks in Odessa.
August 19–September 7. Visits Crimea.
December 23, 1915–March 1916. To Stockholm, where he meets Münter for the last time for Christmas; he remains there until March.

1916

February 1. One-man exhibition of work organized by Walden and Carl Gummeson held at Galerie Gummeson, Stockholm.
February. Kandinsky's essay *Om Konstnären (On the Artist)* published as a brochure by Gummesons Konsthandels Förlag, Stockholm; statement "Konsten utan ämne" ("Art Without Subject") published in periodical *Konst,* Stockholm.
March 17. Galerie Dada (formerly Galerie Corray), Zürich, opens with exhibition of works by Kandinsky and others.
Leaves Stockholm for Moscow via Petrograd.
June. *Klänge* poems read by Ball at Cabaret Voltaire, Zürich; poem "Sehen" ("See") published in review *Cabaret Voltaire,* Zürich.
Summer. Remains in Moscow with visits to Odessa and Kiev.
September. Meets Nina von Andreevskaia.
December 10, 1916–January 14, 1917. Participates in *Vystavka sovremennoi russoi zhivopisi (Exhibition of Contemporary Russian Painting),* Petrograd.

1917

February 11. Marries Nina von Andreevskaia.
Trip to Finland.
April. Ball lectures on Kandinsky at Galerie Dada, Zürich. Ball reads three poems by Kandinsky at second Der Sturm soirée, Zürich.
September. Birth of son Volodia Kandinsky.
Fall. Narkompros (NKP) (People's Commissariat for Enlightenment) established in Moscow shortly after October Revolution. Anatolii Lunacharsky is made Commissar of Enlightenment.
December. Kandinsky's work reproduced in *Dada,* no. 2, published in Zürich.

1918
January 29. Department of Visual Arts (IZO) established within NKP. Vladimir Tatlin, Moscow division emissary for Lunacharsky, visits Kandinsky and requests his participation in IZO; Kandinsky is named member of IZO NKP.
Meets Liubov Popova, Olga Rozanova and Nadezhda Udaltsova through NKP.
April. Svomas (Free State Art Studios), innovative schools, established in Moscow and Petrograd. Antoine Pevsner and Kazimir Malevich teach at Svomas in Moscow; Tatlin teaches in Moscow.
One-man exhibition of Rodchenko's work, *Five Years of Art,* held at Club of the Leftist Federation, Moscow.
July. Becomes director of theater and film sections of IZO NKP and is named editor of journal *Izobrazitel'noe Iskusstvo (Visual Art),* published by IZO NKP, Petrograd. His article "O stesenicheskoi kompozitsii" ("On Stage Composition") appears in first issue.
October. Becomes head of a studio at Moscow Svomas.
Russian edition of "Rückblicke," *Tekst khudozhnika. Stupeni. (Text of the Artist. Steps.)* published by IZO NKP, Moscow.
With critic Nikolai Punin and artists Tatlin and David Shterenberg, appointed to committee in charge of International Bureau of IZO; Kandinsky initiates contact with German artists and architect Walter Gropius.
December 5. Commission on the Organization of the Museums of Painterly Culture, IZO NKP, proposes system of new museums; commission includes artists Altman and Aleksei Karev.

1919
February. "O tochke" ("On the Point") and "O linii" ("On the Line") appear in *Iskusstvo (Art),* no. 3, February 1, and no. 4, February 22.
Museums of Painterly Culture established in Moscow, Petrograd and other cities. Kandinsky becomes first director.
With Rodchenko and others Kandinsky helps organize a system of twenty-two provincial museums.
Works on *Entsiklopediia izobrazitel'nogo iskusstva (Encyclopedia of Fine Arts),* which is never published.
Participates in *Fifth State Exhibition of the Trade Union of Artist-Painters of the New Art (From Impressionism to Nonobjectivity),* Moscow, with Ivan Kliun, Antoine Pevsner, Popova, Rodchenko, Stepanova, Udaltsova and others.
Spring. Gropius founds Bauhaus in Weimar.
June. Kandinsky's article "W. Kandinsky: Selbstcharakteristik" ("Self-Characterization") published by Paul Westheim in periodical *Das Kunstblatt,* Potsdam.

1919–20
Through his administrative duties, Kandinsky is brought into frequent contact with Rodchenko, Stepanova and other artists.

1920
January–April. Three articles by Kandinsky, including "O velikoi utopii" ("On the Great Utopia"), are published in IZO NKP journal *Khudozhestvennaia zhizn' (Artistic Life),* Moscow, which had replaced *Iskusstvo* in 1919.
May. Inkhuk (Institute of Artistic Culture) established in Moscow; affiliated organizations are founded soon thereafter in Petrograd, Vitebsk and other cities in Soviet Union and Europe.
June 16. Death of son Volodia.
June. Kandinsky presents pedagogical program for Inkhuk at First Pan-Russian Conference of Teachers and Students, Moscow Svomas.
Named Honorary Professor at University of Moscow.
Participates in *Exhibition of Four,* Moscow, with Rodchenko, Stepanova and Nikolai Sinezubov.
September. Svomas replaced by Vkhutemas (Higher State Art-Technical Studios), where Kandinsky teaches.
November–December. Participates in Société Anonyme exhibition, New York, and in *Nineteenth Exhibition of the Pan-Russian Central Exhibiting Bureau of the IZO Department of the NKP.*
December 19–25. Reports on activities of Inkhuk at First Pan-Russian Conference of Heads of Art Sections operating under NKP, Moscow.
Kandinsky's program is rejected; at end of year he leaves Inkhuk.
Designs cups and saucers for porcelain factory.

1921
May. Appointed to chair science and art committee, which includes Petr Kogan and A.M. Rodionov, to investigate possibility of establishing Russian Academy of Artistic Sciences. Also serves as chairman of subcommittee on physio-psychology and fine arts.
July. Charles-André Julien interviews Kandinsky in Moscow for article on the arts in post-Revolutionary Russia, which is not published until 1969.
Summer. Delivers lecture on "The Basic Elements of Painting" to science and art committee; special department of fine arts is not established until January 22, 1922.
October. Kandinsky cofounds RAKhN (Russian Academy of Artistic Sciences) with Kogan, and is appointed vice-president.
Participates in his last exhibitions in Russia, *Mir Iskusstva* and *Third Traveling Art Exhibition of the Soviet Regional Subdivision of the Museum Directorship,* Sovetsk (Kirov Province).
December. Kandinsky leaves Soviet Russia for Berlin, where he stays in furnished room on Motzstrasse.
Meets Lyonel Feininger.

1922
March. Gropius offers Kandinsky proffessorship at Weimar Bauhaus.
April 30–June 5. One-man exhibition at Galerie Goldschmidt-Wallerstein, Berlin.
June. Moves to Weimar, lives in furnished room in Cranachstrasse. Kandinsky and Klee reunited. Teaches preliminary course as Elementare Unterricht and is Formmeister of wall painting workshop at Bauhaus.
July. Offered teaching position at Art Academy in Tokyo, which he declines.
September. Vacations with Feininger at home of Gropius's mother at Timmendorfer Strand near Lübeck.
Fall. Wall paintings for entrance room of projected art museum exhibited at *Juryfreie Kunstausstellung* in Glaspalast, Berlin.
October 15–November. Participates in *Erste russische Kunstausstellung* at Galerie van Diemen, Berlin.
Kleine Welten (Small Worlds), portfolio of graphic works, printed in Weimar, published by Propyläen-Verlag, Berlin.

1923
March 23–May 4. First one-man exhibition in New York organized by Société Anonyme, of which he becomes first honorary vice-president; forms close association with Katherine Dreier.
April. Suggests that Schönberg direct Weimar Musikhochschule.
Begins correspondence with Will Grohmann.
August 15–September 30. Bauhaus exhibition in Weimar; Kandinsky's "Die Grundelemente der Form" ("The Basic

Elements of Form"), "Farbkurs und Seminar" ("Color Course and Seminar") and "Über die abstrakte Bühnensynthese" ("Abstract Synthesis on the Stage") published in Bauhaus anthology.
September. Vacations at Müritz and Binz on Baltic Sea.
Fall. Lives in Südstrasse, Weimar.

1924
March. *Blaue Vier (Blue Four),* exhibition group comprised of Feininger, Jawlensky, Kandinsky and Klee, formed by Galka Scheyer who becomes Kandinsky's representative in United States.
August. Vacations in Wennigstedt auf Sylt on North Sea.

1925
February. Visits Dresden and Dessau.
April 1. Bauhaus at Weimar closes.
June. Moves to Dessau where Bauhaus is relocated, rents furnished apartment at Moltkestrasse 7; sublets room to Klee.
Kandinsky's "Abstrakte Kunst" ("Abstract Art") published in *Der Cicerone.*
Summer. Vacations in Binz.
Otto Ralfs forms *Kandinsky Gesellschaft* of eight German art collectors.
November. Completes manuscript of *Punkt und Linie zu Fläche.*

1926
Punkt und Linie zu Fläche published by Albert Langen, Munich; "Tanzkurven: Zu den Tänzen der Palucca" ("Dance Curves: The Dances of Palucca") appears in *Das Kunstblatt.*
Father dies in Odessa.
May. Kandinsky's sixtieth birthday exhibition opens in Braunschweig, travels to Dresden, Berlin, Dessau and other European cities.
Mid-June. Moves to Burgkühnauer Allee 6 (later renamed Stresemann Allee) in Dessau; occupies Masters' double house with Klee and furnishes dining room with Breuer chairs.
Summer. Vacations in Müritz.
November. Participates in *An International Exhibition of Modern Art*, organized by Société Anonyme at The Brooklyn Museum.
December. Periodical *Bauhaus* established. First issue, dedicated to Kandinsky on his sixtieth birthday, includes his "Der Wert des theoretischen Unterrichts in der Malerei" ("The Value of Theoretical Instruction in Painting").

1927
May. Begins to teach Free-Painting class.
Vacations in Austria and Switzerland, visiting the Schönbergs at Wörther See.
Fall. Friendship with Christian Zervos begins.

1928
March. Kandinskys become German citizens.
Designs scenery and costumes for and directs Modest Mussorgsky's *Pictures at an Exhibition,* which opens April 4 at Friedrich-Theater, Dessau.
Kandinsky's "Kunstpädogogik"; "Analytisches Zeichnen" ("Art Pedagogy"; "Analytical Drawing") published in *Bauhaus* magazine.
Meets Rudolf Bauer in Berlin, César Domela in Dessau.
Summer. Vacations at Nice and Juan-les-Pins on French Riviera; Les Sables d'Olonne; Paris.

1929
January 15–31. First one-man exhibition in Paris of watercolors and gouaches at Galerie Zak.
Early May. Marcel Duchamp and Katherine Dreier visit Kandinsky at Bauhaus.
Summer. Meets Hilla Rebay, Mr. and Mrs. Solomon R. Guggenheim.
August. Vacations with Klee at Hendaye (Côte Basque); travels to Belgium, visits James Ensor in Ostend.
November. Visits Erich Mendelsohn and his wife in Berlin.

1930
January. Invited by Michel Seuphor to collaborate on periodical *Cercle et Carré.*
March 14–31. One-man exhibition at Galerie de France, Paris. Travels to Paris, meets Jean Hélion and Gualtieri di San Lazzaro.
Travels to Cattolica, Verona, Bologna, Urbino, Ravenna and Venice; is particularly impressed by mosaics in Ravenna.
Returns to Bauhaus by May 4.
April 18–May 1. Exhibits *Two Sides Red* and *Right* in *Cercle et Carré* exhibition at Galerie 23, Paris.

1931
March. Receives offer of teaching position at Art Students League, New York, which he declines.
Designs ceramic tiles for a music room at *Deutsche Bauausstellung,* Berlin, which opens May 9.
May 26. Visits Klee in Wörlitz; edits *Bauhaus,* vol. V, no. 3, which includes his tribute to Klee.
Summer. Visits Egypt, Palestine, Turkey, Greece and Italy on Mediterranean cruise.
Fall. First contribution to Zervos's *Cahiers d'Art*: "Réflexions sur l'art abstrait" ("Reflections on Abstract Art").

1932
April. Cover design for *Transition,* which also publishes his poetry.
August 22. Dessau city legislature, led by National Socialist Party, decrees dissolution of Dessau Bauhaus, effective October 1.
September. Vacations in Dubrovnik, Yugoslavia.
October. Bauhaus moves to outskirts of Berlin and operates as a private institute.
November. Work exhibited at Valentine Gallery, New York.
December 10. Moves to Bahnstrasse 19, Berlin Südende, where he lives for the next year.

1933
April 11. Bauhaus in Berlin closed by Nazis but negotiates to reopen.
July 20. Bauhaus closes for good, with decision by faculty to dissolve.
August. Paints last work in Germany, *Development in Brown.*
Visits Paris, vacations at Les Sablettes (Var) near Toulon.
October. Stays at Hôtel des Saints-Pères, Paris. Sees Duchamp.
October 27–November 26. Guest of honor in sixth exhibition of *Association Artistique Les Surindépendants,* Surrealist group exhibition.
Late October–December 16. Returns to Berlin.
December 16–21. Travels to Bern.
December 21. Arrives in Paris and by end of year moves into apartment at 135, boulevard de la Seine (now du général Koenig), Neuilly-sur-Seine, suburb of Paris.

1934
February. Resumes work.
March. Meets Joan Miró. About this time meets Piet Mondrian and Alberto Magnelli and sees his old friend Arp.
Works illustrated in *Abstraction-Création,* Paris.
April 24–May 9. Exhibition at Galleria del Milione, Milan.
May 23–June 9. Exhibition at Galerie des "Cahiers d'Art," Paris.
June. Visits Man Ray, Pevsner, Fernand Léger, Constantin Brancusi, Robert

and Sonia Delaunay. Max Ernst visits him.
August. Vacations in Normandy (Calvados).

1935
February. Invited to serve as artist in residence at Black Mountain College, Black Mountain, North Carolina; he declines the offer.
February 24–March 31. Participates in *Thèse-Antithèse- Synthèse* at Kunstmuseum Lucerne.

May. Attends Futurist conference at Galerie Bernheim-Jeune, Paris.
June 14–29. Works exhibited at Castelucho-Diana, Paris.
June 21–September 10. One-man show at Galerie des "Cahiers d'Art," Paris.
Summer. Vacations on French Riviera.
Contributes tribute to catalogue of exhibition of Willi Baumeister, with whom he had corresponded since 1931.
Shows with Max Weber and Klee at J.B. Neumann's New Art Circle, New York: his first exhibition with Neumann, who becomes his representative in eastern United States in July.

1936
February. Exhibitions at J. B. Neumann's New Art Circle in New York, and at Stendahl Galleries in Los Angeles.
Participates in *Abstract and Concrete,* Lefèvre Gallery, London; *Cubism and Abstract Art,* The Museum of Modern Art, New York.
Kandinsky's memoir of Marc published in *Cahiers d'Art.*
Late Summer. Vacations in Genoa, Pisa, Florence, Forte dei Marmi.
December 3–19. First exhibition at Galerie Jeanne Bucher, Paris.

1937
Interviewed by art dealer Karl Nierendorf, who mounts one-man show of his work in New York in March.
Kandinsky exhibition organized by College Art Association of America presented at Nierendorf Gallery, New York, and travels to Cleveland Museum of Art and Germanic Museum at Harvard University, Cambridge, Massachusetts.
February 21–March 29. Kandinsky exhibition at Kunsthalle Bern; he sees it with Klee.
Summer. Vacations in Brittany.
Many of his works in German museums are confiscated by the Nazis.
Included in *Entartete Kunst (Degenerate Art)* exhibition, which opens July 19 at Haus der Kunst, Munich.
July 30–October 1. Participates in *Origines et développement de l'art international indépendant* at Jeu de Paume, Paris.
French museum initiates negotiations to purchase *Composition IX.*
December. Sees work of Arp, Taeuber-Arp and Miró in galleries.

1938
February. Renews relations with André Breton.
Writes "Abstract of Concreet?" for catalogue of exhibition *Abstracte Kunst* at Stedelijk Museum, Amsterdam.
One-man show at Guggenheim Jeune, London.
March. Kandinsky's "L'Art Concret" published in first issue of San Lazzaro's *XXe Siècle.*
April. Four poems and woodcuts published in *Transition.*
June. Meets Otto Freundlich at Freundlich's exhibition at Galerie Jeanne Bucher, Paris.
July 13. Signs petition in support of Freundlich.
Summer. Vacations on French Riviera at Cap Ferrat.
August. Kandinsky's German passport expires.

1939
January. Completes *Composition X,* his last major work in this series.
Begins correspondence with Pierre Bruguière, French official.
February. Negotiations for proposed retrospective at Jeu de Paume.
April. French museum purchases *Composition IX.*
May 10–27. Participates in *Abstract and Concrete Art,* Guggenheim Jeune, London; writes statement for it.
June 1. *Art of Tomorrow,* which includes many Kandinsky paintings, opens at Museum of Non-Objective Painting, New York.
June 2–17. One-man show at Galerie Jeanne Bucher, Paris.
June 30–July 15. Included in first *Réalités Nouvelles* exhibition at Galerie Charpentier, Paris.
French citizenship decreed.
Discusses proposed multimedia ballet with Leonide Massine.
August. Vacations at Croix-Valmer on Mediterranean coast.
September 3. War declared with Germany.
September 27. Sends sixty-five canvases to Emile Redon for storage in Aveyron.

1940
June–August. Following German invasion of France, travels to Cauterets in the Pyrennees; on return trip sees Léger in Vichy.
Autumn. Publication of *Della spiritualità nell'arte,* translated by G. A. Colonna di Cesarò, by Edizioni di Religio, Rome.

1941
May. On behalf of Centre Américain de Secours and various Americans, Varian Fry arranges passage from Marseilles to New York for Kandinskys, but they decide to remain in France.
Late September. Vacations in Marlotte.

1942
Writes short preface for portfolio *10 Origin,* edited by Max Bill.
April 25. Domela visits Kandinsky.
June. Completes *Delicate Tensions,* last large canvas, and henceforth does only small paintings on wood or canvasboard.
July 21–August 4. One-man exhibition at Galerie Jeanne Bucher, held clandestinely because of Nazi occupation.
December–February 1943. Retrospective held at Nierendorf Gallery, New York.

1943
March 3. Severe bombing of Paris.
March 13–April 10. Works included in *15 Early–15 Late* at Peggy Guggenheim's Art of This Century, New York.
June. Writes preface for album of Domela reproductions and tribute to the late Taeuber-Arp.
Mid-September. Vacations at Rochefort-en-Yvelines.
October 19–November 15. Sees Miró exhibition at Galerie Jeanne Bucher.

1944
January. Shows at Galerie Jeanne Bucher with Domela and Nicolas de Staël; exhibits with them and Magnelli at Galerie l'Esquisse, Paris, in April.
March. Completes *Tempered Elan,* last painting catalogued in Handlist. Becomes ill, but continues working until July.
April. Last letters from Kandinsky to Jeanne Bucher and to Domela.
October 11–31. Four works included in exhibition of abstract art at Galerie Berri-Raspail, Paris.
November 7–December 15. Last one-man exhibition during his lifetime held at Galerie l'Esquisse.
December 13. Dies in Neuilly from a sclerosis in cerebellum.

SELECTED BIBLIOGRAPHY

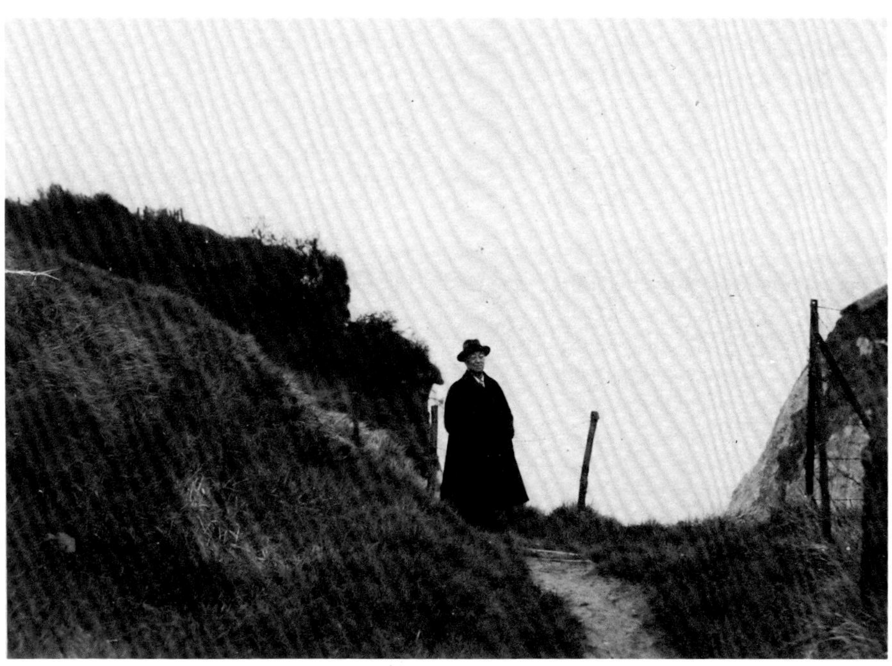

Kandinsky at Varengeville, 1939

1. By Kandinsky

Über das Geistige in der Kunst. Insbesondere in der Malerei [*On the Spiritual in Art and Painting in Particular*], Munich, Piper, December 1911. Second edition April 1912. Third edition Fall 1912

Der Blaue Reiter, Kandinsky and Franz Marc, eds., Munich, Piper, 1912. Second edition 1914. Documentary edition, *The Blaue Reiter Almanac,* Klaus Lankheit, trans., New York, Viking, 1974

Klänge [*Sounds*], Munich, Piper, 1913

"Rückblicke" [Reminiscences] in *Kandinsky, 1901–1913,* Berlin, Der Sturm, 1913. French translation, "Regards sur le passé," in *Wassily Kandinsky: Regards sur le passé et autres textes, 1912–1922,* Paris, Hermann, 1974, pp. 87–132, with introduction by Jean-Paul Bouillon

"Stupeni" in *Tekst khudozhnika* ["Steps" in *Text of the Artist*], Moscow, IZO NKP, 1918. Russian version of "Rückblicke"

Punkt und Linie zu Fläche: Beitrag zur Analyse der malerischen Elemente [*Point and Line to Plane. A Contribution to the Analysis of the Pictorial Elements*], Bauhausbücher 9, Munich, Albert Langen, 1926

"Line and Fish," *Axis,* no. 2, April 1935, p. 6

[Untitled statement] in *Il Milione: Bolletino della Galleria del Milione,* Milan, no. 41, May-June 1935, special issue, "Ommagio a Baumeister"

Interview in *Il lavoro fascista,* vol. XIII, July 28, 1935, p. 4

"L'Art aujourd'hui est plus vivant que jamais," *Cahiers d'Art,* 10e année, no. 1–4, 1935, pp. 53–56. Reply to a questionnaire

"Toile vide, etc.," *Cahiers d'Art,* 10e année, no. 5–6, 1935, p. 117

[Untitled statement] in *Thèse-Antithèse-*

Synthèse, exh. cat., Lucerne, 1935, pp. 15–16

"L'Art concret," *XXe Siècle,* no. 1, March 1938, pp. 9–15

"Blick und Blitz," "Ergo," "S," "Erinnerungen," "Anders," "Immer Zusammen," *Transition,* no. 27, April-May 1938, pp. 104–109

"Mes Gravures sur bois," *XXe Siècle,* vol. 1, July 1938, p. 31

Excerpt from a letter to Irmgard Burchard, December 1937, in Peter Thoene, *Modern German Art,* London, Harmondsworth, 1938, p. 76

"La Valeur d'une oeuvre concrète," *XXe Siècle,* vol. 1, no. 5–6, Winter-Spring 1939, pp. 48–50

"Salongespräch," "Testimonium Paupertatis," "Weiss-Horn," *Plastique,* no. 4, 1939, pp. 14–16

[Untitled statement] in Max Bill, ed., *10 Origin,* Zürich, 1942

[Preface], *Domela, six réproductions en couleurs d'après quelques oeuvres récentes,* Paris, 1943

11 Tableaux et 7 poèmes, Friedrich Vordemberge-Gildewart, ed., Amsterdam, Editions Duwaer, 1945

Concerning the Spiritual in Art and Painting in Particular, M. T. H. Sadler, trans., revisions by Francis Golffing, Michael Harrison and Ferdinand Osterlag, New York, Wittenborn Schultz Inc., 1947. Additional texts by Julia and Lyonel Feininger, Nina Kandinsky and Stanley William Hayter; eight prose poems by Kandinsky, 1912–37, in German with English trans.

"Les reliefs colorés de Sophie Taeuber-Arp" in *Sophie Taeuber-Arp,* Georg Schmidt, ed., Basel, 1948

Du Spirituel dans l'art et dans la peinture en particulier, M. and Mme De Man, trans., Paris, Editions René Drouin, 1949.

Contains original color woodcut by Kandinsky. Limited edition of 300, printed by G. Duval and Imprimerie Union

Du Spirituel dans l'art et dans la peinture en particulier, M. and Mme De Man, trans., Paris, Editions de Beaune, 1954. Postface by Charles Estienne

For Kandinsky's collected writings see:

Kandinsky: Essays über Kunst und Künstler, Max Bill, ed., Stuttgart, 1955. Contains most of Kandinsky's articles published between 1912 and 1943

Wassily Kandinsky: Ecrits complets, Philippe Sers, ed., Paris, Denoël-Gonthier, vol. 2, 1970; vol. 3, 1975; vol. 1 in preparation

Wassily Kandinsky: Tutti gli scritti, Philippe Sers, ed., Milan, Feltrinelli, vol. 1, 1973; vol. 2, 1974

Kandinsky: Die Gesammelten Schriften, Hans K. Roethel and Jelena Hahl-Koch, eds., Bern, Benteli Verlag, vol. 1, 1980

Kandinsky: Complete Writings on Art, Kenneth C. Lindsay and Peter Vergo, eds., 2 vols., Boston, G. H. Hall & Co., 1982

2. On Kandinsky and His Contemporaries

Daniel Abadie, *Hélion ou la force des choses,* Brussels, 1975

Abstraction-Création: art non-figuratif, nos. 1–5, 1932–36, reprint edition, New York, Arno Press, 1968

Abstrakt-Konkret: Bulletin de la Galerie des Eaux Vives, Zürich, no. 10, 1945. Texts by Max Bill, Vasily Kandinsky, Leo Leuppi and Michel Seuphor

Albright-Knox Art Gallery, Buffalo, New York, *Ben Nicholson: Fifty Years of His Art,* 1978. Exhibition catalogue with text by Steven A. Nash

Troels Andersen, "Some Unpublished Letters by Kandinsky," *Artes,* Copenhagen, vol. II, October 1966, pp. 90–110

Louis Aragon, "Expositions: La Peinture au Tournant (1)," *Commune,* 2e année, June 1935, pp. 1181–1182, 1185–1189

Jean Arp and Jean Gorin, "Art Concret," *Arts,* July 6, 1945, p. 2

Art d'aujourd'hui, no. 6, January 1950, special section, "W. Kandinsky," with texts by Charles Estienne, Carola Giedion-Welcker and R. V. Gindertael, n.p.

Axis: A Quarterly Review of Contemporary "Abstract" Painting and Sculpture, nos. 1–8, 1935–37, reprint edition, New York, Arno Press, 1969

Gaston Bachelard, *Le Nouvel esprit scientifique,* Paris, 1936

Vivian Endicott Barnett, "Kandinsky: From Drawing and Watercolor to Oil," *Drawing,* vol. III, July-August 1981, pp. 30–34

Vivian Endicott Barnett, *Kandinsky at the Guggenheim,* New York, 1983

Carlo Belli, *Kn,* Milan, 1935

Berggruen & Cie, Paris, *Kandinsky: aquarelles et dessins,* 1972. Exhibition catalogue with texts by Hans Arp, Paul Klee, Franz Marc, Joan Miró, Christian Zervos et al.

H. Bertram, *Kandinsky,* Copenhagen, 1946. Reprint edition, Copenhagen, 1965, with introduction by Poul Vad

Max Bill, ed., *Wassily Kandinsky,* Boston and Paris, 1951. Texts by Jean Arp, Charles Estienne, Carola Giedion-Welcker, Will Grohmann, Ludwig Grote, Nina Kandinsky and Alberto Magnelli

Anthony Blunt, "The 'Realism' Quarrel," *Left Review,* vol. III, April 1937, pp. 169–171

John E. Bowlt and Rose-Carol Washton Long, eds., *The Life of Vasilii Kandinsky in Russian Art: A Study of "On the Spiritual in Art,"* Newtonville, Massachusetts, 1980

André Breton, *Le Surréalisme et la peinture,* Paris, 1928

André Breton, "Picasso dans son élément," *Minotaure,* no. 1, 1933, pp. 2–37

André Breton, "Introduction," *Constellations,* New York, 1959

André Breton and Paul Eluard, "Enquête," *Minotaure,* no. 3–4, December 12, 1933, pp. 101–116

Herbert Brinkmann, *Wassily Kandinski als Dichter,* Ph.D. dissertation, University of Cologne, 1980

Marcel Brion, "César Domela," *Cahiers d'Art,* vol. XXVIII, no. 1, 1953, pp. 107–111

Marcel Brion, *Art abstrait,* Paris, 1956

Marcel Brion, *Kandinsky,* Paris, 1960. English edition, London, 1961

Bernard Causton, "Art in Germany under the Nazis," *The Studio,* vol. CXII, November 1936, pp. 235–246

"Centenaire de Kandinsky," *XXe Siècle,* vol. XXVII, December 1966, special issue with texts by Charles Estienne, Will Grohmann, Klaus Lankheit, Kenneth C. Lindsay and Paul Volboudt. English edition,

Homage to Wassily Kandinsky, New York, 1975

Centre National d'Art Contemporain, Paris, *Louis Fernandez,* Cnac archives no. 4, 1972. Exhibition catalogue

André Chastel, *Nicolas de Staël,* Paris, 1968. With catalogue raisonné of oil paintings by Jacques Dubourg and Françoise de Staël and letters annotated by Germain Viatte

Alain Clairet, *Catalogue Raisonné de César Domela-Nieuwenhuis (peintures, reliefs, sculptures),* Madelaine Hage, trans., Paris, 1978

The Cleveland Museum of Art, *The Spirit of Surrealism,* 1979. Exhibition catalogue with text by Edward B. Henning

Arthur A. Cohen, *Sonia Delaunay,* New York, 1975

Arthur A. Cohen, ed., *The New Art of Color: The Writings of Robert and Sonia Delaunay,* Arthur A. Cohen, David Shapiro et al., trans., The Documents of 20th-Century Art, New York, 1978

Corcoran Gallery of Art, Washington, D.C., *Georges Vantongerloo,* 1980. Exhibition catalogue with texts by Jane Livingston, Phil Mertens, Angela Thomas-Jankowski and the artist

Salvador Dali, *La Conquête de l'irrationnel,* Paris, 1935. English edition, New York, 1935

Leon Degand, "Le Sens des mots" in *Les Lettres françaises,* June 23, 1945, p. 4

Léon Degand, *Langage et signification de la peinture en figuration et en abstraction,* Boulogne-sur-Seine, 1956

Christian Derouet, "Kandinsky, 'Triumvir' de l'exposition du Jeu de Paume en 1937" in *Paris 1937-Paris 1957: créations en France,* exh. cat., Paris, 1981, pp. 64–67

Christian Derouet, "Vassily Kandinsky: Notes et documents sur les dernières années du peintre," *Cahiers du Musée National d'Art Moderne,* Paris, no. 9, 1982, pp. 84–107

Robert Descharnes, *Salvador Dali,* New York, 1976

Jacques Dupin, *Joan Miró: Life and Work,* Norbert Guterman, trans., New York, 1962

John Elderfield, "Geometric Abstract Painting and Paris in the Thirties, Part II," *Artforum,* vol. VIII, June 1970, pp. 70–75

Encyclopédie de la Pléiade, *Histoire de l'art. 4. Du Réalisme à nos jours,* Bernard Dorival, ed., Paris, 1969

Charles Estienne, *Kandinsky,* Paris, 1950

Charles Estienne, "Deux Eclairages, Kandinsky & Miró," *XXe Siècle,* no. 1, June 1951, pp. 21–26

Denise Fédit, *L'Oeuvre de Kupka,* Paris, 1966

Otto Freundlich, *Schriften. Ein Wegbereiter der gegendstandlosen Kunst,* Cologne, 1982

Galerie Jeanne Bucher, Paris, *Hans Reichel,* 1962. Exhibition catalogue with texts by Bissière, Brassaï, Lawrence Durrell and Henry Miller

Galerie René Drouin, Paris, *Art concret,* 1945. Exhibition catalogue with texts by Hans Arp, Robert Delaunay, Theo van Doesburg, Naum Gabo, Kandinsky and Antoine Pevsner

Galerie René Drouin, Paris, *Kandinsky: Gouaches, aquarelles, dessins,* 1947. Exhibition catalogue with text by Marcel Arland

Galerie René Drouin, Paris, *Kandinsky, époque parisienne,* 1949. Exhibition catalogue with texts by Charles Estienne and Henri-Pierre Roché

Les Galeries Nationales d'Exposition du Grand Palais, Paris, *Hélion: cent tableaux 1928–1970,* 1971. Exhibition catalogue with texts by Francis Ponge, Christian Zervos et al.

Galleria del Milione, Milan, *Kandinsky,* 1934. Exhibition catalogue with statements by Willi Baumeister, Will Grohmann, Michel Seuphor, Christian Zervos et al.

Galleries of the Société Anonyme, New York, *Kandinsky,* 1923. Exhibition brochure with text by Katherine S. Dreier

Malcolm Gee, *Dealers, Critics, and Collectors of Modern Painting: Aspects of the Parisian Art Market Between 1910 and 1930,* New York, 1981

Gemeentemuseum, The Hague, *Max Bill,* 1968. Exhibition catalogue with text by Will Grohmann

Herbert S. Gershman, *The Surrealist Revolution in France,* Ann Arbor, Michigan, 1964

Carola Giedion-Welcker, "Kandinskys Malerei als Ausdruck: eines geistigen Universalismus," *Werk,* vol. 37, April 1950, pp. 119–123

Carola Giedion-Welcker, *Hans Arp,* Stuttgart, 1957

Jürgen Glaesemer, *Paul Klee: Handzeichnungen,* Bern, vol. 1, *Kindheit bis 1920,* 1973; vol. III, *1937–1940,* 1979; vol. II, *1921–1936,* 1984

Jürgen Glaesemer, *Paul Klee: Die farbigen Werke im Kunstmuseum Bern,* Bern, 1976

Laszlo Glozer, *Picasso und der Surrealismus,* Cologne, 1974

Eugen Gomringer, *Josef Albers,* New York, 1968

Clement Greenberg, *Art and Culture: Critical Essays,* Boston, 1961

Jean Grenier, "Kandinsky et Henri Michaux," *Combat,* November 20, 1944

Will Grohmann, "Wassily Kandinsky," *Cahiers d'Art,* 4e année, 1929, pp. 322–329

Will Grohmann, *Wassily Kandinsky,* Paris, 1930. Additional texts by Katherine Dreier, Maurice Raynal, Christian Zervos et al.

Will Grohmann, "Catalogue des oeuvres graphiques," *Sélection,* no. 14, July 1933, pp. 28–32

Will Grohmann, "L'Art non-figuratif en Allemagne," *L'Amour de l'Art,* no. VII, September 1934, pp. 433–440

Will Grohmann, *Paul Klee, 1879–1940,* Basel, Munich and Vienna, 1955

Will Grohmann, *Wassily Kandinsky: Leben und Werk,* Cologne, 1958. English edition, *Wassily Kandinsky: Life and Work,* Norbert Guterman, trans., New York, 1958

Will Grohmann, *Baumeister: Leben und Werk,* Cologne, 1963

Peggy Guggenheim, ed., *Art of this Century: Objects, Drawings, Photographs, Paintings, Sculpture, Collages, 1910–1942,* New York, 1942

The Solomon R. Guggenheim Museum, New York, *Piet Mondrian, 1872–1944: Centennial Exhibition,* 1971. Exhibition catalogue with texts by Max Bill, Nelly van Doesburg, Joop Joosten, Margit Rowell and Robert P. Welsh

The Solomon R. Guggenheim Museum, New York, *Joan Miró: Magnetic Fields,* 1972. Exhibition catalogue with texts by Rosalind Krauss and Margit Rowell

The Solomon R. Guggenheim Museum, New York, *František Kupka 1871–1957: A Retrospective,* 1975. Exhibition catalogue with texts by Meda Mladek and Margit Rowell

The Solomon R. Guggenheim Museum, New York, *Kandinsky Watercolors: A Selection from The Solomon R. Guggenheim Museum and The Hilla von Rebay Foundation,* 1980. Exhibition catalogue with texts by Vivian Endicott Barnett and Louise Averill Svendsen

The Solomon R. Guggenheim Museum, New York, *Kandinsky in Munich: 1896–1914,* 1982. Exhibition catalogue with texts by Peter Jelavich, Carl E. Schorske and Peg Weiss

The Solomon R. Guggenheim Museum, New York, *Julio González: A Retrospective,* 1983. Exhibition catalogue with text by Margit Rowell

The Solomon R. Guggenheim Museum, New York, *Kandinsky: Russian and Bauhaus Years, 1915–1933,* 1983. Exhibition catalogue with text by Clark V. Poling

Werner Haftmann, *Paul Klee: Wege bildnerischen Denkens,* Munich, 1950. English edition, *The Mind and Eye of Paul Klee,* New York, 1967

Werner Haftmann, "Kandinsky 1927–1933," *Derrière le miroir,* no. 154, November 1965, pp. 1–18

Jelena Hahl-Koch, ed., *Arnold Schönberg—Wassily Kandinsky: Briefe, Bilder und Dokumente: einer aussergewöhnlichen Begegnung,* Vienna, 1980. English edition, *Arnold Schoenberg—Wassily Kandinsky: Letters, Pictures and Documents,* John C. Crawford, trans., London, 1984

A. M. Hammacher, *The Sculpture of Barbara Hepworth,* James Brockway, trans., New York, 1968

Erika Hanfstaengl, *Wassily Kandinsky, Zeichnungen und Aquarelle: Katalog der Sammlung in der Städtischen Galerie im Lenbachhaus,* Munich, 1974

Haus der Kunst, Munich, *Wassily Kandinsky 1866–1944,* 1976. Exhibition catalogue with text by Thomas M. Messer

Stanley Hayter, "The Language of Kandinsky," *Magazine of Art,* vol. 38, May 1945, pp. 176–179

Barbara Hepworth, *Barbara Hepworth: A Pictorial Autobiography,* New York, 1970

Robert L. Herbert, Eleanor S. Apter et al., eds., *The Société Anonyme at Yale University: A Catalogue Raisonné,* London and New Haven, 1984

J. P. Hodin, *Barbara Hepworth,* Neuchâtel, 1961

René Huyghe, "L'Allemagne et l'Europe centrale," *L'Amour de l'Art,* no. VII, September 1934, pp. 417–422

Israel Museum, Jerusalem, *Hommage à Otto Freundlich à l'occasion du 100ème anniversaire,* 1978. Exhibition catalogue with texts by Yona Fischer and the artist

H. L. C. Jaffé, *Piet Mondrian,* New York, 1970

Anatole Jakovski, "Alberto Magnelli: à propos de son exposition à la Galerie Pierre," *Cahiers d'Art,* 9e année, 1934, pp. 201–203

Anatole Jakovski, *H. Erni, S. Schiess, K. Seligmann, S. Taeuber-Arp, G. Vulliamy,* Paris, 1934

Anatole Jakovski, "Wassily Kandinsky," *Axis,* no. 2, April 1935, pp. 9–12

Sidney Janis, *Abstract and Surrealist Art in America,* New York, 1944

Ejner Johansson, *Richard Mortensen,* Copenhagen, 1962

Jean-Pierre Jouffroy, *La Mesure de Nicolas de Staël,* Neuchâtel, 1981

Nina Kandinsky, *Kandinsky und ich,* Munich, 1976. French edition, *Kandinsky et moi,* J.M. Gaillard-Paquet, trans., Paris, 1978

"Kandinsky [works 1923–38]," *Derrière le miroir,* no. 60–61, October-November 1953. Issued as catalogue for exhibition at Galerie Maeght, Paris, with text by Will Grohmann

R.C. Kennedy, "Kandinsky's Paris Period," *Art and Artists,* vol. 4, November 1969, pp. 30–33

Kettle's Yard Gallery, Cambridge, England, *Circle: Constructive Art in Britain 1934–1940,* Jeremy Lewison, ed., 1982. Exhibition catalogue

Felix Klee, *Paul Klee: Leben und Werk in Dokumenten,* Zürich, 1960

M. Knoedler and Co., Inc., New York, *Kandinsky: Parisian Period 1934–1944,* 1969. Exhibition catalogue with texts by Nina Kandinsky, Gaëtan Picon and Rose-Carol Washton

Hilton Kramer, "Kandinsky: The Last Decade" in *The Age of the Avant Garde: An Art Chronicle of 1956 to 1972,* New York, 1973, pp. 138–141

Kunsthalle Basel, *Konkrete Kunst,* 1944. Exhibition catalogue with texts by Hans Arp and Max Bill

Michel Conil Lacoste, *Kandinsky,* Paris, 1979. English edition, Shirley Jennings, trans., New York, 1979

Klaus Lankheit, ed., *Wassily Kandinsky–Franz Marc Briefwechsel. Mit Briefen von und an Gabriele Münter und Maria Marc,* Munich, 1983

Jacques Lassaigne, *Kandinsky: Bibliographical and Critical Study,* Geneva, 1964

Jacques Lassaigne and Guy Weelen, *Vieira da Silva,* Paris, 1978

André Lhote, "Kandinsky et ses jeunes censeurs," *Les Lettres françaises,* January 13, 1945

Kenneth C. Lindsay, *An Examination of the Fundamental Theories of Wassily Kandinsky,* Ph. D. dissertation, University of Wisconsin, Madison, 1951

Kenneth C. Lindsay, "*Wassily Kandinsky, Life and Work,* by Will Grohmann," *Art Bulletin,* vol. XLI, December 1959, pp. 348–350

Kenneth C. Lindsay, "Kandinsky and the Compositional Factor," *Art Journal,* vol. 43, Spring 1983, pp. 14–18

Jacques Lipchitz, *12 Dessins pour Prométhée,* Paris, 1940

Giovanni Lista, *Marinetti et le futurisme,* Lausanne, 1977

Anne Lochard, *Magnelli: opere 1907-1939,* Marcella Cartasegna, trans., Rome, 1972. Introduction by F. Le Lionnais

Pierre Loeb, *Voyages à travers la peinture,* Paris, 1945

Rose-Carol Washton Long, *Kandinsky: The Development of an Abstract Style,* New York, 1980

Joan M. Lukach, *Hilla Rebay: In Search*

of the Spirit in Art, New York, 1983

Dougald MacMillan, *Transition: the History of a Literary Era, 1927–1938,* London, 1975

Anne Maisonnier-Lochard, *Catalogue raisonné de l'oeuvre peint d'Alberto Magnelli,* Paris, 1975

Nicole S. Mangin, *Catalogue de l'oeuvre de Georges Braque,* 6 vols., Paris, 1959-82

J. Leslie Martin, Ben Nicholson and Naum Gabo, eds., *Circle: International Survey of Constructive Art,* London, 1937

Joan Miró, *Ceci est la couleur de mes rêves. Entretiens avec Georges Raillard,* Paris, 1977

Reynolds A. Morse, *Dali: A Study of His Life and Works,* Boston, 1958

Musée d'Art Moderne de la Ville de Paris, *Hans Reichel,* 1975. Exhibition catalogue with text by Jacques Lassaigne

Musée du Jeu de Paume, Paris, *Origines et développement de l'art international indépendant,* 1937. Exhibition catalogue

Musée National d'Art Moderne, Centre Georges Pompidou, Paris, *Robert et Sonia Delaunay,* 1967. Exhibition catalogue with text by Michel Hoog

Musée National d'Art Moderne, Centre Georges Pompidou, Paris, *Henri Michaux,* 1978. Exhibition catalogue with texts by Geneviève Bonnefoi, Octavio Paz, Jean Starobinski et al.

Musée National d'Art Moderne, Centre Georges Pompidou, Paris, *Kandinsky, trente peintures des musées soviétiques,* 1979. Exhibition catalogue with text by Christian Derouet

Musée National d'Art Moderne, Centre Georges Pompidou, Paris, *Fernand Léger, la poésie de l'objet 1928–1934,* 1981. Exhibition catalogue with text by Christian Derouet and Maurice Jardot

Musée National d'Art Moderne, Centre Georges Pompidou, Paris, *Paris 1937–Paris 1957: créations en France,* 1981. Exhibition catalogue

Musée National d'Art Moderne, Centre Georges Pompidou, Paris, *Braque: oeuvres de Georges Braque 1882–1963,* 1982. Exhibition catalogue with text by Nadine Pouillon

Musée National d'Art Moderne, Centre Georges Pompidou, Paris, *Hans/Jean Arp: le temps des papiers déchirés,* 1983. Exhibition catalogue with texts by Aimée Bleikasten, Pierre Bruguière, Christian Derouet, Greta Ströh, the artist et al.

Musée National d'Art Moderne, Centre Georges Pompidou, Paris, *Kandinsky: Album de l'exposition,* 1984. Exhibition catalogue with texts by Christian Derouet, Thomas M. Messer, Werner Schmalenbach, Frank Stella, Armin Zweite et al.

Musée National d'Art Moderne, Centre Georges Pompidou, Paris, *Kandinsky,* 1984. Collection catalogue with texts by Christian Derouet and Jessica Boissel

Musée de Peinture, Grenoble, *Andry-Farcy, un conservateur novateur: Le Musée de Grenoble de 1919 à 1949,* 1982. Exhibition catalogue with text by Hélène Vincent

Musée de Pontoise, *La Donation Freundlich au Musée de Pontoise,* 1974. Exhibition catalogue with text by Edda Maillet

Museen der Stadt Köln, *Paul Klee: Das Werk der Jahre 1919–1933, Gemälde, Handzeichnungen, Druckgraphik,* 1979. Exhibition catalogue with texts by Marcel Franciscono, Christian Geelhaar, Siegfried Gohr et al.

The Museum of Fine Arts, Houston, *Miró in America,* 1980. Exhibition catalogue with texts by Duncan MacMillan, Judith McCandless, Barbara Rose, James Johnson Sweeney et al.

The Museum of Modern Art, New York, *Cubism and Abstract Art,* 1936. Exhibition catalogue with text by Alfred H. Barr, Jr.

The Museum of Modern Art, New York, *Bauhaus 1919–1928,* Herbert Bayer, Walter Gropius and Ise Gropius, eds., 1938. Exhibition catalogue

The Museum of Modern Art, New York, *Sophie Taeuber-Arp,* 1981. Exhibition catalogue with text by Carolyn Lanchner

Museum of Non-Objective Painting, New York, *In Memory of Wassily Kandinsky,* Hilla Rebay, ed., 1945. Exhibition catalogue with texts by V. Agrarych, Hilla Rebay and the artist

New Burlington Galleries, London, *The International Surrealist Exhibition,* 1936. Exhibition catalogue with texts by André Breton and Herbert Read; David Gascoyne, trans.

Ben Nicholson, *N. Gabo,* London, 1937. Reprint edition, New York, 1971

Karl Nierendorf, ed., *Paul Klee: Paintings, Watercolors, 1913–1939,* New York, 1941. Introduction by James Johnson Sweeney

"Ommagio a Kandinsky," *Forma,* vol. 2, May 1950. Texts by Charles Estienne, Nina Kandinsky, Kenneth C. Lindsay, E. Prampolini, Hilla Rebay et al.

Eugenio d'Ors and Jacques Lassaigne, *Almanach des Arts: L'Année de l'exposition,* Paris, 1937

Paul Overy, "The Later Painting of Wassily Kandinsky," *Apollo,* no. 78, August 1963, pp. 117–123

Paul Overy, *Kandinsky: The Language of the Eye,* New York, 1969

Pierre Peissi and Carola Giedion-Welcker, *Antoine Pevsner,* Haakon Chevalier, trans., Neuchâtel, 1961

Petit Palais, Paris, *Les Maîtres de l'art indépendant, 1895–1937,* 1937. Exhibition catalogue

Alexei Pevsner, *A Biographical Sketch of my Brothers, Naum Gabo and Antoine Pevsner,* Amsterdam, 1964

Philadelphia Museum of Art, *A.E. Gallatin Collection: "Museum of Living Art,"* 1954. Collection catalogue with texts by Jean Hélion and James Johnson Sweeney

"Picasso de 1930 à 1935," *Cahiers d'Art,* vol. 10, 1935, special issue with texts by Salvador Dali, Louis Fernandez, Julio González, Benjamin Péret, Jaime Sabartes and Christian Zervos, pp. 145–261

Gaëtan Picon, "Préface," *Kandinsky, carnet de dessins, 1941,* Paris, Editions Karl Flinker, 1972

Plastique, no. 1–5, Spring 1937–1939, reprint edition, New York, Arno Press, 1969

Stefanie Poley, *Hans Arp: Die Formensprache in plastischen Werk,* Stuttgart, 1978

Clark V. Poling, *Kandinsky–Unterricht am Bauhaus: Farbenseminar und analytisches Zeichnen dargestellt am Beispiel der Sammlung des Bauhaus-Archivs, Berlin,* Weingarten, 1982

Bernd Rau, *Hans Arp, Die Reliefs: Oeuvre-Katalog,* Stuttgart, 1981. Introduction by Michel Seuphor

Herbert Read, *Art Now,* London, 1934

Herbert Read, *Barbara Hepworth:*

Carvings and Drawings, London, 1952

Herbert Read, ed., *Ben Nicholson*, London, vol. 1, *Work from 1911–1948*, 1955; vol. II, *Work Since 1947*, 1956

Herbert Read, *Kandinsky 1866–1944*, London, 1959

Herbert Read and Leslie Martin, *Gabo: Constructions, Sculpture, Paintings, Drawings and Engravings*, London, 1957

Peter Anselm Riedl, *Wassily Kandinsky in Selbstzeugnissen und Bilddokumenten*, Hamburg, 1983

Sixten Ringbom, "Art in the 'Epoch of the Great Spiritual': Occult Elements in the Early Theory of Abstract Painting," *Journal of the Warburg and Courtauld Institutes*, vol. XXIX, 1966, pp. 386–418

Sixten Ringbom, *The Sounding Cosmos: A Study in the Spiritualism of Kandinsky and the Genesis of Abstract Painting*, Åbo, Finland, 1970

Hans Konrad Roethel, *Kandinsky: Das Graphische Werk*, Cologne, 1970

Hans K. Roethel, *Kandinsky*, Paris, 1977. Revised and translated as Hans K. Roethel in collaboration with Jean K. Benjamin, *Kandinsky*, New York, 1979

Hans K. Roethel and Jean K. Benjamin, *Kandinsky: Catalogue Raisonné of the Oil Paintings*, Ithaca, New York, vol. I., *1900–1915*, 1982; vol. II, *1916-1944*, 1984

Robert Rosenblum, "Picasso as Surrealist," *Artforum*, vol. V, September 1966, special issue on Surrealism, pp. 21–25

Margit Rowell, *Miró*, New York, 1970

Angelica Zander Rudenstine, *The Guggenheim Museum Collection: Paintings 1880–1945*, New York, 1976, vol. 1, pp. 204–391

Serge Sabarsky Gallery, New York, *Paul Klee: The Late Years 1930–1940*, 1977. Exhibition catalogue

Merle Schipper, *Hélion: The Abstract Years, 1929-1939*, Ph. D. dissertation, University of California, 1974

Georg Schmidt, ed., *Sophie Taeuber-Arp*, Basel, 1948. Includes catalogue raisonné by Hugo Weber

Michel Seuphor, *L'Art abstrait, ses origines, ses premiers maîtres*, Paris, 1949

Michel Seuphor, *Mission spirituelle de l'art à propos de l'oeuvre de Sophie Taeuber-Arp et Jean Arp*, Paris, 1953

Michel Seuphor, *Piet Mondrian: Life and Work*, New York, 1956

Michel Seuphor, *Cercle et Carré*, Paris, 1971

James Thrall Soby, *Joan Miró*, New York, 1959. Second edition 1969

Charles Spencer, "Profile of Paule Vézelay," *Arts Review*, vol. XX, October 26, 1968, p. 683

Werner Spies, *Albers*, New York, 1971

Werner Spies, ed., *Max Ernst: Oeuvre Katalog, Cologne*, vol. I, *Das Graphische Werk*, 1975; vol. II, *Werke 1906–1925*, 1975; vol. III, *Werke 1925–1929*, 1976; vol. IV, *Werke 1929–1938*, 1979

Staatsgalerie Stuttgart, *Klee und Kandinsky, Erinnerung an eine Künstlerfreundschaft*, 1979. Exhibition catalogue with text by Magdalena Droste

Margit Stäber, *Sophie Taeuber-Arp*, Lausanne, 1970

Margit Stäber, *Max Bill*, St. Gallen, 1971

Städtische Galerie im Lenbachhaus, Munich, *Kandinsky und München 1896–1914*, 1982. Exhibition catalogue with texts by Peter Jelavich, Johannes Langner, Sixten Ringbom, Carl E. Schorske, Peg Weiss and Armin Zweite

Städtische Galerie im Lenbachhaus, Munich, *Jean Hélion: Abstraktion und Mythen des Alltags: Bilder, Zeichnungen, Gouachen, 1925–1983*, 1984. Exhibition catalogue with texts by Pierre Georges Bruguière, Bernard Dahan, Merle S. Schipper, Armin Zweite and the artist

Le Surréalisme au Service de la Révolution, nos. 1–6, 1930–1933, reprint edition, New York, Arno Press, 1968

Denys Sutton, *De Staël*, Milan, 1966

James Johnson Sweeney, *Plastic Redirections in 20th-Century Painting*, Chicago, 1934

James Johnson Sweeney, *Joan Miró*, New York, 1941. Second edition 1969

The Tate Gallery, London, *Paule Vézelay*, 1983. Exhibition catalogue with introduction by Ronald Alley

Ludmila Vachtová, *Frank Kupka, Pioneer of Abstract Art*, Zdeněk Lederer, trans., Chicago and New York, 1968

Rose Valland, *Le Front de l'art: Défense des collections françaises 1939–1945*, Paris, 1961

Dora Vallier, *Vieira da Silva*, Paris, 1971

Pierre Volboudt, *Kandinsky, 1922–1944*, New York, 1963

Pierre Volboudt, *Die Zeichnungen Wassily Kandinsky*, Cologne, 1974

Gustav Vriesen and Max Imdahl, *Robert Delaunay: Licht und Farbe*, Cologne, 1967

Wallraf-Richartz-Museum, Cologne, *Otto Freundlich, 1878–1943, Gemälde, Graphiken, Skulpturen*, 1960. Exhibition catalogue with text by Gunter Aust

Wallraf-Richartz-Museum, Cologne, *Traum-Zeichen-Raum: Benennung des Unbenannten: Kunst in den Jahren 1924 bis 1939*, 1965. Exhibition catalogue with texts by Horst Keller and Gert von der Osten

Guy Weelen, *Vieira da Silva: les estampes 1929-1976*, Paris, 1977

Peg Weiss, *Kandinsky in Munich: The Formative Jugendstil Years*, Princeton, 1979

Westfälisches Landesmuseum für Kunst und Kulturgeschichte, Münster, and Musée d'Art Moderne de la Ville de Paris, *Abstraction-Création 1931–1936*, 1978. Exhibition catalogue with text by Gladys C. Fabre

Josephine Withers, *Julio González: Sculpture in Iron*, New York, 1978

Jan Würtz Frandsen, *Richard Mortensen ungdomsarene 1930–1940 mellem surrealisme og abstraktion*, Copenhagen, 1984

Zabriskie Gallery, New York, *Paule Vézelay: Paintings, Drawings and Constructions 1933-1980*, 1980. Exhibition catalogue with text by Eric Weiner

Christian Zervos, "L'Oeuvre de Joan Miró de 1917 à 1933," *Cahiers d'Art*, 9e année, no. 1–4, 1934, pp. 11–58

Christian Zervos, "Notes sur Kandinsky: à propos de sa récente exposition à la Galerie des 'Cahiers d'Art,' " *Cahiers d'Art*, 9e année, no. 5–8, 1934, pp. 149–157

Christian Zervos, *Histoire de l'art contemporain*, Paris, 1938

Christian Zervos, "Wassily Kandinsky 1866–1944," *Cahiers d'Art*, 20e–21e années, 1945–46, pp. 114–127

Christian Zervos, *Domela*, Meulon Hoff, trans., Amsterdam, 1966

INDEX OF ARTISTS IN THE CATALOGUE

PHOTOGRAPHIC CREDITS

Color

Courtesy Max Bill, Zürich: cat. no. 154

Carmelo Guadagno: cat. nos. 6, 108, 123, 159

Carmelo Guadagno and David Heald: cat. no. 94

David Heald: cat. no. 117

Fotoatelier Gerhard Howald, Bern: cat. no. 67

Walter Klein, Essen; courtesy Kunstsammlung Nordrhein-Westfalen, Düsseldorf: cat. no. 105

Courtesy Galerie Adrien Maeght, Paris: cat. nos. 86, 130, 148

Robert E. Mates: cat. no. 29

Courtesy Musée National d'Art Moderne, Centre Georges Pompidou, Paris: cat. nos. 7, 62, 116, 127, 134, 139, 168

Courtesy Museum Boymans-van Beuningen, Rotterdam: cat. no. 53

Courtesy The Museum of Modern Art, Seibu Takanawa: cat. no. 47

Courtesy Philadelphia Museum of Art: cat. no. 44

Courtesy The Phillips Collection, Washington, D.C.: cat. no. 57

Courtesy Galerie Rosengart, Lucerne: cat. no. 60

Courtesy Sotheby Parke Bernet, Inc.; © Sotheby Parke Bernet, Inc., 1984: cat. no. 91

Courtesy Thyssen-Bornemisza Collection, Lugano, Switzerland: cat. no. 151

Black and White

Courtesy Anni Albers and the Josef Albers Foundation: cat. nos. 52, 185

Courtesy Fondation Arp, Clamart: cat. no. 175

Courtesy Artcurial, Paris; © A.D.A.G.P., Paris, 1985: cat. no. 183

Courtesy The Baltimore Museum of Art: cat. no. 93

Courtesy Max Bill, Zürich: cat. no. 184

Courtesy Davlyn Gallery, New York: cat. no. 24

Courtesy Collection Domela: cat. no. 189

Courtesy Esbjerg Kunstforening, Esbjerg, Denmark: cat. no. 196

Courtesy Galerie Beyeler, Basel: cat. nos. 136, 146

Courtesy Galerie Jeanne Bucher, Paris: cat. nos. 195, 199

Courtesy Galerie Jan Krugier, Paris: cat. no. 63

Courtesy Galerie Adrien Maeght, Paris: cat. nos. 103, 155, 160, 164

Claude Gaspari; © Galerie Maeght, Paris: cat. no. 143

Carmelo Guadagno: cat. no. 190

Courtesy Haags Gemeentemuseum, The Hague: cat. no. 50

Peter Heman, Basel: cat. no. 153

J. Hyde, Paris: cat. no. 49

Luc Joubert, Paris: cat. nos. 133a, 133c, 199

Courtesy M. Knoedler & Co., Inc., New York: cat. no. 27

Courtesy Mr. and Mrs. David Lloyd Kreeger: cat. no. 28

Courtesy Kunstmuseum Basel: cat. no. 187

Courtesy Kupferstichkabinett, Kunstmuseum Basel: cat. no. 85

Courtesy Öffentliche Kunstsammlung, Kunstmuseum Basel: cat. no. 152

Courtesy Kunstmuseum Bern: cat. no. 150

Courtesy Paul Klee-Stiftung, Kunstmuseum Bern; © COSMOPRESS, Geneva, and A.D.A.G.P., Paris, 1985: cat. no. 65

Courtesy Latner Family Collection: cat. no. 149

Robert E. Mates: cat. nos. 21, 25, 40, 48, 51, 58, 81, 89, 120, 140, 147, 157, 158, 163, 179

Jacques Mer, Antibes; courtesy Musée National Fernand Léger, Biot: cat. no. 181

Courtesy Achim Moeller Fine Art Limited, New York: cat. no. 142

Photo Muller: cat. no. 133b

Courtesy Musée National d'Art Moderne, Centre Georges Pompidou, Paris: cat. nos. 1–4, 8–10, 15–20, 23, 26, 31, 32, 34–39, 41, 42, 54–56, 59, 66, 68–80, 87, 88, 90, 92, 95–102, 106, 107, 109–113, 115, 119, 121, 122, 124, 125, 128, 129, 132, 135, 137, 138, 144, 145, 156, 161, 165, 169–174, 176–178, 182, 193, 194, 198; p. 258

Courtesy Musée National du Louvre, Paris: cat. nos. 11–14

Courtesy The Museum of Modern Art, New York: cat. nos. 61, 84

Courtesy Museum Moderner Kunst, Vienna: cat. no. 180

Hans Petersen: cat. no. 197

Courtesy Philadelphia Museum of Art: cat. no. 64

Photo Routhier, Paris: cat. no. 126

Courtesy Arnold A. Saltzman: cat. no. 141

Courtesy Fotostudio Staatsgalerie Stuttgart: cat. no. 30

Courtesy Städtische Galerie im Lenbachhaus, Munich: cat. no. 118

Soichi Sunami, New York: cat. no. 131

Marc Vaux, Paris: cat. no. 186

Etienne Bertrand Weill, Courbevoie: cat. no. 83

Courtesy Association-Fondation Christian et Yvonne Zervos, Vézelay: cat. nos. 45, 188

Figures in Christian Derouet's text

Courtesy Fondation Arp, Clamart: fig. 16

Courtesy Galerie Jeanne Bucher, Paris: figs. 1, 32

Courtesy Kunsthaus Zürich: fig. 14

Georges Martin; courtesy Librairie Flammarion, Paris: fig. 13

Robert E. Mates: fig. 11

Courtesy Musée National d'Art Moderne, Centre Georges Pompidou, Paris: figs. 2–10, 19, 21, 23–31, 33

Courtesy The Museum of Modern Art, New York: fig. 12

Courtesy Bill J. Strehorn, Dallas: fig. 22

Figures in Vivian Endicott Barnett's text

Courtesy Albright-Knox Art Gallery, Buffalo, New York: fig. 27

Courtesy Galerie Beyeler, Basel: fig. 1

Courtesy Galerie Karl Flinker, Paris: fig. 6

Courtesy Mr. and Mrs. David Lloyd Kreeger: fig. 18

Courtesy Galerie Maeght, Paris: fig. 10

Courtesy M. Knoedler & Co., Inc., New York: figs. 19, 23, 32

Courtesy Öffentliche Kunstsammlung, Kunstmuseum Basel; © COSMOPRESS, Geneva, and A.D.A.G.P., Paris, 1985: fig. 28

Robert E. Mates: figs. 14, 37, 45

Courtesy Menil Foundation, Houston: fig. 5

Courtesy Moderna Museet, Stockholm: fig. 47

Courtesy The Museum of Modern Art, New York: fig. 56

Courtesy The Museum of Modern Art Library, New York: fig. 9

Courtesy Musée National d'Art Moderne, Centre Georges Pompidou, Paris: figs. 25, 33–35, 42, 51, 52

Courtesy Art, Prints and Photographs Division, The New York Public Library, Astor, Lenox and Tilden Foundations: fig. 20

Courtesy General Research Division, The New York Pubic Library, Astor, Lenox and Tilden Foundations: figs. 3, 7, 11-13, 15-17, 21, 22, 24, 26, 30, 31, 38–41, 43, 44, 46, 49, 50, 53, 54

Courtesy The Phillips Collection, Washington, D.C.: fig. 29

Courtesy Stedelijk Museum, Amsterdam: fig. 2

Courtesy Association-Fondation Christian et Yvonne Zervos, Vézelay: fig. 8

KANDINSKY

IN MUNICH: 1896-1914

RUSSIAN AND BAUHAUS YEARS 1915-1933

IN PARIS: 1934-1944

General Commissioner	Thomas M. Messer
Guest Curators	Peg Weiss
	Clark V. Poling
	Christian Derouet
Project Coordinator	Vivian Endicott Barnett
Exhibition Coordinator	Susan B. Hirschfeld
Editor	Carol Fuerstein
Project Sponsors	National Endowment for the Humanities
	National Endowment for the Arts
	Federal Republic of Germany
	Philip Morris Incorporated
	Lufthansa German Airlines
Participating Museums	San Francisco Museum of Modern Art
	Städtische Galerie im Lenbachhaus, Munich
	The High Museum of Art, Atlanta
	Kunsthaus Zürich
	Bauhaus-Archiv, Berlin
	The Museum of Fine Arts, Houston
	Museum des 20. Jahrhunderts, Vienna

Exhibition 85/1

6,000 copies of this catalogue, designed by Malcolm Grear Designers and typeset by Schooley Graphics/Craftsman Type Inc., have been printed by Eastern Press in January 1985 for the Trustees of The Solomon R. Guggenheim Foundation on the occasion of the exhibition *Kandinsky in Paris: 1934–1944*.